THE FOREIGN T[illegible]

A COM[illegible]

ON

THE GOSPEL OF ST. LUKE

BY

F. GODET,

DOCTOR AND PROFESSOR OF THEOLOGY, NEUCHATEL.

VOLUME FIRST.

TRANSLATED FROM THE SECOND FRENCH EDITION BY

E. W. SHALDERS, B.A.,

NEWBURY.

FIFTH EDITION.

EDINBURGH:

T. & T. CLARK, 38 GEORGE STREET.

PRINTED IN ENGLAND BY
THE SCOLAR PRESS LTD.
FOR
T. & T. CLARK LTD., EDINBURGH

ISBN 0 567 27445 4

LATEST IMPRESSION 1976

PREFACE.

A YEAR and half has passed away—and how swiftly!—since the publication of this Commentary, and already a second edition has become necessary. I bless the Lord for the acceptance which this work has met with in the churches of Switzerland and of France, and I hail it as a symptom of that revived interest in exegetical studies, which has always appeared to me one of their most urgent needs. I tender my special thanks to the authors of those favourable reviews which have given effectual aid towards the attainment of this result.

Almost every page of this second edition bears the traces of corrections in the form of my former work; but the substance of its exegesis and criticism remains the same. Of only one passage, or rather of only one term (*second-first*, vi. 1), has the interpretation been modified. Besides that, I have made a number of additions occasioned by the publication of two works, one of which I have very frequently quoted, and the other as often controverted. I refer to M. Gess' book, *Sur la Personne et l'Œuvre de Christ* (first part), and to *La Vie de Jésus* by M. Keim (the last two volumes).

In a recent article of the *Protestantische Kirchenzeitung*, M. Holtzmann has challenged my critical standpoint as being determined by a dogmatic prepossession. But has he forgotten the advantage which Strauss took in his first *Vie de Jésus* of the hypothesis of Gieseler, which I have defended? The reader having the whole before him will judge. He will see for himself whether the attempt to explain in a natural and rational way the origin of the three synoptical texts by means of common written sources is successful. There is one fact especially which still waits for explanation, namely, the *Aramaisms* of Luke. These *Aramaisms* are met with not only in passages which belong exclusively to this Hellenistic writer but also in those which are common to him and the other writers, who were of Jewish origin, and in whose parallel passages nothing of a similar kind is to be found! This fact remains as a rock, against which all the various hypotheses I have controverted are completely shattered, and especially that of Holtzmann. May not the somewhat ungenerous imputation of the Professor of Heidelberg, whose earnest labours no one admires more than myself, have been inspired by a slight feeling of wounded self-esteem?

And now, may this Commentary renew its course with the blessing of the Lord, to whose service it is consecrated; and may its second voyage be as prosperous and short as the first! F. G.

NEUCHATEL, *August* 1870.

EXTRACTS FROM THE PREFACE TO THE FIRST EDITION.

A Commentary on the Gospel of John remains an unfinished work so long as it is left unaccompanied by a similar work on at least one of the synoptical Gospels. Of these three writings, the Gospel of Luke appeared to me best fitted to serve as a complement to the exegetical work which I had previously published, because, as M. Sabatier has well shown in his short but substantial *Essai sur les Sources de la Vie de Jésus*, Luke's writing constitutes, in several important respects, a transition between the view taken by John and that which forms the basis of the synoptical literature.[1]

The exegetical method pursued is very nearly the same as in my preceding Commentary. I have not written merely for professed theologians; nor have I aimed directly at edification. This work is addressed, in general, to those readers of culture, so numerous at the present day, who take a heart-felt interest in the religious and critical questions which are now under discussion. To meet their requirements, a translation has been given of those Greek expressions which it was necessary to quote, and technical language has as far as possible been avoided. The most advanced ideas of modern unbelief circulate at the present time in all our great centres of population. In the streets of our cities, workmen are heard talking about the conflict between St. Paul and the other apostles of Jesus Christ. We must therefore endeavour to place the results of a real and impartial Biblical science within reach of all. I repeat respecting this Commentary what I have already said of its predecessor; it has been written, not so much with a view to its being consulted, as read.

. . . . . .

From the various readings, I have had to select those which had a certain value, or presented something of interest. A commentary cannot pretend to supply the place of a complete critical edition such as all scientific study requires. Since I cannot in any way regard the eighth edition of Tischendorf's text just published as a standard text, though I gratefully acknowledge its aid as absolutely indispensable, I have

[1] The publishers intend, if these volumes on Luke meet with a favourable reception, to bring out M. Godet's celebrated Commentary on John in an English dress. Indeed, they would have followed the author's order of publication, but that they waited to take advantage of a second edition, which is preparing for the press.—TRANS.

adopted the received text as a basis in indicating the various readings; but I would express my earnest desire for an edition of the Byzantine text that could be regarded as a standard authority.

Frequently I have contented myself with citing the *original* text of the ancient manuscripts, without mentioning the changes made in it by later hands; but whenever these changes offered anything that could be of any interest, I have indicated them.

If I am asked with what scientific or religious assumptions I have approached this study of the third Gospel, I reply, With these two only: that the authors of our Gospels were men of *good sense* and *good faith*.

TABLE OF CONTENTS

TO THE FIRST VOLUME.

FIRST PART.

SECOND PART.

THIRD PART.

COMMENTARY ON ST. LUKE.

INTRODUCTION.

THE Introduction of a Biblical Commentary is not designed to solve the various questions relating to the origin of the book under consideration. This solution must be the result of the study of the book itself, and not be assumed beforehand. The proper work of introduction is to *prepare* the way for the study of the sacred book; it should propose questions, not solve them.

But there is one side of the labour of criticism which may and indeed ought to be treated before exegesis—the *historical.* And by this we understand: 1. The study of such facts of ecclesiastical history as may throw light upon the time of publication and the sources of the work which is to engage our attention; 2. The review of the various opinions which have been entertained respecting the origin of this book, particularly in modern times. The first of these studies supplies exegetical and critical labour with its starting-point; the second determines its aim. The possession of these two kinds of information is the condition of the maintenance and advancement of science.

This introduction, then, will aim at making the reader acquainted with—

I. The earliest traces of *the existence of our Gospel,* going back as far as possible in the history of the primitive Church.

II. The statements made by ancient writers as to *the person of the author,* and the opinions current at the present day on this point.

III. The information furnished by tradition respecting *the circumstances in which this writing was composed* (its readers, date, locality, design), as well as the different views which criticism has taken of these various questions.

IV. The ideas which scholars have formed of *the sources* whence the author derived the subject-matter of his narrations.

V. Lastly, the documents by means of which *the text* of this writing has been preserved to us.

An introduction of this kind is not complete without a conclusion in which the questions thus raised find their solution. This conclusion should seek to combine the facts established by tradition with the results obtained from exegesis.

SEC. I.—TRACES OF THE EXISTENCE OF THE THIRD GOSPEL IN THE PRIMITIVE CHURCH.

We take as our starting-point the middle of the second century, and our aim is not to come down the stream, but to ascend it. It is admitted, indeed, that at this epoch our Gospel was universally known and received, not only in *the great Church* (an expression of Celsus, about 150), but also by the sects which were detached from it. This admission rests on some indisputable quotations from this book in Theophilus of Antioch (about 170) and Irenæus (about 180), and in the *Letter of the Churches of Lyons and Vienne* (in 177); on the fact, amply verified by the testimony of Clement of Alexandria, that the Gnostic Heracleon had published a commentary on the Gospel of Luke as well as on the Gospel of John (between 175–195);[1] on the very frequent use which Valentinus, or at least writers of his school, made of this Gospel; lastly, on numerous quotations from Luke, acknowledged by all scholars at the present day, contained in the *Clementine Homilies* (about 160). It is not surprising, therefore, that Origen ranks Luke's work among the number of *those four*

[1] See, for the fact, Grabe, *Spicilegium*, sec. ii. t. i. p. 83; and for the date, Lipsius, *Die Zeit des Marcion und des Heracleon*, in Hilgenfeld's *Zeitschrift*, 1867.

Gospels admitted by all the churches under heaven, and that Eusebius places it among the *homologoumena* of the new covenant. The only matter of importance here is to investigate that obscure epoch, the first half of the second century, for any indications which may serve to prove the presence and influence of our Gospel. We meet with them in four departments of inquiry,—in the field of heresy, in the writings of the Fathers, in the pseudepigraphical literature, and lastly, in the biblical writings.

1. Heresy—*Marcion, Cerdo, Basilides.*

Marcion, a son of a bishop of Pontus, who was excommunicated by his own father, taught at Rome from 140–170.[1] He proposed to purify the Gospel from the Jewish elements which the twelve, by reason of their education and Israelitish prejudices, had necessarily introduced into it. In order more effectually to remove this alloy, he taught that the God who created the world and legislated for the Jews was different from the supreme God who revealed Himself in Jesus Christ, and was only an inferior and finite being; that for this reason the Jewish law rested exclusively on justice, while the gospel was founded on charity. According to him, St. Paul alone had understood Jesus. Further, in the canon which Marcion formed, he only admitted the Gospel of Luke (on account of its affinity with the teaching of Paul), and ten epistles of this apostle. But even in these writings he felt himself obliged to suppress certain passages; for they constantly assume the divine character of the Old Testament, and attribute the creation of the visible universe to the God of Jesus Christ. Marcion, in conformity with his ideas about matter, denied the reality of the body of Jesus; and on this point, therefore, he found himself in conflict with numerous texts of Paul and Luke. The greater part of the modifications of Luke's text which were exhibited, according to the statements of Tertullian and Epiphanius, in the Gospel used by Marcion and his adherents, are to be accounted for in this way.

Notwithstanding this, the relation between the Gospel of Luke and that of this heretic has in modern times been repre-

[1] Lipsius, *Die Zeit des Marcion und des Heracleon*, in Hilgenfeld's *Zeitschr.* 1867.

sented in a totally different light. And the reason for this is not hard to find. The relation which we have just pointed out between these two writings, if clearly made out, is sufficient to prove that, at the time of Marcion's activity, Luke's Gospel existed in the collections of apostolic writings used in the churches, and to compel criticism to assign to this writing both ancient authority and a very early origin. Now this is just what the rationalistic school was not disposed to admit.[1] Consequently, Semler and Eichhorn in the past century, and, with still greater emphasis, Ritschl, Baur, and Schwegler in our time, have maintained that the priority belonged to the Gospel of Marcion, that this work was the true primitive Luke, and that our canonical Luke was the result of a retouching of this more ancient work, accomplished in the second century in the sense of a modified Paulinism. We must do justice, however, to this critical school. No one has laboured more energetically to rectify this erroneous opinion, tentatively brought forward by several of its adherents. Hilgenfeld, and above all Volkmar, have successfully combated it, and Ritschl has expressly withdrawn it (*Theol. Jahrb.* X. p. 528 et seq.); Bleek (*Einl. in. d. N. T.* p. 122 et seq.) has given an able summary of the whole discussion. We shall only bring forward the following points, which seem to us the most essential:—

1. The greater part of the differences which must have distinguished the Gospel of Marcion from our Luke are to be explained either as the result of his Gnostic system, or as mere critical corrections. Thus, Marcion suppressed the first two chapters on the *birth* of Jesus,—a retrenchment which suited his Docetism; also in the passage Luke xiii. 28, "When you shall see *Abraham, Isaac, and Jacob, and all the prophets* in the kingdom of God," he read, "When you shall see *the just* enter into the kingdom of heaven," which alone answered to his theory of the old covenant; in the same way also, for the words of Jesus in Luke xvi. 17, "It is easier for heaven and earth to pass, than one tittle *of the law* to fail"

[1] Hilgenfeld himself points out the purely dogmatic origin of this rationalistic opinion: "This opinion," he says, "has misapprehended the true tendency of the Gospel of Marcion, *through a desire to assign to the canonical text* (to our Luke) *the most recent date possible*" (*Die Evangelien*, p. 27).

Marcion read, "than that one tittle of the letter *of my words* should fail." In both these instances, one must be blind not to see that it was Marcion who modified the text of Luke to suit his system, and not the reverse. Again, we read that the Gospel of Marcion began in this way: "*In the fifteenth year of the reign of the Emperor Tiberius, Jesus descended to Capernaum*" (naturally, from heaven, without having passed through the human stages of birth and youth); then came the narrative of the first sojourn at Capernaum, just as it is related Luke iv. 31 et seq.; and after that, only in the inverse order to that which obtains in our Gospel, the narrative of the visit to Nazareth, Luke iv. 16 et seq. Is it not clear that such a beginning could not belong to the primitive writing, and that the transposition of the two narratives which follow was designed to do away with the difficulty presented by the words of the inhabitants of Nazareth (Luke iv. 23), as Luke places them, *before* the sojourn at Capernaum? The narrative of Marcion was then the result of a dogmatic and critical revision of Luke iii. 1, iv. 31, iv. 16 and 23.

2. It is a well-known fact that Marcion had falsified the epistles of Paul by an exactly similar process.

3. Marcion's sect *alone* availed themselves of the Gospel used by this heretic. This fact proves that this work was not an evangelical writing already known, which the author of our Luke modified, and which Marcion alone had preserved intact.

From all this, a scientific criticism can only conclude that our Gospel of Luke was in existence before that of Marcion, and that this heretic chose this among all the Gospels which enter into the ecclesiastical collection as the one which he could most readily adapt to his system.[1] About 140, then,

[1] Zeller (in his *Apostelgeschichte*) expresses himself thus: "We may admit as proved and generally accepted, not only that Marcion made use of an older Gospel, but further, that he recomposed, modified, and often abridged it, and that this older Gospel was essentially none other than our Luke." This restriction "essentially" refers to certain passages, in which it appears to writers of the Tübingen school that Marcion's reading is more original than that of our canonical text. The latter, according to Baur and Hilgenfeld, must have been introduced with a view to counteract the use which the Gnostics made of the true text. Zeller, however (p. 12 et seq.), considerably reduces the number of those passages in which Marcion is supposed to have preserved the true reading, and those which he retains are far from bearing the marks of proof. Thus, Luke x. 22, Marcion appears to have read οὐδεὶς ἔγνω, no one *hath known*, in-

our Gospel already possessed full authority, the result of a conviction of its apostolic origin.

Marcion did not create his system himself. Before him, Cerdo, according to Theodoret's account (*Hæret. fabulæ,* i. 24), proved *by the Gospels* that the *just* God of the old covenant and the *good* God of the new are different beings; and he founded this contrariety on the precepts of the Sermon on the Mount (Matt. v. 38–48; Luke vi. 27–38). The Gospel of Luke must have sustained the principal part in this demonstration, if at least we credit the testimony of an ancient writer (Pseudo-Tertullian, in the conclusion of the *De præscriptione hæreticorum,* c. 51): "*Solum evangelium Lucæ, nec tamen totum, recipit* [*Cerdo*]." Some years, then, before Marcion, Cerdo sought to prove the opposition of the law to the gospel by the *written Gospels,* especially by that of Luke.

Basilides, one of the most ancient known Gnostics, who is usually said to have flourished at Alexandria about 120, assumed for himself and his son Isidore the title of pupils of the Apostle Matthias. The statement of Hippolytus is as follows: "Basilides, with Isidore, his true son and disciple, said that Matthias had transmitted to them orally some secret instructions which he had received from the mouth of the Saviour in His private teaching."[1] This claim of Basilides implies the circulation of the book of the Acts, in which alone there is any mention of the apostolate of Matthias, and consequently of the Gospel of Luke, which was composed before the Acts.

stead of οὐδεὶς γινώσκει, no one *knoweth;* and because this reading is found in Justin, in the *Clementine Homilies,* and in some of the Fathers, it is inferred that our canonical text has been altered. But Justin himself also reads γινώσκει (*Dial. c. Tryph.* c. 100). There appears to be nothing more here than an ancient variation. In the same passage, Marcion appears to have placed the words which refer to the knowledge of the Father by the Son before those which refer to the knowledge of the Son by the Father,—a reading which is also found in the *Clement. Hom.* But here, again, this can only be a mere variation of reading which it is easy to explain. It is of such little dogmatic importance, that Irenæus, who opposes it critically, himself quotes the passage twice in this form (*Tischend. ad Matth.* xi. 27).

[1] *S. Hippolyti Refutationis omnium hæresium librorum decem quæ supersunt* (ed. Duncker et Schneidewin), L. vii. § 20.

2. THE FATHERS—*Justin, Polycarp, Clement of Rome.*

If it is proved that about 140, and at Rome, Cerdo and Marcion made use of the Gospel of Luke as a book generally received in the Church, it is quite impossible to suppose that this Gospel was not in the hands of Justin, who wrote in this very city some years later. Besides, the writings of Justin allow of no doubt as to this fact; and it is admitted at the present day by all the writers of that school which makes exclusive claims to be *critical*—by Zeller, Volkmar, and Hilgenfeld.[1] With this admission before us, we know what the assertions of M. Nicolas are worth, which he does not scruple to lay before French readers, who have so little acquaintance with questions of this nature,—such an assertion, for instance, as this: "It is impossible to read the comparisons which critics of this school [the orthodox] are accustomed to make between certain passages of Polycarp, Clement of Rome, Ignatius, and *even Justin Martyr,* and analogous passages from our Gospels, without being tempted to think that the cause must be very bad that can need, or that can be satisfied with, such arguments."[2] It appears that Messrs. Zeller, Hilgenfeld, and Volkmar are all implicated together in furbishing up these fallacious arguments in favour of orthodoxy! Here are some passages which prove unanswerably that Justin Martyr used our third Gospel: *Dial.* c. 100, he quotes almost *verbatim* Luke i. 26–30. *Ibid.* c. 78, and *Apol.* i. 34, he mentions the census of Quirinus in the very terms of Luke. *Dial.* c. 41 and 70, and *Apol.* i. 66, he refers to the institution of the Holy Supper according to the text of Luke. *Dial.* c. 103, he says: "In the memoirs which I say were composed by His apostles, and by those that accompanied them, [it is related] that the sweat rolled from Him in drops whilst He

[1] "Justin's acquaintance with the Gospel of Luke is demonstrated by a series of passages, of which some *certainly,* and others *very probably,* are citations from this book" (Zeller, *Apostelgesch.* p. 26). On the subject of a passage from the *Dialogue with Trypho,* c. 49, Volkmar says: "Luke (iii. 16, 17) is quoted here, first in common with Matthew, then, in preference to the latter, *literally*" (*Ursprung unserer Ev.* p. 157). "Justin is acquainted with our three synoptical Gospels, and extracts them almost completely" (*Ibid.* p. 91). "Besides Matthew and Mark . . . Justin also makes use of the Gospel of Luke" (Hilgenfeld, *Der Kanon,* p. 25).

[2] *Etudes critiques sur le N. T.* p. 5.

prayed," etc. (Luke xxii. 44). *Ibid.*, Justin refers to Jesus having been sent to Herod,—an incident only related by Luke. *Ibid.* c. 105, he quotes the last words of Jesus, "Father, into Thy hands I commit my spirit," as taken from *The Memoirs of the Apostles.* This prayer is only recorded by Luke (xxiii. 46). We have only indicated the quotations expressly acknowledged as such by Zeller himself (*Apostelgesch.* pp. 26–37).

It is impossible, then, to doubt that the Gospel of Luke formed part of those *apostolic memoirs* quoted eighteen times by Justin, and from which he has derived the greater part of the facts of the Gospel that are mentioned by him.

The Acts of the Apostles having been written after the Gospel, and by the same author (these two facts are admitted by all true criticism), every passage of the Fathers which proves the existence of this book at a given moment demonstrates *à fortiori* the existence of the Gospel at the same time. We may therefore adduce the following passage from Polycarp, which we think can only be explained as a quotation from the Acts:—

Acts ii. 24.	Polyc. *ad Phil.* c. 1.
Ὃν ὁ Θεὸς ἀνέστησεν, λύσας τὰς ὠδῖνας τοῦ θανάτου.	Ὃν ἤγειρεν ὁ Θεὸς λύσας τὰς ὠδῖνας τοῦ ᾅδου.
"Whom God hath raised up, having loosed the [birth-] pains of death."	"Whom God hath awakened, having loosed the [birth-] pains of Hades."

The identical construction of the proposition in the two writings, the choice of the term λύσας, and the strange expression, *the birth-pains of death* (Acts) or *of Hades* (Polyc.) scarcely permit us to doubt that the passage in Polycarp was taken from that in the Acts.[1]

In the Epistle of Clement of Rome there is an exhortation beginning with these words: "Remember the words of the Lord Jesus, in which He taught equity and generosity;" then comes a passage in which the texts of Matthew and Luke in the Sermon on the Mount appear to be combined, but where, in the opinion of Volkmar,[2] the text of Luke predomi-

[1] It is not impossible, certainly, that the expression ὠδῖνες was taken by both these authors from Ps. xviii. 5, or from Ps. cxvi. 3, where the LXX. translate by this term the word חבל, which signifies at once *bonds* and *pains of childbirth;* but there still remains in the two propositions as a whole an unaccountable similarity.

[2] "The text of Matthew differs most, whilst Luke's text furnishes the substance of the developed thought" (*Urspr.* p. 138).

nates (vi. 31, 36–38). In this same letter the Acts are twice quoted, first at c. 18, where mention is made of a divine testimony respecting King David, and there is an amalgamation of the two following Old Testament passages: 1 Sam. xiii. 14 and Ps. lxxxix. 21. Now a precisely similar fusion, or very nearly so, is found in the book of the Acts (xiii. 22). How could this almost identical combination of two such distinct passages of the Old Testament have occurred spontaneously to the two writers?

1 SAM. xiii. 14.	PS. lxxxix. 20.
"The Lord hath sought him *a man after his own heart.*"	"*I have found David* my servant; with my holy oil have I anointed him."

ACTS xiii. 22.

"*I have found David* the son of Jesse, *a man after mine own heart,* which shall fulfil all my will."

CLEM. *Ep. ad Cor.* c. 18.

"*I have found a man after my own heart, David* son of Jesse; and I have anointed him with eternal oil."

The other quotation is an expression of eulogy which Clement addresses to the Corinthians (c. 2): "Giving more willingly than receiving (μᾶλλον δίδοντες ἢ λαμβάνοντες),"—a repetition of the very words of Jesus cited by Paul, Acts xx. 35: "It is more blessed to give than to receive (διδόναι μᾶλλον ἢ λαμβάνειν)." No doubt these are allusions rather than quotations properly so called. But we know that this is the ordinary mode of quotation in the Fathers.

It is true that the Tübingen school denies the authenticity of the epistles of Clement and Polycarp, and assigns them, the former to the first quarter, and the latter to the second part, of the second century; but the authenticity of the former in particular is guaranteed by the most unexceptionable testimonies. Although in many respects not at all flattering to the church of Corinth, it was deposited in the archives of this church, and, according to the testimony of Dionysius, bishop of Corinth about 170, was frequently read publicly to the congregation. Further, it is quoted by Polycarp, Hegesippus, and Irenæus. Now, if it is authentic, it dates, not from 125, as Volkmar thinks, but at latest from the end of the first century. According to Hase, it belongs to between 80 and

90; according to Tischendorf, it dates from 69, or, less probably, from 96. For our part, we should regard this last date as most probable. In any case, we see that the use of Luke's writings in this letter confers a very high antiquity on their diffusion and authority.

3. The Pseudepigraphical Writings—*Testaments of the Twelve Patriarchs.*

Among the writings of Jewish or Jewish-Christian origin which antiquity has bequeathed to us, there is one which appears to have been composed by a Christian Jew, desirous of bringing his fellow-countrymen to the Christian faith. With this view he represents the twelve sons of Jacob as speaking on their death-beds, and assigns to each of them a prophetic discourse, in which they depict the future lot of their people, and announce the blessings to be conferred by the gospel. Contrary to the opinion of M. Reuss, who places the composition of this work after the middle of the second century,[1] de Groot and Langen think that it belongs to the end of the first or the beginning of the second.[2] As this book alludes to the first destruction of Jerusalem by the Romans in 70, but in no way refers to the second by Adrian in 135, it must, it would seem, date from the interval between these two events. It contains numerous quotations from Luke as well as from the other evangelists, but the following passage is particularly important: "In the last days, said Benjamin to his sons, there shall spring from my race a ruler according to the Lord, who, after having heard His voice, shall spread a new light among the heathen. He shall abide in the synagogues of the heathen to the end of the ages, and shall be in the mouth of their chiefs as a pleasant song. *His work and his word shall be written in the holy books.* He shall be chosen of God for eternity. My father Jacob hath told me about him who is to make up for the deficiencies of my race." The Apostle Paul was of the tribe of Benjamin, and there is an allusion in this passage to his work as described in the book of the Acts, and probably also to his epistles as containing his word.

[1] *Die Gesch. der heil. Schr. N. T.* § 257.

[2] De Groot, *Basilides*, p. 37; Langen, *Das Judenthum in Palest.* p. 148.

There is no doubt, then, that the book of the Acts is here referred to as constituting part of the collection of holy books (ἐν βίβλοις ταῖς ἁγίαις). This passage is thus the parallel of the famous *As it is written*, which is found in the Epistle of Barnabas, and which serves as a preamble, about the same time, to a quotation from the Gospel of St. Matthew.[1] Before the end of the first century, therefore, there were collections of apostolic writings in the churches, the contents of which we cannot exactly describe: they varied, no doubt, in different churches, which were already regarded equally with the Old Testament *as holy;* and in these, the book of the Acts, and consequently the Gospel of Luke, found a place.

4. Biblical Writings—*John, Mark, Acts.*

The whole Gospel of John supposes, as we think has been proved in our *Commentary* upon that book, the existence of our synoptics, and their propagation in the Church. As to Luke in particular, x. 38–42 must be compared with John xi. and xii. 1–8; then xxiv. 1–12 and 36–49 with John xx. 1–18 and 19–23, where John's narrative appears to allude, sometimes even in expression, to Luke's.

The first distinct and indubitable trace of the influence of Luke's Gospel on a book of the New Testament is found in the conclusion of Mark (xvi. 9–20). On the one hand, we hope to prove that, until we come to this fragment, the composition of Mark is quite independent of Luke's narrative. On the other hand, it is evident that from this point the narrative of Mark, notwithstanding some peculiarities, is scarcely anything but an abridged reproduction of Luke's. It is, as it has been called, *the most clearly marked style of extract.* Compare ver. 9*b* and Luke viii. 2; vers. 10, 11, and Luke xxiv. 10–12; ver. 12 and Luke vers. 13–32; ver. 13 and Luke vers. 33–35; ver. 14*a* and Luke vers. 36–43. It is possible also that John xx. 1–17 may have had some influence on ver. 9*a*. As to the dis-

[1] Hilgenfeld, with all fairness, acknowledges this quotation in the Ep. of Barnabas, and the consequences deducible from it: "We meet with the first trace of this application [of the notion of inspiration as in the writings of the Old Testament to those of the apostles] at the close of the first century, in the so-called letter of Barnabas, in which a sentence from the Gospel is quoted as a passage of Scripture" (*Der Kanon*, p. 10).

course vers. 15–18, and the fragment vers. 19, 20, the author of this conclusion must have taken these from materials of his own. Now we know that this conclusion to Mark, from xvi. 9, was wanting, according to the statements of the Fathers, in a great many ancient MSS.; that it is not found at the present day in either of the two most ancient documents, the *Sinaitic* or *Vatican;* that the earliest trace of it occurs in Irenæus; and that an entirely different conclusion, bearing, however, much more evidently the impress of a later ecclesiastical style, is the reading of some other documents. If, then, the conclusion found in the received text is not from the hand of the author, still it is earlier than the middle of the second century. We must also admit that no considerable interval could have elapsed between the composition of the Gospel and the composition of this conclusion; for the discourse, ver. 15 et seq., is too original to be a mere compilation: further, it must have been drawn up from materials dating from the time of the composition of the Gospel; and the remarkable agreement which exists between the ending, vers. 19 and 20, and the general thought of the book, proves that whoever composed this conclusion had fully entered into the mind of the author. The latter must have been suddenly interrupted in his work; for xvi. 8 could never have been the *intended* conclusion of his narrative. An appearance of Jesus in Galilee is announced (v. 1–8), and the narrative ought not to finish without giving an account of this. Besides, ver. 9 is quite a fresh beginning, for there is an evident break of connection between this verse and ver. 8.

From all these considerations, it follows that at ver. 8 the work was suddenly suspended, and that a short time after, a writer, who was still in the current of the author's thought, and who might have had the advantage of some materials prepared by him, drew up this conclusion. Now, if up to xvi. 8 the Gospel of Luke has exercised no influence on Mark's work, and if, on the contrary, from xvi. 9 there is a perceptible influence of the former on the latter, there is only one inference to be drawn,—namely, that the Gospel of Luke appeared in the interval between the composition of Mark and the writing of its conclusion. In order, then, to fix the date of the publication of our Gospel, it becomes important to know by what circumstance the author of the second Gospel was interrupted in his work. The only probable explanation of this fact, as it appears to us, is the unexpected outbreak of Nero's persecution in August 64, just the time when Mark was at Rome with Peter. At the request of the faithful belonging to this church, he had undertaken to write the narratives of this apostle, in other words, the composition of our second Gospel. The persecution which broke out, and the violent death of his master, probably forced him to take precipitous flight from the capital. It is only necessary to suppose that a copy of the yet unfinished work remained in the hands of some Roman Christian, and was deposited in the archives of his church, to explain how the Gospel at first got into circulation in its incomplete form. When, a little while after, some one set to work to complete it, the Gospel of Luke had appeared, and was consulted. The work, finished by help of Luke's Gospel, was copied and circulated in this new form. In this way the existence of the two kinds of copies is explained. The year 64 would then be the *terminus a quo* of the publication of Luke. On the other hand, the writing of the conclusion of Mark must have preceded the publication, or at least the diffusion, of the Gospel of Matthew. Otherwise the continuator of Mark would certainly have given it the preference, because its narrative bears an infinitely closer resemblance than Luke's to the account he was completing. The composition of the canonical conclusion of Mark would then be prior to the diffusion of our Matthew, and consequently before the close of the first century, when this writing was already clothed with a divine authority equal to that of the Old Testament (p. 11). Now, since the conclusion of Mark implies the existence of the Gospel of Luke, we see to what a high antiquity these facts, when taken together, oblige us to refer the composition of the latter.

The other biblical writing which presents a point of connection with our Gospel is the book of the *Acts.* From its opening verses, this writing supposes the Gospel of Luke already composed and known to its readers. When was the book of the Acts composed? From the fact that it terminates so suddenly with the mention of Paul's captivity at Rome (spring 62 to 64), it has often been concluded that events had proceeded just thus far at the time the work was composed. This conclusion, it is true, is hasty, for it may have been the author's intention only to carry his story as far as the apostle's arrival at Rome. His book was not intended to be a biography of the apostles generally, nor of Peter and Paul in particular; it was the work that was important to him, not the workmen. Nevertheless, when we observe the fulness of the narrative, especially in the latter parts of the work; when we see the author relating the minutest details of the tempest and Paul's shipwreck (xxvii.), and mentioning even the sign of the ship which carried the apostle to Italy (xxviii. 11, "A ship of Alexandria, whose sign was *Castor and Pollux*"),—it cannot be reasonably maintained that it was a vigorous adherence to his plan which prevented his giving his readers some details respecting the end of this ministry, and the martyrdom of his master. Or might he have proposed to make this the subject of a third work? Had he a mind to compose a trilogy, after the fashion of the Greek tragedians? The idea of a third work might no doubt be suggested to him afterwards by subsequent events; and this appears to be the sense of certain obscure words in the famous fragment of Muratori. But it is not very probable that such an intention could have determined his original plan, and influenced the composition of his two former works. What matter could appear to the author of sufficient importance to be placed on a level, as the subject of a *τρίτος λόγος*, with the contents of the Gospel or the Acts? Or, lastly, was it the premature death of the author which came and put an end to his labour? There is no ground for this supposition. The conclusion, Acts xxviii. 30 and 31, while resembling analogous conclusions at the end of each narrative in the Gospel and in the Acts, has rather the effect of a *closing period* intentionally affixed to the entire book. We are then, in fact, brought back to the idea that Paul's career was not yet finished when the author of the Acts terminated his narrative, and wrote the last two verses of chap. xxviii.; since, were this not the case, fidelity to his plan would in no way have prevented his giving some details on a subject so interesting to his readers. The book of the Acts, therefore, does not appear to have been written very long after the time which forms the termination of the narrative. This conclusion, if well founded, applies *à fortiori* to the Gospel of Luke.

To sum up: the use which was made of the third Gospel at Rome, in the middle of the second century, by Justin, Marcion, and his master Cerdo, and the apostolic authority implied in the diffusion of this work, and in the respect it enjoyed at this period, oblige us to admit its existence as early as the beginning of this century. A very recent book could not have been known and used thus simultaneously in the Church and by the sects. The place which the Acts held in collections of the sacred writings at the epoch of the *Testaments of the Twelve Patriarchs* (towards the end of the first or the commencement of the second century), sends us back a little further, to about 80-100. Lastly, the relations of the third Gospel to Mark and the Acts carry us to an epoch still more remote, even as far back as the period from 64 to 80.

An objection to this result has been found in the silence of Papias,—a silence which Hilgenfeld has even thought an indication of positive rejection on the part of this Father. But because Eusebius has only preserved the information furnished by Papias respecting the composition of Mark and Matthew—only a few lines altogether—it does not follow that Papias did not know Luke, or that, if he knew, he rejected him. All that can reasonably be inferred from this silence is, that Eusebius had not found anything of interest in Papias as to the origin of Luke's book. And what is there surprising in that? Matthew and Mark had commenced their narratives without giving the smallest detail respecting the composition of their books; Luke, on the contrary, in his preface, had told his readers all they needed to know. There was no tradition, then, current on this point, and so Papias had found nothing new to add to the information given by the author.

We ought to say, in concluding this review, that we do not attach a decisive value to the facts we have just noticed, and that among the results arrived at there are several which we are quite aware are not indisputable.[1] Nevertheless, it has appeared to us that there were some interesting coincidences (*points de repère*) which a careful study of the subject should

[1] We ought to emphasize this reservation, in view of some reviews in which we have been blamed for dealing here too largely in hypothesis.

not overlook. The only fact which appears to us absolutely decisive is the ecclesiastical and liturgical use of our Gospel in the churches in the middle of the second century, as it is established by Justin. If this book really formed part of those *Memoirs of the Apostles,* which he declared to the Emperor were publicly read every Sunday in the Christian assemblies, the apostolic antiquity of this book must have been a fact of public notoriety, and all the more that it did not bear the name of an apostle at the head of it.

SEC. II.—THE AUTHOR.

Under this title are included two distinct questions: I. What do we know of the person designated in the title as the author of our Gospel? II. By what ecclesiastical testimonies is the composition of this book traced to him, and what is their worth?

I.

The person named *Luke* is only mentioned in certain passages of the New Testament, and in some few brief ecclesiastical traditions.

The biblical passages are: Col. iv. 14, "Luke, the beloved physician, and Demas, greet you;" Philem. 24, "There salute thee Epaphras, my fellow-prisoner in Christ Jesus; Marcus, Aristarchus, Demas, Lucas, my fellow-labourers;" 2 Tim. iv. 11, "Only Luke is with me."

These passages, considered in their context, yield these results:—

1. That Luke was a Christian of *pagan* origin. This is proved beyond doubt in the first passage by the distinction between the group of Christians of *the circumcision* (vers. 10, 11), and the following group to which Luke belongs (vers. 12–14). The objection which has been taken to this exegetical inference, on the ground of an Aramæan tincture of style in many passages of Luke, has, so far as we can see, no force. Accordingly, St Luke would be the only author, among those who were called to write the Scriptures, who was not of Jewish origin.

2. The circumstance that his profession was that of *a physician* is not unimportant; for it implies that he must have possessed a certain amount of scientific knowledge, and belonged to the class of educated men. There existed at Rome, in the time of the Emperors, a medical supervision; a superior college (*Collegium archiatrorum*) was charged with the duty of examining in every city those who desired to practise the healing art. Newly admitted men were placed under the direction of older physicians; their modes of treatment were strictly scrutinized, and their mistakes severely punished, sometimes by taking away their diploma.[1] For these reasons, Luke must have possessed an amount of scientific and literary culture above that of most of the other evangelists and apostles.

3. Luke was *the fellow-labourer* of Paul in his mission to the heathen, a fellow-labourer *greatly beloved* (Col. iv. 14) and *faithful* (2 Tim. iv. 9–12).

But here arises an important question. Does the connection which has just been proved between Paul and Luke date, as Bleek thinks, only from the apostle's sojourn at Rome,—a city in which Luke had long been established as a physician and where he had been converted by Paul? Or had Luke already become the companion of the apostle before his arrival at Rome, and had he taken part in his missionary toils in Greece or in Asia? The solution of this question depends on the way in which we regard a certain number of passages in the Acts, in which the author passes all at once from the third person, *they*, to the form of the first person, *we*. If it is admitted (1) that Luke is the author of the Acts (a question which we cannot yet deal with), and (2) that the author, in thus expressing himself, wishes to intimate that at certain times he shared the apostle's work, it is evident that our knowledge of his life will be considerably enriched by these passages. It is only this second question that we shall examine here.

The passages of which we speak are three in number: xvi. 10–17; xx. 5–xxi. 17; xxvii. 1–xxviii. 16. Here several suppositions are possible: Either Luke, the author of the entire book, describes in the first person the scenes in

[1] Tholuck, *Die Glaubwürdigk. der ev. Gesch.* p. 149 (according to Galen).

which he was himself present; or the author, either Luke or some Christian of the first age, inserts in his work such and such fragments of a traveller's journal kept by one of Paul's companions—by Timothy or Silas, for example; or, lastly, a forger of later times, with a view to accredit his work and make it pass for Luke's, to whom he ventures to attribute it, introduces into it some fragments of Luke, changing their substance and remodelling their form, but purposely allowing the first person to stand in these portions. The first supposition is the one that has been most generally admitted from ancient times: the second has been maintained by Schleiermacher and Bleek, who attribute the journal whence these portions are taken to Timothy; also by Schwanbeck, who makes it the work of Silas: the third is the hypothesis defended by Zeller.

If the first explanation is the most ancient, it is because it is that which most naturally occurs to the mind. After the author, at the beginning of his book, had made use of the first person, "The former treatise *have I made,* O Theophilus," would it not be evident to his readers that when, in the course of the narrative, he came to say *we,* it was with the intention of indicating himself as a witness of the facts related? If he had borrowed these fragments from the journal of another, why did he not assimilate them in form to the rest of the narrative? Surely it was not difficult for such a writer as he was to change the first person into the third. It is maintained that the author is an unskilled writer, who does not know how to work up his materials; but Zeller rightly replies that the unity of style, aim, and method which prevails throughout the book of the Acts, proves, on the contrary, that the author has made very skilful use of the documents at his disposal. De Wette himself, although a supporter of Schleiermacher's theory, is obliged to acknowledge this. And if this is so, it is impossible to explain how the author could have allowed this *we* to stand. Besides, this explanation has to contend with other difficulties. If this pronoun *we* emanates from the pen of Timothy, how is it that it does not come in at the moment when Timothy enters on the scene and joins Paul and Silas? How is it, again, that it suddenly disappears, although Timothy continues the journey with Paul (from his departure from Philippi and during his entire stay in Achaia, Acts xviii.; comp. with 1 and 2 Thess. i. 1)? Above all, how is it that this *we* is resumed, xx. 5, in a passage in which the writer who thus designates himself is *expressly opposed* to a number of persons *among whom figures Timothy?* Bleek tries to draw out of this difficulty by applying the pronoun *οὗτοι, these,* ver. 5, simply to the last two of the persons mentioned, Tychicus and Trophimus. But every one must feel that this is a forced explanation. As Zeller says, had this been the case, it would have been necessary to have said *οὗτοι οἱ δύο, these two.*

The same and even greater difficulties prevent our thinking of Silas, since, according to the Epistles, after their stay at Corinth, this missionary no longer appears in company with Paul, yet the *we* goes on to the end of the Acts. As to the opinion of Zeller, it makes the author an impostor, who determined to assume the mask of Luke in order the more easily to obtain credence for his history. But whence comes the unanimous tradition which attributes the Gospel and the Acts to Luke, when he is never once *named* in these works as their author? In order to explain this fact, Zeller is obliged to have recourse to a fresh hypothesis, that the forger in the first instance had inscribed Luke's name at the head of his work, and that afterwards, by some unknown accident, the name was dropped, although the Church had fallen completely into the snare. Can a more improbable supposition be imagined? The ancient explanation, which is that of common sense, is, after all these fruitless attempts, the only one scientifically admissible: the author of the Acts employed the pronoun *we* in every case in which he himself was present at the scenes described.

To this exegetical conclusion only two objections of any value have been offered: 1. The sudden character of the appearance and disappearance of the pronoun *we* in the narrative. A companion of Paul, it is said, would have indicated how it was he happened to be with the apostle, and why he left him. 2. Schleiermacher asks how a new-comer, converted only yesterday, could have expressed himself with so little modesty as: "immediately *we* endeavoured . . .; the Lord had called *us* . . ." (Acts xvi. 10). But how do we know that the author had not been for a long while connected with the apostle when he met with him at Troas (see sec. 3)? Besides, was not Timothy himself also quite a recent convert? That the writer does not explain the circumstances which led to his meetings with Paul and his partings from him, is in accordance with that modest reticence observed by the sacred writers whenever they themselves are concerned. They avoid, with a kind of shame, whatever might direct the attention of the reader to themselves. Obliged by fidelity to truth to indicate his presence wherever he formed part of the missionary company, the author could not do this in a more natural and modest way than that which dispenses with his naming himself.[1]

On the supposition that Luke is the author of the Acts, we may supplement what we know about him by the information supplied by those passages in which the *we* is employed. At Troas, where he was when Paul, whom he had known perhaps long before (p. 21), arrived there, he joined the three missionaries, and passed with them into Europe. He remained at Philippi, the first church founded on this continent, when persecution obliged his three companions to leave the city. For the *we* ceases from this moment. Since this pronoun only reappears when Paul again comes to Philippi, at the end of his third journey (xx. 5), it follows that Luke remained attached to this church during the second and third missionary journey of the apostle, and that then he rejoined him in order to accompany him to Jerusalem. And as the *we* is continued to the end of the book (the interruption, xxi. 17–xxvi. 32, not being really such), Luke must have remained in

[1] Bleek objects, further, that Luke is not mentioned in the Epistles to the Thessalonians, the Corinthians, and the Philippians. But if Luke remained at Philippi, why should he be mentioned in the letters to the Thessalonians, which were written from Achaia a little later? If he is not *named* in the Epistles to the Corinthians, he appears at least to be referred to as one of the most eminent of the evangelists of Greece, 2 Cor. viii. 18 and 22 (though it is not certain that this passage refers to him). And what necessity was there that he should be named in these letters? As to the Epistle to the Philippians, at the time when Paul wrote it, it might very well happen that Luke was neither at Rome nor Philippi. To Bleek's other objection, that the author of the Acts reckons according to the Jewish calendar, which does not suit a writer of heathen origin, Zeller rightly replies that "in the case of a companion of Paul, this was just the only natural mode of reckoning."

Palestine with the apostle during the time of his imprisonment in Cæsarea. This explains the expression (xxvii. 1): "And when it was determined *we should sail* into Italy." Luke, therefore, with Aristarchus (xxvi. 2), was Paul's companion in his journey to Rome. According to the Epistles, from that time to the end, save during those temporary absences when he was called away in the service of the gospel, he faithfully shared Paul's sufferings and toil.

Before leaving the domain of Scripture, we must mention an ingenious conjecture, due to Thiersch, which appears to us open to no substantial objection. From these words, "Only Luke is with me" (2 Tim. iv. 11), compared with what follows almost immediately (ver. 13), "Bring with thee the books, and especially the parchments," this writer has concluded that at the time Paul thus wrote he was occupied in some literary labour for which these manuscripts were required. In this case it must also be admitted that Luke, who was alone with him at the time, was not unacquainted with this labour, if even it was not his own.

These results obtained from Scripture fit in without difficulty with a piece of information supplied by the Fathers Eusebius and Jerome[1] tell us that Luke was originally from Antioch. Meyer and De Wette see in this nothing but an exegetical conclusion, drawn from Acts xiii. 1, where mention is made of one Lucius exercising his ministry in the church at Antioch. But this supposition does very little honour to the discernment of these Fathers, since in this very passage Lucius is described as originally from Cyrene in Africa. Besides, the name Lucius (from the root *lux, lucere*) has quite a different etymology from Lucas, which is an abbreviation from *Lucanus* (as Silas from Silvanus, etc.). If Luke had really found a home at Antioch, we can understand the marked predilection with which the foundation of the church in that city is related in the Acts. In the lines devoted to this fact (xi. 20–24) there is a spirit, animation, and freshness which reveal the charm of delightful recollections. And in this way we easily understand the manner in which the scene at Troas is described (xvi. 10). Paul and the gospel were old acquaintances to Luke when he joined the apostle at Troas.

[1] *Hist. Eccl.* iii. 4; *De vir. illustr.* c. 7.

We cannot, on the other hand, allow any value to the statement of Origen and Epiphanius, who reckon Luke in the number of the seventy disciples; this opinion is contrary to the declaration of Luke himself, i. 2. Could Luke be, according to the opinion referred to by Theophylact, that one of the two disciples of Emmaus whose name is not recorded? This opinion appears to be a conjecture rather than a tradition. The historian Nicephorus Kallistus (fourteenth century) makes Luke the painter who transmitted to the church the portraits of Jesus and His mother. This information rests, perhaps, as Bleek presumes, on a confusion of our evangelist with some ancient painter of the same name.[1] We know absolutely nothing certain respecting the latter part of his life. The passage in Jerome, found in some old editions of the *De viris*, according to which Luke lived a celibate to the age of eighty-four years, is not found in any ancient manuscript; it is an interpolation. Gregory Nazianzen (*Orat.* iii. *Advers. Julian.*) is the first who confers on him the honour of martyrdom; Nicephorus maintains that he was hanged on an olive tree in Greece at the age of eighty years. These are just so many legends, the origin of which we have no means of ascertaining. It appears, however, that there was a widespread tradition that he ended his days in Achaia. For there, according to Jerome (*De vir. ill.* c. 7), the Emperor Constantine sought for his ashes to transport them to Constantinople. Isidore maintains that they were brought from Bithynia.

Is this person really the author of our third Gospel and of the Acts? We have to study the testimonies on which, historically speaking, this opinion rests.

II.

1. At the basis of all the particular testimonies we must place the general opinion of the Church as expressed in its title, *According to Luke.* There was but one conviction on this point in the second century from one extremity of the Church to the other, as we can still prove by the ancient versions in the Syriac and Latin tongues, the *Peschito* and the *Italic.* As

[1] We can only cite as critical fancies the opinion of Kohlreif, which identifies Luke and Silas (*lucus = silva*), and that of Lange, who makes Luke the same person as the Aristion of Papias (*lucere* = ἀριστεύειν).

to the meaning of the prep. *κατά, according to,* in this title, see the exegesis. We will only observe here, that if this preposition could bear the sense of *in the manner of, after the example of,* in the case of Matthew and John, who were apostles, and therefore original authors of an evangelical tradition, this explanation becomes impossible when applied to Mark and Luke, who, since they never accompanied Jesus, could not assume the part of creators of a special tradition, but could only be designated *compilers.*

2. The first special testimony is implied in a passage of Justin Martyr, who, in reference to Jesus' sweat in Gethsemane, says:[1] "As that is related in the memoirs (*ἀπομνημονεύματα*), which I say were composed by His apostles and by their companions." It appears to us indisputable (although criticism has sought other interpretations), that among those books which Justin possessed, and of which he speaks elsewhere as "the memoirs which are called *Gospels,*" there must have been, according to this passage, at least *two* Gospels emanating from apostles, and two proceeding from coadjutors of the apostles. And as the incident to which this Father here alludes is only recorded in Luke, Justin regarded the author of this book as one of the men *who had accompanied the apostles.*

3. In the fragment ascribed to *Muratori,* written about 180, and containing the tradition of the churches of Italy respecting the books of the New Testament, we read as follows: "Thirdly, the book of the Gospel according to St. Luke. This Luke, a physician, when Paul, after the ascension of Christ, had received him among his followers as a person zealous for righteousness (*juris studiosum*), wrote in his own name and according to his own judgment (*ex opinione*). Neither, again, had he himself seen the Lord in the flesh. Carrying his narrative as far back as he could obtain information (*prout assequi potuit*), he commenced with the birth of John." After having spoken of the Gospel of John, the author passes on to the Acts: "The Acts of all the Apostles," he says, "are written in a single book. Luke has included in it, for the excellent Theophilus, all that took place in his presence; as also he clearly points out in a separate form (*semotè*) not only the

[1] *Dial. c. Tryph.* c. 22

suffering of Peter, but further, Paul's departure from Rome for Spain."

With the exception of the name of Luke, which is derived from the tradition received throughout the entire Church, this testimony respecting the Gospel seems to us nothing more than a somewhat bold reproduction of the contents of Luke's preface, combined with the information supplied by Col. iv. 14 as to his profession. *In his own name:* that is to say, in obedience to an inward impulse, on his own personal responsibility; not in the name of an apostle or a church; an allusion to "It hath appeared good to me also" (i. 3). *According to his own judgment:* an allusion to the fact that his narrative was not that of an eye-witness, but in accordance with the opinion he had formed of the facts by help of tradition and his own researches (i. 2). *Neither again* had he himself seen: any more than Mark, of whom the author of the fragment had just spoken. The expression, *as he could obtain information,* refers to what Luke says of the care he had taken to go back as far as possible, and to narrate events in the best order. The term *juris studiosum* (which Hilgenfeld supposes to be the translation of τοῦ δικαίου ζηλωτήν, in the original Greek, which he admits) might also be translated, *a man skilled in questions of legal right;* able, consequently, to make himself useful to Paul whenever he had to deal with the Roman tribunals. But the term ζηλωτής rather favours the sense we have given in our translation. If the passage relating to the Acts has been accurately rendered into Latin, or if the text of it has not been altered, we might infer from it that Luke had narrated, in a third work (*semotè, separately*), the subsequent history of Peter and Paul. In any case, the whole testimony is remarkable for its very sobriety. It does not show the slightest tendency, any more than the preface of the evangelist himself, to ascribe divine authority to this writing. On the contrary, the human aspect of the work comes out very strongly in these expressions: *in his own name, according to his judgment, as far as he was able to obtain information.* Perhaps the author wished to contrast this entirely natural mode of composition with the widely different origin of the Gospel of John, which he describes directly afterwards.

4. At the same period, Irenæus expresses himself thus re-

specting the third Gospel (*Adv. Hær.* iii. 1): "Luke, a companion of Paul, wrote in a book the gospel preached by the latter." Irenæus quotes from our Gospel more than eighty times. This testimony and the preceding are the first two in which Luke is indicated by name as the author of this book.

5. Tertullian, in his book *Against Marcion* (iv. 2), expresses himself thus: "Of the apostles, John and Matthew inspire our faith; of the coadjutors of the apostles, Luke and Mark confirm it." He reminds Marcion "that, not only in the churches founded by the apostles, but in all those which are united to them by the bond of the Christian mystery, this Gospel of Luke has been received without contradiction (*stare*) from the moment of its publication, whilst the greater part are not even acquainted with that of Marcion." He says, lastly (*ibid.* iv. 5), "that several persons of his time have been accustomed to attribute Luke's work to Paul himself, as well as Mark's to Peter." He neither pronounces for nor against this opinion.

6. Origen, in a passage cited by Eusebius (*H. E.* vi. 25), expressed himself thus: "Thirdly, the Gospel according to Luke, cited approvingly (ἐπαινούμενον) by Paul." It appears from the whole passage that he alludes, on the one hand, to the expression *my Gospel*, employed three times by Paul (Rom. ii. 16, xvi. 25; 2 Tim. ii. 8); on the other, to the passage 2 Cor. viii. 18, 19, which he applied to Luke.

7. Eusebius says (*H. E.* iii. 4): "It is maintained that it is of the Gospel according to Luke that Paul is accustomed to speak whenever he makes mention in his writings of *his Gospel.*"

8. Jerome (*De vir. ill.* c. 7) also refers to this opinion, but attributes it to *some persons* only (*quidam suspicantur*).

We have three observations to make on these testimonies.

1. If they are somewhat late,—it is only about A.D. 180 that Luke's name appears,—we must observe, on the other hand, that they are not the expression of the individual opinion of the writers in whose works they occur, but appear incidentally as the expression of the ancient, unbroken, and undisputed conviction of the entire Church. These writers give expression to the fact as a matter of which no one was ignorant. They

would not have dreamed of announcing it, unless some special circumstance had called for it. The ecclesiastical character, at once universal and hereditary, of these testimonies, even when they date only from the second century, enable us to ascertain the conviction of the first. In fact, what prevailed then was not individual criticism, but tradition. Clement of Alexandria, after having quoted a passage from *the Gospel of the Egyptians* (*Strom.* iii. p. 465), immediately adds: "But we have not seen this passage in the four Gospels *which have been transmitted to us* (*ἐν τοῖς παραδεδομένοις ἡμῖν τέσσαρσιν εὐαγγελίοις*)." The bishop Serapion having found, in the parish church of Rhodes, in Cilicia, a so-called Gospel of Peter, containing Gnostic sentiments, wrote a letter to those who made use of it, a portion of which has been preserved by Eusebius (*H. E.* vi. 12, ed. Lœmmer), and it ends with these words: "Knowing well that such writings have not been transmitted (*ὅτι τὰ τοιαῦτα* [*ψευδεπίγραφα*] *οὐ παρελάβομεν*)." The traditional origin of the convictions of the Church respecting the origin of the sacred writings is the only explanation of their stability and universality. An opinion formed upon individual criticism could never have had these characteristics. It is very remarkable that the tradition respecting our Gospel is not disowned even by the ecclesiastical parties most opposed to Paul. Irenæus (iii. 15) declares that the Ebionites made use of our Gospel, and we can prove it ourselves by the quotations from the writings of Luke which we find in the *Clementine Homilies* (ix. 22, xix. 2). The plot even of this religious romance is borrowed from the book of the Acts. Now, in order that parties so opposed to each other, as Marcion on the one hand and the Ebionites on the other, should agree in making use of our Gospel, the conviction of its antiquity and authority must have been very ancient and very firmly established (*stare*, Tert.). There is another fact more striking still. The only sect of the second century which appears to have expressly rejected the book of the Acts, that of the Severians, took no exception to the Gospel of Luke. These results perfectly agree with those to which we were led by the facts enumerated, sec. 1. Thus the blank that exists between the first positive testimonies which we meet with in the second century and the apostolic age is filled up by fact.

2. It is important to observe the gradual change in the tradition which manifests itself during the course of the second and third centuries. The nearer we approach its original sources, the more sober the tradition. In the eyes of Justin, the author of our Gospel is simply *a companion of the apostles.* In the fragment of Muratori the same information reappears without amplification. Strictly speaking, Irenæus does not go beyond this; only he already aims to establish a connection between the writing of Luke and the preaching of Paul. Tertullian notices an opinion prevalent in his time which goes much further,—namely, that Paul himself was the author of this Gospel. Last of all, Origen distinctly declares that when Paul said *my Gospel,* he meant the Gospel of Luke. This progression is just what we want to enable us to verify the real historical character of the tradition in its primitive form. If the original information had been invented under the influence of the apologetic interest which moulded the tradition later on, would it not have begun where it ended?

3 The supposition that the name of Luke, which has been affixed to our Gospel, was merely an hypothesis of the Fathers, gives no explanation why they should have preferred a man so seldom named as Luke, instead of fixing their choice on one of those fellow-labourers of the apostle that were better known, such as Timothy, Silas, or Titus, whom modern criticism has thought of. The obscurity in which this personage would be veiled, if his name did not figure at the head of the writings which are attributed to him, is one of the best guarantees of the tradition which declares him the author of them. We do not see, then, what, in a historic point of view, could invalidate the force of the ecclesiastical testimony on this point; and we agree with Holtzmann (*Die synopt. Evang.* p. 377), when he says that "this tradition is only to be rejected from the point where it proceeds to place the composition of our Gospel under the guarantee of Paul himself."

Three opinions have been put forth by modern criticism on the question under consideration.

1. An "anonymous Saxon,"[1] while declaring that our Gospel is nothing but a tissue of falsehoods, a pamphlet com-

[1] *Die Evangelien, ihr Geist, ihre Verfasser und ihr Verhältniss zu einander,* 1st ed. 1845; 2d, 1852.

posed out of hatred of Peter and the Twelve, boldly attributes it to Paul himself.

2. Hilgenfeld, Zeller, etc., think that this writing is the work of an unknown Christian at the beginning of the second century.

3. Most admit, in conformity with the traditional opinion, that the author is the Luke mentioned in Paul's Epistles. We only mention, to show that we have not forgotten it, the opinion of Mayerhoff, never adopted by any one else, and which was only the very logical consequence of Schleiermacher's on the portions in which *we* occurs in the book of the Acts,—namely, that our Gospel, as well as these portions should be attributed to Timothy.

SEC. III.—COMPOSITION OF THE THIRD GOSPEL.

We possess nothing from tradition but some scanty and uncertain information respecting the origin of our Gospel.

I. As to the *time*, the greater part of the critics are wrong in making Irenæus say that Luke wrote *after the death* (or the departure from Rome) of *Peter and Paul* (*post horum excessum*, iii. 1). This is a false conclusion drawn from the fact that Irenæus speaks of the Gospel of Luke *after* that of Mark, to which this chronological statement applies. The order in which this Father here speaks of the Gospels and their origin may be simply the order of these books in the canon, and in no way of the date of their composition. We find in this same Irenæus (iii. 9, 10) the following order: Matthew, Luke, Mark.

The only real traditional information which we possess on this point is that of Clement of Alexandria, who states it as a fact transmitted by *the presbyters who have succeeded each other from the beginning* (ἀπὸ τῶν ἀνέκαθεν πρεσβυτέρων), "that the Gospels containing the genealogies were written first (προγεγράφθαι τῶν εὐαγγελίων τὰ περιέχοντα τὰς γενεαλογίας)." Eus. *Hist. Eccl.* vi. 14. According to this, Matthew and Luke were composed before Mark. Further, since, according to this very Clement and these same authorities, Mark must have been composed at Rome during Peter's life, it follows that, according to the view embodied in this tradition, Luke was composed prior to the death of this apostle. The sober and original form of the former of these two traditions, the respectable authority on which it rests, the impossibility of its having been deduced from an exegetical combination, seeing that there is no logical connection between the criterion indicated (the presence of a genealogy) and the date which is assigned to it, seem to me to confer a much higher value on this ancient testimony than modern criticism generally accords to it.

The reasons for which so early a date of composition is rejected are purely internal. It is thought that the Gospel itself yields proofs of a later date than would be indicated by this tradition of Clement. Baur, who has fixed it the latest, places the composition after A.D. 130; Hilgenfeld, from 100 to 110; Zeller, at the commencement of the second century or earlier; Volkmar, about 100; Keim, about 90. The other critics, Meyer, De Wette, Bleek, Reuss, who come nearer in general to the traditional opinion, limit themselves to saying, *after* the fall of Jerusalem; Holtzmann, between 70 and 80; Tholuck, Guericke, Ebrard, *before* the fall of Jerusalem. In the concluding dissertation, we shall weigh the exegetical reasons for and against these different opinions. But it appears to us, that the facts mentioned (sec. 1) already make it clear that every opinion which places the composition in the second century is historically untenable. The use which the continuator of Mark and Clement of Rome make of our Gospel, and the use which this same Clement and the author of the *Testaments of the Twelve Patriarchs* make of the Acts, render so late a date of composition quite impossible.

II. As to the *place*, we have only two hints, and we can form no critical judgment of their value. Jerome (*De vir. ill.* c. 7) says: "Luke, a physician, who composed his book in the countries of Achaia and Bœotia." On the other hand, in the *Peschito*, the title of our Gospel runs thus: "Gospel of Luke the Evangelist, which he published and preached in Greek (*quod protulit et evangelisavit græce*) in Alexandria the Great." The two statements are not necessarily contradictory. Luke may have composed his work in Greece and have published it in Alexandria, which was the great centre of the book-world at that time.

Criticism cannot certainly feel itself bound by such late and uncertain information. Hilgenfeld, who on this point differs least from tradition, places the composition in Achaia or Macedonia; Köstlin at Ephesus; the majority at Rome or in Italy. We shall discuss the question in concluding.

III. The author himself announces his *aim* in his preface. He wrote with the design of completing the Christian instruction of a man in high station, named Theophilus. This name could not denote a purely fictitious person, as Origen supposed, who was inclined to apply it to every Christian endowed with spiritual powers. Neither could the Jewish high priest Theophilus, of whom Josephus speaks, be intended (*Antiq.* xviii. 6. 3, xix. 6. 2), nor the Athenian of this name mentioned by Tacitus (*Ann.* ii. 55). The only traditional information we possess about this person is that found in the *Clementine Recognitions* (x. 71), about the middle of the second century: "So that Theophilus, who was at the head of all the men in power at the city (of Antioch), consecrated, under the name of a church, the great basilica (the palace) in which he resided."[1] According to this, Theophilus was a great lord residing in the capital of Syria. We have already referred to the reasons which lead us to think that Luke himself was originally from this city. Did he belong to the household of Theophilus? Had he been his slave, and then his freedman? Lobeck has remarked that the termination ας was a contraction particularly frequent in the names of slaves.[2] Physicians appear to have frequently belonged to the class of slaves or freedmen.[3] If Luke, freed by Theophilus, practised as a physician at Antioch, and if he was brought to the faith at the time of the founding of the church in that city, he might very well have decided to accompany the apostle in his mission. In this case he would have rejoined him at Troas, just as he was about to pass over into Europe; and there would no longer be anything surprising in the pronoun *we*, by which he assigns himself a place in the missionary company.

[1] "*Ita ut Theophilus, qui erat cunctis potentibus in civitate sublimior, domûs suæ ingentem basilicam ecclesiæ nomine consecraret.*"

[2] Wolf's *Analecten*, iii. 49; comp. Tholuck, *Glaubwürd.* p. 148.

[3] Quintilian, *Instit.* vii. 2: *Medicinam factitasse manumissum.* Suet. *Calig.* c. 8: *Mitto cum eo ex servis meis medicum.* Comp. Cic. *pro Cluentio*, c. 63 Seneca, *De Beneficiis*, iii. 24. See Hug, *Einl.* ii. p. 134.

On this supposition, also, we can understand why he should have dedicated his work to his old friend and patron. This dedication does not mean, however, that the book was intended for Theophilus alone. Until the discovery of printing, the publication of a work was a very costly undertaking; and authors were accustomed to dedicate their works to some high personage of their acquaintance, who could procure the writer an opportunity of reading his production in some select circle, and have the first copies prepared at his own expense. In this way he opened to the author the road to publicity. Whoever was obliging enough to undertake this responsibility was called the *patronus libri.* Such, doubtless, was the service which Theophilus was asked to render to Luke's work. In reality, Luke addressed himself, through the medium of this person, to all that part of the Church to which Theophilus belonged, to the churches of the Greek world, and, in a certain sense, to the entire Church.

The object he had in view, according to the Fathers, was simply to make known the history of Jesus, more particularly to converts from the heathen. Modern criticism has found in the preface, and even in the narrative, indications of a more special design connected with the great movement of ecclesiastical polemics which it conceives occupied the first and second centuries. According to Baur (*Marcus Evang.* p. 223 et seq.), the original Luke, of which Marcion has preserved a faithful impression, was intended to oppose the Jewish Christianity of the Twelve, as represented by the Gospel of Matthew in its original form. The author sought to depreciate the apostles in order to exalt Paul; whilst our canonical Luke, which is a later version of this original Luke, was directed rather against the unbelieving and persecuting Judaism. The former part of this proposition has been reproduced and developed in still stronger terms by "the anonymous Saxon," who sees nothing in the third Gospel but a bitter pamphlet of the Apostle Paul against the Twelve, and more especially against Peter. M. Burnouf has made himself the advocate of this view in the *Revue des Deux Mondes.*[1] But even in the Tübingen school a protest has been raised against what have been called the "exaggerations" of Baur. Zeller finds no trace either in the Gospel or the

[1] December 1865.

Acts of this spirit of systematic depreciation of Peter and the Twelve. According to him, the author simply wishes to check excessive admiration for Peter, and to preserve Paul's place *by the side of* this apostle. With this aim, he guards himself from directly opposing the Christianity of the Twelve; he simply places side by side with the views of the Jewish-Christian apostles those of Paul, which he endeavours, as far as possible, to exhibit as identical with the former. That in this attempt at reconciliation real history is sacrificed, appears evident to this critic. He accounts in this way for the fact that in this Gospel Jesus gives utterance alternately to particularist teaching (in the sense of the Twelve), and to universalist passages suited to the thought of Paul.

Volkmar combats this view. Nowhere in our Gospel, not even in the facts and discourses of the first two chapters, does he discover those particularist or Ebionitish elements, by means of which, according to Zeller, the author sought to win the confidence of the Jewish-Christian party. In his judgment. the Gospel of Luke is purely Pauline. In opposition to that fiery manifesto of apostolic Jewish-Christianity, the Apocalypse, composed in A.D. 68, Mark, five years afterwards, published his Gospel, the earliest in point of time, and written in the sense of a moderate Paulinism; later still, Luke re-wrote this book, laying still greater emphasis on the principles of the apostle to the Gentiles. In all these suppositions the idea is, that Jesus speaks in the Gospel, not as He really spoke, but as it suits the evangelist to make Him speak.

All these opinions as to the aim of Luke's work are connected with the great question, suggested by Baur, of a fundamental difference of view between Paul and the Twelve, which is represented as the real starting-point of the development of the Church and of the entire Christian literature. This question, with which that of the origin of the Gospels is now inseparably connected. will be discussed in our concluding paragraphs.

SEC. IV.—SOURCES OF THE THIRD GOSPEL.

There is no room for an inquiry into the sources whence the author of a Gospel derived his knowledge of the facts which he transmits to us, except on two conditions: 1. That the evangelist is not regarded as an eye-witness of the facts related. Now this is a character which the author of the third Gospel expressly disclaims (i. 2). 2. That we are not governed by that false notion of inspiration, according to which the sacred history was revealed and dictated to the evangelists by the Holy Spirit. As far as our third Gospel is concerned, this idea is altogether excluded by what the author says himself of the information he had to obtain to qualify himself to write his book (i. 3).

It is at once, then, the right and the duty of criticism to inquire from what sources the author derived the incidents which he records. This question, however, is immediately complicated with another and more general question, as to the relation between our three synoptics. For many regard it as probable, and even certain, that some one of our Gospels served as a source of information to the writer who composed another of them. It is not our intention to relate here the history of the discussion of this great theological and literary problem.[1] We do not even intend in this place to set forth the numerous and apparently contradictory facts which bring it up afresh after every attempted solution. In view of the exegetical work we have in hand, we shall here bring forward only two matters:—

I. The *elements* of which criticism has availed itself in order to solve the problem.

II. The principal *systems* which it constructs at the present day by means of these elements.

I.

The factors which criticism has hitherto employed for the solution of the problem are four in number:—

1. *Oral tradition* (παράδοσις), or the reproduction of the

[1] We refer our readers to the generally accurate account of M. Nicolas, *Etudes Critiques sur le N. T.* pp. 45–85.

apostolic testimony, as they gave it when they founded the churches. This factor must have borne a very essential part in determining the form of the evangelical historical writings from their very commencement. Luke indicates its importance, i. 2. According to this expression, *even as they delivered them unto us*, this tradition was the original source of the oral or written narratives which were circulated in the churches. It branched out into a thousand channels through the ministry of the *evangelists* (Eph. iv. 11; 2 Tim. iv. 5). Gieseler, with his exquisite historical tact, was the first to bring out all the value of this fact as serving to explain the origin of the Gospels.[1]

2. Separate writings or *memoirs* (*ἀπομνημονεύματα*) on some feature or particular part of the Saviour's life, on a discourse or a miracle which an evangelist related, and which he or one of his hearers put in writing that it might not be forgotten; or, again, some private account preserved amongst their family papers by the persons more immediately interested in the evangelical drama;—we may regard our Gospel as a collection of a number of such detached writings, pieced together by the hand of an editor. Carrying out this view, Schleiermacher made a very ingenious analysis of the Gospel of Luke in a little work[2] which was to be completed by a similar study of the Acts, but the second part never appeared. Thus this scholar thought he could discriminate, in the portion ix. 51–xix. 48, traces of two distinct writings, the first of which would be the journal of a companion of Jesus in His journey to the feast of Dedication, the second the journal of another companion of Jesus when He went up to the feast of the Passover. The truth of this second means of explanation might be supported by the proper meaning of the word *ἀνατάξασθαι*, *to arrange in order*, i. 1, if only it were proved that the arrangement implied by this word refers to the documents, and not to the facts themselves.

Under this category of detached writings would have to be ranged also the various documents which several critics

[1] *Historisch-kritischer Versuch über die Entstehung und die frühesten Schicksale der Schriftlichen Evangelien*, Leipzig 1818.

[2] *Ueber die Schriften des Lucas, ein Kritischer Versuch*, von Schleiermacher. Berlin 1817.

believe they have detected in Luke's work, on account of a kind of literary or dogmatic patchwork which they find in it. Thus Kuinöl, following Marsh, regarded the portion ix. 51–xviii. 14 as a more ancient writing, containing a collection of the precepts of Jesus, to which he gave the name of *gnomonology*. Hilgenfeld[1] also distinguishes from the narrative as a whole, which has the universalist character of the Christianity of St. Paul, certain passages of Jewish-Christian tendency, which he regards as some very early materials, proceeding from the apostolic Church itself. The entire portion ix. 51–xix. 28 rests, according to him, on a more ancient writing which the author introduced into his work, working it up afresh both in substance and form. Köstlin[2] thinks it may be proved that there were some sources of *Judean* origin, and others of *Samaritan* origin, which furnished Luke with a knowledge of the facts of which the two countries of Judea and Samaria are the scene in our Gospel. Keim, while declaring himself for this view, admits besides other sources of *Pauline* origin; for example, the document of the institution of the Holy Supper.[3] It is impossible to doubt that the genealogical document iii. 23 et seq. existed before our Gospel, and, such as it is, was inserted in it by the author (see on iii. 23).

3. We must allow, further, the existence of longer and fuller documents which Luke might have used. Does he not speak himself, in his preface, of writings that were already numerous at the time he was writing (πολλοί), which in respect of contents must have been of very much the same nature as his own, that is to say, veritable Gospels? He designates them by the name of διήγησις, a word which has been wrongly applied to detached writings of the kind that Schleiermacher admitted, and which can only apply to a consecutive and more or less complete narrative. If such works existed in great number, and were known to Luke, it is difficult to think that he has not endeavoured to profit by them. The only question then is, whether, on the supposition that they no longer exist, we can form any idea of them by means

[1] *Die Evangelien*, 1852.
[2] *Der Ursprung und die Compos. der syn. Evang.* 1853.
[3] *Geschichte Jesu.* + i., Zurich 1867.

of our Gospel, for the composition of which they supplied some materials. Keim thinks he recognises, as a general basis of Luke's work, a Jewish-Christian Gospel, which must have been nearly related to our Matthew, very probably its direct descendant, but distinguished from it by an unhealthy tendency to Ebionitism and Dualism. The spirit of this fundamental document would betray itself all through Luke's work. Ewald imagines a whole series of writings of which Luke must have availed himself,—a Hebrew Gospel by Philip the deacon, a collection of the discourses of Jesus by the Apostle Matthew, of which Papias speaks, etc. (see further on). Bleek,[1] reviving in a new form the hypothesis of a primitive Gospel (a manual composed, according to Eichhorn, for the use of evangelists, under apostolic sanction), admits, as a basis of our Gospels of Matthew and Luke, a Greek Gospel, written in Galilee by a believer, who at certain times had himself accompanied Jesus. This earliest account of the Saviour's life would mould all the subsequent evangelical narrations. The writings of the πολλοί, *many* (i. 1), would be only variations of it, and our three synoptics merely different versions of the same. Lastly, we know that many critics at the present day find the principal source of Luke and the two other synoptics (at least of the narrative part) in a supposed Gospel of Mark, older than our canonical Mark, and to which they give the name of Proto-Mark (Reuss, Réville, Holtzmann, etc.).[2] All these writings, anterior to that of Luke, and only known to us by the traces of them discovered in his work, are lost at the present day.

4. Would it be impossible for some writing which we still possess to be one of the sources of Luke—for example, one of our two synoptics, or even both of them? This fourth means of explanation has at all times been employed by criticism. At the present day, it is still used with great confidence by many. According to Baur,[3] Matthew was the direct and sole source of Luke; Mark proceeded from both. Hilgenfeld

[1] *Einleitung in das N. T.* 1862; *Synoptische Erklärung der drei ersten Evangelien*, 1869.

[2] Reuss, *Geschichte der heiligen Schriften N. T.*, 3d ed. 1860; Réville, *Etudes critiques sur l'évang. selon Saint Matthieu*, 1862; Holtzmann, *Die synopt. Ev.* 1863.

[3] Baur, *Das Marcus-Evangelium*, 1851.

also puts Matthew first; but he interposes Mark between Matthew and Luke. According to Volkmar,[1] Mark is the primary source; from him proceeded Luke, and Matthew from both.

To sum up: Oral tradition, detached writings, Gospels more or less complete now lost; last of all, one or other of our existing Gospels,—such are the materials by means of which criticism has made various attempts to solve the problem of the origin both of Luke in particular, and of the synoptics in general. Let us endeavour now to describe the systems which actual criticism labours to construct out of these various kinds of materials.

II.

1. We will commence with the self-styled *critical* school of Baur. The common tendency of writers of this school is to represent the synoptics as deriving their contents from each other. In their view, the contents of our Gospels cannot be historical, because they contain the inadmissible element of miracles.[2] Consequently they regard our Gospels, not as real historical narrations, but as compositions of a poetical or didactic character. The differences between them are not in any way natural divergences proceeding from such undesigned modifications as tradition undergoes in course of oral transmission, or from the diversity of written sources, but result from different dogmatic tendencies in the writers of the Gospels which they perfectly reflect. Each evangelist has reproduced his matter with a free hand, modifying it in accordance with his personal views. In reality, then, our Gospels are the reflection, not of the object they describe, but of the controversial or conciliatory tendencies of their authors. These books make us acquainted, not with the history of Jesus, but with that of the Church, and of the different theories respecting the Founder of the gospel, which have been successively held in it. This common result of the school appears

[1] Volkmar, *Die Evangelien*, 1870.

[2] Hilgenfeld (*Die Evangelien*, p. 530): "The principal argument for the later origin of our Gospels is always this fact, that they relate very many things about the life of Jesus, which certainly could not have taken place as they narrate them."

in its most pronounced form in Baur and Volkmar, in a milder form in Köstlin and Hilgenfeld.

Baur himself, as we have seen, makes, as Griesbach and De Wette did before him, Luke proceed from Matthew, and Mark from Luke and Matthew united. This relationship is made out in this way. There was first of all a strictly legal and particularist Matthew, reflecting the primitive Christianity of the Twelve, and of the church of Jerusalem. From this original Matthew afterwards proceeded our canonical Matthew, the narrative being re-cast in a universalist sense (between 130 and 134). In opposition to the original Matthew there appeared first a Luke, which was altogether Pauline, or anti-legal; this was the writing Marcion adopted, and from which proceeded later on our canonical Luke. The latter was the result of a revision designed to harmonize it with the Jewish-Christian views (about 140). Reconciliation having thus been reached from both sides, Mark followed, in which the original contrast is entirely neutralized. For its matter, the latter is naturally dependent on the other two.

The *anonymous Saxon* [1] starts with the same general notion; but he seasons it in a piquant fashion. According to him, our synoptics, with the exception of Luke, were indeed composed by the authors to whom the Church attributes them; but they intentionally misrepresented the facts. As to the third, Paul, who was its author, composed it with a view to decry the Twelve and their party.

Hilgenfeld denies the opposition, admitted by Baur, between the original Matthew and a Luke which preceded ours. He believes that, in the very bosom of apostolic and Jewish-Christian Christianity, there was an internal development at work from the first century in a Pauline direction, the result partly of the force of events, but more especially of the influence of the fall of Jerusalem, and the conversion of the Gentiles. He finds a proof of this gradual transformation in the numerous universalist passages of our canonical Matthew, which witness to the changes undergone by the original Matthew. This last writing, the oldest of the Gospels, dated from 70–80. The Gospel of Mark, which followed it, went a

[1] *Sendschreiben an Baur über die Abfassungszeit des Lukas und der Synoptiker*, 1848, p. 26 et seq.

step further in the Pauline direction. It was an imitation of the Gospel of Matthew, but at the same time modified by the oral tradition existing in the church at Rome, which was derived from Peter; it dates from the period from 80–100. Hilgenfeld, therefore, does not recognise Luke's influence anywhere in Mark, while Baur discovers it everywhere. Luke proceeds, according to him, from the two former; he takes a fresh step in the universalist and Pauline direction. It was written before Marcion's time, from 100 to 110. Thus, as this theologian himself remarks, "the formation of our canonical Gospels was completely finished before the time when Baur makes it begin" (*Kanon*, p. 172). With this difference as to dates between the master and his disciple, there is connected a more profound difference still. Instead of a sharp dogmatical contrast which was gradually neutralized, Hilgenfeld admits a progressive development in the very bosom of primitive Jewish Christianity.

With Baur, Mark came third; with Hilgenfeld, second; there was only wanted further a theologian of the same school who should assign him the first place; and this is done at the present time by Volkmar, who follows the example of Storr in the last century. According to him, that fiery manifesto of primitive Jewish Christianity, the Apocalypse, had about 68 declared implacable hostility against St. Paul, representing him (chap. xiii.) as *the false prophet* of the last times, and making the churches founded by him, in comparison with the Jewish-Christian churches, a mere *plebs* (chap. vii.). A moderate Paulinian took up the gauntlet, and wrote (about 73) as a reply our second Gospel, the oldest of all the writings of this kind. It was a didactic poem, on a historical basis,[1] designed to defend Paul and the right of the Gentile churches. Beyond the Old Testament and the Epistles of Paul, the author had no other sources than oral tradition, his Christian experience, the Apocalypse which he opposed, and his creative genius. Somewhat later (about the year 100), a Pauline believer of the Church of Rome, who had travelled in Palestine, worked up this book into a new form by the aid of some traditions which he had collected, and by inserting in it first a genealogical document (*Genealogus*

[1] *Die Evangelien*, p. 461: "*Eine selbstbewusste Lehrpoesie auf historischen Grunde.*"

Hebræorum), and then a writing of Essenist tendency (*Evangelium pauperum*). His aim was to win over to Paulinism the Jewish-Christian part of the Church, which was still in a majority. This was our Luke. Matthew is the result of a fusion of the two preceding writings. It is the manifesto of a moderate Jewish-Christian feeling, which desired to gather all the heathen into the Church, but could not see its way to this at the cost of the abolition of the law, as Paul taught; its composition dates from 110. All the other writings, the existence of which has been supposed by modern criticism, such as a Proto-Matthew, the *Logia*, and a Proto-Mark, in Volkmar's judgment, are nothing but empty critical fancies.

The third, second, and first place in succession having been assigned to Mark, no new supposition seemed possible, at least from the same school. Nevertheless Köstlin has rendered possible the impossible, by assigning to Mark all three positions at once. This complicated construction is difficult to follow: The oldest evangelical record would be that Proto-Mark to which Papias must have referred; it represented the moderate universalism of Peter. From this work, combined with oral tradition and the *Logia* of the Apostle Matthew, would proceed our canonical Matthew. These different works are supposed to have given birth to a *Gospel of Peter*, which closely resembled the original Mark, but was still more like our actual Mark. After that must have appeared Luke, to which all the preceding sources contributed; and last of all our actual Mark, which would be the result of a revision of the original Mark by the help of the canonical Matthew and Luke. The principal waymarks of the route thus traversed are these: Mark (I.); Matthew; Mark (II., or the Gospel of Peter); Luke; Mark (III.). We can only say that this hypothesis is the death-blow of the theory of the Tübingen school, as formerly Marsh's system was of the hypothesis of an original Gospel. The complicated and artificial form this hypothesis is compelled to assume, by the difficulties which weigh upon its simpler forms, is its condemnation. Thus, as Hilgenfeld regretfully observes, "after such multiplied and arduous labours, we are still very far from reaching the least agreement even on the most essential points." Let it be observed that this disagreement is evinced by disciples of one and the same school, which advanced into the critical arena with colours flying, and thundering forth the pæan of victory. Is not such a state of things a serious fact, especially for a school the fundamental idea of which is, that there is an intimate connection between the successive appearances of our Gospels and the history of the primitive Church, of which last this school claims to give the world a new conception? Does not such a complete diversity in fixing the order in which the Gospels appeared, exhibit a no less fundamental disagreement in conceiving of the development of the Church? These are evident symptoms not only of the breaking up of this school, but, above all, of the radical error of the original notion on which it was founded. The opposition in principle between Paulinism and Jewish Christianity, which is an axiom with this school, is also its *πρῶτον ψεῦδος*.

2. We will now enumerate the critical systems which have kept independent of the Tübingen school.

If Bleek, who is at once the most discerning and judicious critic of our day, is in several respects the antipodes of Baur, he agrees with him on one point: the entire dependence he attributes to Mark in relation to the two other synoptics. As has been already mentioned, he makes Matthew and Luke proceed from a Gospel written in Greek by a Galilean believer, who was present at several scenes in the ministry of Jesus in this province. This is the reason why this book has given such great preponderance to the Galilean work. The numerous works of which Luke speaks (i. 1) were all different versions of this, as well as our canonical Matthew and Luke. This important book, with all its offshoots, which preceded our synoptics, is lost; these last, the most complete and best accredited, have alone survived. This conception is simple and clear. Whether it renders a sufficient account of the facts, remains to be seen.

Ritschl, in a remarkable article, has pronounced in favour of the absolute priority of our canonical Mark (to the exclusion of any Proto-Mark). Matthew proceeded, according to him, from Mark, and Luke from both.[1] Ritschl endeavours to prove these statements by a very sagacious analysis of the relations between the narratives of Matthew and Mark on

[1] *Ueber den gegenwärtigen Stand der Kritik der syn. Ev.*, in the *Theol Jahrb.* 1851.

certain points of detail. But the impression we have received from this labour is, that both the method followed, and the results obtained, are more ingenious than solid.

Reuss, Réville, Holtzmann, agree in making two writings, now lost, the original sources of our three synoptical Gospels. These were: 1. The Proto-Mark, which furnished our three evangelists with their general outline, and with the narratives common to them all; 2. The *Logia*, or collection of discourses compiled by Matthew, which was the source for those instructions of Jesus related in common by Matthew and Luke. Our canonical Mark is a reproduction (enlarged according to Reuss, abridged according to Holtzmann) of the former of these two writings. Its author made no use of the *Logia*. Matthew and Luke both proceeded from a fusion of these two fundamental writings. Their authors inserted or distributed, in the outline sketch of the Proto-Mark, the sayings and discourses collected in the *Logia*. But here arises a difficulty. If the sayings of Jesus, as Matthew and Luke convey them to us, are drawn from the same source, how does it happen that Matthew transmits them in the form of large masses of discourse (for example, the Sermon on the Mount, chap. v.–vii.; the collection of parables, chap. xiii., etc.), whilst in Luke these very sayings are more frequently presented to us in the form of detached instructions, occasioned by some accidental circumstance? Of these two different forms, which is to be regarded as most faithful to the original document? Matthew, who groups into large masses the materials that lie side by side in the *Logia*? or Luke, who breaks up the long discourses of the *Logia*, and divides them into a number of particular sayings? Holtzmann decides in favour of the first alternative. According to this writer, we ought to allow that the form of the *Logia* was very nearly that presented by the teaching of Jesus in the narrative of travel, Luke ix. 51–xix. 28. Weizsäcker, on the contrary, defends the second view, and thinks that the long discourses of Matthew are more or less faithful reproductions of the form of the *Logia*. This also is the opinion of M. Réville. We shall have to see whether this hypothesis, under either of its two forms, bears the test of facts.

Ewald sets out in the same way with the two hypotheses

of the Proto-Mark and the *Logia;* but he constructs upon this foundation an exceedingly complicated system, according to which our Luke would be nothing less than the combined result of eight anterior writings:—1. A Gospel written by Philip the Evangelist, which described in the Aramæan language the salient facts of the life of Jesus, with short historical explanations. 2. Matthew's *Logia*, or discourses of Jesus, furnished with short historical introductions. 3. The Proto-Mark, composed by the aid of the two preceding writings, remarkable for the freshness and vivacity of its colouring, and differing very little from our canonical Mark. 4. A Gospel treating of certain critical points in our Lord's life (the temptation, for example). Ewald calls this writing the *Book of the Higher History.* 5. Our canonical Matthew, combining the *Logia* of this apostle with all the other writings already named. 6, 7, and 8. Three writings now lost, which Ewald describes as though he had them in his hands: one of a familiar, tender character; another somewhat brusque and abrupt; the third comprising the narratives of the infancy (Luke i. and ii.). Lastly, 9. Our canonical Luke, composed by the aid of all the preceding (with the exception of our Matthew), and which simply combines the materials furnished by the others. We may add, 10. Our canonical Mark, which with very slight modification is the reproduction of No. 3. This construction certainly does not recommend itself by its intrinsic evidence and simplicity. It may prove as fatal to the hypothesis of a Proto-Mark as was formerly that of Marsh to the hypothesis of a primitive Gospel, or as that of Köstlin at the present day to the Tübingen idea.

Lastly, we see a new mode of explanation appearing, which seems destined to replace for a time the theory, so stoutly maintained by and since Wilke, of the priority of Mark or of the Proto-Mark, whenever it has any considerable connection with this last. This opinion has been developed by Weiss in three very elaborate articles,[1] in which he seeks to prove: 1. That the most ancient work was an *apostolical* Matthew, comprising the discourses, some longer and others shorter, with a

[1] In the *Studien und Kritiken*, 1861; *Jahrbücher für Deutsche Theologie*, 1864; *ibid.* 1865. Since then, Weiss has attempted to prove his theory by a detailed exegesis of Mark.

large number of facts, but without any intention on the part of the author to write the entire history of Jesus. 2. Thereupon appeared Mark, written by the aid of recollections which the author had preserved of the recitals of Peter. This was the first attempt to trace the entire course of the ministry of Jesus. He included in this sketch all the sayings of Jesus contained in the preceding work which could be adapted to his narrative. 3. The author of our *canonical* Matthew made use of this work of Mark, re-wrote it, and supplemented it by the aid of the apostolical Matthew. 4. Luke also re-wrote the two more ancient works, the apostolic Matthew and Mark, but in a very free manner, and enriched his narrative with new materials derived from oral or written tradition.

This combination appears to me to come very near the explanation which is the basis of a recent work of Klostermann.[1] By a consecutive, detailed, delicate analysis of the Gospel of Mark, this scholar proves that the author of this work composed it on the basis of Matthew, enamelling the story with explanatory notes, the substance of which evidently emanated from an eye-witness of the ministry of Jesus, which could have been none other than Peter; in general, the additions refer to the relations of Jesus with His apostles. With Klostermann, as with Weiss, Matthew would be the first and principal written source; but with this difference (if we rightly understand), that with the former this Matthew is our canonical Matthew, whilst in the opinion of Weiss, this last writing differed sensibly from the primitive Matthew, which only appears in our canonical Matthew as transformed by means of Mark. The dependence of Mark on Matthew has then much more stress laid upon it by Klostermann than by Weiss. Klostermann announces a second work, in which he will prove a precisely similar dependence of Luke upon Mark. Thus it is clear, that in proportion as criticism dispenses with the hypothesis of a Proto-Mark, it is compelled to attribute to the primitive Matthew, which at the outset was to be only a collection of discourses, more and more of the historical element; so that in Weiss it again becomes a more or less complete Gospel, and lastly in Klostermann approximates closely to our canonical Matthew itself.

[1] *Das Marcus-Evangelium*, Göttingen 1867.

This question of the origin of the synoptics, and of their mutual relations, must not be regarded as unimportant in regard to the substance of the evangelical beliefs. Just as the view defended by the Tübingen school, according to which our synoptics are simply derived from one another, exhibits the contents of these writings, and the degree of confidence they inspired at the time they appeared, in an unfavourable light (since the differences which exist between them could, in such a case, only proceed from the caprice of the copyists, and the slight faith they placed in the story of their predecessors); so does the other opinion, which looks for different sources, oral or written, whence each writing proceeds, and which are adequate to account for their mutual resemblances or differences, tend to re-establish their general credibility, and their genuineness as historical works.

The following is a table of the opinions of which we have just given an account:—

I.—SCHOOL OF TUEBINGEN.

Baur.

Matthew
|
Luke } Mark.

Hilgenfeld.

Matthew
|
Mark } Luke.

Volkmar.

Mark
|
Luke } Matthew.

Koestlin.

Mark (I.); Matthew
Mark (II.) or Gospel of Peter
|
Luke. } Mark (III.).

II.—INDEPENDENT SYSTEMS.

Ritschl.

Mark
|
Matthew } Luke.

Bleek.

Primitive Gospel
Matthew; Luke
Mark.

Reuss, etc.

Mark (I.) Logia
|
Mark (II.); Matthew; Luke.

Ewald.

Gosp. of Phil. Logia
Mark (I.)
|
Matthew. } Luke.

Weiss.

Matthew (I.)
|
Mark
Matthew (II.); Luke.

Klostermann.

Matthew
|
Mark } Luke.

The state of things which this table portrays is not certainly such as to lead us to regard the question as solved, and the door closed against fresh attempts to explain the origin of the synoptics, particularly the origin of Luke, which is the final term of the problem.

SEC. V.—ON THE PRESERVATION OF THE THIRD GOSPEL.

Are we sure that we possess the book which we are about to study as it came from its author's hands? Taken as a whole, yes. As guarantees of it, we have—1. The general agreement of our text with the most ancient versions, the *Peschito* and the *Italic,* which date from the second century, and with the three Egyptian translations made at the beginning of the third; 2. The general agreement of this text with the quotations of the Fathers of the second and third centuries, Justin, Tatian, Irenæus, Clement, Tertullian, Origen, etc.; lastly, 3. The general uniformity of the manuscripts in which the Greek text has been preserved. If any great changes had been introduced into the text, there would inevitably have been much greater differences among all these documents. These different tests prove that the third Gospel, just as we have it, was already in existence in the churches of the second and third centuries. A text so universally diffused could only proceed from the text that was received from the very first.

The manuscripts containing the text of the New Testament consist of *majuscules,* or manuscripts written in uncial letters (until the tenth century), and of *minuscules,* or manuscripts written in small or cursive writing (from the tenth century). The manuscripts known at the present day, containing the whole or part of the Gospels, number nearly 44 *majuscules,* and more than 500 *minuscules.* The former are, for their antiquity and variety, the most important. Of this number, 19 contain the Gospel of Luke more or less complete; of 11 there only remain some fragments, or series of fragments: there are, in all, 30 documents prior to the tenth century.

Two of the fourth century—

1. The *Sinaiticus* (א).
2. The *Vaticanus* (B).

Five of the fifth century—

3. The *Alexandrinus* (A)

4. The *Codex Ephræmi* (C).
5. Twenty-eight palimpsest leaves (I).
6. Palimpsest fragments found at Wolfenbüttel (Q).
7. Different fragments, Greek with a Sahidic version, comprised in the Sahidic collection of Woide (T^w). T^d denotes similar fragments of the seventh century.

Five of the sixth century—

8. The *Cantabrigiensis* (D)
9. Fragments of a manuscript *de luxe*, written in letters of silver and gold (N).
10. The hymns of Luke (chap. i. ii.) preserved in some psalters (O^c). O^{abdef} denote similar portions of the seventh and ninth centuries.
11. Fragments of a palimpsest of London (R).
12. Fragments of Wolfenbüttel (P).

Five of the eighth century—

13. The *Basiliensis* (E).
14. A manuscript of Paris (L).
15. Fragments of the Gospels, of Paris and of Naples (W^a; W^b).
16. Fragment of Luke at St. Petersburg (Θ^d).
17. The *Zacynthius*, a palimpsest manuscript, found at Zante, comprising the first eleven chapters of Luke (Ξ in Tischendorf, Z in our commentary).

Eight of the ninth century—

18. The Codex *Boreeli* (F).
19. The *Cyprius* (K).
20. A manuscript of Paris (M).
21. A manuscript of Munich (X).
22. A manuscript of Oxford (*Γ*).
23. The *San Gallensis* (*Δ*).
24. A manuscript of Oxford (*Λ*).
25. A manuscript found at Smyrna, and deposited at St Petersburg (*Π*).

Five of the tenth century—

26, 27. The two Codd. of *Seidel* (G. H).
28. A manuscript of the Vatican (S).
29. A manuscript of Venice (U).
30. A manuscript of Moscow (V).

Adding together all the various readings which these documents contain, we find from five to six thousand of them. But in general they are of very secondary importance, and involve no change in the matter of the Gospel history.

On a closer study of them, it is observed that certain manuscripts habitually go together in opposition to others, and thus two principal forms of the text are established,—one which is generally found in the most ancient majuscules, another which is met with in the minuscules and in the less ancient of the majuscules. Some manuscripts oscillate between these two forms.

As the text on which Erasmus formed the first edition of the New Testament in Greek was that of certain minuscules in the Bâle library, and this text has continued to form the basis of subsequent editions, of which that of the Elzevirs of 1633 is the most generally diffused, it is evident that this, called the *Received Text*, is rather that of the minuscules and less ancient majuscules than the text of the old majuscules. This text is also called *Byzantine*, because it is probably the one which was uniformly fixed in the churches of the Greek Empire. Those of our majuscules which represent it are the following: E. F. G. H. R. M. S. U. V. *Γ*. *Δ*. *Π*. This form of the text is also called *Asiatic*.

The opposite form, which is found in the older majuscules, B. G. L. R. X. Z., appears to come from Alexandria, where, in the first centuries of the Church, manuscripts were most largely produced. For this reason this text takes the name of *Alexandrine*. Some manuscripts, while ordinarily following the Alexandrine, differ from them more or less frequently; these are א. A. D. *Δ*. The text of א and of D resembles, in many instances, the ancient Latin translation, the *Italic*.

A middle form between these two principal texts is found in the fragments denoted by N. O. W. Y. *Θ*.

It is a constant question, which of the two texts, the Alexandrine or the Byzantine, reproduces with the greatest fidelity the text of the original document. It is a question which, in our opinion, cannot be answered in a general way and *à priori*, and which must be solved in each particular instance by exegetical skill.

ABBREVIATIONS.

The abbreviations we shall use are generally those which Tischendorf has adopted in his eighth edition.

1. Fathers.

Just., Justin; Ir., Irenæus; Or., Origen, etc.

2. Versions.

Vss., versions.

It., the *Italic*, comprising the different Latin translations prior to Jerome's (from the second century): *a*, *b*, *c*, etc., denote the different documents of the *Italic*; *a* the *Vercellensis* (4th c.); *b* the *Veronensis* (5th c.); *c* the *Colbertinus* (11th c.), etc.

Vg., the *Vulgate*, Jerome's translation (4th c.); Am., Fuld., denote the principal documents of this translation,—the *Amiatinus* (6th c.), the *Fuldensis* (*id.*), etc.

Syr., the Syriac translations. Syr^{sch}, the *Peschito*, Schaaf's edition; Syr^{cur}, a more ancient translation than the *Peschito*, discovered and published by Cureton. *Syr.* in brief (in our own use), these two united.

Cop., the Coptic translation (3d c.).

3. Manuscripts.

Mss., the manuscripts; Mjj., the majuscules; Mnn., the minuscules.

The letter denoting a manuscript with the sign * (א*, B*) denotes the original text in opposition to corrections inserted in the text afterwards. The small figures added to this same letter (B^2, C^2, etc.) signify first, second correction. For the manuscript א, which is in a peculiar condition, $א^a$, $א^b$ denote the most ancient corrections, made by at least two different hands according to the text of different MSS. from that from which א was copied, and $א^c$ similar corrections, but made a little later (7th c.), and differing sometimes from each other ($א^{ca}$, $א^{cb}$). F^a, some quotations from the Gospels annotated in the margin of the *Coislinianus* (H. of the Epistles of Paul).

4. Editions.

T. R., the received text, viz. the ed. *Elzevir* of 1633, which is generally the reproduction of the third ed. of Stephens; ϛ (Steph.) denotes the received text and that of Stephens united, where they are identical · $ϛ^e$ (Steph. Elzev.), the received text alone, in the rare instances in which these two texts differ.

THE TITLE OF THE GOSPEL.

THE shortest form is found in ℵ. B. F., *κατὰ Λουκᾶν*. The greater part of the Mjj. read *εὐαγγέλιον κατὰ Λουκᾶν*. The T. R., with some Mnn. only, *τὸ κατὰ Λουκᾶν εὐαγγ*. Some Mnn., *τὸ κατὰ Λουκᾶν ἅγιον εὐαγγ*.

In the opinion of several scholars (Reuss, *Gesch. der heil. Schr. N. T.*, § 177), the prep. *κατὰ*, *according to*, signifies not: *composed by*, but: *drawn up according to the conception of* . . . Thus this title, so far from affirming that our Gospel was composed by the person designated, would rather deny it. This sense does not appear to us admissible. Not only *may* the preposition *κατὰ* apply to the writer himself, as the following expressions prove: *ἡ κατὰ Μωϋσέα πεντάτευχος* (the Pentateuch according to Moses) in Epiphanius; *ἡ καθ' Ἡρόδοτον ἱστορία* (the history according to Herodotus) in Diodorus; *Ματθαῖος . . . γραφῇ παραδοὺς τὸ κατ' αὐτὸν εὐαγγέλιον* (Matthew having *put in writing* the Gospel *according* to him) in Eusebius (*H. Eccl.* iii. 24);—but this preposition *must* have this sense in our title. For, 1. The titles of our four Gospels bear too close a resemblance to each other to have come from the authors of these writings; they must have been framed by the Church when it formed the collection of the Gospels. Now the opinion of the Church, as far as we can trace it, has always been, that these writings were *composed* by the persons named in the titles. 2. With respect to the third Gospel in particular, no other sense is possible. Apostles and eyewitnesses, such as Matthew or John, might have created an original conception of the Gospel, and afterwards a different writer might have produced a narrative of the ministry of Jesus according to this type. But this supposition is not applicable to persons so secondary and dependent as Luke or Mark.

This Luke, whom the title designates as the author of our Gospel, can be no other than the companion of Paul. The evangelical history mentions no other person of this name. As to the term *Gospel*, it appears to us very doubtful whether in our four titles it indicates the *writings* themselves. This term applies rather, as throughout the New Testament, to the facts related, to the contents of the books, to *the coming of Christ*—this merciful message of God to mankind. The complement understood after εὐαγγέλιον is Θεοῦ; comp. Rom. i. 1. This good news, though one in itself, is presented to the world under four different aspects in these four narratives. The meaning then is, "The good news of the coming of Christ, according to the version of . . ." It is the εὐαγγέλιον τετράμορφον, *the Gospel with four faces*, of which Irenæus still speaks towards the end of the second century, even after the term *Gospel* had been already applied by Justin to the *written Gospels*.

PROLOGUE.

CHAP. I. 1–4.

THE first of our synoptic Gospels opens with a genealogy. This mode of entering upon the subject transports us into a completely Jewish world. This preamble is, as it were, a continuation of the genealogical registers of Genesis; in the βίβλος γενέσεως of Matthew (i. 1) we have again the *Ellé Tholedoth* of Moses.

How different Luke's prologue, and in what an entirely different atmosphere it places us from the first! Not only is it written in most classical Greek, but it reminds us by its contents of the similar preambles of the most illustrious Greek historians, especially those of Herodotus and Thucydides. The more thoroughly we examine it, the more we find of that delicacy of sentiment and refinement of mind which constitute the predominant traits of the Hellenic character. Baur, it is true, thought he discerned in it the work of a forger. Ewald, on the contrary, admires its true simplicity, noble modesty, and terse conciseness.[1] It appears to us, as to Holtzmann,[2] "that between these two opinions the choice is not difficult." The author does not seek to put himself in the rank of the Christian authorities; he places himself modestly among men of the second order. He feels it necessary to excuse the boldness of his enterprise, by referring to the numerous analogous attempts that have preceded his own. He does not permit himself to undertake the work of writing a Gospel history until he has furnished himself with all the aids fitted to enable him to attain the lofty aim he sets before him. There is a striking contrast between his frank and modest attitude and that of a forger. It excludes even the ambitious part of a

[1] *Jahrbücher*, ii. p. 128.

[2] *Die Synoptischen Evangelien*, p. 398.

secretary of the Apostle Paul, which tradition has not been slow to claim for the author of our Gospel.

This prologue is not least interesting for the information it contains respecting the earliest attempts at writing histories of the Gospel. Apart from these first lines of Luke, we know absolutely nothing definite about the more ancient narratives of the life of Jesus which preceded the composition of our Gospels. Therefore every theory as to the origin of the synoptics, which is not constructed out of the materials furnished by this preface, runs the risk of being thrown aside as a tissue of vain hypotheses the day after it has seen the light.

This introduction is a dedication, in which Luke initiates the reader into the idea, method, and aim of his work. He is far from being the first who has attempted to handle this great subject (ver. 1). Numerous written narratives on the history of Jesus are already in existence; they all of them rest on the oral narrations of the apostles (ver. 2). But while drawing also on this original source, Luke has collected more particular information, in order to supplement, select, and properly arrange the materials for which the Church is indebted to apostolic tradition. His aim, lastly, is to furnish his readers, by this connected account of the facts, with the means of establishing their certainty (ver. 4).

Vers. 1–4. "*Since, as is known, many have undertaken to compose a narrative of the events which have been accomplished amongst us,* (2) *in conformity with that which they have handed down to us who were eye-witnesses of them from the beginning, and who became ministers of the word,* (3) *I have thought good also myself, after carefully informing myself of all these facts from their commencement, to write a consecutive account of them for thee, most excellent Theophilus,* (4) *in order that thou mightest know the immoveable certainty of the instructions which thou hast received.*"[1]—This period, truly Greek in its style, has been composed with

[1] A literal translation of M. Godet's rendering of Luke's preface is given here, for the sake of harmonizing the text with the verbal comments which follow in the next paragraph; but, except when something turns on our author's rendering, the passages commented on will be given in the words of the A. V. A close and happy translation of the original Greek into French does not always admit of being reproduced literally in English, and a *free* translation of a translation is of little service for purposes of exegesis.—*Note by the Translator.*

particular care. We do not find a style like it in all the New Testament, except at the end of the Acts and in the Epistle to the Hebrews. As to the thought of this prologue, it cannot be better summed up than in these lines of Tholuck: "Although not an immediate witness of the facts that took place, I have none the less undertaken, following the example of many others, to publish an account of them according to the information I have gathered."[1]

The conjunction ἐπειδήπερ is found nowhere else in the New Testament; it has a certain solemnity. To the idea of *since* (ἐπεί), δή adds that of notoriety: "since, as is well known;" περ draws attention to the relation between the great number of these writings and the importance of the events related: It is so (δή), and it could not be otherwise (περ).—The relation between the *since* thus defined and the principal verb, *I have thought good,* is easy to seize: If my numerous predecessors have not been blamed, why should I be blamed, who am only walking in their steps?—The term ἐπεχείρησαν, *have undertaken,* involves no blame of the skill of these predecessors, as several Fathers have thought; the *I have thought good also myself* is sufficient to exclude this supposition. This expression is suggested by the greatness of the task, and contains a slight allusion to the insufficiency of the attempts hitherto made to accomplish it.

The nature of these older writings is indicated by the term ἀνατάξασθαι διήγησιν, *to set in order a narrative.* It is a question, as Thiersch[2] says, of an attempt at arrangement. Did this arrangement consist in the harmonizing of a number of separate writings into a single whole, so as to make a consecutive history of them? In this case, we should have to admit that the writers of whom Luke speaks had already found in the Church a number of short writings on particular events, which they had simply united: their work would thus constitute a *second* step in the development of the writing of the Gospel history. But the expression, *in conformity with that which they have handed down to us,* hardly leaves room

[1] *Glaubwürdigk. der evang. Gesch.* p. 143.

[2] *Versuch zur Herstellung des historischen Standpunkts für die Kritik der Neutestamentl. Schr.* p. 164 (a work which we cannot too strongly recommend to beginners, although we are far from sharing all its views).

for intermediate accounts between the apostolic tradition and the writings of which Luke speaks. The notion of *arrangement*, then, refers rather to the facts themselves which these authors had co-ordinated in such a way as to make a consecutive narrative of them. The term *diegesis* designates not, as Schleiermacher maintained, recitals of isolated facts, but a complete narrative.

What idea should we form of these writings, and are they to be ranked among the sources on which Luke has drawn?—Certain extra-canonical Gospels, which criticism has sometimes regarded as prior to Luke's, may be thought of,—that *of the Hebrews*, for example, in which Lessing was disposed to find the common source of our three synoptics; or that of *Marcion*, which Ritschl and Baur regarded as the principal document reproduced by Luke.[1] But does not tradition exhibit itself in these writings in a form already perceptibly altered, and very far removed from the primitive purity and freshness which characterize our canonical Gospels? They are then later than Luke.

Or does Luke allude to our Gospels of Matthew and Mark? This is maintained by those who think that Luke wrote after Matthew and Mark (Hug), or only after Matthew (Griesbach, etc.). But however little Luke shared in the traditional opinion which attributed the first Gospel to the Apostle Matthew, he could not speak of that writing as he speaks here; for he clearly opposes to *the writers* of the tradition (the πολλοί, ver. 1), the apostles who were the *authors* of it. It may be affirmed, from the connection of ver. 2 with ver. 1, that Luke was not acquainted with a single written Gospel emanating from an apostle. As to the collection of the *Logia* (discourses of the Lord), which some attribute to Matthew, it certainly would not be excluded by Luke's expressions; for the term *diegesis* denotes a recital, a *historical* narrative. Hug, in his desire to save his hypothesis, according to which Luke made use of Matthew, explained vers. 1 and 2 in this sense: "Many have undertaken to compose written Gospels *similar to those which the apostles bequeathed to us* . . ." But this sense would require ὁποῖα (βιβλία) instead of καθώς,[2] and has not

[1] Ritschl has since withdrawn this assertion.
[2] Thiersch, *Versuch*, etc., p. 211.

been accepted by any one.—As to the Gospel of Mark, Luke's expressions might certainly suit this writing. For, according to tradition, Mark made use in his narrative of the accounts of an eye-witness, St. Peter. But still it may be questioned whether Luke would have employed the term *undertake* in speaking of a work which was received in the Church as one of the essential documents of the life of Jesus. For the rest, exegesis alone can determine whether Luke really had Mark before him either in its present or in a more ancient form.—It appears probable, therefore, to me, that the works to which Luke alludes are writings really unknown and lost. Their incompleteness condemned them to extinction, in proportion as writings of superior value, such as our synoptics, spread through the Church.

As to whether Luke availed himself of these writings, and in any way embodied them in his own work, he does not inform us. But is it not probable, since he was acquainted with them, that he would make some use of them? Every aid would appear precious to him in a work the importance of which he so deeply felt.

The subject of these narratives is set forth in expressions that have a touch of solemnity: "the events which have been accomplished amongst us." *Πληροφορεῖν* is a word analogous in composition and meaning to *τελεσφορεῖν* (*to bring to an end, to maturity*, viii. 14). It signifies, when it refers to a *fact*, to bring it to complete accomplishment (2 Tim. iv. 5, to accomplish the ministry; ver. 17, to *accomplish* [to finish rendering] the *testimony*); and when it refers to a *person*, it means to cause him to attain inward fulness [of conviction], that is to say, a conviction which leaves no room for doubt (Rom. iv. 21, xiv. 5; Heb. x. 22, etc.). With a substantive such as *πράγματα*, the second sense is inadmissible. Nevertheless, it has been defended by some of the Fathers, by some modern interpreters, as Beza, Grotius, Olshausen, and by Meyer, who concludes from 2 Tim. iv. 17 that *πληροφεῖσθαι* may also be applied to *things* in the sense of *being believed*. But when Paul says, "In order that the testimony *might be accomplished*, and that all the Gentiles might hear it," the last words plainly show that *accomplished* signifies not *fully believed*, but *fully rendered*. This term, which has more weight than the simple *πληροῦν*, is designedly chosen here to indicate that these events were not simple accidents, but accomplished a preconceived plan; the divine thought carried into execution was, as it were, a measure which filled up itself.—Doubtless, what has led many interpreters to prefer the sense of *fully believed,* is the complement *amongst us.* This is said that the facts of the gospel were *accomplished* not only in the presence of believers, but before the Jewish people and the whole world. This is true; but was not Jesus from the beginning surrounded by a circle of disciples, chosen to be witnesses of His life? It is with this meaning that John says, xx. 30, "Jesus did many other miracles *in the presence of His disciples;*" and i. 14, "He dwelt among us (ἐν ἡμῖν), and we saw His glory,"—a sentence in which the last words limit the *us* to the circle of believers. The meaning is the same here. In ver. 2 the sense of the word *us* is more limited still. Here *us* denotes the Church with the apostles; in ver. 2, the Church apart from the apostles. Bleek extends the meaning of the word *us,* in ver. 1, to the whole contemporary generation both within and without the Church. But Luke, writing for believers, could scarcely use *us* in such a general sense as this.—In this expression, "the events accomplished amongst us," did the author include also the contents of the book of the Acts, and did he intend the preface to apply to the two books, so that the Acts would be just the second volume of the Gospel? The words *amongst us* would be more easily explained in this case, and the mention made of the apostles as *ministers of the word* (ver. 2) might lead us to this supposition. It is not probable, however, that Luke would have applied to the facts related in the Acts the expressions παράδοσις, *tradition* (ver. 2), and κατήχησις, *instruction* (ver. 4). The subject of apostolical tradition and catechetical instruction could only be the history and teaching of Jesus. It is impossible, therefore, to infer from this preface, that when Luke wrote his Gospel he had in view the composition of the book of the Acts.

Ver. 2. Tradition emanating from the apostles was the common source, according to ver. 2, of all the first written narratives. The general accuracy of these accounts follows from καθώς, *in conformity with that which.* This conjunction can only refer to the principal thought of ver. 1, *to compose a narrative*, and not to the secondary idea *πεπληροφορημένων*, as Olshausen thinks, who translates, "fully believed in conformity with the account of the first witnesses."—As the two substantives, *αὐτόπται* and *ὑπηρέται*, *witnesses* and *ministers*, have each certain defining expressions which especially belong to them (the first, *ἀπ' ἀρχῆς*, *from the beginning*, and the second, *γενόμενοι*, *become*, and *τοῦ λόγου*, *of the word*), the most simple construction appears to us to be to regard *οἱ*, *the*, as a pronoun, and make it the subject of the proposition: *they* (the men about to be pointed out). This subject is defined by the two following substantives, which are in apposition, and indicate the qualification in virtue of which these men became the authors of the tradition. 1. *Witnesses from the beginning.* The word *ἀρχή*, *beginning*, in this context, can only refer to the commencement of the ministry of Jesus, particularly to His baptism, as the starting-point of *those things which have been accomplished amongst us.* Comp. Acts i. 21, 22, for the sense; and for the expression, John xv. 27, xvi. 4. Olshausen would extend the application of this title of *witnesses from the beginning* to the witnesses of the birth and infancy of Jesus. But the expression *became ministers of the word* does not allow of this application. 2. *Ministers of the word; become ministers*, as the text literally reads. This expression is in contrast with the preceding. These men began afterwards to be ministers of the word; they only *became* such after Pentecost. It was then that their part as *witnesses* was transformed into that of *preachers.* The sense then is: "Those who were witnesses from the commencement, and who afterwards became ministers of the word."—If *ὑπηρέται*, *ministers*, is thus taken as a second noun of apposition with *οἱ*, parallel to the first, there is no longer any difficulty in referring the complement *τοῦ λόγου*, *of the word*, to *ὑπηρέται*, ministers, alone, and taking this word in its ordinary sense of preaching the gospel. This also disposes of the reason which induced certain Fathers (Origen, Athanasius) to give the term *word* the meaning of the eternal Word (John i. 1), which is very forced in this connection. Only in this way could they make this complement depend simultaneously on the two substantives, *witnesses* and *ministers* The same motive led Beza, Grotius, and Bleek to understand the term *word* here in the sense in which it is frequently taken—*the thing related:* "eye-witnesses and ministers of the Gospel history." But in passages where the term *word* bears this meaning, it is fixed by some defining expression: thus, at ver. 4 by the relative proposition, and in Acts viii. 21, xv. 6 (which Bleek quotes), by a demonstrative pronoun.

With the third verse we reach the principal proposition. Luke places himself by the *κἀμοὶ, myself also,* in the same rank as his predecessors. He does not possess, any more than they, a knowledge of the Gospel history as a witness; he belongs to the second generation of the *ἡμεῖς, us* (ver. 2), which is dependent on the narratives of the apostles.—Some Italic MSS. add here to *mihi, et spiritui sancto* (it has pleased me *and the Holy Spirit*),—a gloss taken from Acts xv. 28, which clearly shows in what direction the tradition was gradually altered.

While placing himself in the same rank as his predecessors, Luke nevertheless claims a certain superiority in comparison with them. Otherwise, why add to their writings, which are already numerous (*πολλοί*), a fresh attempt? This superiority is the result of his not having confined himself to collecting the apostolic traditions current in the Church. Before proceeding to write, he obtained exact information, by means of which he was enabled to select, supplement, and arrange the materials furnished by those oral narratives which his predecessors had contented themselves with reproducing just as they were. The verb *παρακολουθεῖν, to follow step by step,* is not used here in the literal sense; this sense would require *πᾶσιν* to be taken as masculine: *all the apostles,* and thus would lead to an egregiously false idea; the author could not have accompanied *all* the apostles! The verb, therefore, must be taken in the figurative sense which it frequently has in the classics: *to study anything point by point;* thus Demosth. *de coronâ,* 53: *παρακολουθηκὼς τοῖς πράγμασιν ἀπ' ἀρχῆς.* Comp. 2 Tim. iii. 10, where we see the transition from the purely literal to the figurative meaning. The *πάντα, all things,* are the events related (ver. 1). Luke might have put the participle in the accusative: *παρακολουθηκότα*; but then he would only have indicated the *succession* of the two actions, —the acquisition of information, and the composition which followed it. This is not his thought. The dative makes the information obtained a quality inherent in his person, which constitutes his qualification for the accomplishment of this great work.

Luke's information bore particularly on three points: 1. He sought first of all to go back to the origin of the facts, to the very starting-point of this *res christiana* which he desired to describe. This is expressed in the word *ἄνωθεν*, literally *from above, from the very beginning.* The author compares himself to a traveller who tries to discover the source of a river, in order that he may descend it again, and follow its entire course. The apostolic tradition, as current in the Church, did not do this; it began with the ministry of John the Baptist, and the baptism of Jesus. It is in this form that we find it set forth in the Gospel of Mark, and summarized in Peter's preaching at the house of Cornelius, and in Paul's at Antioch in Pisidia (Acts x. 37 et seq., xiii. 23 et seq.). The author here alludes to the accounts contained in the first two chapters of his Gospel.—2. After having gone back to the commencement of the Gospel history, he endeavoured to reproduce as completely as possible its entire course (*πᾶσιν, all things,* all the particular facts which it includes). Apostolic tradition probably had a more or less fragmentary character; the apostles not relating every time the whole of the facts, but only those which best answered to the circumstances in which they were preaching. This is expressly said of St. Peter on the testimony of Papias, or of the old presbyter on whom he relied: *πρὸς τὰς χρείας ἐποιεῖτο τὰς διδασκαλίας* (he chose each time the facts appropriate to the needs of his hearers). Important omissions would easily result from this mode of evangelization. By this word *πᾶσιν, all things,* Luke probably alludes to that part of his Gospel (ix. 51–xviii. 14), by which the tradition, as we have it set forth in our first two synoptics, is enriched with a great number of facts and new discourses, and with the account of a long course of evangelization probably omitted, until Luke gave it, in the public narration.—3. He sought to confer on the Gospel history that exactness and precision which tradition naturally fails to have, after being handed about for some time from mouth to mouth. We know how quickly, in similar narratives, characteristic traits are effaced, and the facts transposed. Diligent and scrupulous care is required afterwards to replace the stones of the edifice in their right position, and give them their exact form and sharpness of edge. Now the third Gospel is distinguished, as we shall see, by the constant effort to trace the continued progressive development of the work of Jesus, to show the connection of the facts, to place each discourse in its historical setting, and to exhibit its exact purport.

By means of this information bearing upon the three points indicated, the author hopes he shall be qualified to draw a *consecutive picture,* reproducing the actual course of events: *καθεξῆς γράψαι, to write in order.* It is impossible in this connection to understand the phrase *in order* in the sense of a systematic classification, as Ebrard prefers; here the term must stand for a chronological order.—The term *καθεξῆς* is not found in the New Testament except in Luke.

Ver. 4. And now, what is the aim of the work thus conceived? To strengthen the faith of Theophilus and his readers in the reality of this extraordinary history.—On Theophilus, see the Introduction, sec. 3.—The epithet *κράτιστος* is applied several times, in the writings of Luke, to high Roman officials, such as Felix and Festus: Acts xxiii. 26, xxiv. 3, xxvi. 25. It is frequently met with in medals of the time. Luke wishes to show his friend and patron, that he is not unmindful of the exalted rank he occupies. But in his opinion, one mention suffices. He does not deem it necessary to repeat this somewhat ceremonious form at the beginning of the book of the Acts.—The work executed on the plan indicated is to give Theophilus the means of ascertaining and *verifying* (*ἐπιγινώσκειν*) *the irrefragable certainty* (*ἀσφάλειαν*) of the instruction which he had already received. The construction of this last phrase has been understood in three ways. The most complicated is to understand a second *περι*: *τὴν ἀσφάλειαν περὶ τῶν λόγων περὶ ὧν κατηχήθης*; the second and more simple, adopted by Bleek, is to make *περί* depend not on *ἀσφάλειαν*, but on *κατηχήθης*: *τὴν ἀσφάλειαν τῶν λόγων περὶ ὧν κατηχήθης.* But the example *κατηχήθησαν περί σου* (Acts xxi. 21), which Bleek quotes, is not analogous; for there the object of *περί* is personal: "they are informed *of thee.*" The simplest construction is this: *τὴν ἀσφάλειαι* περὶ τῶν λόγων οὓς κατηχήθης, certitude touching the instruction which . . . Comp. for this form κατηχεῖσθαί τι, Acts xviii. 25, Gal. vi. 6.—The term κατηχεῖν, to cause a sound to penetrate into the ears, and thereby also a fact, an idea, into the mind, may simply mean that intelligence of the great events of which Luke speaks had reached Theophilus by public report (Acts xxi. 21, 24); or it may denote *instruction* properly so called, as Rom. ii. 18, Acts xviii. 25, Gal. vi. 6; neither the expressions nor the context appear to me to offer sufficient reasons to decide which. Perhaps the truth lies between these two extreme opinions. Theophilus might have talked with Christian evangelists without receiving such catechetical instruction, in the strict sense of the term, as was often given when a church was founded (Thiersch, *Versuch*, p. 122 et seq.); and then have applied to Luke with a view to obtain through his labours something more complete.—The word ἀσφάλειαν is relegated to the end, to express with greater force the idea of the irrefragable certainty of the facts of the Gospel.

It is a very nice question whether the term λόγοι, which we have translated *instruction*, here refers solely to the historical contents of the Gospel, or also to the religious *meaning* of the facts, as that comes out of the subsequent narrative. In the former case, Luke would simply mean that the certainty of each particular fact was established by its relation to the whole, which could not well be invented. An extraordinary fact, which, presented separately, appears impossible, becomes natural and rational when it takes its place in a well-certified sequence of facts to which it belongs.[1] In strictness, this meaning might be sufficient. But when we try to identify ourselves completely with the author's mind, do we not see, in this *instruction* of which he speaks, something more than a simple narrative of facts? Does not the passage in 1 Cor. xv. 1–4 show that, in apostolic instruction,

[1] The Catholic missionaries, Huc and Gabet, in their *Travels in Tartary* (vol. ii. p. 136), relate as follows: "We had adopted [in regard to the Buddhist priests amongst whom they lived] an entirely historical mode of teaching. . . . Proper names and precise dates made much more impression on them than the most logical arguments. . . . The close connection which they remarked in the history of the Old and New Testaments was, in their view, a demonstration." Is not that the καθεξῆς γράψαι ἵνα ἐπιγνῷς . . . τὴν ἀσφάλειαν?

religious comment was inseparable from the historical text? Was it not with a view to faith that facts were related in the preaching of the gospel? and does not faith, in order to appropriate them, require an exposition of their meaning and importance? The instruction already received by Theophilus refers, then, without doubt to the Gospel history, but not as isolated from its religious interpretation; and since we have to do here with a reader belonging to a circle of Christians of heathen origin, the signification given to this history could be none other than that twofold principle of the universality and free grace of salvation which constituted the substance of what Paul calls *his gospel.* Luke's object, then, was to relate the Christian fact in such a way as to show that, from its very starting-point, the work and preaching of Jesus Himself had had no other meaning. This was the only way of making evangelical instruction, as formulated by St. Paul, rest on an immoveable basis. As a consequence, this apostle ceased to appear an innovator, and became the faithful expositor of the teaching of Jesus. To write a Gospel with this view, was to introduce beneath the vast ecclesiastical edifice raised by Paul, the only foundation which could in the end prevent it from falling. For whatever there is in the Church that does not emanate from Jesus, holds a usurped and consequently a transitory place. This would be true even of the spiritualism of St. Paul, if it did not proceed from Jesus Christ. Certainly it does not therefore follow, that the acts and words of Jesus which Luke relates, and in which the universalist tendency of the Gospel is manifested, were invented or modified by him in the interest of this tendency. Is it not important for him, on the contrary, to prove to his readers that this tendency was not infused into the Gospel by Paul, but is a legitimate deduction from the work and teaching of Jesus Christ? The essential truth of this claim will be placed beyond all suspicion when we come to prove, on the one hand, that the author has in no way tried to mutilate the narrative by suppressing those facts which might yield a different tendency from that which he desired to justify; on the other, that the tendency which he favours is inseparable from the course of the facts themselves.

If we have correctly apprehended the meaning of the last

words of the prologue, we must expect to find in the third Gospel the counterpart of the first. As that is *A Treatise on the right of Jesus to the Messianic sovereignty of Israel,* this is *A Treatise on the right of the heathen to share in the Messianic kingdom founded by Jesus.* In regard to the earliest writings on the subject of the Gospel history, we may draw from this preface four important results: 1. The common source from which the earliest written narratives of the history of the ministry of Jesus proceeded was the oral testimony of the apostles,—the *διδαχή τῶν ἀποστόλων,* which is spoken of in Acts ii. 42 as the daily food dispensed by them to the rising Church.—2. The work of committing this apostolic tradition to writing began early, not later than the period of transition from the first to the second Christian generation; and it was attempted by numerous authors at the same time. Nothing in the text of Luke authorizes us to think, with Gieseler, that this was done only amongst the Greeks. From the earliest times, the art of writing prevailed amongst the Jews; children even were not ignorant of it (Judg. viii. 14).—3. In composing his Gospel, Luke possessed the apostolic tradition, not merely in the oral form in which it circulated in the churches, but also reduced to writing in a considerable number of these early works; and these constituted two distinct sources.—4 But he did not content himself with these two means of information; he made use, in addition, of personal investigations designed to complete, correct, and arrange the materials which he derived from these two sources.

Having obtained these definite results, it only remains to see whether they contain the elements required for the solution of the problem of the origin of our synoptics, and of the composition of our Gospel in particular. We shall examine them for this purpose at the conclusion of the work.

FIRST PART.

THE NARRATIVES OF THE INFANCY.

CHAP. I. 5–II. 52.

BOTH the first and the third Gospel open with a cycle of narratives relating to the birth and childhood of Jesus. These narratives do not appear to have formed part of the tradition bequeathed to the Church by the apostles (ver. 2). At least, neither the Gospel of Mark, the document which appears to correspond most nearly with the type of the primitive preaching, nor the oldest example we have of this early preaching, Peter's discourse in the house of Cornelius (Acts x. 37–48), go further back than the ministry of John the Baptist and the baptism of Jesus. The reason, doubtless, for this is, that edification was the sole aim of apostolic preaching. It was intended to lay the foundation of the faith; and in order to do this, the apostles had only to testify concerning what they had *themselves* seen and heard during the time they had been with Jesus (John xv. 27; Acts i. 21, 22).

But these facts with which their preaching commenced supposed antecedent circumstances. Actual events of such an extraordinary nature could not have happened without preparation. This Jesus, whom Mark himself designates from the outset (i. 1) as *the Son of God,* could not have fallen from heaven as a full-grown man of thirty years of age. Just as a botanist, when he admires a new flower, will not rest until he has dug it up by the roots, while an ordinary observer will be satisfied with seeing its blossom; so among believers, among the Greeks especially, there must have been thoughtful minds—Luke and Theophilus are representatives of such—who felt the need of supplying what the narratives of the official witnesses of the ministry of Jesus were deficient in respecting the origin of this history.

The historical interest itself awakened by faith must have tended to dissipate the obscurity which enveloped the first appearance of a being so exceptional as He who was the subject of the evangelical tradition. In proportion as the first enthusiasm of faith gave place, at the transition period between the first and the second generation of Christians, to careful reflection, this need would be felt with growing intensity. Luke felt constrained to satisfy it in his first two chapters. It is evident that the contents of this *Gospel of the Infancy* proceed neither from apostolic tradition (ver. 2), nor from any of the numerous writings to which allusion is made (ver. 1), but that they are derived from special information which Luke had obtained. It is to these two chapters especially that Luke alludes in the third verse of the prologue (*ἄνωθεν, from the beginning*).

A similar need must have been felt, probably at the same time, in the Jewish-Christian world; only it arose out of another principle. There was no demand there for the satisfaction of the historic sense. In those circles, interest in the Messianic question prevailed over all others. They wanted to know whether from the beginning the child, as well as afterwards the grown man, had not been divinely pointed out as the Messiah. The first two chapters of St. Matthew are plainly intended to meet this need.

In this way we obtain a natural explanation of the extension of the Gospel history to the first commencement of the life of Jesus, and just in those different directions which are to be observed in our two Gospels.

But does not this imply consequences somewhat unfavourable to the truth of the narratives comprised in these two cycles, Luke i.–ii. and Matt. i.–ii.? It is admitted: 1. That these narratives of the infancy lack the guarantee of apostolic testimony. 2. That the wants which we have pointed out might easily call into activity the Christian imagination, and, in the absence of positive history, seek their satisfaction in legend. These narratives are actually regarded in this light, not only by Strauss or Baur, but even by such men as Meyer, Weizsäcker, and Keim, who do not generally avow themselves partisans of the mythical interpretation. What in their view renders these narratives suspicious is their poetical character, and the marvels with which they abound (a great number of angelic appearances and of prophetic songs); the complete silence of the other New Testament writings respecting the miraculous birth (there is no mention of it in Paul, or even in John); certain facts of the subsequent history (the unbelief of the brethren of Jesus and of His own mother) which appear incompatible with the miraculous circumstances of this birth; contradictions between Matthew and Luke on several important points; and lastly, historical errors in Luke's narrative, which may be proved by comparing it with the facts of Jewish and Roman history.

We can only examine these various reasons as we pursue in detail the study of the text. As to the way in which the wants we have indicated were satisfied, we would observe: 1. That it is natural to suppose, since the matter in question was regarded as sacred both by the writers and the Church, that the more simple and reverential process of historical investigation would be employed before having recourse to fiction. It is only at a later stage, when the results obtained by this means are no longer sufficient to satisfy curiosity and a corrupted faith, that invention comes in to the aid of history. The apocryphal Gospels, which made their appearance as early as the end of the first century, indicate the time when this change was in operation. Luke, if we may trust his preface, belongs to the first period, that of investigation.—2. It is evident that Luke himself, on the authority of information which he had obtained, believed in the reality of the facts which he relates in his first two chapters as firmly as in that of all the rest of the Gospel history. His narrative bears numerous marks of its strictly historical character: the course of Abia, the city of Galilee named Nazareth, the city of the hill-country of Juda, where dwelt the parents of John the Baptist, the census of Cyrenius, the eighty-four years' widowhood of Anna the prophetess, the physical and moral growth of Jesus as a child and young man, His return to Nazareth and settlement there—all these details leave us no room to doubt the completely historical sense which the author himself attached to these narratives. If, then, this part lacks the authority of apostolic testimony, it is guaranteed by the religious convictions of the author, and by his personal assurance of the value of the oral or written sources whence he derived his knowledge of these facts.

The Gospel of the Infancy in Luke comprises seven narratives :—

1. The announcement of the birth of the forerunner, i. 5–25; 2. The announcement of the birth of Jesus, i. 26–38; 3. The visit of Mary to Elizabeth, i. 39–56. These three narratives form the first cycle.

4. The birth of the forerunner, i. 57–80; 5. The birth of Jesus, ii. 1–20; 6. The circumcision and presentation of Jesus, ii. 21–40. These three narratives form a second cycle.

7. The first journey of Jesus to Jerusalem, ii. 41–52. This seventh narrative is, as it were, the crown of the two preceding cycles.

FIRST NARRATIVE.—CHAP. I. 5–25.

Announcement of the Birth of John the Baptist.

The first words of the narrative bring us back from the midst of Greece, whither we were transported by the prologue, into a completely Jewish world. The very style changes its character. From the fifth verse it is so saturated with Aramaisms, that the contrast with the four preceding verses resulting from it obliges us to admit, either that the author artificially modifies his language in order to adapt it to his subject, and so produces an imitation,—a refinement of method scarcely probable,—or that he is dealing with ancient documents, the Aramaic colouring of which he endeavours to preserve as faithfully as possible. This second supposition alone appears admissible. But it may assume two forms. Either the author simply copies a Greek document which already had the Hebraistic character with which we are struck; or the document in his hands is in the Aramean tongue, and he translates it into Greek. Bleek maintains the first view. We shall examine, at the seventy-eighth verse of chap. i., his principal proof. As all the most characteristic peculiarities of Luke's style are found in these two chapters, the second alternative is by this circumstance rendered more probable.—But in this case it is asked, Why Luke, translating from the Aramean, did not reproduce his document in purer Greek, as he was perfectly competent to do; comp. vers. 1–4. And he is blamed for his servility as a translator.—It is exactly as if M. de Barante were blamed for preserving with all possible fidelity, in his history of the Dukes of Burgundy, the style of the ancient chronicles from which the contents of his narrative are drawn; or M. Augustin Thierry, for "having kept as near as he possibly could to the language of the ancient historians."[1] So far from deserving the blame of his critics, Luke has shown himself a man of exquisite taste, in that he has preserved throughout his narrative all the flavour of the documents he uses, and has availed himself of the incomparable flexibility of the Greek language to reproduce in all their purity of substance and form, and give, as it were, a tracing of the precious documents which had fallen into his hands.

This first narrative describes: 1. The trial of Zacharias and Elizabeth (vers. 5–7). 2. The promise of deliverance (vers. 8–22). 3. The accomplishment of this promise (vers. 23–25).

1. *The trial:* vers. 5–7.[2] For 400 years direct communications between the Lord and His people had ceased. To the lengthened seed-time of the patriarchal, Mosaic, and prophetic periods, had succeeded a season of harvest. A fresh seed-time, the second and last phase of divine revelation, was about to open; this time God would address Himself to the whole world. But when God begins a new work, He does not scornfully break with the instrument by which the past work has been effected. As it is from the seclusion of a convent that in the middle ages He will take the reformer of the Church, so it is from the loins of an Israelitish priest that He now causes to come forth the man who is to introduce the world to the renovation prepared for it. The temple itself, the centre of the theocracy, becomes the cradle of the new covenant, of the worship in spirit and in truth. There is,

[1] *Histoire de la Conquête d'Angleterre*, etc., Introd. p. 9.

[2] Ver. 5. ℵ. B. C. D. L. X. Z. and some Mnn., γυνη αυτω, instead of η γυνη αυτου, the reading of T. R. 15 Mjj. the Mnn. Syr. Itplerique. Ver. 6. ℵ. B. C. X., εναντιον, instead of ενωπιον, the reading of T. R. 18 Mjj. the Mnn.

then, a divine suitability in the choice both of the actors and theatre of the scene which is about to take place.

The *days of Herod* (ver. 5) designate the time of this prince's reign. This fact agrees with Matt. ii. 1 et seq., where the birth of Jesus is also placed in the reign of Herod. It may be inferred from Matt. ii. 19 that this birth happened quite at the end of this reign. According to Josephus, the death of Herod must have taken place in the spring of the year 750 U.C. Jesus, therefore, must have been born at latest in 749, or quite at the beginning of 750. It follows from this, that in the fifth century our era was fixed at least four years too late.

The title of *King of Judea* had been decreed to Herod by the Senate on the recommendation of Antony and Octavius. *The course of Abia* was the eighth of the twenty-four courses or *ephemeriæ* into which, from David's time, the college of priests had been divided (1 Chron. xxiv. 10). Each of these classes did duty for eight days, from one Sabbath to another, once every six months (2 Kings xi. 9). Ἐφημερία, properly *daily service;* thence: in rotation, returning on a fixed day; thence: lastly, the group of persons subject to this rotation. As we know that the day on which the temple of Jerusalem was destroyed was the ninth of the fifth month of the year 823 U.C., that is to say, the 4th of August of the year 70 of our era; and as, according to the Talmud, it was the first ephemeria which was on duty that day, we may reckon, calculating backwards, that in the year which must have preceded that in which Jesus was born, that is to say, probably in 748, the ephemeria of Abia was on duty in the week from the 17th to the 23d of April, and in that from the 3d to the 9th of October. Therefore John the Baptist would be born nine months after one of these two dates, and Jesus six months later, consequently in the month of July 749, or in the month of January 750.[1] In this calculation, however, of *the time* of year to which the births of John and Jesus should be assigned, everything depends on the determination of the year of the birth of Jesus. But this is a question which is not yet decided with any certainty.

The Hebraistic colouring of the style is seen particularly:

[1] Wieseler, *Chronolog. Synopsis der vier Evang.* pp. 141–145.

1*st*, in the expression ἐν ταῖς ἡμέραις (בימי); 2*dly*, in the connection of propositions by means of the particle καί, instead of the Greek syntactical construction by means of relative pronouns and conjunctions; 3*dly*, in the employment of the verb ἐγένετο in the sense of ויהי. The subject of ἐγένετο is not, as is generally thought, the word ἱερεύς, but rather the verb ἦν, which must be understood in the three following propositions (comp. ver. 8, ἐγένετο ἔλαχε).—The Alex. reading γυνὴ αὐτῷ, which is more uncouth and Hebraistic than ἡ γυνὴ αὐτοῦ, is probably the true reading.—The term *righteous* (ver. 6) indicates general conformity of conduct to the divine precepts: this quality does not absolutely exclude sin (comp. vers. 18-20). It simply supposes that the man humbly acknowledges his sin, strives to make amends for it, and, aided from on high, struggles against it.—The Byz. reading ἐνώπιον, *in the presence*, *under the eyes of*, appears preferable to the Alexandrian reading ἐναντίον, *in the face of*, *before*. God and man cannot be represented as being *face to face* in this passage, where God's judgment on man is in question (see at ver. 8). Ἐνώπιον answers to לפני, and expresses the *inward* reality of this righteousness.—The two terms ἐντολαί and δικαιώματα, *commandments* and *ordinances*, have been distinguished in different ways. The former appears to us to refer to the more general principles of the moral law—to the Decalogue, for example; the latter, to the multitude of particular Levitical ordinances. Δικαίωμα properly is, what God has declared righteous.—As the expression *before God* brings out the inward truth of this righteousness, so the following, *walking in* . . ., indicates its perfect fidelity in practice. The term *blameless* no more excludes sin here than Phil. iii. 6. The well-known description in Rom. vii. explains the sense in which this word must be taken. The germ of concupiscence may exist in the heart, even under the covering of the most complete external obedience.

Ver. 7. In the heart of this truly theocratic family, so worthy of the divine blessing, a grievous want was felt. To have no children was a trial the more deeply felt in Israel, that barrenness was regarded by the Jews as a mark of divine displeasure, according to Gen. ii.—Καθότι does not signify *because that* exactly, but *in accordance with this, that*. It is one of those terms which, in the New Testament, only occur in Luke's writings (xix. 9, and four times in the Acts). If, therefore, as Bleek thinks, Luke had found these narratives already composed in Greek, he must nevertheless admit that he has modified their style. The last proposition cannot, it appears, depend on καθότι, *seeing that;* for it would not be logical to say, "*They had no children* . . . seeing that they were both well stricken in years." So, many make these last words an independent sentence. The position, however, of the verb ἦσαν at the end, tends rather to make this phrase depend on καθότι. To do this, it suffices to supply a thought: They had no children, *and they retained but little hope of having any,* seeing that . . ." The expression προβεβηκότες ἐν ταῖς ἡμέραις αὐτῶν is purely Hebraistic (Gen. xviii. 11, xxiv. 1; Josh. xiii. 1; 1 Kings i. 1—בוא בימים).

2. *The promise of deliverance:* vers. 8–22. This portion comprises: 1. vers. 8–17, The promise itself; 2. vers. 18–22, The manner in which it was received.

1. The narrative of the promise includes: the appearance (vers. 8–12), and the message (vers. 13–17), of the angel.

The appearance of the angel: vers. 8–12.[1] — The incense had to be offered, according to the law (Ex. xxx. 7, 8), every morning and evening. There was public prayer three times a day: at nine in the morning (Acts ii. 15 ?), at noon (Acts x. 9), and at three in the afternoon (Acts iii. 1, x. 30). The first and last of these acts of public prayer coincided with the offering of incense (Jos. *Antiq.* xiv. 4. 3).—In the construction ἐγένετο ἔλαχε, the subject of the first verb is the act indicated by the second.—Ἔναντι, *in the face of, before,* is suitable here; for the officiating priest enacts a part *in the front* of the Divinity. The words, *according to the custom of the priest's office* (ver. 8), may be referred either to the established rotation of the courses (ver. 8), or to the use of the lot with a view to the assignment of each day's functions. In both cases, the extraordinary use of the lot would be worthy of mention. The reference of these words to what precedes appears to us more natural; we regard them as a simple

[1] Ver. 8. The Mnn. vary between εναντι and εναντιον.—Ver. 10. ℵ. B. E. and 13 Mjj. put του λαου between ην and προσευχομενον; whilst the T R., with A. C. D. K. Π., put it before ην.

amplification of ἐν τῇ τάξει: "the order of his course, according to the custom of the priest's office."—On the use of the lot Oosterzee rightly observes that it proceeded from this, that nothing in the service of the sanctuary was to be left to man's arbitrary decision. The function of offering incense, which gave the priest the right to enter the holy place, was regarded as the most honourable of all. Further, according to the Talmud, the priest who had obtained it was not permitted to draw the lot a second time in the same week.—*Εἰσελθών*, *having entered*; there was the honour! This fact was at the same time the condition of the whole scene that followed. And that is certainly the reason why this detail, which is correctly understood by itself, is so particularly mentioned. Meyer and Bleek, not apprehending this design, find here an inaccuracy of expression, and maintain that with the infinitive θυμιάσαι the author passes by anticipation from the *notion* of the fact to its historical realization. This is unnecessary; εἰσελθών is a pluperfect in reference to θυμιάσαι: "It fell to him to offer incense *after having entered*." The term ναός, temple, designates the buildings properly so called, in opposition to the different courts; and the complement κυρίου, *of the Lord*, expresses its character in virtue of which the Lord was about to manifest Himself in this house.

The 10th verse mentions a circumstance which brings out the solemnity of the time, as the preceding circumstance brought out the solemnity of the place. The prayer of the people assembled in the court accompanied the offering of incense. There was a close connection between these two acts. The one was the typical, ideal, and therefore perfectly pure prayer; the other the real prayer, which was inevitably imperfect and defiled. The former covered the latter with its sanctity; the latter communicated to the former its reality and life. Thus they were the complement of each other. Hence their obligatory simultaneousness and their mutual connection are forcibly expressed by the dative τῇ ὥρᾳ. The reading which puts τοῦ λαοῦ between ἦν and προσευχόμενον, expresses better the essential idea of the proposition contained in this participle.

Ver. 11. Here, with the appearance of the angel, begins the marvellous character of the story which lays it open to the suspicion of criticism. And if, indeed, the Christian dispensation were nothing more than the natural development of the human consciousness, advancing by its own laws, we should necessarily and unhesitatingly reject as fictitious this supernatural element, and at the same time everything else in the Gospel of a similar character. But if Christianity was *an entirely new beginning* (Verny) in history, the second and final creation of man, it was natural that an interposition on so grand a scale should be accompanied by a series of particular interpositions. It was even necessary. For how were the representatives of the ancient order of things, who had to co-operate in the new work, to be initiated into it, and their attachment won to it, except by this means ?—According to the Scripture, we are surrounded by angels (2 Kings vi. 17 ; Ps. xxxiv. 8), whom God employs to watch over us ; but in our ordinary condition we want the sense necessary to perceive their presence. For that, a condition of peculiar receptivity is required. This condition existed in Zacharias at this time. It had been created in him by the solemnity of the place, by the sacredness of the function he was about to perform, by his lively sympathy with all this people who were imploring Heaven for national deliverance, and, last of all, by the experience of his own domestic trial, the feeling of which was to be painfully revived by the favour about to be shown him. Under the influence of all these circumstances combined, that internal sense which puts man in contact with the higher world was awakened in him. But the necessity of this inward predisposition in no way proves that the vision of Zacharias was merely the result of a high state of moral excitement. Several particulars in the narrative make this explanation inadmissible, particularly these two: the difficulty with which Zacharias puts faith in the promise made to him, and the physical chastisement which is inflicted on him for his unbelief. These facts, in any case, render a simple psychological explanation impossible, and oblige the denier of the objectivity of the appearance to throw himself upon the mythical interpretation.—The term *ἄγγελος κυρίου*, *angel of the Lord,* may be regarded as a kind of proper name, and we may translate *the angel of the Lord,* notwithstanding the absence of the article. But since, when once this personage is introduced, the word angel is preceded by the article (ver. 13), it is more natural to translate here *an angel.*—The entrance to the temple facing the east, Zacharias, on entering, had on his right the table of shew-bread, placed on the north side; on his left the candelabrum, placed on the south side; and before him the golden altar, which occupied the end of the Holy Place, in front of the veil that hung between this part of the sanctuary and the Holy of Holies. The expression, *on the right side of the altar,* must be explained according to the point of view of Zacharias; the angel stood, therefore, between the altar and the shew-bread table. The fear of Zacharias proceeds from the consciousness of sin, which is immediately awakened in the human mind when a supernatural manifestation puts it in direct contact with the divine world. The expression φόβος ἐπέπεσεν is a Hebraism (Gen. xv. 12).—Was it morning or evening? Meyer concludes, from the connection between the entrance of Zacharias into the temple and the drawing of the lot (ver. 9), that it was morning. This proof is not very conclusive. Nevertheless, the supposition of Meyer is in itself the most probable.

The message of the angel: vers. 13–17.[1] "*But the angel said unto him, Fear not, Zacharias: for thy prayer is heard; and thy wife Elizabeth shall bear thee a son, and thou shalt call his name John.* 14. *And thou shalt have joy and gladness; and many shall rejoice at his birth.* 15. *For he shall be great in the sight of the Lord, and shall drink neither wine nor strong drink; and he shall be filled with the Holy Ghost, even from his mother's womb.* 16. *And many of the children of Israel shall he turn to the Lord their God.* 17. *And he shall go before Him in the spirit and power of Elias, to turn the hearts of the fathers to the children, and the disobedient to the wisdom of the just; to make ready a people prepared for the Lord.*"

The angel begins by reassuring Zacharias (ver. 13); then he describes the person of the son of Zacharias (vers. 14, 15), and his mission (vers. 16, 17).

In the 13th verse the angel tells Zacharias that he has not

[1] Ver. 14. Instead of γεννήσει, which T. R. reads with G. X. Γ. and several Mnn., all the others read γενέσει.—Ver. 17. B. G. L. V.: προσελεύσεται, instead of προελεύσεται, the reading of T. R. with 15 Mjj., etc.

come on an errand of judgment, but of favour; comp. Dan x. 12.—The prayer of Zacharias to which the angel alludes would be, in the opinion of many, an entreaty for the advent of the Messiah. This, it is said, is the only solicitude worthy of a priest in such a place and at such a time. But the preceding context (ver. 7) is in no way favourable to this explanation, nor is that which follows (ver. 13[b]); for the sense of the *καί* is most certainly this: "*And so* thy wife Elizabeth . . ." Further, the two personal pronouns, *σοῦ* and *σοί*, "*thy* wife shall bear *thee*," as also the *σοί*, "*thou shalt* have (ver. 14), prove positively the entirely personal character of the prayer and its answer. The objection that, according to ver. 7, he could no longer expect to have a child, and consequently could not pray with this design, exaggerates the meaning of this word.—The phrase *καλεῖν ὄνομα* is a Hebraism; it signifies, properly, to call any one by his name. The name *'Ιωάννης*, John, is composed of יהוה and חנן: *Jehovah shows grace.* It is not the character of the preaching of this person which is expressed by this name; it belongs to the entire epoch of which his appearance is the signal.

The 14th verse describes the joy which his birth will occasion; it will extend beyond the narrow limits of the family circle, and be spread over a large part of the nation. There is an evident rising towards a climax in this part of the message: 1st, a son; 2d, a son great before God; 3d, the forerunner of the Messiah. *'Αγαλλίασις* expresses the transports which a lively emotion of joy produces. The beginning of the fulfilment of this promise is related, vers. 64–66. The reading *γενέσει* is certainly preferable to *γεννήσει*, which is perhaps borrowed from the use of the verb *γεν'âν* (ver. 13).

The ardour of this private and public joy is justified in the 15th verse by the eminent qualities which this child will possess (*γάρ*). The only greatness which can rejoice the heart of such a man as Zacharias is a greatness which the Lord Himself recognises as such: great *before the Lord.* This greatness is evidently that which results from personal holiness and the moral authority accompanying it.—The two *καί* following may be paraphrased by: *and in fact.*—The child is ranked beforehand amongst that class of specially consecrated men, who may be called the heroes of theocratic religion, the *Nazarites.* The ordinance respecting the kind of life to be led by these men is found in Num. vi. 1–21. The vow of the Nazarite was either temporary or for life. The Old Testament offers us two examples of this second form: Samson (Judg. xiii. 5–7) and Samuel (1 Sam. i. 11). It was a kind of voluntary lay priesthood. By abstaining from all the comforts and conveniences of civilised life, such as wine, the bath, and cutting the hair, and in this way approaching the state of nature, the Nazarite presented himself to the world as a man filled with a lofty thought, which absorbed all his interest, as the bearer of a word of God which was hidden in his heart (Lange).—Σικέρα denotes all kinds of fermented drink extracted from fruit, except that derived from the grape. In place of this means of sensual excitement, John will have a more healthful stimulant, the source of all pure exaltation, the Holy Spirit. The same contrast occurs in Eph. v. 18: "*Be not drunk with wine . . . , but be filled with the Spirit.*" And in his case this state will begin from his mother's womb: *ἔτι, even,* is not put for *ἤδη, already;* this word signifies, whilst he is *yet* in his mother's womb. The fact related (vers. 41–44) is the beginning of the accomplishment of this promise, but it in no way exhausts its meaning.

Vers. 16, 17. The mission of the child; it is described (ver. 16) in a general and abstract way: *he will bring back, turn;* this is the הֵשִׁיב of the Old Testament. This expression implies that the people are sunk in estrangement from God. —The 17th verse specifies and developes this mission. The pronoun *αὐτός, he,* brings out prominently the person of John with a view to connect him with the person of the Lord, who is to follow him (*αὐτοῦ*). The relation between these two personages thus set forth is expressed by the two prepositions, *πρό, before* (in the verb), and *ἐνώπιον, under the eyes of;* he who precedes walks under the eyes of him that comes after him. The Alex. reading *προσελεύσεται* has no meaning.—The pronoun *αὐτοῦ* (before *him*) has been referred by some directly to the person of the Messiah. An attempt is made to justify this meaning, by saying that this personage is always present to the mind of the Israelite when he says "*he.*" But this meaning is evidently forced; the pronoun *him* can only refer to the principal word of the preceding verse: *the Lord their God.* The prophecy (Mal. iii. 1), of which this passage is an exact reproduction, explains it: "*Behold, I will send my messenger, and he shall prepare the way before me; and the Lord, whom ye seek, shall suddenly come to His temple, even the Messenger of the Covenant, whom ye delight in.*" According to these words, therefore, in the eyes of the prophet the Messiah is no other than Jehovah Himself. For it is Jehovah who speaks in this prophecy. It is He who causes Himself to be preceded in His appearance as the Messiah by a forerunner who receives (iv. 5) the name of Elijah, and who is to prepare His way. It is He who, under the names of *Adonaï* (the Lord), and *the Angel of the covenant,* comes to take possession of *His temple.* From the Old as well as the New Testament point of view, the coming of the Messiah is therefore the supreme theophany. Apart from this way of regarding them, the words of Malachi and those of the angel in our 17th verse are inexplicable. See an *αὐτοῦ* very similar to this in the strictly analogous passage, John xii. 41 (comp. with Isa. vi.).

It appears from several passages in the Gospels that the people, with their learned men, expected, before the coming of the Messiah, a personal appearance of Elijah, or of some other prophet like him, probably both (John i. 21, 22; Matt. xvi. 14, xvii. 10, xxvii. 47). The angel spiritualizes this grossly literal hope: "Thy son shall be another Elijah." The *Spirit* designates the divine breath in general; and the term *power,* which is added to it, indicates the special character of the Spirit's influence in John, as formerly in Elijah. The preposition *ἐν, in,* makes the Holy Spirit the element into which the ministry of John is to strike its roots.

The picture of the effect produced by this ministry is also borrowed from Malachi, who had said: "*He shall turn the heart of the fathers to the children, and the heart of the children to their fathers, lest I come and smite the earth with a curse.*" The LXX., and, after their example, many modern interpreters, have applied this description to the re-establishment of domestic peace in Israel. But nothing either in the ministry of Elijah or of John the Baptist had any special aim in this direction. Besides, such a result has no direct connection with the preparation for the work of the Messiah, and bears no proportion to the threat which follows in the prophetic word: "*Lest I come and smite the earth with a curse.*" Lastly, the thought, "*and the heart of the children to their fathers,*" taken in this sense, could not have substituted for it in the discourse of the angel, "*and the rebellious to the wisdom of the just,*" unless we suppose that in every Israelitish family the children are necessarily rebellious and their parents just. Some explain it thus: "He will bring back *to God* all together, both the hearts of the fathers and those of the children;" but this does violence to the expression employed. Calvin and others give the word *heart* the sense of *feeling:* "He will bring back the pious feeling of the fathers [faithful to God] to the present generation [the disobedient children], and turn the latter to the wisdom of the former." But can "*to turn their hearts towards*" mean "to awaken dispositions in"? For this sense *εἰς* would have been necessary instead of *ἐπί* (*τέκνα*); besides, we cannot give the verb *ἐπιστρέψαι* such a different sense from *ἐπιστρέψει* in ver. 16. The true sense of these words, it seems to me, may be gathered from other prophetic passages, such as these: Isa. xxix. 22, "*Jacob shall no more be ashamed, neither shall his face wax pale, when he seeth his children become the work of my hands.*" lxiii. 16, "*Doubtless Thou art our Father, though Abraham be ignorant of us, and Israel acknowledge us not; Thou, O Lord, art our Father, our Redeemer!*" Abraham and Jacob, in the place of their rest, had blushed at the sight of their guilty descendants, and turned away their faces from them; but now they would turn again towards them with satisfaction in consequence of the change produced by the ministry of John. The words of Jesus (John viii. 56), "*Abraham rejoiced to see my day, and he saw it, and was glad,*" proves that there is a reality underlying these poetic images. With this meaning the modification introduced into the second member of the phrase is easily explained. The children who will turn towards their fathers (Malachi), are the Jews of the time of the Messiah, *the children of the obedient,* who return to the *wisdom of the pious patriarchs* (Luke). Is not this modification made with a view to enlarge the application of this promise? The expression, *the rebellious,* may, in fact, comprehend not only the Jews, but also the heathen. The term ἀπειθεῖς, *rebellious*, is applied by Paul (Rom. xi.) to both equally.—*Φρόνησις δικαίων, the wisdom of the just*, denotes that healthy appreciation of things which is the privilege of upright hearts.—The preposition of rest, ἐν, is joined to a verb of motion, ἐπιστρέψαι, to express the fact that this wisdom is a state in which men remain when once they have entered it.—It will be John's mission, then, to reconstitute the moral unity of the people by restoring the broken relation between the patriarchs and their descendants. The withered branches will be quickened into new life by sap proceeding from the trunk. This restoration of the unity of the elect people will be their true preparation for the coming of the Messiah.—Some interpreters have proposed to make ἀπειθεῖς the object of ἑτοιμάσαι, and this last a second infinitive of purpose, parallel to ἐπιστρέψαι: "And to prepare, by the wisdom of the just, the rebellious, as a people made ready for the Lord." It is thought that in this way a tautology is avoided between the two words ἑτοιμάσαι, *to prepare*, and κατεσκευασμένον, *made ready, disposed.* But these two terms have distinct meanings. The first bears on the relation of John to the people; the second on the relation of the people to the Messiah. John *prepares* the people in such a way that they are *disposed* to receive the Messiah.—Of course it is the ideal task of the forerunner that is described here. In reality this plan will succeed only in so far as the people shall consent to surrender themselves to the divine action.—Is it probable that after the ministry of Jesus, when the unbelief of the people was already an historical fact, a later writer would have thought of giving such an optimist colouring to the discourse of the angel?

2. Vers. 18–22 relate the manner in which the promise is received; and first, the objection of Zacharias (ver. 18); next, his punishment (vers. 19, 20); lastly, the effect produced upon the people by this latter circumstance.

Vers. 18–20. "*And Zacharias said unto the angel, Whereby shall I know this? for I am an old man, and my wife well stricken in years. And the angel answering, said unto him, I am Gabriel, that stand in the presence of God; and am sent to speak unto thee, and to show thee these glad tidings. And, behold, thou shalt be dumb, and not able to speak, until the day that these things shall be performed, because thou believest not my words, which shall be fulfilled in their season."*—Abraham, Gideon, and Hezekiah had asked for signs (Gen. xv.; Judg. vi.; 2 Kings xx.) without being blamed. God had of Himself granted one to Moses (Ex. iv.), and offered one to Ahaz (Isa. vii.). Why, if this was lawful in all these cases, was it not so in this? There is a maxim of human law which says, *Si duo faciunt idem, non est idem.* There are different degrees of responsibility, either according to the degree of development of the individual or of the age, or according to the character of the divine manifestation. God alone can determine these degrees. It appears from the 19th verse that the appearance of the being who spoke to Zacharias ought of itself to have been a sufficient sign. In any case this difference from the similar accounts in the Old Testament proves that our narrative was not artificially drawn up in imitation of them. The sign requested is designated by the preposition *κατά, according to,* as the *norm* of knowledge. The *γάρ, for,* refers to this idea understood: I have need of such a sign. Yet Zacharias prayed for this very thing which now, when promised by God, appears impossible to him. It is an inconsistency, but one in keeping with the laws of our moral nature. The narrative, Acts xii., in which we see the church of Jerusalem praying for the deliverance of Peter, and refusing to believe it when granted, presents a similar case.

In order to make Zacharias feel the seriousness of his fault, the angel (ver. 19) refers to two things: his dignity as a divine messenger, and the nature of his message.—*'Εγώ, I,* coming first, brings his person into prominence. But he immediately adds, *that stand in the presence of God,* to show that it is not he who is offended, but God who has sent him. —The name *Gabriel* is composed of גבר and אל: *vir Dei,* the mighty messenger of God. The Bible knows of only two heavenly personages who are invested with a name, *Gabriel* (Dan. viii. 16, ix. 21) and *Michael* (Dan. x. 13, 21, xii. 1; Jude 9; Rev. xii. 7). This latter name (מיכאל) signifies, *who is like God?* Here the critic asks sarcastically whether Hebrew is spoken in heaven? But these names are evidently symbolical; they convey to us the character and functions of these personalities. When we speak to any one, it is naturally with a view to be understood. When heaven communicates with earth, it is obliged to borrow the language of earth. According to the name given him, Gabriel is the mighty servant of God employed to promote His work here below. It is in this capacity that he appears to Daniel, when he comes to announce to him the restoration of Jerusalem; it is he also who promises Mary the birth of the Saviour. In all these circumstances he appears as the heavenly *evangelist.* The part of Gabriel is positive; that of Michael is negative. Michael is, as his name indicates, the destroyer of every one who dares to equal, that is, to oppose God. Such is his mission in Daniel, where he contends against the powers hostile to Israel; such also is it in Jude and in the Apocalypse, where he fights, as the champion of God, against Satan, the author of idolatry: Gabriel builds up, Michael overthrows. The former is the forerunner of Jehovah *the Saviour,* the latter of Jehovah *the Judge.* Do not these two heavenly personages remind us of the two angels who accompanied Jehovah (Gen. xviii.) when He came to announce to Abraham, on the one hand, the birth of Isaac, and, on the other, the destruction of Sodom? Biblical angelology makes mention of no other persons belonging to the upper world. But this wise sobriety did not satisfy later Judaism; it knew besides an angel Uriel, who gives good counsel, and an angel Raphael, who works bodily cures. The Persian angelology is richer still. It reckons no less than seven superior spirits or amschaspands. How, then, can it be maintained that the Jewish angelology is a Persian importation? History does not advance from the complicated to the simple. Besides, the narrative, Gen. xviii., in which the two archangels appear, is prior to the contact of Israel with the Persian religion. Lastly, the idea represented by these two personages is essentially Jewish. These two notions, of a work of grace personified in Gabriel, and of a work of judgment personified in Michael, have their roots in the depths of Jewish monotheism.—The term *to stand before God* indicates a permanent function (Isa. vi. 2). This messenger is one of the servants of God nearest His throne. This superior dignity necessarily rests on a higher degree of holiness. We may compare 1 Kings xvii. 1, where Elijah says. "*The Lord before whom I stand.*" Jesus expresses Himself in a similar manner

(Matt. xviii.) respecting the guardian angels of the little ones: "*Their angels do always behold the face of my Father which is in heaven.*"—Such a being deserves to be taken at his word; how much more when he is the bearer of a message which is to fulfil the desires of him to whom he is sent, and answer his earnest supplication (ver. 19^b^)!

The chastisement inflicted on Zacharias (ver. 20) is at the same time to serve as a sign to him. Ἰδού, *behold*, indicates the unexpected character of this dispensation. Σιωπιῶν, *not speaking*, denotes simply the fact; μὴ δυνάμενος, *not being able to speak*, discloses its cause; this silence will not be voluntary.—Οἵτινες, *which, as such*, that is to say, as being the words of such a being as I am. It may seem that with the future *shall be fulfilled*, the preposition ἐν is required, and not εἰς. But εἰς indicates that the performance of the promise will begin immediately in order to its completion at the appointed time; comp. Rom. vi. 22, εἰς ἁγιασμόν. Καιρός, *their season*, refers not only to the time (χρόνος), but to the entire circumstances in which this fulfilment will take place.—There is not a word in this speech of the angel which is not at once simple and worthy of the mouth into which it is put. It is not after this fashion that man makes heaven speak when he is inventing; only read the apocryphal writings!

Vers. 21 and 22. According to the Talmud, the high priest did not remain long in the Holy of Holies on the great day of atonement. Much more would this be true of the priest officiating daily in the Holy Place. The analytical form ἦν προσδοκῶν depicts the lengthened expectation and uneasiness which began to take possession of the people. The text indicates that the event which had just taken place was made known in two ways: on the one hand, by the silence of Zacharias; on the other, by signs by which he himself (αὐτός) indicated its cause. The analytical form ἦν διανεύων denotes the frequent repetition of the same signs, and the imperfect διέμενεν, *he remained dumb*, depicts the increasing surprise produced by his continuing in this state.

3. *The accomplishment of the promise:* vers. 23–25. The subject of ἐγένετο, *it came to pass*, is all that follows to the end of ver. 25. Comp. a similar ἐγένετο, Acts ix. 3.—The active form περιέκρυβεν ἑαυτήν, literally, *she kept herself concealed*,

expresses a more energetic action than that designated by the middle περιεκρύψατο. Elizabeth isolated herself intentionally, rendering herself invisible to her neighbours. Her conduct has been explained in many ways. Origen and Ambrose thought that it was the result of a kind of false modesty. Paulus supposed that Elizabeth wished to obtain assurance of the reality of her happiness before speaking about it. According to De Wette, this retreat was nothing more than a precaution for her health. It was dictated, according to Bleek and Oosterzee, by a desire for meditation and by sentiments of humble gratitude. Of all these explanations, the last certainly appears the best. But it in no way accounts for the term for *five months,* so particularly mentioned. Further, how from this point of view are we to explain the singular expression, *Thus* hath the Lord dealt with me? The full meaning of this word *thus* is necessarily weakened by applying it in a general way to the greatness of the blessing conferred on Elizabeth, whilst this expression naturally establishes a connection between the practice she pursues towards herself from this time, and God's method of dealing with her. What is this connection? Does she not mean, "I will treat myself as God has treated my reproach. He has taken it away from me; I will therefore withdraw myself from the sight of men so long as I run any risk of still bearing it, when I am in reality delivered from it?" Restored by God, she feels that she owes it to herself, as well as to Him who has honoured her in this way, to expose herself no more to the scornful regards of men until she can appear before them *evidently honoured* by the proofs of the divine favour. In this way the term *five months,* which she fixes for her seclusion, becomes perfectly intelligible. For it is after the fifth month that the condition of a pregnant woman becomes apparent. Therefore it is not until then that she can appear again in society, as what she really is, *restored.* In this conduct and declaration there is a mixture of womanly pride and humble gratitude which makes them a very exquisite expression of maternal feeling for one in such a position. We should like to know what later narrator would have invented such a delicate touch as this. But the authenticity of this single detail implies the authenticity of the whole of the preceding narrative.[1] Ὅτι must be taken here in the sense of *because;* Elizabeth wants to justify whatever is unusual in the course of conduct she has just adopted.—Ἐπεῖδεν ἀφελεῖν, "He has regarded me in a manner that takes away;" he has cast on me one of those efficacious looks which, as the Psalmist says, are deliverance itself.—On barrenness as a reproach, comp. Gen. xxx. 23, where, after the birth of her first-born, Rachel cries, "*God has taken away my reproach.*"

This saying of Elizabeth's discloses all the humiliations which the pious Israelite had endured from her neighbours during these long years of barrenness. This also comes out indirectly from ver. 36, in which the angel makes use of the expression, "Her who was *called barren.*" This epithet had become a kind of sobriquet for her in the mouth of the people of the place.

SECOND NARRATIVE.—CHAP. I. 26–38.

Announcement of the Birth of Jesus.

The birth of John the Baptist, like that of Isaac, was due to a higher power; but it did not certainly transcend the limits of the natural order. It is otherwise with the birth of Jesus; it has the character of a creative act. In importance it constitutes the counterpart, not of the birth of Isaac, but of the appearance of the first man; Jesus is the second Adam. This birth is the beginning of the world to come. If this character of the appearance of Jesus be denied, the whole of the subsequent narrative remains unintelligible and inadmissible. Directly it is conceded, all the rest accords with it.

But the creative character of this birth does not destroy the connection between the old and the new era. We have just seen how, in the birth of the greatest representative of the old covenant, God remained faithful to the theocratic past, by

[1] For this beautiful explanation I am indebted to the friend to whom I have had the joy of dedicating my commentary on the Gospel of John, and with whom I have more than once read the Gospel of Luke, Professor Charles Prince, who now beholds face to face Him whom we have so often contemplated together in the mirror of His word. Generally speaking, this commentary is as much his as mine.

making the Israelitish priesthood the cradle of this child. He acts in the same way when the Head of renewed humanity, the Lord of the world to come, is to make His appearance; He causes Him to come forth as a scion from the stock of the ancient royalty of Israel. Further, God has respect in this work to the conditions of the *human* past generally. While creating in Him a new humanity, He is careful to preserve the link which unites Him to the ancient humanity. Just as in the first creation He did not create man's body out of nothing, but formed it out of the dust of the already existing earth, of which Adam was to become the lord; so, at the appearance of the second Adam, He did not properly create His body; He took it from the womb of a human mother, so as to maintain the organic connection which must exist between the Head of the new humanity and that natural humanity which it is His mission to raise to the height of His own stature.

This narrative records: 1. The appearance of the angel (vers. 26–29); 2. His message (vers. 30–33); 3. The manner in which his message is received (ver. 34–38).

1. *The appearance of the angel:* vers. 26–29.[1] From the temple the narrative transports us to the house of a young Israelitish woman. We leave the sphere of official station to enter into the seclusion of private life. Mary probably was in prayer. Her chamber is a sanctuary; such, henceforth, will be the true temple.—The date, the *sixth month,* refers to that given in ver. 24. It was the time when Elizabeth had just left her retirement; all that takes place in the visitation of Mary is in connection with this circumstance. The government ὑπὸ τοῦ θεοῦ, *by God,* or, as some Alex. read, ἀπὸ τοῦ θεοῦ, *on the part of God,* indicates a difference between this message and that in ver. 19. God interposes more directly; it is a

[1] Ver. 26. א. B. L. Wc. and some Mnn., απο instead of υπο, which is the reading of T. R. with 16 Mjj. and almost all the Mnn.—The MSS. vary here between Ναζαρεθ (C. E. G. H. M. S. U. V. Γ. Λ. Itplerique; in addition, א. at ii. 4, and B. at ii. 39, 51), Ναζαραθ (A. Λ.), and Ναζαρετ (K. L. X. Π. and Z. at ii. 4); further, א. B. Z. read Ναζαρα at iv. 16.—Ver. 27. א. B. Fw. L. and 32 Mnn. add after οικου, και πατριας (taken from ii. 4).—Ver. 28. א. B. L. Wc. and some Mnn. omit the words ευλογημενη συ εν γυναιξιν, which is the reading of T. R. with 16 Mjj., almost all the Mnn., Syr. It. Vulg.—Ver. 29. א. B. D. L. X. and some Mnn. omit ιδουσα, which T. R. reads after η δε along with 15 Mjj., the other Mnn., Syr. It.—א. B. D. L. X. and some Mnn. omit αυτου after λογω.

question here of His own Son. The received reading *ὑπο, by*, seems to me for this reason more in accordance with the spirit of the context than the Alex. reading, which lays less emphasis on the divine origin of the message.

The most usual form of the name of the town in the documents is *Nazareth:* it is admitted here by Tischendorf in his eighth edition. He accords, however, some probability to the form *Nazara,* which is the reading of iv. 16 in the principal Alexandrians. In Matt. iii. 23, the MSS. only vary between *Nazareth* and *Nazaret.* Keim, in his *History of Jesus,* has decided for *Nazara.* He gives his reasons, i. p. 319 et seq.: 1. The derived adjectives *Ναζωραῖος*, *Ναζαρηνός* are most readily explained from this form. 2. The form *Nazareth* could easily come from Nazara, as Ramath from Rama (by the addition of the Aramean article). The forms Nazareth and Nazaret may also be explained as forms derived from that. 3. The phrase *ἀπὸ Ναζάρων,* in Eusebius, supposes the nominative Nazara. 4. It is the form preserved in the existing Arabic name *en-Nezirah.* Still it would be possible, even though the true name was Nazara, that Luke might have been accustomed to use the form Nazareth; Tischendorf thinks that this may be inferred from Acts x. 38, where א. B. C. D. E. read *Nazareth.*—The etymology of this name is probably נצר (whence the feminine form נצרת), *a shoot or scion;* this is the form used in the Talmud. The Fathers accordingly perceived in this name an allusion to the *scion of David* in the prophets. Burckhardt the traveller explains it more simply by the numerous shrubs which clothe the ground. Hitzig has proposed another etymology: נוצרה, *the guardian,* the name referring either to some pagan divinity, the protectress of the locality, as this scholar thinks, or, as Keim supposes, to the town itself, on account of its commanding the defile of the valley.

Nazareth, with a population at the present day of 3000 inhabitants, is about three days' journey north of Jerusalem, and about eight leagues west of Tiberias. It is only a short distance from Tabor. It is reached from the valley of Jezreel through a mountain gorge running from S. to N., and opening out into a pleasant basin of some twenty minutes in length by ten in width. A chain of hills shuts in the valley on its northern side. Nazareth occupies its lower slopes, and rises in smiling terraces above the valley. From the summit of the ridge which encloses this basin on the north there is a splendid view.[1] This valley was in Israel just what Israel was in the midst of the earth—a place at once secluded and open, a solitary retreat and a high post of observation, inviting meditation and at the same time affording opportunity for far-reaching views in all directions, consequently admirably adapted for an education of which God reserved to Himself the initiative, and which man could not touch without spoiling it.—The explanation, *a town of Galilee,* is evidently intended for Gentile readers; it is added by the translator to the Jewish document that lay before him.

Do the words, *of the house of David,* ver. 27, refer to Joseph or Mary? Grammatically, it appears to us that the form of the following sentence rather favours the former alternative. For if this clause applied, in the writer's mind, to Mary, he would have continued his narrative in this form: "and *her name* was . . .," rather than in this: "and the *young girl's* name was . . ." But does it follow from this that Mary was not, in Luke's opinion, a descendant of David? By no means. Vers. 32 and 69 have no sense unless the author regarded Mary herself as a daughter of this king. See iii. 23.

The term χαριτοῦν τινα, to make any one the object of one's favour, is applied to believers in general (Eph. i. 6). There is no thought here of outward graces, as the translation *full of grace* would imply. The angel, having designated Mary by this expression as the special object of divine favour, justifies this address by the words which follow: *The Lord with thee.* Supply *is,* and not *be;* it is not a wish. The heavenly visitant speaks as one knowing how matters stood. The words, "Blessed art thou among women," are not genuine; they are taken from ver. 42, where they are not wanting in any document.

The impression made on Mary, ver. 29, is not that of fear; it is a troubled feeling, very natural in a young girl who is suddenly made aware of the unexpected presence of a strange person. The T. R. indicates two causes of trouble: "And when *she saw him,* she was troubled *at his saying.*" By the omission of ἰδοῦσα, *when she saw,* the Alexs. leave only one remaining. But this very simplification casts suspicion on their reading.

[1] See Keim's fine description, *Gesch. Jesu,* t. i. p. 321.

The two ancient Syriac and Latin translations here agree with the T. R. The meaning is, that trouble was joined to the surprise caused by the sight of the angel, as soon as his words had confirmed the reality of his presence. *Ποταπός* denotes properly the origin (*ποῦ τὸ ἀπό*). But this term applies also to the contents and value, as is the case here. *What was the meaning the import of* . . . Having thus prepared Mary, the angel proceeds with the message he has brought.

2. *The message of the angel:* vers. 30–33.[1]—"*And the angel said unto her, Fear not, Mary; for thou hast found favour with God.* 31. *And, behold, thou shalt conceive in thy womb, and bring forth a son, and shalt call His name Jesus.* 32. *He shall be great, and shall be called the Son of the Highest; and the Lord God shall give unto Him the throne of His father David:* 33. *And He shall reign over the house of Jacob for ever; and of His kingdom there shall be no end.*"—By long continuance, Mary's trouble would have degenerated into fear. The angel prevents this painful impression: "Fear not." The term *εὗρες χάριν*, *thou hast found favour,* reproduces the idea of *κεχαριτωμένη*; this expression belongs to the Greek of the LXX. The angel proceeds to enumerate the striking proofs of this assertion, the marks of divine favour: 1*st*, a son; 2*d*, His name, a sign of blessing; 3*d*, His personal superiority; 4*th*, His divine title; *lastly*, His future and eternal sovereignty.—*Ἰδού*, behold, expresses the unexpected character of the fact announced.—*Ἰησοῦς*, *Jesus,* is the Greek form of ישוע, Jeschovah, which was gradually substituted for the older and fuller form יהושוע, Jehoschovah, of which the meaning is, *Jehovah saves.* The same command is given by the angel to Joseph, Matt. i. 21, with this comment: "*For He shall save His people from their sins.*" Criticism sees here the proof of two different and contradictory traditions. But if the reality of these two divine messages is admitted, there is nothing surprising in their agreement on this point. As to the two traditions, we leave them until we come to the general considerations at the end of chap. ii.—The personal quality of this son: *He shall be great*—first of all, in holiness; this is true greatness in the judgment of Heaven; then, and

[1] Ver. 30. D. alone reads μαριαμ instead of μαρια; so at vers. 39, 56, and (with ℵ) at vers. 34, 38, 46, ii. 19, the MSS. are divided between these two readings.

as a consequence, in power and influence.—His title: *Son of the Highest.* This title corresponds with His real nature. For the expression, *He shall be called,* signifies here, universally recognised as such, and that because He is such in fact. This title has been regarded as a simple synonym for that of *Messiah.* But the passages cited in proof, Matt. xxvi. 63 and John i. 50, prove precisely the contrary: the first, because had the title Son of God signified nothing more in the view of the Sanhedrim than that of Messiah, there would have been no *blasphemy* in assuming it, even falsely; the second, because it would be idle to put two titles together between which there was no difference.[1] On the other hand, the Trinitarian sense should not be here applied to the term Son of God. The notion of the pre-existence of Jesus Christ, as the eternal Son of God, is quite foreign to the context. Mary could not have comprehended it; and on the supposition that she had comprehended or even caught a glimpse of it, so far from being sustained by it in her work as a mother, she would have been rendered incapable of performing it. The notion here expressed by the title *Son of God* is solely that of a personal and mysterious relation between this child and the Divine Being. The angel explains more clearly the meaning of this term in ver. 35.—Lastly, the dignity and mission of this child: He is to fulfil the office of Messiah. The expressions are borrowed from the prophetic descriptions, 2 Sam. vii. 12, 13, Isa. ix. 5–7. The *throne of David* should not be taken here as the emblem of the throne of God, nor *the house of Jacob* as a figurative designation of the Church. These expressions in the mouth of the angel keep their natural and literal sense. It is, indeed, the theocratic royalty and the Israelitish people, neither more nor less, that are in question here; Mary could have understood these expressions in no other way. It is true that, for the promise to be realized in this sense, Israel must have consented to welcome Jesus as their Messiah. In that case, the transformed theocracy would have opened its bosom to the heathen; and the empire of Israel would have assumed, by the very fact of this incorporation, the character of a universal monarchy. The unbelief of Israel foiled this plan, and subverted the regular course of history;

[1] See my *Conférences apologétiques*, 6th conférence: the divinity of Jesus Christ, pp. 15–18.

so that at the present day the fulfilment of these promises is still postponed to the future. But is it likely, after the failure of the ministry of Jesus amongst this people, that about the beginning of the second century, when the fall of Jerusalem had already taken place, any writer would have made an angel prophesy what is expressed here? This picture of the Messianic work could have been produced at no other epoch than that to which this narrative refers it—at the transition period between the old and new covenants. Besides, would it have been possible, at any later period, to reproduce, with such artless simplicity and freshness, the hopes of these early days?

3. *The manner in which the message was received:* vers 34–38.[1]—34. "*Then said Mary unto the angel, How shall this be, seeing I know not a man?* 35. *And the angel answered and said unto her, The Holy Ghost shall come upon thee, and the power of the Highest shall overshadow thee; therefore also that holy thing which shall be born of thee shall be called the Son of God.* 36. *And, behold, thy cousin Elizabeth, she hath also conceived a son in her old age; and this is the sixth month with her, who was called barren.* 37. *For with God nothing shall be impossible.* 38. *And Mary said, Behold the handmaid of the Lord; be it unto me according to thy word. And the angel departed from her.*"—Mary's question does not express doubt: it simply asks for an explanation, and this very request implies faith. Her question is the legitimate expression of the astonishment of a pure conscience.—We observe in the angel's reply the parallelism which among the Hebrews is always the expression of exalted feeling and the mark of the poetic style. The angel touches upon the most sacred of mysteries, and his speech becomes a song. Are the terms *come upon, overshadow,* borrowed, as Bleek thinks, from the image of a bird covering her eggs or brooding over her young? Comp. Gen. i. 3. It appears to us rather that these expressions allude to the cloud which covered the camp of the Israelites in the desert. In ix. 34, as here, the evangelist describes the approach

[1] Ver. 34. Some Mjj. Mnn. Vss. and Fathers add μοι to εσται.—Ver. 35. C. several Mnn. It. add εκ σου after γεννωμενον.—Ver. 36. Instead of συγγενης, 9 Mjj. several Mnn. read συγγενις. Instead of συνειληφυια, the reading of T. R. with 16 Mjj., the Mnn. Syr., ℵ. B. L. Z., συνειληφεν.—Ver. 37. Instead of παρα τω Θεω, ℵ. B. L. Z., παρα του Θεου.

of this mysterious cloud by the term ἐπισκιάζειν.—The Holy Ghost denotes here the divine power, the life-giving breath which calls into developed existence the germ of a human personality slumbering in Mary's womb. This germ is the link which unites Jesus to human nature, and makes Him a member of the race He comes to save. Thus in this birth the miracle of the first creation is repeated on a scale of greater power. Two elements concurred in the formation of man: a body taken from the ground, and the divine breath. With these two elements correspond here the germ derived from the womb of Mary, and the Holy Ghost who fertilizes it. The absolute purity of this birth results, on the one hand, from the perfect holiness of the divine principle which is its efficient cause; on the other, from the absence of every impure motion in her who becomes a mother under the power of such a principle.

By the word *also* ("therefore *also*") the angel alludes to his preceding words: *He shall be called the Son of the Highest.* We might paraphrase it: "And it is precisely for this reason that I said to thee, that . . ." We have then here, from the mouth of the angel himself, an authentic explanation of the term *Son of God* in the former part of his message. After this explanation, Mary could only understand the title in this sense: a human being of whose existence God Himself is the immediate author. It does not convey the idea of pre-existence, but it implies more than the term Messiah, which only refers to His mission. The word ὑψίστου, *of the Highest,* also refers to the term υἱὸς ὑψίστου, *Son of the Highest,* ver. 32, and explains it. Bleek, following the *Peschito,* Tertullian, etc., makes **ἅγιον** the predicate of **κληθήσεται,** and **υἱὸς Θεοῦ** in apposition with **ἅγιον**: "Wherefore that which shall be born of thee shall be called holy, Son of God." But with the predicate *holy,* the verb should have been, not "*shall* be called," but *shall be.* For *holy* is not a title. Besides, the connection with ver. 32 will not allow any other predicate to be given to *shall be called* than *Son of God.* The subject of the phrase is therefore the complex term τὸ γεννώμενον ἅγιον, *the holy thing conceived in thee,* and more especially ἅγιον, *the holy;* this adjective is taken as a substantive. As the adjective of γεννώμενον, taken substantively, it would of necessity be preceded by the article

The words ἐκ σοῦ are a gloss.—What is the connection between this miraculous birth of Jesus and His perfect holiness? The latter does not necessarily result from the former. For holiness is a fact of volition, not of nature. How could we assign any serious meaning to the moral struggles in the history of Jesus,—the temptation, for example,—if His perfect holiness was the necessary consequence of His miraculous birth? But it is not so. The miraculous birth was only the *negative* condition of the spotless holiness of Jesus. Entering into human life in this way, He was placed in the normal condition of man before his fall, and put in a position to fulfil the career originally set before man, in which he was to advance from innocence to holiness. He was simply freed from the obstacle which, owing to the way in which we are born, hinders us from accomplishing this task. But in order to change this possibility into a reality, Jesus had to exert every instant His own free will, and to devote Himself continually to the service of good and the fulfilment of the task assigned Him, namely, "the keeping of His Father's commandment." His miraculous birth, therefore, in no way prevented this conflict from being real. It gave Him liberty *not to sin*, but did not take away from Him the liberty of sinning.

Mary did not ask for a sign; the angel gives her one of his own accord. This sign, it is clear, is in close connection with the promise just made to her. When she beholds in Elizabeth the realization of this promised sign, her faith will be thoroughly confirmed. *Ἰδού, behold,* expresses its unexpectedness.—*Καί* before *αὐτή, she also,* brings out the analogy between the two facts thus brought together.—Mary's being related to Elizabeth in no way proves, as Schleiermacher thought, that Mary did not belong to the tribe of Judah. There was no law to oblige an Israelitish maiden to marry into her own tribe; Mary's father, even if he was of the tribe of Judah, might therefore have espoused a woman of the tribe of Levi. Could it be from this passage that Keim derives his assertion, that the priestly origin of Mary is indicated in Luke (i. 334)? The dative γήρᾳ in the T. R. is only found in some MSS. All the other documents have γήρει, from the form γῆρος.

In ver. 37 the angel refers the two events thus announced to the common cause which explains them both—the bound less omnipotence of God. That is the rock of faith. Ἀδυνατεῖν signifies, properly, *to be powerless.* And Meyer maintains that this must be its meaning here, and that ῥῆμα is to be taken in its proper sense of *word.* In that case we should have to give the preference to the Alex. reading τοῦ Θεοῦ: "No word proceeding from God shall remain powerless." But this meaning is far-fetched. Παρὰ τοῦ Θεοῦ cannot depend naturally either on ῥῆμα or ἀδυνατήσει. Matt. xvii. 20 proves that the verb ἀδυνατεῖν also signifies, in the Hellenistic dialect, *to be impossible.* The sense therefore is, "Nothing shall be impossible." Παρὰ τῷ Θεῷ, *with God,* indicates the sphere in which alone this word is true. As though the angel said, The *impossible* is not divine. Ῥῆμα, as דבר, *a thing,* in so far as announced. In reference to this concise vigorous expression of biblical supernaturalism, Oosterzee says: "The laws of nature are not chains which the Divine Legislator has laid upon Himself; they are threads which He holds in His hand, and which He shortens or lengthens at will."

God's message by the mouth of the angel was not a command. The part Mary had to fulfil made no demands on her. It only remained, therefore, for Mary to consent to the consequences of the divine offer. She gives this consent in a word at once simple and sublime, which involved the most extraordinary act of faith that a woman ever consented to accomplish. Mary accepts the sacrifice of that which is dearer to a young maiden than her very life, and thereby becomes pre-eminently the heroine of Israel, the ideal daughter of Zion, the perfect type of human receptivity in regard to the divine work. We see here what exquisite fruits the lengthened work of the Holy Spirit under the old covenant had produced in true Israelites. The word ἰδού, *behold,* does not here express surprise, but rather the offer of her entire being. Just as Abraham, when he answers God with, *Behold, here I am* (Gen. xxii., Behold, I), Mary places herself at God's disposal. The evangelist shows his tact in the choice of the aorist γένοιτο. The present would have signified, "Let it happen to me this very instant!" The aorist leaves the choice of the time to God.

What exquisite delicacy this scene displays! What simplicity and majesty in the dialogue! Not one word too many, not one too few. A narrative so perfect could only have emanated from the holy sphere within which the mystery was accomplished. A later origin would inevitably have betrayed itself by some foreign element. Hear the *Protevangelium* of James, which dates from the first part of the second century: "Fear not, said the angel to Mary; for thou hast found grace before the Master of all things, and thou shalt conceive by His word. Having heard that, she doubted and said within herself: Shall I conceive of the Lord, of the living God, and shall I give birth as every woman gives birth? And the angel of the Lord said to her: No, not thus, Mary, for the power of God . . .," etc.

THIRD NARRATIVE.—CHAP. I. 39–56.

Mary's Visit to Elizabeth.

This narrative is, as it were, the synthesis of the two preceding. These two divinely favoured women meet and pour forth their hearts.

1. Arrival of Mary (vers. 39–41); 2. Elizabeth's salutation (vers. 42–45); 3. Song of Mary (vers. 46–55). Ver. 56 forms the historical conclusion.

1. *The arrival of Mary:* vers. 39–41.[1]—The terms *arose* and *with haste* express a lively eagerness. This visit met what was in fact a deep need of Mary's soul. Since the message of the angel, Elizabeth had become for her what a mother is for her daughter in the most important moment of her life.—The words *in those days* comprise the time necessary for making preparations for the journey. The distance to be traversed being four days' journey, Mary could not travel so far alone.—The word ἡ ὀρεινή, *the hill country*, has sometimes received quite a special meaning, making it a kind of proper name, by which in popular language the mountainous plateau to the south of Jerusalem was designated; but no instance of a similar designation can be given either from the Old or the New Testament. It appears to me that in this expression, *a city of Juda in the mountain*, it is in no way necessary to give the term mountain the force of a proper name. The context makes it sufficiently clear that it is the mountain *of*

[1] Ver. 40. ℵ. and some Mnn. add εν αγαλλιασει after βρεφος (taken from ver. 44)

Juda, in distinction from the plain *of Juda*, that is meant. Comp. Josh. xv. 48, where ἡ ὀρεινή is employed precisely in this way by the LXX. According to Josh. xv. 55, xxi. 16, there was in this country, to the south of Hebron, a city of the name of *Jutha* or *Juttha;* and according to the second passage (comp. ver. 13), this city was a priestly city.[1] From this several writers (Reland, Winer, Renan) have concluded that the text of our Gospel has undergone an alteration, and that the word *Juda* is a corruption of *Jutha*. But no MS. supports this conjecture; and there is nothing in the context to require it. On the contrary, it is probable that, had Luke desired to indicate by name the city in which the parents of John the Baptist lived, he would have done it sooner. The most important priestly city of this country was Hebron, two leagues south of Bethlehem. And although, subsequent to the exile, the priests no longer made it a rule to reside exclusively in the towns that had been assigned to them at the beginning, it is very natural to look for the home of Zacharias at Hebron, the more so that Rabbinical tradition in the Talmud gives express testimony in favour of this opinion.[2] Keim finds further support for it on this ground, that in the context πόλις Ἰούδα can only signify *the* city of Juda, that is to say, the principal priestly city in Juda. But wrongly; the simplest and most natural translation is: *a* city of Juda.

The detail, *she entered into the house*, serves to put the reader in sympathy with the emotion of Mary at the moment of her arrival. With her first glance at Elizabeth, she recognises the truth of the sign that had been given her by the angel, and at this sight the promise she had herself received acquires a startling reality. Often a very little thing suffices to make a divine thought, which had previously only been conceived as an idea, take distinct form and life within us. And the expression we have used is perhaps, in this case, more than a simple metaphor.—It is not surprising that the intense feeling produced in Mary by the sight of Elizabeth should have reacted immediately on the latter. The unex-

[1] According to Robinson, it is at the present day a village named *Jutta*. The name in the LXX. is *Ita*.

[2] Othon. *Lexicon rabbinicum*, p. 324.

pected arrival of this young maiden at such a solemn moment for herself, the connection which she instantly divines between the miraculous blessing of which she had just been the object and this extraordinary visit, the affecting tones of the voice and holy elevation of this person, producing all the impression of some celestial apparition, naturally predisposed her to receive the illumination of the Spirit. The emotion which possesses her is communicated to the child whose life is as yet one with her own; and at the sudden leaping of this being, who she knows is compassed about by special blessing, the veil is rent. The Holy Spirit, the prophetic Spirit of the old covenant, seizes her, and she salutes Mary as the mother of the Messiah.

2. *The salutation of Elizabeth:* vers. 42–45.[1]—"*And she spake out with a loud voice, and said, Blessed art thou among women, and blessed is the fruit of thy womb.* 43. *And whence is this to me, that the mother of my Lord should come to me?* 44. *For, lo, as soon as the voice of thy salutation sounded in mine ears, the babe leaped in my womb for joy.* 45. *And blessed is she that believed: for there shall be a performance of those things which were told her from the Lord.*" — The course of Elizabeth's thought is this: first of all, Mary and the Son of Mary (ver. 42); next, Elizabeth herself and her son (vers. 43, 44); lastly, Mary and her happiness. The characteristic of all true action of the Holy Spirit is the annihilation of the proper individuality of the person who is the instrument of it, and the elevation of his personal feelings to the height of the divine word. This is precisely the character of Elizabeth's salutation; we shall find it the same in the song of Zacharias. Thus the truth of this word, *Elizabeth was filled with the Holy Ghost,* is justified by this very fact. The reading of some Alexandrians, ἀνεβόησεν, would indicate a cry, instead of a simple breaking forth into speech. The reading κραυγῇ of three other Alex. would have the same meaning. They both savour of exaggeration. In any case. both could not be admitted together. We may translate, *Blessed art thou,* or *Blessed be thou.* The former translation is

[1] Ver. 42. ℵ. C. F. several Mnn. read ανεβοησεν instead of ανεφωνησεν, which is the reading of T. R. with all the rest.—B. L. Z. and Origen (three times) read κραυγη in place of φωνη

best; for exclamation is more in place here than a wish.—The superlative form, *blessed among*, is not unknown to classical Greek.—The expression, *the fruit of thy womb*, appears to imply that the fact of the incarnation was already accomplished; so also does the expression, *the mother of my Lord* (ver. 43).—*Ἵνα*, *in order that* (ver. 43), may keep its ordinary meaning: "What have I done *in order that* this blessing might come to me?" This *ἵνα* is used from the standpoint of the divine intention.—From Mary and her Son, her thought glances to herself and her own child. In calling Mary *the mother of my Lord*, she declares herself the servant of the Messiah, and consequently of His mother also.—Everything of a sublime character springs from a deeper source than the understanding. The leaping of John, a prelude of the work of his life, belongs to the unfathomable depths of instinctive life. Elizabeth sees in it a sign of the truth of the presentiment she felt as soon as she saw Mary.

At ver. 45 she reverts to Mary. The expression *blessed* is doubtless inspired by the contemplation of the calm happiness that irradiates the figure of the young mother. *Ὅτι* cannot be taken here in the sense of *because*; for the word *πιστεύσασα*, *she that believed*, in order that it may have its full force, must not govern anything. "Blessed is she that, at the critical moment, could exercise faith (the aorist)!" De Wette, Bleek, Meyer, think that the proposition which follows should depend on *πιστεύσασα*: "she *who believed* that the things . . . would have their accomplishment." The two former, because *σοί* would be necessary in place of *αὐτῇ*; the third, because all that had been promised to Mary was already accomplished. But Elizabeth's thought loses itself in a kind of meditation, and her words, ceasing to be an apostrophe to Mary, become a hymn of faith. This accounts for the use of a pronoun of the third person. As to Meyer, he forgets that the accomplishment is only just begun, and is far from being completed. The glorification of the Messiah and of Israel still remains to be accomplished. *Τελείωσις* denotes this *complete* accomplishment. But how could Elizabeth speak of the kind of things which had been promised to Mary? What had passed between the angel and Zacharias had enlightened her respecting the similar things that must have taken place between heaven and Mary.

3. *The song of Mary:* vers. 46–56. Elizabeth's salutation was full of excitement (*she spake out with a loud voice*), but Mary's hymn breathes a sentiment of deep inward repose. The greater happiness is, the calmer it is. So Luke says simply, εἶπε, *she said.* A majesty truly regal reigns throughout this canticle. Mary describes first her actual impressions (vers. 46–48*a*); thence she rises to the divine fact which is the cause of them (vers. 48*b*–50); she next contemplates the development of the historical consequences contained in it (vers. 51–53); lastly, she celebrates the moral necessity of this fact as the accomplishment of God's ancient promises to His people (vers. 54 and 55).—The tone of the first strophe has a sweet and calm solemnity. It becomes more animated in the second, in which Mary contemplates the work of the Most High. It attains its full height and energy in the third, as Mary contemplates the immense revolution of which this work is the beginning and cause. Her song drops down and returns to its nest in the fourth, which is, as it were, the amen of the canticle.—This hymn is closely allied to that of the mother of Samuel (1 Sam. ii.), and contains several sentences taken from the book of Psalms. Is it, as some have maintained, destitute of all originality on this account? By no means. There is a very marked difference between Hannah's song of triumph and Mary's. Whilst Mary celebrates her happiness with deep humility and holy restraint, Hannah surrenders herself completely to the feeling of personal triumph; with her very first words she breaks forth into cries of indignation against her enemies. As to the borrowed biblical phrases, Mary gives to these consecrated words an entirely new meaning and a higher application. The prophets frequently deal in this way with the words of their predecessors. By this means these organs of the Spirit exhibit the continuity and progress of the divine work. Criticism asks whether Mary turned over the leaves of her Bible before she spoke. It forgets that every young Israelite knew by heart from childhood the songs of Hannah, Deborah, and David; that they sang them as they went up to the feasts at Jerusalem; and that the singing of psalms was the daily

accompaniment of the morning and evening sacrifice, as well as one of the essential observances of the passover meal.

Vers. 46–55.[1] "*And Mary said, My soul doth magnify the Lord,* 47. *And my spirit hath rejoiced in God my Saviour.* 48*a*. *For He hath regarded the low estate of His handmaiden.*

48*b*. *For, behold, from henceforth all generations shall call me blessed.* 49. *For He that is mighty hath done to me great things; and holy is His name.* 50. *And His mercy is on them that fear Him from generation to generation.*

51. *He hath showed strength with His arm; He hath scattered the proud in the imagination of their hearts.* 52. *He hath put down the mighty from their seats, and exalted them of low degree.* 53. *He hath filled the hungry with good things, and the rich He hath sent empty away.*

54. *He hath holpen His servant Israel, in remembrance of His mercy;* 55. *(As He spake to our fathers), to Abraham, and to his seed for ever.*"

Vers. 46–48*a*. The contrast between the tone of this canticle and Elizabeth's discourse forbids the admission of the reading of some Latin authorities which puts it in the mouth of the latter. It is, indeed, Mary's reply to the congratulations of Elizabeth.—Luke does not say that Mary was filled with the Spirit (comp. ver. 41). At this epoch of her life she dwelt habitually in a divine atmosphere, whilst the inspiration of Elizabeth was only momentary. Her first word, μεγαλύνει, *magnifies,* fully expresses this state of her soul. In what, indeed, does the magnifying of the Divine Being consist, if not in giving Him, by constant adoration (the verb is in the present tense), a larger place in one's own heart and in the hearts of men? The present, *magnifies,* is in contrast with the aorist, *rejoiced,* in the following sentence. Some would give the aorist here the sense which this tense some-

[1] Ver. 46. Three MSS. of the *Italic*, a. b. l., read *Elizabeth* instead of *Mary*. Irenæus, at least in the Latin translation, follows this reading; and Origen (Latin translation) speaks of MSS. in which it was found.—Ver. 49. ℵ. B. D. L. read μεγαλα instead of μεγαλεια, the reading of T. R. with 22 Mjj. and all the Mnn. —Ver. 50. B. C. L. Z. read εις γενεας και γενεας; ℵ. F. M. O. and several Mnn., εις γενεας και γενεαν, in place of εις γενεας γενεων, which is the reading of 12 Mjj. and most of the Mnn.—Ver. 51. ℵ[ca] E. F. H. O[a]. O[c]. and some Mnn. read διανοιας instead of διανοια.—Ver. 55. C. F. M. O. S. 60 Mnn. read εως αιωνος instead of εις τον αιωνα.—Ver. 56. ℵ. B. L. Z. read ως instead of ωσει. D. It[plerique]. Or.. omit it.

times has in Greek, that of a repetition of the act. It is more natural, however, to regard it as an allusion to a particular fact, which kindled in her a joy that was altogether peculiar. The seat of this emotion was her spirit—*πνεῦμα, spirit.* When the human spirit is referred to in Scripture, the word indicates the deepest part of our humanity, the point of contact between man and God. The *soul* is the actual centre of human life, the principle of individuality, and the seat of those impressions which are of an essentially personal character. This soul communicates, through the two organs with which it is endowed, the spirit and the body, with two worlds,—the one above, the other below it,—with the divine world and the world of nature. Thus, while the expression, "*My soul* doth magnify," refers to the personal emotions of Mary, to her feelings as a woman and a mother, all which find an outlet in adoration, these words, "My *spirit* hath rejoiced," appear to indicate the moment when, in the profoundest depths of her being, by the touch of the Divine Spirit, the promise of the angel was accomplished in her.—These two sentences contain yet a third contrast: The *Lord* whom she magnifies is the Master of the service to which she is absolutely devoted; the *Saviour* in whom she has rejoiced is that merciful God who has made her feel His restoring power, and who in her person has just saved fallen humanity. Further, it is this divine compassion which she celebrates in the following words, ver. 48. What did He find in her which supplied sufficient grounds for such a favour? One thing alone—her *low estate.* *Ταπείνωσις* does not denote, as *ταπεινότης* does, the moral disposition of humility; Mary does not boast of her humility. It is rather, as the form of the word indicates, an act of which she had been the object, the humbling influence under which she had been brought by her social position, and by the whole circumstances which had reduced her, a daughter of kings, to the rank of the poorest of the daughters of Israel.—Perhaps the interval between the moment of the incarnation, denoted by the aorists *hath rejoiced, hath regarded,* and that in which she thus celebrated it, was not very great. Was not that thrilling moment, when she entered the house of Zacharias, and beheld at a glance in the person of Elizabeth the fulfilment of the sign given her by the angel, the moment of supreme divine manifestation towards herself? The expression, *Behold, henceforth*, which commences the following strophe, thus becomes full of meaning.

Vers. 48*b*–50. The greatness of her happiness appears in the renown which it will bring her; hence the γάρ, *for*. The word *behold* refers to the unexpected character of this dealing. Mary ascribes to God, as its author, the fact which she celebrates, and glorifies the three divine perfections displayed in it. And first *the power*. In calling God the *Almighty*, she appears to make direct allusion to the expression of the angel: *the power of the Highest* (ver. 35). Here is an act in which is displayed, as in no other since the appearance of man, the creative power of God. The received reading μεγαλεῖα answers better than the reading of some Alex., μεγάλα, to the emphatic term נפלאות, which Luke doubtless read in his Hebrew document (comp. Acts ii. 11). But this omnipotence is not of a purely physical character; it is subservient to *holiness*. This is the second perfection which Mary celebrates. She felt herself, in this marvellous work, in immediate contact with supreme holiness; and she well knew that this perfection more than any other constitutes the essence of God: *His name is holy*. The *name* is the sign of an object in the mind which knows it. The *name of God* therefore denotes, not the Divine Being, but the more or less adequate reflection of Him in those intelligences which are in communion with Him. Hence we see how this name can be *sanctified*, rendered holy. The essential nature of God may be more clearly understood by His creatures, and more completely disengaged from those clouds which have hitherto obscured it in their minds. Thus Mary had received, in the experience she had just passed through, a new revelation of the holiness of the Divine Being.—This short sentence is not dependent on the ὅτι, *because*, which governs the preceding. For the καί, *and*, which follows, establishes a close connection between it and ver. 50, which, if subordinated to ver. 49, would be too drawn out.—This feature of holiness which Mary so forcibly expresses, is, in fact, that which distinguishes the incarnation from all the analogous facts of heathen mythologies.

The third divine perfection celebrated by Mary is *mercy*

(ver. 50). Mary has already sung its praise in ver. 48 in relation to herself. She speaks of it here in a more general way. By *them that fear God,* she intends more especially Zacharias and Elizabeth, there present before her; then all the members of her people who share with them this fundamental trait of Jewish piety, and who thus constitute the true Israel. —The received reading εἰς γενεὰς γενεῶν, *from generation to generation,* is a form of the superlative which is found in the expression *to the age of the ages,* the meaning of which is, "to the most remote generations." The two other readings mentioned in the critical notes express continuity rather than remoteness in time. These words, "*on them that fear Him,*" are the transition to the third strophe. For they implicitly contain the antithesis which comes out in the verses following.

Vers. 51–53. A much more strongly marked poetical parallelism characterizes this strophe. Mary here describes with a thrill of emotion, of which even her language partakes, the great Messianic revolution, the commencement of which she was beholding at that very time. In the choice God had made of two persons of such humble condition in life as herself and her cousin, she saw at a glance the great principle which would regulate the impending renewal of all things. It is to be a complete reversal of the human notions of greatness and meanness.—The *poor* and the *hungry* are evidently the Israelites *fearing God* of ver. 50. Such expressions cannot apply to Israel as a whole—to the proud Pharisees and rich Sadducees, for example. The line of demarcation which she draws in these words passes, therefore, not between the Jews and Gentiles, but between the pious Israelites and all that exalt themselves against God, whether in or beyond Israel. The *proud,* the *mighty,* and the *rich,* denote Herod and his court, the Pharisees and the Sadducees, as well as the foreign oppressors, Cæsar and his armies, and all the powers of heathendom. The aorists of these three verses indicate, according to Bleek, the repetition of the act; so he translates them by the present. I rather think that to Mary's eyes the catastrophe presents itself as already consummated in the act which God had just accomplished. Does not this act contain the principle of the rejection of all that is exalted in the world, and of the choice of whatever in human estimation is brought low? All these divine acts which are about to follow, one after another, will only be a further application of the same principle. They are virtually contained in that which Mary celebrates. Consequently the aorists are properly translated by the past.—The first proposition of ver. 51 applies to the righteous and wicked alike. Still the former of these two applications predominates (ver. 50). The *arm* is the symbol of force. The expression ποιεῖν κράτος, *to make strength,* is a Hebraism, עשה חיל (Ps. cxviii. 15). The LXX. translate it by ποιεῖν δύναμιν. If it was Luke who translated the Hebrew document into Greek, it is evident that he kept his version independent of the LXX. —The favour God shows to the righteous has its necessary counterpart in the overthrow of the wicked. This is the connection of the second proposition. The expression ὑπερηφάνους διανοίᾳ, *proud in thought,* answers to אבירי לב (Ps. lxxvi. 6); the LXX. translate this expression by ἀσύνετοι τῇ καρδίᾳ. The dative διανοίᾳ defines the adjective: "the proud in *thought,* who exalt themselves in their thoughts." Mary represents all these as forming an opposing host to men that fear God; hence the expression *scatter.* With the reading διανοίας, ὑπερηφάνους is the epithet of the substantive, *proud thoughts.* This reading is evidently a mistake.

Ver. 52. From the moral contrast between the proud and the faithful, Mary passes to a contrast of their social position, *the mighty* and those of *low degree.* The former are those who reign without that spirit of humility which is inspired by the fear of Jehovah.—The third antithesis (ver. 53), which is connected with the preceding, is that of suffering and prosperity. The *hungry* represent the class which toils for a living—artisans, like Joseph and Mary; the rich are men gorged with wealth, Israelites or heathen, who, in the use they make of God's gifts, entirely forget their dependence and responsibility. The abundance which is to compensate the former certainly consists—the contrast requires it—of temporal enjoyments. But since this abundance is an effect of the divine blessing, it implies, as its condition, the possession of spiritual graces. For, from the Old Testament point of view, prosperity is only a snare, when it does not rest on the foundation of peace with God. And so also, the spoliation which is to befall the rich is without doubt the loss of their temporal advantages. But what makes this loss a real evil is, that it is the effect of a divine curse upon their pride.

The poetic beauty of these three verses is heightened by a crossing of the members of the three antitheses, which is substituted for the ordinary method of symmetrical parallelism. In the first contrast (ver. 51), the *righteous* occupy the first place, the *proud* the second; in the second, on the contrary (ver. 52), the *mighty* occupy the first place, so as to be in close connection with the proud of ver. 51, and the *lowly* the second; in the third (ver. 53), the *hungry* come first, joining themselves with the lowly of ver. 52, and the *rich* form the second member. The mind passes in this way, as it were, on the crest of a wave, from like to like, and the taste is not offended, as it would have been by a symmetrical arrangement in which the homogeneous members of the contrast occurred every time in the same order.

Vers. 54, 55. Mary celebrates in this last strophe the faithfulness of God. That, in fact, is the foundation of the whole Messianic work. If the preceding strophe unveils to us the future developments of this work, this sends us back to its beginning in the remote past.—*Παῖς* signifies here *servant* rather than *son*. It is an allusion to the title of Israel, *servant of the Lord* (Isa. xli. 8). The Master sees His well-beloved servant crushed beneath the burden which his pitiless oppressors have imposed, and He takes it upon *Himself* (middle λαμβάνεσθαι) in order to *comfort* him (ἀντί). This term, *Israel His servant*, seems at first sight to apply to the whole people; and doubtless it is this explanation that has led several interpreters to apply the expressions *proud, mighty, rich,* in the preceding verses, solely to foreign oppressors. If, as we have seen, the latter explanation cannot be maintained, we must conclude that by this Israel, the servant of God, Mary understands the *God-fearing* Israelites of the fiftieth verse, not as individuals, but as the true representatives of the nation itself. The faithful portion of the nation is identified in this expression with the nation as a whole, because it is its true substance; besides, Mary could not know beforehand how far this true Israel would correspond with the actual people. For her own part, she already sees in hope (aorist ἀντελάβετο) the normal Israel transformed into the glorified Messianic nation. Would such a view as this have been possible when once the national unbelief had apparently foiled all these Messianic hopes?—There is nothing here to hinder the infinitive of the end, μνησθῆναι, from preserving its proper meaning. *To remember His promises* signifies, in order not to be unfaithful.—Erasmus, Calvin, and others regard the datives τῷ Ἀβραάμ and τῷ σπέρματι as governed by ἐλάλησε, in apposition with πρὸς τοὺς πατέρας: "As He spake to our fathers, to Abraham, and to his seed . . ." But this construction is forced and inadmissible. Besides, the last words, *for ever,* if referred to the verb *He spake,* would have no meaning. Therefore we must make the proposition, *as He spake to our fathers,* a parenthesis intended to recall the divine faithfulness, and refer the datives, *to Abraham and to his seed,* to the verb, *to remember His mercy.* It is the dative of favour, *to remember towards Abraham and . . .* For Abraham, as well as his race, enjoys the mercy which is shown to the latter (comp. ver. 17). The words *for ever* qualify the idea, not to forget His mercy. Divine forgetfulness will never cause the favour promised to Israel to cease. Would any poet have ever put such words into the mouth of Mary, when Jerusalem was in ruins and its people dispersed?

Ver. 56 is a historical conclusion.—Did the departure of Mary take place before the birth of John the Baptist? We might suppose so from the particle δέ and the aorist ἐπλήσθη (ver. 57), which very naturally imply a historical succession. But, on the other hand, it would be hardly natural that Mary should leave at a time when the expected deliverance of Elizabeth was so near at hand. This verse, therefore, must be regarded as a historical anticipation, such as is frequently found in Luke. Comp. i. 65, iii. 19, 20, etc.

FOURTH NARRATIVE.—CHAP. I. 57–80.

Birth and Circumcision of John the Baptist.

Here opens the second cycle of the narratives of the infancy. This first narration comprises—1. The birth of John (vers. 57, 58); 2. The circumcision of the child (vers. 59–66);

3. The song of Zacharias, with a short historical conclusion (vers. 67–80).

1. *Birth of John:* vers. 57 and 58.—These verses are like a pleasing picture of Jewish home-life. We see the neighbours and relations arriving one after the other,—the former first, because they live nearest. Elizabeth, the happy mother, is the central figure of the scene; every one comes up to her in turn. Ἐμεγάλυνε μετ' αὐτῆς, literally, *He had magnified with her,* is a Hebraistic expression (הגדל עם; comp. 1 Sam. xii. 24 in the LXX.). This use of μετά, *with,* comes from the fact that man is in such cases the material which concurs in the result of the divine action.

2. *Circumcision of John:* vers. 59–66.[1] As an Israelitish child by its birth became a member of the human family, so by circumcision, on the corresponding day of the following week, he was incorporated into the covenant (Gen. xvii.); and it was the custom on this occasion to give him his name. The subject of ἦλθον, *came,* is that of the preceding verse. It has been maintained that the text suggests something miraculous in the agreement of Elizabeth and Zacharias; as if, during the nine months which had just passed away, the father had not made to the mother a hundred times over the communication which he presently makes to all present (ver. 63)! How many times already, especially during Mary's stay in their house, must the names of John and Jesus have been mentioned!—It has been inferred from the words, *they made signs to him* (ver. 62), that Zacharias became deaf as well as dumb. But the case of Zacharias cannot be assimilated to that of deaf mutes from their birth, in whom dumbness ordinarily results from deafness. The whole scene, on the contrary, implies that Zacharias had heard everything. The use of the language of signs proceeds simply from this, that we instinctively adopt this means of communication towards those who can speak in no other way.

Ver. 63. The word λέγων added to ἔγραψεν is a Hebraism

[1] Ver. 61. ℵ. A. B. C. L. Δ. Λ. Z. Π. and some Mnn. read εκ της συγγενειας, in place of εν τη συγγενεια, the reading of T. R., with 11 Mjj., the greater part of the Mnn. Syr. It.—Ver. 62. ℵ. B. D. F. G., αυτο in place of αυτον.—Ver. 65. ℵ* reads δια τα instead of διελαλειτο παντα τα.—Ver. 66. ℵ. B. C. D. L. It. Vg. add γαρ after και.

(ויכתב לאמר, 2 Kings x. 6), the meaning of which is, "deciding the question."—The expression, *his name is,* points to a higher authority which has so determined it; and it is this circumstance, rather than the agreement between the father and mother—a fact so easily explained—which astonishes the persons present. Every one recalls on this occasion the strange events which had preceded the birth of the child.

Ver. 64. Zacharias, thus obedient, recovers his speech, of which his want of faith had deprived him. The verb ἀνεῴχθη, *was opened,* does not agree with the second subject, *the tongue,* for which the verb *was loosed,* taken from the preceding verb, must be supplied.—In the words, *he spake and praised God,* naturally it is on the word *spake* that the emphasis rests, in opposition to his previous dumbness. The last words are only an appendix, serving to introduce the song which follows. We must therefore refrain from translating, with Ostervald, "He spake *by* praising God."

Ver. 65. At the sight of this miracle, surprise changes into fear. And this impression spreads abroad, with the report of these facts, throughout all the country. That is more especially the sense of the reading of א, which, however, from a critical point of view, it is impossible to adopt.—Ver. 66. They not merely told, they laid to heart; these were the first emotions of the Messianic era.—The Alex. reading, καὶ γάρ, *for also the hand of the Lord was with him,* although adopted by Tischendorf, appears to us untenable. Whether, in fact, this *for* be put in the mouth of the narrator, or be assigned to the persons who ask the preceding question, in either case these words, *the hand of the Lord was with him,* must refer to all the circumstances which have just been narrated, while, according to the natural sense of the imperfect ἦν, *was,* they apply to the entire childhood of John the Baptist. This *for* has been wrongly added, with a view of making this reflection the motive of the preceding question. The T. R. is supported by not only the majority of the Mjj., but more especially by the agreement of the *Alexandrinus* and of the *Peschito,* which is always a criterion worthy of attention.—The development of this child was effected with the marked concurrence of divine *power.* The *hand,* here as usually, is the emblem of force.—These last words form the first of those resting-points which we shall often meet with in the course of our Gospel, and which occur in the book of the Acts. It is a picture, drawn with a single stroke of the pen, of the entire childhood of John the Baptist. Comp. ver. 80, which describes, by a corresponding formula, his youth.

3. *The song of Zacharias:* vers. 67–80.—It might be supposed that Zacharias composed this song in view of the religious and moral progress of the child, or on the occasion of some special event in which the divine power within him was displayed during the course of his childhood. We are led, however, to another supposition by the connection between the first words of the song, *Blessed be the Lord,* and the expression which the evangelist has employed in ver. 64, "he spake, *blessing God.*" This song, which was composed in the priest's mind during the time of his silence, broke solemnly from his lips the moment speech was restored to him, as the metal flows from the crucible in which it has been melted the moment that an outlet is made for it. At ver. 64, Luke is contented to indicate the place of the song, in order not to interrupt the narrative, and he has appended the song itself to his narrative, as possessing a value independent of the time when it was uttered.—We observe in the hymn of Zacharias the same order as in the salutation of Elizabeth. The theocratic sentiment breaks forth first: Zacharias gives thanks for the arrival of the *times of the Messiah* (vers. 68–75). Then his paternal feeling comes out, as it were, in a parenthesis: the father expresses his joy at the glorious part assigned to *his son* in this great work (vers. 76 and 77); lastly, thanksgiving for the Messianic *salvation* overflows and closes the song (vers. 78 and 79).—The spiritual character of this passage appears even from this exposition. It is the work of the Holy Spirit alone to subordinate even the legitimate emotions of paternal affection to the theocratic sentiment.

1*st.* Vers. 67–75.—Zacharias gives thanks, first of all, for the coming of the Messiah (vers. 67–70); then for the deliverance which His presence is about to procure for Israel (vers. 71–75).

Vers. 67–75.[1] "*And his father Zacharias was filled with*

[1] Ver. 70. א. B. L. W°. Δ. some Mnn. Or. omit των after αγιων.—Ver. 74. א. B. L. W°. some Mnn. Or. omit ημων.—Ver. 75. B. L., ταις ημεραις, instead of

the Holy Ghost, and prophesied, saying, 68. *Blessed be the Lord God of Israel; for He hath visited and redeemed His people,* 69. *And hath raised up a horn of salvation for us in the house of His servant David;* 70. *As He spake by the mouth of His holy prophets, which have been since the world began;* 71. *That we should be saved from our enemies, and from the hand of all that hate us;* 72. *To perform the mercy promised to our fathers, and to remember His holy covenant,* 73. *The oath which He sware to our father Abraham,* 74. *That He would grant unto us, that we, being delivered out of the hand of our enemies, might serve Him without fear,* 75. *In holiness and righteousness before Him, all the days of our life.*"

The aorists, *hath raised up, hath delivered,* imply a knowledge on Zacharias' part of the fact of the incarnation. The term *visited* refers to the absence of God during the four centuries in which the prophetic voice had been silent and heaven shut. The abstract expressions of the sixty-eighth verse are followed in ver. 69 by one more concrete. Zacharias is emboldened to designate the Messiah Himself. He calls Him *a horn of salvation.* This image of *a horn* is frequent in the Old Testament, where it had been already applied to the Messiah: *I will raise up a horn to David* (Ps. cxxxii. 16). The explanation must be found neither in the horns of the altar on which criminals sought to lay hold, nor in the horns with which they ornamented their helmets; the figure is taken from the horns of the bull, in which the power of this animal resides. It is a natural image among an agricultural people. The term ἤγειρε, *hath raised up,* is properly applied to an organic growth, like a horn. Just as the strength of the animal is concentrated in its horn, so all the delivering power granted to the family of David for the advantage of the people will be concentrated in the Messiah. This verse implies that Zacharias regarded Mary as a descendant of David.—In ver. 70, Zacharias sets forth the greatness of this appearing by referring to the numerous and ancient promises of which it is the subject. Whether with or without the article τῶν, ἁγίων (*holy*) must in any case be taken as an adjective; and it is unnecessary to translate, *of His saints of every age who have*

τας ημερας.—ℵ. A. B. C. D. and 11 other Mjj. 40 Mnn. Syr. It. omit της ζωης which is the reading of T. R. with 7 Mjj. Or.

been prophets which would imply that all the saints have prophesied. If τῶν is retained, the word simply serves as a point of support to the definitive term ἀπ' αἰῶνος. The epithet *holy* characterizes the prophets as organs, not of a human and consequently profane word, but of a divine revelation. Holiness is the distinctive feature of all that emanates from God. We may judge, by the impression which the certain approach of Christ's advent would make on us, of the feeling which must have been produced in the hearts of these people by the thought, The Messiah is there; history, long suspended, resumes its march, and touches its goal.

In vers. 71–75, Zacharias describes the work of this Messiah.—The most natural explanation of σωτηρίαν, *salvation*, is to regard this word as in apposition with the term *horn of salvation* (ver. 69). The notion of salvation is easily substituted for that of a Saviour.—The idea of salvation, brought out in this first word, is exhibited in its full meaning in ver. 74. The two terms, *our enemies*, and *them that hate us*, cannot be altogether synonymous. The former denotes the foreign heathen oppressors; the latter would embrace also the native tyrants, Herod and his party, so odious to true Israelites.—In granting this deliverance, God *shows mercy* (ver. 72) not only to the living, but to the dead, who were waiting with the heart-sickness of deferred hope for the accomplishment of the promises, and especially of the *oaths* of God. On this idea, see i. 17; for the infinitive μνησθῆναι, ver. 54; for the turn of expression ποιεῖν μετά, ver. 58.—Ὅρκον (ver. 73) is in apposition with διαθήκης. The accusative is occasioned by the pronoun ὅν. This attraction is the more easily accounted for, that μνᾶσθαι is construed in the LXX. with the accusative and the genitive indifferently.—The infinitive *to grant* expresses the long-expected end of the development of prophecy, a development which seems designed to typify this long period.—The article τοῦ characterizes the infinitive δοῦναι as the end desired and determined from the beginning. Grammatically, it depends on ὅρκον; logically, on all that precedes.—In the following phrase, the relation of ῥυσθέντας to λατρεύειν should be observed: *after having been delivered, to serve God:* the end is perfect religious service; political deliverance is only a means to it. Perfect worship requires outward security. The

Messiah is about to reign; no Antiochus Epiphanes or Pompey shall any more profane the sanctuary! We find here in all its purity the ideal salvation as it is described in the Old Testament, and as the son of Zacharias himself understood it to the very last. Its leading feature is the indissoluble union of the two deliverances, the religious and the political; it was a glorious theocracy founded on national holiness. This programme prevented John the Baptist from identifying himself with the course of the ministry of Jesus. How, after the unbelief of Israel had created a gulf between the expectation and the facts, could a later writer, attributing to Zacharias just what words he pleased, put into his mouth these fond hopes of earlier days?

Ὁσιότης, *purity*, and δικαιοσύνη, *righteousness* (ver. 75), have been distinguished in several ways. Bleek and others refer the former of these terms to the inward disposition, the latter to the outward conduct. But righteousness, in the Scriptures, comprehends more than the outward act. Others apply the former to relations with God, the latter to relations with men. But righteousness also comprehends man's relations with God. It appears to us rather that *purity*, ὁσιότης, is a negative quality, the absence of stain; and *righteousness*, δικαιοσύνη, a positive quality, the presence of all those religious and moral virtues which render worship acceptable to God. Comp. Eph. iv. 24.—The authorities decide in favour of the excision of the words τῆς ζωῆς, although the French translation cannot dispense with them. —At the time of the captivity, the prophet-priest Ezekiel contemplated, under the image of a *temple* of perfect dimensions, the perfected theocracy (Ezek. xl.–xlviii.). Here the priest-prophet Zacharias contemplates the same ideal under the image of an uninterrupted and undefiled *worship*. The Holy Spirit adapts the form of His revelations to the habitual prepossessions of those who are to be the organs of them.

2*d*. Vers. 76, 77.—From the height to which he has just attained, Zacharias allows his glance to fall upon the little child at rest before him, and he assigns him his part in the work which has begun. Ver. 76 refers to him personally, ver. 77 to his mission.

Vers. 76 and 77.[1] "*And thou, child, shalt be called the Prophet of the Highest, for thou shalt go before the face of the Lord to prepare His ways,* 77 *To give knowledge of salvation unto His people by the remission of their sins.*"

The reading καὶ σύ, *and thou*, connects, by an easy transition, the forerunner with the work of the Messiah. The Alex. reading καὶ σὺ δέ, *but thou*, brings out more strongly, too strongly, doubtless, this secondary personality; it has against it not only the sixteen other Mjj., but further, the *Peschito*, the *Italic*, Irenæus, and Origen, and must therefore be rejected. The title of *prophet of the Highest* simply places John the Baptist in that choir of the prophets of whom Zacharias speaks in ver. 70; later on, Jesus will assign him a higher place.—In saying *the Lord*, Zacharias can only be thinking of the Messiah. This is proved by the πρό, *before Him*, in προπορεύσῃ, and the αὐτοῦ, *His ways*. But he could not designate Him by this name, unless, with Malachi, he recognised in His coming the appearing of Jehovah (comp. i. 17, 43, ii. 11). The second proposition is a combination of the two propositions, Isa. xl. 3 (ἑτοιμάσαι) and Mal. iii. 1 (προπορεύσῃ),—prophecies which are also found combined in Mark i. 2, 3. The article τοῦ before δοῦναι, *to give*, indicates a *purpose*. This word, in fact, throws a vivid light on the aim of John the Baptist's ministry. Why was the ministry of the Messiah preceded by that of another divine messenger? Because the very notion of salvation was falsified in Israel, and had to be corrected before salvation could be realized. A carnal and malignant patriotism had taken possession of the people and their rulers, and the idea of a political deliverance had been substituted for that of a moral salvation. If the notion of salvation had not been restored to its scriptural purity before being realized by the Messiah, not only would He have had to employ a large part of the time assigned to Him in accomplishing this indispensable task; but further, He would certainly have been accused of inventing a theory of salvation to suit His impotence to effect any other. There was needed, then, another person, divinely authorized, to remind the people

[1] Ver. 76. ℵ. B. C. D. L. R. read δε after και συ.—ℵ. B. Or., ενωπιον instead of προ προσωπου.—Ver. 77. A. C. M. O. R. U., some Mnn., read ημων instead of αυτου.

that perdition consisted not in subjection to the Romans, but in divine condemnation; and that salvation, therefore, was not temporal emancipation, but the forgiveness of sins. To implant once more in the hearts of the people this notion of salvation, was indeed to prepare the way for Jesus, who was to accomplish this salvation, and no other. The last words, *by the remission of their sins,* depend directly on the word σωτηρίας, *salvation:* salvation *by,* that is to say, *consisting in.* The article τῆς is omitted before ἐν ἀφέσει, as is the case when the definitive forms, with the word on which it depends, merely one and the same notion.—The pronoun αὐτῶν refers to all the individuals comprehended under the collective idea of *people.* The authorities which read ἡμῶν are insufficient.—The words *to His people* show that Israel, although the people of God, were blind to the way of salvation. John the Baptist was to show to this people, who believed that all they needed was political restoration, that they were not less guilty than the heathen, and that they needed just as much divine pardon. This was precisely the meaning of the baptism to which he invited the Jews.

3*d.* Vers. 78 and 79.—After this episode, Zacharias returns to the principal subject of his song, and, in an admirable closing picture, describes the glory of Messiah's appearing, and of the salvation which He brings.

Vers. 78 and 79.[1] "*Through the tender mercy of our God, whereby the day-spring from on high hath visited us,* 79 *To give light to them that sit in darkness and in the shadow of death, to guide our feet unto the way of peace.*"

Zacharias ascends to the highest source whence this stream of grace pours down upon our earth—the divine mercy. This idea is naturally connected with that of pardon (ver. 77), as is expressed by διά with the accusative, which means properly *by reason of.*—The *bowels* in Scripture are the seat of all the sympathetic emotions. Σπλάγχνα answers to רחמים.—The future ἐπισκέψεται, *will visit,* in some Alex., is evidently a correction suggested by the consideration that Christ was not born at the time Zacharias was speaking. Yet even such instances as these do not disturb the faith of critics in the authority of Alexandrine MSS.!

[1] **Ver. 78. ℵ. B. L.,** ἐπισκέψεται: instead of ἐπεσκέψατο.

All the images in the picture portrayed in vers. 78, 79 appear to be borrowed from the following comparison:—A caravan misses its way and is lost in the desert; the unfortunate pilgrims, overtaken by night, are sitting down in the midst of this fearful darkness, expecting death. All at once a bright star rises in the horizon and lights up the plain; the travellers, taking courage at this sight, arise, and by the light of this star find the road which leads them to the end of their journey.—The substantive ἀνατολή, *the rising*, which by general consent is here translated *the dawn*, has two senses in the LXX. It is employed to translate the noun צמח, *branch*, by which Jeremiah and Zechariah designate the Messiah. This sense of the word ἀνατολή is unknown in profane Greek. The term is also used by the LXX. to express the rising of a heavenly body—the rising of the moon, for instance; comp. Isa. lx. 19. This sense agrees with the meaning of the verb ἀνατέλλειν; Isa. lx. 1, "*The glory of the Lord hath risen* (ἀνατέταλκεν) *upon thee*;" Mal. iv. 2, "*The Sun of righteousness shall rise* (ἀνατελεῖ) *upon you*." This is the meaning of the word ἀνατολή in good Greek. And it appears to us that this is its meaning here. It follows, indeed, from the use of the verb *hath visited us*, which may very well be said of a star, but not of a branch; and the same remark applies to the images that follow, *to light* and *to direct* (ver. 79). Besides, the epithet *from on high* agrees much better with the figure of a star than with that of a plant that sprouts. The regimen *from on high* does not certainly quite agree with the verb *to rise*. But the term *from on high* is suggested by the idea of *visiting* which goes before: it is from the bosom of divine mercy that this star comes down, and it does not *rise* upon humanity until after it has descended and been made man. Bleek does not altogether reject this obvious meaning of ἀνατολή; but he maintains that we should combine it with the sense of *branch*, by supposing a play of words turning upon the double image of a sprouting branch and a rising star; and as there is no Hebrew word which will bear this double meaning, he draws from this passage the serious critical consequence, that this song, and therefore all the others contained in these two chapters, were originally written, not in Aramæan, but in Greek, which of course deprives them of their authenticity.

But this whole explanation is simply a play of Bleek's imagination. There is nothing in the text to indicate that the author intends any play upon words here; and, as we have seen, none of the images employed are compatible with the meaning of *branch*.

The expressions of ver. 79 are borrowed from Isa. ix. 1, lx. 2. *Darkness* is the emblem of alienation from God, and of the spiritual ignorance that accompanies it. This darkness is a *shadow of death*, because it leads to perdition, just as the darkening of sight in the dying is a prelude to the night of death. The term *sit* denotes a state of exhaustion and despair. The sudden shining forth of the star brings the whole caravan of travellers to their feet (τοὺς πόδας), and enables them to find their way.—The *way of peace* denotes the means of obtaining reconciliation with God, the chief of all temporal and spiritual blessings. *Εἰρήνη*, *peace*, answers to שָׁלוֹם, a word by which the Hebrew language designates the bountiful supply of whatever answers to human need—full prosperity.

Ver. 80. The historical conclusion, ver. 80, corresponds with that in ver. 66. As the latter sketches with a stroke of the pen the childhood of John, so this gives a picture of his youth, and carries us forward to the time when he began his ministry. The term *he grew* refers to his physical development, and the expression following, *waxed strong in spirit*, to his spiritual development, that is to say, religious, moral, and intellectual. The predominant feature of this development was force, energy (*he grew strong in spirit*). Luke, doubtless, means by this the power of the will over the instincts and inclinations of the body. The *spirit* is here certainly that of John himself; but when a man developes in a right way, it is only by communion with the Divine Spirit that his spirit unfolds, as the flower only blows when in contact with the light.—This spiritual development of John was due to no human influence. For the child lived *in the deserts*. Probably the desert of Judea is meant here, an inhabited country, whose deeply creviced soil affords an outlet to several streams that empty themselves into the Dead Sea. This country, abounding in caves, has always been the refuge of anchorites. In the time of John the Baptist there were probably Essenıan monasteries there; for history says positively that these cenobites dwelt upon both shores of the Dead Sea. It has been inferred from this passage that John, during his sojourn in the desert, visited these sages, and profited by their teaching. This opinion is altogether opposed to the design of the text which is to attribute to God alone the direction of the development of the forerunner. But more than this. If John was taught by the Essenes, it must be admitted that the only thing their instructions did for him was to lead him to take entirely opposite views on all points. The Essenes had renounced every Messianic expectation; the soul of John's life and ministry was the expectation of the Messiah and the preparation for His work. The Essenes made matter the seat of sin; John, by his energetic calls to conversion, shows plainly enough that he found it in the will. The Essenes withdrew from society, and gave themselves up to mystic contemplation; John, at the signal from on high, threw himself boldly into the midst of the people, and to the very last took a most active and courageous part in the affairs of his country. If, after all, any similarities are found between him and them, John's originality is too well established to attribute them to imitation; such similarities arise from the attempt they both made to effect a reform in degenerate Judaism. The relation of John to the Essenes is very similar to that of Luther to the mystics of the middle ages. On the part of the Essenes, as of the mystics, there is the human effort which attests the need; on the part of John, as well as of Luther, the divine work which satisfies it.—The abstract plural *in the deserts* proves that this observation is made with a moral and not a geographical aim.—The word ἀνάδειξις, *showing*, denotes the installation of a servant into his office, his official institution into his charge. The author of this act, unnamed but understood, is evidently God. It follows from iii. 2, and from John i. 31–33, that a direct communication from on high, perhaps a theophany, such as called Moses from the desert, was the signal for John to enter upon his work. But we have no *account* of this scene which took place between God and His messenger. Our evangelists only relate what they know.

FIFTH NARRATIVE.—CHAP. II. 1–20.

The Birth of the Saviour.

Henceforth there exists in the midst of corrupt humanity a pure Being, on whom God's regard can rest with unmingled satisfaction. Uniting in this divine contemplation, the celestial intelligences already see streaming from this fire those waves of light which will ultimately penetrate to the remotest bounds of the moral universe. The new creation, the union of God with the sanctified creature, begins to find its accomplishment in this Being, in order to extend from Him to the whole of mankind, and to comprehend at last heaven itself, which is to be united with us under one and the same head, and to adore one Lord Jesus Christ as its Lord (Col. i. 20; Eph. i. 10; Phil. ii. 9–11). Such is the point of view we must take in order to appreciate the following narrative:—1. Jesus is born (vers. 1–7); 2. The angels celebrate this birth (vers. 8–14); 3. The shepherds ascertain and publish it (vers. 15–20).

1. *The Birth of Jesus:* vers. 1–7. And first a historical note: vers. 1 and 2.[1]—The words *in those days* refer to the time which followed the birth of John the Baptist, and give the remark in i. 80 an anticipatory character.—*Δόγμα* denotes, in classical Greek, any *edict* of a recognised authority. The use of the word *ἐξελθεῖν, to go forth,* in the sense of *being published,* answers to the meaning of יצא, Dan. ix. 2, 3. The term *ἀπογραφή, description,* denotes among the Romans the inscription on an official register of the name, age, profession, and fortune of each head of a family, and of the number of his children, with a view to the assessment of a tax. The fiscal taxation which followed was more particularly indicated by the term *ἀποτίμησις.*—Criticism raises several objections against the truth of the fact related in ver. 1: 1*st,* No historian of the time mentions such a decree of Augustus. 2*d,* On the supposition that Augustus had issued such an edict, it would not have been applicable to the states of Herod in general, nor to

[1] Ver. 2. ℵ. B. D. omit η after αυτη.—Instead of απογραφη πρωτη εγενετο, ℵ* reads απογραφη εγενετο πρωτη.—Instead of Κυρηνιου, A. Κηρυνιου, B* Κυρεινου, B³. It. Vg. Κυρινου (Cyrino).

Judea in particular, since this country was not reduced to a Roman province until ten or eleven years later—the year 6 of our era. *3d,* A Roman edict, executed within the states of Herod, must have been executed according to Roman forms; and according to these, it would have been in no way necessary for Joseph to put in an appearance at Bethlehem; for, according to Roman law, registration was made at the place of birth or residence, and not at the place where the family originated. *4th,* Even admitting the necessity of removal in the case of Joseph, this obligation did not extend to Mary, who, as a woman, was not liable to registration.—In order to meet some of these difficulties, Hug has limited the meaning of the words, *all the earth,* to Palestine. But the connection of this expression with the name *Cæsar Augustus* will not allow of our accepting this explanation; besides which, it leaves several of the difficulties indicated untouched. The reader who feels any confidence in Luke's narrative, and who is desirous of solving its difficulties, will find, we think, a solution resulting from the following facts:—

From the commencement of his reign, Augustus always aimed at a stronger centralization of the empire. Already, under Julius Cæsar, there had been undertaken, with a view to a more exact assessment of taxation, a great statistical work, a complete survey of the empire, *descriptio orbis.* This work, which occupied thirty-two years, was only finished under Augustus.[1] This prince never ceased to labour in the same direction. After his death, Tiberius caused to be read in the Senate, in accordance with instructions contained in the will of Augustus, a statistical document, which applied not only to the empire properly so called, but also to the allied kingdoms, —a category to which the states of Herod belonged. This document, called *Breviarium totius imperii,* was written entirely by Augustus' own hand.[2] It gave "the number of the citizens and *of allies under arms,* of the fleets, of the kingdoms, of the provinces, of *the tributes or taxes.*" The compilation of such a document as this necessarily supposes a previous statistical labour, comprehending not only the empire proper, but also the

[1] See the recent work of Wieseler, *Beiträge zur richtigen Würdigung der Evangelien,* etc., 1869, p. 23.

[2] Tacitus, *Ann.* i. 11; Suetonius, *Octav.* c. 27, 28, 101.

allied states. And if Augustus had ordered this work, Herod, whose kingdom belonged to the number of *regna reddita*, could not have refused to take part in it.—The silence of historians in regard to this fact proves simply nothing against its reality. Wieseler gives a host of examples of similar omissions. The great statistical work previously accomplished by Julius Cæsar, and about which no one can entertain a doubt, is not noticed by any historian of the time.[1] Josephus, in his *Jewish War*, written before his *Antiquities*, when giving an account of the government of Coponius, does not mention even the census of Quirinius.[2] Then it must not be forgotten that one of our principal sources for the life of Augustus, Dion Cassius, presents a blank for just the years 748–750 U.C.—Besides, this silence is amply compensated for by the positive information we find in later writers. Thus, Tertullian mentions, as a well-known fact, "the census taken in Judea under Augustus by Sentius Saturnius,"[3] that is to say, from 744–748 U.C., and consequently only a short time before the death of Herod in 750. The accounts of Cassiodorus and Suidas leave no doubt as to the great statistical labours accomplished by the orders of Augustus.[4] The latter says expressly: "Cæsar Augustus, having chosen twenty men of the greatest ability, sent them into all the countries of the subject nations (*τῶν ὑπηκόων*), and caused them to make a registration (*ἀπογραφάς*) of men and property (*τῶντε ἀνθρώπων καὶ οὐσιῶν*)." These details are not furnished by Luke. And if the task of these commissioners specially referred, as Suidas says, *to the subject nations*, the omission of all mention of this measure in the historians of the time is more easily accounted for.

Surprise is expressed at an edict of Augustus having reference to the states of Herod. But Herod's independence was only relative. There is no money known to have been coined in his name; the silver coin circulating in his dominions was Roman.[5] From the time of the taking of Jerusalem by

[1] Wieseler, in the work referred to, p. 51.

[2] *Ibid.* p. 95.

[3] *Sed et census constat actos sub Auguste . . . in Judæa per Sentium Saturnium*" (*Adv. Marc.* 19). The word *constat* appears to allude to public documents; and the detail by Sentius Saturnius proves that his source of information was independent of Luke.

[4] Wieseler, p. 53.

[5] Wieseler, p. 86.

Pompey, the Jews paid the Romans a double tribute, a poll-tax and a land-tax.[1] Tacitus also speaks of complaints from Syria and *Judea* against the taxes which burdened them. Further, the Jews had quite recently, according to Josephus, been obliged to take individually an oath of obedience to the emperor (*Antiq.* xvii. 2. 4). The application of a decree of Augustus to the dominions of Herod, a simple vassal of the emperor, presents, therefore, nothing improbable. Only it is evident that the emperor, in the execution of the decree, would take care to respect in form the sovereignty of the king, and to execute it altogether by his instrumentality. Besides, it was the custom of the Romans, especially in their fiscal measures, always to act by means of the local authorities, and to conform as far as possible to national usages.[2] Augustus would not depart from this method in regard to Herod, who was generally an object of favour.—And this observation overthrows another objection, namely, that according to Roman custom, Joseph would not have to present himself in the place where his family originated, since the census was taken at the place of residence. But Roman usage did not prevail here. In conformity with the remnant of independence which Judea still enjoyed, the census demanded by the emperor would certainly be executed according to Jewish forms. These, doubtless, were adapted to the ancient constitution of tribes and families, the basis of Israelitish organization: this mode was at once the simplest, since the greater part of the families still lived on their hereditary possessions, and the surest, inasmuch as families that had removed would be anxious to strengthen a link on which might depend questions of inheritance and other rights besides.[3] That which distinguished the census of Quirinius, ten years later, from all similar undertakings that had preceded it, was just this, that on this occasion the Roman authority *as such* executed it, without the intervention of the national power and Jewish customs. Then, accordingly, the people keenly felt the reality of their subjection, and broke into revolt. And history has

[1] Wieseler, p. 73 and fol.

[2] Comp. on this point the recent works of Huschke (*Ueber den Census der Kaiserzeit*) and of Marquadt (*Handbuch der römischen Alterthümer*).

[3] Wieseler, pp. 66, 67.

preserved scarcely any record of similar measures which preceded this eventful census.

As to Mary, we may explain without any difficulty the reasons which induced her to accompany Joseph. If, at ver. 5, we make the words *with Mary* depend specially on the verb *in order to be enrolled,* the fact may be explained by the circumstance that, according to Roman law, women among conquered nations were subject to the capitation tax. Ulpian expressly says this (*De censibus*): "that in Syria (this term comprehends Palestine) men are liable to the capitation from their fourteenth year, *women* from their twelfth to their sixtieth." Perhaps women were sometimes summoned to appear in person, in order that their age might be ascertained. Or, indeed, we may suppose that Mary was the sole representative of one of the branches of her tribe, *an heiress,* which obliged her to appear in person. Perhaps, also, by the inscription of her name she was anxious to establish anew, in view of her son, her descent from the family of David. But we may join the words *with Mary* to the verb *went up.* The motives which would induce Mary to accompany Joseph in this journey are obvious. If, in the whole course of the Gospel history, we never see the least reflection cast on the reputation of Mary, although only six months had elapsed between her marriage and the birth of Jesus, is not this circumstance explained by the very fact of this journey, which providentially removed Joseph and Mary from Nazareth for a sufficient length of time, just when the birth took place? Mary must have recognised the finger of God in the event which compelled Joseph to leave home, and have been anxious to accompany him.

But a much more serious difficulty than any of the preceding arises relative to ver. 2. If this verse is translated, as it usually is, "*This census, which was the first, took place when Quirinius governed Syria,*" we must suppose, on account of what precedes, that Quirinius filled this office before the death of Herod. But history proves that Quirinius did not become governor of Syria until the year 4, and that he did not execute the enumeration which bears his name until the year 6 of our era, after the deposition of Archelaus, the son and successor of Herod, that is to say, ten years at least after the birth of Jesus. It was Varus who was governor of Syria at the death of Herod.—An attempt has been made to solve this difficulty by correcting the text: Theodore de Beza by making ver. 2 an interpolation; Michaelis by adding the words πρὸ τῆς after ἐγένετο: "This enumeration took place before that which Quirinius executed . . ."[1] These are conjectures without foundation.—Again, it has been proposed to give the word πρώτη, *first*, a meaning more or less unusual. And accordingly, some translate this word as *primus* is sometimes to be taken in Latin, and as *erst* regularly in German: "This census was executed *only* when . . ." (*prima accedit cum, geschah erst als*). Such a Latinism is hardly admissible. And besides, if the execution had *not* followed the decree *immediately* (as the translation supposes), how could the decree have led to the removal of Joseph and the birth of Jesus at Bethlehem while Herod was still reigning?

An interpretation of the word πρώτη which is scarcely less forced, has been adopted by Tholuck, Ewald, Wieseler (who maintains and defends it at length in his last work), and Pressensé (in his *Vie de Jésus*). Relying on John i. 15, πρῶτός μου, xv. 18, πρῶτον ὑμῶν, they give to πρώτη the sense of προτέρα, and explain πρώτη ἡγεμονεύοντος as if it were πρότερον ἢ ἡγεμονεύειν; which results in the following translation: "This enumeration took place *before* Quirinius . . ." They cite from the LXX. Jer. xxix. 2, ὕστερον ἐξελθόντος Ἰεχονίου, "after Jechonias was gone forth;" and from Plato, ὕστεροι ἀφίκοντο τῆς ἐν Μαραθῶνι μάχης γενομένης, "*they arrived after the battle of Marathon had taken place.*" But this accumulation of two irregularities, the employment of the superlative for the comparative, and of the comparative adjective for the adverb, is not admissible in such a writer as Luke, whose style is generally perfectly lucid, especially if, with Wieseler, after having given to πρώτη the sense of a comparative, we want to keep, in addition, its superlative meaning: "This enumeration took place *as a first one, and before that* . . ." This certainly goes beyond all limits of what is possible, whatever the high philological authorities may say for it, upon whose support this author thinks he can

[1] For this sense it would be better to conjecture a reading πρὸ τῆς as a substitute for πρώτη, admitting at the same time the place which the last word occupies in the text of ℵ and D.

rely.[1]—Another attempt at interpretation, proposed by Ebrard, sets out from a distinction between the meaning of *ἀπογράφεσθαι* (ver. 1) and of *ἀπογραφή* (ver. 2). The former of these two interpretations may denote the registration, the second the pecuniary taxation which resulted from it (the *ἀποτίμησις*); and this difference of meaning would be indicated by the pronoun *αυτη*, which it would be necessary to read *αὐτή* (*ipsa*), and not *αὕτη* (*ea*). "As to the taxation *itself* (which followed the registration), it took place only when Quirinius was . . ." But why, in this case, did not Luke employ, in the second verse, another word than *ἀπογραφή*, which evidently recalled the *ἀπογράφεσθαι* of ver. 1? Köhler[2] acknowledged that these two words should have an identical meaning; but, with Paulus, Lange, and others, he thinks he can distinguish between the *publication* of the decree (ver. 1) and its execution (ver. 2), which only took place ten years afterwards, and, with this meaning, put the accent on *ἐγένετο*: "Cæsar Augustus published a decree (ver. 1), and the registration decreed by him *was executed* (only) when Quirinius . . ." (ver. 2). But the difficulty is to see how this decree, if it was not immediately enforced, could induce the removal of Joseph and Mary. Köhler replies that the measure decreed began to be carried into execution; but on account of the disturbances which it excited it was soon suspended, and that it was only resumed and completely carried out (*ἐγένετο*) under Quirinius. This explanation is ingenious, but very artificial. And further, it does not suit the context. Luke, after having positively denied the execution of the measure (ver. 2), would relate afterwards (ver. 3 and ff.), without the least explanation, a fact which has no meaning, but on the supposition of the immediate execution of this decree!

There remain a number of attempted solutions which rely on history rather than philology. As far as the text is concerned, they may be classed with the ordinary explanation which treats the words *ἡγεμονεύοντος Κυρηνίου* as a genitive absolute. Several of the older expositors, as Casaubon, Sanclemente, and more recently Hug and Neander, starting with the fact that before Quirinius was governor of Syria he took a

[1] MM. Curtius at Leipsic and Schömann at Greifswald.

[2] *Encyclopédie de Herzog*, Art. *Schatzung*.

considerable part in the affairs of the East (Tac. *Ann.* iii. 48), supposed that he presided over the census, of which Luke here speaks, in the character of an imperial commissioner. Luke, they think, applied to this temporary jurisdiction the term ἡγεμονεύειν, which ordinarily denotes the function of a *governor* in the proper sense of the term. Zumpt even believed he could prove that Quirinius had been twice *governor of Syria,*[1] in the proper sense of the word, and that it was during the former of these two administrations that he presided over the census mentioned by Luke. Mommsen[2] also admits the fact of the double administration of Quirinius as governor of Syria. He relies particularly on a tumular inscription discovered in 1764,[3] which, if it refers to Quirinius, would seem to say that this person had been governor of Syria on two occasions (*iterum*). But does this inscription really refer to Quirinius? And has the term *iterum* all the force which is given to it? Wieseler clearly shows that these questions are not yet determined with any certainty. And supposing even that this double administration of Quirinius could be proved, the former, which is the one with which we are concerned here, could not have been, as Zumpt acknowledges, until from the end of 750 to 753 U.C. Now it is indisputable that at this time Herod had been dead some months (the spring of 750), and consequently, according to the text of Luke, Jesus was already born. One thing, however, is certain,—that Quirinius, a person honoured with the emperor's entire confidence, took a considerable part, throughout this entire period, in the affairs of the East, and of Syria in particular. And we do not see what objection there is, from a historical point of view, to the hypothesis of Gerlach,[4] who thinks that, whilst Varus was the political and military governor of Syria (from 748), Quirinius administered its financial affairs, and that it was in the capacity of *quæstor* that he presided over the census which took place among the Jews at

[1] By the passage in Tac. iii. 48. *De Syriâ Romanorum provinciâ ab Cæsare Augusto ad Titum Vespasianum*, 1854, and *Ueber den Census des Quirinius, Evang. Kirchenzeitung*, 1865, No. 82.

[2] *Res gestæ Divi Augusti. Ex monumento Ancyrano.*

[3] Published in the last place by Mommsen, *De P. S. Quirinii titulo Tiburtino*, 1865.

[4] *Römische Statthalter in Syrien*, p. 33.

this time. Josephus (*Antiq.* xvi. 9. 1, 2, and *Bell. Jud.* i. 27. 2) designates these two magistrates, the præses and the quæstor, by the titles of ἡγεμόνες and τῆς Συρίας ἐπιστατοῦντες. There is nothing, then, to hinder our giving a somewhat more general meaning to the verb ἡγεμονεύειν, or supposing, we may add, that Luke attributed to Quirinius as governor a function which he accomplished as quæstor. In this case, Quirinius would have already presided over a first enumeration under Herod in 749, before directing the better known census which took place in 759 U.C., and which provoked the revolt of Judas the Galilean.[1]

Those who are not satisfied with any of these attempts at explanation admit an error in Luke, but not all in the same sense. Meyer thinks that ἡγεμονεύειν in Luke's text must keep its ordinary meaning, but that Luke, in employing this term here, confounded the later enumeration of the year 6 with that over which this person presided ten years earlier in the capacity of imperial commissioner. Schleiermacher and Bleek admit a greater error: Luke must have confounded a simple sacerdotal census, which took place in the latter part of Herod's reign, with the famous enumeration of the year 6. Strauss and Keim go further still. In their view, the enumeration of vers. 1 and 2 is a pure invention of Luke's, either to account for the birth of Jesus at Bethlehem, as required by popular prejudice (Strauss), or to establish a significant parallel between the birth of Jesus and the complete subjection of the people (Keim, p. 399). But the text of Luke is of a too strictly historical and prosaic character to furnish the least support to Keim's opinion. That of Strauss might apply to a Gospel like Matthew, which lays great stress on the connection between the birth of Jesus at Bethlehem and Messianic prophecy; but it in no way applies to Luke's Gospel, which does not contain the slightest allusion to the prophecy. Schleiermacher's explanation is a pure conjecture, and one which borders on absurdity. That of Meyer, which in substance is very nearly the opinion of Gerlach, would certainly be the most probable of all these opinions. Only there are two facts which hardly allow of our imputing to Luke a con-

[1] This certainly is only a hypothesis: but we do not see what ground Keim has for characterizing it as [illegible] (Gesch. *Jesu*, t. i. p. 402).

fusion of facts in this place. The first is, that, according to Acts v. 37, he was well acquainted with the later enumeration which occasioned the revolt of Judas the Galilean, and which he calls, in an absolute way, *the enumeration.* Luke could not be ignorant that this revolt took place on the occasion of the definitive annexation of Judea to the empire, and consequently at some distance of time after the death of Herod. Now, in our text, he places the enumeration of which he is speaking in the reign of Herod! The second fact is the perfect knowledge Luke had, according to xxiii. 6–9, of the subsequent political separation between Judea and Galilee. Now, the registration of a Galilean in Judea supposes that the unity of the Israelitish monarchy was still in existence. In the face of these two plain facts, it is not easy to admit that there was any confusion on his part.

May we be permitted, after so many opinions have been broached, to propose a new one? We have seen that the census which was carried out by Quirinius in 759 U.C., ten years after the birth of Jesus, made a deep impression upon all the people, convincing them of their complete political servitude. This census is called *the enumeration* without any qualification, therefore (Acts v. 37); but it might also be designated the *first enumeration,* inasmuch as it was the first census executed by pagan authority; and it would be in this somewhat technical sense that the expression ἡ ἀπογραφὴ πρώτη would here have to be taken. We should accentuate αυτη (as has been already proposed) αὐτή, which presents no critical difficulty, since the ancient MSS. have no accents, and understand the second verse thus: As to the census itself called the *first,* it took place under the government of Quirinius.[1] Luke would break off to remark that, prior to the well-known enumeration which took place under Quirinius, and which history had taken account of under the name of *the first,* there had really been another, generally lost sight of, which was the very one here in question; and thus that it was not unadvisedly that he spoke of a census anterior to the *first.* In this way, 1*st,* the intention of this parenthesis is clear; 2*d,* the *asyndeton* between vers. 1 and 2 is explained quite in a natural

[1] We spell this name Quirinius (not Quirinus) in conformity with the authority of all the documents, B. alone and some MSS. of the It. excepted.

way; and 3*d*, the omission of the article *ἡ* between *ἀπογραφή* and *πρώτη*, which has the effect of making *ἡ ἀπογραφὴ πρώτη* a sort of proper name (like *ἡ ἐπιστολὴ πρώτη, δευτέρα*), is completely justified.

Vers. 3–7.[1] The terms *οἶκος* and *πατριά*, *house* and *family* (ver. 4), have not an invariable meaning in the LXX. According to the etymology and the context, the former appears to have here the wider meaning, and to denote the entire connections of David, comprising his brethren and their direct descendants.—On this journey of Mary, see p. 123. The complement *with Mary* appears to us to depend, not on the verb *ἀπογράψασθαι*, *to be enrolled*, as Meyer, Bleek, etc., decide, but on the entire phrase *ἀνέβη ἀπογράφασθαι*, *he went up to be enrolled*, and more especially on *he went up*. For, as Wieseler observes, the important point for the context is, that she went up, not that she was enrolled. And the words in apposition, *being great with child*, connect themselves much better with the idea of going up than with that of being enrolled.—There is great delicacy in the received reading, which has also the best support critically, his *espoused wife*. The substantive indicates the character in which Mary made the journey; the participle recalls the real state of things. The Alex., not having perceived this shade of thought, have wrongly omitted *γυναικί*.—From the last proposition of ver. 7, in which *φάτνη*, *a manger*, seems opposed to *κατάλυμα*, *an inn*, some interpreters have inferred that the former of these two words should here have a wider sense, and signify *a stable*. But this meaning is unexampled. We have merely to supply a thought: "in the manger, *because they were lodging in the stable*, seeing that . . ." The article *τῇ* designates the manger as *that* belonging to the stable. The Alex., therefore, have wrongly omitted it.—Did this stable form part of the hostelry? or was it, as all the apocryphal writings[2] and Justin[3] allege, a cave near the city? In the time of Origen,[4] a grotto was shown where the birth of Jesus took place. It was on this

[1] Ver. 3. ℵ^{c}. B. D. L. Z., *εαυτου* instead of *ιδιαν*.—Ver. 5. ℵ* A. D. some Mnn. *απογραφεσθαι* in place of *απογραψασθαι*.—ℵ. B. D. L. Z. some Mnn. Syr. omit *γυναικι*.—Ver. 7. ℵ. A. B. D. L. Z. some Mnn. omit *η* before *φατνη*.

[2] Protevangelium of James, History of J seph, Gospel of the Infancy. *Works of Justin*, edit. of Otto, t. i. p. 269, note.

[3] *Dial. c. Tryph.* c. 78.

[4] *Contra Celsum*, i. 11.

place that Helena, the mother of Constantine built a church; and it is probable that the Church *Mariæ de Præsepio* is erected on the same site. The text of Luke would not be altogether incompatible with this idea. But probably it is only a supposition, resulting on the one hand from the common custom in the East of using caves for stables, and on the other from a mistaken application to the Messiah of Isa. xxxiii. 16, "*He shall dwell in a lofty cave,*" quoted by Justin.—The expression *first-born* naturally implies that the writer believed Mary had other children afterwards, otherwise there would be no just ground for the use of this term. It may be said that Luke employs it with a view to the account of the presentation of Jesus in the temple as a *first-born* son (ver. 22 et seq.). But this connection is out of the question in Matt. i. 25.—This expression proves that the composition of the narrative dates from a time posterior to the birth of the brothers and sisters of Jesus.—Thus was accomplished, in the obscurity of a stable, the fact which was to change the face of the world; and Mary's words (i. 51), "*He hath put down the mighty, and exalted the lowly,*" were still further verified. "*The weakness of God is stronger than men,*" says St. Paul; this principle prevails throughout all this history, and constitutes its peculiar character.

2. *The appearing of the angels:* vers. 8–14.—"*The gospel is preached to the poor.*" The following narrative contains the first application of this divine method. Vers. 8 and 9 relate the appearing of the angel to the shepherds; vers. 10–12, his discourse; vers. 13 and 14, the song of the heavenly host.

Vers. 8 and 9.[1] Among the Jews, the occupation of keepers of sheep was held in a sort of contempt. According to the treatise *Sanhedrin,* they were not to be admitted as witnesses; and according to the treatise *Aboda Zara,* succour must not be given to shepherds and heathen.—'Αγραυλεῖν, properly, to make his ἀγρός his αὐλή, his field his abode. Columella (*De re rusticâ*) describes these αὐλαί as enclosures surrounded by high walls, sometimes covered in, and sometimes *sub dio* (open to the sky). As it is said in a passage in the Talmud

[1] Ver. 9. ℵ. B. L. Z. omit ιδου after και.—ℵ[c]. Z. It[aliq]. Vg., Θεου instead of κυριου (second).—ℵ*. επελαμψεν αυτοις instead of περιελαμψεν αυτους.

that the flocks are kept in the open air during the portion of the year between the Passover and the early autumnal rains, it has been inferred from this narrative of the shepherds that Jesus must have been born during the summer. Wieseler, however, observes that this Talmudic determination of the matter applies to the season passed by the flocks out on the steppes, far away from human dwellings. The flocks in this case were not so.—In the expression φυλάσσειν φυλακάς, the plural φυλακάς perhaps denotes that they watched *in turns.* The genitive τῆς νυκτός must be taken adverbially: the watch, such as is kept *by night.* 'Ιδού (ver. 9) is omitted by the Alex. But it is probably authentic; it depicts the surprise of the shepherds.—'Επέστη does not signify that the angel stood above them (comp. ἐπιστᾶσα, ver. 38). It is our *survenir* (*to come unexpectedly*). We must translate, as in i. 11, *an angel,* not *the angel.* This is proved by the article ὁ at ver. 10 (see i. 13). By *the glory of the Lord* must be here understood, as generally, the supernatural light with which God appears. whether personally or by His representatives.

Vers. 10–12.[1] The angel first announces the favourable nature of his message; for at the sight of any supernatural appearance man's first feeling is fear.—"Ητις, "which, *inasmuch as great,* is intended for the whole people."—Ver. 11, the message itself. By the title *Saviour,* in connection with the idea of joy (ver. 10), is expressed the pity angels feel at the sight of the miserable state of mankind. The title *Christ,* anointed, refers to the prophecies which announce this Person, and the long expectation He comes to satisfy. The title *Lord* indicates that He is the representative of the divine sovereignty. This latter title applies also to His relation to the angels. The periphrasis, *the city of David,* hints that this child will be a second David. —Ver. 12, the sign by means of which the shepherds may determine the truth of this message. This sign has nothing divine about it but its contrast with human glory. There could not have been many other children born that night in Bethlehem; and among these, if there were any, no other certainly would have a manger for its cradle.

[1] Ver. 12. B. Z. omit το before σημειον.—ℵ* D. omit κειμενον.—ℵ[c] B. L. P. S. Z. some Mnn. Syr. It[plerique] Or. add και before κειμενον (taken from ver. 16).—T. R. reads τη before φατνη, with F[2]. K. only (taken from ver. 16).

Vers. 13 and 14.[1] The troop of angels issues forth all at once from the depths of that invisible world which surrounds us on every side. By their song they come to give the key-note of the adoration of mankind. The variation of some Alex. and of the Latin translations, which read the gen. εὐδοκίας instead of the nom. εὐδοκία, is preferred in the modern exegesis: "peace to *the men of goodwill.*" In this case the song divides itself into two parallel propositions, whether the words *and on earth* be referred to that which precedes, "Glory to God in the highest places and on earth; peace to the men of goodwill;" or, which is certainly preferable, they be connected with what follows, "Glory to God in the highest places; and on earth peace to the men of goodwill." In this second interpretation the parallelism is complete: the three ideas, *peace, men, on earth,* in the second member, answer to the three ideas, *glory, God, in the highest places,* in the first. Men make their praise arise towards God in the heavens; God makes His peace descend towards them on the earth. The gen. εὐδοκίας, *of goodwill,* may refer to the pious dispositions towards God with which a part of mankind are animated. But this interpretation is hardly natural. Εὐδοκία, from εὐδοκεῖν, *to delight in,* חפץ ב, denotes an entirely gracious goodwill, the initiative of which is in the subject who feels it. This term does not suit the relation of man to God, but only that of God to man. Therefore, with this reading, we must explain the words thus: Peace on earth *to the men who are the objects of divine goodwill.* But this use of the genitive is singularly rude, and almost barbarous; the *men of goodwill,* meaning those on whom goodwill rests . . ., is a mode of expression without any example. We are thus brought back to the reading of the T. R., present also in 14 Mjj., among which are L. and Z., which generally agree with the Alex., the Coptic translation, of which the same may be said, and the *Peschito.* With this reading, the song consists of three propositions, of which two are parallel, and the third forms a link between the two. In the first, *glory to God in the highest places,* the angels demand that, from the lower regions to which they have just come down, from the bosom of humanity, praise shall

[1] Ver. 14. It^plerique Ir. Or., etc., omit εν before ανθρωποις.—א* A. B* D. It. Vg. Ir. and Or. (in the Latin translation) read ευδοκιας in place of ευδοκια.

arise, which, ascending from heavens to heavens, shall reach at last the supreme sanctuary, the *highest places*, and there glorify the divine perfections that shine forth in this birth. The second, *peace on earth*, is the counterpart of the first. While inciting men to praise, the angels invoke on them peace from God. This peace is such as results from the reconciliation of man with God; it contains the cause of the cessation of all war here below. These two propositions are of the nature of a desire or prayer. The verb understood is *ἔστω*, *let it be*. The third, which is not connected with the preceding by any particle, proclaims the fact which is the ground of this two-fold prayer. If the logical connection were expressed, it would be by the word *for*. This fact is the extraordinary favour shown to men by God, and which is displayed in the gift He is bestowing upon them at this very time. The sense is, "for God takes pleasure in men." In speaking thus, the angels seem to mean, God has not bestowed as much on us (Heb. ii. 16). The idea of *εὐδοκία*, *goodwill*, recalls the first proposition, "Glory to God!" whilst the expression *towards men* reminds us of the second, "Peace on earth!" For the word *εὐδοκία*, comp. Eph. i. 5 and Phil. ii. 13.—When the witnesses of the blessing sing, how could they who are the objects of it remain silent?

3. *The visit of the shepherds:* vers. 15–20.—The angel had notified a sign to the shepherds, and invited them to ascertain its reality. This injunction they obey.

Vers. 15–20.[1] The T. R. exhibits in ver. 15 a singular expression: "And it came to pass, when the angels were gone away, . . . *the men, the shepherds*, said . . ." The impression of the shepherds when, the angels having disappeared, they found themselves alone *among men*, could not be better expressed. The omission of the words *καὶ οἱ ἄνθρωποι* in the Alex. is owing to the strangeness of this form, the meaning of which they did not understand. The *καὶ* before *οἱ ἄνθρωποι* is doubtless the sign of the apodosis, like the Hebrew ו; but at the same time it brings out the close connection between

[1] Ver. 15. ℵ. B. L. Z. many Mnn. Syr^{sch}. It^{plerique}, Vg. Or. omit *και οι ανθρωποι*.—ℵ. B. It^{aliq}., *ελαλουν* instead of *ειπον*.—Ver. 17. ℵ. B. D. L. Z., *εγνωρισαν* instead of *διεγνωρισαν*.—Ver. 20. Instead of *επεστρεψαν*, the reading of T. R. and a part of the Mnn., all the other documents, *υπεστρεψαν*.

the disappearance of the angels and the act of the shepherds, as they addressed themselves to the duty of obeying them. The aorist εἶπον of the T. R. is certainly preferable to the imperf. ἐλάλουν of the Alex., since it refers to an act immediately followed by a result: "*They said* (not *they were saying*) one to another, Let us go therefore."—The term ῥῆμα denotes, as דבר so often does, a word in so far as accomplished (γεγονός). We see how the original Aramæan form is carefully preserved even to the minutest details.—'Ανά in ἀνεῦρον expresses the discovery in succession of the objects enumerated. 'Εγνώρισαν or διεγνώρισαν (Alex.), ver. 17, may signify *to verify;* in the fifteenth verse, however, ἐγνώρισαν signifies *to make known,* and in ver. 17 it is the most natural meaning. There is a gradation here: heaven had revealed; and now, by the care of men, publicity goes on increasing. This sense also puts the seventeenth verse in more direct connection with what follows. The compound διαγνωρίζειν, *to divulge,* appears to us for this reason to be preferred to the simple form (in the Alex.).

Vers. 18–20 describe the various impressions produced by what had taken place. In the eighteenth verse, a vague surprise in the greater part (*all those who heard*). On the other hand (δέ), ver. 19, a profound impression and exercise of mind in Mary. First of all, she is careful to store up all the facts in her mind with a view to preserve them (συντηρεῖν); but this first and indispensable effort is closely connected with the further and subordinate aim of comparing and combining these facts, in order to discover the divine idea which explains and connects them. What a difference between this thoughtfulness and the superficial astonishment of the people around her! There is more in the joyful feelings and adoration of the shepherds (ver. 20) than in the impressions of those who simply heard their story, but less than in Mary.—*Δοξάζειν, to glorify,* expresses the feeling of the *greatness* of the work; *αἰνεῖν, to praise,* refers to the *goodness* displayed in it.—Closely connected as they are, the two participles *heard* and *seen* can only refer to what took place in the presence of the shepherds after they reached the stable. They were told the remarkable occurrences that had preceded the birth of Jesus; it is to this that the word *heard* refers. And they beheld the manger and the infant; this is what is expressed by the word *seen.* And the whole was a confirmation of the angel's message to them. They were convinced that they had not been the victims of an hallucination.—The reading ὑπέστρεψαν (they returned *thence*) is evidently to be preferred to the ill-supported reading of the T. R., ἐπέστρεψαν (they returned to *their flocks*).

Whence were these interesting details of the impression made on the shepherds and those who listened to their story, and of the feelings of Mary, obtained? How can any one regard them as a mere embellishment of the author's imagination, or as the offspring of legend? The Aramæan colouring of the narrative indicates an ancient source. The oftener we read the nineteenth verse, the more assured we feel that Mary was the first and real author of this whole narrative. This pure, simple, and private history was composed by her, and preserved for a certain time in an oral form, until some one committed it to writing, whose work fell into the hands of Luke, and was reproduced by him in Greek.

SIXTH NARRATIVE.—CHAP. II. 21–40.

Circumcision and Presentation of Jesus.

This narrative comprises—1. The circumcision of Jesus (ver. 21); 2. His presentation in the temple (vers. 22–38); 3. A historical conclusion (vers. 39, 40).

1. *The Circumcision:* ver. 21.—It was under the Jewish form that Jesus was to realize the ideal of human existence. The theocracy was the surrounding prepared of God for the development of the Son of man. So to His entrance into life by birth succeeds, eight days after, His entrance into the covenant by circumcision. "*Born of a woman, made under the law,*" says St. Paul, Gal. iv. 4, to exhibit the connection between these two facts. There is a brevity in the account of the circumcision of Jesus which contrasts with the fuller account of the circumcision of John the Baptist (chap. i.). This difference is natural; the simply Jewish ceremony of circumcision has an importance, in the life of the latest representative of the theocracy, which does not belong to it in the life of Jesus, who only entered into the Jewish form of existence to pass through it.

Ver. 21.[1] The absence of the article before ἡμέραι ὀκτώ is due to the determinative τοῦ περιτεμεῖν αὐτόν which follows. In Hebrew the construct state (subst. with complement) excludes the article.—The false reading of the T. R., τὸ παιδίον instead of αὐτόν, proceeds from the cause which has occasioned the greater part of the errors in this text, the necessities of public reading. As the section to be read began with this verse, it was necessary to substitute the noun for the pronoun. *Καί*, while marking the apodosis, brings out the intimate connection between the circumcision and the giving of the name. This καί is almost a τότε, *then.*

2. *The presentation:* vers. 22–38.—And first the sacrifice, vers. 22–24.[2] After the circumcision there were two other rites to observe. One concerned the mother. Levitically unclean for eight days after the birth of a son, and for fourteen days after that of a daughter, the Israelitish mother, after a seclusion of thirty-three days in the first case, and of double this time in the second, had to offer in the temple a sacrifice of purification (Lev. xii.). The other rite had reference to the child; when it was a first-born, it had to be redeemed by a sum of money from consecration to the service of God and the sanctuary. In fact, the tribe of Levi had been chosen for this office simply to take the place of the first-born males of all the families of Israel; and in order to keep alive a feeling of His rights in the hearts of the people, God had fixed a ransom to be paid for every first-born male. It was five shekels, or, reckoning the shekel at 2s. 4d.,[3] nearly 12s. (Ex. xiii. 2; Num. viii. 16, xviii. 15).—Vers. 22 and 23 refer to the ransom of the child; ver. 24 to Mary's sacrifice. *Αὐτῶν*, *their purification*, is certainly the true reading. This pronoun refers primarily to Mary, then to Joseph, who is, as it were, involved in her uncleanness, and obliged to go up with her. Every detail of the narrative is justified with the greatest care in the three verses by a legal prescription.—The sacrifice for the mother (ver. 24) consisted properly of the offering of a

[1] ℵ. A. B. and 11 Mjj. 100 Mnn. It^{plerique} read αυτον in place of το παιδιον, the reading of T. R. with 6 Mjj. Syr^{sch}.

[2] Ver. 22. Instead of αυτης, which is the reading of T. R. with only some Mnn., and of αυτου, which is the reading of D. and 6 Mnn., all the other authorities read αυτων.

[3] Meylau, *Dictionnaire Biblique*, p. 353.

lamb as a sin-offering. But when the family was poor, the offering was limited to a pair of pigeons or two turtle-doves (Lev. xii. 8).

From the twenty-fifth verse Simeon becomes the centre of the picture: vers. 25–28 relate his coming in; vers. 29–32, his song; vers. 33–35, his address to the parents.

Vers. 25–28.[1] In times of spiritual degeneracy, when an official clergy no longer cultivates anything but the form of religion, its spirit retires amongst the obscurer members of the religious community, and creates for itself unofficial organs, often from the lowest classes. Simeon and Anna are representatives of this spontaneous priesthood. It has been conjectured that Simeon might be the rabbi of this name, son of the famous Hillel, and father of Gamaliel. But this Simeon, who became president of the Sanhedrim in the year 13 of our era, could hardly be the one mentioned by Luke, who at the birth of Jesus was already an old man. Further, this conjecture is scarcely compatible with the religious character of Luke's Simeon. The name was one of the commonest in Israel.—The term *just* denotes positive qualities; *fearing God* —A. V. *devout* (εὐλαβής appears to be the true reading)—watchfulness with regard to evil.—The separation of **πνεῦμα** from ἅγιον by the verb ἦν in the greater part of the MSS. gives prominence to the idea of the adjective. An influence rested upon him, and this influence was holy.—***Χρηματίζειν,*** properly, to do business; thence, to act officially, communicate a decision, give forth an oracle.—The reading **κύριον** has neither probability nor authority; **κυρίου** is the genitive of possession: the Christ whom Jehovah gives and sends.—There are critical moments in life, when everything depends on immediate submission to the impulse of the Spirit. The words **ἐν τῷ πνεύματι,** *in spirit,* or *by the spirit,* do not denote a state of ecstasy, but a higher impulse.—A contradiction has been found between the term γονεῖς, *parents,* and the preceding narrative of the miraculous birth; and Meyer finds in this fact a proof that

[1] Ver. 25. ℵ* K. Γ. Π. 10 Mnn. read ευσεβης instead of ευλαβης.—Αγιον is placed after ην by ℵ. A. B. L. and 14 other Mjj. and almost all the Mnn., whilst the T. R. places it before ην, with D. some Mnn. It[plerique], Syr.—Ver. 26. Instead of πριν η, ℵ[c]. B. and 4 Mjj., πριν η αν.; ℵ* e., εως αν.—Instead of κυριου, Λ. b. c. Cop., κυοιον. —Ver. 28. ℵ. B. L. Π. It[aliq]. Ir. omit αυτου after αγκαλας.

Luke avails himself here of a different document from that which he previously used. What criticism! The word *parents* is simply used to indicate the character in which Joseph and Mary appeared at this time in the temple and presented the child.—The καί of the twenty-eighth verse indicates the apodosis; exactly as if the circumstantial ἐν τῷ εἰσαγαγεῖν . . . formed a subordinate proposition; this καί, at the same time, brings out the close connection between the act of the parents who present the child and that of Simeon, who is found there opening his arms to receive it. By the term *receive*, the text makes Simeon the true priest, who acts for the time on behalf of God.

Vers. 29–32. "*Lord, now lettest Thou Thy servant depart in peace, according to Thy word:* 30 *For mine eyes have seen Thy salvation,* 31 *Which Thou hast prepared before the face of all people;* 32 *A light to lighten the Gentiles, and the glory of Thy people Israel.*"

The vivid insight and energetic conciseness which characterize this song remind us of the compositions of David. Simeon represents himself under the image of a sentinel whom his master has placed in an elevated position, and charged to look for the appearance of a star, and then announce it to the world. He sees this long-desired star; he proclaims its rising, and asks to be relieved of the post he has occupied so long. In the same way, at the opening of Æschylus' *Agamemnon*, when the sentinel, set to watch for the appearing of the fire that is to announce the taking of Troy, beholds at last the signal so impatiently expected, he sings at once both the victory of Greece and his own release.—Beneath each of these terms in ver. 29 is found the figure which we have just indicated: νῦν, *now*, that is to say, *at last*, after such long waiting! The word ἀπολύειν, *to release, discharge*, contains the two ideas of relieving a sentinel on duty, and delivering from the burden of life. These two ideas are mixed up together here, because for a long time past Simeon's earthly existence had been prolonged simply in view of this special mandate. The term δέσποτα, *lord*, expresses Simeon's acknowledgment of God's absolute right over him. Ῥῆμά σου, *Thy word*, is an allusion to the word of command which the commander gives to the sentinel. The expression, *in peace*, answers to the word *now*, with which the song begins. This soul, which for a long time past has been all expectation, has now found the satisfaction it desired, and can depart from earth in perfect peace.

Vers. 30 and 31 form, as it were, a second strophe. Simeon is now free. For *his eyes have seen.*—The term σωτήριον, which we can only translate by *salvation,* is equivalent neither to σωτήρ, *Saviour,* nor to σωτηρία, *salvation.* This word, the neuter of the adjective σωτήριος, *saving,* denotes an apparatus fitted to save. Simeon sees in this little child *the means of deliverance* which God is giving to the world. The term *prepare* is connected with this sense of σωτήριον: *we make ready* an apparatus. This notion of preparation may be applied to the entire theocracy, by which God had for a long time past been preparing for the appearance of the Messiah. But it is simpler to apply this term to the birth of the infant. The complement, *in the sight of,* must be explained in this case by an intermediate idea, " Thou hast prepared this means *for placing* before the eyes of . . .," that is to say, in order that all may have the advantage of it. It is a similar expression to that of Ps. xxiii. 5, " *Thou hast prepared a table before me.*" Perhaps this expression, *in the sight of all nations,* is connected with the fact that this scene took place in the court of the Gentiles. The universalism contained in these words, *all nations,* in no way goes beyond the horizon of the prophets, of Isaiah in particular (Isa. xlii. 6, lx. 3); it is perfectly appropriate in the mouth of a man like Simeon, to whom the prophetic spirit is attributed.

The collective idea, *all people,* is divided, in the third strophe, into its two essential elements, the Gentiles and Israel. From Genesis to Revelation this is the great dualism of history, the contrast which determines its phases. The Gentiles are here placed first. Did Simeon already perceive that the salvation of the Jews could only be realized after the enlightenment of the heathen, and by this means? We shall see what a profound insight this old man had into the moral condition of the generation in which he lived. Guided by all that Isaiah had foretold respecting the future unbelief of Israel, he might have arrived at the conviction that his people were about to reject the Messiah (ver. 35).—The idea of salvation is presented under two different aspects, according as it is applied to the heathen or to the Jews. To the first this child brings *light,* to the second *glory*. The heathen, in fact, are sunk in ignorance. In Isa. xxv. 7 they are represented as enveloped in a thick mist, and covered with darkness. This covering is taken away by the Messiah. The genitive ἐθνῶν may be regarded as a genitive of the subject, the enlightenment which the heathen receive. The heathen might also be made the object of the enlightenment, the light whereby the covering which keeps them in darkness is done away, and they themselves are brought into open day. But this second sense is somewhat forced.—Whilst the ignorant heathen receive in this child the light of divine revelation, of which they have hitherto been deprived, the humiliated Jews are delivered by Him from their reproach, and obtain the glory which was promised them. Springing from amongst them, Jesus appears their crown in the eyes of mankind. But this will be at the end, not at the commencement of the Messianic drama.—In this song all is original, concise, enigmatical even, as the words of an oracle. In these brief pregnant sentences is contained the substance of the history of future ages. Neither the hackneyed inventions of legend, nor any preconceived dogmatic views, have any share in the composition of this joyous lyric.

Vers. 33–35.[1] A carnal satisfaction, full of delusive hopes, might easily have taken possession of the hearts of these parents, especially of the mother's, on hearing such words as these. But Simeon infuses into his message the drop of bitterness which no joy, not even holy joy, ever wants in a world of sin.—Instead of *Joseph*, which is the reading of T. R., the Alex. read: *his father*. We should have thought that the former of these two readings was a dogmatic correction, but that at ver. 27 the T. R. itself reads the word γονεῖς, *parents*. But the Alexandrian reading is supported by the fact that the ancient translations, the *Peschito* and *Italic*, have it.—Strauss finds something strange in the wonder of Joseph and Mary. Did they not already know all this? But in the first place, what Simeon has just said of the part this child would sustain towards the heathen goes beyond all that had hitherto been

[1] Ver. 33. ℵ. B. D. L. some Mnn., ο πατηρ αυτου και η μητηρ αυτου, instead of Ιωσεφ και η μητηρ αυτου, which is the reading of T. R. with 13 Mjj., the greater part of the Mnn. Syr. It.—Ver. 35. B. L. Z. omit δε after σου.—ℵ* adds πουηρy after διαλsγισμοι.

told them. And then especially, they might well be astonished to hear an unknown person, like Simeon, express himself about this child as a man completely initiated into the secret of His high destiny.

In the expression, *he blessed them,* ver. 34, the word *them* refers solely to the parents: the child is expressly distinguished from them (*this child*).—Simeon addresses himself specially to Mary, as if he had discerned that a peculiar tie united her to the child. Ἰδού, *behold,* announces the revelation of an unexpected truth. In Isa. viii. 14 the Messiah is represented as a rock on which believers find refuge, but whereon the rebellious are broken. Simeon, whose prophetic gift was developed under the influence of the ancient oracles, simply reproduces here this thought. The words, *is set for,* make it clear that this sifting, of which the Messiah will be the occasion, forms part of the divine plan. The images of *a fall* and *a rising again* are explained by that employed by Isaiah. The expression, *signal of contradiction* (*a sign which shall be spoken against,* A. V.), may be understood in two ways: either it is an appearing about which men *argue contradictorily,* or it is a sign which excites *opposition* directly it appears. Taken in the first sense, this expression would reproduce the ideas of a fall and a rising again, and would be a simple repetition of that which precedes; in the second sense, it would merely recall the idea of a fall, and would form the transition to what follows. Will not the general unbelief of the nation be the cause of the sad lot of the Messiah, and of the sufferings that will fill the heart of His mother? The second sense is therefore preferable. The gradation καὶ σοῦ δὲ αὐτῆς, *thy own also,* ver. 35, is in this way readily understood. The δέ of the received reading is well suited to the context. "The opposition excited by this child will go so far, that thine own heart will be pierced by it."—It is natural to refer what follows to the grief of Mary, when she shall behold the rejection and murder of her son. Some such words as those of Isaiah, "*He was bruised for our iniquities,*" and of Zechariah, "*They shall look on me whom they have pierced,*" had enlightened Simeon respecting this mystery. Bleek has proposed another explanation, which is less natural, although ingenious: "Thou shalt feel in thine own heart this contradiction in regard to thy son, when thou thyself shalt be seized with doubt in regard to His mission." But the image of a sword must denote something more violent than simple doubt. *Ψυχή*, the soul, as the seat of the psychical affections, and consequently of maternal love.—It has been thought that the following proposition, *in order that the thoughts of many* . . ., could not be connected with that which immediately precedes; and for this reason some have tried to treat it as a parenthesis, and connect the *in order that* with the idea, *This is set* . . . (ver. 34). But this violent construction is altogether unnecessary. The hatred of which Jesus will be the object (ver. 34), and which will pierce the heart of Mary with poignant grief (ver. 35), will bring out those hostile thoughts towards God which in this people lie hidden under a veil of pharisaical devotion. Simeon discerned, beneath the outward forms of Jewish piety, their love of human glory, their hypocrisy, avarice, and hatred of God; and he perceives that this child will prove the occasion for all this hidden venom being poured forth from the recesses of their hearts. *In order that* has the same sense as *is set for*. God does not will the evil; but He wills that the evil, when present, should show itself: this is an indispensable condition to its being either healed or condemned. *Πολλῶν*, *of many*, appears to be a pronoun, the complement of *καρδιῶν* (*the hearts of many*), rather than an adjective (of *many* hearts); comp. Rom. v. 16.—The term *διαλογισμοί*, *thoughts*, has usually an unfavourable signification in the N. T.; it indicates the uneasy working of the understanding in the service of a bad heart. The epithet *πονηροί*, added by the *Sinaiticus*, is consequently superfluous. These words of Simeon breathe a concentrated indignation. We feel that this old man knows more about the moral condition of the people and their rulers than he has a mind to tell.

Vers. 36–38.[1] Anna presents, in several respects, a contrast to Simeon. The latter came into the temple impelled by the Spirit; Anna lives there. Simeon has no desire but to die;

[1] Ver. 37. ℵ. A. B. L. Z. It[aliq]., *εως* instead of *ως*.—ℵ*, *εβδομηκοντα* instead of *ογδοηκοντα*.—The Alex. omit *απο του ιερου*.—Ver. 38. 9 Mjj. (Alex.) some Mnn., *και αυτη τη*, instead of *και αυτη αυτη τη*.—A. B. D. L. X. Z., *τω Θεω*, instead of *τω κυριω*, the reading of T. R. with 14 Mjj. all the Mnn. Syr. It[plerique].—ℵ. B. Z. some Mnn. It[plerique], Syr[sch]. Ir. omit *εν* between *λυτρωσιν* and *Ιερουσαλημ*, which is the reading of T. R., with 15 Mjj., the greater part of the Mnn., etc.

Anna seems to recover the vigour of youth to celebrate the Messiah. The words ἣ οὐκ ἀφίστατο (ver. 37) might be made the predicate of ἦν, and the two αυτη which separate them, two appositions of Ἄννα. But it is simpler to understand ἦν in the sense of *there was*, or *there was there*, and to regard ἣ οὐκ ἀφιστατο as an appendix intended to bring back the narrative from the description of Anna's person to the actual fact. Meyer, who understands ἦν in the same way, begins a fresh proposition with the αὕτη which immediately follows, and assigns to it ἀνθωμολογεῖτο for its verb (ver. 38). This construction is less natural, especially on account of the intermediate clauses (ver. 37). Προβεβηκυῖα ἐν is a Hebraism (especially with πολλαῖς), i. 7. The moral purity of Anna is expressed by the term παρθενία, *virginity*, and by the long duration of her widowhood. Do the 84 years date from her birth, or from the death of her husband? In the latter case, supposing that she was married at 15, she would have been 106 years old. This sense is not impossible, and it more easily accounts perhaps for such a precise reckoning. Instead of ὡς, *about*, the Alex. read ἕως, *until*, a reading which appears preferable; for the restriction *about* would only be admissible with a round number—80, for example. Did Anna go into the temple in the morning, to spend the whole day there? or did she remain there during the night, spreading her poor pallet somewhere in the court? Luke's expression is compatible with either supposition. What he means is, that she was dead to the outer world, and only lived for the service of God.—We could not, with Tischendorf, following the Alex., erase one of the two αυτη (ver. 38). Both can be perfectly accounted for, and the omission is easily explained by the repetition of the word.—'Αντί, in the compound ἀνθωμολογεῖτο, might refer to a kind of antiphony between Anna and Simeon. But in the LXX. this compound verb corresponds simply to הודה (Ps. lxxix. 13); ἀντί only expresses, therefore, the idea of payment in acknowledgment which is inherent in an act of thanksgiving (as in the French word *reconnaissance*). The Alex. reading τῷ Θεῷ, *to God*, is probably a correction, arising from the fact that in the O. T. the verb ἀνθωμολογεῖσθαι never governs anything but God. It is less natural to regard the received reading as resulting from the pronoun αὐτοῦ, *Him*, which follows.—

We need not refer the imperf., *she spake*, merely to the time then present; she was doing it continually. The reading of some Alex., "those who were looking for the deliverance *of Jerusalem*," is evidently a mistaken imitation of the expression, *the consolation of Israel* (ver. 25). The words, *in Jerusalem*, naturally depend on the participle, *that looked for*. The people were divided into three parties. The Pharisees expected an outward triumph from the Messiah; the Sadducees expected nothing; between them were the true faithful, who expected the *consolation*, that is, deliverance. It was these last, who, according to Ezekiel's expression (chap. ix.), *cried for all the abominations of Jerusalem*, that were represented by Anna and Simeon; and it was amongst these that Anna devoted herself to the ministry of an evangelist. If Luke had sought, as is supposed, occasions for practising his muse, by inventing personages for his hymns, and hymns for his personages, how came he to omit here to put a song into the mouth of Anna, as a counterpart to Simeon's?

3. *Historical conclusion:* vers. 39, 40.[1]—It is a characteristic feature of Luke's narrative, and one which is preserved throughout, that he exhibits the various actors in the evangelical drama as observing a scrupulous fidelity to the law (i. 6, ii. 22–24, xxiii. 56). It is easy also to understand why Marcion, the opponent of the law, felt obliged to mutilate this writing in order to adapt it to his system. But what is less conceivable is, that several critics should find in such a Gospel the monument of a tendency systematically opposed to Jewish Christianity. The fact is, that in it the law always holds the place which according to history it ought to occupy. It is under its safeguard that the transition from the old covenant to the new is gradually effected. It is easy to perceive that ver. 39 has a religious rather than a chronological reference. "They returned to Nazareth *only* after having fulfilled every prescription of the law." Ver. 40 contains a short sketch of the childhood of Jesus, answering to the similar sketch, i. 66, of that of John the Baptist. It is probably

[1] Ver. 39. Some Alex., παντα instead of απαντα. Others, κατα instead of τα κατα.— ℵ. B. Z., επεστρεψαν instead of υπεστρεψαν.—Ver. 40. ℵ. B. D. L. It^plerique^, Vg. Or., omit πνευματι after εκραταιουτο, which is the reading of T. R., with 14 Mjj., all the Mnn. Syr. It^aliq^.—ℵ^c^. B. L., σοφια instead of σοφιας.

from this analogous passage that the gloss *πνεύματι, in spirit,* has been derived. It is wanting in the principal Alex. and Græco-Latin documents. The expression *He grew* refers to His physical development. The next words, *He waxed strong,* are defined by the words *being filled,* or more literally, *filling Himself with wisdom ;* they refer to His spiritual, intellectual, and religious development. The *wisdom* which formed the leading feature of this development (in John the Baptist it was *strength*) comprises, on the one hand, the knowledge of God ; on the other, a penetrating understanding of men and things from a divine point of view. The image (*filling Himself*) appears to be that of a vessel, which, while increasing in size, fills itself, and, by filling itself, enlarges so as to be continually holding more. It is plain that Luke regards the development, and consequently the humanity, of Jesus as a reality. Here we have the normal growth of man from a physical and moral point of view. It was accomplished for the first time on our earth. God therefore regarded this child with perfect satisfaction, because His creative idea was realized in Him. This is expressed by the last clause of the verse. *Χάρις*, the divine *favour.* This word contrasts with *χεὶρ, the hand,* i. 66. The accus. ἐπ' *αὐτό* marks the energy with which the grace of God rested on the child, penetrating His entire being. This government contrasts with that of i. 66, *μετ' αὐτοῦ,* which only expresses simple co-operation. This description is partly taken from that of the young Samuel (1 Sam. ii. 26) ; only Luke omits here the idea of human favour, which he reserves for ver. 52, where he describes the young man.—Let any one compare this description, in its exquisite sobriety, with the narratives of the infancy of Jesus in the apocryphal writings, and he will feel how authentic the tradition must have been from which such a narrative as this was derived.

SEVENTH NARRATIVE.—CHAP. II. 41–52.

The Child Jesus at Jerusalem.

The following incident, the only one which the historian relates about the youth of Jesus, is an instance of that wisdom which marked His development. Almost all great men have some story told about their childhood, in which their future destiny is foreshadowed. Here we have the first glimpse of the spiritual greatness Jesus exhibited in His ministry.—Three facts: 1. The separation (vers. 41–45); 2. The reunion (vers. 46–50); 3. The residence at Nazareth (vers. 51, 52).

1. *The separation:* vers. 41–45.[1]—The idea of fidelity to the law is prominent also in this narrative. According to Ex. xxiii. 17, Deut. xvi. 16, men were to present themselves at the sanctuary at the three feasts of Passover, Pentecost, and Tabernacles. There was no such obligation for women. But the school of Hillel required them to make at least the Passover pilgrimage.—The term γονεῖς, *parents,* is found at ver. 41 in all the MSS., even in those in which it does not occur at vers. 27 and 43, which proves that in these passages it was not altered with any dogmatic design.—Ver. 42. It was at the age of twelve that the young Jew began to be responsible for legal observances, and to receive religious instruction; he became then *a son of the law.*—The partic. pres. of the Alex. reading, ἀναβαινόντων, must be preferred to the aor. partic. of the T. R., ἀναβάντων. The present expresses a habit; the aor. is a correction suggested by the aor. partic. which follows. The words εἰς Ἱεροσόλυμα should be erased, according to the Alex. reading, which evidently deserves the preference. It is a gloss easily accounted for.—The words, *after the custom of the feast,* perhaps allude to the custom of going up in caravans.—Jesus spent these seven days of the feast in holy delight. Every rite spoke a divine language to His pure heart; and His quick understanding gradually discovered their typical meaning. This serves to explain the following incident. An indication of wilful and deliberate disobedience has been found in the term ὑπέμεινεν, *He abode.* Nothing could be further from the historian's intention (ver. 51). The notion of perseverance contained in this verb alludes simply to Jesus' love for the temple, and all that took place there. It was owing to this that, on the day for leaving,

[1] Ver. 41. ℵ*, εθος instead of ετος.—Ver. 42. ℵ. A. B. K. L. X. Π., αναβαινοντων instead of αναβαντων.—ℵ. B. D. L. some Mnn. Syr^{sch}. omit εις Ιεροσολυμα.—Ver. 43. ℵ. B. D. L. some Mnn. read εγνωσαν οι γονεις αυτου instead of εγνω Ιωσεφ και η μητηρ αυτου.—Ver. 45. ℵ. B. C. D. L. some Mnn. omit αυτον.—ℵ^{c}. B. C. D. L., αναζητουντες instead of ζητουντες.

He found Himself unintentionally separated from the band of children to which He belonged.—When once left behind, where was He to go in this strange city? The home of a child is the house of his father. Very naturally, therefore, Jesus sought His in the temple. There He underwent an experience resembling Jacob's (Gen. xxviii.). In His solitude, He learnt to know God more familiarly as His Father. Is not the freshness of a quite recent intuition perceptible in His answer (ver. 49)? The Alex. reading *οἱ γονεῖς* has against it, besides the Alex. A. and C., the *Italic* and *Peschito* translations.—It was only in the evening, at the hour of encampment, when every family was gathered together for the night, that the absence of the child was perceived. When we think of the age of Jesus, and of the unusual confidence which such a child must have enjoyed, the conduct of His parents in this affair presents nothing unaccountable.—The partic. pres. *seeking Him* (ver. 45) appears to indicate that they searched for Him on the road while returning.

2. *The meeting:* vers. 46–50.[1]—As it is improbable that they had sought for Jesus for two or three days without going to the temple, the three days must certainly date from the time of separation. The first was occupied with the journey, the second with the return, and the third with the meeting. —Lightfoot, following the Talmud, mentions three synagogues within the temple enclosure: one at the gate of the court of the Gentiles; another at the entrance of the court of the Israelites; a third in the famous peristyle *lischchat hagasith,* in the S.E. part of the inner court.[2] It was there that the Rabbins explained the law. Desire for instruction led Jesus thither. The following narrative in no way attributes to Him the part of a doctor. In order to find support for this sense in opposition to the text, some critics have alleged the detail: *seated in the midst of the doctors.* The disciples, it is said, listened around. This opinion has been refuted by Vitringa;[3] and Paul's expression (Acts xxii. 3), *seated at the feet of Gamaliel,* would be sufficient to prove the contrary. Never-

[1] Ver. 48. ℵ* B. ζητουμεν instead of εζητουμεν.—Ver. 49. ℵ* b. Syr[cur], ζητειτε instead of εζητειτε.

[2] *Hor. hebr.* ad Luc. ii. 46 (after *Sanhedr.* xi. 2).

[3] *Synag.* p. 167.

theless the expression, *seated in the midst of the doctors,* proves no doubt that the child was for the time occupying a place of honour. As the Rabbinical method of teaching was by questions,—by proposing, for example, a problem taken from the law,—both master and disciples had an opportunity of showing their sagacity. Jesus had given some remarkable answer, or put some original question; and, as is the case when a particularly intelligent pupil presents himself, He had attracted for the moment all the interest of His teachers. There is nothing in the narrative, when rightly understood, that savours in the least of an apotheosis of Jesus. The expressions, *hearing them, and asking them questions,* bear in a precisely opposite direction. Josephus, in his autobiography (c. i.), mentions a very similar fact respecting his own youth. When he was only fourteen years of age, the priests and eminent men of Jerusalem came to question him on the explanation of the law. The apocryphal writings make Jesus on this occasion a professor possessing omniscience.[1] There we have the legend grafted on the fact so simply related by the evangelist. Σύνεσις, *understanding,* is the personal quality of which the answers, ἀποκρίσεις, are the manifestations.—The surprise of His parents proves that Jesus habitually observed a humble reserve.—There is a slight tone of reproach in the words of Mary. She probably wished to justify herself for the apparent negligence of which she was guilty. Criticism is surprised at the uneasiness expressed by Mary; did she not know who this child was? Criticism reasons as if the human heart worked according to logic.—To the indirect reproach of Mary, Jesus replies in such words as she had never heard from Him before: *Wherefore did ye seek me?* He does not mean, "You could very well leave me at Jerusalem." The literal translation is: "What is it, that you sought me?" And the implied answer is: "To seek for me thus was an inadvertence on your part. It should have occurred to you at once that you would find me here."

[1] In the Gospel of Thomas (belonging to the second century; known to Irenæus), Jesus, when on the road to Nazareth, returns of His own accord to Jerusalem; the doctors are stupefied with wonder at hearing Him solve the most difficult questions of the law and the prophecies. In an Arabic Gospel (of later date than the preceding), Jesus instructs the astronomers in the mysteries of the celestial spheres, and reveals to the philosophers the secrets of metaphysics.

The sequel explains why.—The phrase τί ὅτι is found in Acts v. 9. Οὐκ ᾔδειτε, *did ye not know?* not, do ye not know? The expression τὰ τοῦ πατρός μου may, according to Greek usage, have either a local meaning, *the house of*, or a moral, *the affairs of*. The former sense is required by the idea of *seeking;* and if, nevertheless, we are disposed to adopt the latter as wider, the first must be included in it. "Where my Father's affairs are carried on, there you are sure to find me." —The expression *my Father* is dictated to the child by the situation: a child is to be found at his father's. We may add that He could not, without impropriety, have said *God's*, instead of *my Father's;* for this would have been to exhibit in a pretentious and affected way the entirely religious character of His ordinary thoughts, and to put Himself forward as a little saint. Lastly, does not this expression contain a delicate but decisive reply to Mary's words, *Thy father and I?* Any allusion to the Trinitarian relation must, of course, be excluded from the meaning of this saying. But, on the other hand, can the simple notion of moral paternity suffice to express its meaning? Had not Jesus, during those days of isolation, by meditating anew upon the intimacy of His moral relations with God, been brought to regard Him as the sole author of His existence? And was not this the cause of the kind of shudder which He felt at hearing from Mary's lips the word *Thy father*, to which He immediately replies with a certain ardour of expression, *my Father?*—That Mary and Joseph should not have been able to understand this speech appears inexplicable to certain critics,—to Meyer, for instance, and to Strauss, who infers from this detail that the whole story is untrue. But this word, *my Father*, was the first revelation of a relation which surpassed all that Judaism had realized; and the expression, "*to be about the business*" of this Father, expressed the ideal of a completely filial life, of an existence entirely devoted to God and divine things, which perhaps at this very time had just arisen in the mind of Jesus, and which we could no more understand than Mary and Joseph, if the life of Jesus had never come before us. It was only by the light Mary received afterwards from the ministry of her Son, that she could say what is here expressed: that she did not understand this saying at the time.—Does not the original source of this narrative discover itself in this remark? From whom else could it emanate, but from Mary herself?

3. *The residence at Nazareth:* vers. 51, 52.[1]—From this moment Jesus possesses within Him this ideal of a life entirely devoted to the kingdom of God, which had just flashed before His eyes. For eighteen years He applied Himself in silence to the business of His earthly father at Nazareth, where He is called *the carpenter* (Mark vi. 3). The analytical form ἦν ὑποτασσόμενος indicates the permanence of this submission; and the pres. partic. mid., *submitting Himself,* its spontaneous and deliberate character. In this simple word, *submitting Himself,* Luke has summed up the entire work of Jesus until His baptism.—But why did not God permit the child to remain in the temple of Jerusalem, which during the feast-days had been His Eden? The answer is not difficult. He must inevitably have been thrown too early into the theologico-political discussions which agitated the capital; and after having excited the admiration of the doctors, He would have provoked their hatred by His original and independent turn of thought. If the spiritual atmosphere of Nazareth was heavy, it was at least calm; and the labours of the workshop, in the retirement of this peaceful valley, under the eye of the Father, was a more favourable sphere for the development of Jesus than the ritualism of the temple and the Rabbinical discussions of Jerusalem.—The remark at the end of ver. 51 is similar to that at ver. 19; only for the verb συντηρεῖν, which denoted the grouping of a great number of circumstances, to collect and combine them, Luke substitutes here another compound, διατηρεῖν. This δια denotes the permanence of the recollection, notwithstanding circumstances which might have effaced it, particularly the inability to understand recorded in ver. 50. She carefully kept in her possession this profound saying as an unexplained mystery.—The fifty-second verse describes the youth of Jesus, as the fortieth verse had depicted His childhood; and these two brief sketches correspond with the two analogous pictures of John the Baptist

[1] **Ver. 51.** The MSS. and Vss. are divided between και η μητηρ and η δε μητηρ.—ℵ* B. D. M. omit ταυτα.—Ver. 52. ℵ. L. add εν τη, B. εν, before σοφια.—D. L. Syr. Itplerique place ηλικια before σοφια.

(i. 66, 80). Each of these general remarks, if it stood alone, might be regarded, as Schleiermacher has suggested, as the close of a small document. But their relation to each other, and their periodical recurrence, demonstrate the unity of our writing. This form is met with again in the book of the Acts.—*Ἡλικία* does not here denote *age,* which would yield no meaning at all, but *height, stature,* just as xix. 3. This term embraces the entire physical development, all the external advantages; *σοφία, wisdom,* refers to the intellectual and moral development. The third term, *favour with God and men,* completes the other two. Over the person of this young man there was spread a charm at once external and spiritual; it proceeded from the favour of God, and conciliated towards Him the favour of men. This perfectly normal human being was the beginning of a reconciliation between heaven and earth. The term wisdom refers rather to *with God;* the word stature to *with men.* The last words, *with men,* establish a contrast between Jesus and John the Baptist, who at this very time was growing up in the solitude of the desert; and this contrast is the prelude to that which later on was to be exhibited in their respective ministries.—There is no notion for the forgetfulness or denial of which theology pays more dearly than that of a *development* in pure goodness. This positive notion is derived by biblical Christianity from this verse. With it the humanity of Jesus may be accepted, as it is here presented by Luke, in all its reality.

GENERAL CONSIDERATIONS ON CHAP. I. AND II.

It remains for us to form an estimate of the historical value of the accounts contained in these two chapters.

I. *Characteristics of the Narrative.*—We have already observed that Luke thoroughly believes that he is relating facts, and not giving poetical illustrations of ideas. He declares that he only writes in accordance with the information he has collected; he writes with the design of convincing his readers of the unquestionable certainty of the things which he relates (i. 3, 4); and in speaking thus, he has very specially in view the contents of the first two chapters (comp. the ἄνωθεν, ver. 3). In short, the very nature of these narratives admits of no other supposition (p. 68). Was he himself the dupe of false information? Was he not in a much more favourable position than we are for estimating the value of the communications that were made to him? There are not two ways, we imagine, of replying to these preliminary questions. As to the substance of the narrative, we may distinguish between the facts and the discourses or songs. The supernatural element in the facts only occurs to an extent that may be called *natural*, when once the supernatural character of the appearance of Jesus is admitted in a general way. If Mary was to accept spontaneously the part to which she was called, it was necessary that she should be informed of it beforehand. If angels really exist, and form a part of the kingdom of God, they were interested as well as men in the birth of Him who was to be the Head of this organization, and reign over the whole moral universe. It is not surprising, then, that some manifestation on their part should accompany this event. That the prophetic Spirit might have at this epoch representatives in Israel, can only be disputed by denying the existence and action of this Spirit in the nation at any time. *From the point of view presented by the biblical premisses*, the possibility of the facts related is then indisputable. In the details of the history, the supernatural is confined within the limits of the strictest sobriety and most perfect suitability, and differs altogether in this respect from the marvels of the apocryphal writings.[1]

The discourses or hymns may appear to have been a freer element, in the treatment of which the imagination of the author might have allowed itself larger scope. Should not these portions be regarded as somewhat analogous to those discourses which the ancient historians so often put into the mouth of their heroes, a product of the individual or collective Christian muse? But we have proved that, in attributing to the angel, to Mary, and to Zacharias the language which he puts into their mouths, the author would of his own accord have made his characters false prophets. They would be so many oracles *post eventum contra eventum!* Never, after the unbelief of the people had brought about a separation between the Synagogue and the Church, could the Christian muse have celebrated the glories of the Messianic future of Israel, with such accents of artless joyous hope as prevail in these canticles (i. 17, 54, 55, 74, and 75, ii. 10, 32). The only words that could be suspected from this point of view are those which are put into the mouth of Simeon. For they suppose a more distinct view of

[1] In addition to the specimens already given, we add the following, taken from the Gospel of James (2d c.): Zacharias is high priest; he inquires of God respecting the lot of the youthful Mary, brought up in the temple. God Himself commands that she shall be confided to Joseph. The task of embroidering the veil of the temple is devolved upon Mary by lot. When she brings the work, Elizabeth at the sight of her praises the mother of the Messiah, without Mary herself knowing why. Afterwards it is John, more even than Jesus, who is the object of Herod's jealous search. Elizabeth flees to the desert with her child; a rock opens to receive them; a bright light reveals the presence of the angel who guards them. Herod questions Zacharias, who is ignorant himself where his child is. Zacharias is then slain in the temple court; the carpets of the temple cry out; a voice announces the avenger; the body of the martyr disappears; only his blood is found changed into stone.

the future course of things in Israel. But, on the other hand, it is precisely the hymn of Simeon, and his address to Mary, which, by their originality, conciseness, and energy, are most clearly marked with the stamp of authenticity. We have certainly met with some expressions of a *universalist* tendency in these songs ("goodwill *towards men*," ii. 14; "a light *of the Gentiles*," ver. 32); but these allusions in no way exceed the limits of ancient prophecy, and they are not brought out in a sufficiently marked way to indicate a time when Jewish Christianity and Paulinism were already in open conflict. This universalism is, in fact, that of the early days, simple, free, and exempt from all polemical design. It is the fresh and normal unfolding of the flower in its calyx.

The opinion in closest conformity with the internal marks of the narrative, as well as with the clearly expressed intention of the writer, is therefore certainly that which regards the facts and discourses contained in these two chapters as historical.

II. *Relation of the Narratives of Chap.* i. *and* ii. *to the Contents of other parts of the N.T.*—The first point of comparison is the narrative of the infancy in *Matthew*, chap. i. and ii. It is confidently asserted that the two accounts are irreconcilable.—We ask, first of all, whether there are *two* accounts. Does what is called the *narrative* of Matthew really deserve this name? We find in the first two chapters of Matthew five incidents of the infancy of Christ, which are mentioned solely to connect with them five prophetic passages, and thus prove the Messianic dignity of Jesus, in accordance with the design of this evangelist, i. 1: Jesus, *the Christ*. Is this what we should call a narrative? Is it not rather a didactic exposition? So little does the author entertain the idea of *relating*, that in chap. i., while treating of the birth of Jesus, he does not even mention Bethlehem; he is wholly taken up with the connection of the fact of which he is speaking with the oracle, Isa. vii. It is only after having finished this subject, when he comes to speak of the visit of the magi, that he mentions for the first time, and as it were in passing (*Jesus being born in Bethlehem*), this locality. And with what object? With a historical view? Not at all. Simply on account of the prophecy of Micah, which is to be illustrated in the visit of the magi, and in which the place of the Messiah's birth was announced beforehand. Apart from this prophecy, he would still less have thought of mentioning Bethlehem in the second narrative than in the first. And it is this desultory history, made up of isolated facts, referred to solely with an apologetic aim, that is to be employed to criticise and correct a complete narrative such as Luke's! Is it not clear that, between two accounts of such a different nature, there may easily be found blanks which hypothesis alone can fill up? Two incidents are common to Luke and Matthew: the birth of Jesus at Bethlehem, and His education at Nazareth. The historical truth of the latter piece of information is not disputed. Instead of this, it is maintained that the former is a mere legendary invention occasioned by Mic. v. But were it so, the fact would never occur in the tradition entirely detached from the prophetic word which would be the very soul of it. But Luke does not contain the slightest allusion to the prophecy of Micah. It is only natural, therefore, to admit that the first fact is historical as well as the other.—With this common basis, three differences are discernible in which some find contradictions.

1*st.* The account which Matthew gives of the appearance of an angel to Joseph, in order to relieve his perplexity, is, it is said, incompatible with that of the appearance of the angel to Mary in Luke. For if this last appearance had taken place, Mary could not have failed to have spoken of it to Joseph, and in that case his doubts would have been impossible.—But all this is uncertain. For, first, Mary may certainly have told Joseph everything, either before or after her return from Elizabeth; but in this case, whatever confidence Joseph had in her, nothing could prevent his being for a moment shaken by doubt at hearing of a message and a fact so extraordinary. But it is possible also—and this supposition appears to me more probable—that Mary, judging it right in this affair to leave everything to God, who immediately directed it, held herself as dead in regard to Joseph. And, in this case, what might not have been his anxiety when he thought he saw Mary's condition? On either of these two possible suppositions, a reason is found for the appearance of the angel to Joseph.

2*d.* It would seem, according to Matthew, that at the time Jesus was born, His parents were residing at Bethlehem, and that this city was their permanent abode. Further, on their return from Egypt, when they resolved to go and live at Nazareth, their decision was the result of a divine interposition which aimed at the fulfilment of the prophecies (Matt. ii. 22, 23). In Luke, on the contrary, the ordinary abode of the parents appears to be Nazareth. It is an exceptional circumstance, the edict of Augustus, that takes them to Bethlehem. And consequently, as soon as the duties, which have called them to Judæa and detained them there, are accomplished, they return to Nazareth, without needing any special direction (ii. 39).—It is important here to remember the remark which we made on the nature of Matthew's narrative. In that evangelist, neither the mention of the place of birth nor of the place where Jesus was brought up is made as a matter of history; in both cases it is solely a question of proving the fulfilment of a prophecy. An account of this kind without doubt affirms what it actually says, but it in no way denies what it does not say; and it is impossible to derive from it a historical view sufficiently complete, to oppose it to another and more detailed account that is decidedly historical. There is nothing, therefore, here to prevent our completing the information furnished by Matthew from that supplied by Luke, and regarding Nazareth with the latter as the natural abode of the parents of Jesus. What follows will complete the solution of this difficulty.

3*d.* The incidents of the visit of the magi and the flight into Egypt, related by Matthew, cannot be intercalated with Luke's narrative, either *before* the presentation of the child in the temple,—His parents would not have been so imprudent as to take Him back to

Jerusalem after that the visit of the magi had drawn upon Him the jealous notice of Herod; and besides, there would not be, during the six weeks intervening between the birth and the presentation, the time necessary for the journey to Egypt,—or *after* this ceremony; for, according to Luke ii. 39, the parents return directly from Jerusalem to Nazareth, without going again to Bethlehem, where nevertheless they must have received the visit of the magi; and according to Matthew himself, Joseph, after the return from Egypt, does not return to Judæa, but goes immediately to settle in Galilee.—But notwithstanding these reasons, it is not impossible to place the presentation at Jerusalem either after or before the visit of the magi. If this had already taken place, Joseph and Mary must have put their trust in God's care to protect the child; and the time is no objection to this supposition, as Wieseler has shown. For from Bethlehem to Rhinocolure, the first Egyptian town, is only three or four days' journey. Three weeks, then, would, strictly speaking, suffice to go and return. It is more natural, however, to place the visit of the magi and the journey into Egypt *after* the presentation. We have only to suppose that after this ceremony Mary and Joseph returned to Bethlehem, a circumstance of which Luke was not aware, and which he has omitted. In the same way, in the Acts, he omits Paul's journey into Arabia after his conversion, and combines into one the two sojourns at Damascus separated by this journey. This return to Bethlehem, situated at such a short distance from Jerusalem, is too natural to need to be particularly accounted for. But it is completely accounted for, if we suppose that, when Joseph and Mary left Nazareth on account of the census, they did so with the intention of *settling* at Bethlehem. Many reasons would induce them to this decision. It might appear to them more suitable that the child on whom such high promises rested should be brought up at Bethlehem, the city of His royal ancestor, in the neighbourhood of the capital, than in the remote hamlet of Nazareth. The desire of being near Zacharias and Elizabeth would also attract them to Judæa. Lastly, they would thereby avoid the calumnious judgments which the short time that elapsed between their marriage and the birth of the child could not have failed to occasion had they dwelt at Nazareth. Besides, even though this had not been their original plan, after Joseph had been settled at Bethlehem for some weeks, and had found the means of subsistence there, nothing would more naturally occur to his mind than the idea of settling down at the place. In this way the interposition of the angel is explained, who in Matthew induces him to return to Galilee.—Bleek inclines to the opinion that the arrival of the magi preceded the presentation, and that the journey into Egypt followed it. This supposition is admissible also; it alters nothing of importance in the course of things as presented in the preceding explanations, of which we give a sketch in the following recapitulation:—

1. The angel announces to Mary the birth of Jesus (Luke i.). 2. Mary, after or without having spoken to Joseph, goes to Elizabeth (Luke i.). 3. After her return, Joseph falls into the state of per-

plexity from which he is delivered by the message of the angel (Matt. i.). 4. He takes Mary ostensibly for his wife (Matt. i.). 5. Herod's order, carrying out the decree of Augustus, leads them to Bethlehem (Luke ii.). 6. Jesus is born (Matt. i.; Luke ii.). 7. His parents present Him in the temple (Luke ii.). 8. On their return to Bethlehem, they receive the visit of the magi and escape into Egypt (Matt. ii.). 9. Returned from Egypt, they give up the idea of settling at Bethlehem, and determine once more to fix their abode at Nazareth.

Only one condition is required in order to accept this effort to harmonize the two accounts; namely, the supposition that each writer was ignorant of the other's narrative. But this supposition is allowed by even the most decided adversaries of any attempt at harmony,—such, for instance, as Keim, who, although he believes that Luke in composing his Gospel made use of Matthew, is nevertheless of opinion that the first two chapters of Matthew's writing were not in existence at the time when Luke availed himself of it for the composition of his own.

If the solution proposed does not satisfy the reader, and he thinks he must choose between the two writings, it will certainly be more natural to suspect the narrative of Matthew, because it has no proper historical aim. But further, it will only be right, in estimating the value of the facts related by this evangelist, to remember that the more forced in some cases appears the connection which he maintains between the facts he mentions and the prophecies he applies to them, the less probable is it that the former were invented on the foundation of the latter. Such incidents as the journey into Egypt and the massacre of the children must have been well-ascertained facts before any one would think of finding a prophetic announcement of them in the words of Hosea and Jeremiah, which the author quotes and applies to them.

We pass on to other parts of the N. T.—Meyer maintains that certain facts subsequently related by *the synoptics* themselves are incompatible with the reality of the miraculous events of the infancy. How could the brethren of Jesus, acquainted with these prodigies, refuse to believe in their brother? How could even Mary herself share their unbelief? (Mark iii. 21, 31 et seq.; Matt. xii. 46 et seq.; Luke viii. 19 et seq.; comp. John vii. 5.) In reply, it may be said that we do not know how far Mary could communicate to her sons, at any rate before the time of Jesus' ministry, these extraordinary circumstances, which touched on very delicate matters affecting herself. Besides, jealousy and prejudice might easily counteract any impression produced by facts of which they had not been witnesses, and induce them to think, notwithstanding, that Jesus was taking a wrong course. Did not John the Baptist himself, although he had given public testimony to Jesus, as no one would venture to deny, feel his faith shaken in view of the unexpected course which His work took? and did not this cause him to be offended in Him? (Matt. xi. 6.) As to Mary, there is nothing to prove that she shared the unbelief of her sons. If she accompanies them when they go to Jesus, intending to lay hold upon Him (Mark iii.), it is probably from a feeling of anxiety as to what might take place, and from a desire to prevent the conflict she anticipates.—Keim alleges the omission of the narratives of the infancy in Mark and John. These two evangelists, it is true, make the starting-point of their narrative on this side of these facts. Mark opens his with the ministry of the forerunner, which he regards as the true commencement of that of Jesus.[1] But it does not follow from this that he denies all the previous circumstances which he does not relate. All that this proves is, that the original apostolic preaching, of which this Gospel is the simplest reproduction, went no further back; and for this manifest reason, that this preaching was based on the tradition of the apostles as *eye-witnesses* (αὐτόπται, i. 2; Acts i. 21, 22; John xv. 27), and that the personal testimony of the apostles did not go back as far as the early period of the life of Jesus. It is doubtless for the same reason that Paul, in his enumeration of the testimonies to the resurrection of Jesus, omits that of the women, because he regards the testimony of the apostles and of the Church gathered about them as the only suitable basis for the official instruction of the Church. —John commences his narrative at the hour of the birth of his own faith, which simply proves that the design of his work is to trace the history of the development of his own faith and of that of his fellow-disciples. All that occurred previous to this time—the baptism of Jesus, the temptation—he leaves untold; but he does not on that account deny these facts, for he himself alludes to the baptism of Jesus.

Keim goes further. He maintains that there are to be found in the N. T. three theories as to the origin of the person of Christ, which are exclusive of each other:—1*st*. That of the purely *natural birth;* this would be the true view of the apostles and primitive Church, which was held by the Ebionitish communities (*Clement. Homil.*). This being found insufficient to explain such a remarkable sequel as the life of Jesus, it must have been supplemented afterwards by the legend of the descent of the Holy Spirit at the baptism. 2*d*. That of the *miraculous* birth, held by part of the Jewish-Christian communities and the Nazarene churches, and proceeding from an erroneous Messianic application of Isa. vii. This theory is found in the Gospel of Luke and in Matt. i. and ii. 3*d*. The theory of the *pre-existence* of Jesus as a divine being, originated in the Greek churches, of which Paul and John are the principal representatives. —To this we reply:—

1*st*. That it cannot be proved that the apostolic and primitive doctrine was that of the natural birth. Certain words are cited in proof which are put by the evangelists in the mouth of the people: "Is not this *the carpenter's son?*" (Matt. xiii. 55; Luke iv. 22; comp. John vi. 42); next the words of the Apostle Philip in John: "We have found . . . Jesus of Nazareth, *the son of Joseph*" (John i. 45)

[1] These words, *The beginning of the gospel of Jesus Christ, the Son of God* (Mark i. 1), appear to me to be in logical apposition with the subsequent account of the ministry of John (v. 4).

The absence of all protest on the part of John against this assertion of Philip's is regarded as a confirmation of the fact that he himself admitted its truth.—But who could with any reason be surprised that, on the day after Jesus made the acquaintance of His first disciples, Philip should still be ignorant of the miraculous birth? Was Jesus to hasten to tell this fact to those who saw Him for the first time? Was there nothing more urgent to teach these young hearts just opening to His influence? Who cannot understand why Jesus should allow the words of the people to pass, without announcing such a fact as this to these cavilling, mocking Jews? Jesus testifies before all *what He has seen with His Father* by the inward sense, and not outward facts which He had from the fallible lips of others. Above all, He very well knew that it was not faith in His miraculous birth that would produce faith in His person; on the contrary, that it was only faith in His person that would induce any one to admit the miracle of His birth. He saw that, to put out before a hostile and profane people an assertion like this, which He could not possibly prove, would only draw forth a flood of coarse ridicule, which would fall directly on that revered person who was more concerned in this history even than Himself, and that without the least advantage to the faith of any one. Certainly this was a case for the application of the precept, *Cast not your pearls before swine*, if you would not have them *turn again and rend you.* This observation also explains the silence of the apostles on this point in the Acts of the Apostles They could not have done anything more ill-advised than to rest the controversy between the Jews and Christ on such a ground.—If John does not rectify the statements of the people and of Philip, the reason is, that he wrote for the Church already formed and sufficiently instructed. His personal conviction appears from the following facts:—He admitted the *human* birth, for he speaks several times of *His mother*. At the same time he regarded natural birth as the means of the transmission of sin: "That which is born of the flesh *is flesh*." And nevertheless he regarded this Jesus, born of a human mother, as the *Holy One of God*, and the *bread that came down from heaven!* Is it possible that he did not attribute an exceptional character to His birth? As to Mark, we do not, with Bleek, rely upon the name *Son of Mary*, which is given to Jesus by the people of Nazareth (vi. 3); this appellation in their mouth does not imply a belief in the miraculous birth. But in the expression, Jesus Christ, *the Son of God* (i. 1), the latter title certainly implies more, in the author's mind, than the simple notion of *Messiah;* this, in fact, was already sufficiently expressed by the name *Christ.* There can be no doubt, therefore, that this term implies in Mark a relation of mysterious Sonship between the person of Jesus and the Divine Being.[1] All these passages quoted by Keim only prove what is self-apparent, that the notion of the natural birth of Jesus was that of the Jewish people, and also of the apostles in the early days of their faith, before they received fuller information. It is not at all surprising, there-

[1] If the *Sinaiticus* suppresses it, this is one of the numberless omissions, resulting from the negligence of the copyist, with which this manuscript abounds.

fore, that it remained the idea of the Ebionitish churches, which never really broke with the Israelitish past, but were contented to apply to Jesus the popular notion of the Jewish Messiah.—Keim also finds a trace of this alleged primitive theory in the two genealogies contained in Luke and Matthew. According to him, these documents imply, by their very nature, that those who drew them up held the idea of a natural birth. For what interest could they have had in giving the genealogical tree of Joseph, unless they had regarded him as the father of the Messiah? Further, in order to make these documents square with their new theory of the miraculous birth, the two evangelists have been obliged to subject them to arbitrary revision, as is seen in the appendix ἐξ ἧς . . . Matt. i. 16, and in the parenthesis ὡς ἐνομίζετο, Luke iii. 23.—It is very possible, indeed, that the original documents, reproduced in Matt. i. and Luke iii., were of Jewish origin; they were probably the same public registers (δέλτοι δημόσιαι) from which the historian Josephus asserts that his own genealogy was taken.[1] It is perfectly obvious that such documents could contain no indication of the miraculous birth of Jesus, if even they went down to Him. But how could this fact furnish a proof of the primitive opinion *of the Church* about the birth of its Head? It is in these genealogies, as *revised and completed* by Christian historians, that we must seek the sentiments of the primitive Church respecting the person of her Master. And this is precisely what we find in the Gospels of Matthew and Luke. The former, in demonstrating, by the genealogy which he presents to us, the Davidic sonship of Joseph, declares that, as regards Jesus, this same Joseph sustains part of the adoptive, legal father. The extract from the public registers which the second hands down is not another edition of that of Joseph, in contradiction with the former; it is the genealogy of Levi, the father of Mary (see iii. 23). In transmitting this document, Luke is careful to observe that the opinion which made Jesus the son of Joseph was only a popular prejudice, and that the relationship of which he here indicates the links is the only real one. These are not, therefore, Jewish-Christian materials, as Keim maintains, but purely Jewish; and the evangelists, when inserting them into their writings, have imprinted on them, each after his own manner, the Christian seal.

Keim relies further on the silence of *Paul* respecting the miraculous birth. But is he really silent? Can it be maintained that the expression, Rom. i. 3, "*made of the seed of David according to the flesh*," was intended by Paul to describe the entire fact of the human birth of Jesus? Is it not clear that the words, *according to the flesh*, are a restriction expressly designed to indicate another side to this fact, the action of another factor, called in the following clause *the Spirit of holiness*, by which he explains the miracle of the resurrection? The notion of the miraculous birth appears equally indispensable to explain the antithesis, 1 Cor. xv. 47: "The first man is of the earth, earthy; the second, from heaven." But whatever else he is, Paul is a man of logical mind. How then could he affirm,

[1] Jos. *Vita*, c. i.

on the one hand, the hereditary transmission of sin and death by natural generation, as he does in Rom. v. 12, and on the other the truly human birth of Jesus (Gal. iv. 4), whom he regards as the Holy One, if, in his view, the birth of this extraordinary man was not of an exceptional character? Only, as this fact could not, from its very nature, become the subject of apostolical testimony, nor for that reason enter into general preaching, Paul does not include it among the elements of the παράδοσις which he enumerates, 1 Cor. xv. 1 et seq. And if he does not make any special dogmatic use of it, it is because, as we have observed, the miraculous birth is only the *negative* condition of the holiness of Jesus; its *positive* condition is, and must be, His voluntary obedience; consequently it is this that Paul particularly brings out (Rom. viii. 1–4). These reasons apply to the other didactic writings of the N. T.

2d. It is arbitrary to maintain that the narrative of the descent of the Holy Spirit is only a later complement of the theory of the natural birth. Is not this narrative found in two of our synoptics by the side of that of the supernatural birth? And yet this is only a complement of the theory of the natural birth! Further, in all these synoptics alike, it is found closely and organically connected with two other facts, the ministry of John and the temptation, which proves that these three narratives formed a very firmly connected cycle in the evangelical tradition, and belonged to the very earliest preaching.

3d. The idea of the pre-existence of Jesus is in no way a rival theory to that of the miraculous birth; on the contrary, the former implies the latter as its necessary element. It is the idea of the natural birth which, if we think a little, appears incompatible with that of the incarnation. M. Secretan admirably says: "Man represents the principle of individuality, of progress; woman, that of tradition, generality, species. The Saviour could not be the son of a particular man; He behoved to be the son of humanity, *the Son of man.*"[1]

4th. So far from there being in the N. T. writings traces of three opposite theories on this point, the real state of the case is this: The disciples set out, just as the Jewish people did, with the idea of an ordinary birth; it was the natural supposition (John i. 45). But as they came to understand the prophetic testimony, which makes the Messiah the supreme manifestation of Jehovah, and the testimony of Jesus Himself, which constantly implies a divine background to His human existence, they soon rose to a knowledge of the God-man, whose human existence was preceded by His divine existence. This step was taken, in the consciousness of the Church, a quarter of a century after the death of Jesus. The Epistles of Paul are evidence of it (1 Cor. viii. 6; Col. i. 15–17; Phil. ii. 6, 7). Lastly, the mode of transition from the divine existence to the human life, the fact of the miraculous birth, entered a little later into the sphere of the ecclesiastical world, by means of the Gospels of Matthew and Luke, about thirty-five or forty years after the departure of the Saviour.

[1] *La Raison et le Christianisme*, pp. 259 and 277.

III. *Connection between these Narratives and the Christian Faith in general.*—The miraculous birth is immediately and closely connected with the perfect holiness of Christ, which is the basis of the Christology; so much so, that whoever denies the former of these miracles, must necessarily be led to deny the latter; and whoever accepts the second, cannot fail to fall back on the first, which is indeed implied in it. As to the objection, that even if the biblical narrative of the miraculous birth is accepted, it is impossible to explain how it was that sin was not communicated to Jesus through His mother, it has been already answered (p. 93).—The miraculous birth is equally inseparable from the fact of the incarnation. It is true that the first may be admitted and the second rejected, but the reverse is impossible. The necessity for an exceptional mode of birth results from the pre-existence (p. 160). But here we confront the great objection to the miraculous birth: What becomes, from this point of view, of the real and proper humanity of the Saviour? Can it be reconciled with this exceptional mode of birth? "The conditions of existence being different from ours," says Keim, "equality of nature no longer exists."—But, we would ask those who reason in this way, do you admit the theories of Vogt respecting the origin of the human race? Do you make man proceed from the brute? If not, then you admit a *creation* of the human race; and in this case you must acknowledge that the conditions of existence in the case of the first couple were quite different from ours. Do you, on this ground, deny the full and real humanity of the first man? But to deny the *human* character to the being from whom has proceeded by way of generation, that is to say, by the transmission of his own nature, all that is called man, would be absurd. Identity of nature is possible, therefore, notwithstanding a difference in the mode of origin. To understand this fact completely, we need to have a complete insight into the relation of the individual to the species, which is the most unfathomable secret of nature. But there is something here still more serious. Jesus is not only the continuator of human nature as it already exists; He is the elect of God, by whom it is to be renewed and raised to its destined perfection. In Him is accomplished the new creation, which is the true end of the old. This work of a higher nature can only take place in virtue of a fresh and immediate contact of creative power with human nature. Keim agrees with this up to a certain point; for, while holding the paternal concurrence in the birth of this extraordinary man, he admits a divine interposition which profoundly influenced and completely sanctified the appearance of this Being.[1] This attempt at explanation is a homage rendered to the incomparable moral greatness of Jesus, and we think it leaves untouched the great object of faith—Jesus Christ's dignity as the Saviour. But must we not retort upon this explanation the objection which Keim brings against the two notions of the pre-existence and the supernatural birth: "These are theories, not facts established by any documents!" If it is absolutely necessary to acknowledge that Jesus was a man specifically different from all

[1] *Gesch. Jesu*, t. i. pp. 357, 358.

others,[1] and if, in order to explain this phenomenon, it is indispensable to stipulate, as Keim really does, for an exceptional mode of origin, then why not keep to the positive statements of our Gospels, which satisfy this demand, rather than throw ourselves upon pure speculation?

IV. *Origin of the Narratives of the Infancy.*—The difference of style, so absolute and abrupt, between Luke's preface (i. 1–4) and the following narratives, leaves no room for doubt that from i. 5 the author makes use of documents of which he scrupulously preserves the very form. What were these documents? According to Schleiermacher, they were brief family records which the compiler of the Gospel contented himself with connecting together in such a way as to form a continuous narrative. But the modes of conclusion, and the general views which appear as recurring topics, in which Schleiermacher sees the proof of his hypothesis, on the contrary upset it. For these brief summaries, by their resemblance and correspondence, prove a unity of composition in the entire narrative. Volkmar regards the sources of these narratives as some originally Jewish materials, into which the author has infused his own Pauline feeling. According to Keim, their source would be the great Ebionitish writing which constitutes, in his opinion, the original trunk of our Gospel, on which the author set himself to graft his Paulinism. These two suppositions come to the same thing. We are certainly struck with the twofold character of these narratives; there is a spirit of profound and scrupulous fidelity to the law, side by side with a not less marked universalist tendency. But are these really two currents of contrary origin? I think not. The old covenant already contained these two currents,—one strictly legal, the other to a great extent universalist. Universalism is even, properly speaking, the primitive current; legalism was only added to it afterwards, if it is true that Abraham preceded Moses. The narratives of the infancy reflect simply and faithfully this twofold character; for they exhibit to us the normal transition from the old to the new covenant. If the so-called Pauline element had been introduced into it subsequently, it would have taken away much more of the original tone, and would not appear organically united with it; and if it were only the product of a party manœuvre, its polemical character could not have been so completely disguised. These two elements, as they present themselves in these narratives, in no way prove, therefore, two sources of an opposite religious nature.

The true explanation of the origin of Luke's and Matthew's narrative appears to me to be found in the following fact. In Matthew, Joseph is the principal personage. It is to him that the angel appears; he comes to calm his perplexities; it is to him that the name of Jesus is notified and explained. If the picture of the infancy be represented, as in a stereoscope, in a twofold form, in Matthew it is seen on the side of Joseph; in Luke, on the contrary, it is Mary who assumes the principal part. It is she who receives the visit of the angel; to her is communicated the name of the child

[1] *Gesch. Jesu*, t. i. p. 359.

her private feelings are brought out in the narrative; it is she who is prominent in the address of Simeon and in the history of the search for the child. The picture is the same, but it is taken this time on Mary's side.

From this we can draw no other conclusion than that the two cycles of narratives emanate from two different centres. One of these was the circle of which Joseph was the centre, and which we may suppose consisted of Cleopas his brother, James and Jude his sons, of whom one was the first bishop of the flock at Jerusalem; and Simeon, a son of Cleopas, the first successor of James. The narratives preserved amongst these persons might easily reach the ear of the author of the first Gospel, who doubtless lived in the midst of this flock; and his Gospel, which, far more than Luke's, was the record of the official preaching, was designed to reproduce rather that side of the facts which up to a certain point already belonged to the *public.* But a cycle of narratives must also have formed itself round Mary, in the retreat in which she ended her career. These narratives would have a much more private character, and would exhibit more of the inner meaning of the external facts. These, doubtless, are those which Luke has preserved. How he succeeded in obtaining access to this source of information, to which he probably alludes in the ἄνωθεν (i. 3), we do not know. But it is certain that the nature of these narratives was better suited to the *private* character of his work. Does not Luke give us a glimpse, as it were designedly, of this incomparable source of information in the remarks (ii. 19, and 50, 51) which, from any other point of view, could hardly be anything else than a piece of charlatanism?

We think that these two cycles of narratives existed for a certain time,—the one as a public tradition, the other as a family *souvenir*, in a purely *oral* form. The author of the first Gospel was doubtless the first who drew up the former, adapting it to the didactic aim which he proposed to himself in his work. The latter was originally in Aramæan, and under any circumstances could only have been drawn up, as we have shown, after the termination of the ministry of Jesus. It was in this form that Luke found it. He translated it, and inserted it in his work. The very songs had been faithfully preserved until then. For this there was no need of the stenographer. Mary's heart had preserved all; the writer himself testifies as much, and he utters no vain words. The deeper feelings are, the more indelibly graven on the soul are the thoughts which embody them; and the recollection of the peculiar expressions in which they find utterance remains indissolubly linked with the recollection of the thoughts themselves. Every one has verified this experience in the graver moments of his life.

Lastly, in the question which now occupies our attention, let us not forget to bear in mind the importance which these narratives possessed in the view of the two writers who have handed them down to us. They wrote seriously, because they were believers and wrote to win the faith of the world.

SECOND PART

THE ADVENT OF THE MESSIAH.

CHAP. III. 1–IV. 13.

FOR eighteen years Jesus lived unknown in the seclusion of Nazareth. His fellow-townsmen, recalling this period of His life, designate Him *the carpenter* (Mark vi. 3). Justin Martyr—deriving the fact, doubtless, from tradition—represents Jesus as making ploughs and yokes, and teaching men righteousness by these products of His peaceful toil.[1] Beneath the veil of this life of humble toil, an inward development was accomplished, which resulted in a state of perfect receptivity for the measureless communication of the Divine Spirit. This result was attained just when Jesus reached the climacteric of human life, the age of thirty, when both soul and body enjoy the highest degree of vitality, and are fitted to become the perfect organs of a higher inspiration. The forerunner then having given the signal, Jesus left His obscurity to accomplish the task which had presented itself to Him for the first time in the temple, when He was twelve years of age, as the ideal of His life—the establishment of the kingdom of God on the earth. Here begins the second phase of His existence, during which He gave forth what He had received in the first.

This *transition* from private life to public activity is the subject of the following part, which comprises four sections: 1. The ministry of John the Baptist (iii. 1–20); 2. The baptism of Jesus (vers. 21, 22); 3. The genealogy (vers. 23–38); 4. The temptation (iv. 1–13). The corresponding part

[1] *Dial. c. Tryph.* c. 88.

in the two other synoptics embraces only numbers 1, 2, and 4. We shall have no difficulty in perceiving the connection between these three sections, and the reason which induced St. Luke to intercalate the fourth.

FIRST NARRATIVE.—CHAP. III. 1–20.

The Ministry of John the Baptist.

We already know from i. 77 why the Messiah was to have a forerunner. A mistaken notion of salvation had taken possession of Israel. It was necessary that a man clothed with divine authority should restore it to its purity before the Messiah laboured to accomplish it. Perhaps no more stirring character is presented in sacred history than that of John the Baptist. The people are excited at his appearing; their consciences are aroused; multitudes flock to him. The entire nation is filled with solemn expectation; and just at the moment when this man has only to speak the word to make himself the centre of this entire movement, he not only refrains from saying this word, but he pronounces another. He directs all the eager glances that were fixed upon himself to One *coming after* him, whose sandals he is not worthy to carry. Then, as soon as his successor has appeared, he retires to the background, and gives enthusiastic expression to his joy at seeing himself eclipsed. Criticism is fertile in resources of every kind; but with this unexampled moral phenomenon to account for, it will find it difficult to give any satisfactory explanation of it, without appealing to some factor of a higher order.

Luke begins by framing the fact which he is about to relate in a general outline of the history of the time (vers. 1 and 2). He next describes the personal appearance of John the Baptist (vers. 3–6); he gives a summary of his preaching (vers. 7–18); and he finishes with an anticipatory account of his imprisonment (vers. 19, 20).

1. Vers. 1 and 2.[1] In this concise description of the epoch

[1] Ver. 1. ℵ* omits *Ιτουραιας* . . . *Δυσανιου* (confusion of the two *της*).—Ver. **2.** Instead of *αρχιερεων*, which is the reading of T. R with some Mnn. It^{plerique}, **V*v*.**, all the Mjj., etc., read *αρχιερεως*.

at which John appeared, Luke begins with the largest sphere—that of the empire. Then, by a natural transition furnished by his reference to the representative of imperial power in Judæa, he passes to the special domain of the people of Israel; and he shows us the Holy Land divided into four distinct states. After having thus described the political situation, he sketches in a word the ecclesiastical and religious position, which brings him to his subject. It cannot be denied that there is considerable skill in this preamble. Among the evangelists, Luke is the true historian.

And first, the empire. Augustus died on the 19th August of the year 767 U.C., corresponding to the year 14 and 15 of our era. If Jesus was born in 749 or 750 U.C., He must have been at this time about eighteen years of age. At the death of Augustus, Tiberius had already, for two years past, shared his throne. The fifteenth year of his reign may consequently be reckoned, either from the time when he began to share the sovereignty with Augustus, or from the time when he began to reign alone, upon the death of the latter. The Roman historians generally date the reign of Tiberius from the time when he began to reign alone. According to this mode of reckoning, the fifteenth year would be the year of Rome 781 to 782, that is to say, 28 to 29 of our era. But at this time Jesus would be already thirty-two to thirty-three years of age, which would be opposed to the statement iii. 23, according to which He was only thirty years old at the time of His baptism, towards the end of John's ministry. According to the other mode of reckoning, the fifteenth year of the reign of Tiberius would be the year of Rome 779 to 780, 26 to 27 of our era. Jesus would be about twenty-nine years old when John the Baptist appeared; and supposing that the public ministry of the latter lasted six months or a year, He would be "*about thirty years of age*" when He received baptism from him. In this way agreement is established between the two chronological data, iii. 1 and 23. It has long been maintained that this last mode of reckoning, as it is foreign to the Roman writers, could only be attributed to Luke to meet the requirements of harmonists. Wieseler, however, has just proved, by inscriptions and medals, that it prevailed in the East, and particularly at

Antioch,[1] whence Luke appears originally to have come, and where he certainly resided for some time.

The circle narrows. We return to the Holy Land. The title of Pontius Pilate was properly ἐπίτροπος, *procurator.* That of ἡγεμών belonged to his superior, the governor of Syria. But as, in Judæa, the military command was joined to the civil authority, the procurator had a right to the title of ἡγεμών. Upon the deprivation of Archelaus, son of Herod, in the year 6 of our era, Judæa was united to the empire. It formed, with Samaria and Idumea, one of the districts of the province of Syria. Pilate was its fifth governor. He arrived there in the year 26, or sooner, in the autumn of the year 25 of our era; thus, in any case, a very short time before the ministry of John the Baptist. He remained in power ten years.

Herod, in his will, made a division of his kingdom. The first share was given to Archelaus, with the title of *ethnarch,* —an inferior title to that of *king,* but superior to that of *tetrarch.* This share soon passed to the Romans. The second, which comprised Galilee and the Peræa, was that of Herod Antipas. The title of *tetrarch,* given to this prince, signifies properly *sovereign of a fourth.* It was then employed as a designation for dependent petty princes amongst whom had been shared (originally in fourths [2]) certain territories previously united under a single sceptre. Herod Antipas reigned for forty-two years, until the year 39 of our era. The entire ministry of our Lord was therefore accomplished in his reign. The third share was Philip's, another son of Herod, who had the same title as Antipas. It embraced Ituræa (*Dschedur*), a country situated to the south-east of the Libanus, but not mentioned by Josephus amongst the states of Philip, and in addition, Trachonitis and Batanæa. Philip reigned 37 years, until the year 34 of our era. If the title of *tetrarch* be taken in its etymological sense, this term would imply that Herod had made a fourth share of his states; and this would natu-

[1] *Beiträge zur richtigen Würdigung der Evangelien*, etc., 1869, pp. 191–194. As to seeing, with him, in the terms καῖσαρ (instead of Augustus) and ἡγεμονία (instead of μοναρχία) proofs of the *co-regency* of Tiberius, these are subtleties in which it is impossible for us to follow this scholar

[2] Wieseler, work cited, p. 204

rally be that which Luke here designates by the name of *Abilene,* and which he assigns to *Lysanias. Abila* was a town situated to the north-west of Damascus, at the foot of the Anti-Libanus. Half a century before the time of which we are writing, there reigned in this country a certain Lysanias, the son and successor of Ptolemy king of Chalcis. This Lysanias was assassinated thirty-six years before our era by Antony, who gave a part of his dominions to Cleopatra.[1] His heritage then passed into various hands. Profane history mentions no Lysanias after that one; and Strauss is eager to accuse Luke of having, by a gross error, made Lysanias live and reign sixty years after his death. Keim forms an equally unfavourable estimate of the statement of Luke.[2] But while we possess no positive proof establishing the existence of a Lysanias posterior to the one of whom Josephus speaks, we ought at least, before accusing Luke of such a serious error, to take into consideration the following facts: 1. The ancient Lysanias bore the title of king, which Antony had given him (Dion Cassius, xlix. 32), and not the very inferior title of tetrarch.[3] 2. He only reigned from four to five years; and it would be difficult to understand how, after such a short possession, a century afterwards, had Abilene even belonged to him of old, it should still have borne for this sole reason, in all the historians, the name of *Abilene of Lysanias* (Jos. *Antiq.* xviii. 6. 10, xix. 5. 1, etc.; Ptolem. v. 18). 3. A medal and an inscription found by Pococke[4] mention a Lysanias *tetrarch and high priest,* titles which do not naturally apply to the ancient king Lysanias. From all these facts, therefore, it would be reasonable to conclude, with several interpreters, that there was a younger Lysanias,—a descendant, doubtless, of the preceding,—who possessed, not, as his ancestor did, the entire kingdom of Chalcis, but simply the tetrarchate of Abilene. This natural supposition may at the present day be asserted as a fact.[5] Two inscriptions

[1] Jos. *Antiq.* xiv. 7. 4; *Bell. Jud.* i. 9. 2; *Antiq.* xv. 4. 1, xiv. 13. 3.

[2] "In the third tetrarch, Lysanias of Abilene, Luke introduces a personage who did not exist" (*Gesch. Jesu,* t. i. p. 618).

[3] Not one of the numerous passages cited by Keim (i. p. 619, note) proves the contrary.

[4] *Morgenland,* ii. 177.

[5] Wieseler, work quoted, pp. 191 and 202–204.

recently deciphered prove: 1. That at the very time when Tiberius was co-regent with Augustus, there actually existed a tetrarch Lysanias. For it was a freedman of this Lysanias, named Nymphæus (*Νύμφαιος . . . Λυσανίου τετράρχου ἀπελεύθερος*), who had executed some considerable works to which one of these inscriptions refers (Boeckh's *Corpus inscript. Gr.* No. 4521). 2. That this Lysanias was a descendant of the ancient Lysanias.[1] This may be inferred, with a probability verging on certainty, from the terms of the other inscription: "and to the sons of Lysanias" (*ibid.* No. 4523). Augustus took pleasure in restoring to the children what his rivals had formerly taken away from their fathers. Thus the young Jamblichus, king of Emesa, received from him the inheritance of his father of the same name, slain by Antony. In the same way, also, was restored to Archelaus of Cappadocia a part of Cilicia, which had formerly belonged to his father of the same name. Why should not Augustus have done as much for the young Lysanias, whose ancestor had been slain and deprived by Antony? That this country should be here considered by Luke as belonging to the Holy Land, is explained, either by the fact that Abilene had been temporarily subject to Herod, —and it is something in favour of this supposition, that when Claudius restored to Agrippa I. all the dominions of his grandfather Herod the Great, he also gave him Abilene,[2]—or by this, that the inhabitants of the countries held by the ancient Lysanias had been incorporated into the theocracy by circumcision a century before Christ, and that the ancient Lysanias himself was born of a Jewish mother, an Asmonæan, and thus far a Jew.[3] This people, therefore, in a religious point of view, formed part of the holy people as well as the Idumæans.—The intention of Luke in describing the dismemberment of the Holy Land at this period, is to make palpable the political dissolution into which the theocracy had fallen at the time when He appeared who was to establish

[1] It does not follow from the expression of Eusebius (*Hist. Eccl.* i. 9), recapitulating the account of Josephus, that the young Lysanias was a son of Herod. We may, and indeed, as it appears to me, we must, refer the title of ἀδελφοί, *brethren*, only to Philip and Herod the younger, and not to Lysanias: "*The brothers Philip and Herod the younger, with Lysanias,* governed their tetrarchies." The note in the first edition must be corrected accordingly.

[2] Jos. *Antiq.* xix. 5. 1.

[3] Wieseler, work quoted, p. 204.

it in its true form, by separating the eternal kingdom from its temporary covering.

Luke passes to the sphere of religion (ver. 2). The true reading is doubtless the sing. ἀρχιερέως, *the high priest Annas and Caiaphas.* How is this strange phrase to be explained? It cannot be accidental, or used without thought. The predecessor of Pilate, Valerius Gratus, had deposed, in the year 14, the high priest Annas. Then, during a period covering some years, four priestly rulers were chosen and deposed in succession. Caiaphas, who had the title, was son-in-law of Annas, and had been appointed by Gratus about the year 17 of our era. He filled this office until 36. It is possible that, in conformity with the law which made the high-priesthood an office for life, the nation continued to regard Annas, notwithstanding his deprivation and the different elections which followed this event, as the true high priest, whilst all those pontiffs who had followed him were only, in the eyes of the best part of the people, titular high priests. In this way Luke's expression admits of a very natural explanation: "Annas and Caiaphas being the high priests," that is to say, the two high priests,—one by right, the other in fact. This expression would have all the better warrant, because, as history proves, Annas in reality continued, as before, to hold the reins of government. This was especially the case under the pontificate of Caiaphas, his son-in-law. John indicates this state of things in a striking way in two passages relating to the trial of Jesus, xviii. 13 and 24: "And they bound Jesus, and led Him away to *Annas first;* for he was *father-in-law to Caiaphas.* . . . And Annas *sent* Jesus bound to Caiaphas, *the high priest.*" These words furnish in some sort a commentary on Luke's expression. These two persons constituted really one and the same high priest. Add to this, as we are reminded by Wieseler, that the higher administration was then shared officially between two persons whom the Talmud always designates as distinct,—the *nasi,* who presided over the Sanhedrin, and had the direction of public affairs; and the *high priest* properly so called, who was at the head of the priests, and superintended matters of religion. Now it is very probable that the office of *nasi* at that time devolved upon Annas. We are led to this conclusion by the powerful influence which he exerted; by the part which, according to John, he played in the trial of Jesus; and by the passage Acts iv. 6, where he is found at the head of the Sanhedrin with the title of ἀρχιερεύς, while Caiaphas is only mentioned after him, as a simple member of this body. This separation of the office into two functions, which, united, had constituted, in the regular way, the true and complete theocratic high-priesthood, was the commencement of its dissolution. And this is what Luke intends to express by this gen. sing. ἀρχιερέως, in apposition with two proper names. It is just as if he had written: "*under the high priest Annas-Caiaphas.*" Disorganization had penetrated beneath the surface of the political sphere (ver. 1), to the very heart of the theocracy. What a frame for the picture of the appearing of the Restorer!—The expression, *the word came to John* (lit. *came upon*), indicates a positive revelation, either by theophany or by vision, similar to that which served as a basis for the ministry of the ancient prophets: Moses, Ex. iii.; Isaiah, chap. vi.; Jeremiah, chap. i.; Ezekiel, chap. i.–iii.; comp. John i. 33, and see i. 80. The word *in the wilderness* expressly connects this portion with that last passage.

2. Vers. 3–6.[1]—The *country about Jordan*, in Luke, doubtless denotes the arid plains near the mouth of this river. The name *wilderness of Judea*, by which Matthew and Mark designate the scene of John's ministry, applies properly to the mountainous and broken country which forms the western boundary of the plain of the Jordan (towards the mouth of this river), and of the northern part of the basin of the Dead Sea. But as, according to them also, John was baptizing in Jordan, the wilderness of Judea must necessarily have included in their view the lower course of the river. As to the rest, the expression *he came into* supposes, especially if with the Alex. we erase the τήν, that John did not remain stationary, but went too and fro in the country. This hint of the Syn., especially in the form in which it occurs in Luke, agrees perfectly with John x. 40, where the Peræa is pointed out as the principal theatre of John's ministry.

[1] Ver. 3. A. B. L. Or. omit την before περιχωρον.—Ver. 4. ℵ. B. D. L. Δ some Mnn. Syr^cur. It^plerique, omit λεγοντος.—Ver. 5. B. D. Z. some Mnn. It^aliq Or. read ευθειας instead of ευθειαν.

The rite of *baptism*, which consisted in the plunging of the body more or less completely into water, was not at this period in use amongst the Jews, neither for the Jews themselves, for whom the law only prescribed lustrations, nor for proselytes from paganism, to whom, according to the testimony of history, baptism was not applied until after the fall of Jerusalem. The very title *Baptist*, given to John, sufficiently proves that it was he who introduced this rite. This follows also from John i. 25, where the deputation from the Sanhedrin asks him by what right he baptizes, if he is neither the Messiah nor one of the prophets, which implies that this rite was introduced by him; and further, from John iii. 26, where the disciples of John make it a charge against Jesus, that He adopted a ceremony of which the institution, and consequently, according to them, the monopoly, belonged to their master. Baptism was a humiliating rite for the Jews. It represented a complete purification; it was, as it were, a lustration carried to the second power, which implied in him who accepted it not a few isolated faults so much as a radical defilement. So Jesus calls it (John iii. 5) *a birth of water*. Already the promise *of clean water, and of a fountain opened for sin and uncleanness*, in Ezekiel (xxxvi. 25) and Zechariah (xiii. 1), had the same meaning.—The complement μετανοίας, *of repentance*, indicates the moral act which was to accompany the outward rite, and which gave it its value. This term indicates a complete change of mind. The object of this new institution is sin, which appears to the baptized in a new light. According to Matthew and Mark, this change was expressed by a positive act which accompanied the baptism, the confession of their sins (ἐξομολόγησις). Baptism, like every divinely instituted ceremony, contained also a grace for him who observed it with the desired disposition. As Strauss puts it: if, on the part of man, it was a declaration of the renunciation of sin, on the part of God it was a declaration of the pardon of sins.—The words *for the pardon* depend grammatically on the collective notion, *baptism of repentance*.

According to ver. 4, the forerunner of the Messiah had a place in the prophetic picture by the side of the Messiah Himself. It is very generally taken for granted by modern interpreters, that the prophecy Isa. xl. 1–11, applied by the three synoptics to the times of the Messiah and to John the Baptist, refer properly to the return from the exile, and picture the entrance of Jehovah into the Holy Land at the head of His people. But is this interpretation really in accordance with the text of the prophet? Throughout this entire passage of Isaiah the people are nowhere represented as returning to their own country; they are settled in their cities; it is God who comes to them: "*O Zion, get thee up into a high mountain . . . Lift up thy voice with strength! Say to the cities of Judah, Behold your God!*" (ver. 9). So far are the people from following in Jehovah's train, that, on the contrary, they are invited by the divine messenger to prepare, in the country where they dwell, the way by which Jehovah is to come to them: "*Prepare the way of the Lord . . ., and His glory shall be revealed*" (vers. 3 and 5). The desert to which the prophet compares the moral condition of the people is not that of Syria, which had to be crossed in returning from Babylon, a vast plain in which there are neither mountains to level nor valleys to fill up. It is rather the uncultivated and rocky hill-country which surrounds the very city of Jerusalem, into which Jehovah is to make His entry as the Messiah. If, therefore, it is indeed the coming of Jehovah as Messiah which is promised in this passage (ver. 11, "He shall feed His flock like a shepherd . . ., He shall carry the lambs in His arms"), the herald who invites the people to prepare the way of his God is really the forerunner of the Messiah. The image is taken from an oriental custom, according to which the visit of a sovereign was preceded by the arrival of a courier, who called on all the people to make ready the road by which the monarch was to enter.[1]

The text is literally: *A voice of one crying! . . .* There is no finishing verb; it is an exclamation. The messenger is not named; his person is of so little consequence, that it is lost in his message. The words *in the desert* may, in Hebrew as in Greek, be taken either with what precedes: "cries in the desert," or with what follows: "Prepare in the desert." It matters little; the order *resounds* wherever it is to be *executed*. Must we be satisfied with a general applica-

[1] Lowth, *Isaiah*, übers. v. Koppe, ii. p. 207.

tion of the details of the picture? or is it allowable to give a particular application to them,—to refer, for instance, the mountains that must be levelled to the pride of the Pharisees; the valleys to be filled up, to the moral and religious indifference of such as the Sadducees; the crooked places to be made straight, to the frauds and lying excuses of the publicans; and lastly, the rough places, to the sinful habits found in all, even the best? However this may be, the general aim of the quotation is to exhibit repentance as the soul of John's baptism.—It is probable that the plur. εὐθείας was early substituted for the sing. εὐθεῖαν, to correspond with the plur. τὰ σκολιά. With this adj. ὁδόν or ὁδούς must be understood.

When once this moral change is accomplished, Jehovah will appear. *Καί*, and *then*. The Hebrew text is: "*All flesh shall see the glory of God.*" The LXX. have translated it: "The glory of the Lord shall be seen (by the Jews?), and all flesh (including the heathen?) shall see the salvation of God." This paraphrase, borrowed from Isa. lii. 10, proceeded perhaps from the repugnance which the translator felt to attribute to the heathen the sight of the *glory* of God, although he concedes to them a share in the salvation. This term *salvation* is preserved by Luke; it suits the spirit of his Gospel.—Only the end of the prophecy (vers. 5 and 6) is cited by Luke. The two other synoptics limit themselves to the first part (ver. 4). It is remarkable that all three should apply to the Hebrew text and to that of the LXX. the same modification: τὰς τρίβους αὐτοῦ, *His paths*, instead of τὰς τρίβους τοῦ Θεοῦ ἡμῶν, the *paths of our God*. This fact has been used to prove the dependence of two of the synoptics on the third. But the proof is not valid. As Weizsäcker[1] remarks, this was one of the texts of which frequent use was made in the preaching of the Messiah; and it was customary, in applying the passage to the person of the Messiah, to quote it in this form. If Luke had, in this section, one of the two other synoptics before him, how could he have omitted all that refers to the dress and mode of life of the forerunner?

3. Vers 7–17.—The following discourse must not be re

[1] *Untersuchungen*, p. 24, note.

garded as a particular specimen of the preaching, the substance of which Luke has transmitted to us. It is a summary of all the discourses of John the Baptist during the period that preceded the baptism of Jesus. The imperf. ἔλεγεν, *he used to say,* clearly indicates Luke's intention. This summary contains—1. A call to repentance, founded on the impending Messianic judgment (vers. 7–9); 2. Special practical directions for each class of hearers (vers. 10–14); 3. The announcement of the speedy appearance of the Messiah (vers. 15–17).

Vers. 7–9. "*Then said he to the multitude that came forth to be baptized of him, O generation of vipers, who hath warned you to flee from the wrath to come?* 8 *Bring forth therefore fruits worthy of repentance, and begin not to say within yourselves, We have Abraham to our father; for I say unto you, that God is able of these stones to raise up children unto Abraham.* 9 *And now also the axe is laid unto the root of the trees; every tree therefore which bringeth not forth good fruit is hewn down, and cast into the fire.*"—What a stir would be produced at the present day by the preaching of a man, who, clothed with the authority of holiness, should proclaim with power the speedy coming of the Lord, and His impending judgment! Such was the appearance of John in Israel.—The expression *that came forth* (ver. 7) refers to their leaving inhabited places to go into the desert (comp. vii. 24). In Matthew it is a number of Pharisees and Sadducees that are thus accosted. In that Gospel, the reference is to a special case, as the aor. εἶπεν, *he said to them,* shows. But for all this it may have been, as Luke gives us to understand, a topic on which John ordinarily expatiated to his hearers. The reproachful address, *generation of vipers,* expresses at once their wickedness and craft. John compares these multitudes who come to his baptism, because they regard it as a ceremony that is to ensure their admission into the Messianic kingdom, to successive broods of serpents coming forth alive from the body of their dam. This severe term is opposed to the title *children of Abraham,* and appears even to allude to another father, whom Jesus expressly names in another place (John viii. 37–44). Keim observes, with truth, that this figurative language of John (comp. the following images, *stones, trees*) is altogether the language of the desert.[1] What excites such lively indignation in the forerunner, is to see people trying to evade the duty of repentance by means of its sign, by baptism performed as an *opus operatum*. In this deception he perceives the suggestion of a more cunning counsellor than the heart of man. Ὑποδείκνυμι: to address advice to the ear, to suggest. The choice of this term excludes Meyer's sense: "Who has reassured you, persuading you that your title children of Abraham would preserve you from divine wrath?"—The *wrath to come* is the Messiah's judgment. The Jews made it fall solely on the heathen; John makes it come down on the head of the Jews themselves.

Therefore (ver. 8) refers to the necessity of a sincere repentance, resulting from the question in ver. 7. The *fruits worthy of repentance* are not the Christian dispositions flowing from faith; they are those acts of justice, equity, and humanity, enumerated vers. 10–14, the conscientious practice of which leads a man to faith (Acts x. 35). But John fears that the moment their conscience begins to be aroused, they will immediately soothe it, by reminding themselves that they are children of Abraham. Μὴ ἄρξησθε, literally, "do not begin . . .," that is to say: "As soon as my voice awakens you, do not set about saying . . ." The μὴ δόξητε, *do not think*, in Matthew, indicates an illusory claim. On the abuse of this title by the Jews, see John viii. 33–39, Rom. iv. 1, Jas. ii. 21. It is to the posterity of Abraham, doubtless, that the promises are made, but the resources of God are not limited. Should Israel prove wanting, with a word He can create for Himself a new people. In saying, *of these stones*, John points with his finger to the stones of the desert or on the river banks. This warning is too solemn to be only an imaginary supposition. John knew the prophecies; he was not ignorant that Moses and Isaiah had announced the rejection of Israel and the calling of the Gentiles. It is by this threatening prospect that he endeavours to stir up the zeal of his contemporaries. This word contained in germ the

[1] Winer, *Realwörterbuch*, on Jericho: "This place might have passed for a paradise, apart from the venomous serpents found there."—The trees along the course of the Jordan.

whole teaching of St. Paul on the contrast between the carnal and the spiritual posterity of Abraham developed in Rom. ix. and Gal. iii. In Deuteronomy the circumcision of the flesh had already been similarly contrasted with the circumcision of the heart (xxx. 6).

In vers. 7 and 8 Israel is reminded of the incorruptible *holiness* of the judgment awaiting them; ver. 9 proclaims it *at hand.* *Ἤδη δὲ καί*: "*and now also.*" The image is that of an orchard full of fruit trees. An invisible axe is laid at the trunk of every tree. This figure is connected with that of the fruits (ver. 8). At the first signal, the axe will bury itself in the trunks of the barren trees; it will cut them down to the very roots. It is the emblem of the Messianic judgment. It applies at once to the national downfall and the individual condemnation, two notions which are not yet distinct in the mind of John. This fulminating address completely irritated the rulers, who had been willing at one time to come and hear him; from this time they broke all connection with John and his baptism. This explains the passage (Luke vii. 30) in which Jesus declares that the rulers refused to be baptized. This rejection of John's ministry by the official authorities is equally clear from Matt. xxi. 25: "*If we say, Of God; he will say, Why then did ye not believe on him?*" The proceeding of the Sanhedrim, John i. 19 et seq., proves the same thing.

Vers. 10–14.[1]—But what then, the people ask, are those fruits of repentance which should accompany baptism? And, seized with the fear of judgment, different classes of hearers approach John to obtain from him special directions, fitted to their particular social position. It is the confessional after preaching. This characteristic fragment is wanting in Matthew and Mark. Whence has Luke obtained it? From some oral or written source. But this source could not, it is evi-

[1] Ver. 10. Almost all the Mjj., ποιησωμεν instead of ποιησομεν, which is the reading of T. R., with G. K. U. and many Mnn.—Ver. 11. ℵ. B. C. L. X. some Mnn., ελεγεν instead of λεγει.—Ver. 12. Almost all the Mjj., ποιησωμεν instead of ποιησομεν, which is the reading of T. R., with G. U. and many Mnn.—Ver. 13. ℵ* omits ειπεν προς αυτους.—Ver. 14. C. D. It^{aliq}., επηρωτησαν instead of επηρωτων.—Almost all the Mjj., ποιησωμεν instead of ποιησομεν, which A. G. K. V. and many Mnn. read.—ℵ* H. Syr., μηδενα before συκοφαντησητε, instead of μηδε, which T. R. with all the other documents read.

dent, contain simply the five verses which follow; it must have been a narrative of the entire ministry of John. Luke therefore possessed, on this ministry as a whole, a different document from the other two Syn. In this way we can explain the marked differences of detail which we have observed between his writing and Matthew's: *he says,* instead of *he was saying,* ver. 7; *do not begin,* instead of *think not,* ver. 8.

The imperf., *asked,* signifies that those questions of conscience were frequently repeated (comp. ἔλεγεν, ver. 7). To a similar question St. Peter replied (Acts ii. 37) very differently. This was because the kingdom of God had come. The forerunner contents himself with requiring the works fitted to *prepare* his hearers,—those works of moral rectitude and benevolence which are in conformity with the law written in the heart, and which attest the sincerity of the horror of evil professed in baptism, and that earnest desire after good which Jesus so often declares to be the true preparation for faith (John iii. 21). In vain does hypocrisy give itself to the practice of devotion; it is on moral obligation faithfully acknowledged and practised that the blessing depends which leads men to salvation.—There is some hesitation in the form ποιήσωμεν (deliberative subj.); the future ποιήσομεν indicates a decision taken.—Ver. 13. *Πράσσειν, exact;* the meaning is, no overcharge!—Who are the soldiers, ver. 14? Certainly not the Roman soldiers of the garrison of Judæa. Perhaps military in the service of Antipas king of Galilee; for they came also from this country to John's baptism. More probably armed men, acting as police in Judæa. Thus the term συκοφαντεῖν admits of a natural interpretation. It signifies etymologically those who denounced the exporters of figs (out of Attica), and is applied generally to those who play the informer. *Διασείειν* appears to be connected with the Latin word *concutere,* whence comes also our word *concussion.* These are unjust extortions on the part of subordinates. The reading of א. H. *Pesch.,* *μηδένα,* does not deserve the honour Tischendorf has accorded to it of admitting it into his text.—When all the people shall in this way have made ready the way of the Lord, they will be that prepared people of whom the angel spoke to Zacharias (i. 17), and the Lord will be able to bring salvation to them (iii. 6).

Vers. 15–17.[1]—"*And as the people were in expectation, and all men mused in their hearts of John, whether he were the Christ or not;* 16 *John answered, saying unto them all: I indeed baptize you with water; but one mightier than I cometh, the latchet of whose shoes I am not worthy to unloose: He shall baptize you with the Holy Ghost, and with fire:* 17 *Whose fan is in His hand, and He will throughly purge His floor, and will gather the wheat into His garner; but the chaff He will burn with fire unquenchable.*"—This portion is common to the three Syn. But the preamble, ver. 15, is peculiar to Luke. It is a brief and striking sketch of the general excitement and lively expectation awakened by John's ministry. The **ἅπασιν** of the T. R. contains the idea of a solemn gathering; but this scene is not the same as that of John i. 19 et seq., which did not take place till after the baptism of Jesus. In his answer John asserts two things: first, that he is not the Messiah; second, that the Messiah is following him close at hand. The art. **ὁ** before **ἰσχυρότερος** denotes this personage as expected.—To unloose the sandals of the master when he came in (Luke and Mark), or rather to *bring* them to him (**βαστάσαι**, Matt.) when he was disposed to go out, was the duty of the lowest class of slaves. Mark expresses its menial character in a dramatic way: **κύψας λῦσαι**, *to stoop down and unloose.* Each evangelist has thus his own shade of thought. If one of them had copied from the other, these changes, which would be at once purposed and insignificant, would be puerile.—**Ἱκανός** may be applied either to physical or intellectual capacity, or to moral dignity. It is taken in the latter sense here.—The pronoun **αὐτός** brings out prominently the personality of the Messiah. The preposition **ἐν**, which had not been employed before **ὕδατι**, is added before **πνεύματι**; the Spirit cannot be treated as a simple means. One baptizes with water, but not with the Spirit.—If the pardon granted in the baptism of water was not followed by the baptism of the Spirit, sin would soon regain the upper hand, and the pardon would be speedily annulled (Matt.

[1] Ver. 16. ℵ. B. L., πασιν instead of απασιν.—Ver. 17. ℵ* B. a. e. Heracleon, διακαθαραι instead of και διακαθαριει, which is the reading of T. R., with all the other Mjj. and all the Mnn.—ℵ* B. e., συναγαγειν instead of συναξει, which all the others read

xviii. 23–25). But let the baptism of the Spirit be added to the baptism of water, and then the pardon is confirmed by the renewal of the heart and life.—Almost all modern interpreters apply the term *fire* to the consuming ardour of the judgment, according to ver. 17, *the fire which is not quenched.* But if there was such a marked contrast between the two expressions *Spirit* and *fire*, the preposition ἐν must have been repeated before the latter. Therefore there can only be a shade of difference between these two terms. *The Spirit* and *fire* both denote the same divine principle, but in two different relations with human nature: the first, inasmuch as taking possession of all in the natural man that is fitted to enter into the kingdom of God, and consecrating it to this end; the second—the image of *fire* is introduced on account of its contrariness to the water of baptism—inasmuch as consuming everything in the old nature that is out of harmony with the divine kingdom, and destined to perish. The Spirit, in this latter relation, is indeed the principle of judgment, but of an altogether internal judgment. It is the fire symbolized on the day of Pentecost. As to the *fire* of ver. 17, it is expressly opposed to that of ver. 16 by the epithet ἄσβεστον, *which is not quenched.* Whoever refuses to be baptized with the fire of holiness, will be exposed to the fire of wrath. Comp. a similar transition, but in an inverse sense, Mark ix. 48, 49.—John had said, *shall baptize you* (ver. 16). Since this *you* applied solely to the penitent, it contained the idea of a sifting process going on amongst the people. This sifting is described in the seventeenth verse. The *threshing-floor* among the ancients was an uncovered place, where the corn, spread out upon the hardened ground, was trodden by oxen, which were sometimes yoked to a sledge. The straw was burnt upon the spot; the corn was gathered into the garner. This garner, in John's thought, represents the Messianic kingdom, the Church in fact, the earliest historical form of this kingdom, into which all believing Israelites will be gathered. Jewish presumption made the line of demarcation which separates the elect from the condemned pass between Israel and the Gentiles; John makes it pass *across* the theocracy itself, of which the threshing-floor is the symbol. This is the force of the διά in διακαθαριεῖ. Jesus expresses Himself in exactly the same sense, John iii. 18 et seq. The judgment of the nation and of the individual are here mingled together, as in ver. 9; behind the national chastisement of the fall of Jerusalem and the dispersion of the people, is placed in the background the judgment of individuals, under another dispensation. The readings **διακαθᾶραι** and **συναγαγεῖν**, *in order to purify, in order to gather,* cannot be admitted. They rather weaken the force of this striking passage; the authority of ℵ. B. and of the two documents of the *Italic* are not sufficient; lastly, the future **κατακαύσει**, which must be in opposition to a preceding future (δέ), comes in too abruptly.—The pronoun *αὐτοῦ*, twice repeated ver. 17 (*His* threshing-floor, *His* garner), leaves no doubt about the divine dignity which John attributed to the Messiah. The theocracy belongs to Jehovah. Comp. the expression, *His* temple, Mal. iii. 1.

4. **Vers.** 18–20.[1]—We find here one of those general surveys such as we have in i. 66, 80, ii. 40, 52. For the third time the lot of the forerunner becomes the prelude to that of the Saviour. The expression *many other things* (ver. 18) confirms what was already indicated by the imperf. *he used to say* (ver. 7), that Luke only intends to give a summary of John's preaching. The term *he evangelized* (a literal translation) refers to the Messianic promises which his discourses contained (vers. 16 and 17), and the true translation of this verse appears to me to be this: "*while addressing these and many other exhortations to the people, he announced to them the glad tidings.*"—Ver. 19. Herod Antipas, the sovereign of Galilee, is the person already mentioned in ver. 1. The word **Φιλίππου**, rejected by important authorities, is probably a gloss derived from Matthew. The first husband of Herodias was called Herod. He has no other name in Josephus. He lived as a private individual at Jerusalem. But perhaps he also bore the surname of Philip, to distinguish him from Herod Antipas. The brother of Antipas, who was properly called Philip, is the tetrarch of Ituræa (iii. 1). The ambitious Herodias had abandoned her husband to marry Antipas,

[1] Ver. 19. The T. R., with A. C. K. X. Π. many Mnn. Syr., adds, before τοῦ ἀδελφου, Φιλιππου, which is omitted by 16 Mjj. 120 Mnn. It. Vg. (taken from Matthew).—Ver. 20. ℵ* B. D. X. It^{aliq}. omit καὶ before προσέθηκε.

who for love of her sent away his first wife, a daughter of Aretas king of Arabia; this act drew him into a disastrous war.

Luke's expression indicates concentrated indignation. In order to express the energy of the ἐπὶ πᾶσιν, we must say: *to crown all* . . . The form of the phrase προσέθηκε καὶ κατέκλεισε is based on a well-known Hebraism, and proves that this narrative of Luke's is derived from an Aramæan document. This passage furnishes another proof that Luke draws upon an independent source; he separates himself, in fact, from the two other synoptics, by mentioning the imprisonment of John the Baptist here instead of referring it to a later period, as Matthew and Mark do, synchronizing it with the return of Jesus into Galilee after His baptism (Matt. iv. 12; Mark i. 14). He thereby avoids the chronological error committed by the two other Syn., and rectified by John (iii. 24). This notice is brought in here by anticipation, as the similar notices, i. 66*b* and 80*b*. It is intended to explain the sudden end of John's ministry, and serves as a stepping-stone to the narrative vii. 18, where John sends *from his prison* two of his disciples to Jesus.

The *fact* of John the Baptist's ministry is authenticated by the narrative of Josephus. This historian speaks of it at some length when describing the marriage of Herod Antipas with Herodias. After relating the defeat of Herod's army by Aretas, the father of his first wife, Josephus (*Antiq.* xviii. 5. 1, 2) continues thus: "This disaster was attributed by many of the Jews to the displeasure of God, who smote Herod for the murder of John, surnamed the Baptist; for Herod had put to death this good man, who exhorted the Jews to the practice of virtue, inviting them to come to his baptism, and bidding them act with justice towards each other, and with piety towards God; for their baptism would please God if they did not use it to justify themselves from any sin they had committed, but to obtain purity of body after their souls had been previously purified by righteousness. And when a great multitude of people came to him, and were deeply moved by his discourses, Herod, fearing lest he might use his influence to urge them to revolt,—for he well knew that they would do whatever he advised them,—thought that the best course for him to take was to put him to death before he attempted anything of the kind. So he put him in chains, and sent him to the castle of Machærus, and there put him to death. The Jews, therefore, were convinced that his army was destroyed as a punishment for this murder, God being incensed against Herod." This account, while altogether independent of the evangelist's, con firms it in all the essential points: the extraordinary appearance of this person of such remarkable sanctity; the rite of baptism introduced by him; his surname, the *Baptist;* John's protest against the use of baptism as a mere *opus operatum;* his energetic exhortations; the general excitement; the imprisonment and murder of John; and further, the criminal marriage of Herod, related in what precedes. By the side of these essential points, common to the two narratives, there are some secondary differences:—1*st.* Josephus makes no mention of the Messianic element in the preaching of John. But in this there is nothing surprising. This silence proceeds from the same cause as that which he observes respecting the person of Jesus. He who could allow himself to apply the Messianic prophecies to Vespasian, would necessarily try to avoid everything in contemporaneous history that had reference either to the forerunner, *as such,* or to Jesus. Weizsäcker rightly observes that the narrative of Josephus, so far from invalidating that of Luke on this point, confirms it. For it is evident that, apart from its connection with the expectation of the Messiah, the baptism of John would not have produced that general excitement which excited the fears of Herod, and which is proved by the account of Josephus.—2*d.* According to Luke, the determining cause of John's imprisonment was the resentment of Herod at the rebukes of the Baptist; while, according to Josephus, the motive for this crime was the fear of a *political* outbreak. But it is easy to conceive that the cause indicated by Luke would not be openly avowed, and that it was unknown in the political circles where Josephus gathered his information. Herod and his counsellors put forward, as is usual in such cases, the reason of State. The previous revolts—those which immediately followed the death of Herod, and that which Judas the Gaulonite provoked—only justified too well the fears which they affected to feel.—In any case, if, on account of this general agreement, we were willing to admit that one of the two historians made use of the other, it is not Luke that we should regard as the copyist; for the Aramæan forms of his narrative indicate a source independent of that of Josephus.

The *higher origin* of this ministry of John is proved by the two following characteristics, which are inexplicable from a purely natural point of view:—1*st.* His connection, so emphatically announced, with the immediate appearance of the Messiah; 2*d.* The abdication of John, when at the height of his popularity, in favour of the poor Galilean, who was as yet unknown to all. As to the *originality* of John's baptism, the lustrations used in the oriental religions, in Judaism itself, and particularly among the Essenes, have been alleged against it. But this originality consisted less in the outward form of the rite, than—1. In its application to the whole people, thus pronounced defiled, and placed on a level with the heathen; and 2. In the preparatory relation established by the forerunner between this imperfect baptism and that final baptism which the Messiah was about to confer.

We think it useful to give an example here of the way in which Holtzmann tries to explain the composition of our Gospel:—

1. Vers. 1–6 are borrowed from source A. (the original Mark), only Luke leaves out the details respecting the ascetic life of John the Baptist, because he intends to give his discourses at greater length; he *compensates* for this omission by adding the chronological data (vers. 1 and 2), and by extending the quotation from the LXX. (vers. 5 and 6)!—2. Vers. 7–9 are also taken from A., just as are the parallel verses in Matthew; they were left out by the author of our canonical Mark, whose intention was to give only an abridgment of the discourses.—3. Vers. 10–14 are taken from a private source, peculiar to Luke.—Are we then to suppose that this source contained only these four verses, since Luke has depended on other sources for all the rest of his matter?—4. Vers. 15–17 are composed (*a*) of a sketch of Luke's invention (ver. 15); (*b*) of an extract from A., vers. 16, 17.—5. Vers. 18–20 have been compiled on the basis of a fragment of A., which is found in Mark vi. 17–29, a summary of which Luke thought should be introduced here.—Do we not thus fall into that process of manufacture which Schleiermacher ridiculed so happily in his work on the composition of Luke, *à propos* of Eichhorn's hypothesis, a method which we thought had disappeared from criticism for ever?

SECOND NARRATIVE.—CHAP. III. 21, 22.

The Baptism of Jesus.

The relation between John and Jesus, as described by St. Luke, resembles that of two stars following each other at a short distance, and both passing through a series of similar circumstances. The announcement of the appearing of the one follows close upon that of the appearing of the other. It is the same with their two births. This relation repeats itself in the commencement of their respective ministries; and lastly, in the catastrophes which terminate their lives. And yet, in the whole course of the career of these two men, there was but one personal meeting—at the baptism of Jesus. After this moment, when one of these stars rapidly crossed the orbit of the other, they separated, each to follow the path that was marked out for him. It is this moment of their actual contact that the evangelist is about to describe.

Vers. 21 and 22.[1]—This narrative of the baptism is the sequel, not to vers. 18, 19 (the imprisonment of John), which

[1] Ver. 22. ℵ. B. D. L., *ως* instead of *ωσει*.—ℵ. B. D. L. It^plerique^, omit *λεγουσαν*. D. It^aliq^. Justin, and some other Fathers, read, *υιος μου ει συ, εγω σημερον γεγεννηκα σε*, *εν σοι*, etc.

are an anticipation, but to the passage vers. 15–17, which describes the expectation of the people, and relates the Messianic prophecy of John. The expression ἅπαντα τὸν λαόν, *all the people*, ver. 21, recalls the crowds and popular feeling described in ver. 15. But Meyer is evidently wrong in seeing in these words, "When all the people were baptized," a proof that all this crowd was present at the baptism of Jesus. The term *all the people*, in such a connection, would be a strange exaggeration. Luke merely means to indicate the general agreement in time between this movement and the baptism of Jesus; and the expression he uses need not in any way prevent our thinking that Jesus was alone, or almost alone, with the forerunner, when the latter baptized Him. Further, it is highly probable that He would choose a time when the transaction might take place in this manner. But the turn of expression, ἐν τῷ βαπτισθῆναι, expresses more than the simultaneousness of the two facts; it places them in moral connection with each other. In being baptized, Jesus surrenders Himself to the movement which at this time was drawing *all the people* towards God. Had He acted otherwise, would He not have broken the bond of solidarity which He had contracted, by circumcision, with Israel, and by the incarnation, with all mankind? So far from being relaxed, this bond is to be drawn closer, until at last it involve Him who has entered into it in the full participation of our condemnation and death. This relation of the baptism of the nation to that of Jesus explains also the singular turn of expression which Luke makes use of in mentioning the fact of the baptism. This act, which one would have thought would have been the very pith of the narrative, is indicated by means of a simple participle, and in quite an incidental way: "When all the people were baptized, Jesus *also being baptized*, and praying . . ." Luke appears to mean that, granted the national baptism, that of Jesus follows as a matter of course. It is the moral consequence of the former. This turn of thought is not without its importance in explaining the fact which we are now considering.—Luke adds here a detail which is peculiar to him, and which serves to place the miraculous phenomena which follow in their true light. At the time when Jesus, having been baptized, went up out of the water, He was in prayer. The extraordinary manifestations about to be related thus become God's answer to the prayer of Jesus, in which the sighs of His people and of mankind found utterance. The earth is thirsty for the rain of heaven. The Spirit will descend on Him who knows how to ask it effectually; and it will be His office to impart it to all the rest. If, afterwards, we hear Him saying (xi. 9), "*Ask, and it shall be given you; seek, and ye shall find; knock, and it shall be opened to you,*" we know from what personal experience He derived this precept: at the Jordan He Himself first asked and received, sought and found, knocked and it was opened to Him.

The heavenly manifestation.—Luke assigns these miraculous facts to the domain of objective reality: *the heavens opened, the Spirit descended.* Mark makes them a personal intuition of Jesus: *And coming up out of the water, He saw the heavens opened, and the Spirit descending* (i. 10). Matthew corresponds with Mark; for Bleek is altogether wrong in maintaining that this evangelist makes the whole scene a vision of John the Baptist. The text does not allow of the two verbs, *He went up* and *He saw,* which follow each other so closely (Matt. iii. 16), having two different subjects. Bleek alleges the narrative of the fourth Gospel, where also the forerunner speaks merely of what *he saw himself.* But that is natural; for in that passage his object was, not to relate the fact, but simply to justify the testimony which he had just borne. For this purpose he could only mention what he had *seen himself.* No inference can be drawn from this as to the fact itself, and its relation to Jesus, the other witness. Speaking generally, the scene of the baptism does not fall within the horizon of the fourth Gospel, which starts from a point of time six weeks after this event took place. Keim has no better ground than this for asserting that the accounts of the Syn. on this subject are contradictory to that of John, because the former attribute an external reality to these miraculous phenomena, while the latter treats them as a simple vision of the forerunner, and even, according to him, excludes the reality of the baptism.[1] The true relation of these accounts to each other is this: According to the fourth Gospel, *John* saw; according to the first and second, *Jesus* saw. Now, as two persons can hardly be under an hallucination at the same time and in the same manner, this double perception

[1] *Gesch. Jesu,* t. i. p. 535.

supposes a reality, and this reality is affirmed by Luke. *And it came to pass, that . . .*

The divine manifestation comprises three internal facts, and three corresponding sensible phenomena. The three former are the divine communication itself; the three latter are the manifestation of this communication to the consciousness of Jesus and of John. Jesus was a true man, consisting, that is, at once of body and soul. In order, therefore, to take complete possession of Him, God had to speak at once to His outward and inward sense. As to John, he shared, as an official witness of the spiritual fact, the sensible impression which accompanied this communication from on high to the mind of Jesus. The first phenomenon is *the opening of the heavens.* While Jesus is praying, with His eyes fixed on high, the vault of heaven is rent before His gaze, and His glance penetrates the abode of eternal light. The spiritual fact contained under this sensible phenomenon is the perfect understanding accorded to Jesus of God's plan in the work of salvation. The treasures of divine wisdom are opened to Him, and He may thenceforth obtain at any hour the particular enlightenment He may need. The meaning of this first phenomenon is therefore *perfect revelation.*—From the measureless heights of heaven above, thus laid open to His gaze, Jesus sees descend *a luminous appearance,* having the form of a dove. This emblem is taken from a natural symbolism. The fertilizing and persevering incubation of the dove is an admirable type of the life-giving energy whereby the Holy Spirit developes in the human soul the germs of a new life. It is in this way that the new creation, deposited with all its powers in the soul of Jesus, is to extend itself around Him, under the influence of this creative principle (Gen. i. 2). By the organic form which invests the luminous ray, the Holy Spirit is here presented in its absolute totality. At Pentecost the Holy Spirit appears under the form of *divided* (*διαμεριζόμεναι*) tongues of fire, emblems of special gifts, of particular *χαρίσματα,* shared among the disciples. But in the baptism of Jesus it is not a portion only, it is the fulness of the Spirit which is given. This idea could only be expressed by a symbol taken from organic life. John the Baptist understood this emblem: "For God giveth not," he says (John iii. 34), "the Spirit *by measure* unto Him." The vibration of the luminous ray on the head of Jesus, like the fluttering of the wings of a dove, denotes the *permanence* of the gift. "I saw," says John the Baptist (John i. 32), "the Spirit descending from heaven like a dove, and *it abode upon Him.*" This luminous appearance, then, represents an inspiration which is neither partial as that of the faithful, nor intermittent as that of the prophets—*perfect inspiration.*—The third phenomenon, that of the *divine voice*, represents a still more intimate and personal communication. Nothing is a more direct emanation from the personal life than speech, the voice. The voice of God resounds in the ear and heart of Jesus, and reveals to Him all that He is to God—the Being most tenderly beloved, beloved as a father's only son; and consequently all that He is called to be to the world—the organ of divine love to men, He whose mission it is to raise His brethren to the dignity of sons.—According to Luke, and probably Mark also (in conformity with the reading admitted by Tischendorf), the divine declaration is addressed *to* Jesus: "*Thou art* my Son . . .; *in Thee* I am . . ." In Matthew it has the form of a testimony addressed to a third party touching Jesus: "*This is* my Son . . . *in whom* . . ." The first form is that in which God spoke to Jesus; the second, that in which John became conscious of the divine manifestation. This difference attests that the two accounts are derived from different sources, and that the writings in which they are preserved are independent of each other. What writer would have deliberately changed the *form* of a saying which he attributed to God Himself?—The pronoun σύ, *Thou*, as well as the predicate ἀγαπητος, with the article, *the well-beloved*, invest this filial relation with a character that is altogether *unique*; comp. x. 22. From this moment Jesus must have felt Himself the supreme object of the love of the infinite God. The unspeakable blessedness with which such an assurance could not fail to fill Him was the source of the witness He bore concerning Himself,—a witness borne not for His own glory, but with a view to reveal to the world the love wherewith God loves those to whom He imparts such a gift. From this moment dates the birth of that unique consciousness Jesus had of God as *His own Father*,—the rising of that radiant sun which henceforth illuminates His life, and which since Pentecost has risen upon mankind. Just as, by the instrumentality of His Word and Spirit, God communicates to believers, when the hour has come, the certainty of their adoption, so answering *both inwardly* and *outwardly* the prayer of Jesus, He raises Him in His human consciousness to a sense of His dignity as the only-begotten Son. It is on the strength of this revelation that John, who shared it, says afterwards, "The Father *loveth the Son*, and hath given *all things* into His hands" (John iii. 35). The absence of the title *Christ* in the divine salutation is remarkable. We see that the principal fact in the development of the consciousness of Jesus was not the feeling of His Messianic dignity, but of His close and personal relation with God (comp. already ii. 49), and of His divine origin. On that alone was based His conviction of His Messianic mission. The religious fact was first; the official part was only its corollary. M. Renan has reversed this relation, and it is the capital defect of his work.—The quotation of the words of Ps. ii., "*To-day have I begotten Thee*," which Justin introduces into the divine salutation, is only supported by D. and some Mss. of the Italic. It contrasts with the simplicity of the narrative. God does not quote Himself textually in this way! The *Cantabrigiensis* swarms with similar interpolations which have not the slightest critical value. It is easy to understand how this quotation, affixed at an early period as a marginal gloss, should have found its way into the text of some documents; but it would be difficult to account for its suppression in such a large number of others, had it originally formed part of the text. Justin furnishes, besides, in this very narrative of the baptism, several apocryphal additions.

By means of a perfect revelation, Jesus contemplates the plan of God. Perfect inspiration gives Him strength to realize it. From the consciousness of His dignity as Son He derives the assurance of His being the supreme ambassador of God, called to accomplish this task. These were the positive conditions of His ministry.

THE BAPTISM OF JESUS.

We shall examine—1*st*. The baptism itself; 2*d*. The marvellous circumstances which accompanied it; 3*d*. The different accounts of this fact.

1*st. The Meaning of the Baptism.*—Here two closely connected questions present themselves: What was the object of Jesus in seeking baptism? What took place within Him when the rite was performed?

To the former question Strauss boldly replies: The baptism of Jesus was an avowal on His part of defilement, and a means of obtaining divine pardon. This explanation contradicts all the declarations of Jesus respecting Himself. If there is any one feature that marks His life, and completely separates it from all others, it is the entire absence of remorse and of the need of personal forgiveness.—According to Schleiermacher, Jesus desired to endorse the preaching of John, and obtain from him consecration to His Messianic ministry. But there had been no relation indicated beforehand between the baptism of water and the mission of the Messiah, nor was any such known to the people; and since baptism was generally understood as a confession of defilement, it would rather appear incompatible with this supreme theocratic dignity.—Weizsäcker, Keim, and others see in it a personal engagement on the part of Jesus to consecrate Himself to the service of holiness. This is just the previous opinion shorn of the Messianic notion, since these writers shrink from attributing to Jesus, thus early, a fixed idea of His Messianic dignity. It is certain that baptism was a vow of moral purity on the part of him who submitted to it. But the form of the rite implies not only the notion of progress in holiness, but also that of the removal of actual defilement; which is incompatible with the idea which these authors have themselves formed of the person of Jesus.—Lange sees in this act the indication of Jesus' guiltless participation in the collective defilement of mankind, by virtue of the solidarity of the race, and a voluntary engagement to deliver Himself up to death for the salvation of the world. This idea contains substantially the truth. We would express it thus: In presenting Himself for baptism, Jesus had to make, as others did, His ἐξομολόγησις, His confession of sins.[1] Of what sins, if not of those of His people and of the world in general? He placed before John a striking picture of them, not with that pride and scorn with which the Jews spoke of the sins of the heathen, and the Pharisees of the sins of the publicans, but with the humble and compassionate tones of an Isaiah (chap. lxiii.), a Daniel (chap. ix.), or a Nehemiah (chap. ix.), when they confessed the miseries of their people, as if the burden were their own. He could not have gone down into the water after such an act of communion with our misery, unless resolved to give Himself up entirely to the work of putting an end to the reign of sin. But He did not content Himself with making a vow. *He prayed*, the text tells us; He besought God for all that He needed for the accomplishment of this great task, *to take away the sin of the world.* He asked for wisdom, for spiritual strength, and particularly for the solution of the mystery which family records, the Scriptures, and

[1] Matthew (iii. 6) and **Mark (i. 7)**: "And they were baptized by him in **Jordan**, *confessing their sins.*"

His own holiness had created about His person. We can understand how John, after hearing Him *confess and pray* thus, should say, "Behold the Lamb of God, which taketh away the sin of the world!" This is what Jesus did by presenting Himself for baptism.

What took place within Him during the performance of the rite? According to Schleiermacher, nothing at all. He knew that He was the Messiah, and, by virtue of His previous development, He already possessed every qualification for His work. John, His forerunner, was merely apprised of his vocation, and rendered capable of proclaiming it. Weizsäcker, Keim, and others admit something more. Jesus became at this time conscious of His redemptive mission. It was on the banks of the Jordan that the grand resolve was formed; there Jesus felt Himself at once the man of God and the man of His age; there John silently shared in His solemn vow; and there the "God wills it" sounded through these two elect souls.[1] Lastly, Gess and several others think they must admit, besides a communication of strength from above, the gift of the Holy Spirit, but solely as a *spirit of ministry*, in view of the charge He was about to fulfil. These ideas, although just, are insufficient. The texts are clear. If Jesus was revealed to John, it was because He was revealed to Himself; and this revelation could not have taken place without being accompanied by a new gift. This gift could not refer to His work simply; for in an existence such as His, in which all was *spirit and life*, it was impossible to make a mechanical separation between work and life. The exercise of the functions of His office was an emanation from His life, and in some respects the atmosphere of His very personality. His entrance upon the duties of His office must therefore have coincided with an advance in the development of His personal life. Does not the power of giving imply possession in a different sense from that which holds when this power is as yet unexercised? Further, our documents, accepting the humanity of Jesus more thoroughly than our boldest theologians, overstep the bounds at which they stop. According to them, Jesus really received, not certainly as Cerinthus, going beyond the limits of truth, taught, a heavenly Christ who came and united Himself to him for a time, but *the Holy Spirit*, in the full meaning of the term, by which Jesus became the Lord's anointed, the *Christ*, the perfect man, the second Adam, capable of begetting a new spiritual humanity. This Spirit no longer acted *on* Him simply, on His will, as it had done from the beginning; it became His proper nature, His personal life. No mention is ever made of the action of the Holy Spirit on Jesus during the course of His ministry. Jesus was more and better than inspired. Through the Spirit, whose life became His life, God was in Him, and He in God. In order to His being completely glorified as man, there remained but one thing more, that His earthly existence be transformed into the divine state. His transfiguration was the prelude to this transformation. In the development of

[1] See the fine passage in Keim's *Gesch. Jesu*, t. i. pp. 543-549.

Jesus, the baptism is therefore the intermediate point between the miraculous birth and the ascension.

But *objections* are raised against this biblical notion of the baptism of Jesus. Keim maintains that, since Jesus already possessed the Spirit through the divine influence which sanctified His birth, He could not receive it in His baptism. But would he deny that, if there is one act in human life which is free, it is the acquisition of the Spirit? The Spirit's influence is too much of the nature of fellowship to force itself on any one. It must be desired and sought in order to be received; and for it to be desired and sought, it must be in some measure known. Jesus declares (John xiv. 17), "that the world cannot receive the Holy Spirit, because it seeth Him not, neither knoweth Him." The possession of the Spirit cannot therefore be the starting-point of moral life; it can only be the term of a more or less lengthened development of the soul's life. The human soul was created as the betrothed of the Spirit; and for the marriage to be consummated, the soul must have beheld her heavenly spouse, and learnt to love Him and accept Him freely. This state of energetic and active receptivity, the condition of every Pentecost, was that of Jesus at His baptism. It was the fruit of His previous pure development, which had simply been rendered *possible* by the interposition of the Holy Spirit in His birth (p. 94).

Again, it is said that it lessens the moral greatness of Jesus to substitute a sudden and magical illumination, like that of the baptism, for that free acquisition of the Spirit,—that spontaneous discovery and conquest of self which are due solely to personal endeavour.—But when God gives a soul the inward assurance of adoption, and reveals to it, as to Jesus at His baptism, the love He has for it, does this gift exclude previous endeavour, moral struggles, even anguish often bordering on despair? No; so far from grace excluding human preparatory labour, it would remain barren without it, just as the human labour would issue in nothing apart from the divine gift. Every schoolmaster has observed marked stages in the development of children,—crises in which past growth has found an end, and from which an entirely new era has taken its date. There is nothing, therefore, out of harmony with the laws of psychology in this apparently abrupt leap which the baptism makes in the life of Jesus.

2*d. The Miraculous Circumstances.*—Keim denies them altogether. Everything in the baptism, according to him, resolves itself into a heroic decision on the part of Jesus to undertake the salvation of the world. He alleges—1. The numerous differences between the narratives, particularly between that of John and those of the Syn. This objection rests on misapprehensions (see above).—2. The legendary character of the prodigies related. But here one of two things must be true. Either our narratives of the baptism are the reproduction of the original evangelical tradition circulated by the apostles (i. 2), and repeated during many years under their eyes; and in this case, how could they contain statements positively false? Or these accounts are legends of later invention; but if so, how is their all but literal agreement to be accounted for, and the well-defined and fixed type which they exhibit?—3. The internal struggles of Jesus and the doubts of John the Baptist, mentioned in the subsequent history, are not reconcilable with this supernatural revelation, which, according to these accounts, both must have received at the time of the baptism. But it is impossible to instance a single struggle in the ministry of Jesus respecting the reality of His mission; it is to pervert the meaning of the conversation at Cæsarea Philippi (see ix. 18 et seq.), and of the prayer in Gethsemane, to find such a meaning in them. And as to the doubts of John the Baptist, they certainly did not respect *the origin* of the mission of Jesus, since it is to none other than Jesus Himself that John applies for their solution, but solely to the *nature* of this mission. The unostentatious and peaceful progress of the work of Jesus, His miracles purely of mercy ("*having heard of the works of Christ,*" Matt. xi. 2), contrasted so forcibly with the terrible Messianic judgment which he had announced as imminent (iii. 9, 17), that he was led to ask himself whether, in accordance with a prevalent opinion of Jewish theology,[1] Jesus was not the messenger of grace, the instrument of salvation; whilst another, a *second* (ἕτερος, Matt. xi. 3), to come after Him, would be the agent of divine judgment, and the temporal restorer of the people purified from every corruption. John's doubt therefore respects, not the divinity of Jesus' mission, but the *exclusive* character of His Messianic dignity.—4. It is asked why John, if he believed in Jesus, did not from the hour of the baptism immediately take his place among His adherents? But had he not a permanent duty to fulfil in regard to Israel? Was he not to continue to act as a mediating agent between this people and Jesus? To abandon his special position, distinct as it was from that of Jesus, in order to rank himself amongst His disciples, would have been to desert his official post, and to cease to be a mediator for Israel between them and their King.

We cannot imagine for a moment, especially looking at the matter from a Jewish point of view, according to which every holy mission proceeds from above, that Jesus would determine to undertake the unheard-of task of the salvation of the world and of the destruction of sin and death, and that John could share this determination, and proclaim it in God's name a heavenly mission, without some positive sign, some sensible manifestation of the divine will. Jesus, says Keim, is not a man of visions; He needs no such signs; there is no need of a dove between God and Him. Has Keim, then, forgotten the real humanity of Jesus? That there were no visions during the course of His ministry, we concede; there was no room for ecstasy in a man whose inward life was henceforth that of the Spirit Himself. But that there had been none in His preceding life up to the very threshold of this new state, is more than any one can assert. Jesus *lived over again,* if we may venture to say so, the whole life of humanity and the whole life of Israel, so far as these two lives were of a normal character; and this was how it was that He so well

[1] See my *Commentary on the Gospel of John,* i. p. 311.

understood them. Why should not the preparatory educational method of which God made such frequent use under the old covenant,—the vision,—have had its place in His inward development, before He reached, physically and spiritually, the stature of complete manhood?

3*d*. *The Narratives of the Baptism.*—Before we pronounce an opinion on the origin of our synoptical narratives, it is important to compare the apocryphal narrations. In the *Gospel of the Nazarenes*, which Jerome had translated,[1] the mother and brethren of Jesus invite Him to go and be baptized by John. He answers: "Wherein have I sinned, and why should I go to be baptized by him,—unless, perhaps, this speech which I have just uttered be [a sin of] ignorance?" Afterwards, a heavenly voice addresses these words to Him: "My Son, in all the prophets I have waited for Thy coming, in order to take my rest in Thee: for it is Thou who art my rest; Thou art my first-born Son, and Thou shalt reign eternally."—In the *Preaching of Paul*,[2] Jesus actually confesses His sins to John the Baptist, just as all the others.—In the Ebionitish recension of the *Gospel of the Hebrews*, cited by Epiphanius,[3] a great light surrounds the place where Jesus has just been baptized: then the plenitude of the Holy Spirit enters into Jesus under the form of a dove, and a divine voice says to Him: "Thou art my well-beloved Son; on Thee I have bestowed my good pleasure." It resumes: "To-day have I begotten Thee." In this Gospel also, the dialogue between Jesus and John, which Matthew relates before the baptism, is placed after it. John, after having seen the miraculous signs, says to Jesus, "Who then art Thou?" The divine voice replies, "This is my beloved Son, on whom I have bestowed my good pleasure." John falls at His feet, and says to Him, "Baptize me!" and Jesus answers him, "Cease from that."—Justin Martyr relates,[4] that when Jesus had gone down into the water, a fire blazed up in the Jordan; next, that when He came out of the water, the Holy Spirit, like a dove, descended upon Him; lastly, that when He had ascended from the river, the voice said to Him, "Thou art my Son; to-day have I begotten Thee."—Who cannot feel the difference between prodigies of this kind—between these theological and amplified discourses attributed to God—and the holy sobriety of our biblical narratives? The latter are the text; the apocryphal writings give the human paraphrase.—The comparison of these two kinds of narrative proves that the type of the apostolic tradition has been preserved pure, as the impress of a medal, in the common tenor of our synoptical narratives.—As to the difference between these narratives, they are not without importance. The principal differences are these: Matthew has, over and above the two others, the dialogue between Jesus and John which preceded the baptism, and which was only a continuation of the act of confession which Jesus had just made. The Ebionite Gospel places it after, because it did not understand this connection. The prayer of

[1] *Adv. Pet.* iii. 1.
[2] See *De rebaptismate*, in the works of Cyprian. Grabe, *Spicil.* t. i. p. 69.
[3] *Hær.* xxx. 13.
[4] *Dial. c. Tryph.* c. 88 and 103.

Jesus is peculiar to Luke, and he differs from the other two in the remarkable turn of the participle applied to the fact of the baptism of Jesus, and in the more objective form in which the miraculous facts are mentioned. Mark differs from the others only in the form of certain phrases, and in the expression, "He saw the heavens *open*." Holtzmann derives the accounts of Matthew and Luke from that of the alleged original Mark, which was very nearly an exact fac-simile of our canonical Mark. But whence did the other two derive what is peculiar to them? Not from their imagination, for an earnest writer does not treat a subject which he regards as sacred in this way. Either, then, from a document or from tradition? But this document or tradition could not contain merely the detail peculiar to each evangelist; the detail implies the complete narrative. If the evangelist drew the detail from it, he most probably took from it the narrative also. Whence it seems to us to follow, that at the basis of our Syn. we must place certain documents or oral narrations, emanating from the primitive tradition (in this way their common general tenor is explained), but differing in some details, either because in the oral tradition the secondary features of the narrative naturally underwent some modification, or because the private documents underwent some alterations, owing to additional oral information, or to writings which might be accessible.

THIRD NARRATIVE.—III. 23–38.

The Genealogy of Jesus.

In the first Gospel the genealogy of Jesus is placed at the very beginning of the narrative. This is easily explained. From the point of view indicated by theocratic forms, scriptural antecedents, and, if we may so express it, Jewish etiquette, the Messiah was to be a descendant of *David* and *Abraham* (Matt. i. 1). This relationship was the *sine quâ non* of His civil status. It is not so easy to understand why Luke thought he must give the genealogy of Jesus, and why he places it just here, between the baptism and the temptation. Perhaps, if we bear in mind the obscurity in which, to the Greeks, the origin of mankind was hidden, and the absurd fables current among them about *autochthonic* nations, we shall see how interesting any document would be to them, which, following the track of actual names, went back to the first father of the race. Luke's intention would thus be very nearly the same as Paul's when he said at Athens (Acts xvii. 26), "*God hath made of one blood the whole human race.*" But from a strictly religious point of view, this genealogy possessed still greater importance. In carrying it back not only, as Matthew does, as far as Abraham, but even to Adam, Luke lays the foundation of that universality of redemption which is to be one of the characteristic features of the picture he is about to draw. In this way he places in close and indissoluble connection the imperfect image of God created in Adam, which reappears in *every* man, and His perfect image realized in Christ, which is to be reproduced in all men.

But why does Luke place this document *here?* Holtzmann replies (p. 112), "because hitherto there had been no suitable place for it." This answer harmonizes very well with the process of *fabrication,* by means of which this scholar thinks the composition of the Syn. may be accounted for. But why did this particular place appear more suitable to the evangelist than another? This is what has to be explained. Luke himself puts us on the right track by the first words of ver. 23. By giving prominence to the person of Jesus in the use of the pronoun *αὐτός*, *He,* which opens the sentence, by the addition of the name *Jesus,* and above all, by the verb ἦν which separates this pronoun and this substantive, and sets them both in relief ("*and Himself was, He, Jesus . . .*"), Luke indicates this as the moment when Jesus enters personally on the scene to commence His proper work. With the baptism, the obscurity in which He has lived until now passes away; He now appears detached from the circle of persons who have hitherto surrounded Him and acted as His patrons; namely, His parents and the forerunner. He henceforth becomes the *He,* the principal personage of the narrative. This is the moment which very properly appears to the author most suitable for giving His genealogy. The genealogy of Moses, in the Exodus, is placed in the same way, not at the opening of his biography, but at the moment when he appears on the stage of history, when he presents himself before Pharaoh (vi. 14 et seq.).—In crossing the threshold of this new era, the sacred historian casts a general glance over the period which thus reaches its close, and sums it up in this document, which might be called the mortuary register of the earlier humanity.

There is further a difference of form between the two genealogies. Matthew comes down, whilst Luke ascends the stream of generations. Perhaps this difference of method depends on the difference of religious position between the Jews and the Greeks. The Jew, finding the basis of his thought in a revelation, proceeds synthetically from cause to effect; the Greek, possessing nothing beyond the fact, analyzes it, that he may proceed from effect to cause. But this difference depends more probably still on another circumstance. Every official genealogical register must present the *descending* form; for individuals are only inscribed in it as they are born. The *ascending* form of genealogy can only be that of a private instrument, drawn up from the public document with a view to the particular individual whose name serves as the starting-point of the whole list. It follows that in Matthew we have the exact copy of the official register; while Luke gives us a document extracted from the public records, and compiled with a view to the person with whom the genealogy commences.

Ver. 23 is at once the transition and preamble; vers. 24–38 contain the genealogy itself. 1*st.* Ver. 23.[1]—The exact translation of this important and difficult verse is this: "*And Himself, Jesus, was* [aged] *about thirty years when He began* [or, if the term may be employed here, *made His début*], *being a son, as was believed, of Joseph.*"—The expression *to begin* can only refer in this passage to the entrance of Jesus upon His Messianic work. This idea is in direct connection with the context (baptism, temptation), and particularly with the first words of the verse. Having fully become *He,* Jesus *begins.* We must take care not to connect ἀρχόμενος and ἦν as parts of a single verb (*was beginning* for *began*). For ἦν has a complement of its own, *of thirty years;* it therefore signifies here, *was of the age of.* Some have tried to make τριάκοντα ἔτων depend on ἀρχόμενος, He began *His thirtieth year;* and it is perhaps owing to this interpretation that we find this participle placed first in the Alex. But for this sense, τριακοστοῦ ἔτους would have been necessary; and the limitation *about* cannot have reference to the *commencement of the year.*—(On the

[1] ℵ. B. L. X. some Mnn. Italiq. Or. place αρχομενος before ωσει ετων τριακοντα, whilst T. R., with all the rest of the documents, place it after these words.—ℵ. B. L. some Mnn. read in this order: ων υιος ως ενομιζετο Ιωσηφ, instead of ων ως ενομιζετο υιος Ιωσηφ in T. R. and the other authorities.—H. Γ. (not B.) some Mnn. add του before Ιωσηφ.

agreement of this chronological fact with the date, ver. 1, see p. 166.)—We have already observed that the age of thirty is that of the greatest physical and psychical strength, the *ἀκμη* of natural life. It was the age at which, among the Jews, the Levites entered upon their duties (Num. iv. 3, 23), and when, among the Greeks, a young man began to take part in public affairs.[1]—The participle *ὤν*, *being*, makes a strange impression, not only because it is purely and simply in juxtaposition with *ἀρχόμενος* (*beginning, being*), and depends on *ἦν*, the very verb of which it is a part, but still more because its connection with the latter verb cannot be explained by any of the three logical relations by which a participle is connected with a completed verb, *when, because*, or *although*. What relation of simultaneousness, causality, or opposition, could there be between the filiation of Jesus and the age at which He had arrived? This incoherence is a clear indication that the evangelist has with some difficulty effected a soldering of two documents,—that which he has hitherto followed, and which for the moment he abandons, and the genealogical register which he wishes to insert in this place.

With the participle *ὤν*, *being*, there begins then a transition which we owe to the pen of Luke. How far does it extend, and where does the genealogical register properly begin? This is a nice and important question. We have only a hint for its solution. This is the absence of the article *τοῦ*, *the*, before the name *Joseph*. This word is found before all the names belonging to the genealogical series. In the genealogy of Matthew, the article *τόν* is put in the same way before each proper name, which clearly proves that it was the ordinary form in vogue in this kind of document. The two MSS. H. and I. read, it is true, *τοῦ* before *Ἰωσήφ*. But since these unimportant MSS. are unsupported by their ally the *Vatican*, to which formerly the same reading was erroneously attributed (see Tischend. 8th ed.), this various reading has no longer any weight. On the one hand, it is easily explained as an imitation of the following terms of the genealogy; on the other, we could not conceive of the suppression of the article in all the most ancient documents, if it had originally belonged to the

[1] See the two passages from Xenophon (*Memor.* 1) and from Dionysius of Halicarnassus (*Hist.* iv. 6), cited by Wieseler, *Beiträge*, etc., pp. 165, 166.

text. This want of the article puts the name Joseph outside the genealogical series properly so called, and assigns to it a peculiar position. We must conclude from it—1*st.* That this name belongs rather to the sentence introduced by Luke; 2*d.* That the genealogical document which he consulted began with the name of Heli; 3*d.* And consequently, that this piece was not originally the genealogy of Jesus or of Joseph, but of Heli.

There is a second question to determine: whether we should prefer the Alexandrine reading, "*being a son, as it was believed, of Joseph;*" or the Byzantine text, "*being, as it was believed, a son of Joseph.*" There is internal probability that the copyists would rather have been drawn to connect the words *son* and *Joseph,* in order to restore the phrase frequently employed in the Gospels, *son of Joseph,* than to separate them. This observation appears to decide for the Alexandrine text.

It is of importance next to determine the exact meaning of the τοῦ which precedes each of the genealogical names. Thus far we have supposed this word to be the article, and this is the natural interpretation. But we might give it the force of a pronoun, *he, the one,* and translate: "Joseph, *he* [the son] of Heli; Heli, *he* [the son] of Matthat," etc. Thus understood, the τοῦ would each time be in apposition with the preceding name, and would have the following name for its complement. But this explanation cannot be maintained; for—1*st.* It cannot be applied to the last term τοῦ Θεοῦ, in which τοῦ is evidently an article; 2*d.* The recurrence of τόν in the genealogy of Matthew proves that *the article* belonged to the terminology of these documents; 3*d.* The τοῦ thus understood would imply an intention to distinguish the individual to which it refers from some other person bearing the same name, but not having the same father, "Heli, *the one* of Matthat, [and not one of another father];" which could not be the design of the genealogist. The τοῦ is therefore undoubtedly an article. But, admitting this, we may still hesitate between two interpretations, we may *subordinate* each genitive to the preceding name, as is ordinarily done: "Heli, son of Matthat, [which Matthat was a son] of Levi, [which Levi was a son] of . . .;" or, as Wieseler proposed, we may *co-ordinate* all the genitives, so as to make each of them depend directly on the word *son* placed at the head of the entire series: "Jesus, son of Heli; [Jesus, son] of

Matthat . . ." So that, according to the Jewish usage, which permitted a grandson to be called the *son* of his *grandfather*, Jesus would be called the son of each of His ancestors in succession. This interpretation would not be, in itself, so forced as Bleek maintains. But nevertheless the former is preferable, for it alone really expresses the notion of a *succession of generations*, which is the ruling idea of every genealogy. The genitives in Luke merely supply the place of ἐγέννησε, as repeated in the original document, of which Matthew gives us the text.—Besides, we do not think that it would be necessary to supply, between each link in the genealogical chain, the term υἱοῦ, *son of*, as an apposition of the preceding name. Each genitive is also the complement of the name which precedes it. The idea of filiation resides in the grammatical *case*. We have the *genitive* here in its essence.

There remains, lastly, the still more important question: On what does the genitive τοῦ Ἡλί (*of Heli*) precisely depend? On the name Ἰωσήφ which immediately precedes it? This would be in conformity with the analogy of all the other genitives, which, as we have just proved, depend each on the preceding name. Thus Heli would have been the father of Joseph, and the genealogy of Luke, *as well as that of Matthew*, would be the genealogy of Jesus through Joseph. In that case we should have to explain how the two documents could be so totally different. But this view is incompatible with the absence of the article before *Joseph*. If the name Ἰωσήφ had been intended by Luke to be the basis of the entire genealogical series, it would have been fixed and determined by the article with much greater reason certainly than the names that follow. The genitive τοῦ Ἡλί, *of Heli*, depends therefore not on *Joseph*, but on the word *son*. This construction is not possible, it is true, with the received reading, in which the words *son* and *Joseph* form a single phrase, *son of Joseph*. The word *son* cannot be separated from the word it immediately governs: *Joseph*, to receive a second and more distant complement. With this reading, the only thing left to us is to make τοῦ Ἡλί depend on the participle ὤν: "Jesus . . . *being* . . . [born] *of Heli*." An antithesis might be found between the real fact (ὤν, *being*) and the apparent (ἐνομίζετο, *as was thought*). "being, as was thought, a son of

Joseph, [in reality] born of Heli." But can the word ὤν signify both *to be* (in the sense of the verb substantive) and *to be born of?* Everything becomes much more simple if we assume the Alex. reading, which on other grounds has already appeared to us the more probable. The word *son*, separated as it is from its first complement, *of Joseph*, by the words *as was thought*, may very well have a second, *of Heli.* The first is only noticed in passing, and in order to be denied in the very mention of it: "Son, as was thought, of Joseph." The official information being thus disavowed, Luke, by means of the second complement, substitutes for it the truth, *of Heli;* and this name he distinguishes, by means of the article, as the first link of the genealogical chain properly so called. The text, therefore, to express the author's meaning clearly, should be written thus: "being a son—as was thought, of Joseph—of Heli, of Matthat . . ." Bleek has put the words ὡς ἐνομίζετο into a parenthesis, and rightly; only he should have added to them the word Ἰωσήφ.

This study of the text in detail leads us in this way to admit—1. That the genealogical register of Luke is that of Heli, the grandfather of Jesus; 2. That, this affiliation of Jesus by Heli being expressly opposed to His affiliation by Joseph, the document which he has preserved for us can be nothing else in his view than the genealogy of Jesus through Mary. But why does not Luke name Mary, and why pass immediately from Jesus to His grandfather? Ancient sentiment did not comport with the mention of the mother as the genealogical link. Among the Greeks a man was the son of his father, not of his mother; and among the Jews the adage was: "*Genus matris non vocatur genus*" (*Baba bathra,* 110, *a*). In lieu of this, it is not uncommon to find in the O. T. the grandson called the son of his grandfather.[1]

If there were any circumstances in which this usage was applicable, would not the wholly exceptional case with which Luke was dealing be such? There was only one way of filling up the hiatus, resulting from the absence of the father, between

[1] Comp., for example, 1 Chron. viii. 3 with Gen. xlvi. 21; Ezra v. 1, vi. 14, with Zech. i. 1, 7; and in the N. T., Matt. i. 8 with 1 Chron. iv. 11, 12,—a passage in which King Joram is even recorded as having begotten the son of his grandson

the grandfather and his grandson; namely, to introduce the name of the presumed father, noting at the same time the falseness of this opinion. It is remarkable that, in the Talmud, Mary the mother of Jesus is called *the daughter of Heli* (*Chagig.* 77. 4). From whence have Jewish scholars derived this information? If from the text of Luke, this proves that they understood it as we do; if they received it from tradition, it confirms the truth of the genealogical document Luke made use of.[1]

If this explanation be rejected, it must be admitted that Luke as well as Matthew gives us the genealogy of Joseph. The difficulties to be encountered in this direction are these:—1. The absence of τοῦ before the name Ἰωσήφ, and before this name alone, is not accounted for.—2. We are met by an all but insoluble contradiction between the two evangelists,—the one indicating Heli as the father of Joseph, the other Jacob,—which leads to two series of names wholly different. We might, it is true, have recourse to the following hypothesis proposed by Julius Africanus (third century):[2] Heli and Jacob were brothers; one of them died without children; the survivor, in conformity with the law, married his widow, and the first-born of this union, Joseph, was registered as a son of the deceased. In this way Joseph would have had two fathers,—one real, the other legal. But this hypothesis is not sufficient; a second is needed. For if Heli and Jacob were brothers, they must have had the same father; and the two genealogies should coincide on reaching the name of the grandfather of Joseph, which is not the case. It is supposed, therefore, that they were brothers on the mother's side only, which explains both the difference of the fathers and that of the entire genealogies. This superstructure of coincidences is not absolutely inadmissible, but no one can think it natural. We should be reduced, then, to admit an absolute contradiction between the two evangelists. But can it be supposed that both or either of them could have been capable of fabricating such a register, heaping name upon name quite arbitrarily, and at the mere pleasure of their caprice? Who could credit a proceeding so absurd, and that in two genealogies, one of which sets out from Abraham, the venerated ancestor of the people, the other terminating in God Himself! All these names must have been taken from documents. But is it possible in this case to admit, in one or both of these writers, an entire mistake?—3. It is not only with Matthew that Luke would be in contradiction, but with himself. He admits the miraculous birth (chap. i. and ii.). It is conceivable that, from the theocratic point of view which Matthew takes, a certain interest might, even on this supposition,

[1] The relationship of Jesus to the royal family is also affirmed by the Talmud (Tr. *Sanhedrim*, 43).
[2] Eus. *Hist. Eccl.* i. 7.

be assigned to the genealogy of Joseph, as the *adoptive*, legal father of the Messiah. But that Luke, to whom this official point of view was altogether foreign, should have handed down with so much care this series of seventy-three names, after having severed the chain at the first link, as he does by the remark, *as it was thought;* that, further, he should give himself the trouble, after this, to develope the entire series, and finish at last with God Himself;—this is a moral impossibility. What sensible man, Gfrörer has very properly asked (with a different design, it is true), could take pleasure in drawing up such a list of ancestors, after having declared that the relationship is destitute of all reality? Modern criticism has, last of all, been driven to the following hypothesis:—Matthew and Luke each found a genealogy of Jesus written from the Jewish-Christian standpoint: they were both different genealogies of Joseph; for amongst this party (which was no other than the primitive Church) he was without hesitation regarded as the father of Jesus. But at the time when these documents were published by the evangelists another theory already prevailed, that of the miraculous birth, which these two authors embraced. They published, therefore, their documents, adapting them as best they could to the new belief, just as Luke does by his *as it was thought,* and Matthew by the periphrasis i. 16.—But, 1. We have pointed out that the opinion which attributes to the primitive apostolic Church the idea of the natural birth of Jesus rests upon no solid foundation. 2. A writer who speaks of apostolic tradition as Luke speaks of it, i. 2, could not have knowingly put himself in opposition to it on a point of this importance. 3. If we advance no claim on behalf of the sacred writers to inspiration, we protest against whatever impeaches their good sense. The first evangelist, M. Reville maintains,[1] *did not even perceive the incompatibility* between the theory of the miraculous birth and his genealogical document. As to Luke, this same author says: "The third *perceives very clearly* the contradiction; nevertheless he writes his history *as if it did not exist.*" In other words, Matthew is more foolish than false, Luke more false than foolish. Criticism which is obliged to support itself by attributing to the sacred writers absurd methods, such as are found in no sensible writer, is self-condemned. There is not the smallest proof that the documents used by Matthew and Luke were of Jewish-*Christian* origin. On the contrary, it is very probable, since the facts all go to establish it, that they were simply copies of the official registers of the *public tables* (see below), referring, one to Joseph, the other to Heli, both consequently of *Jewish* origin. So far from there being any ground to regard them as monuments of a *Christian* conception differing from that of the evangelists, it is these authors, or those who transmitted them to them, who set upon them for the first time the Christian seal, by adding to them the part which refers to Jesus. 4. Lastly, after all, these two series of completely different names have in any case to be explained. Are they fictitious? Who can maintain this, when

[1] *Histoire du Dogme de la Divinité de Jésus Christ*, p. 27.

writers so evidently in earnest are concerned? Are they founded upon documents? How then could they differ so completely? This difficulty becomes greater still if it is maintained that these two different genealogies of Joseph proceed from the same ecclesiastical quarter—from the Jewish-Christian party.

But have we sufficient proofs of the existence of genealogical registers among the Jews at this epoch? We have already referred to the *public tables* (δέλτοι δημόσιαι) from which Josephus had extracted his own genealogy: "I relate my genealogy as I find it recorded in the public tables."[1] The same Josephus, in his work, *Contra Apion* (i. 7), says: "From all the countries in which our priests are scattered abroad, they send to Jerusalem (in order to have their children entered) documents containing the names of their parents and ancestors, and countersigned by witnesses." What was done for the priestly families could not fail to have been done with regard to the royal family, from which it was known that the Messiah was to spring. The same conclusion results also from the following facts. The famous Rabbi Hillel, who lived in the time of Jesus, succeeded in proving, by means of a genealogical table in existence at Jerusalem, that, although a poor man, he was a descendant of David.[2] The line of descent in the different branches of the royal family was so well known, that even at the end of the first century of the Church, the grandsons of Jude, the brother of the Lord, had to appear at Rome as *descendants of David*, and undergo examination in the presence of Domitian.[3] According to these facts, the existence of two genealogical documents relating, one to Joseph, the other to Heli, and preserved in their respective families, offers absolutely nothing at all improbable.

In comparing the two narratives of the infancy, we have been led to assign them to two different sources: that of Matthew appeared to us to emanate from the relations of Joseph; that of Luke from the circle of which Mary was the centre (p. 163). Something similar occurs again in regard to the two genealogies. That of Matthew, which has Joseph in view, must have proceeded from his family; that which Luke has transmitted to us, being that of Mary's father, must have come from this latter quarter. But it is manifest that this difference of production is connected with a moral cause. The meaning of one of the genealogies is certainly hereditary, Messianic; the meaning of the other is universal redemption. Hence, in the one, the relationship is through Joseph, the representative of the civil, national, theocratic side; in the other, the descent is through Mary, the organ of the real human relationship.—Was not Jesus at once *to appear* and *to be* the son of David?—to appear such, through him whom the people regarded as His father; to be such, through her from whom He really derived His human existence? The two affiliations answered to these two requirements.

[1] Jos. *Vita*, c. i.
[2] *Bereschit rabba*, 98.
[3] Hegesippus, in Eusebius' *Hist. Eccl.* iii. 19 and 20 (ed. Lœmmer).

2*d*. Vers 24–38.[1]—And first, vers. 24–27: from Heli to the captivity. In this period Luke mentions 21 generations (up to Neri); only 19, if the various reading of Africanus be admitted; Matthew, 14. This last number is evidently too small for the length of the period. As Matthew omits in the period of the kings four well-known names of the O. T., it is probable that he takes the same course here, either through an involuntary omission, or for the sake of keeping to the number 14 (i. 17). This comparison should make us appreciate the exactness of Luke's register.—But how is it that the names Zorobabel and Salathiel occur, connected with each other in the same way, in both the genealogies? And how can Salathiel have Neri for his father in Luke, and in Matthew King Jechonias? Should these names be regarded as standing for different persons, as Wieseler thinks? This is not impossible. The Zorobabel and the Salathiel of Luke might be two unknown persons of the obscurer branch of the royal family descended from Nathan; the Zorobabel and the Salathiel of Matthew, the two well-known persons of the O. T. history, belonging to the reigning branch, the first a son, the second a grandson of King Jechonias (1 Chron. iii. 17; Ezra iii. 2; Hag. i. 1). This is the view which, after all, appears to Bleek most probable. It is open, however, to a serious objection from the fact that these two names, in the two lists, refer so exactly to the same period, since in both of them they are very nearly halfway between Jesus and David. If the identity of these persons in the two genealogies is admitted, the explanation must be found in 2 Kings xxiv. 12, which proves that King Jechonias had no son at the time when he was carried into captivity. It is scarcely probable that he had one while in prison, where he remained shut up for thirty-eight years. He or they whom the passage 1 Chron. iii. 17 assigns to him (which, besides, may be translated in three different ways) must be regarded as adopted sons or as sons-in-law; they would be spoken of as sons, because they would be unwilling to allow the reigning branch of the royal family to become extinct. Salathiel, the first of them, would thus have some other father than Jechonias;

[1] We omit the numerous orthographical variations connected with these proper names.—Ver. 24. Jul. Afric. Eus. Ir. (probably) omit the two names Ματθατ and Λευει.

and this father would be Neri, of the Nathan branch, indicated by Luke. An alternative hypothesis has been proposed, founded on the Levirate law. Neri, as a relative of Jechonias, might have married one of the wives of the imprisoned king, in order to perpetuate the royal family; and the son of this union, Salathiel, would have been *legally* a son of Jechonias, but *really* a son of Neri. In any case, the numerous differences that are found in the statements of our historical books at this period prove that the catastrophe of the captivity brought considerable confusion into the registers or family traditions.[1] Rhesa and Abiud, put down, the one by Luke, the other by Matthew, as sons of Zorobabel, are not mentioned in the O. T., according to which the sons of this restorer of Israel should have been Meshullam and Hananiah (1 Chron. iii. 19). Bleek observes, that if the evangelists had fabricated their lists, they would naturally have made use of these two names that are furnished by the sacred text; therefore they have followed their documents.

Vers. 28–31.—From the captivity to David, 20 names. Matthew for the same period has only 14. But it is proved by the O. T. that he omits four; the number 20, in Luke, is a fresh proof of the accuracy of his document. On Nathan, son of David, comp. 2 Sam. v. 14, Zech. xii. 12. The passage in Zechariah proves that this branch was still flourishing after the return from the captivity. If Neri, the descendant of Nathan, was the *real* father of Salathiel, the adopted son or son-in-law of Jechonias, we should find here once more the characteristic of the two genealogies: in Matthew, the legal, official point of view; in Luke, the real, human point of view.

Vers. 32–34*a*.—From David to Abraham. The two genealogies agree with each other, and with the O. T.

Vers. 34*b*–38.—From Abraham to Adam. This part is peculiar to Luke. It is compiled evidently from the O. T., and according to the text of the LXX., with which it exactly coincides. The name Cainan, ver. 36, is only found in the

[1] According to 1 Chron. iii. 16, 2 Chron. xxxvi. 10 (Heb. text), Zedekiah was son of Jehoiakim and brother of Jehoiachin; but, according to 2 Kings xxiv. 17 and Jer. xxxvii. 1, he was son of Josiah and brother of Johoiakim. According to 1 Chron. iii. 19, Zorobabel was son of Pedaiah and grandson of Jeconiah, and consequently *nephew* of Salathiel; while, according to Ezra iii. 2, Neh. xii. 1, Hag. i. 1, he was *son* of Salathiel, etc.

LXX., and is wanting in the Heb. text (Gen. x. 24, xi. 12). This must be a very ancient variation.—The words, *of God*, with which it ends, are intended to inform us that it is not through ignorance that the genealogist stops at Adam, but because he has reached the end of the chain, perhaps also to remind us of the truth expressed by Paul at Athens: "We are the offspring of God." The last word of the genealogy is connected with its starting-point (vers. 22, 23). If man were not the offspring of God, the incarnation (ver. 22) would be impossible. God cannot say to *a man*: "Thou art my beloved son," save on this ground, that humanity itself is His issue (ver. 38).[1]

FOURTH NARRATIVE.—CHAP. IV. 1–13.

The Temptation.

Every free creature, endowed with various faculties, must pass through a conflict, in which it decides either to use them for its own gratification, or to glorify God by devoting them to His service. The angels have passed through this trial; the first man underwent it; Jesus, being truly human, did not escape it. Our Syn. are unanimous upon this point. Their testimony as to the time when this conflict took place is no less accordant. All three place it immediately after His baptism, at the outset of His Messianic career. This date is important for determining the true meaning of this trial.

The temptation of the first man bore upon the use of the powers inherent in our nature. Jesus also experienced this kind of trial. How many times during His childhood and early manhood must He have been exposed to those temptations which address themselves to the instincts of the natural life! The lust of the flesh, the lust of the eyes, and the pride of life,—these different forms of sin, separately or with united force, endeavoured to besiege His heart, subjugate His will, enslave His powers, and invade this pure being as they had invaded the innocent Adam. But on the battle-field on which Adam had succumbed Jesus remained a victor. The "conscience without a scar," which He carried from the first part

[1] See the valuable applications which Riggenbach makes of these genealogies, *Vie de Jésus*, ninth lesson, at the commencement.

of His life into the second, assures us of this. The new trial He is now to undergo belongs to a higher domain—that of the spiritual life. It no longer respects the powers of the natural man, but His filial position, and the supernatural powers just conferred upon Him at His baptism. The powers of the Spirit are in themselves holy, but the history of the church of Corinth shows how they may be profaned when used in the service of egotism and self-love (1 Cor. xii.–xiv.) This is that *filthiness of the spirit* (2 Cor. vii. 1), which is more subtle, and often more pernicious, than that of the flesh. The divine powers which Jesus had just received had therefore to be sanctified in His experience, that is, to receive from Him, in His inmost soul, their consecration to the service of God. In order to this, it was necessary that an opportunity to apply them either to His own use or to God's service should be offered Him. His decision on this critical occasion would determine for ever the tendency and nature of His Messianic work. Christ or Antichrist was the alternative term of the two ways which were opening before Him. This trial is not therefore a repetition of that of Adam, the father of the old humanity; it is the special trial of the Head of the new humanity. And it is not simply a question here, as in our conflicts, whether a given individual shall form part of the kingdom of God; it is the very existence of this kingdom that is at stake. Its future sovereign, sent to found it, struggles in close combat with the sovereign of the hostile realm.

This narrative comprises—1*st*. A general view (vers. 1, 2); 2*d*. The first temptation (vers. 3, 4); 3*d*. The second (vers. 5–8); 4*th*. The third (vers. 9–12); 5*th*. An historical conclusion (ver. 13).

1*st*. Vers. 1, 2.[1]—By these words, *full of the Holy Ghost*, this narrative is brought into close connection with that of the baptism. The genealogy is therefore intercalated.—While the other baptized persons, after the ceremony, went away to their own homes, Jesus betook Himself into solitude. This He did not at His own prompting, as Luke gives us to understand by the expression *full of the Holy Ghost*, which proves that the

[1] Ver. 1. ℵ. B. D. L. It[aliq]., εν τη ερημω instead of εις την ερημον, the reading of T. R. with 15 Mjj., all the Mnn. Syr. It[aliq]. Vg.—Ver. 2. The same omit υστερον (taken from Matthew).

Spirit directed Him in this, as in every other step The two other evangelists explicitly say it. Matthew, *He was led up of the Spirit;* Mark, still more forcibly, *Immediately the Spirit driveth Him into the wilderness.* Perhaps the human inclination of Jesus would have been to return to Galilee and begin at once to teach. The Spirit detains Him; and Matthew, who, in accordance with his didactic aim, in narrating the fact explains its object, says expressly: "He was led up of the Spirit . . . *to be tempted.*"—The complement of the verb *returned* would be: *from the Jordan* (ἀπό) *into Galilee* (εἰς). But this complex government is so distributed, that the first part is found in ver. 1 (the ἀπό without the εἰς), and the second in ver. 14 (the εἰς without the ἀπό). The explanation of this construction is, that the temptation was an interruption in the return of Jesus from the Jordan into Galilee. The Spirit detained Him in Judæa.—The T. R. reads εἰς, "led *into* the wilderness;" the Alex. ἐν, "led (carried hither and thither) *in* the wilderness." We might suppose that this second reading was only the result of the very natural reflection that, John being already in the desert, Jesus had not *to repair thither.* But, on the other hand, the received reading may easily have been imported into Luke from the two other Syn. And the prep. of rest (ἐν) in the Alex. better accords with the imperf. ἤγετο, *was led,* which denotes a continuous action.—The expression, *was led by,* indicates that the severe exercises of soul which Jesus experienced under the action of the Spirit absorbed Him in such a way, that the use of His faculties in regard to the external world was thereby suspended. In going into the desert, He was not impelled by a desire to accomplish any definite object; it was only, as it were, a cover for the state of intense meditation in which He was absorbed. Lost in contemplation of His personal relation to God, the full consciousness of which He had just attained, and of the consequent task it imposed upon Him in reference to Israel and the world, His heart sought to make these recent revelations wholly its own. —If tradition is to be credited, the *wilderness* here spoken of was the mountainous and uninhabited country bordering on the road which ascends from Jericho to Jerusalem. On the right of this road, not far from Jericho, there rises a limestone peak, exceedingly sharp and abrupt, which bears the name of

Quarantania. The rocks which surround it are pierced by a number of caves. This would be the scene of the temptation. We are ignorant whether this tradition rests upon any historical fact. This locality is a continuation of the desert of Judæa, where John abode.

The words *forty days* may refer either to *was led* or to *being tempted;* in sense both come to the same thing, the two actions being simultaneous. According to Luke and Mark, Jesus was incessantly besieged during this whole time. Suggestions of a very different nature from the holy thoughts which usually occupied Him harassed the working of His mind. Matthew does not mention this secret action of the enemy, who was preparing for the final crisis. How can it be maintained that one of these forms of the narrative has been borrowed from the other?

The term *devil,* employed by Luke and Matthew, comes from *διαβάλλειν, to spread reports, to slander.* Mark employs the word Satan (from שטן, to oppose; Zech. iii. 1, 2; Job i. 6, etc.). The first of these names is taken from the relation of this being to men; the second from his relations with God.

The possibility of the existence of moral beings of a different nature from that of man cannot be denied *à priori.* Now if these beings are free creatures, subject to a law of probation, as little can it be denied that this probation might issue in a fall. Lastly, since in every society of moral beings there are eminent individuals who, by virtue of their ascendency, become centres around which a host of inferior individuals group themselves, this may also be the case in this unknown spiritual domain. Keim himself says: "We regard this question of the existence of an evil power as altogether an open question for science." This question, which is an open one from a scientific point of view, is settled in the view of faith by the testimony of the Saviour, who, in a passage in which there is not the slightest trace of accommodation to popular prejudice, John viii. 44, delineates in a few graphic touches the moral position of Satan. In another passage, Luke xxii. 31, "*Satan hath desired to have you, that he may sift you as wheat; but I have prayed for thee, that thy faith fail not,*" Jesus lifts the veil which hides from us the scenes of the invisible world; the relation which He maintains between the accuser Satan, and Himself the intercessor, implies that in His eyes this personage is no less a personal being than Himself. The part sustained by this being in the temptation of Jesus is attested by the passage, Luke xi. 21, 22. It was necessary that *the strong man,* Satan, the prince of this world, should be vanquished by his adversary, *the stronger than he,* in a personal conflict, for the latter to be able to set about spoiling the world, which is Satan's stronghold. Weizsäcker and Keim[1] acknowledge an allusion in this passage to the fact of the temptation. It is this victory in single combat which makes the deliverance of every captive of Satan possible to Jesus.

Luke mentions Jesus' abstinence from food for six weeks as a fact which was only the natural consequence of His being absorbed in profound meditation. To Him, indeed, this whole time passed like a single hour; He did not even feel the pangs of hunger. This follows from the words: "And when they were ended, *He afterward hungered.*" By the term νηστεύσας *having fasted,* Matthew appears to give this abstinence the character of a deliberate ritual act, to make it such a fast as, among the Jews, ordinarily accompanied certain seasons devoted specially to prayer. This shade of thought is not a contradiction, but accords with the general character of the two narrations, and becomes a significant indication of their originality.—The fasts of Moses and Elijah, in similar circumstances, lasted the same time. In certain morbid conditions, which involve a more or less entire abstinence from food, a period of six weeks generally brings about a crisis, after which the demand for nourishment is renewed with extreme urgency. The exhausted body becomes a prey to a deathly sinking. Such, doubtless, was the condition of Jesus; He felt Himself dying. It was the moment the tempter had waited for to make his decisive assault.

2*d*. Vers. 3, 4.[2]—First Temptation.—The text of Luke is very sober: *The devil said to Him.* The encounter exhibited under this form may be explained as a contact of *mind* with *mind;* but in Matthew, the expression *came to Him* seems to imply a bodily appearance. This, however, is not necessarily its meaning. This term may be regarded as a symbolical expression of the moral sensation experienced by Jesus at the moment when He felt the attack of this spirit so alien from His own. In this sense, the coming took place only in the spiritual sphere. Since Scripture does not mention any visible appearance of Satan, and as the angelophanies are facts the

[1] *Untersuch.* p. 330; *Gesch. Jesu,* t. i. p. 570.

[2] Ver. 4. ℵ. B. L. omit λεγων.—9 Mjj. 70 Mnn. Or. omit ο before ανθρωπος.—ℵ. B. L. Cop. omit the words, αλλ' επι παντι ρηματι Θεου, which is the reading of T. R. with 15 Mjj., all the Mnn. Syr. It. Vg. (taken from Matthew).

perception of which always implies a co-operation of the inner sense, the latter interpretation is more natural.—The words, *if thou art,* express something very different from a doubt; this *if* has almost the force of *since:* "If thou art really, as it seems . . ." Satan alludes to God's salutation at the baptism. M. de Pressensé is wrong in paraphrasing the words: "If thou art the Messiah." Here, and invariably, the name *Son of God* refers to a personal relation, not to an office (see on ver. 22).—But what criminality would there have been in the act suggested to Jesus? It has been said that He was not allowed to use His miraculous power for His own benefit. Why not, if He was allowed to use it for the benefit of others? The moral law does not command that one should love his neighbour better than himself. It has been said that He would have acted from His own will, God not having commanded this miracle. But did God direct every act of Jesus by means of a positive command? Had not divine direction in Jesus a more spiritual character? Satan's address and the answer of Jesus put us on the right track. In saying to Him, *If thou art the Son of God,* Satan seeks to arouse in His heart the feeling of His divine greatness; and with what object? He wishes by this means to make Him feel more painfully the contrast between His actual destitution, consequent on His human condition, and the abundance to which His divine nature seems to give Him a right. There was indeed, especially after His baptism, an anomaly in the position of Jesus. On the one hand, He had been exalted to a distinct consciousness of His dignity as the Son of God; while, on the other, His condition as Son of man remained the same. He continued this mode of existence wholly similar to ours, and wholly dependent, in which form it was His mission to realize here below the filial life. Thence there necessarily resulted a constant temptation to elevate, by acts of power, His miserable condition to the height of His conscious Sonship. And this is the first point of attack by which Satan seeks to master His will, taking advantage for this purpose of the utter exhaustion in which he sees Him sinking.—Had Jesus yielded to this suggestion, He would have violated the conditions of that earthly existence to which, out of love to us, He had submitted, denied His title as Son of man, in order to realize before the time His condition as Son of God, retracted in some sort the act of His incarnation, and entered upon that false path which was afterwards formulated by *docetism* in a total or partial denial of *Christ come in the flesh.* Such a course would have made His humanity a mere appearance.

This is precisely what is expressed in His answer. The word of holy writ, Deut. viii. 3, in which He clothes His thought, is admirably adapted, both in form and substance, to this purpose: *Man shall not live by bread alone.* This term, *man,* recalls to Satan the form of existence which Jesus has accepted, and from which He cannot depart on His own responsibility.—The omission of the article ὁ before ἄνθρωπος in nine Mjj. gives this word a generic sense which suits the context. But Jesus, while thus asserting His entire acceptance of human nature, reminds Satan that man, though he be but man, is not left without divine succour. The experience of Israel in the wilderness, to which Moses' words refer, proves that the action of divine power is not limited to the ordinary nourishment of bread. God can support human existence by other material means, such as manna and quails; He can even, if He pleases, make a man live by the mere power of His will. This principle is only the application of a living monotheism to the sphere of physical life. By proclaiming it in this particular instance, Jesus declares that, in His career, no physical necessity shall ever compel Him to deny, in the name of His exalted Sonship, the humble mode of existence He adopted in making Himself man, until it shall please God Himself to transform His condition by rendering it suitable to His essence as Son of God. Although Son, He will nevertheless remain subject, subject unto the weakness even of death (Heb. v. 8).—The words, *but by every word of God,* are omitted by the Alex.; they are probably taken from Matthew. What reason could there have been for omitting them from the text of Luke? By their suppression, the answer of Jesus assumes that brief and categorical character which agrees with the situation.—The sending of the angels to minister to Jesus, which Matthew and Mark mention at the close of their narrative, proves that the expectation of Jesus was not disappointed; God sustained Him, as He had sustained Elijah in the desert in similar circumstances (1 Kings xix.)

The first temptation refers to *the person* of Jesus; the second, to *His work.*

3*d.* Vers. 5–8.[1]—Second Temptation.—The occasion of this fresh trial is not a physical sensation; it is an aspiration of the soul. Man, created in the image of God, aspires to reign. This instinct, the direction of which is perverted by selfishness, is none the less legitimate in its origin. It received in Israel, through the divine promises, a definite aim—the supremacy of the elect people over all others; and a very precise form—the Messianic hope. The patriotism of Jesus was kindled at this fire (xiii. 34, xix. 41); and He must have known, from what He had heard from the mouth of God at His baptism, that it was He who was destined to realize this magnificent expectation. It is this prospect, open before the gaze of Jesus, of which Satan avails himself in trying to fascinate and seduce Him into a false way.—The words *the devil,* and *into an high mountain,* ver. 5, are omitted by the Alex. It might be supposed that this omission arises from the confusion of the two syllables *ον* which terminate the words *αὐτόν* and *ὑψηλόν.* But is it not easier to believe there has been an interpolation from Matthew? In this case, the complement understood to *taking Him up,* in Luke, might doubtless be, as in Matthew, a mountain. Still, where no complement is expressed, it is more natural to explain it as "taking Him *into the air.*" It is not impossible that this difference between the two evangelists is connected with the different order in which they arrange the two last temptations. In Luke, Satan, after having taken Jesus up into the air, set Him down on a pinnacle of the temple. This order is natural.—We are asked how Jesus could be given over in this way to the disposal of Satan. Our reply is: Since the Spirit led Him into the wilderness in order that He might be tempted, it is not surprising that He should be given up for a time, body and soul, to the power of the tempter.—It is not said that Jesus really *saw* all the kingdoms of the earth, which would be absurd; but

[1] Ver. 5. ℵ. B. D. L. some Mnn. omit ὁ διαβολος.—ℵ. B. L. It^aliq^. omit εις ορος υψηλον, which is the reading of T. R. with 14 Mjj. the Mnn. Syr. It^aliq^.—Ver. 7. All the Mjj. read πασα instead of παντα, the reading of T. R. with only some Mnn.—Ver. 8. ℵ. B. D. L. Z. several Mnn. Syr. It^plerique^, Vg. omit the words υπαγε οπισω μου Σατανα.—Γαρ, in the T. R., has in its favour only U. Wb. Δ. Λ.

that Satan *showed* them to Him. This term may very well signify that he made them appear before the view of Jesus, in instantaneous succession, by a diabolical phantasmagoria. He had seen so many great men succumb to a similar mirage, that he might well hope to prevail again by this means.—The Jewish idea of Satan's rule over this visible world, expressed in the words which two of the evangelists put into his mouth, may not be so destitute of foundation as many think. Has not Jesus endorsed it, by calling this mysterious being *the prince of this world?* Might not Satan, as an archangel, have had assigned to him originally as his domain the earth and the system to which it belongs? In this case, he uttered no falsehood when he said, All this power *has been delivered unto me* (ver. 6). The truth of this asssertion appears further from this very expression, in which he does homage to the sovereignty of God, and acknowledges himself His vassal. Neither is it necessary to see imposture in the words: *And to whomsoever I will, I give it.* God certainly leaves to Satan a certain use of His sovereignty and powers; he reigns over the whole extra-divine sphere of human life, and has power to raise to the pinnacle of glory the man whom he favours. The majesty of such language was doubtless sustained by splendour of appearance on the part of him who used it; and if ever Satan put on his form of *an angel of light* (2 Cor. xi. 14), it was at this moment which decided his empire.—The condition which he attaches to the surrender of his power into the hands of Jesus, ver. 7, has often been presented as a snare far too coarse for it ever to have been laid by such a crafty spirit. Would not, indeed, the lowest of the Israelites have rejected such a proposal with horror? But there is a little word in the text to be taken into consideration—*οὖν*, *therefore*—which puts this condition in logical connection with the preceding words. It is not as an individual, it is as the representative of divine authority on this earth, that Satan here claims the homage of Jesus. The act of prostration, in the East, is practised towards every lawful superior, not in virtue of his personal character, but out of regard to the portion of divine power of which he is the depositary. For behind every power is ever seen the power of God, from whom it emanates. As man, Jesus formed part of the domain entrusted to Satan. As called to succeed him, it seemed He could only do it, in so far as Satan himself should transfer to Him the investiture of his office. The words, *if thou wilt worship me,* are not therefore an appeal to the ambition of Jesus; they express the condition *sine quâ non* laid down by the ancient Master of the world to the installation of Jesus in the Messianic sovereignty. In speaking thus, Satan deceived himself only in one point; this was, that the kingdom which was about to commence was in any respect a continuation of his own, or depended on a transmission of power from him. It would have been very different, doubtless, had Jesus proposed to realize such a conception of the Messianic kingdom as found expression in the popular prejudice of His age. The Israelitish monarchy, thus understood, would really have been only a new and transient form of the kingdom of Satan on this earth,—a kingdom of external force, a kingdom *of this world.* But what Jesus afterwards expressed in these words, "I am a King; to this end was I born, but my kingdom is not of this world" (John xviii. 37, 36), was already in His heart. His kingdom was the beginning of a rule of an entirely new nature; or, if this kingdom had an antecedent, it was that established by God in Zion (Ps. ii.). Jesus had just at this very time been invested with this at the hands of the divine delegate, John the Baptist. Therefore He had nothing to ask from Satan, and consequently no homage to pay him. This refusal was a serious matter. Jesus thereby renounced all power founded upon material means and social institutions. He broke with the Messianic Jewish ideal under the received form. He confined Himself, in accomplishing the conquest of the world, to spiritual action exerted upon souls; He condemned Himself to gain them one by one, by the labour of conversion and sanctification,—a gentle, unostentatious progress, contemptible in the eyes of the flesh, of which the end, the visible reign, was only to appear after the lapse of centuries. Further, such an answer was a declaration of war against Satan, and on the most unfavourable conditions. Jesus condemned Himself to struggle, unaided by human power, with an adversary having at his disposal all human powers; to march with ten thousand men against a king who was coming against Him with twenty thousand (xiv. 31). Death inevitably awaited Him in this path. But He unhesitatingly accepted all this, that He might remain faithful to God, from whom alone He determined to receive everything. To render homage to a being who had broken with God, would be to honour him in his guilty usurpation, to associate Himself with his rebellion. —This time again Jesus conveys His refusal in a passage of holy writ, Deut. vi. 13; He thereby removes every appearance of answering him on mere human authority. The Hebrew text and the LXX. merely say: "Thou shalt fear the Lord, and thou shalt *serve Him*." But it is obvious that this word *serve* includes adoration, and therefore the act of *προσκυνεῖν*, *falling down in worship*, by which it is expressed. The words, *Get thee behind me, Satan,* in Luke, are taken from Matthew; so is the *for* in the next sentence.—But in thus determining to establish His kingdom without any aid from material force, was not Jesus relying so much the more on a free use of the supernatural powers with which He had just been endowed, in order to overcome, by great miraculous efforts, the obstacles and dangers to be encountered in the path He had chosen? This is the point on which Satan puts Jesus to a last proof. The third temptation then refers to the use which He intends to make of divine power in the course of His Messianic career.

4*th*. Vers. 9–12.[1]—Third Temptation.—This trial belongs to a higher sphere than that of physical or political life. It is of a purely religious character, and touches the deepest and most sacred relations of Jesus with His Father. The dignity of a son of God, with a view to which man was created, carries with it the free disposal of divine power, and of the motive forces of the universe. Does not God Himself say to His child: "Son, thou art ever with me, *and all that I have is thine*"? (xv. 31). But in proportion as man is raised to this filial position, and gradually reaches divine fellowship, there arises out of this state an ever-increasing danger,—that of abusing his great privilege, by changing, as an indiscreet inferior is tempted to do, this fellowship into familiarity. From this giddy height to which the grace of God has raised him, man falls, therefore, in an instant into the deepest abyss —into a presumptuous use of God's gifts and abuse of His

[1] Ver. 9. The *ὁ* before *υἱος* in the T. R. is omitted in all the Mjj. and in 150 Mnn.

confidence. This pride is more unpardonable than that called in Scripture *the pride of life.* The abuse of God's help is a more serious offence than not waiting for it in faith (first temptation), or than regarding it as insufficient (second temptation).—The higher sphere to which this trial belongs is indicated by the scene of it—the most sacred place, Jerusalem (*the holy city,* as Matthew says) and the temple. The term πτερύγιον τοῦ ἱεροῦ, translated *pinnacle of the temple,* might denote the anterior extremity of the line of meeting of two inclined planes, forming the roof of the sacred edifice. But in this case, ναοῦ would have been required rather than ἱεροῦ (see i. 9). Probably, therefore, it is some part of the court that is meant,—either *Solomon's Porch,* which was situated on the eastern side of the temple platform, and commanded the gorge of the Kedron, or the *Royal Porch,* built on the south side of this platform, and from which, as Josephus says, the eye looked down into an abyss. The word πτερύγιον would denote the *coping* of this peristyle. Such a position is a type of the sublime height to which Satan sees Jesus raised, and whence he would have Him cast Himself down into an abyss.

The idea of this incomparable spiritual elevation is expressed by these words: *If thou art a Son of God.* The Alex. rightly omit the art. before the word *Son.* For it is a question here of the *filial character,* and not of the personality of the Son. "If thou art a being to whom it appertains to call God *thy Father* in a unique sense, do not fear to do a daring deed, and give God an opportunity to show the particular care He takes of thee." And as Satan had observed that Jesus had twice replied to him by the word of God, he tries in his turn to avail himself of this weapon. He applies here the promise (Ps. xci. 11, 12) by an *à fortiori* argument: "If God has promised thus to keep the righteous, how much more His well-beloved Son!" The quotation agrees with the text of the LXX., with the exception of its omitting the words *in all thy ways,* which Matthew also omits; the latter omits, besides, the preceding words, *to keep thee.* It has been thought that this omission was made by Satan himself, who would suppress these words with a view to make the application of the passage more plausible, unduly generalizing the promise of the Psalm, which, according to the context, applies to the righteous only in so far as he walks *in the ways of obedience.* This is very subtle.—What was the real bearing of this temptation? With God, power is always employed in the service of goodness, of love; this is the difference between God and Satan, between divine miracle and diabolical sorcery. Now the devil in this instance aims at nothing less than making Jesus pass from one of these spheres to the other, and this in the name of that most sacred and tender element in the relationship between two beings that love each other—confidence. If Jesus succumbs to the temptation by calling on the Almighty to deliver Him from a peril into which He has not been thrown in the service of goodness, He puts God in the position of either refusing His aid, and so separating His cause from His own—a divorce between the Father and the Son—or of setting free the exercise of His omnipotence, at least for a moment, from the control of holiness,—a violation of His own nature. Either way, it would be all over with Jesus, and even, if we dare so speak, with God.

Jesus characterizes the impious nature of this suggestion as a *tempting God*, ver. 12. This term signifies putting God to the alternative either of acting in a way opposed to His plans or His nature, or of compromising the existence or safety of a person closely allied to Him. It is confidence carried to such presumption, as to become treason against the divine majesty. It has sometimes been thought that Satan wanted to induce Jesus to establish His kingdom by some miraculous demonstration, by some prodigy of personal display, which, accomplished in the view of a multitude of worshippers assembled in the temple, would have drawn to Him the homage of all Israel. But the narrative makes no allusion to any effect to be produced by this miracle. It is a question here of a whim rather than of a calculation, of divine force placed at the service of caprice rather than of a deliberate evil purpose.—For the third time, Jesus borrows the form of His reply from Scripture, and, which is remarkable, again from Deuteronomy (vi. 16). This book, which recorded the experience of Israel during the forty years' sojourn in the desert, had perhaps been the special subject of Jesus' meditations during His own sojourn in the wilderness. The plural, *ye shall not tempt*, in the O. T. is changed by Jesus into the singular, *thou shalt not tempt.* Did this change proceed from a double meaning which Jesus designedly introduced into this passage? While applying it to Himself in His relation to God, He seems, in fact, to apply it at the same time to Satan in relation to Himself; as if He meant to say: Desist, therefore, now from tempting *me*, thy God.

Almost all interpreters at the present day disapprove the order followed by Luke, and prefer Matthew's, who makes this last temptation the second. It seems to me, that if the explanation we have just given is just, there can be no doubt that Luke's order is preferable. The man who is no longer man, the Christ who is no longer Christ, the Son who is no longer Son,—such are the three degrees of the temptation.[1] The second might appear the most exalted and dangerous to men who had grown up in the midst of the theocracy; and it is intelligible that the tradition found in the Jewish-Christian Churches, the type of which has been preserved in the first Gospel, should have made this peculiarly Messianic temptation (the second in Luke) the crowning effort of the conflict. But in reality it was not so; the true order *historically*, in a moral conflict, must be that which answers to the moral essence of things.

5th. Ver. **13**. Historical Conclusion.—The expression *πάντα πειρασμόν* does not signify *all the* temptation (this would require *ὅλον*), but *every kind* of temptation. We have seen that the temptations mentioned refer, one to the person of Jesus, another to the nature of His work, the third to His use of the divine aid accorded to Him for this work; they are therefore very varied. Further, connected as they are, they form a complete cycle; and this is expressed in the term *συντελέσας*, *having finished, fulfilled.* Nevertheless Luke announces, in the conclusion of his narrative, the future return of Satan to subject Jesus to a fresh trial. If the words *ἄχρι καιροῦ* signified, as they are often translated, *for a season,* we might think that this future temptation denotes in general the trials to which Jesus would be exposed during the course of His ministry. But these words signify, *until a favourable time.* Satan expects, therefore, some new opportunity, just such a special occasion as the

[1] [M. Godet is not as perspicuous here as usual The original is: "*L'homme qui n'est plus homme, le Christ qui n'est plus Christ, le Fils qui n'est plus Fils, voila . . .*"]

previous one. This conflict, foretold so precisely, can be none other than that of Gethsemane. "This is *the hour and power of darkness*," said Jesus at that very time (xxii. 53); and a few moments before, according to John (xiv. 30), He had said. "*The prince of this world* cometh." Satan then found a new means of acting on the soul of Jesus, through the fear of suffering. Just as in the desert he thought he could dazzle this heart, that had had no experience of life, with the *éclat* of success and the intoxication of *delight;* so in Gethsemane he tried to make it swerve by the nightmare of punishment and the anguish of grief. These, indeed, are the two levers by which he succeeds in throwing men out of the path of obedience.

Luke omits here the fact mentioned by Matthew and Mark, of the approach of angels to minister to Jesus. It is no dogmatic repugnance which makes him omit it, for he mentions an instance wholly similar, xxii. 43. Therefore he was ignorant of it; and consequently he was not acquainted with the two other narratives.

THE TEMPTATION

We shall examine—1*st.* The nature of this fact; 2*d.* Its object, 3*d.* The three narratives.

1*st. Nature of the Temptation.* —The ancients generally understood this account *literally.* They believed that the devil appeared to Jesus in a bodily form, and actually carried Him away to the mountain and to the pinnacle of the temple. But, to say nothing of the impossibility of finding anywhere a mountain from which all the kingdoms of the world could be seen, the Bible does not mention a single visible appearance of Satan; and in the conflict of Gethsemane, which, according to Luke, is a renewal of this, the presence of the enemy is not projected into the world of sense.—Have we to do then here, as some moderns have thought, with a *human* tempter designated metaphorically by the name Satan, in the sense in which Jesus addressed Peter, "Get thee behind me, Satan," with an envoy from the Sanhedrim, *ex gr.*, who had come to test Him (Kuinoel), or with the deputation from the same body mentioned in John i. 19 et seq., who, on their return from their interview with the forerunner, met Jesus in the desert, and there besought His Messianic co-operation, by offering Him the aid of the Jewish authorities (Lange)? But it was not until after Jesus had already left the desert and rejoined John on the banks of the Jordan, that He was publicly pointed out by the latter as the Messiah.[1] Up to this time

[1] See my *Commentary on the Gospel of John,* on i. 29.

no one knew Him as such. Besides, if this hypothesis affords a sufficient explanation of the second temptation (in the order of Luke), it will not explain either the first or the third.

Was this narrative, then, originally nothing more than a moral lesson conveyed in the form of a *parable*, in which Jesus inculcated on His disciples some most important maxims for their future ministry? Never to use their miraculous power for their personal advantage, never to associate with wicked men for the attainment of good ends, never to perform a miracle in an ostentatious spirit,—these were the precepts which Jesus had enjoined upon them in a figurative manner, but which they took literally (Schleiermacher, Schweizer, Bleek). But, first of all, is it conceivable that Jesus should have expressed Himself so awkwardly as to lead to such a mistake? Next, how could He have spoken to the apostles of an external empire to be founded by them? Further, the Messianic aspect, so conspicuous in the second temptation, is completely disguised in that one of the three maxims which, according to the explanation of these theologians, ought to correspond with it. Baumgarten-Crusius, in order to meet this last objection, applies the three maxims, not to that from which the apostles were to abstain, but to that which they must not expect from Jesus Himself: "As Messiah, Jesus meant to say, I shall not seek to satisfy your sensual appetites, your ambitious aspirations, nor your thirst for miracles." But all this kind of interpretation meets with an insurmountable obstacle in Mark's narrative, where mention is made merely of the sojourn in the desert, and of the temptation *in general*, without the three particular tests, that is, according to this opinion, without the really significant portion of the information being even mentioned. According to this, Mark would have lost the kernel and retained only the shell, or, as Keim says, "kept the flesh while rejecting the skeleton." In transforming the parable into history, the evangelist would have omitted precisely that which contained the idea of the parable.—Usteri, who had at one time adopted the preceding view, was led by these difficulties to regard this narrative as a *myth* emanating from the Christian consciousness; and Strauss tried to explain the origin of this legend by the Messianic notions current among the Jews. But the latter has not succeeded in producing, from the Jewish theology, a single passage earlier than the time of Jesus in which the idea of a personal conflict between the Messiah and Satan is expressed. As to the Christian consciousness, would it have been capable of creating complete in all its parts a narrative so mysterious and profound? Lastly, the remarkably fixed place which this event occupies in the three synoptics between the baptism of Jesus and the commencement of His ministry, proves that this element of the evangelical history belongs to the earliest form of Christian instruction. It could not therefore be the product of a later legendary creation.

Unless all these indications are delusive, the narrative of the temptation must correspond with a real fact in the life of the Saviour. But might it not be the description of a purely *moral* struggle—of a struggle that was confined to the soul of Jesus? Might not the temptation be a vision occasioned by the state of exaltation resulting from a prolonged fast, in which the brilliant image of the Jewish Messiah was presented to His imagination under the most seductive forms? (Eichhorn, Paulus.) Or might not this narrative be a condensed summary of a long series of intense meditations, in which, after having opened His soul with tender sympathy to all the aspirations of His age and people, Jesus had decidedly broken with them, and determined, with a full knowledge of the issue, to become solely the Messiah of God? (Ullmann.) In the first case, the heart whence came this carnal dream could no longer be the heart of the Holy One of God, and the perfectly pure life and conscience of Jesus become inexplicable. As to the second form in which this opinion is presented, it contains undoubtedly elements of truth. The last two temptations certainly correspond with the most prevalent and ardent aspirations of the Jewish people—the expectation of a political Messiah, and the thirst for external signs (σημεῖα αἰτεῖν, 1 Cor. i. 22). 1. But how, from this point of view, is the first temptation to be explained? 2. How could the figure of a personal tempter find its way into such a picture? How did it become its predominating feature, so as to form almost the entire picture in Mark's narrative? 3. Have we not the authentic comment of Jesus Himself on this conflict in the passage xi. 21, 22, already referred to (p. 210)? In describing this victory over *the strong man* by *the man stronger than he*, and laying it down as a condition absolutely indispensable to the spoiling of the stronghold of the former, did not Jesus allude to a *personal* conflict between Himself and the prince of this world, such as we find portrayed in the narrative of the temptation? For these reasons, Keim, while he recognises in the temptation, with Ullmann, a sublime fact in the moral life of Jesus, an energetic determination of His will by which He absolutely renounced any deviation whatever from the divine will, notwithstanding the insufficiency of human means, confesses that he cannot refuse to admit the possibility of the existence and interposition of the representative of the powers of evil.

Here we reach the only explanation which, in our opinion, can account for the narrative of the temptation. As there is a mutual contact of bodies, so also, in a higher sphere than that of matter, there is an action and reaction of spirits on each other. It was in this higher sphere to which Jesus was raised, that He, the representative of voluntary dependence and filial love to God, met that spirit in whom the autonomy of the creature finds its most resolute representative, and in every way, and notwithstanding all this spirit's craft, maintained by conscientious choice His own ruling principle. This victory decided the fate of mankind; it became the foundation of the establishment of God's kingdom upon earth. This is the essential significance of this event. As to the narrative in which this mysterious scene has been disclosed to us, it must be just a symbolical picture, by means of which Jesus endeavoured to make His disciples understand a fact which, from its very nature, could only be fitly described in figurative language. Still we must remember, that Jesus being really man, having His spirit united to a body, He needed, quite as much as we do, sensible representations as a means of apprehending spiritual facts. Metaphorical language was as natural in His case as in ours. In all probability, therefore, it was necessary, in order to His fully entering into the conflict between Himself and the tempter, that it should assume the scenic (*plastique*) form in which it has been preserved to us. While saying this, we do not think that Jesus was transported bodily by Satan through the air. We believe that, had He been observed by any spectator whilst the temptation was going on, He would have appeared all through it motionless upon the soil of the desert. But though the conflict did not pass out of the *spiritual* sphere, it was none the less real, and the value of this victory was not less incalculable and decisive. This view, with some slight shades of difference, is that advocated by Theodore of Mopsuestia in the ancient Church, by some of the Reformers, and by several modern commentators (Olshausen, Neander, Oosterzee, Pressensé, etc.).

But could Jesus be really *tempted*, if He was holy? could He *sin*, if He was the Son of God? *fail* in His work, if He was the Redeemer appointed by God? As a holy being, He could be tempted, because a conflict might arise between some legitimate bodily want or normal desire of the soul, and the divine will, which for the time forbade its satisfaction. The Son could sin, since He had renounced His divine mode of existence *in the form of God* (Phil. ii. 6), in order to enter into a human condition altogether like ours. The Redeemer might succumb, if the question be regarded from the standpoint of His personal liberty; which is quite consistent with God being assured by His foreknowledge that He would stand firm. This foreknowledge was one of the factors of His plan, precisely as the foreknowledge of the faith of believers is one of the elements of His eternal πρόθεσις (Rom. viii. 28).

2*d*. *Object of the Temptation.*—The temptation is the complement of the baptism. It is the *negative* preparation of Jesus for His ministry, as the baptism was His *positive* preparation. In His baptism Jesus received impulse, calling, strength. By the temptation He was made distinctly conscious of the errors to be shunned, and the perils to be feared, on the right hand and on the left. The temptation was the last act of His moral education; it gave Him an insight into all the ways in which His Messianic work could possibly be marred. If, from the very first step in His arduous career, Jesus kept the path marked out by God's will without deviation, change, or hesitancy, this bold front and stedfast perseverance are certainly due to His experience of the temptation. All the wrong courses possible to Him were thenceforth known; all the rocks had been observed; and it was the enemy himself who had rendered Him this service. And it was for this reason that God apparently delivered Him for a brief time into his power. This is just what Matthew's narrative expresses so forcibly: "He was led up of the Spirit . . . *to be tempted.*" When He left this school, Jesus distinctly understood that, as respects His *person*, no act of His ministry was to have any tendency to lift it out of His human condition; that, as to His work, it was to be in no way assimilated to the action of the powers of this world; and that in the *employment* of divine power, filial liberty was never to become caprice, not even under a pretext of blind trust in the help of God. And this programme was carried out. His material wants were supplied by the gifts of charity (viii. 3), not by miracles; His mode of life was nothing else than a perpetual humiliation—a prolongation, so to speak, of His incarnation. When labouring to establish His kingdom, He unhesitatingly refused the aid of human power,—as, for instance, when the multitude wished to make Him a king (John vi. 15); and His ministry assumed the character of an exclusively spiritual conquest. He abstained, lastly, from every miracle which had not for its immediate design the revelation of moral perfection, that is to say, of the glory of His Father (Luke xi. 29). These supreme rules of the Messianic activity were all learnt in that school of trial through which God caused Him to pass in the desert.

3*d*. *The Narratives of the Temptation.*—It has been maintained that, since John does not relate the temptation, he *de facto* denies it. But, as we have already observed, the starting-point of his narrative belongs to a later time.—The narrative of Mark (i. 12, 13) is very summary indeed. It occupies in some respects a middle place between the other two, approaching Matthew's in the preface and close (the ministration of the angels), and Luke's in the extension of the temptation to forty days. But it differs from both in omitting the three particular temptations, and by the addition of the incident of the wild beasts. Here arises, for those who maintain that one of our Gospels was the source of the other, or of both the others, the following dilemma: Either the original narrative is Mark's, which the other two have amplified (Meyer), or Mark has given a summary of the two others (Bleek). There is yet a third alternative, by which Holtzmann escapes this dilemma: There was an original Mark, and its account was transferred *in extenso* into Luke and Matthew, but abridged by our canonical Mark. This last supposition appears to us inadmissible; for if Matthew and Luke drew from *the same* written source, how did the strange reversal in the order of the two temptations happen? Schleiermacher supposes — and modern criticism approves the suggestion (Holtzmann, p. 213)—that Luke altered the order of Matthew in order not to change the scene so frequently, by making Jesus leave the desert (for the temple), and then return to it (for the mountain). We really wonder how men can seriously put forward such puerilities. Lastly, if the three evangelists drew from the same source, the Proto-Mark, whence is the mention of the wild beasts in our canonical Mark derived? The evangelist cannot have imagined it without any authority; and if it was mentioned in the common source, it could not have been passed over, as Holtzmann admits (p. 70), by Luke and Matthew. The explanation of the latter critic being set aside, there remains the original dilemma. Have Matthew and Luke amplified Mark? How then does it happen that they coincide, not only in that part which they have in common with Mark, but quite as much, and even more, in that which is wanting in Mark (the detail of the three temptations)? How is it, again, that Matthew confines the temptation to the last moment, in opposition to the narrative of Mark and Luke; that Luke omits the succour brought to Jesus by the angels, contrary to the account of Mark and Matthew; and that Luke and Matthew omit the detail of the wild beasts, in opposition to their source, the narrative of Mark? They amplify, and yet they abridge! On the other hand, is Mark a compiler from Matthew and Luke? How, then, is it that he says not a word about the forty days' fast? It is alleged that he desires to avoid long discourses. But this lengthened fast belongs to the facts, not to the words. Besides, whence does he get the fact about the wild beasts? He abridges, and yet he amplifies!

All these difficulties which arise out of this hypothesis, and which can only be removed by supposing that the evangelists used their authorities in an inconceivably arbitrary way, disappear of themselves, if we admit, as the common source of the three narratives, an oral tradition which circulated in the Church, and reproduced, more or less exactly, the original account given by Jesus and transmitted by the apostles. Mark only wished to give a brief account, which was all that appeared to him necessary for his readers. The preaching of Peter to Cornelius (Acts x. 37 et seq.) furnishes an example of this mode of condensing the traditional accounts. Mark had perhaps heard the detail relative to the wild beasts from the mouth of Peter himself. The special aim of his narrative is to show us in Jesus the holy man raised to his original dignity, as Lord over nature (the wild beasts), and the friend of heaven (the angels). Matthew has reproduced the apostolic tradition, in the form which it had specially taken in the Jewish-Christian churches. Of this we have two indications: 1. The *ritualistic* character which is given in this narrative to the fasting of Jesus (*having fasted*); 2. The order of the last two temptations, according to which the peculiarly Messianic temptation is exhibited as the supreme and decisive act of the conflict. As to Luke, the substance of his narrative is the same apostolic tradition; but he was enabled by certain written accounts, or means of information, to give some details with greater exactness,—to restore, for example, the actual order of the three temptations. We find him here, as usual, more complete than Mark, and more exact, historically speaking, than Matthew.

And now, His position thus made clear, with God for His sure ally, and Satan for His declared adversary, Jesus advances to the field of battle.

THIRD PART.

THE MINISTRY OF JESUS IN GALILEE.

CHAP. IV. 14–IX. 50.

THE three Synoptics all connect the narrative of the Galilæan ministry with the account of the temptation. But the narrations of Matthew and Mark have this peculiarity, that, according to them, the motive for the return of Jesus to Galilee must have been the imprisonment of John the Baptist: "Now when Jesus had heard that John was cast into prison, He departed into Galilee" (Matt. iv. 12); "Now, after that John was put in prison, Jesus came into Galilee" (Mark i. 14). As the temptation does not appear to have been coincident with the apprehension of John, the question arises, Where did Jesus spend the more or less lengthened time that intervened between these two events, and what was He doing during the interval? This is the first difficulty. There is another: How could the apprehension of John the Baptist have induced Jesus to return to Galilee, to the dominions of this very Herod who was keeping John in prison? Luke throws no light whatever on these two questions which arise out of the narrative of the Syn., because he makes no mention in this place of the imprisonment of John, but simply connects the commencement of the ministry of Jesus with the victory He had just achieved in the desert. It is John who gives the solution of these difficulties. According to him, there were *two returns* of Jesus to Galilee, which his narrative distinguishes with the greatest care. The first took place immediately after the baptism and the temptation (i. 44). It was then that He called some young Galilæans to follow Him, who were attached to the forerunner, and shared his expectation of the Messiah. The second is related in chap. iv. 1; John connects it with the Pharisees' jealousy of John the Baptist, which explains the account of the first two Syn. It appears, in fact, according to him, that some of the Pharisees were party to the blow which had struck John, and therefore we can well understand that Jesus would be more distrustful of them than even of Herod.[1] That the Pharisees had a hand in John's imprisonment, is confirmed by the expression *delivered,* which Matthew and Mark employ. It was they who had caused him to be seized and delivered up to Herod.

The two returns mentioned by John were separated by quite a number of events: the transfer of Jesus' place of residence from Nazareth to Capernaum; His first journey to Jerusalem to attend the Passover; the interview with Nicodemus; and a period of prolonged activity in Judæa, simultaneous with that of John the Baptist, who was still enjoying his liberty (John ii. 12–iv. 43). The second return to Galilee, which terminated this long ministry in Judæa, did not take place, according to iv. 35, until the month of December in this same year, so that at least twelve months elapsed between it and the former. The Syn., relating only a single return, must have blended the two into one. Only there is this difference between them, that in Matthew and Mark it is rather the idea of the second which seems to predominate, since they connect it with John's imprisonment; whilst Luke brings out more the idea of the first, for he associates it with the temptation exclusively. The mingling of these two analogous facts—really, however, separated by almost a year—must have taken place previously in the oral tradition, since it passed, though not without some variations, into our three Synoptics. The narrative of John was expressly designed to re-establish this lost distinction (comp. John ii. 11, iii. 24, iv. 54). In this way in the Syn. the interval between these two returns to Galilee disappeared, and the two residences in Galilee, which were separated from each other by this ministry in Judæa, form in them one continuous whole. Further, it is difficult to determine in which of the two to place the several

[1] Bäumlein, *Comment. über das Evang. Joh.* p. 8.

facts which the Syn. relate at the commencement of the Galilæan ministry.

We must not forget that the apostolic preaching, and the popular teaching given in the churches, were directed not by any historical interest, but with a view to the foundation and confirmation of faith. Facts of a similar nature were therefore grouped together in this teaching until they became completely inseparable. We shall see, in the same way, the different journeys to Jerusalem, fused by tradition into a single pilgrimage, placed at the end of Jesus' ministry. Thus the great contrast which prevails in the synoptical narrative between Galilee and Jerusalem is explained. It was only when John, not depending on tradition, but drawing from his own personal recollections, restored to this history its various phases and natural connections, that the complete picture of the ministry of Jesus appeared before the eyes of the Church.

But why did not Jesus commence His activity *in Galilee,* as, according to the Syn., He would seem to have done? The answer to this question is to be found in John iv. 43–45. In that country, where He spent His youth, Jesus would necessarily expect to meet, more than anywhere else, with certain prejudices opposed to the recognition of His Messianic dignity. "A prophet hath no honour *in his own country*" (John iv. 44). This is why He would not undertake His work among His Galilæan fellow-countrymen until after He had achieved some success elsewhere. The reputation which preceded His return would serve to prepare His way amongst them (John iv. 45). He had therefore Galilee in view even during this early activity in Judæa. He foresaw that this province would be the cradle of His Church; for the yoke of pharisaical and sacerdotal despotism did not press so heavily on it as on the capital and its neighbourhood. The chords of human feeling, paralyzed in Judæa by false devotion, still vibrated in the hearts of these mountaineers to frank and stirring appeals, and their ignorance appeared to Him a medium more easily penetrable by light from above than the perverted enlightenment of rabbinical science. Comp. the remarkable passage, x. 21.

It is not easy to make out the *plan* of this part, for it describes a continuous progress without any marked breaks.

it is a picture of the inward and outward progress of the work of Jesus in Galilee. Ritschl is of opinion that the progress of the story is determined by the growing hostility of the adversaries of Jesus; and accordingly he adopts this division: iv. 16–vi. 11, absence of conflict; vi. 12–xi. 54, the hostile attitude assumed by the two adversaries towards each other. But, 1*st*, the first symptoms of hostility break out before vi. 12; 2*d*, the passage ix. 51, which is passed over by the division of Ritschl, is evidently, in the view of the author, one of the principal connecting links in the narrative; 3*d*, the growing hatred of the adversaries of Jesus is only an accident of His work, and in no way the governing motive of its development. It is not there, therefore, that we must seek the principle of the division. The author appears to us to have marked out a route for himself by a series of facts, in which there is a gradation easily perceived. At first Jesus preaches without any following of regular disciples; soon He calls about Him some of the most attentive of His hearers, to make them His permanent disciples; after a certain time, when these disciples had become very numerous, He raises twelve of them to the rank of apostles; lastly, He entrusts these twelve with their first mission, and makes them His evangelists. This gradation in the position of His helpers naturally corresponds, 1*st*, with the internal progress of His teaching; 2*d*, with the local extension of His work; 3*d*, with the increasing hostility of the Jews, with whom Jesus breaks more and more, in proportion as He gives organic form to His own work. It therefore furnishes a measure of the entire movement.—We are guided by it to the following division:—

First Cycle, iv. 14–44, extending to the call of the first disciples.

Second Cycle, v. 1–vi. 11, to the nomination of the twelve.

Third Cycle, vi. 12–viii. 56, to their first mission.

Fourth Cycle, ix. 1–50, to the departure of Jesus for Jerusalem.

At this point the work of Jesus in Galilee comes to an end; He bids adieu to this field of labour, and, setting His face towards Jerusalem, He carries with Him into Judæa the result of His previous labours, His Galilæan Church.

FIRST CYCLE.—CHAP. IV. 14–44.

Visits to Nazareth and to Capernaum.

The following narratives are grouped around two names—*Nazareth* (vers. 14–30) and *Capernaum* (vers. 31–44).

1. *Visit to Nazareth:* vers. 14–30.—This portion opens with a general glance at the commencement of the active labours of Jesus in Galilee: 14, 15. Then, resting on this foundation, but separable from it, as a particular example, we have the narrative of His preaching at Nazareth: vers. 16–30.

1*st.* Vers. 14, 15.—The 14th verse is, as we have shown, the complement of ver. 1 (see ver. 1).—The verb, *he returned,* comprehends, according to what precedes, the two returns mentioned John i. 44 and iv. 1, and even a third, understood between John v. and vi. The words, *in the power of the Spirit,* do not refer, as many have thought, to an impulse from above, which urged Jesus to return to Galilee, but to His possession of the divine powers which He had received at His baptism, and with which He was now about to teach and act; comp. *filled with the Spirit,* ver. 1. Luke evidently means that He returned *different* from what He was when He left. Was this supernatural power of Jesus displayed solely in His preaching, or in miracles also already wrought at this period, though not related by Luke? Since the miracle at Cana took place, according to John, just at this time, we incline to the latter meaning, which, considering the term employed, is also the more natural. In this way, what is said of His fame, which immediately spread *through all the region round about,* is readily explained. Preaching alone would scarcely have been sufficient to have brought about this result. Meyer brings in here the report of the miraculous incidents of the baptism; but these probably had not been witnessed by any one save Jesus and John, and no allusion is made to them subsequently. —The 15th verse relates how, after His reputation had prepared the way for Him, He came *Himself* (αὐτός); then how they all, after hearing Him, ratified the favourable judgment which His fame had brought respecting Him (*glorified of all*). —The synagogues, in which Jesus fulfilled His itinerant ministry, were places of assembly existing from the return of the captivity, perhaps even earlier. (Bleek finds the proof of an earlier date in Ps. lxxiv. 8.) Wherever there was a somewhat numerous Jewish population, even in heathen countries, there were such places of worship. They assembled in them on the Sabbath-day, also on the Monday and Tuesday, and on court and market days. Any one wishing to speak signified his intention by rising (at least according to this passage; comp. also Acts xiii. 16). But as all teaching was founded on the Scriptures, to speak was before anything else *to read.* The reading finished, he taught, sitting down (Acts xiii. 16, Paul speaks standing). Order was maintained by the ἀρχισυνάγωγοι, or presidents of the synagogue. — Vers. 14 and 15 form the fourth definite statement in the account of the development of the person and work of Jesus; comp. ii. 40, 52, and iii. 23.

2*d.* Vers. 16–30.—Jesus did not begin by preaching at Nazareth. In His view, no doubt, the inhabitants of this city stood in much the same relation to the people of the rest of Galilee as the inhabitants of Galilee to the rest of the Jewish people; He knew that in a certain sense His greatest difficulties would be encountered there, and that it would be prudent to defer His visit until the time when His reputation, being already established in the rest of the country, would help to counteract the prejudice resulting from His former lengthened connection with the people of the place.

Vers. 16–19.[1] — *The Reading.* — Ver. 16. *Καί.* "And in these itinerancies He came *also.*" John (ii. 12) and Matthew (iv. 13) refer to this time the transfer of the residence of Jesus (and also, according to John, of that of His mother and brethren) from Nazareth to Capernaum, which naturally implies a visit to Nazareth. Besides, John places the miracle at the marriage at Cana at the same time. Now, Cana being such a very short distance from Nazareth, it would have been an affectation on the part of Jesus to be staying so near His

[1] Ver. 16. T. R., with K. L. Π. many Mnn., Ναζαρετ (ϛ°—ρεθ with 11 Mjj.); D., Ναζαρεδ; ℵ. B.* Z. Ναζαρα; A., Ναζαρατ; Δ., Ναζαραθ.—Ver. 17. A. B. L. Z. Syr. read ανοιξας instead of αναπτυξας, which is the reading of 16 Mjj. Mnn. B. It.—Ver. 18. Twenty Mjj. read ευαγγελισασθαι instead of ευαγγελιζεσθαι, which is the reading of T. R. with merely some Mnn.—Ver. 19. ℵ. B. D. L. Z. It. omit the words ιασασθαι τ. συντετρ. τ. καρδιαν, which is the reading of T. R. with 15 Mjj., the greater part of the Mnn. Syr.

native town, and not visit it.—The words, *where He had been brought up*, assign the motive of His proceeding. The expression, *according to His custom*, cannot apply to the short time which had elapsed since His return to Galilee, unless, with Bleek, we regard it as an indication that this event is of later date, which indeed is possible, but in no way necessary. It rather applies to the period of His childhood and youth. This remark is in close connection with the words, *where He had been brought up.* Attendance at the synagogue was, as Keim has well brought out (t. i. p. 434), a most important instrument in the religious and intellectual development of Jesus. Children had access to this worship from the age of five or six; they were compelled to attend it when they reached thirteen (Keim, t. i. p. 431). But it was not solely by means of these Scripture lessons, heard regularly in the synagogue several times a week, that Jesus learned to know the O. T. so well. There can be no doubt, as Keim says, that He possessed a copy of the sacred book Himself. Otherwise He would not have known how to read, as He is about to do here.—The received reading, *having unrolled*, ver. 17, is preferable to the Alex. var., *having opened.* The sacred volumes were in the form of rectangular sheets, rolled round a cylinder. By the expression, *He found*, Luke gives us to understand that Jesus, surrendering Himself to guidance from above, read at the place where the roll opened of itself.—We cannot then infer, as Bengel does, from the fact of this passage being read by the Jews on the day of atonement, that this feast was being observed on that very day. Besides, the present course of the Haphtaroth, or readings from the prophets, dates from a later period.

This passage belongs to the second part of Isaiah (lxi. 1 et seq.). This long consecutive prophecy is generally applied to the return from the captivity. The only term which would suggest this explanation in our passage is αἰχμαλώτοις, properly *prisoners of war*, ver. 19. But this word is used with a more general meaning. St. Paul applies it to his companions in work and activity (Col. iv. 10). The term πτωχός, *poor*, rather implies that the people are settled in their own country. The remarkable expression, *to proclaim the acceptable year of the Lord*, makes the real thought of the prophet sufficiently clear. There was in the life of the people of Israel a year of grace, which might very naturally become a type of the Messianic era. This was the year of jubilee, which returned every fifty years (Lev. xxv.). By means of this admirable institution, God had provided for a periodical social restoration in Israel. The Israelite who had sold himself into slavery regained his liberty; families which had alienated their patrimony recovered possession; a wide amnesty was granted to persons imprisoned for debt,—so many types of the work of Him who was to restore spiritual liberty to mankind, to free them from their guilt, and restore to them their divine inheritance. Jesus, therefore, could not have received from His Father a text more appropriate to His present position—the inauguration of His Messianic ministry amidst the scenes of His previous life.

The first words, *The Spirit of the Lord is upon me*, are a paraphrase of the term משיח, Messiah (Χριστός, Anointed). Jesus, in reading these words, could not but apply them to His recent baptism.—The expression ἕνεκεν οὗ cannot signify here *wherefore:* "The Spirit is upon me; wherefore God hath anointed me;"—this would be contrary to the meaning. The LXX. have used this conjunction to translate יען, which in the original signifies, just as יען אשר, *because*, a meaning which the Greek expression will also bear (*on this account that, propterea quod*).—On the first day of the year of jubilee, the priests went all through the land, announcing with sound of trumpets the blessings brought by the opening year (*jubilee*, from יבל, *to sound a trumpet*). It is to this proclamation of grace that the words, *to announce good news to the poor*, undoubtedly allude, Lev. xxv. 6, 14, 25.—The words, *to heal the broken in heart*, which the Alex. reading omits, might have been introduced into the text from the O. T.; but, in our view, they form the almost indispensable basis of the word of Jesus, ver. 23. We must therefore retain them, and attribute their omission to an act of negligence occasioned by the long string of infinitives. —The term κηρύξαι ἄφεσιν, *to proclaim liberty*, employed ver 19, also alludes to the solemn proclamation of the jubilee. This word ἄφεσιν is found at almost every verse, in the LXX., in the statute enjoining this feast. Bleek himself observes that the formula קרא דרור, which corresponds to those two Greek terms, is that which is employed in connection with the jubilee; but notwithstanding, this does not prevent his applying the passage, according to the common prejudice, to the return from the captivity! The *prisoners* who recover their freedom are amnestied malefactors as well as slaves set free at the beginning of this year of grace. The image of the *blind* restored to sight does not, at the first glance, accord with that of the jubilee; but it does not any better suit the figure of the return from the captivity. And if this translation of the Hebrew text were accurate, we should have in either case to allow that the prophet had departed from the general image with which he had started. But the term in Isaiah (אסורים, properly *bound*) denotes *captives*, not blind persons. The expression פקח קוח signifies, it is true, the opening of the eyes, not the opening of a prison. But the captives coming forth from their dark dungeon are represented under the figure of blind men suddenly restored to sight.—The words, *to set at liberty them that are bruised*, are taken from another passage in Isaiah (lviii. 6). Probably in Luke's authority this passage was already combined with the former (as often happens with Paul). The figurative sense of **τεθραυσμένοι**, *pierced through*, is required by the verb to *send away*. The *acceptable year* of the Lord is that in which He is pleased to show mankind extraordinary favours. Several Fathers have inferred from this expression that the ministry of Jesus only lasted a single year. This is to confound the type and the antitype.

Vers. 20–22. *The Preaching.*—The description of the assembly, ver. 20, is so dramatic, that it appears to have come from an eye-witness.—The sense of *ἤρξατο*, He began (ver. 21), is not that these were the *first words* of His discourse; this expression describes the solemnity of the moment when, in the midst of a silence resulting from universal attention, the voice of Jesus sounded through the synagogue.—The last words of the verse signify literally, "This word is accomplished in your ears;" in other words, "This preaching to which you are now listening is itself the realization of this prophecy." Such was the text of Jesus' discourse. Luke, without going into His treatment of His theme (comp., for example, Matt. xi. 28–30), passes (ver. 22) to the impression produced. It was generally favourable. The term *bare witness* alludes to the favourable reports which had reached them; they proved for themselves that His fame was not exaggerated. **'Εθαύμαζοι** signifies here, *they were astonished* (John vii. 21; Mark vi. 6), rather than *they admired.* Otherwise the transition to what follows would be too abrupt. So the term *gracious words* describes rather the matter of Jesus' preaching—its description of the works of divine grace—than the impression received by His hearers. They were astonished at this enumeration of marvels hitherto unheard of. The words, *which proceeded forth out of His mouth,* express the fulness with which this proclamation poured forth from His heart.

Two courses were here open to the inhabitants of Nazareth: either to surrender themselves to the divine instinct which, while they listened to this call, was drawing them to Jesus as the Anointed of whom Isaiah spake; or to give place to an intellectual suggestion, allow it to suppress the emotion of the heart, and cause faith to evaporate in criticism. They took the latter course: *Is not this Joseph's son?* Announcements of such importance appeared to them altogether out of place in the mouth of this young man, whom they had known from his childhood. What a contrast between the cold reserve of this question, and the enthusiasm which welcomed Jesus everywhere else (glorified *of all,* ver. 15)! For them this was just such a critical moment as was to occur soon after for the inhabitants of Jerusalem (John ii. 13–22). Jesus sees at a glance the bearing of this remark which went round amongst His hearers: when the impression He has produced ends in a question of curiosity, all is lost; and He tells them so.

Vers. 23–27.[1] *The Colloquy.*—"*And He said to them, Ye will surely say unto me this proverb, Physician, heal thyself; whatsoever we have heard done in Capernaum, do also here in thy country.* 24 *And He said, Verily I say unto you, No prophet is accepted in his own country.* 25 *But I tell you of a truth, many widows were in Israel in the days of Elias, when the heaven was shut up three years and six months, when great famine was throughout all the land;* 26 *But unto none of them was Elias sent, save unto Sarepta, a city of Sidon, unto a woman*

[1] Ver. 23. ℵ. B. D. L. some Mnn. read εις την instead of εν τη.—Ver. 24. Καφαρναουμ in ℵ. B. D. X. It. Vg. instead of Καπερναουμ, which is the reading of T. R. with 15 other Mjj. the Mnn. and Vss. Very nearly the same in the other passages.—Ver. 27. The Mss. are divided between Σιδωνιας (Alex.) and Σιδωνος (T. R. Byz.). Marcion probably placed this verse after xvii. 19.

that was a widow. 27 *And many lepers were in Israel in the time of Eliseus the prophet; and none of them was cleansed, saving Naaman the Syrian.*" The meaning *surely,* which πάντως often has, would be of no force here; it rather means *wholly, nothing less than:* "The question which you have just put to me is only the first symptom of unbelief. From surprise you will pass to derision. Thus you will quickly arrive at the end of the path in which you have just taken the first step."—The term παραβολή, *parable,* denotes any kind of figurative discourse, whether a complete narrative or a short sentence, couched in an image, like proverbs. Jesus had just attributed to Himself, applying Isaiah's words, the office of a restorer of humanity. He had described the various ills from which His hearers were suffering, and directed their attention to Himself as the physician sent to heal them. This is what the proverb cited refers to. (Comp. ἰατρός, a physician, with ἰάσασθαι, *to heal,* ver. 18.) Thus: "You are going even to turn to ridicule what you have just heard, and to say to me, Thou who pretendest to save humanity from its misery, begin by delivering thyself from thine own." But, as thus explained, the proverb does not appear to be in connection with the following proposition. Several interpreters have proposed another explanation: "Before attempting to save mankind, raise *thy native town* from its obscurity, and make it famous by miracles like those which thou must have wrought at Capernaum." But it is very forced to explain the word *thyself* in the sense of *thy native town.* The connection of this proverb with the following words is explained, if we see in the latter a suggestion of *the means* by which Jesus may yet prevent the contempt with which He is threatened in His own country: "In order that we may acknowledge you to be what you claim, the Saviour of the people, do here some such miracle as it is said thou hast done at Capernaum." This speech betrays an ironical doubt respecting those marvellous things which were attributed to Him.

It appears from this passage, as well as from Matt. xiii. 58 and Mark vi. 5, that Jesus performed no miracles at Nazareth. It is even said that "*He could do no miracle* there." It was a moral impossibility, as in other similar instances (Luke xi. 16, 29, xxiii. 35). It proceeded from the spirit in which the demand was made: it was a miracle of ostentation that was required of Him (the third temptation in the desert); and it was what He could not grant, without *doing what the Father had not shown Him* (John v. 19, 30).—The allusion to the miracles at Capernaum creates surprise, because none of them have been recorded; and modern interpreters generally find in these words a proof of the chronological disorder which here prevails in Luke's narrative. He must have placed this visit much too soon. This conclusion, however, is not so certain as it appears. The expression, *in the power of the Spirit* (ver. 14), contains by implication, as we have seen, an indication of miracles wrought in those early days, and amongst these we must certainly rank the miracle at the marriage feast at Cana (John ii.). This miracle was followed by a residence at Capernaum (John ii. 12), during which Jesus may have performed some miraculous works; and it was not till after that that He preached publicly at Nazareth. These early miracles have been effaced by subsequent events, as that at Cana would have been, if John had not rescued it from oblivion. If this is so, the twenty-third verse, which seems at first sight not to harmonize with the previous narrative, would just prove with what fidelity Luke has preserved the purport of the sources whence he drew his information. John in the same way makes allusion (ii. 12) to miracles which he has not recorded.—The preposition εἰς before the name *Capernaum* appears to be the true reading: "done *at* and *in favour of* Capernaum."

The δέ (ver. 24) indicates opposition. "So far from seeking to obtain your confidence by a display of miracles, I shall rather accept, as a prophet, the fate of all the prophets." The proverbial saying here cited by Jesus is found in the scene Matt. xiii. and Mark vi., and, with some slight modification, in John iv. 44. None have more difficulty in discerning the exceptional character of an extraordinary man than those who have long lived with him on terms of familiarity.—The δέ (ver. 25) is again of an adversative force: If by your unbelief you prevent my being your physician, there are others whom you will not prevent me from healing. The expression *verily* announces something important; and it is evident that the application of the saying, ver. 24, in the mind of Jesus, has a much wider reference than the instance before Him; Nazareth becomes, in His view, a type of unbelieving Israel. This is proved by the two following examples, which refer to the relations of Israel with the heathen.—He speaks of a famine of three years and a half. From the expressions of the O. T., *during these years* (1 Kings xvii. 1), and *the third year* (xviii. 1), we can only in strictness infer a drought of two years and a half. But as this same figure, *three years and a half*, is found in Jas. v. 17, it was probably a tradition of the Jewish schools. The reasoning would be this: The famine must have lasted for a certain time after the drought. There would be a desire also to make out the number which, ever since the persecution of Antiochus Epiphanes, had become the emblem of times of national calamity. The expression, *all the land*, denotes the land of Israel, with the known countries bordering upon it. The Alex. reading **Σιδωνίας**, *the territory of Sidon*, may be a correction derived from the LXX. The reading Σιδῶνος, the city of Sidon itself, makes the capital the centre on which the surrounding cities depend.—The somewhat incorrect use of **εἰ μή**, *except*, is explained by the application of this restriction not to the special notion of *Israelitish* widowhood, but to the idea of *widowhood* in general; the same remark applies to ver. 27, Matt. xii. 4, Gal. i. 19, and other passages.—The second example (ver. 27) is taken from 2 Kings v. 14. The passage 2 Kings vii. 3 and some others prove how very prevalent leprosy was in Israel at this time. The prophecy contained in these examples is being fulfilled to this hour: Israel is deprived of the works of grace and marvels of healing which the Messiah works among the Gentiles.

Vers. 28–30.[1] *Conclusion.*—The threat contained in these examples exasperates them: "Thou rejectest us: we reject thee," was their virtual reply. The term ἐκβάλλειν, *to cast out*, denotes that they set upon Him with violence.—About forty minutes distant from Nazareth, to the south-east, they show a wall of rock 80 feet high, and (if we add to it a second declivity which is found a little below) about 300 feet above the plain of Esdraelon. It is there that tradition places this scene. But Robinson regards this tradition as of no great antiquity. Besides, it does not agree with the expression: *on*

[1] Ver. 29. ℵ. B. D. L. some Mnn., ὥστε instead of εἰς τό.

which the city was built. Nazareth spreads itself out upon the eastern face of a mountain, where there is a perpendicular wall of rock from 40 to 50 feet high. This nearer locality agrees better with the text.—The ὥστε of the Alex. reading signifies: *so as to be able* to cast Him down. It was for that purpose that they took the trouble of going up so high. This reading is preferable to the T. R.: εἰς τό, *for the purpose of*.—The deliverance of Jesus was neither a miracle nor an escape; He passed through the group of these infuriated people with a majesty which overawed them. The history offers some similar incidents. We cannot say, as one critic does: "In the absence of any other miracle, He left them this."

The greater part of modern critics regard this scene as identical with that of Matt. xiii. and Mark vi., placed by these evangelists at a much later period. They rely, 1*st*, On the expression of surprise: *Is not this the son of Joseph?* and on the proverbial saying, ver. 24, which could not have been repeated twice within a few months; 2*d*, On the absence of miracles common to the two narratives; 3*d*, On the words of ver. 23, which suppose that Jesus had been labouring at Capernaum prior to this visit to Nazareth. But how in this case are the following differences to be explained?—1. In Matthew and Mark there is not a word about the attempt to put Jesus to death. All goes off peaceably to the very end. 2. Where are certain cases of healing recorded by Matthew (ver. 58) and Mark (ver. 5) to be placed? Before the preaching? This is scarcely compatible with the words put into the mouth of the inhabitants of Nazareth (ver. 23, Luke). After the preaching? Luke's narrative absolutely excludes this supposition. 3. Matthew and Mark place the visit which they relate at the culminating point of the Galilæan ministry, and towards its close, whilst Luke commences his account of this ministry with the narrative which we have just been studying. An attempt has been made to explain this difference in two ways: Luke may have wished, in placing this narrative here, to make us see the reason which induced Jesus to settle at Capernaum instead of Nazareth (Bleek, Weizsäcker); or he may have made this scene the opening of Jesus' ministry, because it prefigures the rejection of the Jews and the salvation of the Gentiles, which is the leading idea of his book (Holtzmann). But how is such an arbitrary transposition to be harmonized with his intention of *writing in order*, so distinctly professed by Luke (i. 4)? These difficulties have not yet been solved. Is it then impossible, that after a first attempt among His fellow-citizens at the beginning of His ministry, Jesus should have made a second later on? On the contrary, is it not quite natural that, before leaving Galilee for ever (and thus at the very time to which Matthew and Mark refer their account), He should have addressed Himself once more to the heart of His fellow-countrymen, and that, if He had again found it closed against Him, the shock would nevertheless have been less violent than at the first encounter! However this may be, if the two narratives refer to the same event, as present criticism decides, Luke's appears to me to deserve the preference, and for two reasons: 1. The very dramatic and detailed picture he has drawn leaves no room for doubting the accuracy and absolute originality of the source whence he derived his information; whilst the narratives of Matthew and Mark betray, by the absence of all distinctive features, their traditional origin. 2. John (iv. 4) cites, *at the beginning* of his account *of the Galilæan ministry*, the saying recorded by the three evangelists as to the rejection which every prophet must undergo from his own people. He quotes it as a maxim already previously announced by Jesus, and which had influenced from the first the course of His ministry. Now, as the three Syn. are agreed in referring this saying to a visit at Nazareth, this quotation in John clearly proves that the visit in question took place at the commencement (Luke), and not in the middle or at the end of the Galilæan ministry (Matthew and Mark). We are thus brought to the conclusions: 1. That the visit related by Luke is historical; 2. That the recollection of it was lost to tradition, in common with many other facts relating to the beginning of the ministry (marriage at Cana, etc.); 3. That it was followed by another towards the end of the Galilæan ministry, in the traditional account of which several incidents were introduced belonging to the former. As to the sojourn at Capernaum, implied in Luke iv. 23, we have already seen that it is included in the general description, ver. 15. John ii. 12 proves that from the first the attention of Jesus was drawn to this city as a suitable place in which to reside. His first disciples lived near it. The synagogue of Capernaum must then have been one of the first in which He preached, and consequently one of those mentioned in ver. 15.

2. *Residence at Capernaum:* vers. 31–44. Five sections: 1*st.* A general survey (vers. 31 and 32); 2*d.* The healing of a demoniac (vers. 33–37); 3*d.* That of Peter's mother-in-law (vers. 38 and 39); 4*th.* Various cures (vers. 40–42); 5*th.* Transition to the evangelization of Galilee generally.

1*st.* Vers. 31 and 32.—The term, *He went down,* refers to the situation of Capernaum on the sea-shore, in opposition to that of Nazareth on the high land.—We have to do here with a permanent abode; comp. John ii. 12 and Matt. iv. 13 (ἐλθὼν κατῴκησεν εἰς K.), as well as the term, *His own city* (Matt. ix. 1). The name Capernaum or Capharnaum (see critical note, ver. 23) does not occur in the O. T. From this it would seem that it was not a very ancient place. The name may signify, *town of Nahum* (alluding to the prophet of this name), or (with more probability) *town of consolation.*

The name, according to Josephus, belonged properly to a fountain;[1] in the only passage in which he mentions this town, he calls it Κεφαρνώμη.[2] Until lately, it was very generally admitted that the site of Capernaum was marked by the ruins of Tell-Hum towards the northern end of the lake of Gennesareth, to the west of the embouchure of the Jordan. Since Robinson's time, however, several, and among the rest M. Renan, have inclined to look for it farther south, in the rich plain where stands at the present day the town of Khan-Minyeh, of which Josephus has left us such a fine description. Keim pronounces very decidedly in favour of this latter opinion, and supports it by reasons of great weight.[3]—Agriculture, fishing, and commerce, favoured by the road from Damascus to Ptolemais, which passed through or near Capernaum, had made it a flourishing city. It was therefore the most important town of the northern district of the lake country. It was the Jewish, as Tiberias was the heathen, capital of Galilee (a similar relation to that between Jerusalem and Cæsarea).

The 31st and 32d verses form the fifth resting-place or general summary in the narrative (see vers. 14, 15). The analytical form ἦν διδάσκων indicates habit. In the parallel place in Mark, the imperf. ἐδίδασκεν puts the act of teaching in direct and special connection with the following fact. By the authority (ἐξουσία) which characterized the words of Jesus, Luke means, not the power employed in the healing of the demonaic (to express this he would rather have used δύναμις, *force*), but the commanding character which distinguished His teaching. Jesus did not dissect texts, like the Rabbis; He laid down truths which carried with them their own evidence. He spoke as a legislator, not as a lawyer (Matt. vii. 28, 29).—The following incident proves the right He had to teach in this way.—It appears that it was with this 31st verse that Marcion commenced his Gospel, prefacing it with the fixing of the date, iii. 1: "In the 15th year of

[1] *Bell. Jud.* iii. 10. 8: "To the mildness of the climate is added the advantage of a copious spring, which the inhabitants call Capharnaum.'

[2] Jos. *Vita*, § 72.

[3] Delitzsch, in his little tractate, *Ein Tag in Capernaüm*, does not hesitate to recognise in the great field of ruins of Tell-Hum the remains of Capernaum.

the government of Tiberius, Jesus went down into the town of Galilee called Capernaum."[1] The complement understood of *went down* was evidently: from heaven. As to the visit to Nazareth, Marcion places it after the scene which follows; this transposition was certainly dictated by ver. 23.

2*d*. Vers. 33–37.[2] Should the possessed mentioned by the evangelists be regarded simply as persons afflicted after the same manner as our lunatics, whose derangement was attributed by Jewish and heathen superstition to supernatural influence? Or did God really permit, at this extraordinary epoch in history, an exceptional display of diabolical power? Or, lastly, should certain morbid conditions now existing, which medical science attributes to purely natural causes, either physical or psychical, be put down, at the present day also, to the action of higher causes? These are the three hypotheses which present themselves to the mind. Several of the demoniacs healed by Jesus certainly exhibit symptoms very like those which are observed at the present day in those who are simply afflicted; for example, the epileptic child, Luke ix. 37 et seq., and parall. These strange conditions in every case, therefore, were based on a real disorder, either physical or physico-psychical. The evangelists are so far from being ignorant of this, that they constantly class the demoniacs under the category of the sick (vers. 40 and 41), never under that of the vicious. The possessed have nothing in common with the *children of the devil* (John viii.). Nevertheless these afflicted persons are constantly made a class by themselves. On what does this distinction rest? On this leading fact, that those who are simply sick enjoy their own personal consciousness, and are in possession of their own will; while in the possessed these faculties are, as it were, confiscated to a foreign power, with which the sick person identifies himself (ver. 34, viii. 30). How is this peculiar symptom to be explained? Josephus, under Hellenic influence, thought that it should be attributed to the souls of wicked men who came after death seeking a domicile in the living.[3] In the eyes

[1] Tertullian, *Contra Marc.* iv. 7.

[2] Ver. 33. ℵ. B. L. V. Z. omit λεγων.—Ver. 35. ℵ. B. D. L. V. Z. several Mnn. read απο instead of εξ.

[3] *Bell. Jud.* vii. 6. 3.

of the people the strange guest was a demon, a fallen angel This latter opinion Jesus must have shared. Strictly speaking, His colloquies with the demoniacs might be explained by an accommodation to popular prejudice, and the sentiments of those who were thus afflicted; but in His private conversations with His disciples, He must, whatever was true, have disclosed His real thoughts, and sought to enlighten them. But He does nothing of the kind; on the contrary, He gives the apostles and disciples power to *cast out devils* (ix. 1), and to tread on *all the power of the enemy* (x. 19). In Mark ix. 29, He distinguishes a certain class of demons that can only be driven out by prayer (and fasting?). In Luke xi. 21 and parall., He explains the facility with which He casts out demons by the personal victory which He had achieved over Satan at the beginning. He therefore admitted the intervention of this being in these mysterious conditions. If this is so, is it not natural to admit that He who exercised over this, as over all other kinds of maladies, such absolute power best understood its nature, and that therefore His views upon the point should determine ours?

Are there not times when God permits a superior evil power to invade humanity? Just as God sent Jesus at a period in history when moral and social evil had reached its culminating point, did not He also permit an extraordinary manifestation of diabolical power to take place at the same time? By this means Jesus could be proclaimed externally and visibly as the conqueror of the enemy of men, as He who came to destroy *the works of the devil* in the moral sense of the word (1 John iii. 8). All the miracles of healing have a similar design. They are signs by which Jesus is revealed as the author of spiritual deliverances corresponding to these physical cures.—An objection is found in the silence of the fourth Gospel; but John in no way professed to relate all he knew. He says himself, xx. 30, 31, *that there are besides many miracles,* and *different* miracles (πολλὰ καὶ ἄλλα), which he does not relate.

As to the present state of things, it must not be compared with the times of Jesus. Not only might the latter have been of an exceptional character; but the beneficent influence which the gospel has exercised in restoring man to himself, and bringing his conscience under the power of the holy and true God, may have brought about a complete change in the spiritual world. Lastly, apart from all this, is there nothing mysterious, from a scientific point of view, in certain cases of mental derangement, particularly in those conditions in which the will is, as it were, confiscated to, and paralyzed by, an unknown power? And after deduction has been made for all those forms of mental maladies which a discriminating analysis can explain by moral and physical relations, will not an impartial physician agree that there is a residuum of cases respecting which he must say: *Non liquet?*

Possession is a caricature of inspiration. The latter, attaching itself to the moral essence of a man, confirms him for ever in the possession of his true self; the former, while profoundly opposed to the nature of the subject, takes advantage of its state of morbid passivity, and leads to the forfeiture of personality. The one is the highest work of God; the other of the devil.

The question has been asked, How could a man in a state of mental derangement, and who would be regarded as unclean (ver. 33), be found in the synagogue? Perhaps his malady had not broken out before as it did at this moment —Luke says literally: *a man who had a spirit* (*an afflatus*) *of an unclean devil.* In this expression, which is only found in Rev. xvi. 14, the term *spirit* or *afflatus* denotes the influence of the *unclean devil,* of the being who is the author of it.— The crisis which breaks out (ver. 34) results from the opposing action of those two powers which enter into conflict with each other,—the influence of the evil spirit, and that of the person and word of Jesus. A *holy* power no sooner begins to act in the sphere in which this wretched creature lives, than the *unclean* power which has dominion over him feels its empire threatened. This idea is suggested by the contrast between the epithet *unclean* applied to the diabolical spirit (ver. 33), and the address: Thou art *the Holy One of God* (ver. 34). The exclamation *ἔα, ah!* (ver. 34) is properly the imperative of *ἐάω, let be!* It is a cry like that of a criminal who, when suddenly apprehended by the police, calls out: Loose me! This is also what is meant in this instance by the expression, in frequent use amongst the Jews with different applications: *What is there between us and thee?* of which the meaning here is: What have we to contend about? What evil have we done thee? The plural *we* does not apply to the devil and to the possessed, since the latter still identifies himself altogether with the former. The devil speaks in the name of all the other spirits of his kind which have succeeded in obtaining possession of a human being.—The *perdition* which he dreads is being sent into the abyss where such spirits await the judgment (viii. 31). This abyss is the emptiness of a creature that possesses no point of support outside itself,—neither in God, as the faithful angels have, nor in the world of sense, as sinful men endowed with a body have. In order to remedy this inward destitution, they endeavour to unite themselves to some human being, so as to enter through this medium into contact with sensible realities. Whenever a loss of this position befalls them, they fall back into the abyss of their empty self-dependence (*vide subjectivité*).—The term *Holy One of God* expresses the character in which this being recognised his deadly enemy. We cannot be surprised that such homage should be altogether repugnant to the feelings of Jesus. He did not acknowledge it as the utterance of an individual whose will is free, which is the only homage that can please Him; and He sees what occasion may be taken from such facts to exhibit His work in a suspicious light (xi. 15). He therefore puts an end to this scene immediately by these two peremptory words (ver. 35): *Silence!* and *Come out.* By the words ἐξ αὐτοῦ, *of him,* Jesus forcibly distinguishes between the two beings thus far mingled together. This divorce is the condition of the cure.—A terrible convulsion marks the deliverance of the afflicted man. The tormentor does not let go his victim without subjecting him to a final torture. The words, *without having done him any hurt,* reproduce in a striking manner the impression of eyewitnesses: they ran towards the unhappy man, expecting to find him dead; and to their surprise, on lifting him up, they find him perfectly restored.

We may imagine the feelings of the congregation when they beheld such a scene as this, in which the two powers that dispute the empire of mankind had in a sensible manner just come into conflict. Vers. 36 and 37 describe this feeling. Several have applied the expression *this word* (What a word *is* this! A. V.) to the command of Jesus which the devil had just obeyed. But a reference to ver. 32 obliges us to take the term *word* in its natural sense, the preaching of Jesus in general. The authority with which He taught (ver. 32) found its guarantee in the authority backed by *power* (δύναμις), with which He forced the devils themselves to render obedience. The power which Jesus exercises by His simple word is opposed to the prescriptions and pretences of the exorcists; His cures differed from theirs, just as His teaching did from that of the scribes. In both cases He speaks as a master.

The account of this miracle is omitted by Matthew. It is found with some slight variations in Mark (i. 23 et seq.). It is placed by him, as by Luke, at the beginning of this sojourn of Jesus at Capernaum. Instead of ῥίψαν, *having thrown him*, Mark says, σπαράξαν, *having torn, violently convulsed him.*—Instead of *What word is this?* Mark makes the multitude say: *What new doctrine is this?*—an expression which agrees with the sense which we have given to λόγος in Luke. The meaning of the epithet *new* in the mouth of the people might be rendered by the common exclamation: Here is something new! According to Bleek, Mark borrowed his narrative from Luke. But how very paltry and insignificant these changes would seem! According to Holtzmann, the original source was the primitive Mark (A.), the narrative of which has been reproduced exactly by our Mark; whilst Luke has modified it with a view to exalt the miracle, by changing, for example, *having torn* into *having thrown*, and by adding on his own authority the details, *with a loud voice*, and *without having done him any hurt.* Holtzmann congratulates himself, after this, on having made Luke's dependence on the Proto-Mark *quite evident.* But the simple term *word*, which in Luke (ver. 36) supplies the place of Mark's emphatic expression, *this new doctrine*, contradicts this explanation. And if this miracle was in the primitive Mark, from which, according to Holtzmann, Matthew must also have drawn his narrative, how came the latter to omit an incident so striking? Holtzmann's answer is, that this evangelist thought another example of a similar cure, that of the demoniac at Gadara, the *more striking;* and to compensate for the omission of the healing at Capernaum, he has put down two demoniacs, instead of one, to Gadara . . .! How can such a childish procedure be imputed to a grave historian?

3*d*. Vers. 38 and 39.[1]—Peter, according to our narrative, seems to have lived at Capernaum. According to John i. 45, he was originally of Bethsaida. The two places were very

[1] Ver. 38. The Mss. are divided between απο and εκ.

near, and might have had a common synagogue; or, while originally belonging to the one, Peter might have taken up his abode at the other.—The term πενθερά (not μητρυῖα) proves that Peter was married, which agrees with 1 Cor. ix. 5. It is possible that from this time Jesus took up His abode in Peter's house, Matt. xvii. 24 et seq.—According to Mark i. 29, His train of disciples consisted, not only of Simon and Andrew, but also of James and John. This already existing association supposes a prior connection between Jesus and these young fishermen, which is explained in John i. Luke does not name the companions of Jesus. We only see by the words, *she arose and ministered unto them* (ver. 39), that He was not alone.—The expression πυρετὸς μέγας does not appear to be used here in the technical sense which it has in ancient books of medicine, where it denotes a particular kind of fever. —In Luke, Jesus *bends down* over the sick woman. This was a means of entering into spiritual communication with her; comp. Peter's words to the impotent man (Acts iii. 4): *Look on me.* In Matthew, He *touches* the sick woman with His hand. This action has the same design. In Mark, He *takes her by the hand* to lift her up. How are these variations to be explained, if all three drew from the same source, or if one derived his account from the other?—Luke says, literally, *He rebuked the fever;* as if He saw in the disease some principle hostile to man. This agrees with John viii. 44, where the devil is called *the murderer of man.*—It was doubtless at the time of the evening meal (ver. 40). The first use which the sick woman makes of her recovered strength was to serve up a repast for her guests. Holtzmann finds a proof in the plur. αὐτοῖς, "she served *them*," that Luke's narrative depends on Mark; for thus far Luke has only spoken of Jesus: *He came down* (ver. 31), *He entered* (ver. 38). But this proof is weak. In the description of the public scene, Luke would only present the principal person, Jesus; while in the account of the domestic scene he would naturally mention also the other persons, since they had all the same need of being waited upon.

In Luke and Mark the position of this narrative is very nearly the same, with merely this difference, that in the latter it follows the calling of the four disciples, while in Luke it precedes it. In

Matthew, on the contrary, it is placed very much later—after the Sermon on the Mount. As to the details, Matthew is almost identical with Mark. Thus the two evangelists which agree as to the time (Luke and Mark) differ most as to the details, and the two which come nearest to each other in details (Matthew and Mark) differ considerably as to time. How can this singular relation be explained if they drew from common written sources, or if they copied from each other? Luke here omits Andrew, whom Mark mentions. Why so, if he copied from the primitive Mark? Had he any animosity against Andrew? Holtzmann replies: Because he does not speak of Andrew in what follows. As if, in Mark himself, he was any the more mentioned in the incidents that follow!

4*th*. Vers. 40 and 41.[1]—Here we have one of those periods when the miraculous power of Jesus was most abundantly displayed. We shall meet again with some of these culminating points in the course of His ministry. A similar rhythm is found in the career of the apostles. Peter at Jerusalem (Acts v. 15, 16), and Paul at Ephesus (xix. 11, 12), exercise their miraculous power to a degree in which they appear to have exhibited it at no other time in their life; it was at the same time the culminating point of their ministry of the word.

The memory of this remarkable evening must have fixed itself indelibly in the early tradition; for the account of this time has been preserved, in almost identical terms, in our three Syn. The sick came in crowds. The expression, *when the sun was setting*, shows that this time had been waited for. And that not "because it was the cool hour," as many have thought, but because it was the end of the Sabbath, and carrying a sick person was regarded as work (John v. 10). The whole city, as Mark, in his simple, natural, and somewhat emphatic style, says, was gathered together at the door.—According to our narrative, Jesus made use on this occasion of the laying on of hands. Luke cannot have invented this detail himself; and the others would not have omitted it if it had belonged to their alleged common source of information. Therefore Luke had some special source in which this detail was found, and not

[1] Ver. 40. B. D. Q. X. επιτιθεις instead of επιθεις.—B. D. It. Syr., εθεραπευει instead of εθεραπευσεν.—Ver. 41. The Mss. are divided between κραυγαζοντα and κραζοντα.—The T. R., with 14 Mjj. almost all the Mnn. Syr., reads ο Χριστος before ο υιος του Θεου, contrary to ℵ. B. C. D. F. L. R. X. Z. It[plerique], which omit it.

this alone. This rite is a symbol of any kind of transmission, whether of a gift or an office (Moses and Joshua, Deut. xxxiv. 9), or of a blessing (the patriarchal blessings), or of a duty (the transfer to the Levites of the natural functions of the eldest sons in every family), or of guilt (the guilty Israelite laying his hands on the head of the victim), or of the sound vital strength enjoyed by the person who imparts it (cures). It is not certainly that Jesus could not have worked a cure by His mere word, or even by a simple act of volition. But, in the first place, there is something profoundly human in this act of laying the hand on the head of any one whom one desires to benefit. It is a gesture of tenderness, a sign of beneficial communication such as the heart craves. Then this symbol might be *morally* necessary. Whenever Jesus avails Himself of any material means to work a cure, whether it be the sound of His voice, or clay made of His spittle, His aim is to establish, in the form best adapted to the particular case, a personal tie between the sick person and Himself; for He desires not only to heal, but to effect a restoration to God, by creating in the consciousness of the sick a sense of union with Himself, the organ of divine grace in the midst of mankind. This moral aim explains the variety of the means employed. Had they been curative means,—of the nature of magnetic passes, for example,—they could not have varied so much. But as they were addressed to the sick person's soul, Jesus chose them in such a way that His action was adapted to its character or position. In the case of a deaf mute, He put His fingers into his ears; He anointed the eyes of a blind man with His spittle, etc. In this way their healing appeared as an emanation from His person, and attached them to Him by an indissoluble tie. Their restored life was felt to be dependent on His. The repetition of the act of laying on of hands in *each* case was with the same view. The sick person, being thus visibly put into a state of physical dependence, would necessarily infer his moral dependence. — The Alex. readings ἐπιτίθεις, *laying on*, ἐθεράπευε, *He healed*, must be preferred. The aor. (in the T. R.) indicates the completed act, the imperf. its indefinite continuation: "*Laying* His hands *on* each of them, He *healed*, and kept on healing, as many as came for it."

The demoniacs are mentioned in ver. 41 among the sick, but as forming a class by themselves. This agrees with what we have stated respecting their condition. There must have been some physico-psychical disorganization to afford access to the malign influence. The words ὁ Χριστός are correctly omitted by the Alex.; they have been taken from the second part of the verse.—From the fact that the multitude translated the exclamation of the devils, *Thou art the Son of God,* into this, *It is the Christ,* we have no right to conclude that the two titles were identical. By the former, the devils acknowledged the divine character of this man, who made them feel so forcibly His sovereign power. The latter was the translation of this homage into ordinary speech by the Jewish multitude. Was it the design of the devil to compromise Jesus by stirring up a dangerous excitement in Israel in His favour, or by making it believed that there was a bond of common interest between His cause and theirs? It is more natural to regard this exclamation as an involuntary homage, an anticipation of that compulsory adoration which all creatures, even those which are *under the earth,* as St. Paul says (Phil. ii. 10), shall one day render to Jesus. They are before the representative of Him *before whom they tremble* (Jas. ii. 19). Jesus, who had rejected in the desert all complicity with their head, could not think of deriving advantage from this impure homage.

5*th.* Vers. 42–44.[1]—The more a servant of God exerts himself in outward activity, the more need there is that he should renew his inward strength by meditation. Jesus also was subject to this law. Every morning He had to obtain afresh whatever was needed for the day; for *He lived by the Father* (John vi. 57). He went out before day from Peter's house, where no doubt He was staying. Instead of, *And when it was day,* Mark says, *While it was still very dark* (ἔννυχον λίαν). Instead of, *the multitude sought Him,* Mark says, *Simon and they that were with him followed after Him . . ., and said unto Him, All men seek Thee.* Instead of, *I must preach,* Mark makes Jesus say, *Let us go, that I may preach . . .,* etc. These

[1] Ver. 43. א. B. C. D. L. X. some Mnn., απισταλην instead of απισταλμαι.—א. B. L. some Mnn., επι τουτο instead of εις τουτο.—Ver. 44. א. B. D. Q., εις τας συναγωγας instead of εν ταις συναγωγαις.—א. B. C. L. Q. R. several Mnn., της Ιουδαιας, instead of της Γαλιλαιας

shades of difference are easily explained, if the substance of these narratives was furnished by oral tradition; but they become childish if they are drawn from the same written source. Holtzmann thinks that Luke generalizes and obscures the narrative of the primitive Mark. The third evangelist would have laboured very uselessly to do that! Bleek succeeds no better in explaining Mark by Luke, than Holtzmann Luke by Mark. If Mark listened to the narrations of Peter, it is intelligible that he should have added to the traditional narrative the few striking features which are peculiar to him, and particularly that which refers to the part taken by Simon on that day. As we read Mark i. 36, 37, we fancy we hear Peter telling the story himself, and saying: "And we found Him, and said to Him, All men seek Thee." These special features, omitted in the general tradition, are wanting in Luke. —The words of Jesus, ver. 43, might be explained by a tacit opposition between the ideas of *preaching* and healing. "If I stayed at Capernaum, I should soon have nothing else to do but work cures, whilst I am sent that I may preach also." But in this case the verb εὐαγγελίσασθαι should commence the phrase. On the contrary, the emphasis is on the words, *to other cities* . . . Jesus opposes to the idea of a stationary ministry at Capernaum, that of *itinerant* preaching. The term εὐαγγελίσασθαι, *to tell news*, is very appropriate to express this idea. The message ceases to be *news* when the preacher remains in the same place. But in this expression of Jesus there is, besides, a contrast between Capernaum, the large city, to which Jesus in no way desires to confine His care, and the smaller towns of the vicinity, designated in Mark by the characteristic term κωμοπόλεις, which are equally entrusted to His love.—It is difficult to decide between the two readings, ἀπεστάλην, *I have been sent in order to* . . ., and ἀπέσταλμαι, *my mission is to* . . . The second perhaps agrees better with the context. A very similar various reading is found in the parallel passage, Mark i. 38 (ἐξῆλθον or ἐξελήλυθα). Mark's term appears to allude to the incarnation; Luke's only refers to the mission of Jesus.—The readings εἰς τὰς συναγωγάς and ἐν ταῖς συναγωγαῖς, ver. 44, recur in Mark i. 39. The former appears less regular, which makes it more probable: Jesus *carried* the preaching into the synagogues.—The absurd reading τῆς Ἰουδαίας, which is found in the six principal Alex., should be a caution to blind partisans of this text.

THE MIRACLES OF JESUS.

We shall here add a few thoughts on the miracles of Jesus in general. Four methods are used to get rid of the miraculous element in the Gospel history :—1*st.* The explanation called *natural*, which upholds the credibility of the narrative, but explains the text in such a way that its contents offer nothing extraordinary. This attempt has failed ; it is an expedient repudiated at the present day, rationalistic criticism only having recourse to it in cases where other methods are manifestly ineffectual.—2*d.* The *mythical* explanation, according to which the accounts of the miracles would be owing to reminiscences of the miraculous stories of the O. T.,—the Messiah could not do less than the prophets,—or would be either the product of spontaneous creations of the Christian consciousness, or the accidental result of certain words or parables of Jesus that were misunderstood (the resurrection of Lazarus, *e.g.*, the result of the passage Luke xvi. 31 ; the cursing of the barren fig-tree, a translation into fact of the parable, Luke xiii. 6–9). But the simple, plain, historical character of our Gospel narratives, so free from all poetical adornment and bombast, defends them against this suspicion. Besides, several accounts of miracles are accompanied by words of Jesus, which in such a case would lose their meaning, but which are nevertheless beyond doubt authentic. For example, the discourse, Matt. xii. 26 et seq., where Jesus refutes the charge, laid against Him by His adversaries, of casting out devils by the prince of the devils, would have no sense but on the supposition, fully conceded by these adversaries, of the reality of His cures of the possessed. His address to the cities of Galilee, Luke x. 12–15, implies the notorious and undisputed reality of numerous miraculous facts in His ministry ; for we know of no exegesis which consents to give the term δυνάμεις in this passage the purely moral meaning which M. Colani proposes.[1] —3*d.* The *relative* hypothesis, according to which these facts must be ascribed to natural laws as yet unknown. This was the explanation of Schleiermacher ; in part also it was the explanation of M. Renan : "The miraculous is only the unexplained." It is in conflict with two insurmountable difficulties : 1. If certain cures may be explained after a fashion, we may be perfectly sure that no one will ever discover a natural law capable of producing a multiplication of loaves and of cooked fish, a resurrection of the dead, and above all, such an event as the resurrection of Jesus Himself. 2. We must, according to this explanation, attribute to Jesus miracles of scientific knowledge quite as inexplicable as the miracles of power which are

[1] See on this subject the fine chapter of Holtzmann, *Die Synopt. Evangelien*, § 30 ; *Die Synoptischen Wunderberichte ;* and my lecture on the *Miracles de Jésus*, second edition, p. 11 et seq.

now in question.—*4th.* The *psychological* explanation. After having got rid of the miracles wrought on external nature (the multiplication of the loaves and the stilling of the storm) by one of the three methods indicated, Keim admits a residuum of extraordinary and indisputable facts in the life of Jesus. These are the cures wrought upon the sick and the possessed. Before him, M. Renan had spoken of the influence exerted on suffering and nervous people by *the contact of a person of finely organized nature* (*une personne exquise*). Keim merely, in fact, amplifies this expression. The only real miracles in the history of Jesus—the cures—are to be ascribed, according to him, to moral influence (*ethico-psychological,* t. ii. p. 162).—We reply —1. That the miracles wrought on nature, which are set aside as mythical, are attested in exactly the same manner as the cures which are admitted. 2. That Jesus wrought these cures with an absolute certainty of success ("Now, in order that ye may know, I say unto thee . . ." "I will; be thou clean." "Be it unto thee as thou wilt"), and that the effect produced was *immediate.* These two features are incompatible with the psychological explanation. 3. That if Jesus had known that these cures did not proceed from an order of things above nature, it is inconceivable that He would have offered them as *God's* testimony in His favour, and as signs of His Messianic dignity. Charlatanism, however slight, is incompatible with the moral character of Jesus. On the possessed, see pp. 243–5.

Jewish legends themselves bear witness to the reality of Jesus' miracles. "The Son of Stada (a nickname applied to Jesus in the Talmud) brought charms from Egypt in an incision which he had made in his flesh." This is the accusation of the Talmud against Him. Surely, if the Jews had been able to deny His miracles, it would have been a simpler thing to do than to explain them in this way. Lastly, when we compare the miracles of the Gospels with those attributed to Him in the apocryphal writings, we feel what a wide difference there is between tradition and legend.

SECOND CYCLE.—CHAP. V. 1–VI. 11.

From the Call of the First Disciples to the Choice of the Twelve.

Up to this time Jesus has been preaching, accompanied by a few friends, but without forming about Him a circle of permanent disciples. As His work grows, He feels it necessary to give it a more definite form. The time has arrived when He deems it wise to attach to Himself, as regular disciples, those whom the Father has given Him. This new phase coincides with that in which His work begins to come into conflict with the established order of things.

This cycle comprises six narratives: 1. The call of the first four disciples (v. 1–11); 2 and 3. Two cures of the leper and the paralytic (v. 12–14 and 15–26); 4. The call of Levi, with the circumstances connected with it (v. 27–39); 5 and 6. Two conflicts relating to the Sabbath (vi. 1–11).

1. *The Call of the Disciples*: v. 1–11.—The companions of Jesus, in the preceding scene, have not yet been named by Luke (*they* besought Him, iv. 38; she ministered unto *them*, iv. 39). According to Mark (i. 29), they were Peter, Andrew, James, and John. These are the very four young men whom we find in this narrative. They had lived up to this time in the bosom of their families, and continued their old occupations. But this state of things was no longer suitable to the part which Jesus designed for them. They were to treasure up all His instructions, be the constant witnesses of His works, and receive from Him a daily moral education. In order to this, it was indispensable that they should be continually with Him. In calling them to leave their earthly occupation, and assigning them in its place one that was wholly spiritual, Jesus founded, properly speaking, the Christian *ministry*. For this is precisely the line of demarcation between the simple Christian and the minister, that the former realizes the life of faith in any earthly calling; while the latter, excused by his Master from any particular profession, can devote himself entirely to the spiritual work with which he is entrusted. Such is the new position to which Jesus raises these young fishermen. It is more than simple faith, but less than apostleship; it is the ministry, the general foundation on which will be erected the apostolate.

The call related here by Luke is certainly the same as that which is related, in a more abridged form, by Matthew (iv. 18–22) and Mark (i. 16–20). For can any one suppose, with Riggenbach, that Jesus twice addressed the same persons in these terms, "*I will make you fishers of men*," and that they could have twice *left all* in order to follow Him? If the miraculous draught of fishes is omitted in Matthew and Mark, it is because, as we have frequent proof in the former, in the traditional narratives, the whole interest was centred in the word of Jesus, which was the soul of every incident. Mark has given completeness to these narratives wherever he could avail himself of Peter's accounts. But here this was not the case, because, as many facts go to prove, Peter avoided giving prominence to himself in his own narrations.

Vers. 1–3.[1]—*The General Situation.*—This description furnishes a perfect frame to the scene that follows. The words, *καὶ αὐτός* . . ., *He was also standing there,* indicate the inconvenient position in which He was placed by the crowd collected at this spot.—The details in ver. 2 are intended to explain the request which Jesus makes to the fishermen. The night fishing was at an end (ver. 5). And they had no intention of beginning another by daylight; the season was not favourable. Moreover, they had washed their nets (*ἀπέπλυναν* is the true reading; the imperf. in B. D. is a correction), and their boats were drawn up upon the strand (*ἑστῶτα*). If the fishermen had been ready to fish, Jesus would not have asked them to render a service which would have interfered with their work. It is true that Matthew and Mark represent them as actually engaged in casting their nets. But these two evangelists omit the miraculous draught altogether, and take us to the final moment when Jesus says to them: "*I will make you fishers of men.*" Jesus makes a pulpit of the boat which His friends had just left, whence He casts the net of the word over the crowd which covers the shore. Then, desiring to attach henceforth these young believers to Himself with a view to His future work, He determines to give them an emblem they will never forget of the magnificent success that will attend the ministry for the love of which He invites them to forsake all; and in order that it may be more deeply graven on their hearts, He takes this emblem from their daily calling.

Vers. 4–10*a*.[2] *The Preparation.*—In the imperative, *launch out* (ver. 4), Jesus speaks solely to Peter, as director of the embarkation; the order, *let down,* is addressed to all. Peter, the head of the present fishing, will one day be head also of the mission.—Not having taken anything during the night, the most favourable time for fishing, they had given up the idea

[1] Ver. 1. ℵ. A. B. L. X., και ακουειν instead of του ακουειν.—Ver. 2. B. D., επλυνον, instead of επλυναν or απεπλυναν, which is the reading of all the others.

[2] Ver. 6. ℵ. B. L. διερησσετο, C. διερρητο, instead of διερρηγνυτο (or διερηγνυτο), which is the reading of T. R. and the rest.—Ver. 8. ℵ. omits κυριε.—Ver. 9. B. D. X., ων instead of η.

of fishing in the day. Peter's reply, so full of docility, indicates faith already existing. "*I should not think of letting down the net; nevertheless at Thy word . . .*" He calls Jesus ἐπιστάτης, properly *Overseer, Master.* This word frequently occurs in Luke; it is more general than ῥαββί or διδάσκαλος; it refers to any kind of oversight.—The miraculous draught may be only a miracle of knowledge; Jesus had a supernatural knowledge of a large shoal of fish to be found in this place. There are numerous instances of a similar abundance of fish appearing in an unexpected way.[1] Jesus may, however, have wrought by His own will what is frequently produced by physical circumstances.—The imperf., *was breaking,* ver. 6, indicates a beginning to break, or at least a danger of it. The arrival of their companions prevented this accident. The term μέτοχοι denotes merely participation in the same employment. —In Matthew and Mark, John and James were mending their nets. Luke contains nothing opposed to this.—Meyer thinks Peter's astonishment (ver. 8) incomprehensible after all the miracles he had already seen. But whenever divine power leaves the region of the abstract, and comes before our eyes in the sphere of actual facts, does it not appear new? Thus, in Peter's case, the emotion produced by the draught of fishes effaces for the time every other impression. Ἔξελθε ἀπ' ἐμοῦ. *Go out* [of the boat, and depart] *from me.* Peter here employs the more religious expression *Lord,* which answers to his actual feeling.—The word ἀνήρ, *a man,* strongly individualizes the idea of sinner.—If the reading ᾗ be preferred to ὧν (Alex.), we must take the word ἄγρα, *catch,* in the passive sense.—The term κοινωνοί, *associates* (ver. 10), implies more than μέτοχοι, companions (ver. 7); it denotes association in a common undertaking.

[1] Tristram, *The Natural History of the Bible,* p. 285: "The thickness of the shoals of fish in the lake of Gennesareth is almost incredible to any one who has not witnessed them. They often cover an area of more than an acre; and when the fish move slowly forward in a mass, and are rising out of the water, they are packed so close together, that it appears as if a heavy rain was beating down on the surface of the water."—A similar phenomenon was observed some years ago, and even in the spring of this year, in several of our Swiss lakes. "At the end of February, in the lakes of Constance and Wallenstadt, the fish crowded together in such large numbers at certain places by the banks, that the water was darkened by them. At a single draught, 35 quintals of different kinds of fish were taken."—(*Bund,* 6th March 1872.)

Vers. 10*b*, 11.[1] *The Call.*—In Matthew and Mark the call is addressed to the four disciples present; in Luke, in express terms, to Peter only. It results, doubtless, from what follows that the call of the other disciples was implied (comp. *launch out*, ver. 4), or that Jesus extended it to them, perhaps by a gesture. But how can criticism, with this passage before them, which brings the person of Peter into such prominence, while the other two Syn. do not in any way, attribute to our evangelist an intention to underrate this apostle?[2]

The analytical form *ἔσῃ ζωγρῶν, thou shalt be catching,* expresses the *permanence* of this mission; and the words, *from henceforth,* its altogether new character.—Just as the fisherman, by his superior intelligence, makes the fish fall into his snares, so the believer, restored to God and to himself, may seize hold of the natural man, and lift it up with himself to God.

This whole scene implies certain previous relations between Jesus and these young men (ver. 5), which agrees with Luke's narrative; for in the latter this incident is placed after the healing of Peter's mother-in-law, when the newly called disciples were present. We must go further back even than this; for how could Jesus have entered into Peter's house on the Sabbath-day (iv. 38), unless they had already been intimately acquainted? John's narrative easily explains all: Jesus had made the acquaintance of Peter and his friends when they were with John the Baptist (John i.). As for Matthew and Mark, their narrative has just the fragmentary character that belongs to the traditional narrative. The facts are simply put into juxtaposition. Beyond this, each writer follows his own bent: Matthew is eager after the words of Christ, which in his view are the essential thing; Mark dwells somewhat more on the circumstances; Luke enriches the traditional narrative by the addition of an important detail—the miraculous fishing—obtained from private sources of information. His narrative is so simple, and at the same time so picturesque, that its accuracy is beyond suspicion. John does not mention this incident, because it was already sufficiently known through the tradition; but, in accordance with his method, he places before us the *first commencement* of the connection which terminated in this result.—Holtzmann thinks that Luke's narrative is made up partly from that of Mark and Matthew, and partly from the account of the miraculous fishing related in John xxi.

[1] Ver. 11. ℵ. B. D. L., παντα instead of απαντα.

[2] "Luke underrates Peter," says M. Burnouf, following M. de Bunsen, jun., *Revue des Deux-Mondes*, 1st December 1865.—Is it not time to have done with this bitter and untruthful criticism, of which the *Anonymous Saxon* has given the most notorious example, and which belongs to a phase of science now passed away!

It would be well to explain how, if this were the case, the thrice repeated reply of Peter, *Thou knowest that I love Thee*, could have been changed by Luke into the exclamation, *Depart from me!* Is it not much more simple to admit that, when Jesus desired to restore Peter to his apostleship, after the denial, He began by placing him in a similar situation to that in which he was when first called, in the presence of another miraculous draught of fishes; and that it was by awakening in him the fresh impressions of earlier days that He restored to him his ministry? Besides, in John xxi., the words, *on the other side of the ship*, seem to allude to the mission *to the heathen.*

The course of events therefore was this: Jesus, after having attached to Himself in Judæa these few disciples of John the Baptist, took them back with Him into Galilee; and as He wished Himself to return to His own family for a little while (John ii. 1–12; Matt. iv. 13), He sent them back to theirs, where they resumed their former employments. In this way those early days passed away, spent in Capernaum and the neighbourhood, of which John speaks (οὐ πολλὰς ἡμέρας), and which Luke describes from iv. 14. But when the time came for Him to go to Jerusalem for the feast of the Passover (John ii. 13 et seq.), where Jesus determined to perform the solemn act which was to inaugurate His Messianic ministry (John ii. 13 et seq.), He thought that the hour had come to attach them to Him altogether; so, separating Himself finally from His family circle and early calling, He required the same sacrifice from them. For this they were sufficiently prepared by all their previous experiences; they made it therefore without hesitation, and we find them from this time constantly with Him, both in the narrative of John (ii. 17, iv. 2–8) and in the Synoptics.

2. *The Lepers:* vers. 12–14.[1]—In Mark (i. 40), as in Luke, the cure of the lepers took place during a preaching tour. Matthew connects this miracle with the Sermon on the Mount; it is as He comes down from the hill that Jesus meets and heals the leper (viii. 1 et seq.). This latter detail is so precise, that it is natural to give Matthew the preference here, rather than say, with Holtzmann, that Matthew wanted to fill up the return from the mountain to the city with it.

Leprosy was in every point of view a most frightful malady. 1*st.* In its physical aspects it was a whitish pustule, eating away the flesh, attacking member after member, and at last eating away the very bones; it was attended with burning fever, sleeplessness, and nightmare, without scarcely the slightest hope of cure. Such were its physical characteristics; it was a living death. 2*d.* In the social point of

[1] Ver. 13. The Mss. are divided between ειπων and λεγων (Alex.).

view, in consequence of the excessively contagious nature of his malady, the leper was separated from his family, and from intercourse with men, and had no other company than that of others as unhappy as himself. Lepers ordinarily lived in bands, at a certain distance from human habitations (2 Kings vii. 3; Luke xvii. 12). Their food was deposited for them in convenient places. They went with their head uncovered, and their chin wrapped up; and on the approach of any persons whom they met, they had to announce themselves as lepers. *3d.* In the religious point of view, the leper was Levitically unclean, and consequently excommunicate. His malady was considered a direct chastisement from God. In the very rare case of a cure, he was only restored to the theocratic community on an official declaration of the priest, and after offering the sacrifice prescribed by the law (Lev. xiii. and xiv., and the tract *Negaïm* in the Talmud).

The Greek expression is: *And behold, a man!* There is not a verb even. His approach was not seen; it has all the effect of an apparition. This dramatic form reproduces the impression made on those who witnessed the scene; in fact, it was only by a kind of surprise, and as it were by stealth, that a leper could have succeeded in approaching so near. The construction of the 12th verse (καὶ ἐγένετο . . . καὶ . . . καὶ) is Hebraistic, and proves an Aramæan document. There is nothing like it in the other Syn.; the eye-witness discovers himself in every feature of Luke's narrative. The diseased man was *full of leprosy;* that is to say, his countenance was lividly white, as is the case when the malady has reached an advanced stage. The unhappy man looks for Jesus in the crowd, and *having discovered Him* (ἰδών) he rushes towards Him; the moment he recognises Him, he is at His feet. Luke says, *falling on his face;* Mark, *kneeling down;* Matthew, *he worshipped.* Would not these variations in terms be puerile if this were a case of copying, or of a derivation from a common source? The dialogue is identical in the three narratives; it was expressed in the tradition in a fixed form, while the historical details were reproduced with greater freedom.—All three evangelists say *cleanse* instead of *heal,* on account of the notion of uncleanness attached to this malady. In the words, *if Thou wilt, Thou canst,* there is at once deep anguish and great faith. Other sick persons had been cured, —this the leper knew,—hence his faith; but he was probably the first man afflicted with his particular malady that succeeded in reaching Jesus and entreating His aid,—hence his anxiety. The older rationalism used to explain this request in this way: "Thou canst, as Messiah, *pronounce me clean.*" According to this explanation, the diseased person, already in the way of being cured naturally, simply asked Jesus to verify the cure and pronounce him clean, in order that he might be spared a costly and troublesome journey to Jerusalem. But for the term *καθαρίζειν, to purify,* comp. vii. 22, Matt. x. 8, where the simply declarative sense is impossible; and as to the context, Strauss has already shown that it comports just as little with this feeble meaning. After the words, *be thou clean* (pronounced pure), these, *and he was cleansed* (pronounced pure), would be nothing but absurd tautology.—Mark, who takes pleasure in portraying the feelings of Jesus, expresses the deep compassion with which He was moved by this spectacle (σπλαγχνισθείς). The three narratives concur in one detail, which must have deeply impressed those who saw it, and which, for this reason, was indelibly imprinted on the tradition: *He put forth His hand, and touched him* Leprosy was so contagious,[1] that this courageous act excited the liveliest emotion in the crowd. Throughout the whole course of His life, Jesus confronted the touch of our impure nature in a similar manner.—His answer is identical in the three narratives; but the result is variously expressed. Matthew says: *his leprosy was cleansed,* regarding it from a ceremonial point of view. Luke simply says: *the leprosy departed from him,* looking at it from a human point of view. Mark combines the two forms. This is one of the passages on which they rely who make Mark a compiler from the other two; but if Mark was anxious to adhere so slavishly to the minutest expressions of his predecessors, to the point even of reproducing them without any object, how are we to explain the serious and important modifications which in so

[1] It probably was regarded as contagious in popular apprehension, which would justify the remark in the text; but the man who was so completely covered with the disease that it could find no further range was clean, according to Lev. xiii. 13. See Smith's *Dict. of Bible, sub voce.*—TR.

many other cases he introduced into their narratives, and the considerable omissions which he is continually making of the substance of what they relate? The fact is, that there were two sides to this cure, as to the malady itself, the physical and the religious; and Mark combines them, whilst the other two appear to take one or the other.

The prohibition which Jesus lays on the leper appears in Luke v. 14, in the form of indirect discourse; but in relating the injunction which follows it, Luke passes to the direct form. This form is peculiar to his narrative. Luke and Matthew omit the threat with which Jesus, according to Mark, accompanied this injunction (ἐμβριμησάμενος). What was the intention of Jesus? The cure having been public, He could not prevent the report of it from being spread abroad. This is true; but He wanted to do all in His power to diminish its fame, and not give a useless impetus to the popular excitement produced by the report of His miracles. Comp. Luke viii. 56; Matt. ix. 30, xii. 16; Mark i. 34, iii. 12, v. 43, vii. 36, viii. 26. All these passages forbid our seeking a particular cause for the prohibition He lays on the leper; such as a fear that the priests, having had notice of his cure before his reaching them, would refuse to acknowledge it; or that they would pronounce Jesus unclean for having touched him; or that the sick man would lose the serious impressions which he had received; or that he would allow himself to be deterred from the duty of offering the sacrifice. —Jesus said, "Show *thyself*," because the person is here the convincing proof. In Luke we read, *according as Moses* . . .; in Matthew, *the gift which Moses* . . .; in Mark, *the things which Moses* . . . Most puerile changes, if they were designed!—What is the testimony contained in this sacrifice, and to whom is it addressed? According to Bleek, the word *them* would refer to the people, who are to be apprised that every one may henceforth renew his former relations with the leper. But is not the term *testimony* too weighty for this meaning? Gerlach refers the pronoun *them* to the priests: in order that thou, by thy cure, mayest be a witness to them of my almightiness; but according to the text, the testimony consists not in the cure being verified, but in the sacrifice being offered. The word *them* does indeed refer to the priests, who are all represented by the one who will verify the cure; but the testimony respects Jesus Himself, and His sentiments in regard to the law. In the Sermon on the Mount, Jesus repels the charge already preferred against Him of despising the law (Matt. v. 17: "*Think not that I am come to destroy the law*"). It is to His respect, therefore, for the Mosaic legislation, that this offering will testify to the priests. During His earthly career, Jesus never dispensed His people from the obligation to obey the prescriptions of the law; and it is an error to regard Him as having, under certain circumstances, set aside the law of the Sabbath as far as He Himself was concerned. He only transgressed the arbitrary enactments with which Pharisaism had surrounded it.—We see by these remarkable words that Jesus had already become an object of suspicion and serious charges at Jerusalem. This state of things is explained by the narrative of the fourth Gospel, where, from the 2d chapter, we see Jesus exposed to the animosity of the dominant party, and accords to iv. 1. He is even obliged to leave Judæa in order that their unfavourable impressions may not be aggravated before the time. In chap. v., which describes a fresh visit to Jerusalem (for the feast of Purim), the conflict thus prepared breaks forth with violence, and Jesus is obliged to testify solemnly His respect for this Moses, who will be the Jews' accuser, and not His (v. 45–47). This is just the state of things with which the passage we are explaining agrees, as well as all the facts which are the sequel of it. Notwithstanding apparent discrepancies between the Syn. and John, a substantial similarity prevails between them, which proves that both forms of narrative rest on a basis of historic reality.

The leper, according to Mark, did not obey the injunction of Jesus; and this disobedience served to increase that concourse of sick persons which Jesus endeavoured to lessen.

This cure is a difficulty for Keim. A purely moral influence may calm a fever (iv. 39), or restore a frenzied man to his senses (iv. 31 et seq.); but it cannot purify vitiated blood, and cleanse a body covered with pustules. Keim here resorts to what is substantially the explanation of Paulus. The leper already cured simply desired to be *pronounced* clean by authorized lips, that he might not have to go to Jerusalem. It must be acknowledged. on this view of the matter, that the three narratives (Matthew as well as Luke and Mark, whatever Keim may say about it) are completely falsified by the legend. Then how came it to enter into the mind of this man to substitute Jesus for a priest? How could Jesus have accepted such an office? Having accepted it, why should He have sent the afflicted man to Jerusalem? Further, for what reason did He impose silence upon him, and enforce it with threats? And what could the man have had to publish abroad, of sufficient importance to attract the crowd of people described Mark i. 45?

Holtzmann (p. 432) concludes, from the words ἐξέβαλεν and ἐξελθών, literally, *He cast him out,* and *having gone forth* (Mark i. 43, 45), that according to Mark this cure took place in a house, which agrees very well with the leper being prohibited from making it known; and that consequently the other two Syn. are in error in making it take place in public,—Luke *in a city,* Matthew on the road from the mountain to Capernaum (viii. 1). He draws great exegetical inferences from this. But when it is said in Mark (i. 12) that the Spirit *drove out* (ἐκβάλλει) Jesus into the wilderness, does this mean out *of a house?* And as to the verb ἐξέρχεσθαι, is it not frequently used in a broad sense: to go out of the midst of that in which one happens to be (here: the circle formed around Jesus)? Comp. Mark vi. 34 (Matt. xiv. 14), vi. 12; John i. 44, etc. A leper would hardly have been able to make his way into a house. His taking them by surprise in the way he did could scarcely have happened except in the open country; and, as we have seen, the prohibition of Jesus can easily be explained, taking this view of the incident. The critical consequences of Holtzmann, therefore, have no substantial basis.

3. *The Paralytic:* vers. 15–26.—1*st.* A general description of the state of the work, vers. 15, 16; 2*d.* The cure of the paralytic, vers. 17–26.

1*st.* Vers. 15 and 16.[1]—While seeking to calm the excitement produced by His miracles, Jesus endeavoured also to preserve His energies from any spiritual deterioration by devoting part of His time to meditation and prayer. As Son of man, He had, in common with us all, to draw from God the strength He needed for His hours of activity. Such touches as these in the narrative certainly do not look like an apotheosis of Jesus, and they constitute a striking difference between the evangelical portrait and the legendary caricature. —This thoroughly original detail suffices also to prove the independence of Luke's sources of information.—After this general

[1] ℵ. B. C. D. L. some Mnn. It. omit υπ' αυτου.

description (the seventh), the narrative is resumed with a detached and special incident, given as an example of the state of things described.

2*d*. Vers. 17–19.[1] *The Arrival.*—The completely Aramæan form of this preface (the *καί* before *αὐτός*, the form *καὶ ἦσαν . . . οἳ ἦσαν*, and especially the expression *ἦν εἰς τὸ ἰᾶσθαι*) proves that Luke's account is not borrowed from either of the two other Synoptics.—This was one of those solemn hours of which we have another instance in the evening at Capernaum (iv. 41, 42). The presence of the Pharisees and scribes from Jerusalem is easily explained, if the conflict related John v. had already taken place. The scribes did not constitute a theological or political party, like the Pharisees and Sadducees. They were the professional lawyers. They were designedly associated with the Pharisees sent to Galilee to watch Jesus (ver. 21). — The narrative in the first Gospel is extremely concise. Matthew does not tell the story ; he is intent upon his object, the word of Jesus. Mark gives the same details as Luke, but without the two narratives presenting *one* single term in common. And yet they worked on the same document, or one on the text of the other !—The roof of the house could be reached by a flight of steps outside built against the wall, or by a ladder, or even from the next house, for the houses frequently communicated with each other by the terraces. Does Luke's expression, *διὰ τῶν κεράμων*, signify simply *by the roof,*—that is to say, by the stairs which conducted from the terrace to the lower storeys, or down over the balustrade which surrounded the terrace ; or is it just equivalent to Mark's description : " they uncovered the ceiling of the place where He was, and having made an opening, let down the pallet " ? This term, *through the tiles,* would be strange, if it was not to express an idea similar to that of Mark. Strauss objects that such an operation as that of raising the tiles could not have been effected without danger to those who were below ; and he concludes from this that the narrative is only a legend. But in any case, a legend would have been invented in conformity with the mode of construction then adopted and known to everybody. — Jesus

[1] Ver. 17. ℵ. B. L. Z., *αυτον* instead of *αυτους*. — Ver. 19. All the Mjj. omit *δια* before *ποιας*.

was probably seated in a hall immediately beneath the terrace.[1]

Vers. 20 and 21.[2] *The Offence.*—The expression *their faith,* in Luke, applies evidently to the perseverance of the sick man and his bearers, notwithstanding the obstacles they encountered; it is the same in Mark. In Matthew, who has not mentioned these obstacles, but who nevertheless employs the same terms, *and seeing their faith,* this expression can only refer to the simple fact of the paralytic's coming. The identical form of expression indicates a common source; but at the same time, the different sense put upon the common words by their entirely different reference to what precedes proves that this source was not *written.* The oral tradition had evidently so stereotyped this form of expression, that it is found in the narrative of Matthew, though separated from the circumstances to which it is applied in the two others.—Jesus could not repel such an act of faith. Seeing the persevering confidence of the sick man, recognising in him one of those whom *His Father draws to Him* (John vi. 44), He receives him with open arms, by telling him that he is forgiven.—The three salutations differ in our Syn.: *Man* (Luke); *My son* (Mark); *Take courage, my son* (Matthew). Which of the evangelists was it that changed in this arbitrary and aimless manner the words of Jesus as recorded in his predecessor? *Ἀφέωνται* is an Attic form, either for the present *ἀφίενται,* or rather for the perf. *ἀφεῖνται.* It is not impossible that, by speaking in this way, Jesus intended to throw down the gauntlet to His inquisitors. They took it up. The scribes are put before the Pharisees; they were the experts. A blasphemy! How welcome to them! Nothing could have sounded more agreeably in their ears. We will not say, in

[1] Delitszch represents the fact in this way (*Ein Tag in Capernaum,* pp. 40–46): Two bearers ascend the roof by a ladder, and by means of cords they draw up by the same way the sick man after them, assisted by the other two bearers. In the middle of the terrace was a square place open in summer to give light and air to the house, but closed with tiles during the rainy season. Having opened this passage, the bearers let down the sick man into the large inner court immediately below, where Jesus was teaching near the cistern fixed as usual in this court. The trap-stairs which lead down from the terrace into the house would have been too narrow for their use, and would not have taken them into the court, but into the apartments which overlooked it from all sides.

[2] Ver. 20. ℵ B. L. X. omit *αυτω* after *ειπεν.*

regard to this accusation, with many orthodox interpreters, that, as God, Jesus had a right to pardon; for this would be to go directly contrary to the employment of the title Son of man, in virtue of which Jesus attributes to Himself, in ver. 24, this power. But may not God delegate His gracious authority to a man who deserves His confidence, and who becomes, for the great work of salvation, His ambassador on earth? This is the position which Jesus takes. The only question is, whether this pretension is well founded; and it is the demonstration of this moral fact, already contained in His previous miracles, that He proceeds to give in a striking form to His adversaries.

Vers. 22–24.[1] *The Miracle.*—The miraculous work which is to follow is for a moment deferred. Jesus, without having heard the words of those about Him, understands their murmurs. His mind is, as it were, the mirror of their thoughts. The form of His reply is so striking, that the tradition has preserved it to the very letter; hence it is found in identical terms in all three narratives. The proposition, *that ye may know*, depends on the following command: *I say to thee . . .* The principal and subordinate clauses having been separated by a moment of solemn silence, the three accounts fill up this interval with the parenthesis: *He saith to the paralytic.* This original and identical form must necessarily proceed from a common source, oral or written.—It is no easier, certainly, to pardon than to heal; but it is much easier to convict a man of imposture who falsely claims the power to heal, than him who falsely arrogates authority to pardon. There is a slight irony in the way in which Jesus gives expression to this thought. "You think these are empty words that I utter when I say, Thy sins are forgiven thee. See, then, whether the command which I am about to give is an empty word." The miracle thus announced acquires the value of an imposing demonstration. It will be *seen* whether Jesus is not really what He claims to be, the *Ambassador of God* on earth to forgive sins. Earth, where the pardon is granted, is opposed to heaven, where He dwells from whom it proceeds.

It is generally acknowledged at the present day, that the

[1] The Mss. vary between παραλελυμένω and παραλυτικῷ.

title *Son of man,* by which Jesus preferred to designate Himself, is not simply an allusion to the symbolical name in Dan. vii., but that it sprang spontaneously from the depths of Jesus' own consciousness. Just as, in His title of *Son of God,* Jesus included whatever He was conscious of being for God, so in that of *Son of man* He comprehended all He felt He was for men. The term *Son of man* is generic, and denotes each representative of the human race (Ps. viii. 5; Ezek. xxxvii. 3, 9, 11). With the art. (*the* Son of man), this expression contains the notion of a superiority in the equality. It designates Jesus not simply as man, but as the normal man, the perfect representative of the race. If this title alludes to any passage of the O. T., it must be to the ancient prophecy, "*The seed of the woman* shall bruise the serpent's head" (Gen. iii. 15).[1]—There is a tone of triumph in this expression, ver. 25: *He took up that whereon he lay.* The astonishment of the people, ver. 26, is expressed differently in the three narratives: *We never saw it on this fashion* (Mark); *They glorified God, which had given such power unto men* (Matthew). This remarkable expression, *to men,* is doubtless connected with *Son of man.* Whatever is given to the normal man, is in Him given to all. Matthew did not certainly add this expression on his own authority, any more than the others arbitrarily omitted it. Their sources were different.

Παράδοξα, strange things, in Luke, is found in Josephus' account of Jesus. By the term *to-day* the multitude allude not only to the miracle,—they had seen others as astounding on previous days,—but more particularly to the divine prerogative of pardon, so magnificently demonstrated by this miracle with which Jesus had just connected it.—The different expressions by which the crowd give utterance to their surprise in the three Syn. might really have been on the lips of different witnesses of this scene.

Keim, applying here the method indicated, pp. 253–4, thinks that the paralysis was overcome by the moral excitement which

[1] M. Gess, in his fine work, *Christi Zeugniss von seiner Person und seinem Werk,* 1870, understands by *the Son of man,* He who represents the divine majesty in a human form. The idea in itself is true; the normal man is called to share in the divine estate, and to become the supreme manifestation of God. But the notion of divine majesty does not belong to the term *Son of man.* It is contained in the term *Son of God.* The two titles are in antithetical connection, and for this reason they complete each other.

the sick man underwent. Examples are given of impotent persons whose power of movement has been restored by a mighty internal shock. Therefore it is just possible that the physical fact might be explained in this way. But the moral fact, the absolute assurance of Jesus, the challenge implied in this address, "In order that ye may know, . . . arise and walk!"—a speech the authenticity of which is so completely guaranteed by the three narratives and by its evident originality,—how is this to be explained from Keim's standpoint? Why, Jesus, in announcing so positively a success so problematical, would have laid Himself open to be palpably contradicted by the fact! At the commencement of His ministry He would have based His title to be the Son of man, His authority to forgive sins, His mission as the Saviour, His entire spiritual work, on the needle's point of this hazardous experiment!—If this were the case, instead of a divine demonstration (and this is the meaning which Jesus attaches to the miracle), there would be nothing more in the fact than a fortunate coincidence.

4. *The Call of Levi:* vers. 27–39.—This section relates: 1*st.* The call of Levi; 2*d.* The feast which followed, with the discourse connected with it; 3*d.* A double lesson arising out of a question about fasting.

1*st.* Vers. 27 and 28.[1] *The Call.*—This fact occupies an important place in the development of the work of Jesus, not only as the complement of the call of the first disciples (ver. 1 et seq.), but especially as a continuation of the conflict already entered into with the old order of things.

The *publicans* of the Gospels are ordinarily regarded as Jewish *sub-collectors* in the service of Roman knights, to whom the tolls of Palestine had been let out at Rome. Wieseler, in his recent work,[2] corrects this view. He proves, by an edict of Cæsar, quoted in Josephus (*Antiq.* xiv. 10. 5), that the tolls in Judæa were remitted direct to the Jewish or heathen collectors, without passing through the hands of the Roman financiers. The publicans, especially such as, like Matthew, were of Jewish origin, were hated and despised by their fellow-countrymen more even than the heathen themselves. They were excommunicated, and deprived of the right of tendering an oath before the Jewish authorities. Their conduct, which was too often marked by extortion and fraud, generally justified the opprobrium which public opinion cast

[1] Ver. 28. The Mss. vary between καταλιπων and καταλειπων, as well as between απαντα and παντα, ηκολουθει and ηκολουθησεν.

[2] *Beiträge zur richtigen Würdigung der Evangelien*, p. 78.

upon them.—Capernaum was on the road leading from Damascus to the Mediterranean, which terminated at Ptolemais (St. Jean d'Acre). It was the commercial highway from the interior of Asia. In this city, therefore, there must have been a tax-office of considerable importance. This office was probably situated outside the city, and near the sea. This explains the expression, *He went out* (Luke); *He went forth in order to go to the sea-side* (Mark). In the three Syn. this call immediately follows the healing of the paralytic (Matt. ix. 9; Mark ii. 13 et seq.).

Jesus must have had some very important reason for calling a man from the class of the publicans to join the circle of His disciples; for by this step He set Himself at open variance with the theocratic notions of decorum. Was it His deliberate intention to throw down the gauntlet to the numerous Pharisees who had come from a distance to watch Him, and to show them how completely He set Himself above their judgment? Or was it simply convenient to have among His disciples a man accustomed to the use of the pen? This is quite possible; but there is something so abrupt, so spontaneous, and so strange in this call, that it is impossible to doubt that Jesus spoke to him in obedience to a direct impulse from on high. The higher nature of the call appears also in the decision and promptness with which it was accepted. Between Jesus and this man there must have been, as it were, a flash of divine sympathy. The relation between Jesus and His first apostles was formed in this way (John i.). The name *Levi* not occurring in any of the lists of apostles,—it is impossible to identify it with *Lebbæus,* which has a different meaning and etymology,—it might be thought that this Levi never belonged to the number of the twelve. But in this case why should his call be so particularly related? Then the expression, *having left all, he followed Him* (ver. 28), forbids our thinking that Levi ever resumed his profession as a toll-collector, and puts him in the same rank as the four older disciples (ver. 11). We must therefore look for him among the apostles. In the catalogue of the first Gospel (x. 3), the Apostle Matthew is called the *publican;* and in the same Gospel (ix. 9) the call of Matthew the publican is related, with details identical with those of our narrative. Must we admit two different but similar incidents? This was the supposition of the Gnostic Heracleon and of Clement of Alexandria. Sieffert, Ewald, and Keim prefer to admit that our first Gospel applies by mistake to the apostle and older publican Matthew, the calling of another less known publican, who should be called Levi (Mark and Luke). This opinion naturally implies that the first Gospel is unauthentic. But is it not much simpler to suppose that the former name of this man was *Levi*, and that Jesus, perceiving the direct hand of God in this event, gave him the surname of *Matthew, gift of God*, just as He gave Simon, at His first meeting with him, the surname of Peter?[1] This name, which Matthew habitually bore in the Church, was naturally that under which he figured afterwards in the catalogues of the apostles. Were Luke and Mark unaware that the apostle so named was the publican whom they had designated by the name of Levi? Or have they neglected to mention this identity in their lists of the apostles, because they have given these just as they found them in their documents? We do not know. We are continually struck by seeing how the evangelical tradition has left in the shade the secondary personages of this great drama, in order to bestow exclusive attention on the principal actor. —Ἐθεάσατο does not signify merely *He saw*, but *He fixed His eyes upon him*. This was the moment when something peculiar and inexplicable took place between Jesus and the publican.—The expression καθήμενον ἐπὶ τὸ τελώνιον cannot signify seated *in* the office; ἐπὶ or ἐν τῷ τελωνίῳ would be necessary. As the accusative after ἐπί, the word *toll* might mean, seated at his *work of toll-collecting*; but this sense of τελώνιον is unexampled. Might not the prep. ἐπί have the sense here in which it is sometimes employed in the classics, —in Herodotus, for example, when he says of Aristides that he kept ἐπὶ τὸ συνέδριον in front of the place where the chiefs were assembled (viii. 79)? Levi must have been *seated in front of his office*, observing what was passing. How, indeed, if he had been seated *in* the office, could his glance have met that of Jesus?—Without even re-entering, he follows Him, forsaking all.

[1] Comp. the Ματθαῖον λεγόμενον, Matt. ix. 9, with Σίμων ὁ λεγόμενος Πέτρος, x. 2.—John i. 43.

2*d*. Vers. 29–32.[1] *The Feast.* — According to Luke, the repast was spread in the house of Levi; the new disciple seeks to bring his old friends and Jesus together. It is his first missionary effort. Meyer sees a contradiction to Matthew here. Matthew says, " as Jesus sat at meat *in the house*,"—an expression which, in his opinion, can only mean the dwelling of Jesus. He decides in favour of Matthew's narrative. But (1) how came the crowd of publicans and people of ill-fame at meat all at once in the house of Jesus? (2) Where is there ever any mention of *the house of Jesus?* (3) The repetition of Jesus' name at the end of the verse (ver. 10 in Matthew) excludes the idea that the complement understood of *the house* is *Jesus.* As to Mark, the pron. *αὐτοῦ, his* house, refers to Levi; this is proved (1) by the opposition of *αὐτοῦ* to the preceding *αὐτόν*, and (2) by the repetition of the name *Ἰησοῦ* in the following phrase.[2] The expression *in the house,* in Matthew, denotes therefore the house, wherever it was, in which the meal took place, in opposition to the *outside,* where the call, with the preaching that followed it, occurred. As usual, Matthew passes rapidly over the external circumstances of the narrative; it is the word of Jesus in which he is interested.—The repast, doubtless, took place on the ground-floor, and the apartment or gallery in which the table was spread could easily be reached from the street. While Jesus was surrounded by His new friends, His adversaries attacked His disciples. The T. R. places *their scribes* before *the Pharisees.* In this case, they would be the scribes *of the place,* or those *of the nation.* Neither meaning is very natural; the other reading, therefore, must be preferred: *the Pharisees and their scribes,* the defenders of strict observance, and the learned men sent with them from Jerusalem as experts (vers. 17–21). The *Sinait.* and some others have omitted *αὐτῶν*, doubtless on account of the difficulty and apparent uselessness of this pronoun.

Eating together is, in the East, as with us, the sign of very

[1] Part of the Mss. put *οι Φαρισαιοι* before *οι γραμματεις αυτων*; T. R., with the others, *οι γραμμ. αυτων* before *οι Φαρισ.* — Αυτον is omitted by א. D. F. X. some Mnn. Ita
liq. ; T. R. omits *των*, with S. V. Π. only.

[2] I am happy to find myself in accord here with Klostermann in his fine and conscientious study of the second Gospel, *Das Marcus-Evangelium*, pp. 43, 44.

close intimacy. Jesus, therefore, went beyond all the limits of Jewish decorum in accepting the hospitality of Matthew's house, and in such company. His justification is partly serious and partly ironical. He seems to concede to the Pharisees that they are perfectly well, and concludes from this that for them He, the physician, is useless; so far the irony. On the other hand, it is certain that, speaking ritually, the Pharisees were right according to the Levitical law, and that being so, they would enjoy the means of grace offered by the old covenant, of which those who have broken with the theocratic forms are deprived. In this sense the latter are really in a more serious condition than the Pharisees, and more urgently need that some one should interest himself in their salvation; this is the serious side of the answer. This word is like a two-edged sword: first of all, it justifies Jesus from His adversaries' point of view, and by an argument *ad hominem*; but, at the same time, it is calculated to excite serious doubts in their minds as to whether this point of view be altogether just, and to give them a glimpse of another, according to which the difference that separates them from the publicans has not all the worth which they attributed to it (see on xv. 1–7).—The words *to repentance* are wanting in Matthew and Mark, according to the best authorities; the words understood in this case are: to the kingdom of God, to salvation. In Luke, where these words are authentic, they continue the irony which forms the substance of this answer: come to call *to repentance just persons!*—It is for the Pharisees to ask themselves, after this, whether, because they meet the requirements of the temple, they satisfy the demands of God.—The discussion here takes a new turn; it assumes the character of a conversation on the use of fasting in the old and new order of things.

3*d*. Vers. 33–39. *Instruction concerning Fasting.*

Vers. 33–35.[1] In Luke they are the same parties, particularly the scribes, who continue the conversation, and who allege, in favour of the regular practice of fasting, the example

[1] Ver. 33. ℵ[a] (?) B. L. X. omit διατι.—Ver. 34. ℵ* D. It[plerique], μη δυνανται εις υιο. . . . νηστευσαι (or νηστευειν) instead of μη δυνασθε τους υιους . . . ποιησαι νηστευσαι (or νηστευειν).—Ver. 35. ℵ. C. F. L. M. some Mnn. Syr. It[plerique], omit και before οταν. The same (with the exception of C. L.) and Δ. place it before τοτε.

of the disciples of John and of the Pharisees. The scribes express themselves in this manner, because they themselves, as scribes, belong to no party whatever. In Matthew it is the disciples of John who appear all at once in the midst of this scene, and interrogate Jesus in their own name and in that of the Pharisees. In Mark it is the disciples of John and of the Pharisees united who put the question. This difference might easily find its way into the oral tradition, but it is inexplicable on any of the hypotheses which deduce the three texts from one and the same written source, or one of them from another.—Mark says literally: *the disciples of John and the Pharisees were fasting;* and we may understand *that day.* Devout persons in Israel fasted, in fact, twice a week (Luke xviii. 12), on Mondays and Fridays, the days on which it was said that Moses went up Sinai (see Meyer on Matt. vi. 16); this particular day may have been one or other of these two days. But we may also explain it: *fasted habitually.* They were *fasting persons,* addicted to religious observances in which fasting held an important place. It is not easy to decide between these two senses: with the first, there seems less reason for the question; with the second, it conveys a much more serious charge against Jesus, since it refers to His habitual conduct; comp. vii. 34, "Ye say, He is a glutton and a winebibber (an eater and a drinker)." The word διατί, omitted by the Alex., appears to have been taken from Matthew and Mark.

Whether the disciples of John were present or not, it is to their mode of religious reformation that our Lord's answer more especially applies. As they do not appear to have cherished very kindly feelings towards Jesus (John iii. 25, 26), it is very possible that they were united on this occasion with His avowed adversaries (Matthew).—Jesus compares the days of His presence on the earth to a nuptial feast. The Old Testament had represented the Messianic coming of Jehovah by this figure. If John the Baptist had already uttered the words reported by John (iii. 29): "*He that hath the bride is the bridegroom; but the friend of the bridegroom, which standeth and heareth him, rejoiceth greatly because of the bridegroom's voice: this my joy therefore is fulfilled,*"—what appropriateness there was in this figure by which He replied to his disciples!

Perhaps the Pharisees authorized a departure from the rule respecting fasting during the nuptial weeks. In this case Jesus' reply would become more striking still. *Νυμφών* signifies *the nuptial chamber*, and not the *bridegroom* (*νυμφίος*), as Martin, Ostervald, and Crampon translate. The true Greek term to indicate the nuptial friend would have been *παρανύμφιος*; John says: *φίλος τοῦ νυμφίου.* The expression of the Syn., *son of the nuptial chamber*, is a Hebraism (comp *son* of the kingdom, of wisdom, of perdition, etc.). The received reading, "*Can you make the marriage friends fast?*" (notwithstanding the joy with which their hearts are full), is preferable to that of the *Sinait.* and of the Græco-Latin Codd., "Can they fast?" which is less forcible, and which is taken from Matthew and Mark. In the midst of this feast of publicans the heart of Jesus is overflowing with joy; it is one of the hours when His earthly life seems to His feeling like a marriage day. But suddenly His countenance becomes overcast; the shadow of a painful vision passes across His brow: *The days will come* . . . said He in a solemn tone. At the close of this nuptial week, the bridegroom Himself will be suddenly smitten and cut off; then will come the time of fasting for those who to-day are rejoicing; there will be no necessity to enjoin it. In this striking and poetic answer Jesus evidently announces His violent death. The passive aor. cannot, as Bleek admits, be explained otherwise. This verb and tense indicate a stroke of violence, by which the subject of the verb will be smitten (comp. 1 Cor. v. 2). This saying is parallel to the words found in John ii. 19, "*Destroy this temple;*" and iii. 14, "As Moses lifted up the serpent, *so* must the Son of man *be lifted up.*" The fasting which Jesus here opposes to the prescribed fasting practised in Israel is neither a state of purely inward grief, a moral fast, in moments of spiritual depression, nor, as Neander thought, the life of privation and sacrifice to which the apostles would inevitably be exposed after the departure of their Master; it is indeed, according to the context, fasting in the proper sense of the term. Fasting has always been practised in the Church at certain solemn seasons, but it is not a rite imposed on it from without, but the expression of a sentiment of real grief. It proceeds from the sorrow which the Church feels in the absence of its Head, and is designed to lend intensity to its prayers, and to ensure with greater certainty that assistance of Jesus which alone can supply the place of His visible presence (comp. Mark. ix. 29 (?); Acts xiii. 2, 3, xiv. 23).—This remarkable saying was preserved with literal exactness in the tradition; accordingly we find it in identical words in the three Syn. It proves, first, that from the earliest period of His ministry Jesus regarded Himself as the Messiah; next, that He identified His coming with that of Jehovah, the husband of Israel and of mankind (Hos. ii. 19);[1] lastly, that at that time He already foresaw and announced His violent death. It is an error, therefore, to oppose, on these three points, the fourth Gospel to the other three.

Vers. 36–39. Here we have the second part of the conversation. The expression ἔλεγε δὲ καί, *and He said also*, indicates its range. This expression, which occurs so frequently in Luke, always indicates the point at which Jesus, after having treated of the particular subject before Him, rises to a more general view which commands the whole question. Thus, from this moment He makes the particular difference respecting fasting subordinate to the general opposition between the old and new order of things,—an idea which carries Him back to the occasion of the scene, the call of a publican.

Ver. 36.[2] *First Parable.*—The T. R. says: "No man putteth a piece of new cloth unto an old garment." The Alex. var. has this: "No man, *rending a piece from a new garment*, putteth it to an old garment." In Matthew and Mark the new piece is taken from *any piece of cloth;* in Luke, according to two readings, it is cut out of a whole *garment;* the Alex. reading only puts this in a somewhat stronger form.—The verb σχίζει, rends (Alex. σχίσει, will rend), in the second proposition, might have the intransitive sense: "Otherwise the new [piece] *maketh a rent* [in the old]," which would come to the same meaning as the passage has in Matthew and Mark: "The new piece *taketh away a part of the old*, and the rent is made worse."

[1] See Gess, *Christi Zeugniss*, pp. 19, 20.

[2] Ver. 36. ℵ. B. D. L. X. Z. several Mnn. Syr. It^{aliq}. omit απο before ιματιου.—ℵ. B. D. L. Z. some Mnn. add σχισας before επιβαλλει.—ℵ. B. C. D. L. X., σχισει, συμφωνησει, instead of σχιζει, συμφωνει.—ℵ. B. C. L. X. Δ. add το επιβλημα before το απο του καινου.

But in Luke the context requires the active sense: "Otherwise *it* [the piece used to patch with] rendeth the *new* [garment]." This is the only sense admissible in the Alex. reading, after the partic. *σχίσας, rending,* in the preceding proposition. The received reading equally requires it: for, 1*st*. The second inconvenience indicated, "the new agreeth not with the old," would be too slight to be placed after that of the enlargement of the rent. 2*d*. The evident correlation between the two *καί, both . . . and . . .*, contains the following idea: the two garments, *both* the new *and* the old, are spoiled together; the new, because it has been rent to patch the old; the old, because it is disfigured by a piece of different cloth. Certainly it would still be possible to refer the expression, *not agree,* not to the incongruity in appearance of the two cloths, but to the stronger and more resisting quality of the new cloth,—an inequality which would have the effect of increasing the rent. This would be the untoward result intended in Matthew and Mark. But the term *συμφονεῖν, to harmonize,* refers much more naturally to a contrast *in appearance* between the two cloths.—The futures, *will rend, will agree,* in the Alex. reading, may be defended; but are they not a correction proceeding from the use of the future in the second parable (*will break, will be spilled, will perish,* ver. 37)? The corrector, in this case, could not have remembered that, in the case of the wine and the leathern bottles, the damage is only produced after a time, whilst in the garment it is immediate. To sum up: in Matthew and Mark there is only a single damage, that which befalls the old garment, the rent of which is enlarged; in Luke the damage is twofold: in one case affecting the new garment, which is cut into to patch the other; in the other, affecting the old garment, as in Matthew and Mark, but consisting in the patchwork appearance of the cloths, and not in the enlargement of the rent.

In the application it is impossible not to connect this image of the piece of new cloth with the subject of the previous conversation, the rite of fasting, while we admit that Jesus generalizes the question. Moses had nowhere prescribed monthly or weekly fasts. The only periodical fast commanded in the law was annual—that on the day of atonement. The regular fasts, such as those which the adversaries of Jesus would have had Him impose on His disciples, were one of those pharisaical inventions which the Jews called *a hedge about the law*, and by which they sought to complete and maintain the legal system. John the Baptist himself had been unable to do anything better than attach himself to this method. This is the *patching-up* process which is indicated in Matthew and Mark, and which is opposed to the mode of action adopted by Jesus—the total substitution of a new for an old garment. In Luke the image is still more full of meaning: Jesus, alluding to that new, unconstrained, evangelical fasting, of which He has spoken in ver. 34, and which He cannot at present require of His disciples, makes the general declaration that it is necessary to wait for the new life before creating its forms; it is impossible to anticipate it by attempting to adapt to the legal system, under which His disciples are as yet living, the elements of the new state which He promises them. His mission is not to labour to repair and maintain an educational institution, *now decaying* and *waxing old* (*παλαιούμενον καὶ γηράσκον*). He is not a patcher, as the Pharisees were, nor a reformer, like John the Baptist. *Opus majus!* It is a new garment that He brings. To mix up the old work with the new, would be to spoil the latter without preserving the former. It would be a violation of the unity of the spiritualism which He was about to inaugurate, and to introduce into the legal system an offensive medley. Would not the least particle of evangelical freedom suffice to make every legal observance fall into disuse? Better then let the old garment remain as it is, until the time comes to substitute the new for it altogether, than try to patch it up with strips taken from the latter! As Lange says (*Leben Jesu*, ii. p. 680): "The work of Jesus is too good to use it in repairing the worn garment of pharisaical Judaism, which could never thereby be made into anything better than the assumed garb of a beggar." This profound idea of the mingling of *the new holiness* with the ancient legalism comes out more clearly from Luke's simile, and cannot have been introduced into the words of Jesus by him.—Neander thinks that the old garment must be regarded as the image of the old *unregenerate nature* of the disciples, on which Jesus could not impose the forms of the new life. But the moral nature of man cannot be compared to a garment; it is the man himself.'[1]—Gess applies the image of the piece of *new cloth* to the asceticism of John the Baptist. This meaning might suffice for the form of it in Matthew and Mark; but it leaves Luke's form of it (a piece of the *new garment*) unexplained.

What a view of His mission this word of Jesus reveals! What a lofty conception of the work He came to accomplish! From what a height He looks down, not only on the Pharisees, but on John himself, the great representative of the old covenant, the greatest of those born of women! And all this is expressed in the simplest, homeliest manner, thrown off with the greatest facility! He speaks as a being to whom nothing is so natural as the sublime. All that has been called *the system of Paul*, all that this apostle himself designates *his gospel*,—the decisive contrast between the two covenants, the mutual exclusiveness of the systems of law and grace, of *the oldness of the letter* and *the newness of the spirit* (Rom. vii. 6), this inexorable dilemma: "*If by grace, then is it no more of works; if it be of works, then is it no more grace*" (Rom. xi. 6), which constitutes the substance of the Epistles to the Romans and the Galatians,—all is contained in this homely figure of a garment patched with a piece of cloth, or with part of a new garment! How can any one, after this, maintain that Jesus was not conscious from the beginning of the bearing of His work, as well of the task He had to accomplish in regard to the law, as of His Messianic dignity? How can any one contend that the Twelve, to whom we owe the preservation of this parable, were only narrow Jewish Christians, as prejudiced in favour of their law as the most extreme men of the party? If they perceived the meaning of this saying alone, the part attributed to them becomes impossible. And if they had no comprehension of it, how was it that they thought it worthy of a place in the teaching of Jesus, which they handed down with such care to the Church?

Often, after having presented an idea by means of a parable, from a feeling that the figure employed fails to represent it completely, Jesus immediately adds a second parable, designed to set forth another aspect of the same idea. In this way are formed what may be called the *pairs of parables*, which are

[1] Eph. iv. 22, 24, is a metaphor, not a parable.

so often met with in the Gospels (the grain of mustard seed and the leaven; the treasure and the pearl; the unwise builder and the imprudent warrior; the sower and the tares). Following the same method, Jesus here adds to the parable of the piece of cloth that of the leathern bottles.

Vers. 37, 38.[1] *The Second Parable.*—The figure is taken from the Oriental custom of preserving liquids in leathern bottles, made generally of goat-skins. "No one," says M. Pierotti, "travels in Palestine without having a leathern bottle filled with water amongst his luggage. These bottles preserve the water for drinking, without imparting any ill taste to it; also wine, oil, honey, and milk."[2] In this parable there is evidently an advance on the preceding, as we always find in the case of *double parables.* This difference of meaning, misapprehended by Neander and the greater part of interpreters, comes out more particularly from two features: 1. The opposition between the *unity* of the garment in the first, and the *plurality* of the bottles in the second; 2. The fact that, since the new *wine* answers to the new garment, the new *bottles* must represent a different and entirely new idea. In fact, Jesus here is no longer opposing the evangelical *principle* to the legal *principle,* but the *representatives* of the one to those of the other. Two complaints were raised against Jesus: 1*st.* His negligence of the legal forms; to this accusation He has just replied. 2*d.* His contempt for the representatives of legalism, and His sympathy with those who had thrown off the theocratic discipline. It is to this second charge that He now replies. Nothing can be more simple than our parable from this point of view. The new wine represents that living and healthy spirituality which flows so abundantly through the teaching of Jesus; and the bottles, the men who are to become the depositaries of this principle, and to preserve it for mankind. And whom in Israel will Jesus choose to fulfil this part? The old practitioners of legal observance? Pharisees puffed up with the idea of their own merit? Rabbis jaded with textual discussions? Such persons have nothing to learn, nothing to receive from Him! If associated with

[1] Ver. 38. ℵ. B. L. and some Mnn. omit the words, και αμφοτεροι συντηρουνται.

[2] *Macpelah,* p. 78. The author gives a detailed description of the way in which these bottles are made.

His work, they could not fail to falsify it, by mixing up with His instructions the old prejudices with which they are imbued; or even if they should yield their hearts for a moment to the lofty thought of Jesus, it would put all their religious notions and routine devotion to the rout, just as new and sparkling wine bursts a worn-out leathern bottle. Where, then, shall He choose His future instruments? Among those who have neither merit nor wisdom of their own. He needs fresh natures, souls whose only merit is their receptivity, new men in the sense of the *homo novus* among the Romans, fair tablets on which His hand may write the characters of divine truth, without coming across the old traces of a false human wisdom. "God, I thank Thee, because Thou hast hidden these things from the wise and prudent, and hast revealed them to these babes" (Luke x. 21). These babes will save the truth, and it will save them; this is expressed by these last words: "*and both*, the wine and the bottles, are preserved." These words are omitted in Luke by some Alex. They are suspected of having been added from Matthew, where they are not wanting in any document; Meyer's conjecture, that they have been suppressed, in accordance with Mark, is less probable.

It has been thought that the old bottles represent the unregenerate nature of man, and the new bottles, hearts renewed by the Gospel. But Jesus would not have represented the destruction of the old corrupt nature by the gospel as a result to be dreaded; and He would scarcely have compared new hearts, the *works* of His Holy Spirit, to bottles, the existence of which *precedes* that of the wine which they contain. Lange and Gess see in the old bottles a figure of the legal forms, in the new bottles the image of the evangelical forms. But Christian institutions are an emanation of the Christian spirit, while the bottles exist independently of the wine with which they are filled. And Jesus would not have attached equal importance to the preservation of the wine and of the bottles, as He does in the words: "And *both* are preserved." It is a question, then, here of the preservation of the gospel, and of the salvation of the individuals who are the depositaries of it. Jesus returns here to the fact which was the occasion of the whole scene, and which had called forth the dissatisfaction of

His adversaries, the call of Levi the publican. It is this bold act which He justifies in the second parable, after having vindicated, in the first, the principle on which it was based. A new system demands new persons. This same truth will be applied on a larger scale, when, through the labours of St. Paul, the gospel shall pass from the Jews to the Gentiles, who are the new men in the kingdom of God.

Ver. 39.[1] *The Third Parable.*—The thorough opposition which Jesus has just established between the legal system and the evangelical system (first parable), then between the representatives of the one and those of the other (second parable), must not lead the organs of the new principles to treat those of the ancient order with harshness. They must remember that it is not easy to pass from a system, with which one has been identified from childhood, to an entirely different principle of life. Such men must be allowed time to familiarize themselves with the new principle that is presented to them; and we must beware how we turn our backs upon them, if they do not answer, as Levi the publican did, to the first call. The conversion of a publican may be sudden as lightning, but that of a scrupulous observer of the law will, as a rule, be a work of prolonged effort. This figure, like that of the preceding parable, is taken from the actual circumstances. Conversation follows a meal; the wine in the bottles circulates amongst the guests. With the figure of the bottles, which contain the wine, is easily connected the idea of the individuals who drink it. The new wine, however superior may be its quality, owing to its sharper flavour, is always repugnant to the palate of a man accustomed to wine, the roughness of which has been softened by age. In the same way, it is natural that those who have long rested in the works of the law, should at first take alarm—Jesus can well understand it—at the principle of pure spirituality. It is altogether an error in the Alex. that has erased here the word εὐθεώς, *immediately.* The very idea of the parable is concentrated in this adverb. We must not judge such people by their first impression. The antipathy which they experience *at the first moment* will perhaps give place to a contrary feeling. We

[1] D. It^{plerique}, and probably Eusebius, omit this verse.—ℵ. B. C. L. omit εὐθέως.—ℵ. B. L. two Mnn. Syr^{sch}., χρηστος instead of χρηστοτερος.

must give them time, as Jesus did Nicodemus.—There is a tone of kindly humour in these words: *for he saith,* "Attempt to bring over to gospel views these old followers of legal routine, and immediately they tell you . . ."—If, with the Alex., the positive χρηστός is read: "the old is *mild,*" the repugnance for the new wine is more strongly marked than if we read, with the T. R., the comparative: χρηστότερος, *milder;* for in the first case the antithesis implied is: "The new is not mild *at all.*" As the idea of comparison runs through the entire phrase, the copyists were induced to substitute the comparative for the positive. The Alex. reading is therefore preferable.

"It was a great moment," as Gess truly says, "when Jesus proclaimed in a single breath these three things: the absolute *newness* of His Spirit, His dignity as the *Husband,* and the nearness of *His violent death.*"—If the first parable contains the germ of Paul's *doctrine,* and the second foreshadows His *work* among the Gentiles, the third lays down the principle whence He derived His *mode of acting* towards His fellow-countrymen: making Himself *all things to all* by subjecting Himself to the law, in order to gain them that were under the law (1 Cor. ix. 19, 20).—What gentleness, condescension, and charity breathe through this saying of Jesus! What sweetness, grace, and appropriateness characterize its form! Zeller would have us believe (*Apostelgesch.* p. 15) that Luke invented this touching saying, and added it on his own authority, in order to render the decided Paulinism of the two preceding parables acceptable to Jewish-Christian readers. But does he not see that in saying this he vanquishes himself by his own hand? If the two former parables are so Pauline, that Luke thought he must soften down their meaning by a corrective of his own invention, how comes it to pass that the two other Syn., the Gospels which are in the main Jewish-Christian, have transmitted them to the Church, without the slightest softening down? Criticism sometimes loses its clear-sightedness through excessive sharpness.—That the ultra-Pauline Marcion should have omitted this third parable is perfectly natural; it proves that he thoroughly understood it, for it carries with it the condemnation of his system. But no consequence unfavourable to its authenticity can be drawn from this. The omission of this verse in D., and some versions, is no less easily explained by its omission in the two other synoptics.

The independence of Luke's text, and the originality of its sources, come out clearly from this last passage, which forms such an excellent close to this portion. The difference which we have pointed out in the purport of the first parable, a difference which is entirely in Luke's favour, also attests the excellence of the document from which he has drawn. As to the others, they are no more under obligation to Luke than Luke is to them; would they, of their own accord, have made the teaching of Jesus more anti-legal than it was?

5. *A Sabbath Scene:* vi. 1–5.—The two Sabbath scenes which follow, provoke, at last, the outbreak of the conflict, which, as we have seen, has long been gathering strength. We have already noted several symptoms of the hostility which was beginning to be entertained towards Jesus: ver. 14 (*for a testimony unto them*); ver. 21 (*he blasphemeth*); vers. 30–33 (the *censure* implied in both questions). It is the apparent contempt of Jesus for the ordinance of the Sabbath, which in Luke as well as in John (chap. v. and ix.), alike in Galilee and in Judæa, provokes the outbreak of this latent irritation, and an open rupture between Jesus and the dominant party. Is there not something in this complete parallelism that abundantly compensates for the superficial differences between the synoptical narrative and John's?

Vers. 1–5.[1]—The term *second-first* is omitted by the Alex. But this omission is condemned by Tischendorf himself. Matthew and Mark presented nothing at all like it, and they did not know what meaning to give to the word, which is found nowhere else in the whole compass of sacred and profane literature. There are half a score explanations of it. Chrysostom supposed that when two festival and Sabbath days followed each other, the first received the name of *second-first:* the first of the two. This meaning does not give a natural explanation of the expression.—Wetstein and Storr say that the first Sabbath of the first, second, and third months of the year were called first, second, and third; the second-first Sabbath would thus be the *first* Sabbath of the *second* month. This meaning, although not very natural, is less forced.—Scaliger thought that, as they reckoned seven Sabbaths from the 16th Nisan, the second day of the Passover feast, to Pentecost, the second-first Sabbath denoted the first of these seven Sabbaths: the *first* Sabbath after the *second* day of the Passover. This explanation, received by De Wette,

[1] Ver. 1. א. B. L. some Mnn. Syr^{sch}. It^{aliq}. omit δευτεροπρωτω.—Ver. 2. א. B. C. L. X. some Mnn. omit αυτοις.—Ver. 3. א. B. D. L. X. Syr. omit οντες.—Ver. 4. א. D. K. Π. some Mnn. omit ελαβε και; B. C. L. X. read λαβων.—Ver. 5. D. places this verse after ver. 10. See at ver. 5 (the end).

Neander, and other moderns, agrees very well with the season when the following scene must have taken place. But the term does not correspond naturally with the idea.—Wieseler supposes that the first Sabbath of each of the seven years which formed a Sabbatic cycle was called first, second, third Sabbath: thus the second-first Sabbath would denote the *first* Sabbath of the *second* year of the septenary cycle. This explanation has been favourably received by modern exegesis. —It appears to us, however, less probable than that which Louis Cappel was the first to offer: The civil year of the Israelites commencing in autumn, in the month Tizri (about mid-September to mid-October), and the ecclesiastical year in the month Nisan (about mid-March to mid-April), there were thus every year two first Sabbaths: one at the commencement of the civil year, of which the name would have been *first-first;* the other at the beginning of the religious year, which would be called *second-first.* This explanation is very simple in itself, and the form of the Greek term favours it: *second-first* signifies naturally a *first* doubled or *twice over* (*bissé*).—But there is yet another explanation which appears to us still more probable. Proposed by Selden,[1] it has been reproduced quite lately by Andreæ in his excellent article on the day of Jesus' death.[2] When the observers entrusted with the duty of ascertaining the appearance of the new moon, with a view to fixing the first day of the month, did not present themselves before the commission of the Sanhedrim assembled to receive their deposition until after the sacrifice, this day was indeed declared the first of the month, or *monthly* Sabbath (*σάββατον πρῶτον, first Sabbath*); but as the time of offering the sacrifice of the new moon was passed, they sanctified the following day, or second of the month (*σάββατον δευτερόπρωτον, second-first* Sabbath), as well. This meaning perfectly agrees with the idea naturally expressed by this term (a first *twice over*), and with the impression it gives of having been taken from the subtleties of the Jewish calendar.

Bleek, ill-satisfied with these various explanations, supposes an interpolation. But why should it have occurred in Luke rather than in Matthew and Mark? Meyer thinks that a

[1] *De anno civili et calendario veteris ecclesiæ judaicæ.*
[2] In the journal: *Beweis des Glaubens*, September 1870.

copyist had written in the margin *πρώτῳ, first,* in opposition to *ἑτέρῳ, the other* (Sabbath), ver. 6; that the next copyist, wishing, in consideration of the Sabbath indicated iv. 31, to correct this gloss, wrote *δευτέρῳ, second,* in place of *πρώτῳ, first;* and that, lastly, from these two glosses together came the word *second-first,* which has made its way into the text. What a tissue of improbabilities! Holtzmann thinks that Luke had written *πρώτῳ, the first,* dating from the journey recorded in iv. 44, and that in consideration of iv. 31 some over-careful corrector added *the second;* whence our reading. But is not the interval which separates our narrative from iv. 44 too great for Luke to have employed the word *first* in reference to this journey? And what object could he have had in expressing so particularly this quality of first? Lastly, how did the gloss of this copyist find its way into such a large number of documents? Weizsäcker (*Unters.* p. 59) opposes the two first Sabbaths mentioned in iv. 16, 33 to the two mentioned here (vers. 1, 6), and thinks that the name *second-first* means here the *first* of the *second* group. How can any one attribute such absurd trifling to a serious writer! This strange term cannot have been invented by Luke; neither could it have been introduced accidentally by the copyists. Taken evidently from the Jewish vocabulary, it holds its place in Luke, as a witness attesting the originality and antiquity of his sources of information. Further, this precise designation of the Sabbath when the incident took place points to a narrator who witnessed the scene.

From Mark's expression *παραπορεύεσθαι, to pass by the side of,* it would seem to follow that Jesus was passing *along the side of,* and not, as Luke says, *across* the field (*διαπορεύεσθαι*). But as Mark adds: *through the corn,* it is clear that he describes two adjacent fields, separated by a path.—The act of the disciples was expressly authorized by the law (Deut. xxiii. 25). But it was done on the Sabbath day; there was the grievance. To gather and rub out the ears was to harvest, to grind, to labour! It was an infraction of the thirty-nine articles which the Pharisees had framed into a Sabbatic code. *Ψώχοντες, rubbing out,* is designedly put at the end of the phrase: this is the labour!—Meyer, pressing the letter of Mark's text, *ὁδὸν ποιεῖν, to make a way,* maintains that the disciples were not thinking of eating, but simply wanted to make themselves a passage across the field by plucking the ears of corn. According to him, the middle *ποιεῖσθαι*, not the active *ποιεῖν*, would have been necessary for the ordinary sense. He translates, therefore: they cleared a way by *plucking* (*τίλλοντες*) the ears of corn (Mark omits *ψώχοντες*, *rubbing them out*). He concludes from this that Mark alone has preserved the exact form of the incident, which has been altered in the other two through the influence of the next example, which refers to food. Holtzmann takes advantage of this idea to support the hypothesis of a proto-Mark. But, 1. What traveller would ever think of clearing a passage through a field of wheat by plucking ear after ear? 2. If we were to lay stress on the active *ποιεῖν*, as Meyer does, it would signify that the disciples made a road *for the public*, and not for themselves alone; for in this case also the middle would be necessary! The ordinary sense is therefore the only one possible even in Mark, and the critical conclusions in favour of the proto-Mark are without foundation.—The Hebraistic form of Luke's phrase (*ἐγένετο . . . καὶ ἔτιλλον*) which is not found in the other two proves that he has a particular document. As to who these accusers were, comp. v. 17–21, 30–33.—The word *αὐτοῖς*, which the Alex. omits, has perhaps been added on account of the plural that follows: *Why do ye . . .?*—It follows from this incident that Jesus passed a spring, and consequently a Passover also, in Galilee before His passion. A remarkable coincidence also with the narrative of John (vi. 4).—The illustration taken from 1 Sam. xxi. cited in vers. 3 and 4 is very appropriately chosen. Jesus would certainly have had no difficulty in showing that the act of the disciples, although opposed perhaps to the Pharisaic code, was in perfect agreement with the Mosaic commandment. But the discussion, if placed on this ground, might have degenerated into a mere casuistical question; He therefore transfers it to a sphere in which He feels Himself master of the position. The conduct of David rests upon this principle, that in exceptional cases, when a moral obligation clashes with a ceremonial law, the latter ought to yield. And for this reason. The rite is a means, but the moral duty is an end; now, in case of conflict, the end has priority over the means. The absurdity of Pharisaism is just this, that it subordinates the end to the means. It was the duty of the high priest to preserve the life of David and his companions, having regard to their mission, even at the expense of the ritual commandment; for the rite exists for the theocracy, not the theocracy for the rite. Besides, Jesus means to clinch the nail, to show His adversaries—and this is the sting of His reply—that when it is a question of *their own particular advantage* (saving a head of cattle for instance), they are ready enough to act in a similar way, sacrificing the rite to what they deem a higher interest (xiii. 11 et seq.).—De Wette understands οὐδέ in the sense of *not even:* "Do you *not even* know the history of your great king?" This sense would come very near to the somewhat ironical turn of Mark: "Have you *never* read . . .—never once, in the course of your profound biblical studies?" But it appears more simple to explain it as Bleek does: "Have you not *also* read . . .? Does not this fact appear in your Bible *as well as* the ordinance of the Sabbath?" The detail: *and to those who were with him,* is not distinctly expressed in the O. T.; but whatever Bleek may say, it is implied; David would not have asked for five loaves for himself alone. Jesus mentions it because He wishes to institute a parallel between His apostles and David's followers.—The pron. οὓς does not refer to τοῖς μετ' αὐτοῦ, as in Matthew (the present ἔξεστι does not permit of it), but to ἄρτους, as the object of φαγεῖν; εἰ μή is therefore taken here in its regular sense. It is not so in Matthew, where εἰ μή is used as in Luke iv. 26, 27. Mark gives the name of the high priest as Abiathar, while according to 1 Sam. it was Ahimelech, his son (comp. 2 Sam. viii. 17; 1 Chron. xviii. 16), or his father (according to Josephus, *Antiq.* vi. 12. 6). The question is obscure.—In Matthew, Jesus gives a second instance of transgression of the Sabbath, the labour of the priests in the temple on the Sabbath day, in connection with the burnt-offerings and other religious services. If the work of God in the temple liberates man from the law of the Sabbath rest, how much more must the service of Him who is Lord even of the temple raise him to the same liberty!

The Cod. D. and one Mn. here add the following narrative. "The same day, Jesus, seeing a man who was working on the

Sabbath, saith to him: O man, if thou knowest what thou art doing, blessed art thou; but if thou knowest not, thou art cursed, and a transgressor of the law." This narrative is an interpolation similar to that of the story in John of the woman taken in adultery, but with this difference, that the latter is probably the record of a real fact, while the former can only be an invention or a perversion. Nobody could have laboured publicly in Israel on the Sabbath day without being instantly punished; and Jesus, who never permitted Himself the slightest infraction of a true commandment of Moses (whatever interpreters may say about it), certainly would not have authorized this premature emancipation in any one else.

After having treated the question from a legal point of view, Jesus rises to the principle. Even had the apostles broken the Sabbath rest, they would not have sinned; for the Son of man has the disposal of the Sabbath, and they are in His service. We find again here the well-known expression, *καὶ ἔλεγεν, and He said to them,* the force of which is (see at ver. 36): "Besides, I have something more important to tell you." The Sabbath, as an educational institution, is only to remain until the moral development of mankind, for the sake of which it was instituted, is accomplished. When this end is attained, the means naturally fall into disuse. Now, this moment is reached in the appearance of the Son of man. The normal representative of the race, He is Himself the realization of this end; He is therefore raised above the Sabbath as a means of education; He may consequently modify the form of it, and even, if He think fit, abolish it altogether.—*Καί*: *even* of the Sabbath, this peculiar property of Jehovah; with how much greater reason, of all the rest of the law![1]—How can any one maintain, in the face of such a saying as this, that Jesus only assumed the part of the Messiah after the conversation at Cæsarea-Philippi (ix. 18), and when moved to do so by Peter?

[1] It is not without justification that Ritschl, in his fine work, *Entstehung der altkathol. Kirche*, 2d ed., sets out to prove from this passage, which is common to the three Syn., that the abolition of the law, the necessary condition of Christian universalism, is not an idea imported into the religion of Jesus by Paul, but an integral element of the teaching of Jesus Himself. It belongs to that common foundation on which rest both the work of Paul and that of the Twelve; this is already proved by the parable of the two garments (ver. 36).

Mark inserts before this declaration one of those short and weighty sayings (he has preserved several of them), which he cannot have invented or added of his own authority, and which the other two Syn. would never have left out, had they made use of his book or of the document of which he availed himself (the proto-Mark): "*The Sabbath is made for man, and not man for the Sabbath.*" God did not create man for the greater glory of the Sabbath, but He ordained the Sabbath for the greater welfare of man. Consequently, whenever the welfare of man and the rest of the Sabbath happen to clash, the Sabbath must yield. *So that* (ὥστε, Mark ii. 28) the Son of man, inasmuch as He is head of the race, has a right to dispose of this institution. This thought, distinctly expressed in Mark, is just what we have had to supply in order to explain the argument in Luke.

Are we authorized to infer from this saying the immediate abolition of every Sabbatic institution in the Christian Church? By no means. Just as, in His declaration, vers. 34, 35, Jesus announced not the abolition of fasting, but the substitution of a more spiritual for the legal fast, so this saying respecting the Sabbath foreshadows important modifications of the form of this institution, but not its entire abolition. It will cease to be a slavish observance, as in Judaism, and will become the satisfaction of an inward need. Its complete abolition will come to pass only when redeemed mankind shall all have reached the perfect stature of the Son of man. The principle: *The Sabbath is made for man,* will retain a certain measure of its force as long as this earthly economy shall endure, for which the Sabbath was first established, and to the nature of which it is so thoroughly fitted.

6. *A Second-Sabbath Scene:* vi. 6–11.—Vers. **6–11.**[1]—Do Matthew and Mark place the following incident on the same

[1] Ver. 7. 14 Mjj. several Mnn. It. omit αυτον after δε.—ℵ. A. D. L. Π. : θεραπευει instead of θεραπευσει.—ℵ* B. S. X. some Mnn. Syr. It[aliq]. : κατηγορειν instead of κατηγοριαν.—Ver. 8. ℵ. B. L. some Mnn. : ανδρι instead of ανθρωπω.—Ver. 9. ℵ. B. L. : επερωτω instead of επερωτησω.—ℵ. B. D. L. It[plerique] : υμας ει instead of υμας τι.—ℵ. B. D. L. X. Syr[sch]. It[plerique] : απολεσαι instead of αποκτειναι.—Ver. 10. 13 Mjj. : αυτω instead of τω ανθρωπω, which is the reading of T. R. with ℵ. D. L. X. It.—T. R. with K. Π. several Mnn.: εποιησεν ουτως; 12 Mjj. 80 Mnn. omit ουτως.—ℵ. D. X. several Mnn. It. εξετεινεν.—11 Mjj. several Mnn Syr. It. omit υγιης.—13 Mjj. many Mnn. read ως η αλλη, which T. R. with ℵ. B. L omit.

day as the preceding? It is impossible to say (πάλιν, in Mark, does not refer to ii. 23, but to i. 21). Luke says positively, on *another* Sabbath. He has therefore His own source of information. This is confirmed by the character of the style, which continues to be decidedly Hebraistic (καὶ . . . καὶ . . . instead of the relative pronoun).—The withering of the hand denotes paralysis resulting from the absence of the vital juices, the condition which is commonly described as *atrophy.*—In Matthew, the question whether it is right to heal on the Sabbath day is put to the Lord by His adversaries, which, taken literally, would be highly improbable. It is evident that Matthew, as usual, condenses the account of the fact, and hastens to the words of Jesus, which he relates at greater length than the others. His adversaries, no doubt, did put the question, but, as Luke and Mark tell us, simply in intention and by their looks. They watch to see how He will act.—The present θεραπεύει, *whether He heals,* in the Alex., would refer to the habit of Jesus, to His principle of conduct. This turn of expression is too far-fetched. The spies want more particularly to ascertain what He will do now; from the fact they will easily deduce the principle. The received reading, θεραπεύσει, *whether He will heal,* must therefore be preferred.—The Rabbis did not allow of any medical treatment on the Sabbath day, unless delay would imperil life; the strictest school, that of Shammai, forbade even the consolation of the sick on that day (*Schabbat* xii. 1).

Ver. 8. Jesus penetrates at a glance the secret spy system organized against Him, and seems to take pleasure in giving the work He is about to perform the greatest publicity possible. Commanding the man to place himself in the midst of the assembly, He makes him the subject of a veritable theological demonstration. Matthew omits these dramatic details which Mark and Luke have transmitted to us. Would he have omitted them had he known them? He could not have had the alleged proto-Mark before him, unless it is supposed that the author of our canonical Mark added these details on his own authority. But in this case, how comes Mark to coincide with Luke, who, according to this hypothesis, had not our actual Mark in his hands, but simply the primitive Mark (the common source of our three Syn.)? Here plainly is a labyrinth from which criticism, having once entered on a wrong path, is unable to extricate itself.—The skilfulness of the question proposed by the Lord (ver. 9) consists in its representing good *omitted* as evil *committed.* The question thus put answers itself; for what Pharisee would venture to make the prerogative of the Sabbath to consist in a permission to torture and kill with impunity on that day? This question is one of those marks of genius, or rather one of those inspirations of the heart, which enhance our knowledge of Jesus. By reason of His compassion, He feels Himself responsible for all the suffering which He fails to relieve. But, it may be asked, could He not have put off the cure until the next day? To this question He would have given the same answer as any one of us: To-morrow belongs to God; only to-day belongs to me. The present ἐπερωτῶ, *I ask you* (Alex.), is more direct and severe, and consequently less suited to the Lord's frame of mind at this moment, than the future of the T. R.: *I will ask you.* For the same reason, we think, we must read not εἰ, *if*, or *is it*, with the Alex., but τί, and make this word not a complement: "I ask you *what* is allowable," a form in which the intentional sharpness of His address is softened down too much (see the contrary case, vii. 40), but the subject of ἔξεστι: "*I ask* you; answer me! *What is* permitted, to . . . or to . . .; for in my position I must do one or the other." Matthew places here the illustration of the sheep fallen into a ditch, an argument which, as we shall see, is better placed in Luke (xiv. 5, 6).—Ver. 10. A profound silence (Mark iii. 4) is the only answer to this question. Those who laid the snare are taken in it themselves. Jesus then surveys His adversaries, ranged around Him, with a long and solemn gaze. This striking moment, omitted in Matthew, is noticed in Luke; in Mark it is described in the most dramatic manner. We feel here how much Mark owes to some source of information closely connected with the person of the Saviour; he describes the feeling of sorrowful indignation which eye-witnesses could read in His glance: "with anger, being grieved at the hardness of their hearts."—The command Jesus gives the sick man to stretch forth his hand, affords room for surprise. Is it not precisely what he was unable to do? But, like every call addressed to faith, this command contained a promise of the strength necessary to accomplish it, provided the will to obey was there. He must make the attempt, depending on the word of Jesus (ver. 5), and divine power will accompany the effort. The word ὑγιής is probably taken from Matthew; it is omitted by six Mjj. It would be hazardous, perhaps, to erase also the words ὡς ἡ ἀλλή with the three Mjj. which omit them.—It is here that Cod. D. places the general proposition, ver. 5.

The Jewish-Christian Gospel which Jerome had found among the Nazarenes relates in detail the prayer of this sick man: "I was a mason, earning my livelihood with my own hands; I pray thee, Jesus, to restore me to health, in order that I may not with shame beg my bread." This is an instance of how amplification and vulgarity meet us directly we step beyond the threshold of the canonical Gospels. Apostolical dignity has disappeared.

The word ἄνοια (ver. 11), properly *madness*, by which Luke expresses the effect produced on the adversaries of Jesus, denotes literally the absence of νοῦς, of the power to discriminate the true from the false. They were *fools through rage*, Luke means. In fact, passion destroys a man's sense of the good and true. Matthew and Mark notice merely the external result, the plot which from this moment was laid against the life of Jesus: "*They took counsel to kill Him;*" Mark adds to the Pharisees, the Herodians. The former, in fact, could take no effectual measures in Galilee against the person of Jesus without the concurrence of Herod; and in order to obtain this, it was necessary to gain over his counsellors to their plans. Why should they not hope to induce this king to do to Jesus what he had already done to John the Baptist?

Holtzmann thinks it may be proved, by the agreement of certain words of Jesus in the three narratives, that they must have had a common *written* source. As if words so striking as these: *The Son of man is Lord also of the Sabbath day*, could not be preserved by oral tradition! The characteristic divergences which we have observed at every line in the historical sketch of the narrative, are incompatible, as we have seen, with the use of a common document.

THIRD CYCLE.—CHAP. VI. 12–VIII. 56.

From the Election of the Twelve to their First Mission.

In the following section we shall see the Galilean ministry reach its zenith; it begins with the institution of the apostolate and the most important of Jesus' discourses during His sojourn in Galilee, the Sermon on the Mount; and it ends with a cycle of miracles that display the extraordinary power of Jesus in all its grandeur (viii. 22–56). The hostility against Him seems to moderate; but it is sharpening its weapons in secret; in a very little while it will break out afresh.

This section comprises eleven portions: 1*st,* the choosing of the Twelve, and the Sermon on the Mount (vi. 12–49); 2*d,* the healing of the centurion's servant (vii. 1–10); 3*d,* the raising of the widow's son at Nain (vii. 11–17); 4*th,* the question of John the Baptist, and the discourse of Jesus upon it (vii. 18–35); 5*th,* the woman that was a sinner at the feet of Jesus (vii. 36–50); 6*th,* the women who ministered to Jesus' support (viii. 1–3); 7*th,* the parable of the sower (viii. 4–18); 8*th,* the visit of the mother and brethren of Jesus (viii. 19–21); 9*th,* the stilling of the storm (viii. 22–25); 10*th,* the healing of the demoniac of Gadara (viii. 26–39); 11*th,* the raising of Jaïrus' daughter (viii. 40–56).

1. *The Choosing of the Twelve, and the Sermon on the Mount:* vi. 12–49.—Our affixing this title to this portion implies two things: 1*st,* that there is a close connection between the two facts contained in this title; 2*d,* that the discourse, Luke vi. 20–49, is the same as that we read in Matt. v.–vii. The truth of the first supposition, from Luke's point of view, appears from ver. 20, where he puts the discourse which follows in close connection with the choosing of the Twelve which he has just narrated. The truth of the second is disputed by those who think that in consequence of this choice Jesus spoke *two* discourses,—one on the summit of the mountain, addressed specially to His disciples,—the second lower down on level ground, addressed to the multitude; the former, which was of a more private character, being that of Matthew;

the latter, of a more popular aim, that of Luke.[1] They rely on the differences in substance and form between the two discourses in our two Gospels. In regard to the substance, the essential matter in the discourse of Matthew, the opposition between the righteousness of the Pharisees and the true righteousness of the kingdom of heaven, is not found at all in Luke. As to the form, in Matthew Jesus *ascends* the mountain to preach it, while in Luke He *comes down*, after having spent the night on the summit. Further, there He is seated *καθίσαντος αὐτοῦ*, Matt. v. 1); here He appears to be standing (ἔστη, Luke vi. 17). Notwithstanding these reasons, we cannot admit that there were two distinct discourses. They both begin in the same way, with the beatitudes; they both treat of the same subject, the righteousness of the kingdom of God, —with this shade of difference, that the essence of this righteousness, in Matthew, is spirituality; in Luke, charity. They both have the same conclusion, the parable of the two buildings. This resemblance in the plan of the discourse is so great, that it appears to us decidedly to take precedence of the secondary differences. As to the differences of form, it should be observed that Luke's expression, *ἐπὶ τόπου πεδινοῦ*, literally, *on a level place*, denotes a flat place *on the mountain*. To denote *the plain*, Luke would have said, *ἐπὶ πεδίου*. Luke's expression is not, therefore, contradictory to Matthew's. The latter, as usual, giving a summary narrative, tells us that Jesus preached this time on *the mountain*, in opposition to *the plain*, the sea-side that is, where He usually preached; while Luke, who describes in detail all the circumstances of this memorable day, begins by mentioning the night which Jesus spent alone on the summit of the mountain; next he tells how He descended to a level place situated on the mountain side, where He stayed to speak to the people. This plateau was still *the mountain* in Matthew's sense. On the relation of ἔστη (Luke) to *He sat down* (Matthew), see on ver. 17.

In order to understand the Sermon on the Mount, it is necessary to form a correct view of the historical circumstances which were the occasion of it; for this sermon is something more than an important piece of instruction de-

[1] Lange, *Leben Jesu*, Book ii. pp. 567–570. St. Augustine and the greater part of the Latin Fathers of the Church hold that there were two discourses.

livered by Jesus; it is one of the decisive acts of His ministry. We have pointed out in the preceding section the symptoms of a growing rupture between Jesus and the hierarchical party (vers. 14, 17, 21–23, vi. 1 seq.). The bold attitude which Jesus assumes towards this party, challenging its hostility by calling a publican, by emphasizing in His teaching the antithesis between the old and new order of things, and by openly braving their Sabbatarian prejudices,—all this enables us to see that a crisis in the development of His work has arrived. It is an exactly corresponding state of things for Galilee to that which was brought about in Judæa after the healing of the impotent man on the Sabbath (John v.). The choice of the Twelve and the Sermon on the Mount are the result and the solution of this critical situation. Up to this time Jesus had been satisfied with gathering converts about Him, calling some of them to accompany Him habitually as disciples. Now He saw that the moment was come to give His work a more definite form, and to organize His adherents. The hostile army is preparing for the attack; it is time to concentrate His own forces; and consequently He begins, if I may venture to say so, by drawing up His list of officers. The choosing of the Twelve is the first constitutive act accomplished by Jesus Christ. It is the first measure, and substantially (with the sacraments) the only measure, of organization which He ever took. It sufficed Him, since the college of the Twelve, once constituted, was in its turn to take what further measures might be required when the time came for them.—The number 12 was significant. Jesus set up in their persons the twelve patriarchs of a new people of God, a spiritual Israel, that was to be substituted for the old. Twelve new tribes were to arise at their word and form the holy humanity which Jesus came to install in the earth. An act more expressly Messianic it is impossible to conceive; and the criticism which maintains that it was only at Cæsarea-Philippi, and at the instigation of Peter, that Jesus decisively accepted the part of Messiah, must begin by effacing from history the choosing of the Twelve, with its manifest signification. Further, this act is the beginning of the divorce between Jesus and the ancient people of God. The Lord does not begin to frame a new Israel until He sees the necessity of breaking with the old. He has laboured in vain to *transform;* nothing now remains but to *substitute.* This attentive crowd which surrounds Him on the mountain is the nucleus of the *new people;* this discourse which He addresses to them is the promulgation of the *new law* by which they are to be governed; this moment is the solemn inauguration of the people of Jesus Christ upon the earth,—of that people which, by means of individual conversions, is eventually to absorb into itself all that belongs to God among all other peoples. Hence this discourse has a decidedly inaugural character,—a character which, whatever Weizsäcker[1] may say about it, belongs no less to its form in Luke than to its form in Matthew. In the latter, Jesus addresses Himself, if you will, to the apostles, but as representing the entire new Israel. In Luke, He rather speaks, if you will, to the new Israel, but as personified in the person of the apostles. In reality this makes no difference. The distinction between apostles and believers is nowhere clearly asserted. Every believer is to be *the salt of the earth, the light of the world* (Matthew); every apostle is to be one of those *poor, hungry, weeping, persecuted* ones of which the new people is to be composed (Luke). Just as, at Sinai, Jehovah makes no distinction between priests and people, so it is His people, with all the constitutive elements of their life, whose appearance Jesus hails, whose new character He portrays, and whose future action on the world He proclaims. Further, He felt most deeply the importance of this moment, and prepared Himself for it by a whole night of meditation and prayer. The expressions of Luke upon this point (ver. 12) have, as we shall see, quite a special character.

The Sermon on the Mount occupies quite a different place in Matthew to that which it holds in Luke. That evangelist has made it the opening of the Galilean ministry, and he places it, therefore, immediately after the call of the four first disciples. Historically speaking, this position is a manifest anachronism. How, at the very commencement of His work, could Jesus speak of persecutions for His name, as He does, Matt. v. 10, 11, or feel it necessary to justify Himself against the charge of destroying the law (ver. 17), and to give a solemn warning to false disciples (vii. 21–23)? The posi-

[1] *Untersuchungen über die evang. Gesch.* pp. 45 and 46, note.

tion of the Sermon on the Mount in Matthew is only to be understood from the *systematic* point of view from which this evangelist wrote. There was no better way in which the author could show the Messianic dignity of Jesus than by opening the history of His ministry with this discourse, in which was laid down the basis of that spiritual kingdom which the Messiah came to found. If the *collection of the discourses* composed by Matthew, of which Papias speaks, really existed, and served as a foundation for our Gospel, the position which this discourse occupies in the latter is fully accounted for.

As to Mark, we can easily perceive the precise point in his sketch where the Sermon on the Mount should come in (iii. 13 et seq.). But the discourse itself is wanting, doubtless because it was no part of his design to give it to his readers. Mark's narrative is nevertheless important, in that it substantiates that of Luke, and confirms the significance attributed by this evangelist to the act of the choosing of the Twelve. This comparison with the two other Syn. shows how well Luke understood the development of the work of Jesus, and the superior chronological skill with which he compiled his narrative (*καθεξῆς γράψαι*, i. 3).

Gess has replied to our objections against the chronological accuracy of Matthew's narrative (*Litter. Anzeiger* of Andreæ, September 1871) in the following manner: The mention of the persecutions might refer to the fact mentioned John iv. 1, and to the fate of John the Baptist; the charge of undermining the law had already been made in Judæa (comp. John v.); the false disciples might have been imitators of the man who wrought cures in the name of Jesus (Luke ix. 49; Mark ix. 38), although of a less pure character. And, in any case, the time of the discourse indicated by Luke does not differ sensibly from that at which Matthew places it.—But neither the hostility which Jesus had met with in Judæa, nor the accusations which had been laid against Him there, could have induced Him to speak as He did in the Sermon on the Mount, unless some similar events, such as those which St. Luke has already related, had taken place in this province, and within the knowledge of the people. It is quite possible that the facts related by Luke do not prove any very great interval between the time to which he assigns this discourse and the beginning of the Galilean ministry, at which Matthew places it. But they serve at least as a preparation for it, and give it just that historical foundation which it needs, whilst in Matthew it occurs *ex abrupto*, and without any historical framework. — The fact that the call of Matthew is placed in the first Gospel (ix. 9) *after* the Sermon on the Mount, which supposes this call already accomplished (Luke vi. 12 et seq.), would be sufficient, if necessary, to show that this discourse is detached, in this Gospel, from its true historical context.

1*st.* Vers. 12–19. *Choosing of the Twelve.*—Ver. 12.[1] Luke has already brought before us more than once the need of prayer, which so often drew Jesus away into solitude (iv. 42, v. 16). But the expressions he makes use of here are intended to carry special weight. *Διαννκτερεύειν, to pass the night in watching,* is a word rarely used in Greek, and which in all the N. T. is only found here. The choice of this unusual term, as well as the analytical form (the imperf. with the participle), express the persevering energy of this vigil. The term *προσευχὴ τοῦ Θεοῦ,* literally, *prayer of God,* is also an unique expression in the N. T. It does not denote any special request, but a state of wrapt contemplation of God's presence, a prayer arising out of the most profound communion with Him. The development of the work of Jesus having now reached a critical point, during this night He laid it before God, and took counsel with Him. The choosing of the twelve apostles was the fruit of this lengthened season of prayer; in that higher light in which Jesus stood, it appeared the only measure answering to the exigencies of the present situation.—The reading *ἐξελθεῖν* is a correction of the Alexandrian purists for *ἐξῆλθεν,* which, after *ἐγένετο,* offended the Greek ear.

Vers. 13–17*a.*[2] In the execution, as in the choice, of this important measure, Jesus no doubt submitted Himself to divine direction. His numerous disciples spent the night not far from the mountain-top to which He withdrew. During this lengthened communion, He presented them all, one by one, to His Father; and God's finger pointed out those to whom He was to entrust the salvation of the world. When at last all had been made perfectly clear, towards morning He called them to Him, and made the selection which had thus been pre-arranged. The *καί, also,* indicates that the title

[1] ℵ. Δ. B. D. L., εξελθειν αυτον instead of εξηλθεν.

[2] Ver. 14. ℵ. B. D. K. L. Δ. Π. 20 Mnn. Syr^{sch}. It^{aliq}. read και before Ιακωβον. —ℵ. B. D. L. Syr^{sch}. It^{aliq}. read και before Φιλιππον.—Ver. 15. The same, or nearly so: και before Ματθαιον and Ιακωβον.—Ver. 16. The same, or nearly so: και before Ιουδαν.—ℵ. B. D. L., Ισκαριωθ instead of Ισκαριωτην.—ℵ. B. L. It. omit και after ος.

proceeded from Jesus, as well as the commission. Schleiermacher thought that this nomination was made simply in reference to the following discourse, of which these twelve were to be the official hearers, and that the name *apostles* (ver. 13, "whom He also named apostles") might have been given them on some other occasion, either previous or subsequent. The similar expression relative to Peter, ver. 14, might favour this latter opinion. Nevertheless, it is natural to suppose that He entitled them apostles when He first distinguished them from the rest of the disciples, just as He gave Simon the surname *Peter* when He met him for the first time (John i.). And if these twelve men had been chosen to attend Jesus officially simply on this occasion, they would not be found the same in all the catalogues of apostles. The fact of this choice is expressly confirmed by Mark (iii. 13, 14), and indirectly by John (vi. 70): "*Have not I chosen you twelve* (ἐξελεξάμην)?"—The function of the apostles has often been reduced to that of simple witnesses. But this very title of apostles, or ambassadors, expresses more, comp. 2 Cor. v. 20, "*We are ambassadors for Christ . . .; and we beseech you to be reconciled to God.*" When Jesus says, "*I pray for them who shall believe on me through their word,*" the expression *their word* evidently embraces more than the simple narration of the facts about Jesus and His works.—The marked prominence which Luke, together with Mark, gives to the choosing of the Twelve, is the best refutation of the unfair criticism which affects to discover throughout his work indications of a design to depreciate them.

According to Keim (t. ii. p. 305), the choice of the Twelve must have taken place later on, at the time of their first mission, ix. 1 et seq. It is then, in fact, that Matthew gives the catalogue, x. 1 et seq. His idea is that Luke imagined this entire scene on the mountain in order to refer the choosing of the apostles to as early a period as possible, and thus give a double and triple consecration to their authority, and that thus far Mark followed him. But Luke, he believes, went much further still. Wanting to put some discourse into the mouth of Jesus on this occasion, he availed himself for this purpose of part of the Sermon on the Mount, though it was a discourse which had nothing in common with the occasion. Mark, however, rejected this amplification, but with the serious defect of not being able to assign any adequate reason for the choosing of the apostles at this time. Thus far Keim.—But, 1. The preface to the account of the first apostolic mission in Matthew (x. 1), "and having called to Him *the twelve disciples*, He gave them . . . ," does away with the idea of their having been chosen just at this time, and implies that this event had already taken place. According to Matthew himself, the college of *the Twelve* is already in existence; Jesus calls them to set them to active service. 2. A scene described in such solemn terms as that of Luke (Jesus spending a night *in prayer to God*), cannot be an invention on his part, consistently with the slightest pretensions to good faith. 3. The narrative of Mark is an indisputable confirmation of Luke's; for it is independent of it, as appears from the way, so completely his own, in which he defines the object of choosing the apostles. 4. We have seen how exactly this measure was adapted to that stage of development which the work of Jesus had now reached. 5. Does not rationalistic criticism condemn itself, by attributing to Luke here the entire invention of a scene designed to confer the most solemn consecration on the apostolic authority of the Twelve, and by asserting elsewhere that this same Luke labours to depreciate them (the Tübingen school, and, to a certain extent, Keim himself; see on ix. 1)?

The four catalogues of apostles (Matt. x. 2 et seq.; Mark iii. 16 et seq.; Luke vi.; and Acts i. 13) present three marks of resemblance: 1*st.* They contain the same names, with the exception of Jude the son of James, for whom in Mark *Thaddæus* is substituted, and in Matthew *Lebbæus, surnamed Thaddæus* (according to the received reading), Thaddæus (according to ℵ. B.), Lebbæus (according to D.). 2*d.* These twelve are distributed in the four lists into three groups of four each, and no individual of either of these groups is transferred to another. We may conclude from this that the apostolical college consisted of three concentric circles, of which the innermost was in the closest relations with Jesus. 3*d.* The same three apostles are found at the head of each quaternion, Peter, Philip, and James.—Besides this quaternary division, Matthew and Luke indicate a division into pairs, at least (according to the received reading, in Luke, and certainly in Matthew) for the last eight apostles. In the Acts, the first four apostles are connected with each other by καί; the remaining eight are grouped in pairs.

Luke places at the head of them the two brothers, Simon and Andrew, with whom Jesus became acquainted while they were with the Forerunner (John i.). At the first glance, Jesus had discerned that power of taking the lead, that promptness of view and action, which distinguished Peter

He pointed him out at the time by the surname כֵּף, in Aramæan כֵּיפָא, *Cephas* (properly a *mass of rock*), as he on whom He would found the edifice of His Church. If the character of Peter was weak and unstable, he was none the less for that the bold confessor on whose testimony the Church was erected in Israel and among the heathen (Acts ii. and x.). There is nothing in the text to indicate that this surname was given to Peter at this time. The aor. ὠνόμασε indicates the act simply, without reference to time. The καί merely serves to express the identity of the person (ver. 16).—Andrew was one of the first believers. At the time when Jesus chose the Twelve, he was no doubt appointed at the same time as Peter; but he gradually falls below James and John, to whom he appears to have been inferior; he is placed after them in Mark and in the Acts. The order followed by Luke indicates a very primitive source. Andrew is very often found associated with Philip (John vi. 7–9, xii. 21, 22). In their ordinary life, he formed the link between the first and the second group, at the head of which was Philip.

The second pair of the first group is formed by the two sons of Zebedee, *James* and *John*. Mark supplies (iii. 17) a detail respecting them which is full of interest: Jesus had surnamed them *sons of thunder*. This surname would have been offensive had it expressed a fault; it denoted, therefore, rather the ardent zeal of these two brothers in the cause of Jesus, and their exalted affection for His person. This feeling which burned within their hearts, came forth in sudden flashes, like lightning from the cloud. John i. 42[1] contains a delicate trace of the calling of James; this, therefore, must have taken place while he was with John the Baptist, immediately after that of his brother. James was the first martyr from the number of the apostles (Acts xii.). This fact is only to be explained by the great influence which he exerted after Pentecost. John was the personal *friend* of Jesus, who doubtless felt Himself better understood by him than by any

[1] Probably it is ver. 41 that is meant. M. Godet, following the usual opinion that the unnamed disciple of ver. 40 is John, the writer of the Gospel, seems to understand the next verse as intimating that Andrew found *his* brother Simon before John found *his* brother James. Alford's view is, that both disciples (John and Andrew) went to seek Simon, but that Andrew found him first.—TRANSLATOR.

of the others. Whilst the other disciples were especially impressed by His miracles, and stored up His moral teaching, John, attracted rather by His person, treasured up in his heart those sayings in which Jesus unfolded His consciousness of Himself.—Wieseler has tried to prove that these two brothers were first-cousins of Jesus, by Salome, their mother, who would have been the sister of the Virgin Mary. Comp. Matt. xxvii. 56, Mark xv. 40, with John xix. 25. But this interpretation of the passage in John is hardly natural.

The second quaternion, which no doubt comprised natures of a second order, contained also two pairs. The first consists, in all three Gospels, of Philip and Bartholomew. In the Acts, Philip is associated with Thomas. Philip was the fifth believer (John i.); he was originally from Bethsaida, as were also the preceding four. John vi. 5 seems to show that Jesus was on terms of special cordiality with him.—The name Bartholomew signifies *son of Tolmai;* it was therefore only a surname. It has long been supposed that the true name of this apostle was Nathanael. John xxi. 2, where Nathanael is named amongst a string of apostles, proves unquestionably that he was one of the Twelve. Since, according to John i., he had been drawn to Jesus by Philip, it is natural that he should be associated with him in the catalogues of the apostles.

Matthew and *Thomas* form the second pair of the second group in the three Syn., whilst in the Acts Matthew is associated with Bartholomew. One remarkable circumstance, all the more significant that it might easily pass unperceived, is this, that whilst in Mark and Luke Matthew is placed first of the pair, in our first Gospel he occupies the second place. Further, in this Gospel also, the epithet *the publican* is added to his name, which is wanting in the two others. Are not these indications of a personal participation, more or less direct, of the Apostle Matthew in the composition of the first Gospel? Having been formerly a toll-collector, Matthew must have been more accustomed to the use of the pen than his colleagues. It is not surprising, therefore, that he should be the first among them who felt called to put into writing the history and instructions of Jesus. The account of his calling implies that he possessed unusual energy, decision, and strength of faith. Perhaps it was for that reason Jesus saw fit to associate him with Thomas, a man of scruples and doubts. The name of the latter signifies *a twin.* The circumstances of his call are unknown. He was doubtless connected with Jesus first of all as a simple disciple, and then his serious character attracted the attention of the Master. If the incident ix. 59, 60 was not placed so long after the Sermon on the Mount, we might be tempted with some writers to apply it to Thomas.

The third quaternion contains the least striking characters in the number of the Twelve. All these men, however, not excepting Judas Iscariot, have had their share in the fulfilment of the apostolic task, the transmission of the holy figure of the Christ to the Church through all time. The stream of oral tradition was formed by the affluents of all these sources together. The last pair comprises here, as in the Acts, *James the son of Alphæus,* and *Simon the Zealot.* But the distribution is different in the two other Syn.—It has been generally allowed since the fourth century that this James is the person so often mentioned, in the Acts and the Galatians, as the *brother of the Lord,* the first head of the flock at Jerusalem. This identity is made out, (1) by applying to him the passage Mark xv. 40, according to which his surname would have been *the less* or *the younger* (relatively to James the son of Zebedee), and his mother would have been a Mary, whom, according to John xix. 25, we should have to regard as *a sister* (*probably sister-in-law*) of the mother of Jesus; (2) by identifying the name of his father *Alphæus* with the name Clopas (חלפי = Κλωπᾶς), which was borne, according to Hegesippus, by a brother of Joseph; (3) by taking the term *brother* in the sense of *cousin* (of the Lord). But this hypothesis cannot, in our judgment, be maintained: (1) The word *ἀδελφός, brother,* used as it is by the side of *μήτηρ, mother* ("*the mother and brethren of Jesus*"), can only signify *brother* in the proper sense. The example often cited, Gen. xiii. 8, when Abraham says to Lot, "*We are brethren,*" is not parallel. (2) John says positively (vii. 5) that the brethren of Jesus *did not believe on Him,* and this long after the choice of the Twelve (John vi. 70). This is confirmed by Luke viii. 19 et seq.; comp. with Mark iii. 20–35. One of them could not, therefore, be found among His apostles. A comparison of all the passages leads us to distinguish, as is generally done at the present day, three Jameses: the first, the son of Zebedee (ver. 14); the second, the son of Alphæus indicated here, whom there is nothing to prevent our identifying with James the less, the son of Clopas and Mary, and regarding him as the first-cousin of Jesus; the third, the brother of the Lord, not a believer before the death of Jesus, but afterwards first bishop of the flock at Jerusalem.

The surname *Zealot*, given to Simon, is probably a translation of the adj. *kanna* (in the Talmud, *kananit*), *zealous.* If this be correct, this apostle belonged to that fanatical party which brought about the ruin of the people, by leading them into war against the Romans. This sense corresponds with the epithet **Καvavίτης**, which is applied to him in the Byz. reading of Matthew and Mark, confirmed here by the authority of the *Sinait.* This name is simply the Hebrew term, *translated* by Luke, and Hellenized by Matthew and Mark. The reading **Καναναῖος** in some Alex. may signify either *Canaanite* or *citizen of Cana.* This second etymology is not very probable. The first would be more so, if in Matt. xv. 22 this word, in the sense of Canaanite, were not written with an X instead of a K. Luke has therefore given the precise meaning of the Aramæan term employed in the document of which he availed himself (Keim, t. ii. p. 319).

The last pair comprises the two Judes. There were in fact two men of this name in the apostolic college, although Matthew and Mark mention but one, Judas Iscariot. This is very clear from John xiv. 22: "*Judas, not Iscariot, saith to Him.*" The names Lebbæus and Thaddæus, in Matthew and Mark, are therefore surnames, derived, the former from לֵב, *heart*, the latter either from תַּד, *mamma*, or from שַׁדִּי, *potens.* The name *Thaddaï* is of frequent occurrence in the Talmud. These surnames were probably the names by which they were usually designated in the Church. The genitive Ἰακώβου must, according to usage, signify *son of James;* this was to distinguish this Judas from the next. With the desire to make this apostle also a cousin of Jesus, the phrase has frequently been translated *brother* of James, that is to say, of the son of Alphæus, mentioned ver. 15. But there is no instance of the genitive being used in this sense. In the

14th verse, Luke himself thought it necessary to use the full expression, τὸν ἀδελφὸν αὐτοῦ. And would not the two other Syn., who join Lebbæus immediately to James, have indicated this relationship?

As there was a town called *Kerijoth* in Judæa, it is probable that the name *Iscariot* signifies *a man of Kerijoth* (at the present day *Kuriut*), towards the northern boundary of Judæa. The objections which De Wette has raised against this etymology are without force. He proposes, with Lightfoot, the etymology *ascara, strangulation.* Hengstenberg prefers *isch schéker, man of falsehood,* from which it would follow that this surname was given *post eventum.* These etymologies are all the more untenable, that in the fourth Gospel, according to the most probable reading (*Ἰσκαριώτου,* vi. 71 and elsewhere), this surname *Iscariot* must have been originally that of the father of Judas. The character of this man appears to have been cold, reserved, and calculating. He was so very reserved that, with the exception perhaps of John, none of the disciples guessed his secret hatred. In the coolness of his audacity, he ventured to cope with Jesus Himself (John xii. 4, 5). With what motive did Jesus choose a man of this character? He had spontaneously joined himself, as did so many others, to the number of His disciples; there was therefore a germ of faith in him, and perhaps, at the outset, an ardent zeal for the cause of Jesus. But there also existed in him, as in all the others, the selfish views and ambitious aspirations which were almost inseparable from the form which the Messianic hope had taken, until Jesus purified it from this alloy. In the case of Judas, as of all the others, it was a question which of the two conflicting principles would prevail in his heart: whether faith, and through this the sanctifying power of the spirit of Jesus, or pride, and thereby the unbelief which could not fail eventually to result from it. This was, for Judas, a question of moral liberty. As for Jesus, He was bound to submit in respect to him, as in respect to all the others, to God's plan. On the one hand, He might certainly hope, by admitting Judas into the number of His apostles, to succeed in purifying his heart, whilst by setting him aside He might irritate him and estrange him for ever. On the other hand, He certainly saw through him sufficiently well to perceive the risk He ran in giving him a place in that inner circle which He was about to form around His person. We may suppose, therefore, that, during that long night which preceded the appointment of the Twelve, this was one of the questions which engaged His deepest solicitude; and certainly it was not until the will of His Father became clearly manifest, that He admitted this man into the rank of the Twelve, notwithstanding His presentiment of the heavy cross He was preparing for Himself (John vi. 64 and 71). Still, even Judas fulfilled his apostolic function; his despairing cry, "*I have betrayed the innocent blood!*" is a testimony which resounds through the ages as loudly as the preaching of Peter at Pentecost, or as the cry of the blood of James, the first martyr.—The *καί, also,* after ὅς (ver. 16), omitted by some authorities, is perhaps taken from the two other Syn. If it is authentic, it is intended to bring out more forcibly, through the identity of the person, the contradiction between his mission and the course he took.

Surrounded by the Twelve and the numerous circle of disciples from which He had chosen them, Jesus descends from the summit of the mountain. Having reached a level place on its slopes, He stops; the crowd which was waiting for Him towards the foot of the mountain, ascends and gathers about Him. Τόπος πεδινός, a level place on an inclined plane. Thus the alleged contradiction with the expression, *the mountain,* in Matthew disappears (see above).—The ἔστη, *He stood still,* in opposition to *having come down,* does not in any way denote *the attitude* of Jesus during the discourse. There is therefore no contradiction between this expression and Matthew's, *having sat down.*—What are we to say of the discovery of Baur, who thinks that, by substituting *having come down,* ver. 16, for *He went up,* Matt. v. 1, Luke intended *to degrade the Sermon on the Mount!*[1]

Vers. 17*b*–19.[2]—We might make ὄχλος πλῆθος, *the crowd, the multitude,* etc., so many subjects of ἔστη: "He stood still, along with the crowd . . ." But it is more natural to understand some verb: "And there was with Him the crowd . . ."

[1] *Die Evangelien,* p. 457.

[2] Ver. 17. ℵ. B. L. Syr[sch]. read πολυς after οχλος.—Ver. 18. ℵ. A. B. D. L Q. some Mnn. It. omit και before θεραπευομενοι.

In any case, even if, with the Alex., we omit the *καί* before *ἐθεραπεύοντο*, *were healed* (ver. 18), we could not think of making these subst. nominatives to this last verb; for the crowd of disciples, etc., was not composed of sick people. Three classes of persons, therefore, surrounded Jesus at this time: occasional hearers (the *multitude* come together from all parts), the permanent disciples (the *crowd of disciples*), and the apostles. The first represent the people in so far as they are called to the kingdom of God; the second, the Church; the third, the ministry in the Church. The term *crowd*, to denote the second, is not too strong. Did not Jesus take out of them, only a little while after, seventy disciples (x. 1)?—If, at the 18th verse, we read *and* before *they were healed*, the idea of healing is only accessory, and is added by way of parenthesis; but the prevailing idea is that of gathering together: "Demoniacs also were there; and what is more, they were healed." If the *and* is omitted, the idea of healing alone remains, and we must translate: "And the possessed *even* were healed." With *παραλίου* we must understand *χώρας*; *Τύρου* and *Σιδῶνος* are complements.—Ver. 19 describes the mighty working of miraculous powers which took place that day. It was a time similar to that which has been described iv. 40 et seq., but to a far higher degree. *Ἰᾶτο* depends on *ὅτι*, and has for its subject *δύναμις*.

2*d*. Vers. 20–49. *The Sermon.*—The aim, prevailing thought, and plan of this discourse have been understood in many different ways. The solution of these questions is rendered more difficult by the difference between the two accounts given by Matthew and Luke. As to its aim, Weizsäcker regards the Sermon on the Mount as a grand proclamation of the kingdom of God, addressed *to the whole people;* and it is in Matthew's version that he finds the best support for this view of it. He acknowledges, nevertheless, that the fact stated in the preface (v. 1, 2: "He taught them [*His disciples*], saying . . .") is not in harmony with this design. Luke, according to him, has deviated further even than Matthew from its original aim, by modifying the entire discourse, to make it an address to the *disciples* alone. Ritschl and Holtzmann, on the contrary, think that the discourse was addressed originally to the disciples alone, and that Luke's version of it has preserved with greater accuracy its real tenor; only the situation described vers. 17–19 would not, according to Holtzmann, accord with its being addressed to them. Keim reconciles all these different views by distinguishing two principal discourses, one addressed to *all the people,* about the time of the Passover feast, of which we have fragments in Matt. vi. 19–34, vii. 7–11, 1-5, 24–27. This inaugural discourse would be on the *chief care of human life.* The second is supposed to have been addressed somewhat later to the *disciples* only, about the time of Pentecost. Matt. v. is a summary of it. This would be a word of welcome addressed by Jesus to His disciples, and an exposition of the new law as the fulfilment of the old. As to the criticism on the Pharisaical virtues, Matt. vi. 1–18, it is doubtless closely related, both in substance and time, to the preceding discourse; but it did not form part of it.

The prevailing idea, in Matthew, is certainly an exposition of the new law in its relations with the old. In Luke, the subject is simply the law of charity, as the foundation of the new order of things. Many critics deny that any agreement can be found between these two subjects. According to Holtzmann, the 5th chapter of Matthew should be regarded as a separate dissertation which the author of the first Gospel introduced into the Sermon; Keim thinks that Luke, as a disciple of Paul, wanted to detach the new morality completely from the old. The anonymous Saxon even sets himself to prove that the Sermon on the Mount was transformed by Luke into a cutting satire against—Saint Peter!

As to the plan of the discourse, many attempts have been made to systematize it. Beck: (1) the doctrine of *happiness* (beatitudes); (2) that of *righteousness* (the central part in Matthew and Luke); (3) that of *wisdom* (conclusion). Oosterzee: (1) the *salutation* of love (Luke, vers. 20–26); (2) the *commandment* of love (vers. 27–38); (3) the *impulse* of love (vers. 39–49). The best division, regarding it in this abstract way, and taking Matthew as a basis, is certainly that of Gess: (1) the happiness of those who are fit to enter into the kingdom (Matt. v. 3–12); (2) the lofty vocation of the disciples (Matt. v. 13–16); (3) the righteousness, superior to that of the Pharisees, after which they must strive who would enter into the kingdom (v. 17–vi. 34); the rocks on which they run a risk of striking (the disposition to judge, intemperate proselytizing, being led away by false prophets); next, the help against these dangers, with the conclusion (vii. 1–27).

The solution of these different questions, as it seems to us, must be sought first of all in the position of affairs which gave rise to the Sermon on the Mount. In order to see it reproduced, as it were, before our eyes, we have only to institute a comparison. Picture a leader of one of those great social revolutions, for which preparations seem making in our day. At an appointed hour he presents himself, surrounded by his principal adherents, at some public place; the crowd gathers; he communicates his plans to them. He begins by indicating the class of persons to which he specially addresses himself: you, poor working people, loaded with suffering and toil! and he displays to their view the hopes of the era which is about to dawn. Next, he proclaims the new principle which is to govern humanity in the future: "The mutual service of mankind; justice, universal charity!" Lastly, he points out the sanction of the law which he proclaims, the penalties that await those who violate it, and the rewards of those who faithfully keep it. This is the caricature; and by the aid of its exaggerations, we are able to give some account of the features of the original model. What, in fact, does the Sermon on the Mount contain? Three things: 1*st.* An indication of the persons to whom Jesus chiefly addresses Himself, in order to form the new people (Luke, vers. 20–26; Matt. v. 1–12); 2*d.* The proclamation of the fundamental principle of the new society (Luke, vers. 27–45; Matt. v. 13–vii. 12); 3*d.* An announcement of the judgment to which the members of the new kingdom of God will have to submit (Luke, vers. 46–49; Matt. vii. 13–27). In other words: the call, the declaration of principles, and their sanction. This is the *order* of the discourse. There is nothing artificial about this plan. It is not a logical outline forcibly fitted to the discourse; it is the result of the actual position of the work of Jesus, just as we have stated it. The discourse itself explains for whom it is intended. Jesus addresses the mass of the people present, as forming the circle within which the new order of things is to be realized, and at the same time the disciples and apostles, by means of whom this revolution is to be brought about Luke and Matthew, therefore, are not at variance in this matter, either with each other or with themselves. As to the fundamental idea of this discourse, see ver. 27.

First part: vers. 20–26. *The Call.*—This solemn invitation describes: (1*st.*) Those who are qualified to become members of the order of things inaugurated by Jesus (vers. 20–23); (2*d.*) Their adversaries (vers. 24–26).—Matthew begins in the same way; but there are two important differences between him and Luke: 1*st.* The latter has only four beatitudes; Matthew has eight (not seven or nine, as is often said). 2*d.* To the four beatitudes of Luke are joined four woes, which are wanting in Matthew. In Luke's form, Keim sees nothing but an artificial construction. That would not in any case be the work of Luke, but of his document. For if there is any one portion which from its contents should be assigned to the primitive document (of an Ebionitish colour), evidently it is this. But the context appears to us decisive in favour of Luke's version. This call deals with the conditions which qualify for *entering* into the kingdom. These are clearly indicated in the first four beatitudes of Matthew; but the next four (mercy, purity of heart, a peaceable spirit, and joy under persecution) indicate the dispositions by means of which men will *remain* in the kingdom, and consequently their natural place is not in this call. It is only the eighth (Luke's fourth) which can belong here, as a transition from the persecuted disciples to the persecutors, who are the objects of the following woes. Two of the last four beatitudes of Matthew find their place very naturally in the body of the discourse. As to the woes, they perfectly agree with the context. After having proclaimed the blessedness of those who are qualified to enter, Jesus announces the unhappiness of those who are animated by contrary dispositions. Schleiermacher says: a harmless addition of Luke's. But, as we have just seen, Luke is here certainly only a copyist. A Gentile Christian would not have dreamed of identifying, as Judaism did, the two ideas of piety and poverty; nor, on the other hand, riches and violence. De Wette says: the first manifestation of the fixed (Ebionitish) idea of Luke. But see xii. 32, xvi. 27, and xviii. 18–30.

Vers. 20 and 21.—"*And He lifted up His eyes on His disciples, and said, Blessed be ye poor: for yours is the kingdom of God.* 21. *Blessed are ye that hunger now: for ye shall be filled. Blessed are ye that weep now: for ye shall laugh.*"—The *disciples* are the constant hearers of Jesus, amongst whom He has just assigned a distinct place to His apostles. Luke does not say that Jesus spoke to *them* alone. He spoke to all the people, but regarding them as the representatives of the new order of things which He was about to institute. In Matthew, *αὐτούς*, ver. 2 (He taught *them*), comprises *both the people and the disciples,* ver. 1.—This commencement of the Sermon on the Mount breathes a sentiment of the deepest joy. In these disciples immediately about Him, and in this multitude surrounding Him in orderly ranks, all eager to hear the word of God, Jesus beholds the first appearance of the true Israel, the true people of the kingdom. He surveys with deep joy this congregation which His Father has brought together for Him, and begins to speak. It must have been a peculiarly solemn moment; comp. the similar picture, Matt. v. 1, 2.

This assembly was chiefly composed of persons belonging to the poor and suffering classes. Jesus knew it; He recognises in this a higher will, and in His first words He does homage to this divine dispensation. *Πτωχός*, which we translate *poor,* comes from *πτώσσω*, *to make oneself little, to crouch,* and conveys the idea of humiliation rather than of poverty (*πένης*). *Πεινῶντες*, *the hungry* (a word connected with *πένης*), denotes rather those whom poverty condemns to a life of toil and privation. This second term marks the transition to the third, *those who weep,* amongst whom must be numbered all classes of persons who are weighed down by the trials of life. All those persons who, in ordinary language, are called unhappy, Jesus salutes with the epithet *μακάριοι*, *blessed.* This word answers to the אשרי, *felicitates,* of the O. T. (Ps. i. 1 and elsewhere). The idea is the same as in numerous passages in which the poor and despised are spoken of as God's chosen ones, not because poverty and suffering are in themselves a title to His blessing; but they dispose the soul to those meek and lowly dispositions which qualify them to receive it, just as, on the other hand, prosperity and riches dispose the heart to be proud and hard. In the very composition of this congregation, Jesus sees a proof of this fact of experience so often expressed in the O. T. The joy which He feels at this sight arises from the magnificent promises which He can offer to such hearers.

The *kingdom of God* is a state of things in which the will of God reigns supreme. This state is realized first of all in the hearts of men, in the heart it may be of a single man, but speedily in the hearts of a great number; and eventually there will come a day when, all rebellious elements having been vanquished or taken away, it will be found in the hearts of all. It is an order of things, therefore, which, from being inward and individual, tends to become outward and social, until at length it shall take possession of the entire domain of human life, and appear as a distinct epoch in history. Since this glorious state as yet exists in a perfect manner only in a higher sphere, it is also called the kingdom *of heaven* (the ordinary term in Matthew).—Luke says: *is*—not *shall be*—yours; which denotes partial present possession, and a right to perfect future possession.—But are men members of this kingdom simply through being poor and suffering? The answer to this question is to be found in what precedes, and in such passages as Isa. lxvi. 2: "To whom will I look? saith the Lord. To *him who is poor* (עני) *and of a broken spirit, and who trembles at my word.*" It is to hearts which suffering has broken that Jesus brings the blessings of the kingdom.—These blessings are primarily spiritual—pardon and holiness. But outward blessings cannot fail to follow them; and this notion is also contained in the idea of a *kingdom of God*, for glory is the crown of grace. The words of Jesus contain, therefore, the following succession of ideas: temporal abasement, from which come humiliation and sighing after God; then spiritual graces, crowned with outward blessings. The same connection of ideas explains the beatitudes that follow. Ver. 21*a*: temporal poverty (being hungry) leads the soul to the need of God and of His grace (Ps. xlii. 1); then out of the satisfaction of this spiritual hunger and thirst arises full outward satisfaction (being filled). Ver. 21*b*: with tears shed over temporal misfortunes, is easily connected the mourning of the soul for its sins; the latter draws down the unspeakable consolations of divine love, which eventually raise the soul to the triumph of perfect joy. The terms *κλαίειν*, *to sob*, *γελᾶν*, *to laugh*, cannot well be literally rendered here. They denote a grief and joy which find outward demonstration; comp. Ps. cxxvi. 2, "Our mouth was *filled with laughter*," and Paul's *καυχᾶσθαι ἐν Θεῷ*, *to joy in God* (Rom. v. 11). The text of Matthew presents here two important differences. 1*st.* He employs the third person instead of the second: "Blessed are *the* poor, for *theirs* is the kingdom of heaven; *they that mourn, for they shall be comforted*," etc. The beatitudes, which in Luke are addressed directly to the hearers, are presented here under the form of general maxims and moral sentences. 2*d.* In Matthew, these maxims have an exclusively spiritual meaning: "the poor *in spirit*, they who hunger *after righteousness*." Here interpreters are divided, some maintaining that Matthew has spiritualized the words of Jesus; others (as Keim), that Luke, under the influence of a prejudice against riches, has given to these blessings a grossly temporal meaning. Two things appear evident to us: (1) That the direct form of address in Luke, "*Ye*," can alone be *historically* accurate: Jesus was speaking *to* His hearers, not discoursing *before* them. (2) That this first difference has led to the second; having adopted the third person, and given the beatitudes that *Maschal* form so often found in the didactic parts of the O. T. (Psalms, Proverbs), Matthew was obliged to bring out expressly in the text of the discourse those moral aims which are inherent in the very persons of the poor whom Jesus addresses directly in Luke, and without which these words, in this abstract form, would have been somewhat too unqualified. How could one say, without qualification, Blessed are *the* poor, *the* hungry? Temporal sufferings of themselves could not be a pledge of salvation. On the other hand, the form, Blessed are *ye* poor, *ye* hungry, in Luke, renders all such explanation superfluous. For Jesus, when He spoke thus, was addressing particular concrete poor and afflicted, whom He already recognised as His disciples, as believers, and whom He regarded as the representatives of that new people which He was come to install in the earth. That they were such attentive hearers sufficiently proved that they were of the number of those in whom temporal sufferings had awakened the need of divine consolation, that they belonged to those labouring and heavy-laden souls whom He was sent to lead to rest (Matt. xi. 29), and that they hungered, not for material bread only, but for the bread of life, for the word of God, for God Himself. The qualification which Matthew was necessarily obliged to add, in order to limit the application of the beatitudes, in the general form which he gives to them, is in Luke then implied in this *ye*, which was only addressed to poor *believers*. These two differences between Matthew and Luke are very significant. They seem to me to prove: (1) that the text of Luke is a more exact report of the discourse than Matthew's; (2) that Matthew's version was originally made with a *didactic* rather than a *historical* design, and consequently that it formed part of a collection of discourses in which the teaching of Jesus was set forth without regard to the particular circumstances under which He gave it, before it entered into the historical framework in which we find it contained at the present day.

Vers. 22 and 23.[1]—"*Blessed are ye when men shall hate you, and when they shall separate you* from their company, *and shall reproach* you, *and cast out your name as evil, for the Son of man's sake.* 23. *Rejoice ye in that day, and leap for joy; for, behold, your reward* is *great in heaven: for in like manner did their fathers unto the prophets.*"—This fourth beatitude is completely accounted for, in Luke, by the scenes of violent hostility which had already taken place. It is not so well accounted for in Matthew, who places the Sermon on the Mount at the opening of the ministry of Jesus.—In Matthew, this saying, like the preceding, has the abstract form of a moral maxim: "Blessed are *they* which are *persecuted* for righteousness' sake; for *theirs* is the kingdom of heaven." But Jesus was certainly not giving utterance here to abstract principles of Christian morality; He spoke as a living man to living men. Besides, Matthew himself passes, in the next verse, to the form of address adopted by Luke from the commencement.—The explanatory adjunct, *for righteousness' sake*, in Matthew, is to be ascribed to the same cause as the similar qualifications in the preceding beatitudes.—By the pres. ἔστε,

[1] Ver. 23. All the Mjj., χαρητε instead of χαιρετε, the reading of T. R. with some Mnn.—B. D. Q. X. Z. Syr^{sch} It^{aliq}., κατα τα αυτα instead of κατα ταυτα.

"happy *are ye*," Jesus transports His hearers directly into this immediate future.—The term ἀφορίζειν, *to separate*, refers to exclusion from the synagogue (John ix. 22).—The strange expression, *cast out your name*, is explained in very *jejune* fashion, both by Bleek, to pronounce the name *with disgust*, and by De Wette and Meyer, *to refuse* altogether to pronounce it. It refers rather to the expunging of the name from the synagogue roll of membership. There is not, on this account, any tautology of the preceding idea. *To separate, to insult*, indicated acts of unpremeditated violence; *to erase the name* is a permanent measure taken with deliberation and coolness. —Πονηρόν, *evil*, as an epitome of every kind of wickedness. In their accounts of this saying, this is the only word left which Matthew and Luke have in common.—Instead of *for the Son of man's sake*, Matthew says *for my sake*. The latter expression denotes attachment to the person of Jesus; the former faith in His Messianic character, as the perfect representative of humanity. On this point also Luke appears to me to have preserved the true text of this saying; it is with His work that Jesus here wishes to connect the idea of persecution. This idea of submission to persecution along with, and for the sake of, *the Messiah*, was so foreign to the Jewish point of view, that Jesus feels He must justify it. The sufferings of the adherents of Jesus will only be a continuation of the sufferings of the prophets of Jehovah. This is the great matter of consolation that He offers them. They will be, by their very sufferings, raised to the rank of the old prophets; the recompense of the Elijahs and Isaiahs will become theirs.—The reading κατὰ τὰ αὐτά, *in the same manner*, appears preferable to the received reading κατὰ ταῦτα, *in this manner*. Τά and αὐτά have probably been made into one word. The imperf. ἐποίουν (treated) indicates habit.—The pronoun αὐτῶν, *their* fathers, is dictated by the idea that the disciples belong already to a new order of things. The word *their* serves as a transition to the woes which follow, addressed to the heads of the existing order of things.

Vers. 24–26.[1]—"*But woe unto you that are rich! for ye have received your consolation.* 25. *Woe unto you that are full!*

[1] Ver. 25. 9 Mjj. some Mnn. read νυν after εμπεπλησμενοι.—ℵ. B. K. L. S. X. Z. and some Mnn. omit the second υμιν.—Ver. 26. 20 Mjj. omit υμιν, which is

for ye shall hunger. Woe unto you that laugh now! for ye shall mourn and weep. 26. *Woe unto you when all men shall speak well of you! for so did their fathers to the false prophets.*" —Jesus here contemplates in spirit those adversaries who were sharpening against Him only just before (ver. 11) the sword of persecution: the rich and powerful at Jerusalem, whose emissaries surrounded Him in Galilee. Perhaps at this very moment He perceives some of their spies in the outer ranks of the congregation. Certainly it is not the rich, as such, that He curses, any more than He pronounced the poor as such blessed. A Nicodemus or a Joseph of Arimathea will be welcomed with open arms as readily as the poorest man in Israel. Jesus is dealing here with historical fact, not with moral philosophy. He takes the fact as it presented itself to Him at that time. Were not the rich and powerful, as a class, already in open opposition to His mission? They were thus excluding themselves from the kingdom of God. The fall of Jerusalem fulfilled only too literally the maledictions to which Jesus gave utterance on that solemn day. —The πλήν, *except, only,* which we can only render by *but* (ver. 24), makes the persons here designated an exception as regards the preceding beatitudes.—The term *rich* refers to social position, *full* to mode of living; the expression, *you that laugh,* describes a personal disposition. All these outward conditions are considered as associated with an avaricious spirit, with injustice, proud self-satisfaction, and a profane levity, which did indeed attach to them at that time. It was to the Pharisees and Sadducees more particularly that these threatenings were addressed.—The word νῦν, *now,* which several MSS. read in the first proposition, is a faulty imitation of the second, where it is found in all the documents. It is in place in the latter; for the notion of *laughing* contains something more transient than that of being full.—The expression ἀπέχετε, which we have rendered by *ye have received,* signifies: you have taken and carried away everything; all therefore is exhausted. Comp. xvi. 25.—The terms hunger, weeping, were literally realized in the great national catastrophe which followed soon after this malediction; but they

the reading of T. R. with B. Δ. only.—8 Mjj. 100 Mnn. omit παντες.—The Mss. are divided between κατα ταυτα (T. R.) and κατα τα αυτα.

also contain an allusion to the privations and sufferings which await, after death, those who have found their happiness in this world.—In ver. 26 it is more particularly the Pharisees and scribes, who were so generally honoured in Israel, that Jesus points out as continuing the work of the false prophets. These four woes would be incompatible with the *spiritual* sense of the terms *poor, hungry,* etc., in the beatitudes.

The second part of the discourse: vers. 27–45. *The New Law.*—Here we have the body of the discourse. Jesus proclaims the supreme law of the new society. The difference from Matthew comes out in a yet more striking manner in this part than in the preceding. In the first Gospel, the principal idea is the opposition between legal righteousness and the new righteousness which Jesus came to establish. He Himself announces the text of the discourse in this saying (ver. 20): "*Except your righteousness exceed* the righteousness *of the scribes and Pharisees, ye shall in no case enter into the kingdom of heaven.*" The law, in the greater number of its statutes, seemed at first sight only to require outward observance. But it was evident to every true heart, that by these commandments the God of holiness desired to lead His worshippers, not to hypocritical formalism, but to spiritual obedience. The tenth commandment made this very clear, as far as respected the decalogue. Israelitish teaching should have laboured to explain the law in this truly moral sense, and to have carried the people up from the letter to the spirit, as the prophets had endeavoured to do. Instead of that, Pharisaism had taken pleasure in multiplying indefinitely legal observances, and in regulating them with the minutest exactness, urging the letter of the precept to such a degree as sometimes even to make it contradict its spirit. It had stifled morality under legalism. Comp. Matt. xv. 1–20 and xxiii. In dealing with this crying abuse, Jesus breaks into the heart of the letter with a bold hand, in order to set free its spirit, and displaying this in all its beauty, casts aside at once the letter, which was only its imperfect envelope, and that Pharisaical righteousness, which rested on nothing else than an indefinite amplification of the letter. Thus Jesus finds the secret of the abolition of the law in its very fulfilment. Paul understood and developed this better than anybody. What in fact, is the legislator's intention in imposing the letter? Not the letter, but the spirit. The letter, like the thick calyx under the protection of which the flower, with its delicate organs, is formed, was only a means of preserving and developing its inward meaning of goodness, until the time came when it could bloom freely. This time had come. Jesus on the mountain proclaims it. And this is why this day is the counterpart of the day of Sinai. He opposes the letter of the divine commandment, understood *as letter*, to the spirit contained in it, and developes this contrast, Matt. v., in a series of antitheses so striking, that it is impossible to doubt either their authenticity, or that they formed the real substance, the centre of the Sermon on the Mount. Holtzmann will never succeed in persuading any one to the contrary; his entire critical hypothesis as to the relations of the Syn. will crumble away sooner than this conviction. The connection of the discourse in Matthew is this: 1. Jesus discloses wherein the Pharisaical righteousness fails, its want of inward truth (vers. 13–48). 2. He judges, by this law, the three positive manifestations of this boasted righteousness: almsgiving, prayer, and fasting (vi. 1–18). 3. He attacks two of the most characteristic sins of Pharisaism: covetousness and censoriousness (vi. 19–34, vii. 1–5). 4. Lastly there come various particular precepts on prayer, conversion, false religious teaching, etc. (vii. 6–20). But between these precepts it is no longer possible to establish a perfectly natural connection. Such is the body of the Sermon in Matthew: at the commencement, an unbroken chain of thought; then a connection which becomes slighter and slighter, until it ceases altogether, and the discourse becomes a simple collection of detached sayings. But the fundamental idea is still the opposition between the formalism of the ancient righteousness and the spirituality of the new.

In Luke also, the subject of the discourse is the perfect law of the new order of things; but this law is exhibited, not under its abstract and polemical relation of *spirituality*, but under its concrete and positive form of *charity*. The plan of this part of the discourse, in Luke, is as follows: 1*st*. Jesus describes the practical *manifestations* of the new principle (vers. 27–30); then, 2*d*. He gives concise *expression* to it (ver. 31); *3d.* He indicates the distinctive characteristics of charity, by contrasting this virtue with certain natural analogous sentiments (vers. 32–35*a*); *4th.* He sets forth its *model* and *source* (vers. 35*b* and 36); *5th.* Lastly, He exhibits this gratuitous, disinterested love as the principle of all sound judgment and salutary religious teaching, contrasting in this respect the new ministry, which He is establishing in the earth in the presence of His disciples, with the old, which, as embodied in the Pharisees, is vanishing away (vers. 37–45).

At the first glance, there seems little or nothing in common between this body of the discourse, and that which, as we have just seen, Matthew gives us. We can even understand, to a certain extent, the odd notion of Schleiermacher, that these two versions emanated from two hearers, of whom one was more favourably situated for hearing than the other! The difference, however, between these two versions may be accounted for by connecting the fully-developed subject in Luke with the subject of the last two of the six antitheses, by which Jesus describes (Matt. v.) the contrast between legal righteousness and true righteousness. Jesus attacks, vers. 38–48, the Pharisaical commentary on these two precepts of the law: *an eye for an eye . . . ;* and, *thou shalt love* thy *neighbour as thyself.* This commentary, by applying the *lex talionis,* which had only been given as a rule for the judges of Israel, to private life, and by deducing from the word *neighbour* this consequence: therefore thou mayest hate him who is not thy neighbour, that is to say, the foreigner, or thine enemy, had entirely falsified the meaning of the law on these two points. In opposition to these caricatures, Jesus sets forth, in Matthew, the inexhaustible and perfect grace of charity, as exhibited to man in the example of his heavenly Benefactor; then He proceeds to identify this charity in man with the divine perfection itself: "Be ye perfect [through charity], as your Father which is in heaven is perfect." Now it is just at this point that Luke begins to appropriate the central part of the discourse. These last two antitheses, which terminate in Matthew in the lofty thought (ver. 48) of man being elevated by love to the perfection of God, furnish Luke with the leading idea of the discourse as he presents it, namely, charity as the law of the new life. Its theme is in this way modified in form, but it is not altered in substance. For if, as St. Paul says, Rom. xiii. 10, "*charity* is the fulfilling of the law;" if perfect spirituality, complete likeness to God, consists in charity; the fundamental agreement between these two forms of the Sermon on the Mount is evident. Only Luke has deemed it advisable to omit all that specially referred to the ancient law and the comments of the Pharisees, and to preserve only that which has a universal human bearing, the opposition between charity and the natural selfishness of the human heart.

The two accounts being thus related, it follows, that as regards the original structure of the discourse, in so far as this was determined by opposition to Pharisaism, Matthew has preserved it more completely than Luke. But though this is so, Matthew's discourse still contains many details not originally belonging to it, which Luke has very properly assigned to entirely different places in other parts of his narrative. We find here once more the two writers following their respective bent: Matthew, having a *didactic* aim, exhibits in a general manner the teaching of Jesus on the *righteousness of the kingdom*, by including in this outline many sayings spoken on other occasions, but bearing on the same subject; Luke, writing as a historian, confines himself more strictly to the actual words which Jesus uttered at this time. Thus each of them has his own kind of superiority over the other.

1*st.* The *manifestations* of charity: vers. 27–30.—To describe the manifestations of this new principle, which is henceforth to sway the world, was the most popular and effectual way of introducing it into the consciences of his hearers. Jesus describes, first of all, charity in its active form (vers. 27 and 28)· then in its passive form of endurance (vers. 29 and 30).

Vers. 27, 28.[1] "*But I say unto you which hear, Love your enemies, do good to them which hate you.* 28. *Bless them that curse you, and pray for them which despitefully use you.*"—There is a break in the connection between ver. 26 and ver. 27. De Wette and Meyer think that the link is to be found

[1] Ver. 28. The Mss. are divided between υμας and υμιν.—All the Mjj. omit και before προσευχεσθε, which is the reading of T. R. with merely some Mnn.—The Mss. are divided between περι and υπερ.

in this thought understood: "Notwithstanding these curses which I pronounce upon the rich, your persecutors, I command you not to hate, but to love them." But in the verses that follow, it is not the rich particularly that are represented as the enemies whom His disciples should love. The precept of love to enemies is given in the most general manner. Rather is it the *new law* which Jesus announces here, as in Matthew. The link of connection with what goes before is this: In the midst of this hatred of which you will be the objects (ver. 22), it will be your duty to realize in the world the perfect law which I to-day proclaim to you. Tholuck, in his *Explanation of the Sermon on the Mount* (p. 498), takes exception to Luke for giving these precepts a place here, where they have no connection; but he thus shows that he has failed to understand the structure of this discourse in our Gospel, as we have exhibited it. In this form of expression: *But I say unto you which hear,* there is an echo as it were of the antithesis of Matthew: "Ye have heard . . . *But I say unto you.*" By this expression, *you which hear,* Jesus opposes the actual hearers surrounding Him to those imaginary hearers to whom the preceding woes were addressed.—We must conceive of the words, ver. 27 and ver. 28, as having been pronounced with some kind of enthusiasm. These precepts overflow with love. You have only to meet every manifestation of hatred with a fresh manifestation of love. Love! Love! You can never love too much! The term *love* denotes the essence of the new principle. Then come its manifestations: first, in acts (*do good*); then in words (*bless*); lastly, the highest manifestation, which is at once act and word (*pray for*). These manifestations of love correspond with the exhibitions of hatred by which they are called forth: ἔχθρα, *hatred,* the inward feeling; μισεῖν, *to hold in abhorrence,* the acts; καταρασθαι, *to curse,* the words. Ἐπηρεάζειν (probably from ἐπί and αἴρεσθαι, *to rise against, to thwart*) corresponds with intercession. Jesus therefore here requires more than that which to natural selfishness appears the highest virtue: not to render evil for evil. He demands from His disciples, according to the expression of St. Paul (Rom. xii. 21), that they shall *overcome evil with good;* Jesus could not yet reveal the source whence His disciples were to derive this entirely new passion, this divine charity which displays its riches of forgiveness and salvation towards a rebellious world at enmity with God (Rom. v. 8-10).—In the parallel passage in Matthew, the two intervening propositions have probably been transferred from Luke.

Vers. 29 and 30.[1] Patient Charity.—"*And unto him that smiteth thee on the one cheek, offer also the other; and him that taketh away thy cloak, forbid not to take thy coat also.* 30. *Give to every man that asketh of thee; and of him that taketh away thy goods ask them not again.*"—Paul also regards *μακροθυμεῖν, to be long-suffering,* as on a par with *χρηστεύεσθαι, to do good* (Charity suffereth long, and is kind, 1 Cor. xiii. 4). The natural heart thinks it does a great deal when it respects a neighbour's rights; it does not rise to the higher idea of sacrificing its own. Jesus here describes a charity which seems to ignore its own rights, and knows no bounds to its self-sacrifice. He exhibits this sublime ideal in actual instances (*lit.* in the most concrete traits) and under the most paradoxical forms. In order to explain these difficult words, Olshausen maintained that they only applied to the members of the kingdom of God among themselves, and not to the relations of Christians with the world. But would Jesus have entertained the supposition of strikers and thieves among His own people? Again, it has been said that these precepts expressed nothing more than an emphatic condemnation of revenge (Calvin), that they were hyperboles (Zwingle), a portrayal of the general disposition which the Christian is to exemplify in each individual case, according as regard for God's glory and his neighbour's salvation may permit (Tholuck); which comes to St. Augustine's idea, that these precepts concern the *præparatio cordis* rather than the *opus quod in aperto fit.* Without denying that there is some truth in all these explanations, we think that they do not altogether grasp the idea. Jesus means that, *as far as itself* is concerned, charity know no limits to its self-denial. If, therefore, it ever puts a stop to its concessions, it is in no way because it feels its patience exhausted; true charity is infinite as God Himself, whose essence it is. Its limit, if it has any, is not that which its rights draw around it; it is a limit like that which the

[1] Ver. 29. ℵ. D., εἰς τὴν for ἐπὶ τήν.—Ver. 30. ℵ. B. omit τῷ after παντί.

beautiful defines for itself, proceeding from within. It is in charity that the disciple of Jesus yields, when he yields; it is in charity also that he resists, when he resists. CHARITY HAS NO OTHER LIMIT THAN CHARITY ITSELF, that is to say, it is boundless.—Σιαγών does not properly mean, as it is ordinarily translated, the *cheek* (παρειά), but the *jaw;* the blow given, therefore, is not a slap, but a heavy blow. Consequently it is an act of violence, rather than of contempt, that is meant.—The disciple who has completely sacrificed his person, naturally will not refuse his clothes. As ἱμάτιον denotes the upper garment, and χιτῶν the under garment or tunic which is worn next the skin, it would seem that here also it is an act of violence that is meant, a theft perpetrated by main force; the thief first snatches away the upper garment. Matthew presents the reverse order: "He who would take away *thy coat,* let him have *thy cloak* also." This is because with him it is an affair of legal process (*if any man will sue thee at the law*). The creditor begins by possessing himself of the coat, which is less valuable; then, if he is not sufficiently compensated, he claims the under garment. This juridical form stands connected in Matthew with the article of the Mosaic code which Jesus has just cited: *an eye for an eye, a tooth for a tooth.* Matthew, therefore, appears to have preserved the original words of this passage. But is it possible to conceive, that if Luke had had Matthew's writing before him, or the document made use of by the author of this Gospel, he would have substituted, on his own authority, a totally different thought from that of his predecessor?

Ver. 30. Another form of the same thought. A Christian so far as he is concerned, would neither refuse anything nor claim anything back. If, therefore, he does either one or the other, it is always out of charity. This sentiment regulates his refusals as well as his gifts, the maintenance as well as the sacrifice of his rights.

2*d.* After having described the applications of the new principle, Jesus gives a formal enunciation of it, ver. 31: "*And as ye would that men should do to you, do ye also to them likewise.*"—The natural heart says, indeed, with the Rabbins. "What is disagreeable to thyself, do not do to thy neighbour." But charity says, by the mouth of Jesus: "Whatsoever thou desirest for thyself, that do to thy neighbour." Treat thy neighbour in everything as thine other self. It is obvious that Jesus only means desires that are reasonable and really salutary. His disciples are regarded as unable to form any others for themselves. *Καί, and,* may be rendered here by, *in a word.* In Matthew this precept is found in chap. vii. towards the end of the discourse, between an exhortation to prayer and a call to conversion, consequently without any natural connection with what precedes and follows. Notwithstanding this, Tholuck prefers the position which it has in Matthew. He regards this saying as a summary of the whole discourse (p. 498). But is it not manifest that it is more naturally connected with a series of precepts on charity, than with an exhortation to prayer?

3*d.* The *distinguishing characteristic* of charity, disinterestedness: vers. 32–35*a.*[1] "*And if ye love them which love you, what thank have ye? For sinners also love those that love them.* 33. *And if ye do good to them which do good to you, what thank have ye? For sinners also do even the same.* 34. *And if ye lend to those of whom ye hope to receive, what thank have ye? For sinners also lend to sinners, to receive the same service.* 35*a.* *But love your enemies, and do them good, and lend, without hoping for anything again.*"—Human love seeks an object which is congenial to itself, and from which, in case of need, it may obtain some return. There is always somewhat of self-interest in it. The new love which Jesus proclaims will be completely gratuitous and disinterested. For this reason it will be able to embrace even an object entirely opposed to its own nature. *Χάρις*: the favour which comes from God; in Matthew: *τίνα μισθόν, what matter of recompense?* *Ἀπολαμβάνειν τὰ ἴσα* may signify, *to withdraw the capital lent,* or indeed, *to receive* some day *the same service.* The preposition *ἀπό* would favour the first sense. But the Alex. reading renders this prep. doubtful. The covert selfishness of this conduct comes out better in the second sense, only to lend to those who, it is hoped, will lend in their turn. It is a

[1] Ver. 33. ℵ* B. add γαρ between και and εαν.—ℵ. B. Λ. omit γαρ after και.—Ver. 34. Instead of απολαβειν, which is the reading of T.R. with 14 Mjj., ℵ. B. L. Z. read λαβειν.—ℵ. B. L. Z. omit γαρ.—Ver. 35. ℵ. Z. Π Syr., μηδενα instead of μηδεν.

shrewd calculation, selfishness in instinctive accord with the law of retaliation, utilitarianism coming forward to reap the fruits of morality. What fine irony there is in this picture! What a criticism on natural kindness! The new principle of wholly disinterested charity comes out very clearly on this dark background of ordinary benevolence. This paradoxical form which Jesus gives His precepts, effectually prevents all attempts of a relaxed morality to weaken them.—*Πλήν* (ver. 35): "This false love cast aside; for you, my disciples, there only remains this."—*Ἀπελπίζειν* means properly, *to despair*. Meyer would apply this sense here: "not despairing of divine remuneration in the dispensation to come." But how can the object of the verb *μηδέν*, *nothing*, be harmonized with this meaning and the antithesis in ver. 34? The sense which the Syriac translation gives, reading probably with some MSS. *μηδένα*, no one, "causing no one to despair by a refusal," is grammatically inadmissible. The only alternative is to give the *ἀπό* in *ἀπελπίζειν* the sense which this prep. already has in *ἀπολαβεῖν*, *hoping for nothing in return from* him who asks of you.

4*th*. ***The*** *model and source* of the charity which Jesus has just depicted: vers. 35*b* and 36.[1] "*And your reward shall be great, and ye shall be the children of the Highest: for He is kind to the unthankful and to the evil.* 36. *Be ye therefore merciful, as your Father also is merciful.*"—Having referred to the love which His disciples are to surpass, that of man by nature a sinner, Jesus shows them what they must aspire to reach,—that divine love which is the source of all gratuitous and disinterested love. The promise of a reward is no contradiction to the perfect disinterestedness which Jesus has just made the essential characteristic of love. And, in fact, the reward is not a payment of a nature foreign to the feeling rewarded, the prize of merit; it is the feeling itself brought to perfection, the full participation in the life and glory of God, who is love!—***Καί***, *and in fact*. This disinterested love, whereby we become like God, raises us to the glorious condition of His sons and heirs, like Jesus Himself. The seventh beatitude in Matthew, "*Blessed are the peacemakers, for they shall be called the children of God,*" is probably a general maxim taken from this saying.

[1] Ver. 36. ℵ. B. D. L. Z. It^plerique omit *οὖν*.—ℵ. B. L. Z. omit *καί*.

—If the ungrateful and the wicked are the object of divine love, it is because this love is compassionate (*οἰκτίρμων*, ver. 36). In the wicked man God sees the unhappy man. Matt. v. 45 gives this same idea in an entirely different form: "*For He maketh His sun to rise on the evil and on the good, and sendeth rain on the just and on the unjust.*" How could these two forms have been taken from the same document? If Luke had known this fine saying in Matthew, would he have suppressed it? Matthew concludes this train of thought by a general maxim similar to that in Luke v. 36: "*Be ye therefore perfect, as your Father in heaven is perfect.*" These two different forms correspond exactly with the difference in the body of the discourse in the two evangelists. Matthew speaks of the inward righteousness, the perfection (to which one attains through charity); Luke, of charity (the essential element of perfection; comp. Col. iii. 14).

5*th. Love, the principle of all beneficent moral action on the world:* vers. 37–45.—The disciples of Jesus are not only called to practise what is good themselves; they are charged to make it prevail in the earth. They are, as Jesus says in Matthew, immediately after the beatitudes, *the light of the world, the salt of the earth.* Now they can only exercise this salutary influence through love, which manifests itself in this sphere also (comp. ver. 27), either by what it refrains from (vers. 37–42), or by action (vers. 43–45). Above all things, love refrains from *judging.*

Vers. 37 and 38.[1] "*And judge not, and ye shall not be judged; condemn not, and ye shall not be condemned; forgive, and ye shall be forgiven.* 38. *Give, and it shall be given unto you; good measure, pressed down, and shaken together, and running over, shall men give into your bosom; for with the same measure that ye mete withal, it shall be measured to you again.*"—There is no reference here to the pardon of personal offences; the reference is to charity, which, in a general way, refuses to judge. Jesus evidently has in view in this passage the judgment which the scribes and Pharisees assumed the right to exercise in Israel, and which their harshness and

[1] Ver. 37. A. C. Λ. It[aliq]., *ινα μη* instead of *και ου μη*. — Ver. 38. ℵ. B. D. L. Ξ., *ω γαρ μετρω* instead of *τω γαρ αυτω μετρω ω*, which is the reading of T. R. with all the other Mss.

arrogance rendered more injurious than useful, as was seen in the effect it produced on the publicans and other such persons (v. 30, xv. 28–30). — *Καί* indicates the transition to a new but analogous subject: *And further.* *Κρίνειν, to judge,* is not equivalent to *condemn;* it means generally to set oneself up as a judge of the moral worth of another. But since, wherever this disposition prevails, judgment is usually exercised in an unkindly spirit, the word is certainly employed here in an unfavourable sense. It is strengthened by the following term: *condemn,* to condemn pitilessly and without taking into account any reasons for forbearance. *Ἀπολύειν, to absolve,* does not refer, therefore, to the pardon of a personal offence; it is the anxiety of love to find a neighbour innocent rather than guilty, to excuse rather than to condemn. The Lord does not forbid all moral judgments on the conduct of our neighbour; this would contradict many other passages, for example 1 Cor. v. 12: "*Do not ye judge them that are within?*" The true judgment, inspired by love, is implied in ver. 42. What Jesus desires to banish from the society of His disciples is the judging *spirit,* the tendency to place our faculty of moral appreciation at the service of natural malignity, or more simply still: judging for the pleasure of judging. The reward promised: *not to be judged or condemned, to be sent away absolved,* may refer either to this world or the other, to the conduct of men or of God. The latter is the more natural meaning, it enforces itself in the next precept.—It is probably from here that the fifth beatitude in Matthew has been taken: "*Blessed are the merciful; for they shall obtain mercy.*"

With a disposition to absolve those that are accused, is naturally connected that of *giving,* that is to say, of rendering service to all, even to the greatest sinners. This idea is introduced here only as an accessory to the other. There is some feeling in these successive imperatives, and a remarkable affluence of expression in the promise. Some one has said: "Give with a full hand to God, and He will give with a full hand to you." The idea of this boundless liberality of God is forcibly expressed by the accumulation of epithets. The *measure,* to which Jesus alludes, is one for solids (*pressed, shaken together*); the epithet, *running over,* is not at all opposed to this.—The expression, *into your bosom,* refers to the form of the oriental garment, which allows of things being heaped together in the large pocket-shaped fold above the girdle (Ruth iii. 15).—The plur. *δώσουσιν, they will give,* corresponds to the French indef. pron. *on;* it denotes the instruments of divine munificence, whoever they may be (xii. 20, 48).—This precept is found, in very nearly the same terms, in Matt. vii. 1 et seq., immediately following an exhortation to confidence in Providence, and before an invitation to prayer,—in a context, therefore, with which it has no connection. In Luke, on the contrary, all is closely connected.

Vers. 39 and 40. "*And He spake a parable unto them, Can the blind lead the blind? Shall they not both fall into the ditch?* 40. *The disciple is not above his master: but every one that is perfect shall be as his master.*"—Meyer, Bleek, and Holtzmann can see no natural connection between this little parable and the preceding precept. The form, *He said to them also,* seems of itself to indicate an interruption, and to betray the interpolation of a passage foreign to the original context. Is not, however, the figure of a *blind man* leading *another man* (ver. 39) evidently connected with that of the man who, while he has a *beam* in his own eye, wants to take a straw out of his brother's eye (ver. 41)? And who can fail to perceive the connection between the idea contained in this last illustration and the precept which precedes (vers. 37, 38) respecting judgments? A man's presuming to correct his neighbour, without correcting himself,—is not this altogether characteristic of that mania for judging others which Jesus has just forbidden? The whole passage (vers. 37–42) is just, therefore, a piece of consecutive instruction respecting judgments. Jesus continues the contrast between that normal and salutary judgment which He expects from His disciples, in regard to the world, based partly on the love of one's neighbour, and partly on unsparing judgment of oneself, and that injurious judgment which the Pharisees, severe towards others, and altogether infatuated with themselves, were exercising in the midst of Jewish society. The sole result of the ministry of the Pharisees was to fit their disciples for the same perdition as themselves! Jesus prays His disciples not to repeat such achievements in the order of things which He is about to establish. In Matt. xv. 14 and xxiii. 15, 16 we have some precisely similar words addressed to the Pharisees. We are not mistaken, therefore, in our application of this figure.—As to the phrase, *And He saith to them also* (ver. 39), comp. vi. 5. This break in the discourse represents a moment's pause to collect His thoughts. Jesus seeks for an illustration that will impress His hearers with the deplorable consequences of passing judgment on others, when it is done after the fashion of the Pharisees.—*Ὁδηγεῖν, to point out the way,* combines the two notions of correction and instruction. The disciple, in so far as he is a disciple, not being able to excel his master (ver. 40), it follows that the disciple of a Pharisee will not be able at best to do more than equal his master, that is to say, fall into the same ditch with him.—Ver. 40 justifies this idea. Here we see what will happen to the whole people, if they remain under the direction of the Pharisees. The further they advance in the school of such masters, the nearer they will come . . . to perdition. The proverbial saying, ver. 40*a*, is used in Matt. x. 24, 25 and John xv. 20 in this sense: The servants of Jesus must not expect to be *treated better* than their Master. In Luke xxii. 27 and John xiii. 16 it is applied to *the humility* which befits the servant of such a Master. It is obvious that Jesus made various applications of these general maxims.—Whatever, then, modern criticism may think, the context of Luke is unexceptionable. How can Weizsäcker so disregard this connection, as actually to make ver. 39 the commencement of a new part, "the second section of the discourse"! (p. 153).

Vers. 41 and 42. "*And why beholdest thou the mote that is in thy brother's eye, but perceivest not the beam that is in thine own eye? 42. Either how canst thou say to thy brother, Brother, let me pull out the mote that is in thine eye, when thou thyself beholdest not the beam that is in thine own eye? Thou hypocrite, cast out first the beam out of thine own eye, and then shalt thou see clearly to pull out the mote that is in thy brother's eye.*"—In order to be useful in correcting another, a man must begin by correcting himself. Love, when sincere, never acts otherwise. Beyond the limits of this restraint, all judgment is the fruit of presumption and blindness. Such was the judgment of the Pharisees. The *mote*, the bit of straw which has slipped into the eye, represents a defect of secondary importance. A *beam* in the eye is a ludicrous image which ridicule uses to describe a ridiculous proceeding,—a man's assuming, as the Pharisee did, to direct the moral education of his less vicious neighbour, when he was himself saturated with avarice, pride, and other odious vices. Such a man is rightly termed a hypocrite; for if it was hatred of evil that inspired his judgment, would he not begin by showing this feeling in an unsparing judgment of himself? Ordinarily, διαβλέψεις is understood in this sense: Thou wilt be able *to think to, to see to* . . . But can βλέπειν, *to see,* be used in this connection in an abstract sense? The connection between ἔκβαλλε, *take away,* and διαβλέψεις, *thou shalt see,* should suffice to prove the contrary: "Take away the beam which takes away thy sight, and then thou shalt see clearly to . . ." The verb διαβλέπειν, *to see through,* to see distinctly, is only found in this passage, and in its parallel in Matthew, in all the N. T. This has been held to prove that the two evangelists both employed the same Greek document. But characteristic expressions such as these doubtless originated in the first rendering of the oral tradition into the Greek tongue; precepts then took a fixed form, certain features of which were preserved in the preaching, and thence passed into our Syn.

In vers. 43–45, the idea of *teaching,* which is perceptible in ver. 40, takes the place altogether of the idea of *judging,* with which it is closely connected.

Vers. 43–45.[1] "*For a good tree bringeth not forth corrupt fruit; neither doth a corrupt tree bring forth good fruit.* 44. *For every tree is known by his own fruit: for of thorns men do not gather figs, nor of a bramble-bush gather they grapes.*"—In order that our words may have a good influence on our neighbour, we must be good ourselves. In this passage, therefore, the fruits of the tree are neither the moral conduct of the individual who teaches, nor his doctrines. They are the results of his labour in others. In vain will a proud man preach humility, or a selfish man charity; the injurious influence of example will paralyze the efforts of their words. The *corrupt tree* (σαρπόν) is a tree infected with canker, whose juices are incapable of producing palatable fruit.—The connection be-

[1] Ver. 43. ℵ. B. L. Z. and several Mnn. add παλιν after ουδε.—Ver. 45. ℵ. B omit αυτου after καρδιας.—ℵ. B. D. L. omit ανθρωπος after πονηρος.—ℵ. B. D L. Z. omit the words θησαυρου της καρδιας αυτου.

tween vers. 43 and 44*a* is this: "*This principle is so true*, that every one, without hesitation, infers the nature of a tree from its fruits."—In Palestine there are often seen, behind hedges of thorns and brambles, fig-trees completely garlanded with the climbing tendrils of *vine branches*.[1]—Ver. 45 gives expression to the general principle on which the whole of the preceding rests. A man's word is the most direct communication of his being. If a man desires to reform others by his word, he must reform himself; then his word will change the world. Jesus Himself succeeded in depositing a germ of goodness in the world by His word alone, because He was a perfectly good man. It is for His disciples to continue His work by this method, which is the antipodes of that of the Pharisees.—An analogous passage is found in Matthew, at the end of the Sermon on the Mount (vii. 15–20). There Jesus is exhorting His hearers to beware of false prophets, who betray their real character by their evil fruits. These false prophets may indeed be, in this precept, as in that of Luke, the Pharisees (comp. our ver. 26). But their *fruits* are certainly, in Matthew, their moral conduct, their pride, avarice, and hypocrisy, and not, as in Luke, the effects produced by their ministry. On the other hand, we find a passage in Matthew (xii. 33–35) still more like ours. As it belongs to a warning against blaspheming the Holy Ghost, the *fruits* of the tree are evidently, as in Luke, the words themselves, in so far as they are good or bad in their nature and in their effect on those who receive them. From this, is it not evident that this passage is the true parallel to ours, and that the passage which Matthew has introduced into the Sermon on the Mount is an importation, occasioned probably by the employment of the same image (that of the trees and their fruits) in both?—Thus Jesus has risen by degrees from the conditions of the Christian life (the beatitudes) to the life itself; first of all to its principle, then to its action on the world. He has made His renewed disciples instruments for the renewal of humanity. It now only remains for Him to bring this inaugural discourse to a close.

Third part of the discourse: vers. 46–49. *The Sanction.*—

[1] Konrad Furrer, *die Bedeutung der biblischen Geographie für die bibl. Exegese*, p. 34.

Here we have the conclusion, and, so to speak, the peroration of the discourse. The Lord enjoins His disciples, for the sake of their own welfare, to put in practice the new principle of conduct which He has just laid down.

Ver. 46. "*And why call ye me Lord, Lord, and do not the things which I say.*"—This saying proves that Jesus was already recognised as Lord by a large part of this multitude, but that even then He would have been glad to find in many of those who saluted Him by this title a more scrupulous fidelity to the law of charity. This warning is connected, doubtless, with the preceding context, by this idea: "Do not be guilty, in the dispensation now commencing, of the same hypocrisy as the scribes and Pharisees have been guilty of in that which is coming to an end; they render homage to Jehovah, and, at the same time, perpetually transgress His law. Do not deal with my word in this way." The same idea is found in Matthew, at the corresponding place in the Sermon on the Mount (vii. 21 et seq.), but under that abstract and sententious form already observed in the Beatitudes: "*Not every one that saith unto me:* Lord, Lord," etc. In this passage in Matthew, Jesus expressly claims to be the Messiah and Supreme Judge. The same idea is expressed in the *Lord, Lord,* of Luke.

Vers. 47–49.[1] "*Whosoever cometh to me, and heareth my sayings, and doeth them, I will show you to whom he is like:* 48. *He is like a man which built an house, and digged deep, and laid the foundation on a rock: and when the flood arose, the stream beat vehemently upon that house, and could not shake it; for it was founded upon a rock.* 49. *But he that heareth, and doeth not, is like a man that, without a foundation, built a house upon the earth; against which the stream did beat vehemently, and immediately it fell; and the ruin of that house was great.*"—The two evangelists coincide in this closing illustration. On the shelving lands which surround the Lake of Genesareth, there are some hills on which the rock is covered with only a thin layer of earth (γῇ, Luke) or sand (ἄμμος, Matthew). A prudent man digs through this moveable soil,

[1] Ver. 48. א. B. L. Z., *δια το καλως οικοδομησθαι αυτην* instead of *τεθεμελιωτο γαρ επι την πετραν*, which is the reading of T. R. with all the other authorities.—Ver. 49. C. and some Mnn., *οικοδομουντι* instead of *οικοδομησαντι*.

digs deep down (ἔσκαψε καὶ ἐβάθυνε), even into the rock, upon and in which (ἐπί with the accusative) he lays the foundation.—Luke only mentions one cause of destruction, the waterspout (πλήμμυρα), that breaks on the summit of the mountain and creates the torrents which carry away the layer of earth and sand, and with it the building that is not founded on the rock. Matthew adds the hurricane (ἄνεμοι) that ordinarily accompanies these great atmospheric disturbances, and overthrows the building which the torrent undermines. Though the differences between these two descriptions in Matthew and Luke are for the most part insignificant, they are too numerous to suppose that both could have been taken from the same document.—To build on the earth, is to admit the Lord's will merely into the understanding, that most superficial and impersonal part of a man's self, while closing the conscience against Him, and withholding the acquiescence of the will, which is the really personal element within us. The trial of our spiritual building is brought about by temptation, persecution, and, last of all, by judgment. Its overthrow is accomplished by unbelief here below, and by condemnation from above.—The Alex. reading, *because it had been well built* (ver. 48), is to be preferred to that of the T. R., *for it was founded on a rock*, which is taken from Matthew.—A single lost soul is *a great ruin* in the eyes of God. Jesus, in closing His discourse, leaves His hearers under the impression of this solemn thought. Each of them, while listening to this last word, might think that he heard the crash of the falling edifice, and say within himself: This disaster will be mine if I prove hypocritical or inconsistent.

The Sermon on the Mount, therefore, as Weizsäcker has clearly seen, is: *the inauguration of the new law.* The order of the discourse, according to the two documents, is this: Jesus addresses His hearers as belonging to a class of people who, even according to the Old Testament, have the greatest need of heavenly compensations. Treating them as disciples, either because they were already attached to Him as such, or in their character as voluntary hearers, He regards this audience, brought together without previous preparation, as representing the new order of things, and promulgates before this new Israel the principle of the perfect law. Then, substituting His disciples for the doctors of the ancient economy, He points out to them the sole condition on which they will be able to accomplish in the world the glorious work which He confides to them. Lastly, He urges them, in the name of all they hold most precious, to fulfil this condition by making their life agree with their profession, in order that, when tested by the judgment, they may not come to ruin. In what respect does this discourse lack unity and regular progression? How can Weizsäcker say that these precepts, in Luke, are for the most part thrown together, without connection, and detached from their natural context? It is in Matthew rather, as Weizsäcker, among others, acknowledges, that we find foreign elements interwoven with the tissue of the discourse; they are easily perceived, for they break the connection, and the association of ideas which has occasioned the interpolation is obvious. Thus: vers. 23–26, reconciliation (*apropos* of hatred and murder); vers. 29, 30, a precept, which is found elsewhere in Matthew itself (xviii. 8, 9); vers. 31 and 32 (a passage which is found xix. 3–9); vi. 7–15, the Lord's Prayer, an evident interruption in His treatment of the three principal Pharisaic virtues (alms, vers. 2–4; prayer, vers. 5, 6; fasting, vers. 16–18); vi. 24 (if not even 19) –34, a passage on providence (in connection with the avarice of the Pharisees); vii. 6–11, and 13, 14, precepts, simply juxtaposited; vii. 15–20, a passage for which xii. 33–35 should be substituted; lastly, vii. 22, 23, where allusion is made to facts which lie out of the horizon of that early period. It is remarkable that these passages, whose foreign character is proved by the context of Matthew, are the very passages that are found dispersed over different places in the Gospel of Luke, where their appropriateness is easily verified. The author of the first Gospel could not be blamed for this combination of heterogeneous elements within one and the same outline, unless his compilation of the discourse had been made from the first with an historical aim. But if we admit, as we are authorized by the testimony of Papias to admit, that this discourse belonged originally to a collection of discourses compiled with a didactic or liturgical aim, and that the author wanted to give a somewhat complete exposition of the new moral law proclaimed by Jesus, there is nothing more natural than this agglomerating process. It is evident that the author found, in this way, a means of producing in his readers, just as any other evangelist, the thrilling impression which the word of Jesus had made on the hearts of His hearers (Matt. vii. 28, 29).—The way in which these two versions stand related to each other, will not allow of their being deduced from a proto-Mark as a common source, according to Holtzmann and Weizsäcker. And besides, how, in this case, did it happen that this discourse was omitted in our canonical Mark? The species of *logophobia* which they attribute to him, in order to explain this fact, is incompatible with Mark ix. 39–51, and xiii.

A religious party has made a party-banner of this discourse. According to them, this discourse is a summary of the teaching of Jesus, who merely spiritualized the Mosaic law. But how are we to harmonize with this view the passages in which Jesus makes

[1] *Untersuchungen*, p. 154.

attachment to His person the very centre of the new righteousness (*for my sake*, Matt. v. 11; *for the sake of the Son of man*, Luke vi. 22), and those in which He announces Himself as the Final and Supreme Judge (Matt. vii. 21–23, comp. with Luke vi. 46: Lord, Lord!)? The true view of the religious import of this discourse, is that which Gess has expressed in these well-weighed words: "The Sermon on the Mount describes that earnest piety which no one can cultivate without an increasing feeling of the need of *redemption*, by means of which the righteousness required by such piety may at last be realized" (p. 6).

2. *The Centurion's Servant:* **vii. 1–10.**—This was the most striking instance of faith that Jesus had met with up to this time; and what was more astonishing, He was indebted for this surprise to a Gentile. Jesus instantly perceives the deep significance of this unexpected incident, and cautiously indicates it in ver. 9, while in Matt. viii. 11, 12 it is expressed with less reserve. We should have expected the reverse, according to the dogmatic prepossessions which criticism imputes to our evangelists. It is obliged, therefore, to have recourse to the hypothesis of subsequent interpolations.

This cure is connected, in Matthew as well as in Luke, with the Sermon on the Mount. This resemblance in no way proves, as some think, a common written source. For, 1. The two passages are separated in Matthew by the healing of the leper, which Luke assigns to another time; 2. The narratives of the two evangelists present very considerable differences of detail; lastly, 3. There was nothing to prevent certain groups of narrative, more or less fixed, being formed in the oral teaching of the gospel, which passed in this way into our written narratives. As to Mark, he omits this miracle, an omission difficult to account for, if he copied Matthew and Luke (Bleek), and equally difficult if, with them, he derived his narrative from an original Mark (Ewald and Holtzmann). Holtzmann (p. 78), with Ewald, thinks that "if he cut out the Sermon on the Mount, he might easily omit also the passage which follows, and which opens a new section." But on other occasions it is asserted that Mark purposely omits the discourses, to make room for facts. Now, are we not here concerned with a fact? Bleek does not even attempt to explain this omission.

Vers. 1–6*a*.[1] *The First Deputation.*—The Alex. reading ἐπειδή,

[1] **Ver. 1. A. B. C. X. Π.,** ἐπειδὴ instead of ἐπεὶ δέ.

since assuredly, has no meaning.—There is something solemn in these expressions : ἐπλήσωσε, *had fulfilled*, and εἰς τὰς ἀκοάς, *in the ears of the people.* The proclamation which had just taken place is given as something complete. The circumstance that this miracle took place just when Jesus returned to Capernaum, after this discourse, was remembered in the traditional account, and has been faithfully preserved in our two evangelical narratives.—The centurion (ver. 2) was probably a Roman soldier in the service of Herod ; he was a proselyte, and had even manifested special zeal on behalf of his new faith (ver. 5).—Instead of δοῦλος, *a slave*, Matthew says παῖς, a word which may signify either a *son* or a *servant*, and which Luke employs in the latter sense at ver. 7. Bleek and Holtzmann prefer the meaning *son* in Matthew, "because otherwise it would be necessary to admit that the centurion had only one slave." As if a man could not say : "My servant is sick," though he had several servants ! The meaning *servant* is more probable in Matthew, because it better explains the reluctance which the centurion feels to trouble the Lord. If it had been his son, he would doubtless have been bolder. —The malady must have been, according to Matthew's description, ver. 6, acute rheumatism. And whatever criticism may say, this malady, when it affects certain organs, the heart for instance, may become mortal.—The words : *who was very dear to him*, serve to explain why a step so important as a deputation of the elders should have been taken.—The latter are doubtless the rulers of the synagogue, whose duty it was to maintain order in the congregation. They could more easily explain to Jesus the honourable facts which made in favour of the centurion, than he could himself.

Vers. 6*b*–8.[1] *The Second Deputation.*—The centurion, from his house, sees Jesus approaching with His retinue of disciples. The veneration with which this mysterious person inspires him makes him afraid even to receive Him under his roof ; he sends, therefore, a second deputation. Strauss sees in this a contradiction of his former proceeding. But it was simply a deeper humility and stronger faith that had dictated this course. Ἱκανός here denotes *moral worth*, as in iii. 16 and

[1] Ver. 6. B. L., εκατονταρχης instead of εκατονταρχος.—ℵ* B. omit προς αυτον. —Ver. 7. B. L., ιαθητω instead of ιαθησεται

elsewhere.—Faith vies with humility in this man. The expression εἰπὲ λόγῳ, *say in a word,* suggests this means in preference to His coming in person.—In Matthew's narrative all these proceedings are united in a single act; the centurion comes himself to tell Jesus of the sickness, and to the offer of Jesus to visit his house, returns the answer which we find in Luke v. 8. Bleek regards the details in Luke as an amplification of the original narrative; others consider Matthew's account an abridgment of Luke's. But how could Luke exaggerate in this way the plain statement of Matthew, or Matthew mangle the description of Luke? Our evangelists were earnest believers. All that tradition had literally preserved was the characteristic reply of the centurion (ver. 8), and our Lord's expression of admiration (ver. 9). The historical outline had been created with greater freedom in the oral narration. This explains in a very natural manner the difference between our two narratives.—Although he was only an ordinary man (ἄνθρωπος), and a man in a dependent position, the centurion had some subordinates through whom he could act without always going himself to the place. Could not Jesus, who stood far above him in the hierarchy of being, having the powers of the invisible world at His disposal, make use, if He pleased, of a similar power? We may compare here Jesus' own words respecting the angels which ascend and descend (John i. 52).—How are we to explain the existence of such faith in this man? We must bear in mind the words of ver. 3: *having heard of Jesus.* The fame of the miracles of Jesus had reached even him. There was one cure especially, which Jesus had wrought at Capernaum itself, and since Cana, which presented a remarkable similarity to that which the centurion besought—the cure of the nobleman's son (John iv.). Perhaps his knowledge of this miracle is the most natural mode of explaining the faith implied in the message which he addresses to Jesus by the mouth of his friends.—The expression, *such faith,* refers not to the request for a cure, but for a cure without the aid of His bodily presence. It was, as it were, a paroxysm of faith!

Vers. 9 and 10.[1] *The Cure.*—The severe words respecting the Jews, which in Matthew Jesus adds to the praise be-

[1] Ver. 10. ℵ. B. L. It^plerique. omit ασθενουντα before δουλον.

stowed on the centurion's faith, seem to prove that Matthew makes use of a different source of information from Luke's. These words are found, in fact, in Luke in a totally different connection (xiii. 28), at a more advanced period, when they are certainly more appropriate.

Several ancient and modern critics identify this cure with that of the nobleman's son (John iv.). The differences, however, are considerable: here we have a soldier of Gentile origin, there a courtier of Jewish origin; here the place is Capernaum, there Cana; here we have a man who in his humility is reluctant that Jesus should enter his house, there a man who comes a long way seeking Jesus that he may induce Him to go with him to his home; lastly, and in our view this difference is most decisive, here we have a Gentile given as an example to all Israel, there a Jew, whose conduct furnishes occasion for Jesus to throw a certain amount of blame on all his Galilean fellow-countrymen. In truth, if these two narratives referred to the same fact, the details of the Gospel narratives would no longer deserve the least credence.—According to Keim, the miracle is to be explained, on the one hand, by the faith of the centurion and the sick man, which already contained certain healing virtues, and on the other, by the moral power of the word of Jesus, which word was something between a *wish* and a *command*, and completed the restoration. But does not this ethico-psychical mode of action require the *presence* of him who effects a cure in this way? Now this presence is unmistakeably excluded here in both narratives by the prayer of the centurion, and by this word of Jesus: *so great faith!* And what is this something between a wish and a command?

3. *The Son of the Widow of Nain:* vii. 11-17.—The following narrative is one of those which clearly reveal our Lord's tenderness of heart, and the power which human grief exerted over Him. The historical reality of this fact has been objected to on the ground that it is only related by Luke. Criticism always reasons as if the evangelists were swayed by the same historical prepossessions as itself. The life of Jesus presented such a rich store of miraculous incidents, that no one ever dreamed of giving a complete record of them. Jesus alludes to miracles performed at Chorazin, none of which are related in our Gospels. With a single exception, we are equally ignorant of all that were wrought at Bethsaida. It is very remarkable that, amongst all the miracles which are indicated summarily in our Gospels (iv. 23, 40, 41, vi. 18, 19 and parall., vii. 21, etc.; John ii. 23,

iv. 45, vi. 1, xx. 30, xxi. 25), one or two only *of each class* are related in detail. It appears that the most striking example of each class was chosen, and that from the first no attempt was made to preserve any detailed account of the others. For edification, which was the sole aim of the popular preaching, this was sufficient. Ten cures of lepers would say no more to faith than one. But it might happen that some of the numerous miracles passed over by the tradition, came, through private sources of information, to the knowledge of one of our evangelists, and that he inserted them in his work. Thus, under the category of resurrections, the raising of Jairus' daughter had taken the foremost place in the tradition,—it is found in the three Syn.,—whilst other facts of the kind, such as that before us, had been left in the background, without, however, being on that account denied.

Vers. 11 and 12.[1] *The Meeting.*—The reading ἐν τῷ ἑξῆς (χρόνῳ), *in the following time*, does not connect this narrative so closely with the preceding as the reading ἐν τῇ ἑξῆς (ἡμέρᾳ), *the following day.* This is a reason for preferring the former; it is only natural that the more precise should be substituted for the less definite connection. Robinson found a hamlet named *Neïn* to the south-west of Capernaum, at the northern foot of the little Hermon. It is in this locality, moreover, that Eusebius and Jerome place the city of Nain. Jesus would only have to make a day's journey to reach it from Capernaum. Josephus (*Bell. Jud.* iv. 9. 4) mentions a city of Nain, situated on the other side of Jordan, in the south part of the Peræa; and Köstlin, relying on the expressions in ver. 17, applied this name to this town in the immediate neighbourhood of Judæa, and thought that Luke's narrative must have come from a *Judæan source.* But we shall see that ver. 17 may be explained without having recourse to this supposition, which is not very natural.—The καὶ ἰδού, *and behold*, expresses something striking in the unexpected meeting of the two processions,—the train which accompanied the Prince of Life, and that which followed the victim of death. This seems to be ex-

[1] Vers. 11–14. Mjj. 70 Mnn. Italiq. read, *εν τω εξης* instead of *εν τη εξης*, which is the reading of T. R. with א. C. D. K. M. S. Π. many Mnn. Syr. Italiq.—א. B. D. F. L. Z. Syrsch. Itplerique, omit *ικανει*.—Ver. 12. 7 Mjj. add *ην* after *αυτη*—א. B. L. Z. add *ην* before *συν αυτη*.

pressed also by the relation of ἱκανοί in ver. 11 to ἱκανός in ver. 12. The first of these words has been omitted by many MSS., because the expression: *his disciples,* appeared to refer to the apostles alone.—At ver. 12 the construction is Aramæan. The dative τῇ μητρί expresses all the tenderness of the relationship which had just been severed.

Vers. 13–15.[1] *The Miracle.*—The expression: *the Lord,* is seldom met with in our Gospels except in Luke, and principally in the passages which are peculiar to him: x. 1, xi. 39, xii. 42, xiii. 15, xvii. 5, 6, xviii. 6, xxii. 31, 61 (Bleek).—The whole circumstances enumerated ver. 12: an only son, a widowed mother, and the public sympathy, enable us to understand what it was that acted with such power upon the heart of Jesus. It seems that He could not resist the silent appeal presented by this combination of circumstances. His heart is completely subdued by the sobs of the mother. Hence the word, at once tender and authoritative: *Weep not.* Prudence perhaps would have dictated that He should not work such a striking miracle at this time. But when pity speaks so loud (ἐσπλαγχνίσθη), there is no longer any room for prudence Besides, He feels Himself authorized to comfort. For in this very meeting He recognises the will of His Father.—Among the Jews the bier was not covered; it was a simple plank, with a somewhat raised edge. The body, wrapped in its shroud, was therefore visible to all. Jesus lays His hand on the bier, as if to arrest this fugitive from life. The bearers, struck by the majesty of this gesture, which was at once natural and symbolical, stopped. There is a matchless grandeur in this σοὶ λέγω: "*I say to thee,* . . . to thee who seemest no longer able to hear the voice of the living . . ." There is absolutely nothing in the text to justify the sarcasm of Keim: "Faith in a force which penetrates to the dead, even *through the wood of the bier,* evidently belongs to the evangelist, but it is not ours." The resurrection is in no way attributed to the touching of the bier, but to the command of Jesus.—The interruption of the connection between the soul and the body in death, as in sleep, is only relative; and as man's voice suffices to re-establish this connection in any one who is wrapt in slumber, so the word of *the Lord* has power to restore this

[1] Ver. 13. The Mss. vary between ἐπ' αὐτῇ and ἐπ' αὐτήν.

interrupted connection even in the dead. The advocates of the natural interpretation have maintained that the young man was only in a lethargic sleep. But if this were so, the miracle of power would only disappear to be replaced by a miracle of knowledge quite as incomprehensible. How could Jesus know that this apparently dead man was still living, and that the moment of his awaking was imminent?[1]—As soon as the soul returned to animate the body, motion and speech indicated its presence. Jesus certainly has acquired a right over the resuscitated man; He asserts this right, but simply to enjoy the happiness of restoring to the afflicted mother the treasure which He has rescued from death. The expression: *He gave him to his mother*, corresponds to this: *He was moved with compassion*, ver. 13.

Vers. 16, 17.[2] *The Effect produced.*—On the feeling of fear, see chap. v. 8.—*A great prophet:* a greater than John the Baptist himself, a prophet of the first rank, such as Elijah or Moses. The second expression: *God hath visited* . . ., is more forcible still; it suggests more than it expresses. The expression: *this saying* [*this rumour*, A. V.], might be referred to the fame of the miracle which was immediately spread abroad. But the words περὶ αὐτοῦ, *concerning Him*, which depend, as in ver. 15, on λόγος οὗτος, rather incline us to refer this expression to the two preceding exclamations (ver. 16): "This manner of thinking and speaking about Jesus spread abroad." It is an indication of progress in the development of the work of Jesus. In order to explain *into Judæa*, Keim (i. p. 72) unceremoniously says: Luke just makes Nain a city of Judæa. But the term ἐξῆλθεν, literally: *went out*, signifies the very contrary; it intimates that these sayings, *after having filled Galilee* (their first sphere, understood without express mention), this time passed beyond this natural limit, and resounded as far as the country of Judæa, where they filled every mouth.

[1] Zeller (*Apostelgesch.* p. 177) replies with some smartness to this ancient rationalistic explanation. "In order to admit it," he says, "it must be thought credible that, within the short period embraced by the evangelical and apostolic history, there took place five times over, thrice in the Gospels and twice in the Acts, this same circumstance, this same remarkable chance of a lethargy, which, though unperceived by those who were engaged about the dead, yields to the first word of the divine messenger, and gives rise to a belief in a real resurrection."

[2] Ver. 16. A. B. C. L. Z., ηγερθη for εγηγερται.

There is no necessity, therefore, to give the word *Judæa* here the unusual meaning of the entire Holy Land, as Meyer and Bleek do. The reason why this detail is added, is not in any way what Köstlin's acute discernment surmised in order to build upon it the critical hypothesis that the narrative is of Judæan origin. These words are intended to form the transition to the following passage. John was in prison in the south of the Holy Land, in the neighbourhood of Judæa (in Peræa, in the castle of Machærus, according to Josephus). The fame of the works of Jesus, therefore, only reached him in his prison by passing through Judæa. The words: *and throughout all the region round about,* which refer especially to the Peræa, leave no doubt as to the intention of this remark of Luke. It forms the introduction to the following narrative.

There is a difficulty peculiar to this miracle, owing to the absence of all moral receptivity in the subject of it. Lazarus was a believer; in the case of the daughter of Jairus, the faith of the parents to a certain extent supplied the place of her personal faith. But here there is nothing of the kind. The only receptive element that can be imagined is the ardent desire of life with which this young man, the only son of a widowed mother, had doubtless yielded his last breath. And this, indeed, is sufficient. For it follows from this, that Jesus did not dispose of him arbitrarily. And as to faith, many facts prove that not in any miracle is it to be regarded as a dynamical factor, but only as a simple *moral* condition related to the spiritual aim which Jesus sets before Himself in performing the wonderful work.

Keim, fully sensible of the incompetency of any psychological explanation to account for such a miracle, has recourse to the mythical interpretation of Strauss in his first *Life of Jesus.* We are supposed to have here an imitation of the resurrection of dead persons in the Old Testament, particularly of that wrought by Elisha at Shunem, which is only a short league from Nain. These continual changes of expedients, with a view to get rid of the miracles, are not calculated to recommend rationalistic criticism. And we cannot forbear reminding ourselves here of what Baur urged with so much force against Strauss on the subject of the resurrection of Lazarus: that a myth that was a creation of the Christian consciousness must have been generally diffused, and not have been found in only one of our Gospels. Invention by *the author* (and consequently imposture) or history, is the only alternative.

From the omission of this miracle in Matthew and Mark, the advocates of the opinion that a proto-Mark was the common source of the Syn., conclude that this narrative was wanting in the primitive document, and that Luke added it from special sources. But if this were only a simple *intercalation* of Luke's, his narrative would coincide immediately afterwards with those of Mark and Matthew. Unfortunately there is no such coincidence. Matthew, after the cure of the centurion's servant, relates the cure of Peter's mother-in-law, and a number of incidents which have nothing in common with those which follow in Luke. And Mark, who has already omitted the preceding fact, although it should have been found, according to this hypothesis, in the proto-Mark,—for that is where Matthew must have taken it from,—does not fall, after this omission, into the series of facts related by Luke. After the day of the Sermon on the Mount, he places a series of incidents which have no connection with those that follow in Luke. And yet the boast is made, that the dependence of the three Syn. on a primitive Mark has been *shown to demonstration!* As to Bleek, who makes Mark depend on the other two, he does not even attempt to explain how Mark, having Luke before his eyes, omitted incidents of such importance.

4. *The Deputation from John the Baptist:* vii. 18–35.—This incident, related only by Matthew (chap. xi.) and Luke, and by them differently placed, is in both accounted for in the same manner. The fame of the works of Jesus reached even John. If Luke does not expressly say, as Matthew does, that the forerunner was in prison, it is because, whatever Bleek may say, this position of affairs was sufficiently known from the remark, iii. 19, 20.—But how should the fame of the miracles of Jesus, of *the works of the Christ* (Matthew), awaken in his mind the doubt which his question appears to imply? Strauss has maliciously expressed his surprise that no manufacturer of conjectures has as yet proposed to substitute in Matthew: *οὐκ ἀκούσας, not having heard,* for *ἀκούσας, having heard.* But this apparent contradiction is the very key to the whole incident. Most assuredly John

does not doubt whether Jesus is a divine messenger, for he interrogates Him. He does not appear even to deny Him all participation in the Messianic work: "*John having heard in his prison of the works of the Christ*" (Matthew). What he cannot understand is just this, that these *works of the Christ* are not accompanied by the realization of all the rest of the Messianic programme which he had formerly proclaimed himself, and especially by the theocratic judgment. "His fan is in His hand . . .; the axe is already laid at the root of the trees." Jesus in no way recognised it as His duty to become the Messiah-*judge* whom John had announced in such solemn terms, and whose expected coming had so unsettled the people. On the contrary, He said: "I am come *not to judge*, but to save" (John iii. 17). This contrast between the form of the Messianic work as it was being accomplished by Jesus, and the picture which John had drawn of it himself, leads him to inquire whether the Messianic work was to be divided between two different persons,—the one, Jesus, founding the kingdom of God in the heart by His word and by miracles of benevolence; the other commissioned to execute the theocratic judgment, and by acts of power to build up on the earth the national and social edifice of the kingdom of God. This is the real meaning of John's question: "Should we look for [not properly *another*, but] a different one (ἕτερον in Matthew, and perhaps in Luke also)?" We know in fact that several divine messengers were expected. Might not Jesus be *that prophet* whom some distinguished from the Christ (ix. 19; John i. 20, 21, 25), but whom others identified with Him (John vi. 14, 15)? Doubtless, if this was the thought of the forerunner, it indicated weakness of faith, and Jesus characterizes it as such (*is offended in Him*, ver. 23). But there is nothing improbable in it. Not without reason had John said concerning himself: "He that is of the earth speaketh as being of the earth" (John iii. 31); and Jesus, that he was less than the least of believers. Such alternations between wonderful exaltation and deep and sudden depression are characteristic of all the men of the old covenant; lifted for a moment above themselves, but not as yet inwardly renewed, they soon sank back to their natural level. There is no need, therefore, to have recourse to the hypothesis of Chrysostom, accepted by

Calvin, Grotius, etc., that John desired to give *his disciples* an opportunity to convince themselves of the dignity of Jesus, or to suppose, with Hase, that John's design was to stimulate Jesus, and accelerate the progress of His work. These explanations do not correspond with either the letter or the spirit of the text.

This portion comprises: 1*st*, the question of John, and the reply of Jesus, vers. 18-23; 2*d*, the discourse of Jesus upon the person and ministry of John, vers. 24–35.

1*st*. Vers. 18–23: *The Question and the Reply.*

Vers. 18 and 19.[1] *The Question.*—Thus far, according to Holtzmann (pp. 135, 143), Luke had followed the first of his sources, the proto-Mark (*A.*); now he leaves it to make use of the second (of which the author of our Matthew has also availed himself), the Logia or *discourses* of Matthew (*Λ.*).—The expression: ὁ ἐρχόμενος, *He who cometh*, is taken from Malachi (iii. 1): "Behold, He cometh, saith the Lord." The reading **ἕτερον**, which is certain in Matthew, is probable in Luke. This pronoun, taken in its strict meaning: *a second*, attributes to Jesus in any case the office of the Christ.

Vers. 20–23.[2] *The Reply.*—As Matthew does not mention the miracles which were wrought, according to Luke, in the presence of John's messengers, criticism has suspected the latter of having invented this scene himself. This conclusion is logical if it be admitted that he makes use of Matthew, or of the same document as Matthew. But by what right are such charges preferred against a historian whose narrative indicates at every step the excellence of his own information, or of the sources upon which he drew? Do we not see Matthew continually abridging his historical outline, in order to give the fullest possible report of the words of Jesus? In the present case, do not the words: "Go, tell John *what ye do see and hear*," imply the historical fact which Matthew omits? It is precisely because the word implied the fact, that this evangelist thought he might content himself with the former. The

[1] Ver. 19. B. L. R. Z. some Mnn. It^{aliq}., κυριον instead of Ιησουν.—ℵ. B. L. R. X. Z. 16 Mnn., ετερον instead of αλλον.

[2] Ver. 20. ℵ. B., απεστειλεν instead of απεσταλκεν.—ℵ. D. L. X. Z. 12 Mnn., ετερον instead of αλλον.—Ver. 21. ℵ. B. L. some Mnn., εκεινη instead of αυτη.—ℵ. L., ημερα instead of ωρα.—Ver. 22. ℵ. B. D. Z. omit ο Ιησους.

demonstrative force of Jesus' reply appears not only from the miracles, but still more from the connection between these facts and the signs of the Messiah, as foretold in the Old Testament (Isa. xxxv. 4, 5, lxi. 1 et seq.). Jesus does not mention the cure of demoniacs, because, perhaps, no mention is made of them in the O. T. Neander and Schweitzer take the words: *the dead are raised up,* in a figurative sense. Keim thinks that the evangelists have taken all these miracles in the literal sense, but that Jesus understood them in the spiritual sense: the people, blinded by the Pharisees, gain knowledge; the publicans (the lepers) are cleansed from their defilement, etc. The *works of the Christ* should be understood in the same spiritual sense (his instructions and missionary efforts). But the spiritual fruits of the ministry of Jesus are not facts which fall under the cognizance of the senses. "What ye do *see* and *hear*" can only denote bodily cures and resurrections, which they either witness or have related.—The preaching of the gospel is intentionally placed at the end; it is the characteristic feature of the Messianic work, as it was being accomplished by Jesus, in opposition to the idea which John had formed of it. Jesus, at the same time, thereby reminds His forerunnner of Isa. lxi. 1. These words form the transition to the warning of the 23d verse: "*Blessed is he who shall not be offended in me,*" who shall not ask for any other proof than those of my Messianic dignity; who shall not, in the humble, gentle, and merciful progress of my work, despise the true characteristics of the promised Christ! Isaiah had said of the Messiah (viii. 14, 15): "*He shall be for a stone of stumbling; and many among them shall stumble and fall.*" It is this solemn warning of which Jesus reminds both John and his disciples, as well as the people who witnessed the scene; σκανδαλίζεσθαι: *to hurt oneself by stumbling.*—To what a height Jesus here soars above the greatest representative of the past! But, at the same time, what sincerity is manifested by the sacred authors, who do not fear to exhibit in the clearest light the infirmities of their most illustrious heroes!

2*d.* Vers. 24–35. *The Discourse of Jesus.*—Jesus had a debt to discharge. John had borne striking testimony to Him; He avails Himself of this occasion to pay public homage in His turn to His forerunner. He would not allow this opportunity to pass without doing it, because there was a strict solidarity between John's mission and His own. This discourse of Jesus concerning John is, as it were, the funeral oration of the latter; for he was put to death soon after. Jesus begins by declaring the *importance* of John's appearing (vers. 24–28); he next speaks of the *influence* exerted by his ministry (vers. 29, 30); lastly, He describes *the conduct of the people* under these two great divine calls—John's ministry and His own (vers. 31–35). The same general order is found in Matt. xi.: 1*st*, vers. 7–11; 2*d*, vers. 12–15; 3*d*, vers. 16–20.

Vers. 24–28.[1] *The Importance of John's Appearing.*—"*And when the messengers of John were departed, He began to speak unto the people concerning John: What went ye out into the wilderness to see? A reed shaken with the wind?* 25. *But what went ye out for to see? A man clothed in soft raiment? Behold, they which are gorgeously apparelled, and live delicately, are in kings' courts.* 26. *But what went ye out for to see? A prophet? Yea, I say unto you, and much more than a prophet.* 27. *This is he of whom it is written, Behold, I send my messenger before Thy face, which shall prepare Thy way before Thee.* 28. *For I say unto you, Among those that are born of women, there is not a greater [prophet] than John the Baptist: but he that is least in the kingdom of God is greater than he.*"—Ἤρξατο, *He began to*, as iv. 21; this term intimates the solemnity of the discourse which it introduces. The people themselves, by crowding to the baptism of John, showed that they recognised him as an extraordinary person; and they were right. Is the reed shaken by the wind an emblem here of moral instability? The meaning in this case would be: "Yes, John is really as vacillating as a reed" (Ewald); or else: "No, you must not draw this conclusion from what has just taken place" (Meyer, Neander, Bleek). But this reed shaken by the wind

[1] Ver. 24. The Mss. are divided between προς τους οχλους and τους οχλους.—Vers. 24 and 25. Instead of εξεληλυθατε, which is the reading of T. R. with 12 Mjj. and the greater part of the Mnn., ℵ. A. B. D. L. X. and some Mnn. read εξηλθατε; K. Π. 30 Mnn., εξηλθετε.—Ver. 26. Just as vers. 24 and 25, except with A. K. Π., which here read εξεληλυθατε with T. R.—Ver. 27. ℵ. B. D. L. X. some Mnn. It. omit εγω after ιδου.—Ver. 28. B. Z., λεγω; ℵ. L. X., αμην λεγω instead of λεγω γαρ, which is the reading of T. R. with 13 Mjj. and the Mnn. —ℵ. B. K. L. M. X. Z. Π. 25 Mnn. It^plerique, omit προφητης, which is the reading of T. R. with 10 Mjj. It^aliq. Syr^sch.—ℵ. B. L. X. omit του Βαπτιστου.

may be regarded simply as the emblem of something of ordinary, every-day occurrence. "It was not certainly to behold something which may be seen every day that you flocked to the desert." The verb ἐξελθεῖν, *to go out*, expresses the great commotion caused by such a pilrimage. The perf. ἐξεληλύθατε signifies: "What impression have you retained from what you went to see?" whilst the aor. (Alex.) would signify: "What motive induced you to go . . . ?" Tischendorf acknowledges that the perf. is the true reading. The aor. is taken from Matthew. — The verb θεάσασθαι depends on ἐξεληλύθατε, and must not be joined to the following proposition: they went out in search of a spectacle. This expression reminds us of the saying of Jesus (John v. 35): "*John was a burning and a shining light: and ye were willing for a season to rejoice in his light.*"—In any case, therefore, John is something great—the popular opinion is not deceived here. But there are two kinds of greatness—earthly greatness, and heavenly. Of which is John's? If it had been, Jesus continues, of an earthly nature, John would not have dwelt in a wilderness, but in a palace. His greatness, therefore, was of a divine order. But, according to Jewish opinion, all greatness of this kind consists in a prophetic mission. Hence the conclusion at which the people arrived respecting John, which Jesus begins by confirming, "*Yea, I say unto you;*" and then going beyond this, *and more than a prophet.* Is it not greater, indeed, to be the subject of prediction than to predict—to figure, in the picture of the Messianic times, as a person foreseen by the prophets, than oneself to hold the prophetic glass? This is why John is more than a prophet: his appearing is a γεγραμμένον, an event *written.*

The quotation from Mal. iii. 1 is found in the three Syn.; in Matthew, in the parallel passage (xi. 10); in Mark (i. 2), at the opening of the Gospel, but with this difference, that he omits the words, *before Thee.* On the ἐγώ, *I* (after ἰδού), the various readings do not permit us to pronounce. This general agreement is remarkable; for the quotation is identical neither with the Hebrew text nor with the LXX. Neither Malachi nor the LXX. have the words, *before my face,* in the proposition; but in the second, the former says, *before me,* and the latter, *before my face.* Further, the LXX. read ἐξαποστέλλω instead of ἀποστέλλω, and ἐμβλέψεται instead of κατασκευάσει. This might be an argument in favour of a common written source, or of the use of one of the Syn. by the rest; but it would not be decisive. For, 1. If the common source is the Proto-Mark, how could Mark himself place this quotation in quite a different context? 2. If it is the *Logia,* why does Mark, instead of simply copying it, omit the words, *before Thee?* 3. It would be just the same if Mark copied one of the other Syn. 4. Neither do these copy Mark, which does not contain the discourse. The coincidences in the Syn. must therefore be explained in a different way. The substitution in Luke and Matthew of *before Thee* for *before me* (in Malachi), results from the way in which Jesus Himself had cited this passage. In the prophet's view, He who was sending, and He before whom the way was to be prepared, were one and the same person, Jehovah. Hence the *before me* in Malachi. But for Jesus, who, in speaking of Himself, never confounds Himself with the Father, a distinction became necessary. It is not Jehovah who speaks of Himself, but Jehovah speaking to Jesus; hence the form *before Thee.* From which evidence, does it not follow from this quotation that, in the prophet's idea, as well as in that of Jesus, Messiah's appearing is the appearing of Jehovah? (See Gess, pp. 39, 40.) As to the other expressions in common, Weizsäcker correctly explains them by saying that, since "this quotation belonged to the Messianic demonstration in habitual use," it acquired in this way the fixed form under which we find it in our Syn.

The *for*, ver. 28, refers to the words, *of whom it is written.* The person whose lot it has been to be mentioned along with the Messiah, must be of no ordinary distinction. The T. R., with the Byz. Mjj., reads: "I say unto you, that among them which are born of woman, there hath arisen no greater *prophet* than John the Baptist." The Alex. omit the word *prophet,* and rightly; for there is tautology. Is not every prophet born of woman? The superiority of John over all other theocratic and human appearances, refers not to his personal worth, but to his position and work. Did his inward life surpass that of Abraham, Elijah, etc. . . . ? Jesus does not say it did. But his mission is higher than theirs. And nevertheless, Jesus adds, the ancient order of things and the new are separated by such a gulph, that the least in the latter has a higher position than John himself. The weakest disciple has a more spiritual intuition of divine things than the forerunner. He enjoys in Jesus the dignity of a son, while John is only a servant. The least believer is one with this Son whom John announces. It does not follow from this, that this believer is more faithful than John. John may be further advanced *on his line,* but none the less for that the line of the believer is higher than his. There is an element of a higher life in the one, which is wanting in the other. This reflection is added by Jesus not with a view to depreciate John, but to explain and excuse the unstedfastness of his faith, the σκανδαλίζεσθαι (ver. 23). Several of the ancients understood by *the least* Jesus Christ, as being either John's junior, or, for the time, even less illustrious than he. The only way of supporting this interpretation would be to refer the words, *in the kingdom of God,* to *is greater,* which is evidently forced.—We have given to the comparative, *less,* a superlative meaning, *least.* Meyer, pressing the idea of the comparative, gives this explanation: " he who, in the new era, has a position relatively less lofty than that which John had in the old." This meaning is far-fetched; Matt. xviii. 1 shows us how the sense of the comparative becomes superlative: he who is greater [than the other]; whence: the greatest of all. Comp. also Luke ix. 48.—This saying, the authenticity of which is beyond suspicion, shows how fully conscious Jesus was of introducing a principle of life superior to the most exalted element in Judaism.

Vers. 29 and 30. *Retrospective Survey of the Ministry of John.*—" *And all the people that heard Him, and the publicans, justified God, being baptized with the baptism of John.* 30. *But the Pharisees and lawyers rejected the counsel of God against themselves* [*the Pharisees and scribes rendered God's design vain in their case.* M. Godet's trans.], *being not baptized of him.*"—These verses form the transition from the testimony which Jesus has just borne to John, to the application which He desires to make to the persons present. He attributes to the ministry of John a twofold result: a general movement amongst the lower classes of the people, ver. 29; an open opposition on the part of the rulers who determine the fate of the nation, ver. 30. Several interpreters (Knapp, Neander) have been led by the historical form of these verses to regard them as a reflection of the evangelist introduced into the discourse of Jesus. But such a mention of a fact interrupting a discourse would be unexampled. In any case it would be indicated, and the resumption of the discourse pointed out in ver. 31; the formula, *And the Lord said*, at the commencement of this verse, is not authentic. Had John been still at liberty, the words *all that heard* might, strictly speaking, have referred to a fact which had taken place at that time, to a resolution which His hearers had formed to go and be baptized by John that very hour. But John was no longer baptizing (iii. 19, 20; Matt. xi. 2). These words are therefore the continuation of the discourse. The meaning of Jesus is: John's greatness (28*b* is only a parenthesis) was thoroughly understood by the people; for a time they did homage to his mission, whilst (δέ, ver. 30) the rulers rejected him. And thus it is that, notwithstanding the eagerness of the people in seeking baptism from John, his ministry has nevertheless turned out a decided failure, in regard to the nation as such, owing to the opposition of its leaders. The object understood after *all that heard* is John the Baptist and his preaching. *To justify God* is to recognise and proclaim by word and deed the excellence of His ways for the salvation of men. The expression: *they have annulled for themselves the divine decree*, signifies that, although man cannot foil God's plan for the world, he may render it vain *for himself*.—On this conduct of the rulers, see iii. 7. The indirect reproof addressed by Jesus to the Pharisee Nicodemus (John iii. 5) for having neglected *the baptism of water*, coincides in a remarkable manner with this passage in Luke.

In place of these two verses, we find in Matthew (xi. 12–15) a passage containing the following thoughts: The appearing of John was the close of the legal and prophetical dispensation; and the opening of the Messianic kingdom took place immediately after. Only, men must know how to use a holy violence in order to enter into it (vers. 12, 13). John was therefore the expected Elijah: Blessed is he who understands it (vers. 14, 13)! These last two verses occur again in Matt. xvii. 12, where they are brought in more naturally; it is probable that some similarity in the ideas led the compiler to place them here. As to vers. 12 and 13, they are placed by Luke in a wholly different and very obscure connection, xvi. 16. According to Holtzmann, it would be Matthew who faithfully reproduces here the common source, the Logia; while Luke, not thinking the connection satisfactory, substitutes for this passage from the Logia another taken from the proto-Mark, which Matthew introduces at xxi. 31, 32. Since, however, he was unwilling to lose the passage omitted here, he gives it another place, in a very incomprehensible context, it is true, but with a reversal of the order of the two verses, in order to make the connection more intelligible. Holtzmann quite prides himself on this explanation, and exclaims: "All the difficulties are solved. . . . This example is very instructive as showing the way in which such difficulties should be treated" (pp. 143–5). The only thing proved, in our opinion, is, that by attempting to explain the origin of the Syn. by such manipulations we become lost in a labyrinth of improbabilities. Luke, forsooth, took the passage v. 12–15 (Matthew) away from its context, because the connection did not appear to him satisfactory, and inserted this same passage in his own Gospel, xvi. 16, in a context where it becomes more unintelligible still! Is it not much more natural to suppose that Matthew's discourse was originally composed for a collection of *Logia*, in which it bore the title: *On John the Baptist*, and that the compiler collected under this head all the words known to him which Jesus had uttered at different times on this subject? As to Luke, he follows his own sources of information, which, as he has told us, faithfully represent the oral tradition, and which furnish evidence of their accuracy at every fresh test.

Gess endeavours, it is true, to prove the superiority of Matthew's text. The *violent* (Matt. xi. 12) would be, according to him, the messengers of John the Baptist, thus designated on account of the abruptness with which they had put their question to Jesus before all the people. And Jesus declared this zeal laudable in comparison with the indifference shown by the people (vers. 31–35). But, 1. How could Jesus say of the disciples of John that they were forcing an entrance into the kingdom, whilst they frequently assumed a hostile attitude towards Him (Matt. ix. 14; John iii. 26)? 2. There would be no proportion between the gravity of this saying thus understood, and that of the declarations which precede and follow it upon the end of the prophetic and the opening of the Messianic era.

Vers. 31–35.[1] *The Application.—" Whereunto then shall I liken the men of this generation? and to what are they like?* 32. *They are like unto children sitting in the market-place, and*

[1] Ver. 31. The T. R. at the commencement of the verse, with some Mnn., ειπε δε ο κυριος.—Ver. 32. Instead of και λεγουσιν, ℵ* B. read α λεγει, D. L. some Mnn. λεγοντες.—ℵ. B. D. L. Z. omit υμιν.—Ver. 35. Some Mjj. several Mnn. omit παντων. ℵ. B. some Mnn. It. place it before των.—ℵ. reads εργων instead of τεκνων.

calling one to another, and saying, We have piped unto you, and ye have not danced; we have mourned to you, and ye have not wept. 33. *For John the Baptist came neither eating bread nor drinking wine, and ye say, He hath a devil.* 34. *The Son of man is come eating and drinking, and ye say, Behold a gluttonous man and a wine-bibber, a friend of publicans and sinners.* 35. *But Wisdom is justified of all her children."*—Here it is no longer the ministry of John simply that is the subject. Jesus is expressing His judgment of the conduct of the generation then living, with respect to the two great divine messages with which it had just been favoured. There is something severe in the double question of ver. 31. Jesus has a difficulty in finding a comparison that will adequately set forth the senseless conduct which He has witnessed. At last His mind fixes on an image which answers to His thought. He recalls a game at which the children of His time were accustomed to play, and in which perhaps He had Himself in His youth taken part of an evening, in the market-place of Nazareth. This game bore some resemblance to that which we call a *charade*. The players divided themselves into two groups, of which each one in turn commences the representation of a scene in ordinary life, while the other, taking up the scene thus begun, finishes the representation of it. It is not therefore, as with us, the mere guessing of a *word*; but, in conformity with the more dramatic character of the oriental genius, a passing from the position of spectators to that of actors, so as to finish the representation commenced by the players who imagined the scene. In this case two attempts are made alternatively. one by each of the two groups of children (προσφανοῦσιν ἀλλήλοις, *calling one to another*, ver. 32); but with equal want of success. Each time the actors whose turn it is to start the game are foiled by the disagreeable humour of their companions, whose part it is to take up the representation and finish the scene. The first company comes playing a dance tune; the others, instead of rising and forming a dance, remain seated and indifferent. The latter, in their turn, indicate a scene of mourning; the others, instead of forming themselves into a funeral procession, assume a weary, sullen attitude. And thus, when the game is over, each company has reason to complain of the other, and say: "*We have . . . , you have not . . .*"—The general meaning is obvious, the actors, in both cases, represent the two divine messengers joined by the faithful followers who gathered about them from the first: John, with his call to repentance, and his train of penitents; Jesus, with His promises of grace, and attended by a company of happy believers. But while the means they employ are so different, and so opposed even, that it seems that any man who resists the one must submit to the other, moral insensibility and a carping spirit have reached such a height in Israel that they paralyze their effects.[1] De Wette, Meyer, and Bleek give quite a different application of the figure. According to them, the company which begins the game represents the people, who want to make the divine messengers act according to their fancy; the other company, which refuses to enter into their humour, represents John and Jesus, who persevere, without deviation, in the path God has marked out for them. But, in this case, the blame in the parable should fall not on the second company, which would be justified in not entering into a part imposed upon them, but on the first, which tries to exact a tyrannical compulsion on the other. Now it is not so at all. It is evident that those on whom the blame falls are the dissatisfied and peevish spectators, who each time refuse to enter into the proposed game (and ye say . . ., and ye say . . ., vers. 33, 34). Besides, when did the people seek to exert such an influence on John and Jesus as would be indicated here? Lastly, there is an evident correspondence between the two reproaches: "*We have piped . . ., we have mourned . . .;*" and the two facts: "*John came . . . The Son of man is come . . .*" What has led these interpreters astray is the somewhat inaccurate form in which the parable is introduced at ver. 32: "This generation is like to children *calling one to another.*" But in these preambles the connection between the image and the idea is often indicated in a concise and somewhat inaccurate manner. Thus Matt. xiii. 24: "*The kingdom of heaven is like unto a man*

[1] The figure, as explained by M. Godet, would rather illustrate a want of sympathy between the disciples of John and those of Jesus, than the waywardness and indifference of the Jewish people to God's messengers. Surely the difficulty which the commentators find here arises from pressing the correspondence of the figure beyond the single point of the *untowardness* of the generation to which John and Jesus preached.—Tr.

which sowed," and elsewhere. The meaning, therefore, of ver. 32 is simply this: "The conduct of the present generation towards the messengers sent to it by God is like that which takes place amongst children who . . ." By the repetition of "*and ye say*" (vers. 33 and 34), Jesus translates, so to speak, *into words* the refusal of the people to enter into the feeling of holy grief or holy joy with which God would impress them.

But, notwithstanding this general resistance, divine wisdom finds some hearts which open to its different solicitations, and which justify by their docility the contrary methods it adopts. These Jesus calls *the children of wisdom,* according to an expression used in the book of Proverbs. *Καί* (ver. 35): "*And nevertheless.*" The preposition *ἀπό, from,* indicates that God's justification is derived from these same men, that is to say, from their repentance on hearing the reproof and threatenings of John, and from their faith, resembling a joyous amen, in the promises of Jesus. *Πάντων, all:* not one of these children of wisdom remain behind . . .; all force their way into the kingdom.—The term *wisdom* recalls the word *counsel* (ver. 30); the expression *is justified,* the *justified* of ver. 29. This connection will not allow of the meaning being given to ver. 35, which some have proposed: "Divine wisdom has been justified from the accusations (*ἀπό*) brought against it by its own children, the Jews." This meaning is also excluded by the word *all,* which would contain an inadmissible exaggeration (ver. 29).[1]—Instead of *τέκνων, children,* ℵ reads *ἔργων, works*: "Wisdom has derived its justification from the excellent works which it produces in those who submit to it." But the epithet *πάντων, all,* does not suit this sense. The reading *ἔργων* is taken from the text of Matthew, in certain documents (ℵ. B. Syr. Cop.). It would be more allowable in that Gospel,

[1] Holtzmann, following Hitzig, regards the word *πάντων, all,* as *added* by Luke, who wrongly applied (as we have done) this expression, *children of wisdom,* to believers. What wonderful sagacity our critics have! Not only do they know more than the evangelists did respecting the meaning of the words of the Master, but they have a more accurate knowledge of their exact terms!—For Holtzmann's sense *ὑπό* would have been needed instead of *ἀπό.*—It is unnecessary to refute the opinion of Weizsäcker and others, who regard the question of John the Baptist as the first sign of a new-born faith. This opinion gives the lie to the scene of the baptism, to the testimonies of John the Baptist, and to the answer even of Jesus (vers. 23 and 28*b*).

in which the word πάντων is omitted. But even then it is improbable.

This discourse is one of those which best show what Jesus was as a popular speaker. The understanding is brought into play, and the curiosity stimulated by the interrogative form (vers. 24, 26, and 31); and the imagination excited by lively images, full of charm (vers. 24, 25, and 32). Lastly, there is a striking application to the conscience: John failed through his austerity; I shall fail through my gentleness; neither under one form nor another will you obey God. Nevertheless there are those whose conduct by condemning you justifies God.

5. *The Gratitude of the Woman who was a Sinner:* vii. 36–50.—The following narrative seems to have been placed here as an illustration of wisdom being justified by her children (ver. 35), and particularly of this last word: *all.*

Vers. 36–39.[1] *The Offence.*—We are still in that epoch of transition, when the rupture between our Lord and the Pharisees, although already far advanced, was not complete. A member of this party could still invite Him without difficulty. It has been supposed that this invitation was given with a hostile intention. But this Pharisee's own reflection, ver. 39, shows his moral state. He was hesitating between the holy impression which Jesus made upon him, and the antipathy which his caste felt against Him. Jesus speaks to him in a tone so friendly and familiar, that it is difficult to suppose him animated by malevolent feelings. Further, ver. 42 proves unanswerably that he had received some spiritual benefit from Jesus, and that he felt a certain amount of gratitude towards Him; and ver. 47 says expressly that he loved Jesus, although feebly.—The entrance of the woman that was a sinner into such society was an act of great courage, for she might expect to be ignominiously sent away. The power of a gratitude that knew no bounds for a priceless benefit which she had received from the Saviour can alone explain her conduct. Ver. 42 shows what this benefit was. It was the pardon of her

[1] Ver. 36. ℵ. B. D. L. Z. It^{aliq}. some Mnn., τον οικον instead of την οικιαν.—ℵ. B. D. L. X. Z. some Mnn., κατεκλιθη instead of ανεκλιθη.—Ver. 37. ℵ. B. L Z. It^{aliq}. place ητις ην after γυνη, and not after εν τη πολει.—Ver. 38. ℵ* A. D. L. X., εξεμασσεν instead of εξεμαξεν.

numerous and fearful sins. Was it on hearing Him preach, or in a private interview, or through one of those looks of Jesus which for broken hearts were like a ray from heaven...? She had received from Him the joy of salvation; and the perfume which she brought with her was the emblem of her ardent gratitude for this unspeakable gift. If we adopt the Alex. reading, the sense is: "A woman who was a sinner in that city," that is to say, who practised in that very city her shameful profession. The received reading: "There was in the city a woman that was a sinner," is less harsh.—*Ἁμαρτωλός*, *a sinner*, in the same superlative sense in which the Jews thought they might apply this epithet to the Gentiles (Gal. ii. 15).—*Μύρον* denotes any kind of odoriferous vegetable essence, particularly that of the myrtle.—As it was the custom when at table to recline upon a couch, the feet being directed backwards, and without their sandals, there was nothing to prevent this woman from coming up to Jesus and anointing His feet. But just when she was preparing to pay Him this homage, she burst into tears at remembrance of her faults. Her tears streamed down upon the Saviour's feet, and having no cloth to wipe them, she promptly loosed her hair, and with that supplied its place. In order to duly appreciate this act, we must remember that among the Jews it was one of the greatest humiliations for a woman to be seen in public with her hair down.[1]—The *τίς*, *who* (ver. 39), refers to the name and family, and the *ποταπή*, *what*, to the character and conduct.

Vers. 40–43.[2] *The Parable.*—If this man wanted a proof of the prophetic gift of Jesus, he received it instantly in the following parable, which so exactly meets his thoughts and secret questions. The form of the following conversation is kindly, familiar, and even slightly humorous. It is just the tone of the Socratic irony. The denarius was equivalent to about three farthings; the larger of the two sums amounted, therefore, to about £16, the smaller to 32s. The former represents the enormous amount of sins to which this sinful woman pleaded guilty, and which Jesus had pardoned; the latter, the few infractions of the law for which the Pharisee reproached himself, and from the burden of which Jesus had also released him

[1] See my *Commentaire sur l'Evangile de Saint Jean*, chap. xii. 3.
[2] Ver. 42. ℵ. B. L. Z. some Mnn. Syr. omit εἰπέ.

—Ὀρθῶς ἔκρινας: "*thou hast rightly judged;* and in judging so rightly, thou hast condemned thyself." It is the πάνυ ὀρθῶς of Socrates, when he had caught his interlocutor in his net. But that which establishes such an immeasurable distance between Jesus and the Greek sage, is the way in which Jesus identifies Himself, both here and in what follows, with the offended God who pardons and who becomes the object of the sinner's grateful love.

Vers. 44–47.[1] *The Application.*—Jesus follows an order the inverse of that which He had taken in the parable. In the latter He descends from the cause to the effect, from the debt remitted to the gratitude experienced. In the application, on the contrary, He ascends from the effect to the cause. For the effect is evident, and comes under the observation of the senses (βλέπεις).—Jesus describes it, vers. 44–46, whilst the cause is concealed (ver. 47), and can only be got at by means of the principle which forms the substance of the parable.—During the first part of the conversation, Jesus was turned towards Simon. He now turns towards the woman whom He is about to make the subject of His demonstration. Jesus had not complained of the want of respect and the impoliteness of His host. But He had noticed them, and felt them deeply. And now what a contrast He draws between the cold and measured welcome of the Pharisee, who appeared to think that it was honour enough to admit Him to his table, and the love shown by this woman that was a sinner! The customary bath for the feet had been omitted by the one, while copious tears were showered upon His feet by the other; the usual kiss with which the host received his guests Simon had neglected, while the woman had covered His feet with kisses; the precious perfume with which it was usual to anoint an honoured guest on a festive day (Ps. xxiii. 5) he had withheld, but she had more than made up for the omission. In fact, it is not Simon, it is she who has done Jesus the honours of the house! The omission of τῆς κεφαλῆς (ver. 44) in the Alex., "[the hairs] *of her head,*" is probably the result of negligence. The word perfectly suits the context; the *head,*

[1] Ver. 44. της κεφαλης, which is the reading of T. R. with 11 Mjj. after θριξιν, is omitted by 11 Mjj. 25 Mnn. Syr[sch]. It., etc.—Ver. 45. L* some Mnn. It[aliq] read εισηλθεν instead of εισηλθον.—Ver. 47. א*, ειπον instead of λεγω.

as the most noble part of the body, is opposed to the *feet* of Jesus.—The reading εἰσῆλθεν, "[ever since] *she entered,*" found in one Mn., has at first glance something taking about it. But it has too little support; and the T. R., "ever since *I entered,*" is in reality preferable. Jesus thereby reminds Simon of the moment when He came under his roof, and when He had a right to expect those marks of respect and affection which had been neglected. The woman had followed Jesus so closely that she had all but entered with Him; there she was, the moment He was set at the table, to pay Him homage. —From this visible effect—the total difference between the love of the one and the love of the other, Jesus ascends, ver. 47, to its hidden cause—the difference in the measure of forgiveness accorded to them respectively. *Οὗ χάριν, wherefore;* properly, *an account of which,* that is to say, of this contrast between the respective exhibitions of your gratitude (vers. 44–46). This conjunction is the inverse of the *therefore* in ver. 42, which led from the cause to the foreseen effect.—We might make this *wherefore* bear upon the principal idea, "Her sins are forgiven her." In that case we should have to regard the words λέγω σοί, *I say unto thee,* as an inserted phrase, and the last proposition as an epexegetical explanation of this *wherefore:* "Wherefore I say unto thee, her many sins are forgiven, and that because she loved much." But we may also make the *wherefore* bear directly on "I say unto thee," and make all the rest of the verse the complement of this verb: "Wherefore I say unto thee, that her many sins are forgiven her, because that . . ." The latter is evidently the more simple construction. The reading, *I said unto thee,* of א, would indicate that this truth was already contained in this parable. It has neither authority nor probability. — How should we understand the words, *for she loved much?* Is love, according to Jesus, the cause of forgiveness? Catholic interpreters, and even many Protestants, understand the words in this sense: God forgives us much when we love much; little, if we love little. But, 1. In this case there is no coherence whatever between the parable and its application. On this principle, Jesus should not have asked, ver. 42, "Which of them *will love* Him most?" but, "Which then *loved* Him most?" The remission of the two debts of such different amounts *would result* from the different degrees of love in the two debtors; while, on the contrary, it is the difference between the debts remitted which produces the different amount of gratitude. 2. There would be, if possible, a more striking incoherence still between the first part of the application, ver. 47*a*, and the second, ver. 47*b*: "To whom little is forgiven, the same loveth little." To be logical, Jesus should have said precisely the contrary: "Who loves little, to him little is forgiven." 3. The words, *Thy faith hath saved thee* (ver. 50), clearly show what, in Jesus' view, was the principle on which forgiveness was granted to this woman; it was faith, not love. We must not forget that ὅτι, *because*, frequently expresses, just as our *for* does, not the relation of the effect to its cause, but the relation (purely logical) of the proof to the thing proved. We may say, It is light, for the sun is risen; but we may also say, The sun is risen, for [I say this because] it is light. So in this passage the ὅτι, *because*, *for*, may, and, according to what precedes and follows, *must* mean: "I say unto thee that her many sins are forgiven, *as thou must infer from this*, that she loved much." Thus all is consistent, the application with the parable, this saying with the words that follow, and Jesus with Himself and with St. Paul.—Ver. 47*b* contains the other side of the application of this same principle: the less forgiveness, the less love. This is addressed to Simon. But with delicacy of feeling Jesus gives this severe truth the form of a general proposition, "*He to whom . . .*;" just as He also did with Nicodemus, "*Except a man* be born . . ." (John iii. 3).

The thought expressed in this ver. 47 raises two difficulties: 1. May forgiveness be only partial? Then there would be men half-saved and half-lost! 2. Is it necessary to have sinned deeply in order to love much?—The real forgiveness of the least sin certainly contains in germ a complete salvation, but only in germ. If faith is maintained and grows, this forgiveness will gradually extend to all the sins of a man's life, just as they will then become more thoroughly known and acknowledged. The first forgiveness is the pledge of all the rest. In the contrary case, the forgiveness already granted will be withdrawn, just as represented in the parable of the wicked debtor, Matt. xviii.; and the work of grace, instead of becoming complete, will prove abortive. All is transition here below, free transition, either to perfect salvation or to complete condemnation. As to the great amount of sin necessary in order to loving much, we need add nothing to what each of us already has; it is sufficient to estimate accurately what we have. What is wanting to the best of us, in order to love much, is not sin, but the knowledge of it.

Vers. 48–50. *Conclusion.*—Bleek has inferred from ver. 48, *thy sins are forgiven thee,* that until this moment the woman had not obtained forgiveness. This supposition is excluded by all that precedes. Bleek forgets that ἀφέωνται is a perfect indicating an actual state resulting from an act accomplished at some indefinite time in the past. Having regard to the pharisaical denials of the persons composing the assembly, and to the doubts which might arise in the heart of the sinning woman herself, Jesus renews to her the assurance of the divine fact of which she had within her the witness and warrant. This direct and personal declaration corresponds with the inward witness of the Divine Spirit in our own experience, after we have embraced the promises of the Word (Eph. i. 13).—On the objection, ver. 49, comp. ver. 21. **Καί**, *even;* besides all the other extraordinary things He does.—Jesus continues as if He had not heard, but all the while taking account of what was being said around Him (εἶπε δέ, "*but* He said"). While addressing the woman, He shows the people assembled the firm foundation on which her forgiveness rests. She has the benefit of this decree: Whosoever believeth is saved. Let her go away, then, with her treasure, her peace, in spite of all their pharisaical murmurs! **Εἰς** εἰρήνην, in peace, and to enjoy peace.

This beautiful narrative, preserved by Luke alone, contains the two essential elements of what is called Paulinism—the freeness and universality of salvation. Does it follow from this that it was invented posterior to Paul in order to set forth these great principles? It simply proves that it was Luke's intention, as he said at the beginning (i. 4), to show by his Gospel, that the doctrine so clearly expressed and so earnestly preached by Paul was already contained in germ in all the acts and teaching of Jesus; that *the gospel of Paul* is nothing but the application of the principles previously laid down by the Lord Himself.

A very similar narrative to this is found in the other three Gospels, but assigned to a much later time—to the Passion week. Mary, a sister of Lazarus, anoints Jesus at a repast which is given Him by the people of Bethany (Matt. xxvi. 6 et seq.; Mark xiv. 3 et seq.; John xii. 1 et seq.). A great number of interpreters agree that this incident is the same as that we have just been considering in Luke. They rely on the similarity of the act, on the circumstance that Luke does not relate the anointing at Bethany; and that, on the other hand, the three other evangelists do not mention this in Galilee; and lastly, on the fact that in both cases the owner of the house where the repast is given bears the name of Simon (Luke vii. 40; Matt. xxvi. 6; Mark xiv. 3). These reasons, doubtless, have their weight; but they are not decisive. The act of anointing was associated with such a common usage on festive occasions (Luke vii. 46; Ps. xxiii. 5), that there can be no difficulty in supposing that it was repeated. The causes of the omission of a narrative in one or two of the evangelists are too accidental for us to be able to base any solid conclusion upon it. We need only refer to the omission in Matthew of the healing of the possessed at Capernaum, and of the healing of the centurion's servant in Mark, omissions which it is impossible to account for. As to the name Simon, it was so common, that out of the small number of persons designated by name in the N. T., there are no less than fifteen Simons! The reasons in favour of the difference of the two incidents are the following: 1*st.* The difference of place—Galilee in Luke; in the other three, Judæa. This reason is of secondary value, it is true, because in chap. x. Luke appears to place the visit of Jesus to Martha and Mary in the midst of the Galilean ministry. 2*d.* The difference of time. 3*d.* The difference of persons: the woman that was a sinner, in Luke, is a stranger in the house of the host (ver. 37, "*a woman of the city*"), and Simon himself regards her as such, and as altogether unknown to Jesus (ver. 39); Mary, on the contrary, belongs to a beloved family, which habitually received Jesus under their roof. Besides, we must always feel a repugnance to identify Mary, the sister of Lazarus, as we know her in John xi. and Luke x. 38–42, with a woman of ill fame. 4*th.* The most important difference respects what was said: at Bethany, a complaint from Judas on behalf of the poor, and a reply from Jesus announcing His approaching death; in Galilee, the great evangelical declaration, that love is the fruit of forgiveness, which is bestowed on the simple condition of faith. What agreement can be discovered between these two conversations? We may conceive of very considerable alterations being made by tradition in the historical framework of a narrative. But by what marvellous process could one of these two conversations have been transformed into the other?

6. *The Women who ministered to Jesus:* viii. 1–3.—By the side of the high religious problems raised by the life of Jesus, there is a question, seldom considered, which neverthe-

less possesses some interest: How did Jesus find the means of subsistence during the two or three years that His ministry lasted? He had given up His earthly occupation. He deliberately refrained from using His miraculous power to supply His necessities. Further, He was not alone; He was constantly accompanied by twelve men, who had also abandoned their trade, and whose maintenance He had taken on Himself in calling them to follow Him. The wants of this itinerant society were met out of a common purse (John xiii. 29); the same source furnished their alms to the poor (John xii. 6). But how was this purse itself filled? The problem is partly, but not completely, explained by hospitality. Had He not various needs, of clothing, etc.? The true answer to this question is furnished by this passage, which possesses, therefore, considerable interest. Jesus said: "*Seek first the kingdom of God, and other things shall be added unto you.*" He also said: "*There is none that leaves father, mother . . ., house, lands for the kingdom of God, who does not find a hundred times more.*" He derived these precepts from His daily experience. The grateful love of those whom He filled with His spiritual riches provided for His temporal necessities, as well as for those of His disciples. Some pious women spontaneously rendered Him the services of mother and sisters.

This passage would suffice to prove the excellence of Luke's sources; their originality, for the other evangelists furnish no similar information; their exactness, for who would have invented such simple and positive details with the names and rank of these women? and their purity, for what can be further removed from false marvels and legendary fictions than this perfectly natural and prosaic account of the Lord's means of subsistence during the course of His ministry?

Vers. 1–3.[1] Luke indicates this time as a distinctly marked epoch in the ministry of the Lord. He ceases to make Capernaum, His *ἰδία πόλις, His own city* (Matt. ix. 1), the centre of His activity; He adopts an altogether itinerant mode of life, and literally has no place where to lay His head. It is this change in His mode of living, carried out at this time,

[1] Ver. 3. Instead of *αυτω*, which is the reading of T. R. with ℵ. A. L. M. X. Π. several Mnn. It^aliq^., *αυτοις* is read in 13 Mjj. 90 Mnn. Syr. It^aliq^. Or. Aug.—The Mss. vary between *εκ* and *απο*.

which induces Luke to place here this glimpse into the means of His material support. The aor. ἐγένετο, *it came to pass* (ver. 1), indicates a definite time. The καί before αὐτός, as the sign of the apodosis, betrays an Aramæan source. The imperf. διώδευε, *He went throughout*, denotes a slow and continuous mode of travelling. The preposition κατά expresses the particular care which He bestowed on every place, whether large (*city*) or small (*village*). Everywhere He gave Himself time to stay. To the general idea of a proclamation, expressed by the verb κηρύσσειν, *to preach*, the second verb, *to evangelize*, to announce the glad tidings of the kingdom, adds the idea of a proclamation of *grace* as the prevailing character of His teaching.—The Twelve accompanied Him. What a strange sight this little band presented, passing through the cities and country as a number of members of the heavenly kingdom, entirely given up to the work of spreading and celebrating salvation! Had the world ever seen anything like it?—Among the women who accompanied this band, filling the humble office of servants, Luke makes special mention first of *Mary*, surnamed *Magdalene*. This surname is probably derived from her being originally from Magdala, a town situated on the western shore of the sea of Galilee (Matt. xv. 39), the situation of which to the north of Tiberias is still indicated at the present day by a village named *El-Megdil* (*the tower*). The seven demons (Mark xvi. 9) denote, without doubt, the culminating point of her possession, resulting from a series of attacks, each of which had aggravated the evil (Luke xi. 24–26). It is without the least foundation that tradition identifies Mary Magdalene with the penitent sinner of chap. vii. Possession, which is a disease (see iv. 33), has been wrongly confounded with a state of moral corruption. The surname, *of Magdala*, is intended to distinguish this Mary from all the others of this name, more particularly from her of Bethany.—*Chuza* was probably entrusted with some office in the household of Herod Antipas. Might he not be that βασιλικός, *court lord*, whose son Jesus had healed (John iv.), and who had believed *with all his house?*—We know nothing of Susanna and the other women.—Αἵτινες reminds us that it was in the capacity of servants that they accompanied Him.—Διακονεῖν, *to serve*, here denotes pecuniary assistance, as Rom

xv. 25, and also the personal attentions which might be rendered by a mother or sisters (ver. 21). The reading of the T. R., *αὐτῷ*, who served *Him*, may be a correction in accordance with Matt. xxvii. 55, Mark xv. 41; but the reading *αὐτοῖς*, who served *them*, is the more probable one according to ver. 1 (the Twelve) and iv. 39.

What a Messiah for the eye of flesh, this being living on the charity of men! But what a Messiah for the spiritual eye, this Son of God living on the love of those to whom His own love is giving life! What an interchange of good offices between heaven and earth goes on around His person!

7. *The Parable of the Sower:* viii. 4–18.—The preceding passage indicated a change in the mode of the Lord's outward life. The following passage indicates a change in His mode of teaching; a crisis, therefore, has been reached. The sequel will make us acquainted with its nature. Before this, Jesus had spoken a few parables (v. 36–39, vi. 39, 47 et seq.). From now, and for a very long time, He habitually makes use of this method. The parable possesses the double property of making an indelible impression of the truth on the mind of him who is able to perceive it through the figure in which it is clothed, and of veiling it from the observation of the inattentive or indolent hearer whose mind makes no effort to penetrate this covering. It is thus admirably fitted for making a selection from the hearers.—The term *parable* (from *παραβάλλειν, to place side by side*) denotes a form of instruction in which, by the side of the truth, is placed the image which represents it. This is also the meaning of *παροιμία*, a path by the side of the high road. The parable bears a close resemblance to the fable; but it differs from it in two respects, one of substance, the other of form. Whilst the fable refers to the relations of men with one another, and to the moral laws which regulate these relations, the parable deals with man's relations with God, and with the lofty principles by which they are governed. The loftier sphere in which the parable moves determines the difference of form which distinguishes it from the fable. The fable partakes of a humorous character; it is quite allowable, therefore, in it to make plants and animals speak. The aim of the parable is too serious to comport with such fictions. There must be

nothing in the picture to violate probability. Animals and material objects may be employed in the parable (sheep, leaven); but they must not assume a character contrary to their actual nature.—The parable was the most natural mode of teaching for Jesus to adopt. Living in the incessant contemplation of the divine world, which lay open to His inward sense, finding Himself at the same time also in constant intercourse with the external world, which He observed with intelligent and calm attention, He was necessarily led to make constant comparisons of these two spheres, and to perceive the innumerable analogies which exist between them.

The first parable He uttered that was fully worked out, appears to have been this of the sower. Matthew makes it the opening parable of the large collection in chap. xiii. Mark assigns it a similar place at the head of a more limited collection, chap. iv. It is the only one, besides that of the vine-dressers, a parable belonging to our Lord's last days, which has been preserved in all the three Syn. In all three, the general explanation, which Jesus gives His disciples once for all, as to why He employs this form of teaching, is connected with the account of this parable. It appears, therefore, that it was the first complete similitude that He offered them. Moreover, it was the one which seems to have struck the disciples the most, and which was most frequently told in the oral tradition; this explains its reproduction by our three evangelists.

The following passage contains: 1*st.* The parable (vers. 4–8); 2*d.* The explanations given by Jesus respecting this mode of teaching (vers. 9 and 10); 3*d.* The exposition of the parable (vers. 11–15); 4*th.* A warning to the apostles as to the course they must pursue in regard to truths which Jesus teaches them in this way (vers. 16–18).

1*st.* Vers. 4–8.[1] *The Parable.*—Matthew and Mark place this parable after the visit of the mother and brethren of Jesus (Matt. xiii. 1; Mark iv. 1). In Luke it immediately precedes the same narrative (ver. 19 et seq.). This connection may be the result of a real chronological relation, or of a moral

[1] Ver. 4. ℵ. some Mnn., συνοντος.—Ver. 6. B. L. R. Z., κατεπεσεν instead of επεσεν.—Ver. 8. Almost all the Mjj. read εις instead of επι, which is the reading of T. R. with D. and some Mnn.

relation as well; comp. ver. 15, "those who keep the word and bring forth fruit," with ver. 21, "those who hear the word of God and practise it."—We might make τῶν ἐπιπορευομένων, *coming together unto Him,* the complement of ὄχλου, *a multitude,* by giving καί the sense of *even.* But this construction is forced; the two genitives are parallel. Luke's meaning is: "As a great multitude was gathered about Him, and as it was continually increasing, owing to fresh additions, which were arriving more or less from every city." This prefatory remark contains a great deal. Jesus goes through the country, stopping at every place; the Twelve are His immediate attendants; the cities are emptied, so to speak; their entire populations accompany Him. We have evidently reached a crisis. But the more the number of His hearers increases, the more clearly Jesus sees that the time has come to set some sifting process to work amongst them; if, on the one hand, it is necessary to draw the spiritual into closer attachment, on the other, it is of importance to keep the carnal at a distance. The parables, in general, have this tendency; that of the sower, by its very meaning, has a direct application to this state of things.—It appears from Matthew and Mark that Jesus was seated in a vessel on the sea-shore, and that from this kind of pulpit He taught the people who stood upon the banks. He could therefore easily discern the various expressions of the persons composing the multitude.—The art. ὁ before σπείρων designates that one of the servants who has been entrusted with this work. Gess points out the contrast between this sower, who commences the work of establishing the kingdom of God by means of the Word alone, and the Messiah, as pictured by John the Baptist, *having His fan in His hand.*—Jesus divides His hearers into four classes, and compares them to four kinds of soil, of which the surrounding country furnished Him with illustrations at the very time He was speaking. From the edge of the lake the soil rises very rapidly; now, on such slopes, it easily happens that the higher portion of a field has only a thin layer of mould, whilst, going down towards the plain, the bed of earth becomes deeper. Hence the differences indicated. The first soil (*by the wayside*) is the part nearest the path which is freely used by passers-by. The second (*on the rock,* according to Luke; *in stony places,* in Matthew and Mark) does not denote, as is often thought, a soil full of stones; but, as is well expressed by Luke, and confirmed by the explanation, *because there was no depth of earth* (Matthew and Mark), that portion of the field where the rock is only covered with a thin layer of earth. The third is a fertile soil, but already choke-full of the seeds of thorns and briars. There remains the *good soil* (Mark and Matthew, *καλή*). This last land is neither *hard* as the first, nor *thin* as the second, nor *unclean* as the third; it is soft, deep, and free from other seeds. The four prep. employed by Luke well describe these different relations of the seed with the soil: *παρά, by the side; ἐπί, upon; ἐν μέσῳ, in the midst; εἰς, into* (*ἐπί* in the T. R., ver. 8, has only very insufficient authorities).

The fate of the seed is determined by the nature of the soil. On the first soil it does not even spring up. The *φυέν, having sprung up* (vers. 6–8), is passed over in silence in the 5th verse. Not having germinated, the seed is destroyed by external causes, the passers-by and the birds. Matthew and Mark mention only the latter. On the second soil the seed springs up; but the root, immediately meeting with the rock, cannot develope itself in proportion to the stem, and, as soon as the sun has dried up the thin layer of earth, the plant perishes. The seed on the third soil grows into ear; but briars choke it before the grain is formed. Thus in the first case there are two external causes of destruction; in the second, an external and an internal cause; in the third, a single cause, and this altogether internal. On the fourth soil the plant successfully accomplishes the entire cycle of vegetation. Luke only mentions the highest degree of fertility, a hundred-fold. Matthew and Mark speak of lesser degrees; Mark in an ascending, and Matthew in a descending order. How puerile and unworthy of earnest men these trifling variations would be, if the evangelists worked upon a common document!

The Lord invites the serious attention of the multitude to this result; *ἐφώνει, He raises His voice* [*He cried,* A.V.], these are the words which He emphasizes. He endeavours to awaken that inward sense for divine things, without which religious teaching is only an empty sound.—The design of

Jesus is, first of all, to show that He is not deceived by the sight of this crowd, which is apparently so attentive; then to put His disciples on their guard against the expectations which such a large concourse might create in their minds; lastly, and more than all, to warn His hearers of the perils which threatened the holy impressions they were then experiencing.

2*d.* Vers. 9 and 10.[1] *The Parables in general.*—"*And His disciples asked Him, saying, What might this parable be?* 10. *And He said, Unto you it is given to know the mysteries of the kingdom of God: but to others in parables; that seeing they might not see, and hearing they might not understand.*"—The question of the disciples referred solely to the meaning of the preceding parable; but Jesus takes advantage of it to give them a general explanation of this mode of teaching. It is the same in Mark, who only adds this detail: *when they were alone with Him.* In Matthew the question of the disciples is altogether general: "*Wherefore speakest Thou unto them in parables?*" This form of the question appears to us less natural.—The reply of Jesus is more extended in Matthew. He quotes *in extenso* the prophecy of Isaiah (chap. vi.) to which Luke's text alludes, and which Mark incorporates into the discourse of Jesus. Bleek professes to find in the *because* of Matthew (xiii. 13) a less harsh thought than the *in order that* of Mark and Luke. He is wrong; the thought is absolutely the same. In both cases, Jesus distinctly declares that the object of His parables is not to make divine truths intelligible to all, but to veil them from those who are indifferent to them. And it is for this very reason that He avails Himself of this mode of teaching just from this time. By such preaching as the Sermon on the Mount He had accomplished the first work of His spiritual fishing; He had cast the net. Now begins the second, the work of selection; and this He accomplishes by means of teaching in parables. As we have seen, the parable possesses the double property of attracting some, while it repels others. The veil which it throws over the truth becomes transparent to the attentive mind, while it remains impenetrable to the careless. The

[1] Ver. 9. ℵ. B. D. L. R. Z. some Mnn. Syr. Itplerique, omit λεγοντες before τις.—Ver. 10. ℵ. R. some Mnn., ακουσωσιν instead of συνιωσιν.

opposition between these two results is expressed in Luke by these words, designedly placed at the beginning of the phrase, *to you* and *to others.* It is the same in Matthew, *to you* and *to those;* in Mark, more forcibly still, *to you* and *to those who are without.* The perf. δέδοται does not refer to any antecedent decree (the aor. would have been required), but to the actual condition of the disciples, which renders them fit to receive the revelation of divine things. It is the inward drawing due to divine teaching, of which Jesus speaks in John vi.—The term *mystery,* in Scripture, denotes the plan of salvation, in so far as it can only be known by man through a higher revelation (μυέω, *to initiate*). Used in the plural (*the mysteries*), it denotes the different parts of this great whole. These are the heavenly things of which Jesus spoke to Nicodemus (John iii. 12), and which He contrasted with the *earthly things* which He had preached at the commencement. The verb understood before ἐν παραβολαῖς is λαλεῖται. —But how, when God makes a revelation, can it be His will not to be understood, as Isaiah says (chap. vi.), and as is repeated here by Jesus? That is not, as Riggenbach says, either His first will or His last. It is an intermediate decree; it is a chastisement. When the heart has failed to open to the first beams of truth, the brighter beams which follow, instead of enlightening, dazzle and blind it; and this result is willed by God; it is a judgment. Since Pharaoh refuses to humble himself under the first lessons he receives, subsequent lessons shall harden him; for, if he is unwilling to be converted himself, he must at least subserve the conversion of others by the conspicuousness of his punishment. The Jewish people themselves, in the time of Isaiah, were just in this position. God makes them feel this by calling them, not *my people,* but *this people.* God already sees that the nation is incapable of fulfilling the part of an apostle to the world which had departed from Him. This part it shall accomplish, nevertheless; only it shall not be by its missionary action, but by its ruin. This ruin, therefore, becomes necessary; and *because* this ruin is necessary (Matthew), or *in order that* it may take place (Mark and Luke), Israel must be hardened. A similar state of things recurred at the period in Jesus' ministry which we have now reached. Israel rejected as a nation the light which shone in Jesus; and this light covered itself under the veil of the parable. But through this veil it sent out still more brilliant rays into the hearts of those who, like His disciples, had welcomed with eagerness its first beams. —The terms, *see, hear,* refer to the description in the parable; *not seeing,* and *not understanding,* to its real meaning.

3*d*. Vers. 11–15.[1] *The Explanation of the Parable.*—The expression, *Now the parable is this* (ver. 11), signifies that the essence of the picture is not in its outward form, but in its idea. The point of resemblance between the word and the seed, is the living power contained in a vehicle which conceals it.—By *the word* Jesus doubtless means primarily His own teaching, but He also comprehends in it any preaching that faithfully represents His own.—Amongst the multitude Jesus discerned four kinds of expression: countenances expressing thoughtlessness and indifference; faces full of enthusiasm and delight; others with a careworn, preoccupied expression; and lastly, expressions of serene joy, indicating a full acceptance of the truth that was being taught.—In the explanation which follows, the word is sometimes identified with the new life which is to spring from it, and the latter with the individuals themselves, in whom it is found. This accounts for the strange expressions: *those which are sown by the wayside* (ver. 12; comp. vers. 13, 14, 15); *these have no root* (ver. 13); *they are choked* (ver. 14). The first class contains those who are wholly insensible to religion, who are conscious of no need, have no fear of condemnation, no desire of salvation, and consequently no affinity with the gospel of Christ. In their case, therefore, the word becomes a prey to external agents of destruction. Only one is mentioned in the application, *the devil* (Luke), *Satan* (Mark), *the evil one* (Matthew), who employs various means of diverting their minds, in order to make them forget what they have heard. Had not Jesus believed in the existence of Satan, He would never have spoken of him as a reality answering to the figure of the parable.—*Οἱ ἀκούοντες, who hear,* must be thus explained: "who hear, and *nothing more.*" This implies Matthew's *do not understand.*

The second are the superficial but excitable natures, in

[1] Ver. 12. ℵ. B. L. U. Z. some Mnn., ακουσαντες instead of ακουοντες.—Ver. 13. ℵ* D. Fw. X., την πετραν instead of της πετρας.

whom imagination and sensibility for the moment make up for the absence of moral feeling. They are charmed with the novelty of the gospel, and the opposition which it offers to received ideas. In every awakening, such men form a considerable portion of the new converts. But in their case the word soon comes into conflict with an internal hindrance: a heart of stone which the humiliation of repentance and the love of holiness have never broken. Thus it finds itself given over to external agents of destruction, such as *temptation* (Luke), *tribulation* and *persecution* (Matthew and Mark); the enmity of the rulers, the rage of the Pharisees, the danger of excommunication, in a word, the necessity of suffering in order to remain faithful. Those who have merely sought for spiritual enjoyment in the gospel are therefore overcome.—In ver. 13 the verb εἰσὶν must be understood, and οἳ ὅταν must be made the predicate: *are those who, when* . . . The οἵ at the end of the verse is a development of **οὗτοι,** and signifies *who, as such.*

The third are persons with a measure of earnestness, but their heart is divided; they seek salvation and acknowledge the value of the gospel, but they are bent also upon their earthly welfare, and are not determined to sacrifice everything for the truth. These persons are often found at the present day among those who are regarded as real Christians. Their worldly-mindedness maintains its ground notwithstanding their serious interest in the gospel, and to the end hinders their complete conversion.—The miscarriage of the seed here results from an inward cause, which is both one and threefold: *cares* (in the case of those who are in poverty), *riches* (in those who are making their fortune), and *the pleasures of life* (in those who are already rich). These persons, like Ananias and Sapphira, have overcome the fear of persecution, but, like them, they succumb to the inward obstacle of a divided heart. —*Πορευόμενοι, go forth,* describes the bustle of an active life, coming and going in the transaction of business (2 Sam. iii. 1). It is in this verse especially that the seed is identified with the new life in the believer. The form differs completely in the three Syn.

In the fourth their spiritual wants rule their life. Their conscience is not asleep, as in the first; it is that, and not, as in the case of the second, imagination or sensibility, which rules the will; it prevails over the earthly interests which have sway in the third. These are the souls described by Paul in Rom. vii. *'Εν καρδίᾳ* and *τὸν λόγον* depend on the two verbs *ἀκούσαντες κατέχουσιν* combined, which together denote one and the same act: *to hear* and *to keep*, for such persons, are the same thing. The term *perseverance* refers to the numerous obstacles which the seed has had to overcome in order to its full development; comp. the *καθ' ὑπομονὴν ἔργου ἀγαθοῦ* (Rom. ii. 7). Jesus was certainly thinking here of the disciples, and of the devoted women who accompanied Him. Luke makes no mention either in the parable or the explanation of the different degrees of fertility indicated by Matthew and Mark, and the latter mention them here also in a contrary order.

We do not think that a single verse of this explanation of the parable is compatible with the hypothesis of the employment of a common text by the evangelists, or of their having copied from each other; at least it must be admitted that they allowed themselves to trifle, in a puerile and profane way, with the words of the Lord. The constant diversity of the three texts is, on the other hand, very naturally explained if their original source was the traditional teaching.

4*th*. Vers. 16–18.[1] *Practical Conclusion.*—"*No man, when he hath lighted a candle, covereth it with a vessel, or putteth it under a bed; but setteth it on a candlestick, that they which enter in may see the light.* 17. *For nothing is secret that shall not be made manifest; neither anything hid that shall not be known and come abroad.* 18. *Take heed therefore how ye hear; for whosoever hath, to him shall be given; and whosoever hath not, from him shall be taken even that which he seemeth to have.*" —Bleek can perceive no connection between these reflections and the preceding parable. But they are closely connected with the similar reflections in vers. 9 and 10. There is even a designed antithesis between the growth of the light (vers. 16 and 17) and the increase of the darkness (ver. 10). Jesus is speaking to the disciples. The word which is translated

[1] Ver. 16. The Mss. vary between *επι λυχνιας* and *επι την λυχνιαν* (a reading derived from Matthew and Mark, and from xi. 33).—Ver. 17. ℵ. B. L. Z., *ο ου μη γνωσθη* instead of *ο ου γνωσθησεται*.

candle denotes simply a lamp, just a saucer filled with oil in which a wick is placed—the mode of lighting most used in the East. It may therefore be placed without any danger under such a vessel as a bushel, which serves at once for measure, table, and dish amongst the poor, or under the divan (κλίνη), a bench furnished with cushions and raised from the floor from one to three feet, on which it is customary to rest while engaged in conversation or at meals. Beds properly so called are not used in the East; they generally lie on the ground, on wraps and carpets.[1] The lighted lamp might denote *the apostles,* whom Jesus enlightens with a view to make them the teachers of the world. *Covering their light* would be not putting them into a position of sufficient influence in regard to other men; and *setting it on a candlestick* would signify, conferring on them the apostolic office, in virtue of which they will become the light of the world. Those who see the light on entering the house would be their converts from the Jews and heathen. Ver. 17 would be an allusion, as in xii. 3, to that law according to which truth is to be fully revealed to the world by the apostolic preaching. Lastly, the 18th verse would refer to that growth of inward light which is the recompense of the preacher for the faithfulness of his labours. But it is just this last verse which upsets the whole of this interpretation. For, 1. With this meaning, Jesus ought to have said, not: *Take heed how ye hear,* but, *how ye preach.* 2. *To have,* in the sense of the 18th verse, is not certainly to produce fruits in others, but to possess the truth oneself. We must therefore regard the term λύχνος, *the lamp,* as denoting *the truth* concerning the kingdom of God which Jesus unveils to the apostles in His parables. If He clothes the truth in sensible images, it is not to render it unintelligible (*to put it under a bushel*); on the contrary, in explaining it to them, as He has just done, He places it on the candlestick; and they are the persons who are illuminated *on entering into the house.* All will gradually become clear to them. Whilst the night thickens over Israel on account of its unbelief, the disciples will advance into even fuller light, until there is nothing left in the plan of God (*His mysteries,* ver. 11) which *is obscure or hidden* (ver. 17). The heart of

[1] Félix Boret, *Voyage en Terre-Sainte,* pp. 348 and 349.

Jesus is lifted up at this prospect. This accounts for the poetical rhythm which always appears at such moments. Here we see why it behoves the disciples to hear with the greatest care; it is in order that they may really hold what He gives them, like the good soil which receives and fertilizes the seed (ver. 18). He alone who assimilates His teaching by an act of living comprehension, who really *hath* (the opposite of seeing without seeing, ver. 10), can receive continually more. Acquisitions are made only by means of, and in proportion to, what is already possessed. The Spirit Himself only makes clear what has been kept (John xiv. 26). If, therefore, any one amongst them contents Himself with hearing truth without appropriating it, by and by he will obtain nothing, and at last even lose everything. Mark (iv. 21–25) says: *that which he hath;* Luke: *that which he thinketh he hath.* It comes to the same thing; for, as to what is heard without comprehending it, it is equally true to say that he *hath* (in a purely external sense), or that he *thinks* he hath (in the real sense of the word *have*). Comp. Luke xix. 26. This very apophthegm is found several times in Matthew. It expresses one of the profoundest laws of the moral world.—Baur and Hilgenfeld thought they found in the word δοκεῖ, *thinks* he hath, a censure of Luke on the haughty pretensions of the Twelve! Our evangelists could never have anticipated that they would ever have such perverse interpreters.—Nothing could more effectually allay any undue elation which the sight of these multitudes might excite in the minds of the disciples, than their being reminded in this way of their responsibility. The similar reflections in Mark (iv. 25) are too different in form to have been drawn from the same source.

Mark goes on to narrate the parable of the ear of corn, which he alone records. In Matthew there are six parables respecting the kingdom of God given along with that of the sower. They form an admirable whole. After the foundation of the kingdom described in the parable of the sower, there follows the mode of its *development* in that of the tares; then its *power*, presented under two aspects (extension and transformation)—in those of the grain of mustard seed and the leaven; next, its incomparable *value* in the parables of the treasure and the pearl; lastly, its *consummation* in that of the net. Is this systematic plan to be attributed to Jesus? I think not. He was too good a teacher to relate in this way seven parables all in a breath.[1] On the other hand, did He only utter on this occasion the parable of the sower? Certainly not, for Matthew says respecting this very time (xiii. 3): "*And He spake many things unto them in parables,*" and Mark (iv. 2): "*He taught them many things in parables.*" Probably, therefore, Jesus spoke on this day, besides the parable of the sower, that of the tares (Matthew), and that of the ear of corn (Mark), the images of which are all taken from the same sphere, and which immediately follow the first, the one in one Gospel, the other in the other. As to the other parables, Matthew has united them with the preceding, in accordance with his constant method of grouping the sayings of our Lord around a given subject. Such different arrangements do not appear compatible with the use of the same written document.

8. *Visit of the Mother and Brethren of Jesus:* viii. 19–21.—We should have been ignorant of the real object of this visit, unless, in this as in several other cases, Mark's narrative had come in to supplement that of the other two. According to Mark, a report had reached the brethren of Jesus that He was in a state of excitement bordering on madness; it was just the echo of this accusation of the Pharisees: "*He casteth out devils by Beelzebub.*" Comp. Mark iii. 21, 22. His brethren therefore came, intending to *lay hold on Him* (*κρατῆσαι αὐτόν*, ver. 21), and take Him home. Matthew also connects this visit (xii. 46) with the same accusation. In John, the brethren of Jesus are represented in a similar attitude in regard to Him (vii. 5): "*His brethren also did not believe on Him.*" As to Mary, it is not said that she shared the sentiments of her sons. But when she saw them set out under the influence of such feelings, she would naturally desire to be present at the painful scene which she anticipated would take place. Perhaps also, like John the Baptist, she was unable to explain to herself the course which her Son's work was taking, and was distracted between contrary impressions.

Vers. 19–21.[2] The word *without* (ver. 20) might be under-

[1] I abide by this statement, notwithstanding the contrary assertion of Gess.

[2] Ver. 20. ℵ. B. D. L. Δ. Z. some Mnn. Syr. It. omit λεγοντων.—Ver. 21. The Alex. omit αυτου.

stood to mean: "outside the circle which surrounded Jesus." But Mark expressly mentions a house in which He was receiving hospitality (ver. 20), and where a large crowd *was seated around Him* (vers. 32 and 34).—Are these brethren of Jesus younger sons of Joseph and Mary, or sons of Joseph by a previous marriage; or are they cousins of Jesus, sons of Cleopas (the brother of Joseph), who would be called his brethren, as having been brought up in the house of their uncle Joseph? We cannot discuss this question here. (See our *Commentary on the Gospel of John*, ii. 12.) One thing is certain, that the literal interpretation of the word *brother*, placed, as it is here, by the side of the word *mother*, is the most natural.—The answer of Jesus signifies, not that family ties are in His eyes of no value (comp. John xix. 26), but that they are subordinate to a tie of a higher and more durable nature. In those women who accompanied Him, exercising over Him a mother's care (vers. 2 and 3), and in those disciples who so faithfully associated themselves with Him in His work, He had found a family which supplied the place of that which had deliberately forsaken Him. And this new spiritual relationship, eternal even as the God in whom it was based, was it not superior in dignity to a relationship of blood, which the least accident might break? In this saying He expresses a tender and grateful affection for those faithful souls whose love every day supplied the place of the dearest domestic affection. He makes no mention of father; this place belongs in His eyes to God alone. We see how the description of the actual circumstances, given by Mark, enables us to understand the appropriateness of this saying. This fact proves that Luke knew neither the narrative of this evangelist, nor that of the alleged proto-Mark. How could he in sheer wilfulness have neglected the light which such a narrative threw upon the whole scene?

9. *The Stilling of the Storm:* viii. 22–25.—We come now to a series of narratives which are found united together in the three Syn. (Matt. viii. 18 et seq.; Mark iv. 35 et seq.): the storm, the demoniac, the daughter of Jairus, together with the woman afflicted with an issue of blood. From the connection of these incidents in our three Gospels, it has frequently been inferred that their authors made use of a common written

source. But, 1. How, in this case, has it come to pass that this cycle fills quite a different place in Matthew (immediately after the Sermon on the Mount) from that which it occupies in the other two? And 2. How came Matthew to intercalate, between the return of Jesus and the account of the daughter of Jairus, two incidents of the greatest importance—the healing of the paralytic (ix. 1 et seq.), and the call of Matthew—with the feast and the discourse which follow it (ver. 9 et seq.), incidents which in Mark and Luke occupy quite a different place? The use of a written source does not accord with such independent arrangement. It is a very simple explanation to maintain that, in the traditional teaching, it was customary to relate these three facts together, probably for the simple reason that they were chronologically connected, and that to this natural cycle there were sometimes added, as in Matthew, other incidents which did not belong historically to this precise time. —That which renders this portion particularly remarkable is, that in it we behold the miraculous power of Jesus at its full height: power over the forces of nature (the storm); over the powers of darkness (the demoniacs); lastly, over death (the daughter of Jairus).

Vers. 22–25.[1] Miracles of this kind, while manifesting the original power of man over nature, are at the same time the prelude of the regeneration of the visible world which is to crown the moral renovation of humanity (Rom. viii.).—From Matthew's narrative it might be inferred that this voyage took place on the evening of the same day on which the Sermon on the Mount was spoken. But, on the other hand, too many things took place, according to Matthew himself, for the limits of a single day. Mark places this embarkation on the evening of the day on which Jesus spoke the parable of the sower; this note of the time is much more probable. Luke's indication of the time is more general: *on one of these days*, but it does not invalidate Mark's.—The object of this excursion was to preach the gospel in the country situated on the other side of the sea, in accordance with the plan drawn out in viii. 1.—According to Mark, the disciples' vessel was accompanied by

[1] Ver. 24. ℵ[a] X. Γ. several Mnn. Syr[cur]. It[plerique], omit ἐπιστατα ἐπιστατα. D. reads κυριε κυριε.—ℵ. E. F. G. H. some Mnn. It[aliq]., ἐπαυσατο instead of ἐπαυσαντο.—K. Δ. Π. several Mnn. add μεγαλη to γαληνη (taken from the parallel passages).

other boats. When they started, the weather was calm, and Jesus, yielding to fatigue, fell asleep. The pencil of Mark has preserved this never-to-be-forgotten picture: the Lord reclining on the hinder part of the ship, with His head upon a pillow that had been placed there by some friendly hand. It often happens on lakes surrounded by mountains, that sudden and violent storms of wind descend from the neighbouring heights, especially towards evening, after a warm day. This well-known phenomenon is described by the word κατέβη, *came down.*[1]—In the expression συνεπληροῦντο, *they were filled,* there is a confusion of the vessel with those whom it carries. —The term ἐπιστάτα is peculiar to Luke; Mark says διδάσκαλε, Matthew κύριε. How ridiculous these variations would be if all three made use of the same document!—The 24th verse describes one of the sublimest scenes the earth has ever beheld: man, calmly confident in God, by the perfect union of his will with that of the Almighty, controlling the wild fury of the blind forces of nature. The term ἐπετίμησε, *rebuked,* is an allusion to the hostile character of this power in its present manifestation. Jesus speaks not only to the wind, but to the water; for the agitation of the waves (κλύδων) continues after the hurricane is appeased.

In Mark and Luke, Jesus first of all delivers His disciples from danger, then He speaks to their heart. In Matthew, he first upbraids them, and then stills the storm. This latter course appears less in accordance with the wisdom of the Lord. —But why did the apostles deserve blame for their want of faith? Ought they to have allowed the tempest to follow its course, in the assurance that with Jesus with them they ran no danger, or that in any case He would awake in time? Or did Jesus expect that one of them, by an act of prayer and commanding faith, would still the tempest? It is more natural to suppose that what He blames in them is the state of trouble and agitation in which He finds them on awaking. When faith possesses the heart, its prayer may be passionate

[1] On these hurricanes, to which the Lake of Gennesareth is particularly exposed, comp. W. Thompson, *The Land and the Book*, London 1868, p. 375 (cited by M. Furrer): "Storms of wind rush wildly through the deep mountain gorges which descend from the north and north-east, and are not only violent, but sudden; they often take place when the weather is perfectly clear."

and urgent, but it will not be full of trouble. There is nothing surprising, whatever any one may say, in the exclamation attributed to those who witnessed this scene (ver. 25): first, because there were other persons there besides the apostles (Mark iv. 36); next, because such incidents, even when similar occurrences have been seen before, always appear new; lastly, because this was the first time that the apostle saw their Master contend with the blind forces of nature.

Strauss maintains that this is a pure myth. Keim, in opposition to him, alleges the evident antiquity of the narrative (the sublime majesty of the picture of Jesus, the absence of all ostentation from His words and actions, and the simple expression of wonder on the part of the spectators). The narrative, therefore, must have some foundation in fact, in some natural incident of water-travel, which has been idealized in accordance with such words as Ps. cvii. 23 et seq., and the appeal to Jonah (i. 4–6): "Awake, O sleeper." There, says criticism, you see how this history was made. We should rather say, how the trick was done.

10. *The Healing of the Demoniac:* viii. 26–39.—This portion brings before us a storm no less difficult to still, and a yet more striking victory. Luke and Mark mention only one demoniac; Matthew speaks of two. The hypothesis of a common written source here encounters a difficulty which is very hard for it to surmount. But criticism has expedients to meet all cases: according to Holtzmann, Matthew, who had omitted the healing of the demoniac at Capernaum, here repairs this omission, "by grouping the possessed who had been neglected along with this new case" (p. 255). This is a sample of what is called at the present day critical sagacity. As if the evangelists had no faith themselves in what they wrote with a view to win the faith of others! Why should it be deemed impossible for the two maniacs to have lived together, and for the healing of only one of the two to have presented the striking features mentioned in the following narrative? However it was, we have here a proof of the independence of Matthew's narratives on the one hand, and of those of Mark and Luke on the other.

Vers. 26–29.[1] *The Encounter.*—There are three readings of

[1] Ver. 26. T. R., with A. R. Γ. Δ. Λ. and 10 other Mjj. many Mnn. Syr., reads

the name of the inhabitants, and unfortunately they are also found in both the other Syn. Epiphanius mentions the following forms: **Γεργεσηνῶν** in Mark and Luke (but it is probable that, in the case of the Luke, we should read **Γερασηνῶν** in this Father); **Γαδαρηνῶν** in Matthew (**Γεργεσαίων** in some manuscripts). It would seem to follow from a passage in Origen (*Ad Joh.* t. vi. c. 24) that the most widely-diffused reading in his time was **Γερασηνῶν**, that **Γαδαρηνῶν** was only read in a small number of manuscripts, and that **Γεργεσηνῶν** was only a conjecture of his own. He states that *Gerasa* is a city of Arabia, and that there is neither sea nor lake near it; that *Gadara*, a city of Judæa, well known for its warm baths, has neither a deep-lying piece of water with steep banks in its neighbourhood, nor is there any sea; whilst, near the lake of Tiberias, the remains are to be seen of a city called *Gergesa*, near which there is a precipice overlooking the sea, and at which the place is still shown where the herd of swine cast themselves down. The MSS. are divided between these readings after the most capricious fashion. The great majority of the Mnn. in Matthew read **Γερασηνῶν**, in Mark and Luke **Γεργεσηνῶν**. The Latin documents are almost all in favour of **Γεργεσηνῶν**. Tischendorf (8th edition) reads **Γαδαρηνῶν** in Matthew, **Γερασηνῶν** in Mark, **Γεργεσηνῶν** in Luke. Bleek thinks that the primitive Gospel on which, in his opinion, our three Syn. are based, read **Γερασηνῶν**, but that, owing to the improbability of this reading, it was changed by certain copyists into **Γαδαρηνῶν**, and by Origen into **Γεργεσηνῶν**. Looking simply at the fact, this last name appears to him to agree with it best. In fact, *Gerasa* was a large city situated at a considerable distance to the south-east, on the borders of Arabia; and the reading **Γερασηνῶν** can only be admitted by supposing that the district dependent on this city extended as far as to the sea of Galilee, which is inadmissible, although Stephen of Byzantium calls Gerasa a city of Decapolis. *Gadara* is nearer,

Γαδαρηνων. B. D. It. Vg., Γερασηνων. ℵ. L. X. Z. some Mnn. Cop. Epiph., Γεργεσηνων.—Ver. 27. ℵ. B. E. Z. some Mnn. omit αυτω.—ℵ. B., εχων instead of ειχεν.—ℵ. B. L. Z. some Mnn., και χρονω ικανων instead of εκ χρονων ικανων και.—Ver. 28. ℵ. B. L. X. Z. some Mnn. Syr. It. omit και before ανακραξας.—Ver. 29. B. F. M. Λ. Z., παρηγγειλε instead of παρηγγελλεν, which is the reading of T. R. with 16 Mjj. several Mnn. Syr., etc.—Ver. 29. The Mss. vary between ηδεσμευετο and εδεσμευετο.—The Mss. vary between δαιμονος and του δαιμονιου.

being only a few leagues from the south-east end of the sea of Galilee. Josephus calls it the metropolis of the Peræa; Pliny reckons it among the cities of Decapolis. Its suburbs might extend as far as the sea. But it is highly natural to suppose, that these two cities being so well known, the copyists substituted their names for that of *Gergesa*, which was generally unknown. It is a confirmation of this view, that the existence of a town of this name is attested not only by Origen, Eusebius, and Jerome, but by the recent discovery of ruins bearing the name of *Gersa* or *Khersa*, towards the embouchure of the Wady Semakh. The course of the walls is still visible, according to Thompson (p. 375). This traveller also says, that "the sea is so near the foot of the mountain at this spot, that animals having once got fairly on to the incline, could not help rolling down into the water" (p. 377). Wilson (*Athenæum*, 1866, i. p. 438) states that this place answers all the conditions of the Bible narrative.[1] The true reading, therefore, would be *Γεργεσηνῶν* or *Γεργεσαίων*. This name, so little known, must have been altered first into *Γερασηνῶν*, which has some resemblance to it, and then into *Γαδαρηνῶν*.[2]

On the demoniacs, see iv. 33.—The 27th verse gives a description of the demoniac, which is afterwards finished in the 29th. This first description (ver. 27) only contains that which presented itself *immediately* to the observation of an eye-witness of the scene. The second and fuller description (ver. 29) is accounted for by the command of Jesus, which, to be intelligible, required a more detailed statement of the state of the possessed. This interruption, which is not found in Mark, reflects very naturally the impression of an eye-witness; it demonstrates the independence of the respective narratives of Matthew and Luke. The plural δαιμόνια (*demons*), explained afterwards (ver. 30) by the afflicted man himself, refers doubtless to the serious nature and multiplicity of the symptoms—melancholy, mania, violence, occasioned by a number of relapses

[1] We cite these two authors from M. Konrad Furrer: *Die Bedeutung der bibl. Geographie*, p. 19.

[2] M. Heer has recently proposed (*Der Kirchenfreund*, 13th May 1870) a view which would more easily account for the reading *Gerasa* found in the MSS. by Origen: The original name of the place *Gergesa*, abbreviated into *Gersa*, might be altered in popular speech into *Gerasa*, which it would be necessary not to confound with the name of the Arabian city.

(see on viii. 2 and xi. 24–26). His refusing to wear clothes or remain in a house is connected with that alienation from society which characterizes such states. The Alex. reading: "who for a long while past had worn no clothes," is evidently an error. The note of time cannot refer to a circumstance altogether so subordinate as that of clothing.—The Levitical uncleanness of the tombs ensured to this man the solitude he sought.—The sight of Jesus appears to have produced an extraordinary impression upon him. The holy, calm, gentle majesty, tender compassion, and conscious sovereignty which were expressed in the aspect of our Lord, awakened in him, by force of contrast, the humbling consciousness of his own state of moral disorder. He felt himself at once attracted and repelled by this man; this led to a violent crisis in him, which revealed itself first of all in a cry. Then, like some ferocious beast submitting to the power of his subduer, he runs and kneels, protesting all the while, in the name of the spirit of which he is still the organ, against the power which is exerted over him. Luke says: προσπίπτειν, not προσκυνεῖν (Mark). The former term does not imply any religious feeling.—On the expression: *What have I to do with thee?* see on iv. 24. The name *Jesus* is wanting in Matthew, and it looks strange. How did he know this name? Perhaps he had heard Jesus talked of, and instinctively recognised Him. Or perhaps there was a supernatural knowledge appertaining to this extraordinary state. The expression: *Son of the most high God,* is explained by the prevalence of polytheism in those countries where there was a large heathen population. Josephus calls Gadara *a Greek city.* We must not infer from this that this man was a heathen.

In his petition, ver. 28, the demoniac still identifies himself with the alien spirit which holds him in his power. The torment which he dreads is being sent away *into the abyss* (ver. 31); Matthew adds, *before the time.* The power of acting on the world, for beings that are alienated from God and move only within the void of their own subjectivity, is a temporary solace to their unrest. To be deprived of this power is for them just what a return to prison is for the captive. If we read παρήγγειλε, we must give this aor. the meaning of a plus-perfect: For He *had commanded.* But MS. authority is rather in favour of the imperf. παρήγγελλεν: "For *He was commanding him.*" This tense indicates a continuous action, which does not immediately produce its effect. The demon's cry of distress, *Torment me not,* is called forth by the strong and continued pressure which the command of Jesus put upon him. This imperf. corresponds with Mark's ἔλεγε γάρ. We find in these two analogous forms the common type of the traditional narration.—The *for,* which follows, explains this imperfect. The evil did not yield instantly, because it had taken too deep root. Συνηρπάκει, *it kept him in its possession.* Πολλοῖς χρόνοις may signify *for a long time past* or *oftentimes.* With the second sense, there would be an allusion to a series of relapses, each of which had aggravated the evil.

Vers. 30–33.[1] *The Cure.*—To this prayer, in which the victim became involuntarily the advocate of his tormentor, Jesus replies by putting a question: He asks the afflicted man his name. For what purpose? There is nothing so suitable as a calm and simple question to bring a madman to himself. Above all, there is no more natural way of awakening in a man who is beside himself the consciousness of his own personality, than to make him tell his own name. A man's name becomes the expression of his character, and a summary of the history of his life. Now, the first condition of any cure of this afflicted man was a return to the distinct feeling of his own personality.—There was at this time a word which, more than any other, called up the idea of the resistless might of the conqueror under whom Israel was then suffering oppression. This was the word Legion. The sound of this word called up the thought of those victorious armies before which the whole world bowed down. So it is by this term that this afflicted man describes the power which oppresses him, and with which he still confounds himself. The expression, *many demons,* is explained by the multiplicity and diversity of the symptoms (ver. 29).—To this answer the demoniac adds, in the name of his tyrant, a fresh request. The demon understands that he must release his prey; but he does not want to enter forthwith into a condition in which contact

[1] Ver. 30. ℵ. B. Syr[sch]. It. omit λεγων.—Ver. 31. The Mss. vary between παρεκαλουν and παρεκαλει.—Ver. 32. The Mss. vary between βοσκομενη and βοσκομενων.—ℵ[c] B. C. L. Z. some Mnn. It[plerique], παρεκαλεσαν instead of παρεκαλουν.

with terrestrial realities would be no longer possible to him.—In Mark there is here found the strange expression: " not to send them *out of the country*," which may mean, *to the desert*, where unclean but not captive spirits were thought to dwell, or into *the abyss*, whence they went forth to find a temporary abode upon the earth. The sequel shows that the second meaning must be preferred. Jesus makes no answer to this request. His silence is ordinarily regarded as signifying consent. But the silence of Jesus simply means that He insists on the command which He has just given. When He wishes to reply in the affirmative,—as, for instance, at the end of ver. 32,—he does so distinctly. This explanation is confirmed by Matthew, " *If thou cast us out* . . ." Their request to enter into the swine only refers, therefore, to the way by which they were suffered to go into the abyss. What is the explanation of this request, and of the permission which Jesus accorded to it? As to these evil spirits, we can understand that it might be pleasant to them, before losing all power of action, to find one more opportunity of doing an injury. Jesus, on his part, has in view a twofold result. The Jewish exorcists, in order to assure their patients that they were cured, were accustomed to set a pitcher of water or some other object in the apartment where the expulsion took place, which the demon took care to upset in going out. What they were accustomed to do as charlatans, Jesus sees it good to do as a physician. The identification of the sick man with his demon had been a long-existing fact of consciousness (vers. 27 and 29). A decisive sign of the reality of the departure of the evil power was needed to give the possessed perfect assurance of his deliverance. Besides this reason, there was probably another. The theocratic feeling of Jesus had been wounded by the sight of these immense herds of animals which the law declared unclean. Such an occupation as this showed how completely the line of demarcation between Judaism and paganism was obliterated in this country. Jesus desired, by a sensible judgment, to reclaim the people, and prevent their being still more unjudaized.

The influence exerted by the demons on the herd was in no sense a possession. None but a moral being can be morally possessed. But we know that several species of animals are accessible to collective influences,—that swine, in particular, readily yield to panics of terror. The idea that it was the demoniac himself who frightened them, by throwing himself into the herd, is incompatible with the text.—Mark, whose narrative is always distinguished by the exactness of its details, says that the number of the swine was about two thousand. An item of his own invention, says De Wette; an appendix of later tradition, according to Bleek: here we see the necessary consequence of the critical system, according to which Mark is supposed to have made use of the text of the other two, or of a document common to them all.—The number 2000 cannot serve to prove the *individual* possession of the swine by the demons (*legion,* ver. 30), for a legion comprised 4000 men.—The question has been asked, Had Jesus the right to dispose in this way of other people's property? One might as well ask whether Peter had the right to dispose of the lives of Ananias and Sapphira! It is one of those cases in which the power, by its very nature, guarantees the right.

Vers. 34–39.[1] *The Effect produced.*—First, on the people of the country; next, on the afflicted man. The owners of the herd dwelt in the city and neighbourhood. They came to convince themselves with their own eyes of the loss of which they had been informed by the herdsmen. On reaching the spot, they beheld a sight which impressed them deeply. The demoniac was known all through the country, and was an object of universal terror. They found him calm and restored. So great a miracle could not fail to reveal to them the power of God, and awaken their conscience. Their fears were confirmed by the account given them of the scene which had just occurred by persons who were with Jesus, and had witnessed it (*οἱ ἰδόντες*, ver. 36). These persons were not the herdsmen; for the cure was wrought at a considerable distance from the place where the herd was feeding (Matt. viii. 30). They were the apostles and the people who had passed over the sea with them (Mark iv. 36). The *καί, also,* is undoubtedly authentic;

[1] Ver. 34. The Mss. vary between γεγονος and γεγενημενον.—Απελθοντες, in the T. R., is only read in a few Mnn.—Ver. 35. ℵ* B., εξηλθεν instead of εξεληλυθει.—Ver. 36. ℵ. B. C. D. L. P. X. some Mnn. and Vss. omit και before οι ιδοντες.—Ver. 37. The Mss. vary between ηρωτησαν (Byz.) and ηρωτησεν (Alex.).—ℵ* L. P. X., Γεργεσηνων. B. C. D. It. Vg., Γερασηνων instead of Γαδαρηνων, which is the reading of T. R. with 14 Mjj. many Mnn. Syr.

the latter account was supplementary to that of the herdsmen, which referred principally to the loss of the herd.—The fear of the inhabitants was doubtless of a superstitious nature. But Jesus did not wish to force Himself upon them, for it was still the season of grace, and grace limits itself to making its offers. He yielded to the request of the inhabitants, who, regarding Him as a judge, dreaded further and still more terrible chastisement at His hand. He consents, therefore, to depart from them, but not without leaving them a witness of His grace in the person of him who had become a living monument of it. The restored man, who feels his moral existence linked as it were to the person of Jesus, begs to be permitted to accompany Him. Jesus was already in the ship, Mark tells us. He does not consent to this entreaty. In Galilee, where it was necessary to guard against increasing the popular excitement, He forbade those He healed publishing abroad their cure. But in this remote country, so rarely visited by Him, and which He was obliged to leave so abruptly, He needed a missionary to testify to the greatness of the Messianic work which God was at this time accomplishing for His people. There is a fine contrast between the expression of Jesus: "What *God* hath done for thee," and that of the man: "What *Jesus* had done for him." Jesus refers all to God; but the afflicted man could not forget the instrument. The whole of the latter part of the narrative is omitted in Matthew. Mark indicates the field of labour of this new apostle as comprising not his own city merely, but the whole of the Decapolis.

Volkmar applies here his system of allegorical interpretation. This incident is nothing, according to him, but the symbolical representation of the work of Paul amongst the Gentiles. The demoniac represents the heathen world; the chains with which they tried to bind him are legislative enactments, such as those of Lycurgus and Solon; the swine, the obscenities of idolatry; the refusal of Jesus to yield to the desire of the restored demoniac, when he wished to accompany Him, the obstacles which Jewish-Christians put in the way of the entrance of the converted heathen into the Church; the request that Jesus would withdraw, the irritation caused in heathen countries by the success of Paul (the riot at Ephesus, *ex. gr.*). Keim is opposed to this unlimited allegorizing, which borders, indeed, on absurdity. He very properly objects, that the demoniac is not even (as is the case with the Canaanitish woman) spoken of as a heathen; that the precise locality, so little known, to which the incident is referred, is a proof of its historical reality; that the request to Jesus to leave the country is a fact without any corresponding example, which does not look like imitation, but has the very features of truth. In short, he only objects to the episode of the swine, which appears to him to be a legendary amplification. But is it likely that the preachers of the gospel would have admitted into their teaching an incident so remarkable, if it could be contradicted by the population of a whole district, which is distinctly pointed out? If possession is only, as Keim thinks, an ordinary malady, this conclusion is certainly inevitable. But if there is any degree of reality attaching to the mysterious notion of possession, it would be difficult to determine *à priori* what might not result from such a state. The picture forms a whole, in which each incident implies all the rest. The request made to Jesus to leave the country, in which Keim acknowledges a proof of authenticity, is only explained by the loss of the swine. Keim admits too much or too little. Either Volkmar and his absurdities, or the frank acceptance of the narrative,—this is the only alternative (comp. Heer's fine work, already referred to, *Kirchenfreund*, Nos. 10 and 11, 1870).

11. *The Raising of Jairus' Daughter:* viii. 40–56.—In Mark and Luke, the following incident follows immediately on the return from the Decapolis. According to Luke, the multitude which He had left behind Him when He went away had not dispersed; they were expecting Him, and received Him on His landing. According to Mark, it collected together again as soon as His arrival was known. In Matthew, two facts are interposed between His arrival and the resurrection of Jairus' daughter—the healing of the paralytic of Capernaum, and the calling of the Apostle Matthew. As the publican's house was probably situated near the port, the second of these facts might certainly have happened immediately on His landing; but, in any case, the feast given by the publican could not have taken place until the evening, and after what occurred in the house of Jairus. But the same supposition will not apply to the healing of the paralytic, which must be assigned to quite another time, as is the case with Mark and Luke.

Vers. 40–42.[1] *The Request.*—The term ἀποδέχεσθαι in-

[1] Ver. 40. ℵ^ca. B. L. R. some Mnn. Syr., εν δε τω instead of εγενετο δε εν τω. —Ver. 42. C. D. P., πορευεσθαι instead of υπαγειν.—C. L. U., συνεθλιβον for συνεπνιγον.

dicates a warm welcome.—Mark and Luke mention the age of the young girl, which Matthew omits.—The circumstance of her being an only daughter, added by Luke, more fully explains the father's distress. Criticism, of course, does not fail to draw its own conclusions from the same circumstance being found already in vii. 12. As if an only son and an only daughter could not both be found in Israel! According to Mark and Luke, the young girl was dying; in Matthew, she is already dead. This evangelist tells the story here, as elsewhere, in a summary manner; he combines in a single message the arrival of the father, and the subsequent arrival of the messenger announcing her death. The process is precisely similar to that already noticed in the account of the healing of the centurion's servant. Matthew is interested simply in the fact of the miracle and the word of Jesus.

Vers. 43–48.[1] *The Interruption.*—The preposition πρός, in **προσαναλώσασα**, expresses the fact that, *in addition to* these long sufferings, she now found herself destitute of resources. Mark expresses with a little more force the injury which the physicians had done her. Hitzig and Holtzmann maintain that Luke, being a physician himself, intentionally tones down these details from the proto-Mark. We find nothing here but Mark's characteristic amplification.—The malady from which this woman suffered rendered her Levitically unclean; it was even, according to the law, a sufficient justification for a divorce (Lev. xv. 25; Deut. xxiv. 1). Hence, no doubt, her desire to get cured as it were by stealth, without being obliged to make a public avowal of her disorder. The faith which actuated her was not altogether free from superstition, for she conceived of the miraculous power of Jesus as acting in a purely physical manner. The word κράσπεδον, which we translate by *the hem* (of the garment), denotes one of the four tassels or tufts of scarlet woollen cord attached to the four corners of the outer robe, which were intended to remind the Israelites of their law. Their name was *zitzit*

[1] Ver. 43. All the Mjj., ιατροις instead of εις ιατρους, which is the reading of T. R. with some Mnn.—Ver. 45. The Mss. vary between οι συν αυτω (Alex.) and οι μετα αυτου (T. R. Byz.).—ℵ. B. L. some Mnn. omit the words και λεγει . . . μου.—Ver. 46. ℵ. B. L., εξεληλυθυιαν instead of εξελθουσαν.—Ver. 47. 9 Mjj. Syr. It. Vg. omit αυτω after απηγγειλεν.—Ver. 48. ℵ. B. D. L. Z. some Mnn. and Vss. omit θαρσει.

(Num. xv. 38). As this robe, which was of a rectangular form, was worn like a woman's shawl, two of the corners being allowed to hang down close together on the back, we see the force of the expression *came behind.* Had it been, as is ordinarily understood, the lower hem of the garment which she attempted to touch, she could not have succeeded, on account of the crowd which surrounded Jesus. This word κράσπεδον, according to Passow, comes from κέρας and πέδον, the forward part of a plain; or better, according to Schleusner, from κεκραμένον εἰς πέδον, *that which hangs down towards the ground.*—Both Mark and Luke date the cure from the moment that she touched. Matthew speaks of it as taking place a little later, and as the effect of Jesus' *word.* But this difference belongs, as we shall see, to Matthew's omission of the following details, and not to any difference of view as to the efficient cause of the cure.

The difficulty about this miracle is, that it seems to have been wrought outside the consciousness and will of Jesus, and thus appears to be of a magical character.—In each of Jesus' miracles there are, as it were, two poles: the receptivity of the person who is the subject of it, and the activity of Him by whom it is wrought. The maximum of action in one of these factors may correspond with the minimum of action in the other. In the case of the impotent man at the pool of Bethesda, in whom it was necessary to excite even the desire to be cured, as well as in the raising of the dead, the human receptivity was reduced to its minimum. The activity of the Lord in these cases reached its highest degree of initiation and intensity. In the present instance it is the reverse. The receptivity of the woman reaches such a degree of energy, that it snatches, as it were, the cure from Jesus. The action of Jesus is here confined to that willingness to bless and save which always animated Him in His relations with men.—He did not, however, remain unconscious of the virtue which He had just put forth; but He perceives that there is a tincture of superstition in the faith which had acted in this way towards Him; and, as Riggenbach admirably shows (*Leben Jesu,* p. 442), His design in what follows is to purify this incipient faith. But in order to do this, it is necessary to discover the author of the deed. There is no reason for not attributing to Jesus the ignorance implied in the question, "Who touched me?" Anything like feigning ignorance ill comports with the candour of His character.—Peter shows his usual forwardness, and ventures to remonstrate with Jesus. But, so far from this detail implying any ill-will towards this apostle, Luke attributes the same fault to the other apostles, and equally without any sinister design, since Mark does the same thing (ver. 31). Jesus does not stop to rebuke His disciple; He pursues His inquiry; only He now substitutes the assertion, *Somebody hath touched me,* for the question, *Who touched me?* Further, He no longer lays stress upon the person, but upon the *act,* in reply to the observation of Peter, which tended to deny it. The verb *ἅψασθαι, to feel about,* denotes a voluntary, deliberate touch, and not merely an accidental contact. Mark adds that, while putting this question, He cast around Him a scrutinizing glance. The reading **ἐξεληλυθυῖαν** (Alex.) signifies properly: "I feel myself in the condition of a man from whom a force has been withdrawn." This is somewhat artificial. The received reading, *ἐξελθοῦσαν,* merely denotes the outgoing of a miraculous power, which is more simple. Jesus had been inwardly apprised of the influence which He had just exerted.

The joy of success gives the woman courage to acknowledge both her act and her malady; but the words, *before all the people,* are designed to show how much this avowal cost her. Luke says *trembling,* to which Mark adds *fearing;* she feels afraid of having sinned against the Lord by acting without His knowledge. He reassures her (ver. 48), and confirms her in the possession of the blessing which she had in some measure taken by stealth. This last incident is also brought out by Mark (ver. 34). The intention of Jesus, in the inquiry He had just instituted, appears more especially in the words, *Thy faith hath saved thee;* thy faith, and not, as thou wast thinking, the material touch. Jesus thus assigns to the moral sphere (in Luke and Mark as well as in Matthew) the virtue which she referred solely to the physical sphere. The word *θάρσει, take courage,* which is wanting in several Alex., is probably taken from Matthew. The term *saved* implies more than the healing of the body. Her recovered health is a link which henceforth will attach her to Jesus as the personification of salvation; and this link is to her the beginning of salvation in the full sense of the term.—The words in Matthew, "And the woman was healed *from that same hour*," refer to the time occupied by the incident, taken altogether.

Eusebius says (*H. E.* vii. 18, ed. Lœmmer) that this woman was a heathen and dwelt at Paneas, near the source of the Jordan, and that in his time her house was still shown, having at its entrance two brass statues on a stone pedestal. One represented a woman on her knees, with her hands held out before her, in the attitude of a suppliant; the other, a man standing with his cloak thrown over his shoulder, and his hand extended towards the woman. Eusebius had been into the house himself, and had seen this statue, which represented, it was said, the features of Jesus.

Vers. 49–56.[1] *The Prayer granted.*—We may imagine how painful this delay had been for the father of the child. The message, which just at this moment is brought to him, reduces him to despair. Matthew, in his very summary account, omits all these features of the story; and interpreters, like De Wette, who maintain that this Gospel was the source of the other two, are obliged to regard the details in Mark and Luke as just so many embellishments of their own invention! The present πίστευε, in the received reading, signifies: "Only persevere, without fainting, in the faith which thou hast shown thus far." Some Alex. read the aor. πιστεῦσον: "Only exercise faith! Make a new effort in view of the unexpected difficulty which has arisen." This second meaning seems to agree better with the position of μόνον, *only*, before the verb. Perhaps the other reading is taken from Mark, where all the authorities read πίστευε.

The reading of the T. R., εἰσελθών, *having entered*, ver. 51, is not nearly so well supported as the reading ἐλθών, *having come.* But with either reading there is a distinction observed

[1] Ver. 49. ℵ. B. L. X. Z. some Mnn. omit αυτω.—ℵ. B. D., μηκετι instead of μη.—Ver. 50. 6 Mjj. some Mnn. Syr. It. omit λεγων after αυτω.—B. L. Z., πιστευσον instead of πιστευε.—Ver. 51. T. R., with D. V. some Mnn., εισελθων instead of ελθων.—The Mss. vary between τινα and ουδενα.—The Mss. vary between Ιωαννην και Ιακωβον and Ιακωβον και Ιωαννην (taken from Mark).—Ver. 52. 8 Mjj. some Mnn. Syr. It., ου γαρ instead of ουκ before απεθανεν.—Ver. 54. ℵ. B. D. L. X. some Mnn. and Vss. omit εκβαλων εξω παντας και, which is the reading of T. R. with all the rest (taken from Matthew).

between the arrival (ἐλθών) or entrance (εἰσελθών) into the *house* and the entrance into the chamber of the sick girl, to which the εἰσελθεῖν which follows refers: "He suffered no man *to go in*." What obliges us to give this sense to this infinitive, is the mention of *the mother* amongst the persons excepted from the prohibition; for if here also entrance *into the house* was in question, this would suppose that the mother had left it, which is scarcely probable, when her daughter had only just expired. Jesus' object in only admitting just the indispensable witnesses into the room, was to diminish as far as possible the fame of the work He was about to perform. As to the three apostles, it was necessary that they should be present, in order that they might be able afterwards to testify to what was done.

The following scene, vers. 52, 53, took place at the entrance of the sick chamber. The πάντες, *all*, are the servants, neighbours, relations, and professional mourners (αὐληταί, Matthew) assembled in the vestibule, who also wanted to make their way into the chamber. Olshausen, Neander, and others infer from Jesus' words, that the child was simply in a lethargy; but this explanation is incompatible with the expression εἰδότες, *knowing well*, ver. 53. If this had been the idea of the writer, he would have employed the word δοκοῦντες, *believing that* . . . On the rest of the verse, see vii. 14. By the words, "*She is not dead, but sleepeth*," Jesus means that, in the order of things over which He presides, death is death no longer, but assumes the character of a temporary slumber (John xi. 11, explained by ver. 14). Baur maintains that Luke means, ver. 53, that the apostles also joined in the laugh against Jesus, and that it is with this in view that the evangelist has chosen the general term *all* (ver. 52; *Evang.* p. 458). In this case it would be necessary to include amongst the πάντες the father and mother!!—The words, *having put them all out*, in the T. R., are a gloss derived from Mark and Matthew. It has arisen in this way: Mark expressly mentions *two* separate dismissals, one of the crowd and nine apostles at the entrance of the house, and another of the people belonging to the house not admitted into the chamber of the dead (ver. 40). As in Luke the word *enter* (ver. 51) had been wrongly referred to the first of these acts it was thought necessary to mention here the second, at first in the margin, and afterwards in the text, in accordance with the parallel passages.—The command to give the child something to eat (ver. 55) is related by Luke alone. It shows the perfect calmness of the Lord when performing the most wonderful work. He acts like a physician who has just felt the pulse of his patient, and gives instructions respecting his diet for the day.—Mark, who is fond of local colouring, has preserved the Aramæan form of the words of Jesus, also the graphic detail, *immediately the child began to walk about.* In these features of the narrative we recognise the account of an eye-witness, in whose ear the voice of Jesus still sounds, and who still sees the child that had been brought to life again moving about. Matthew omits all details. The fact itself simply is all that has any bearing on the Messianic demonstration, which is his object. Thus each follows his own path while presenting the common substratum of fact as tradition had preserved it. On the prohibition of Jesus, ver. 56, see on v. 14 and viii. 39.

According to Volkmar, the woman with an issue would be only the personification of the *believing* Jews, in whom their rabbis (the *physicians* of ver. 43) had been unable to effect a moral cure, but whom Jesus will save after having healed the heathen (the return from Gadara); and the daughter of Jairus represents the dead Judaism of the synagogue, which the gospel alone can restore to life. Keim acknowledges the insufficiency of symbolism to explain such narratives. He admits the cure of the woman as a fact, but maintains that she herself, by her faith, was the sole contributor towards it. In the resurrection of the daughter of Jairus, he sees either a myth, modelled after the type of the resurrection of the Shunammite widow's son by Elisha (a return to Strauss), or a natural awaking from a lethargy (a return to Paulus). But is not the local colouring quite as decided in this narrative as in that of the possessed of Gadara, of which Keim on this ground maintains the historical truth? And as to an awakening from a lethargy, what has he to reply to Zeller? (See p. 342, note.)

FOURTH CYCLE.—IX. 1–50.

From the Mission of the Twelve to the Departure from Galilee.

This cycle describes the close of the Galilean ministry. It embraces six narrations: 1*st.* The mission of the Twelve, and the impression made on Herod by the public activity of

Jesus (ix. 1–9). *2d.* The multiplication of the loaves (vers 10–17). *3d.* The first communication made by Jesus to His apostles respecting His approaching sufferings (vers. 18–27). *4th.* The transfiguration (vers. 28–36). *5th.* The cure of the lunatic child (vers. 37–43*a*). *6th.* Some circumstances which preceded the departure from Galilee (vers. 43*b* to 50).

1. *The Mission of the Twelve, and the Fears of Herod:* ix. 1–9. —The mission with which the Twelve were entrusted marks a twofold advance in the work of Jesus. From the first Jesus had attached to Himself a great number of pious Jews as *disciples* (a first example occurs, v. 1–11; a second, ver. 27); from these He had chosen twelve to form a permanent college of *apostles* (vi. 13 et seq.). And now this last title is to become a more complete reality than it had hitherto been. Jesus sends them forth to the people of Galilee, and puts them through their first apprenticeship to their future mission, as it were, under His own eyes. With this advance in their position corresponds another belonging to the work itself. For six months Jesus devoted Himself almost exclusively to Galilee. The shores of the lake of Gennesaret, the western plateau, Decapolis itself on the eastern side, had all been visited by Him in turn. Before this season of grace for Galilee comes to an end, He desires to address one last solemn appeal to the conscience of this people on whom such lengthened evangelistic labours have been spent; and He does it by this mission, which He confides to the Twelve, and which is, as it were, the close of His own ministry. Mark also connects this portion with the preceding cycle by introducing between the two the visit to Nazareth (vi. 1–6), which, as a last appeal of the Saviour to this place, so dear to his heart, perfectly agrees with the position of affairs at this time.

Matthew, chap. x., also mentions this mission of the Twelve, connecting with it the catalogue of apostles and a long discourse on the apostolate, but he appears to place this fact earlier than Luke. Keim (ii. p. 308) thinks that Luke assigns it a place in nearer connection with the mission of the seventy disciples, in order that this second incident (a pure invention of Luke's) may be more certain to eclipse the former. In imputing to Luke this Machiavellian design against the Twelve, Keim forgets two things: 1. That, according to him, Luke invented the scene of the election of the Twelve (vi.) with the view of conferring on their ministry a *double and triple* con secration. After having had recourse to invention to exalt them, we are to suppose that he now invents to degrade them! 2. That the three Syn. are agreed in placing this mission of the Twelve just after the preceding cycle (the tempest, Gadara, Jairus), and that as Matthew places this cycle, as well as the Sermon on the Mount, which it closely follows, earlier than Luke, the different position which the mission of the Twelve occupies in the one from that which it holds in the other, results very naturally from this fact. It is to be observed that Mark, whose account of the sending forth of the Twelve fully confirms that of Luke, is quite independent of it, as is proved by a number of details which are peculiar to him (vi. 7, *two and two;* ver. 8, *save one staff only; ibid., put on two coats;* ver. 13, *they anointed with oil*).

1*st.* Vers. 1, 2.[1] *The Mission.*—There is something greater than preaching—this is to make preachers; there is something greater than performing miracles—this is to impart the power to perform them. It is this new stage which the work of Jesus here reaches. He labours to raise His apostles up to His own level. The expression *συγκαλεσάμενος, having called together,* indicates a solemn meeting; it expresses more than the term *προσκαλεῖσθαι, to call to Him,* used in Mark and Matthew. What would Baur have said if the first expression had been found in Matthew and the second in Luke, when throughout Luke's narrative as it is he sees an intention to depreciate this scene in comparison with that which follows, x. 1 et seq.?

In Jewish estimation, the most divine form of power is that of working miracles. It is with this, therefore, that Jesus begins: *δύναμις,* the power of execution; *ἐξουσία,* the authority which is the foundation of it; the demons will therefore *owe* them obedience, and will not fail, in fact, to *render* it. These two terms are opposed to the anxious and laboured practices of the exorcists.—*Πάντα*: all the different maladies coming under this head—melancholy, violence, mania, etc. . . . —*Θεραπεύειν, to heal,* depends neither on *δύναμις* nor *ἐξουσία,* but on *ἔδωκεν, He gave them;* there is no *ἐξουσία* in regard to diseases.—Such will be their power, their weapon. But these cures are not the end; they are only the means designed to

[1] Ver. 1. T. R., with E. F. H. U. several Mnn. It^{aliq}., reads *μαθητας αυτου* after *δωδεκα* (taken from Matthew); 11 Mjj. 100 Mnn. Syr. omit these words; ℵ. C* L. X. Λ. Z. some Mnn. It^{aliq}. substitute *αποστολους* for them.—Ver. 2. B. Syr^{cu} omit *τους ασθενουντας*; ℵ. A. D. L. X. read *τους ασθενεις*.

lend support to their message. The end is indicated in ver. 2. This is to proclaim throughout Galilee the coming of the kingdom of God, and at the same time to make the people feel the grave importance of the present time. It is a return to the ministry of John the Baptist, and of our Lord's at its commencement (Mark i. 15). This undertaking was within the power of the Twelve. "*To preach and to heal*" means "*to preach while healing.*" Only imagine the messengers of the Lord at the present day traversing our country with the announcement of His second coming being at hand, and confirming their message by miracles. What a sensation such a mission would produce!—According to Mark, the Lord sent them *two and two,* which recalls their distribution into pairs, Luke vi. 13–15; Matt. x. 2–4.

2*d.* Vers. 3–5.[1] *Their Instructions.*—"*And He said unto them, Take nothing for your journey, neither staves, nor scrip, neither bread, neither money; neither have two coats apiece.* 4. *And whatsoever house ye enter into, there abide and thence depart.* 5. *And whosoever will not receive you, when ye go out of that city, shake off the very dust from your feet for a testimony against them.*"—Ver. 3 contains instructions for their setting out; ver. 4, instructions respecting their arrival and stay; ver. 5, instructions for leaving each place.

Ver. 3. The feeling of confidence is the key to the injunctions of this verse: "Make no preparations, such as are ordinarily made on the eve of a journey; set out just as you are. God will provide for all your wants." The reply of the apostles, xxii. 35, proves that this promise was not unfulfilled. —Μηδέν, *nothing,* is a general negative, to which the subsequent μήτε, neither . . . nor . . . are subordinate. Mark, who commences with a simple μή, naturally continues with the negative μηδέ, *nor further.* Each writer, though expressing the same idea as the other, has his own particular way of doing it. Luke says, *neither staff,* or, according to another reading, *neither staves;* Matthew is like Luke; Mark, on the

[1] Ver. 3. ℵ. B. C* D. E* F. L. M. Z. several Mnn. Syr. It. Eus. read ῥαβδον instead of ῥαβδους, which is the reading of T. R. with 10 Mjj. many Mnn., but which appears taken from Matthew.—ℵ. B. C* F. L. Z. omit ανα.—Ver. 4. Vg., according to C., adds μη after εκειθεν.—Ver. 5. ℵ. B. C. D. L. X. Z. some Mnn. It[aliq]. omit και.

contrary, *save one staff only.* The contradiction in terms could not be greater, yet the agreement in idea is perfect. For as far as the sentiment is concerned which Jesus wishes to express, it is all one to say, "nothing, not even a staff" (Matthew and Luke), or, "nothing, except it be simply (or at most) a staff" (Mark). Ebrard makes the acute observation, that in Aramæan Jesus probably said, כי אם מטה, *for if . . . a staff*, an elliptical form also much used in Hebrew, and which may be filled up in two ways: For *if* you take *a staff, this of itself is quite sufficient* (Mark); or, *this of itself is too much* (Matthew and Luke). This saying of Jesus might therefore be reproduced in Greek either in one way or the other. But in no case could these two opposite forms be explained on the hypothesis of a common written Greek source. Bleek, who prefers the expression given in Matthew and Luke, does not even attempt to explain how that in Mark could have originated.—If we read *staves*, according to a various reading found in Luke and Matthew, the plural must naturally be applied to the two apostles travelling together.—Luke says, *Do not have each* (ἀνά, distributive) two coats, that is to say, each a change of coat, beyond what you wear. As they were not to have a travelling cloak (πήρα), they must have worn the second coat on their person; and it is this idea, implied by Luke, that is exactly expressed by Mark, "*neither put on two coats.*" The infinitive μὴ ἔχειν depends on εἶπε: "He said to them . . . not to have . . ."

As an unanswerable proof of an opposite tendency in Matthew and Luke, it is usual to cite the omission in this passage of the prohibition with which in Matthew this discourse commences (x. 5): "*Go not into the way of the Gentiles, and into any city of the Samaritans enter ye not: but go rather to the lost sheep of the house of Israel.*" But even in Matthew this prohibition is not absolute (*rather*) nor permanent (xxviii. 19, "Go and teach *all nations*"). It was therefore a restriction temporarily imposed upon the disciples, in consideration of the privilege accorded to the Jewish nation of being the cradle of the work of the Messiah. With some exceptions, for which there were urgent reasons, Jesus Himself was generally governed by this rule. He says, indeed, in reference to His earthly ministry: "*I am not sent save to the lost sheep of the house of Israel*" (Matt. xv. 24); nevertheless, He is not ignorant that it is His mission to seek and to save *all that which is lost*, and consequently the heathen. He affirms it in the Gospels of Matthew and Mark, no less than in that of Luke. Paul himself does homage to this divine fidelity, when he recalls the fact that Jesus, during His earthly life, consented to become *a minister of the circumcision* (Rom. xv. 8). But, 1. What reason could Luke have, in the circle for which he was writing, to refer to this restriction temporarily imposed upon the Twelve for the purpose of this particular mission? 2. Mark, no less than Luke, omits these words in the account he gives of this discourse, but the harmony of his leaning with that of the first evangelist is not suspected. 3. This last circumstance makes it all but certain that this detail had already been omitted in the sources whence these two evangelists drew their narratives, and must completely exculpate Luke from all anti-Jewish prejudice in his reproduction of this discourse.

Ver. 4. On their arrival at a city, they were to settle down in the first house to which they obtained access (εἰς ἣν ἄν, *into whatever house*), which, however, was not to exclude prudence and well-ascertained information (Matthew); and, once settled in a house, they were to keep to it, and try to make it the centre of a divine work in that place. To accept the hospitality of several families in succession would be the means of creating rivalry. It would therefore be from this house also, which was the first to welcome them, that they would have to set out on leaving the place: "till ye go *thence.*" The reading of the Vulg.: "Go *not* out of this house," is an erroneous correction. In the primitive churches, Christian work was concentrated in certain houses, which continued to be centres of operation (comp. the expression in Paul's epistles, "*The church which is in his house*").

Ver. 5. The gospel does not force itself upon men; it is an elastic power, penetrating wherever it finds access, and retiring wherever it is repulsed. This was Jesus' own mode of acting all through His ministry (viii. 37; John iii. 22).—The Jews were accustomed, on their return from heathen countries to the Holy Land, to shake off the dust from their feet at the frontier. This act symbolized a breaking away from all joint-participation in the life of the idolatrous world. The apostles were to act in the same way in reference to any Jewish cities which might reject in their person the kingdom of God. *Καί, even* the dust. By this symbolical act they relieved themselves of the burden of all further responsibility on account of the people of that city.—The expression, *for a testimony,* with the complement ἐπ' αὐτούς, *upon them,* has evidently reference to the judgment to come; in Mark, the complement *αὐτοῖς, for them,* makes the testimony an immediate appeal to their guilty consciences.

3*d.* Ver. 6. *The Result.*—*Διά,* in διήρχοντο (*they went through*), has for its complement the country in general, and denotes the *extent* of their mission. *Κατά,* which is distributive, expresses the accomplishment of it in detail: "staying in *every* little town."—Only Mark makes mention here of the use of oil in healing the sick,—a remarkable circumstance, with which the precept, Jas. v. 14, is probably connected. In Matthew, the discourse absorbs the attention of the historian to such a degree, that he does not say a word, at the end of chap. x., about the execution of their mission.

This short address, giving the Twelve their instructions, is only the preamble in Matthew (chap. x.) to a much more extended discourse, in which Jesus addresses the apostles respecting their future ministry in general. Under the influence of his fixed idea, Baur maintains that Luke purposely abridged the discourse in Matthew, in order to diminish the importance of the mission of the Twelve, and bring out in bolder relief that of the seventy disciples (Luke x.) "We see," he says, "that every word here, so to speak, is too much for the evangelist" (*Evangel.* p. 435). But, 1. If Luke had been animated by the jealous feeling which this criticism imputes to him, and so had allowed himself to tamper with the history, would he have put the *election* of the Twelve (chap. vi.), as distinct from their first mission, into such prominence, when Matthew appears to confound these two events (x. 1–4)? Would he mention so expressly the *success* of their mission, as he does, ver. 6, while Matthew himself preserves complete silence upon this point? It is fortunate for Luke that their respective parts were not changed, as they might have been, and very innocently, so far as he is concerned. He would have had to pay smartly for his omission in the hands of such critics! 2. Mark (vi. 8–10) gives this discourse in exactly the same form as Luke, and not at all after Matthew's manner; he, however, is not suspected of any antipathy to the Twelve. It follows from this, that Mark and Luke have simply given the discourse as they found it, either in a common document (the primitive Mark, according to Holtzmann), or in documents of a very similar character, to which they had access. There is sufficient proof, from a comparison of ver. 6 in Luke with ver. 13 in Mark, that of these two suppositions the latter must be preferred. 3. We may add, lastly, that in the discourse *on the apostolate* (Matt. x.) it is easy to recognise the same characteristics already observed in the Sermon on the Mount. It is a composition of a *didactic* nature on a definite subject, in which fragments of very different discourses, speaking chronologically, are collected into a single discourse. "The instructions it contains," Holtzmann rightly observes (p. 183), "go far beyond the actual situation, and imply a much more advanced state of things. . . ." Bleek, Ewald, and Hilgenfeld also recognise the more evident indications of anticipation. We find the true place for the greater part of the passages grouped together in Matthew, under the heading, *general instructions on the apostolate*, in Luke xii. and xxi.—For all these reasons, we regard the accusation brought against Luke respecting this discourse as scientifically untenable.

4*th*. Vers. 7–9.[1] *The Fears of Herod.*—This passage in Matthew (ch. xiv.) is separated by several chapters from the preceding narrative; but it is connected with it both chronologically and morally by Luke and Mark (vi. 14 et seq.). It was, in fact, the stir created by this mission of the Twelve which brought the fame of Jesus to Herod's ears ("*for His name was spread abroad*," Mark vi. 14).—The idea of this prince, which Luke mentions, that Jesus might be John risen from the dead, is the only indication which is to be found in this evangelist of the murder of the forerunner. But for the existence of this short passage in Luke, it would have been laid down as a critical axiom, that Luke was ignorant of the murder of John the Baptist! The saying, Elias or one of the old prophets, meant a great deal—nothing less, in the language of that time, than the Messiah is at hand (Matt. xvi. 14; John i. 21 et seq.).—In Matthew and Mark, the supposition that Jesus is none other than the forerunner risen from the dead proceeds from Herod himself. In Luke this apprehension is suggested to him by popular rumour, which is certainly more natural. The repetition of ἐγώ, *I*, is, as Meyer says, the echo of an alarmed conscience.—The remarkable detail, which Luke alone has preserved, that Herod sought to have a private interview with Jesus, indicates an original source of information closely connected with this king. Perhaps it reached Luke, or the author of the document of which he availed himself, by means of some one of those persons whom Luke describes so exactly, viii. 3 and Acts xiii. 1, and who belonged to Herod's household.

2. *The Multiplication of the Loaves:* ix. 10–17.—This narrative is the only one in the entire Galilean ministry which is common to the four evangelists (Matt. xiv. 13 et seq.;

[1] Ver. 7. ℵ. B. C. D. L. Z. omit υπ' αυτου.—The same and 10 Mnn., ηγερθη instead of εγηγερται.—Ver. 8. The Alex., τις instead of εις.—Ver. 9. ℵ. B. C. L. Z. omit εγω before απεκεφαλισα.

Mark vi. 30 et seq.; John vi.). It forms, therefore, an important mark of connection between the synoptical narrative and John's. This miracle is placed, in all four Gospels alike, at the apogee of the Galilean ministry. Immediately after it, in the Syn., Jesus begins to disclose to His apostles the mystery of His approaching sufferings (Luke ix. 18–27; Matt. xvi. 13–28; Mark viii. 27–38); in John this miracle leads to an important crisis in the work of Jesus in Galilee, and the discourse which follows alludes to the approaching violent death of the Lord (vi. 53–56).

1*st*. Vers. 10, 11.[1] *The Occasion.*—According to Luke, the motive which induced Jesus to withdraw into a desert place was His desire for more privacy with His disciples, that He might talk with them of their experiences during their mission. Mark relates, with a slight difference, that His object was to secure them some rest after their labours, there being such a multitude constantly going and coming as to leave them no leisure. According to Matthew, it was the news of the murder of the forerunner which led Jesus to seek solitude with His disciples; which, however, could in no way imply that He sought in this way to shield Himself from Herod's violence. For how could He, if this were so, have entered the very next day into the dominions of this sovereign (Matt. xiv. 34; comp. with Mark and John)? All these facts prove the mutual independence of the Syn.; they are easily harmonized, if we only suppose that the intelligence of the murder of John was communicated to Jesus by His apostles on their return from their mission, that it made Him feel deeply the approach of His own end (on the relation between these two deaths, see Matt. xvii. 12), and that it was while He was under these impressions that He desired to secure a season of retirement for His disciples, and an opportunity for more private intercourse with them.

The reading of the T. R.: *in a desert place of the city called Bethsaïda*, is the most complete, but for this very reason the most doubtful, since it is probably made up out of the others.

[1] **Ver. 10.** T. R. with 14 Mjj. several Mnn., τοπον ερημον πολεως καλουμενης Βηθσαιδα. ℵ[ca]. B. L. X. Z. (Tisch. 8th ed.), πολιν καλουμενην Βηθσαιδα. Syr[sch]. It. Vulg., τοπον ερημον καλουμενον Βηθσαιδα. ℵ* Syr[cur]., τοπον ερημον.—**Ver. 11.** The Mss. are divided between δεξαμενος and αποδεξαμενος.

The reading of the principal Alex., *in a city called Bethsaïda*, omits the notion, so important in this passage, of *a desert place*, probably because it appeared inconsistent with the idea of a *city*, and specially of Bethsaïda, where Jesus was so well known. The reading of ℵ and of the Cureton Syriac translation, *in a desert place*, is attractive for its brevity. But whence came the mention of Bethsaïda in all the other variations? Of the two contradictory notions, the desert and Bethsaïda, this reading sacrifices the proper name, as the preceding had sacrificed the desert. The true reading, therefore, appears to me to be that which is preserved in the Syriac version of Schaaf and in the Italic, *in a desert place called Bethsaïda*. This reading retains the two ideas, the apparent inconsistency of which has led to all these alterations of the text, but in a more concise and, at the same time, more correct form than that of the received reading. It makes mention not of a city, but of an inhabited country on the shore of the lake, bearing the name of Bethsaïda. If by this expression Luke had intended to denote the city of Bethsaïda, between Capernaum and Tiberias, on the western side of the lake, the country of Peter, Andrew, and Philip, he would be in open contradiction to Matthew, Mark, and John, who place the multiplication of the loaves on the eastern side, since in all three Jesus crosses the sea the next day to return to Galilee (*into the country of Gennesareth*, Matt. xiv. 34; *to Bethsaïda*, on the western shore, Mark vi. 45;[1] *to Capernaum*, John vi. 17). But in this case Luke would contradict himself as well as the others. For Bethsaïda, near Capernaum, being situated in the centre of the sphere of the activity of Jesus, how could the Lord repair thither with the intention of finding a place of retirement, a desert place? The meaning of the name Bethsaïda (*fishing place*) naturally leads us to suppose that there were several fisheries along the lake of this name. The term Bethsaïda of *Galilee*, John xii. 21, confirms this supposition; for this epithet must have served to distinguish this Bethsaïda from some other. Lastly, Josephus (*Antiq.* xviii. 2. 1; *Bell. Jud.* iii. 10. 7) and

[1] It is really incredible that Klostermann should have been induced to adopt an interpretation so forced as that which connects the words πρὸς Βηθσαϊδάν with the following proposition, by making them depend on ἀπολύσῃ: "*until He had sent away the people to Bethsaida!*"

Pliny (v. 15) expressly mention another Bethsaïda, situated in Gaulonitis, at the north-east extremity of the sea of Galilee, near the embouchure of the Jordan. The tetrarch Philip had built (probably in the vicinity of a district of this country called Bethsaïda) a city, which he had named, after a daughter of Augustus, Bethsaïda-*Julias*, the ruins of which Pococke believes he has discovered on a hill, the name of which (*Telui*) seems to signify *mountain of Julia* (*Morgenl.* ii. p. 106[1]). There Jesus would more easily find the solitude which He sought.

The term *ὑπεχώρησε*, *He withdrew*, does not inform us whether Jesus made the journey on foot or by boat. Luke doubtless did not know; he confines himself to reproducing his information. The three other narratives apprise us that the journey was made by water, but that the crowds which, contrary to the intention of Jesus, knew of His departure, set out to follow Him *πεζῇ*, *on foot* (Matthew and Mark), by land, and that the more eager of them arrived almost as soon as Jesus, and even, according to the more probable reading in Mark, *before* Him. The bend of the lake at the northern end approximates so closely to a straight line, that the journey from Capernaum to Julias might be made as quickly by land as by sea.[2]—The unexpected arrival of the people defeated the plan of Jesus. But He was too deeply moved by the love shown for Him by this multitude, like sheep without a shepherd (Mark), to give them anything but a tender welcome

[1] Winer, *Realwörterbuch.*

[2] Konrad Furrer, in the work cited, p. 24, maintains that John (in his view, the romancing Pseudo-John of the second century) places the multiplication of the loaves very much more to the south, *opposite Tiberias.* The proof of this assertion? John vi. 23: "Howbeit there came other boats from Tiberias nigh unto the place where they did eat bread." It appears, according to M. Furrer, that a large lake can only be traversed in the direction of its width and through the middle of it! Pray, why could not boats, setting out from Tiberias, visit Bethsaïda-Julias, where it was understood that a great multitude had gone? Comp. the account which Josephus gives of the transport of a body of troops from Tarichese, at the southern extremity of the lake, to Julias, and of the transport of Josephus, wounded, from Julias to Tarichese (Jos. *Vita*, § 72). Keim himself says: "The multitude, in order to rejoin Jesus, must have made a journey of six leagues round the lake" (on the hypothesis of Furrer); and how could Jesus say to His disciples, when He sent them away to the other side, after the multiplication of the loaves, that He should very soon join them (John vi. 17; Matt. xiv. 22; Mark vi. 45)?—It is on such grounds (*auf topographische Beweise gestützt*) that the evangelist John is made out to be an artist and romancer!

(*δεξάμενος*, Luke); and while these crowds of people were flocking up one after another (John vi. 5), a loving thought ripened in His heart. John has disclosed it to us (vi. 4). It was the time of the Passover. He could not visit Jerusalem with His disciples, owing to the virulent hatred of which He had become the object. In this unexpected gathering, resembling that of the nation at Jerusalem, He discerns a signal from on high, and determines to celebrate a feast in the desert, as a compensation for the Passover feast.

2*d*. Vers. 12–15.[1] *The Preparations.*—It was absolutely impossible to find sufficient food in this place for such a multitude; and Jesus feels Himself to some extent responsible for the circumstances. This miracle was not, therefore, as Keim maintains, a purely ostentatious prodigy. But in order to understand it thoroughly, it must be looked at from the point of view presented by John. In the Syn. it is the disciples who, as evening draws near, call the attention of Jesus to the situation of the people; He answers them by inviting them to provide for the wants of the multitude themselves. In John it is Jesus who takes the initiative, addressing Himself specially to Philip; then He confers with Andrew, who has succeeded in discovering a young lad furnished with some provisions. It is not difficult to reconcile these two accounts; but in the first we recognise the blurred lines of tradition, in the second the recollections of an eyewitness full of freshness and accuracy.—The *two hundred pennyworth* of bread forms a remarkable mark of agreement between the narrative of John and that of Mark. John does not depend on Mark; his narrative is distinguished by too many marks of originality. Neither has Mark copied from John; he would not have effaced the strongly-marked features of the narrative of the latter. From this coincidence in such a very insignificant detail we obtain a remarkable confirmation of all those little characteristics by which Mark's narrative is so often distinguished, and which De Wette, Bleek, and others regard as amplifications.

Jesus has no sooner ascertained that there are five loaves and two fishes than He is satisfied. He commands them to

[1] Ver. 12. ℵ. A. B. C. D. L. R. Z., πορευθεντες instead of απελθοντες.—Ver. 14. ℵ. L. It^aliq. Vg., δε instead of γαρ.—ℵ. B. C. D. L. R. Z., ωσει ανα instead of ανα

make the multitude sit down. Just as though He had said: I have what I want; the meal is ready; let them be seated! But He takes care that this banquet shall be conducted with an order worthy of the God who gives it. Everything must be calm and solemn; it is a kind of passover meal. By the help of the apostles, He seats His guests in rows of fifty each (Matthew), or in double rows of fifty, by hundreds (Mark). This orderly arrangement allowed of the guests being easily counted. Mark describes in a dramatic manner the striking spectacle presented by these regularly-formed companies, each consisting of two equal ranks, and all arranged upon the slope of the hill (*συμπόσια συμπόσια, πρασιαὶ πρασιαί*, vers. 39, 40). The pastures at that time were in all their spring splendour, and John and Mark offer a fresh coincidence here, in that they both bring forward the beauty of this natural carpet (*χόρτος πολύς*, John; *χλωρὸς χόρτος*, Mark; Matthew says, *οἱ χόρτοι*). In conformity with oriental usage, according to which women and children must keep themselves apart, the men alone (*οἱ ἄνδρες*, John vi. 10) appear to be seated in the order indicated. This explains why, according to the Syn., they *alone* were counted, as Luke says (ver. 14), also Mark (ver. 44), and, more emphatically still, Matthew (ver. 21, "without women and children").

3*d*. Vers. 16, 17.[1] *The Repast.*—The pronouncing of a blessing by Jesus is an incident preserved in all four narratives. It must have produced a special impression on all the four witnesses. Each felt that this act contained the secret of the marvellous power displayed on this occasion. To bless God for a little is the way to obtain much. In Matthew and Mark, *εὐλόγησε*, He *blessed*, is absolute; the object understood is *God.* Luke adds *αὐτούς*, *them* (the food), a word which the *Sinaïticus* erases (wrongly, it is clear), in accordance with the two other Syn. It is a kind of sacramental consecration. John uses the word *εὐχαριστεῖν*, which is chosen, perhaps, not without reference to the name of the later paschal feast (*eucharist*). — The imperfect *ἐδίδου* in Luke and Mark is graphic: "He gave, and kept on giving."—The mention of the *fragments* indicates the complete satisfaction of their hunger. In John it is Jesus who orders them to be gathered up. This

[1] Ver. 16. ℵ. X. Syr^{sch}. omit *αυτους*.

act must therefore be regarded as an expression of filial respect for the gift of the Father.—The *twelve baskets* are mentioned in all the four narratives. The baskets belonged to the furniture of a caravan. Probably they were what the apostles had provided themselves with when they set out. The number of the persons fed is given by Matthew and Mark here. Luke had mentioned it already in the 14th verse, after the reply of the disciples; John a little later (ver. 10), at the moment when the companies were being seated. What unaccountable caprice, if these narratives were taken from each other, or even from the same written source!

The criticism which sets out with the denial of the supernatural is compelled to erase this fact from the history of Jesus; and this miracle cannot, in fact, be explained by the "hidden forces of spontaneity," by the "charm which a person of fine organization exercises over weak nerves." It is not possible either to fall back, with some commentators, on the process of vegetation, by supposing here an unusual acceleration of it; we have to deal with bread, not with corn; with cooked fish, not with living creatures. The fact is miraculous, or it is nothing. M. Renan has returned to the ancient interpretation of Paulus: Every one took his little store of provisions from his wallet; they lived on very little. Keim combines with this explanation the mythical interpretation in two ways,—imitation of the O. T. (the manna; Elisha, 2 Kings iv. 42), and the Christian idea of the multiplication of the Word, the food of the soul. With the explanation of Paulus, it is difficult to conceive what could have excited the enthusiasm of the people to the point of making them instantly resolve to proclaim Jesus as their King! The mythical interpretation has to contend with special difficulties. Four parallel and yet original narratives wonderfully supplementing each other, a number of minute precise details quite incompatible with the nebulous character of a myth (the five loaves and the two fishes, the 5000 persons, the ranks of fifty, and the companies of a hundred, the twelve baskets),—all these details, preserved in four independent and yet harmonious accounts, indicate either a *real* event or a *deliberate* invention. But the hypothesis of invention, which Baur so freely applies to the miracles recorded in the fourth Gospel, finds an insurmountable obstacle here in the accounts of the three other evangelists. How is criticism to get out of this network of difficulties? When it has exhausted its ingenuity, it will end by laying down its arms before the holy simplicity of this narrative.

3. *First Announcement of the Passion:* ix. 18–27.—Up to the first multiplication of the loaves, it is impossible to make out any continuous synchronism between the synoptics, as the following table of the series of preceding incidents shows:—

MATTHEW.	MARK.	LUKE.
Gadara.	Accusation (Beelzebub).	Parable of the sower.
The Paralytic.		
Call of Matthew.	Mother and brethren of Jesus.	Mother and brethren of Jesus.
Jaïrus.		
The blind and dumb.	Parable of the sower.	
Mission of the Twelve.		
Deputation of John Bapt.	Gadara.	Gadara.
Sabbatic scenes.	Jaïrus.	Jaïrus.
Accusation (Beelzebub).		
Mother and brethren of Jesus.	Nazareth.	
The seven parables.	Mission of the Twelve.	Mission of the Twelve.
Nazareth.		
Murder of John Baptist.	Murder of John Baptist.	
Desert and first multiplication.	Desert and first multiplication.	Desert and first multiplication.

Numbers might be thrown into a bag and taken out again hap-hazard thrice over, without obtaining an order apparently more capricious and varied. Yet of these three narratives one is supposed to be copied from the other, or to have emanated from the same written source!

Nevertheless, towards the end a certain parallelism begins to show itself, first of all between Mark and Luke (Gadara, Jaïrus, Mission of the Twelve), then between Matthew and Mark (Nazareth, murder of John, desert and first multiplication). This convergence of the three narratives into one and the same line proceeds from this point, after a considerable omission in Luke, and becomes more decidedly marked, until it reaches Luke ix. 50, as appears from the following table:—

MATTHEW.	MARK.	LUKE.
Desert and first multiplication.	As Matthew.	As Matthew.
Tempest (Peter on the water).	Tempest (without Peter).	Wanting.
Purifying and clean food.	As Matthew.	*Id.*
Canaanitish woman.	*Id.*	*Id.*
Second multiplication.	*Id.*	*Id.*
Sign from heaven (Decapolis).	*Id.*	*Id.*
Leaven of the Pharisees.	*Id.*	*Id.*
First announcement of the Passion.	*Id.*	As Matthew.
Transfiguration.	*Id.*	*Id.*
Lunatic child.	*Id.*	*Id.*
Second announcement of the Passion.	*Id.*	*Id.*
The Didrachma.	Wanting.	Wanting.
The example of the child.	As Matthew.	As Matthew.
Ecclesiastical discipline.	*Id.*	*Id.*
Wanting.	Intolerance.	As Mark.
Forgiveness of offences.	Wanting.	Wanting.

How is the large omission to be explained which Luke's narrative exhibits from the storm following the first multiplication to the last announcement of the Passion, corresponding to two whole chapters of Matthew (xiv. 22–xvi. 12) and of Mark (vi. 45–viii. 26)? How is the tolerably exact synchronism which shows itself from this time between all three to be accounted for? Meyer gives up all attempts to explain the omission; it was due to an unknown chance. Reuss (§ 189) thinks that the copy of Mark which Luke used presented an omission in this place. Bleek attributes the omission to the original Greek Gospel which Matthew and Luke made use of; Matthew, he supposes, filled it up by means of certain documents, and Mark copied Matthew. Holtzmann (p. 223) contents himself with saying that Luke here breaks the thread of A. (primitive Mark), in order to connect with his narrative the portion which follows; but he says nothing that might serve to explain this strange procedure.—But the hypothesis upon which almost all these attempted solutions rest is that of a common original document, which, however, is continually contradicted by the numerous differences both in form and matter which a single glance of the eye discovers between Matthew and Mark. Then, with all this, the difficulty is only removed a step further back. For it becomes necessary to explain the omission in the original document. And whenever this is done satisfactorily, it will be found necessary to have recourse to the following idea, which, for our own part, we apply directly to Luke. In the original preaching of the gospel, particular incidents were naturally grouped together in certain cycles more or less fixed, determined sometimes by chronological connection (the call of Matthew, the feast and the subsequent conversations, the tempest, Gadara, and Jaïrus), sometimes by the similarity of the subjects (the Sabbatic scenes, vi. 1–11).[1] These cycles were first of all put in writing, with considerable freedom and variety, sometimes by the preachers for their own use, and in other cases by their hearers, who were anxious to fix their recollection of them. The oldest writings of which Luke speaks (i. 1) were probably collections more or less complete

[1] For the working out of a similar idea, see Lachmann's fine work, *Stud. u. Kritiken*, 1835.

of these groups of narratives (ἀνατάξασθαι διήγησιν). And what in this case can be more readily imagined than the omission of one or the other of these cycles in any of these collections? An accident of this kind is sufficient to explain the great omission which we meet with in Luke. The cycle wanting in the document he used extended a little further than the second multiplication of the loaves, whilst the following portions belong to a part of the Galilean ministry, which, from the beginning, had taken a more definite form in the preaching. This was natural; for the facts of which this subsequent series is composed are closely connected by a double tie, both chronological and moral. The subject is the approaching sufferings of Jesus. The announcement of them to the disciples is the aim of the following discourse; and to strengthen their faith in view of this overwhelming thought is evidently the design of the transfiguration. The cure of the lunatic child, which took place at the foot of the mountain, was associated with the transfiguration in the tradition; the second announcement of the Passion naturally followed the first, and all the more since it took place during the return from Cæsarea to Capernaum; which was the case also with certain manifestations of pride and intolerance of which the apostles were then guilty, and the account of which terminates this part. In the tradition, this natural cycle formed the close of the Galilean ministry. And this explains how the series of facts has been preserved in almost identical order in the three narratives.

The following conversation, reported also by Matthew (xvi. 13 et seq.) and Mark (viii. 27 et seq.), refers to three points: 1*st. The Christ* (vers. 18–20); 2*d. The suffering Christ* (vers. 21 and 22); 3*d. The disciples* of the suffering Christ (vers. 23–27).

Jesus lost no time in returning to His project of seeking a season of retirement, a project which had been twice defeated, at Bethsaïda-Julias, by the eagerness of the multitude to follow Him, and again in Tyre and Sidon, where, notwithstanding His desire to *remain hid* (Mark vii. 24), His presence had been discovered by the Canaanitish woman, and afterwards noised abroad through the miracle which took place. After that He had returned to the south, had visited a second time that Decapolis which he had previously been obliged to quit almost as soon as He entered it. Then He set out again for the north, this time directing His steps more eastward, towards the secluded valleys where the Jordan rises at the foot of Hermon. The city of Cæsarea Philippi was situated there, inhabited by a people of whom the greater part were heathen (Josephus, *Vita*, § 13). Jesus might expect to find in this secluded country the solitude which He had sought in vain in other parts of the Holy Land. He did not visit the city itself, but remained in the *hamlets* which surround it (Mark), or generally *in those quarters* (Matthew).

1*st*. Vers. 18–20. *The Christ.*—According to Mark, the following conversation took place during the journey (ἐν τῇ ὁδῷ); Mark thus gives precision to the vaguer indication of Matthew. The name of Cæsarea Philippi is wanting in Luke's narrative. Will criticism succeed in finding a dogmatic motive for this omission? In a writer like Luke, who loves to be precise about places (ver. 10) and times (ver. 28), this omission can only be accounted for by ignorance; therefore he possessed neither Mark nor Matthew, nor the documents from which these last derived this name. The description of the moral situation belongs, however, to Luke: Jesus had just been alone praying. "Arbitrary and ill-chosen scenery," says Holtzmann (p. 224). One would like to know the grounds of this judgment on the part of the German critic. Would not Jesus, at the moment of disclosing to His disciples for the first time the alarming prospect of His approaching death, foreseeing the impression which this communication would make upon them, having regard also to the manner in which He must speak to them under such circumstances, be likely to prepare Himself for this important step by prayer? Besides, it is probable that the disciples took part in His prayer. The imperfect συνῆσαν, *they were gathered together with Him*, appears to indicate as much. And the term καταμόνας (ὁδούς understood), *in solitude*, in no way excludes the presence of the disciples, but simply that of the people. This appears from the antithesis, ver. 23: "And He said to them *all*," and especially from Mark, ver. 34: "Having called *the multitude*."—The expression, *they were gathered together*, indicates something of importance. Jesus first of all elicits from His disciples the different opinions which they had gathered from the lips of the people during their mission. The object of this first question is evidently to prepare the way for the next (ver. 20).—On the opinions here enumerated, see ver. 8 and John i. 21. They amount to this: Men generally regard thee as one of the forerunners of the Messiah. The question addressed to the disciples is designed, first of all, to make them distinctly conscious of the wide difference between the popular opinion and the conviction at which they have themselves arrived; next, to serve as a starting-point for the fresh communication which Jesus is about to make respecting the manner in which the work of the Christ is to be accomplished.—The confession of Peter is differently expressed in the three narratives: *the Christ, the Son of the living God* (Matthew); *the Christ* (Mark); *the Christ of God* (Luke). The form in Luke holds a middle place between the other two. The genit., *of God,* signifies, as in the expression *Lamb of God:* He who belongs to God, and whom God sends

It has been inferred from this question, that up to this time Jesus had not assumed His position as the Messiah amongst His disciples, and that His determination to accept this character dates from this point; that this resolution was taken partly in concession to the popular idea, which required that His work of restoration should assume this form, and partly to meet the expectation of the disciples, which found emphatic expression through the lips of Peter, the most impatient of their number. But, 1. The question in ver. 20 has not the character of a concession; on the contrary, Jesus thereby takes the initiative in the confession which it calls forth. 2. If this view be maintained, all those previous sayings and incidents in which Jesus gives Himself out to be the Christ, must be set aside as unauthentic; and there are such not only in John (i. 39–41, 49–51, iii. 14, iv. 26), but in the Syn. (the election of the Twelve as heads of a new Israel; the parallel which Jesus institutes, Matt. v., between Himself and the lawgiver of Sinai: "You have heard that it hath been said . . ., but *I* . . .;" the title of *bridegroom* which He gives Himself, Luke v. 35, and parallels). The resolution of Jesus to assume the character of the Messiah, and to accomplish under this national form His universal task as Saviour of the world, was certainly matured within His soul from the first day of His public activity. The scenes of the baptism and temptation forbid any other supposition; hence the entire absence of anything like feeling His way in the progress of His ministry. The import of His question is therefore something very different

The time had come for Him to pass, if we may so express it, to a new chapter in His teaching. He had hitherto, especially since He began to teach in parables, directed the attention of His disciples to the near approach of the kingdom of God. It was now necessary to turn it towards Himself as Head of this kingdom, and especially towards the future, wholly unlooked for by them, which awaited Him in this character. They knew that He was the Christ; they had yet to learn *how* He was to be it. But before commencing on this new ground, He is anxious that they should express, in a distinct declaration, the result of His instructions and of their own previous experiences. As an experienced teacher, before beginning the new lesson He makes them recapitulate the old. With the different forms and vacillations of opinion, as well as the open denials of the rulers before them, He wants to hear from their own lips the expression of their own warm and decided conviction. This established result of His previous labour will serve as a foundation for the new labour which the gravity of His situation urges Him to undertake. The murder of John the Baptist made Him sensible that His own end was not far off; the time, therefore, was come to substitute for the brilliant form of the Christ, which as yet filled the minds of His disciples, the mournful image of the Man of sorrows. Thus the facts which, as we have seen (p. 403), led Jesus to seek retirement in the desert of Bethsaïda-Julias, that He might be alone with His disciples, furnished the motives for the present conversation.

We read in John, after the multiplication of the loaves (chap. vi.), of a similar confession to this, also made by Peter in the name of the Twelve. Is it to be supposed, that at the same epoch two such similar declarations should have taken place? Would Jesus have called for one so soon after having heard the other? Is it not striking that, owing to the omission in Luke, the account of this confession, in his narrative as in John's, follows immediately upon that of the multiplication of the loaves? Certainly the situation described in the fourth Gospel is very different. In consequence of a falling away which had just been going on amongst His Galilean disciples, Jesus puts the question to His apostles of their leaving Him. But the questions which Jesus addresses to them in the Syn. might easily have found a place in the conversation of which John gives us a mere outline. At the first glance, it is true, John's narrative does not lead us to suppose such a long interval between the multiplication of the loaves and this conversation as is required for the journey from Capernaum to Cæsarea Philippi. But the desertion of the Galilean disciples, which had begun immediately, was not completed in a day. It might have extended over some time (John vi. 66: ἐκ τούτου, *from that time*). Altogether, the resemblance between these two scenes appears to us to outweigh their dissimilarity.

Keim admirably says: "We do not know which we must think the greatest; whether the spirit of the disciples, who shatter the Messianic mould, set aside the judgment of the priests, rise above all the intervening degrees of popular appreciation, and proclaim as lofty and divine that which is abased and down-trodden, because to their minds' eye it is and remains great and divine,—or this personality of Jesus, which draws from these feeble disciples, notwithstanding the pressure of the most overwhelming experiences, so pure and lofty an expression of the effect produced upon them by His whole life and ministry." Gess: "The sages of Capernaum remained unmoved, the enthusiasm of the people was cooled, on every side Jesus was threatened with the fate of the Baptist . . . , it was then that the faith of His disciples shone out as genuine, and came forth from the furnace of trial as an energetic conviction of truth."

2*d*. Vers. 21, 22.[1] *The suffering Christ.*—The expression of Luke, *He straitly charged and commanded them,* is very energetic. The general reason for this prohibition is found in the following announcement of the rejection of the Messiah, as is proved by the participle εἰπών, *saying.* They were to keep from proclaiming Him openly as the Christ, on account of the contradiction between the hopes which this title had awakened in the minds of the people, and the way in which this office was to be realized in Him. But this threatening prohibition had a more special nature, which appears from John's narrative. It refers to the recent attempt of the people, after the multiplication of the loaves (John vi. 14, 15), to proclaim Him king, and the efforts which Jesus was then obliged to make to preserve His disciples from this mistaken enthusiasm, which might have seriously compromised His work. It is the recollection of this critical moment which induces Jesus to use this severe language (ἐπιτιμήσας). It was only after the idol of the carnal Christ had been for ever nailed to the cross, that the apostolic preaching could safely connect this title Christ with the name of Jesus. "See how," as Riggenbach says (*Vie de Jésus,* p. 318), "Jesus was obliged in the very moment of self-revelation to veil Himself, when He had lighted the fire to cover it again."—Δέ (ver. 21) is adversative: "Thou sayest truly, I am the Christ; *but* . . ."—*Must,* on account of the prophecies and of the divine purpose, of which they are the expression.—The members composing the Sanhedrim consisted of three classes of members: the *elders,* or presidents of synagogues; the *high*

[1] The Mss. vary between εἰπεῖν (T. R.) and λέγων (Alex.).—Ver. 22. The Mss vary between ἐγερθῆναι (T. R.) and ἀναστῆναι.

priests, the heads of twenty-four classes of priests; and *scribes*, or men learned in the law. All three Syn. give here the enumeration of these official classes. This paraphrase of the technical name invests the announcement of the rejection with all its importance. What a complete reversal of the disciples' Messianic ideas was this rejection of Jesus by the very authorities from whom they expected the recognition and proclamation of the Messiah! Ἀποδοκιμασθῆναι indicates deliberate rejection, after previous *calculation*.—There was a crushing contradiction between this prospect and the hopes of the disciples; but, as Klostermann truly says, the last words, "*And He shall rise again the third day*," furnish the solution of it.

Strauss and Baur contented themselves with denying the details of the prediction in which Jesus foretold His death. Volkmar and Holsten at the present day refuse to allow that He had any knowledge of this event before the last moments. According to Holsten, He went to Jerusalem full of hope, designing to preach there as well as in Galilee, and confident, in case of need, of the interposition of God and of the swords of His adherents. . . . The holy Supper itself was occasioned simply by a passing presentiment. . . . His terrible mistake took Jesus by surprise at the last moment. Keim (ii. p. 556) acknowledges that it is impossible to deny the authenticity of the scene and conversation at Cæsarea Philippi. According to him, Jesus could not have failed to have foreseen His violent death long before the catastrophe came. This is proved by the bold opposition of St. Peter, also by such sayings as those referring to the *bridegroom who is to be taken away*, to *death* as *the way of life* (Luke ix. 23, 24), to Jerusalem which kills the prophets; lastly, by the reply to the two sons of Zebedee. We may add ix. 31, xii. 50; John ii. 20, iii. 14, vi. 53, xii. 7, 24,—words at once characteristic and inimitable. And as to the details of this prediction, have we not a number of facts which leave no room for doubt as to the supernatural knowledge of Jesus (xxii. 10–34; John i. 49, iv. 18, vi. 64, etc.)? What the modern critics more generally dispute, is the announcement of the resurrection. But if Jesus foresaw His death, He must have equally foreseen His resurrection, as certainly as a prophet believing in the mission of Israel could not announce the captivity without also predicting the return. And who would ever have dreamed of putting into the mouth of Jesus the expression *three days and three nights* after the event, when in actual fact the time spent in the tomb did not exceed one day and two nights?—It is asked how it came to pass, if Jesus had so expressly predicted His resurrection, that this event should have been such an extraordinary surprise to his apostles? There we have a psychological problem, which the disciples themselves found it difficult to explain.

Comp. the remarks of the evangelists, ix. 45, xviii. 34, and parallels, which can only have come from the apostles. The explanation of this problem is perhaps this: the apostles never thought, before the facts had opened their eyes, that the expressions death and resurrection used by Jesus should be taken literally. Their Master so commonly spoke in figurative language, that up to the last moment they only saw in the first term the expression of a sad separation, a sudden disappearance; and in the second, only a sudden return, a glorious reappearing. And even after the death of Jesus, they in no way thought they should see Him appear again in His old form, and by the restoration to life of the body laid in the tomb. If they expected anything, it was His return as a heavenly King (see on xxiii. 42).—Luke has omitted here the word of approval and the severe reprimand which Jesus, according to Matthew, addressed to Peter on this occasion. If any one is determined to see in this omission of Luke's a wilful suppression, the result of ill-will towards the Apostle Peter, or at least towards the Jewish Christians (Keim), what will he say of Mark, who, while omitting the words of praise, expressly refers to those of censure?

We can quite understand that the people could not yet bear the disclosure of a suffering Messiah; but Jesus might make them participate in it indirectly, by initiating them into the *practical consequences* of this fact for His true disciples. To describe the moral crucifixion of His servants, vers. 23–27, was to give a complete revelation of the spirituality of the Messianic kingdom.

3*d*. Vers. 23–27.[1]—"*And He said to them all, If any man will come after me, let him deny himself, and take up his cross daily, and follow me.* 24. *For whosoever will save his life shall lose it; but whosoever will lose his life for my sake, the same shall save it.* 25. *For what is a man advantaged, if he gain the whole world, and lose himself, or be cast away?* 26. *For whosoever shall be ashamed of me, and of my words, of him shall the Son of man be ashamed, when He shall come in His own glory, and in His Father's, and of the holy angels.* 27. *But I tell you of a truth, there be some standing here, which shall not taste of death, till they see the kingdom of God.*"—The preceding conversation had taken place within the privacy of the

[1] Ver. 23. The Mss. vary between ελθειν (T. R., Byz.) and ερχεσθαι (Alex.).—ℵ[ca]. C. D. and 11 Mjj. 120 Mnn. It[plerique], omit καθ' ημεραν, which is the reading of T. R. with ℵ* A. B. K. L. M. R. Z. Π. Syr. Vg.—Ver. 26. D. Syr[cur]. It[aliq]. omit λογους.—Ver. 27. ℵ. B. L. X., αυτου instead of ωδε.—13 Mjj., οιτινες instead of οι.

apostolic circle (ver. 18). The following words are addressed *to all*, that is to say, to the multitude, which, while Jesus was praying with His disciples, kept at a distance. According to Mark, Jesus calls them to Him to hear the instruction which follows. Holtzmann maintains that this *to all* of Luke must have been taken from Mark. But why could not the same remark, if it resulted from an actual fact, be reproduced in two different forms, in two independent documents?—Jesus here represents all those who attach themselves to Him under the figure of a train of crucified persons, ver. 23. The aor. ἐλθεῖν of the T. R. means: make in general part of my following; and the present ἔρχεσθαι in the Alex.: range themselves about me at this very moment. The figure employed is that of a journey, which agrees with their actual circumstances as described by Mark: ἐν τῇ ὁδῷ.—The man who has made up his mind to set out on a journey, has first of all to say farewell; here he has to bid adieu to his own life, to deny himself. Next there is luggage to carry; in this case it is *the cross*, the sufferings and reproach which never fail to fall on him who pays a serious regard to holiness of life. By the word *αἴρειν, to take up*, to burden oneself with, Jesus alludes to the custom of making criminals carry their cross to the place of punishment. Further, there is in this term the idea of a voluntary and cheerful acceptance. Jesus says *his* cross, that which is the result of a person's own character and providential position. There is nothing arbitrary about it; it is given from above. The authenticity of the word *daily*, which is wanting in some MSS., cannot be doubted. Had it been a gloss, it would have been inserted in Matthew and Mark as well. This voluntary crucifixion is carried on every day to a certain degree. Lastly, after having taken farewell and shouldered his burden, he must set out on his journey. By what road? By that which the steps of his Master have marked out. The chart of the true disciple directs him to renounce every path of his own choosing, that he may put his feet into the print of his leader's footsteps. Thus, and not by arbitrary mortifications actuated by self-will, is the death of self completely accomplished.—The term *follow*, therefore, does not express the same idea as *come after me*, at the beginning of the verse; the latter would denote *outward* adherence to the followers of Jesus. The other refers to practical fidelity in the fulfilment of the consequences of this engagement.

The 24th verse demonstrates (*for*) the necessity for the crucifixion described, ver. 23. Without this death to self, man loses himself (24*a*); whilst by this sacrifice he saves himself (24*b*). We find here the paradoxical form in which the Hebrew *Maschal* loves to clothe itself. Either of the two ways brings the just man to the antipodes of the point to which it seemed likely to lead him. This profound saying, true even for man in his innocence, is doubly true when applied to man as a sinner.—*Ψυχή, the breath of life,* denotes the soul, with its entire system of instincts and natural faculties. This psychical life is unquestionably good, but only as a point of departure, and as a means of acquiring a higher life. To be anxious to *save* it, to seek to preserve it as it is, by doing nothing but care for it, and seek the utmost amount of self-gratification, is a sure way of losing it for ever; for it is wanting to give stability to what in its essence is but transitory, and to change a means into an end. Even in the most favourable case, the natural life is only a transient flower, which must soon fade. That it may be preserved from dissolution, we must consent to *lose* it, by surrendering it to the mortifying and regenerating breath of the Divine Spirit, who transforms it into a higher life, and imparts to it an eternal value. To keep it, therefore, is to lose both it and the higher life into which, as the blossom into its fruit, it should have been transformed. To lose it is to gain it, first of all, under the higher form of spiritual life; then, some day, under the form even of natural life, with all its legitimate instincts fully satisfied. Jesus says, "for *my sake;*" and in Mark, "for my sake *and the gospel's.*" It is, in fact, only as we give ourselves to Christ that we satisfy this profound law of human existence; and it is only by the gospel, received in faith, that we can contract this personal relationship to Christ. *Self* perishes only when affixed to the cross of Jesus, and the divine breath, which imparts the new life to man, comes to him from Christ alone.—No axiom was more frequently repeated by Jesus; it is, as it were, the substance of His moral philosophy. In Luke xvii. 33 it is applied to the time of the Parousia; it is then, in fact, that it will be fully realized. In John xii. 25 Jesus makes it the law of His own existence; in Matt. x. 39 He applies it to the apostolate.

Vers. 25–27 are the confirmation (*for*) of this *Maschal*, and first of all, vers. 25 and 26, of the first proposition. Jesus supposes, ver. 25, the act of *saving one's own life*, accomplished with the most complete success . . . ., amounting to a gain of the whole world. But in this very moment the master of this magnificent domain finds himself condemned to perish! What gain! To draw in a lottery a gallery of pictures . . ., and at the same time to become blind! The expression ἢ ζημιωθείς, *or suffering loss*, is difficult. In Matthew and Mark this word, completed by ψυχήν, corresponds to ἀπολέσας in Luke; but in Luke it must express a different idea. We may understand with it either *the world* or ἑαυτόν, *himself*, "suffering the loss of this world already gained," or (which is more natural) "losing himself altogether (ἀπολέσας), or even merely suffering some small loss in his own person." It is not necessary that the chastisement should amount to total perdition; the smallest injury to the human personality will be found to be a greater evil than all the advantages accruing from the possession of the whole world.

The losing oneself [the loss of the personality] mentioned in ver. 25 consists, according to ver. 26 (*for*), in being denied by Jesus in the day of His glory. The expression, *to be ashamed of Jesus*, might be applied to the Jews, because fear of their rulers hindered them from declaring themselves for Him; but in this context it is more natural to apply it to disciples whose fidelity gives way before ridicule or violence. The *Cantabrigiensis* omits the word λόγους, which leads to the sense: "ashamed of me *and mine*." This reading would recommend itself if better supported, and if the word λόγους (*my words*) was not confirmed by the parallel expression of Mark (viii. 35): "for my sake *and the gospel's*." The glory of the royal advent of Jesus will be, first, that of His own personal appearing; next, the glory of God; lastly, the glory of the angels,—all these several glories will be mingled together in the incomparable splendour of that great day

(2 Thess. i. 7–10). "Thus," says Gess, "to be worthy of this man is the new and paramount principle. This is no mere spiritualization of the Mosaic law; it is a revolution in the religious and moral intuitions of mankind."

Ver. 27 is the justification of the promise in ver. 24*b* (find his life by losing it), as vers. 25 and 26 explained the threatening of 24*a*. It forms in the three Syn. the conclusion of this discourse, and the transition to the narrative of the transfiguration; but could any of the evangelists have applied to such an exceptional and transitory incident this expression: *the coming of the kingdom of Christ* (Matthew), or *of God* (Mark and Luke)?—Meyer thinks that this saying can only apply to the Parousia, to which the preceding verse referred, and which was believed to be very near. But could Jesus have laboured under this misconception (see the refutation of this opinion at chap. xxi.)? Or has the meaning of His words been altered by tradition? The latter view only would be tenable. Many, urging the difference between Matthew's expression (until they have seen *the Son of man coming in His kingdom*) and that of Mark ("*. . . the kingdom of God come with power*") or of Luke ("*. . . the kingdom of God*"), think that the notion of the Parousia has been designedly erased from the text of Matthew by the other two, because they wrote after the fall of Jerusalem. Comp. also the relation between Matt. xxiv., where the confusion of the two events appears evident, and Luke xxi., where it is avoided. But, 1. It is to be observed that this confusion is found in Mark (xiii.) exactly the same as in Matthew (xxiv.). Now, if Mark had corrected Matthew for the reason alleged in the passage *before us*, how much more would he have corrected him in chap. xiii., where it is not a single isolated passage that is in question, but where the subject of the Parousia is the chief matter of discourse! And if the form of expression in Mark is not the result of an intentional correction, but of a simple difference in the mode of transmission, why might it not be the same also with the very similar form that occurs in Luke? 2. There is a very marked distinction both in Mark and Luke, a sort of gradation and antithesis between this saying and the preceding—in Luke by means of the particle δέ, *and further*: "And I *also* say that this recompense promised to the faithful confessors shall be enjoyed by some of you before you die;" and in Mark, in a still more striking manner, by the interruption of the discourse and the commencement of a new phrase: "*And He said to them*" (ix. 1). So that the idea of the Parousia must be set aside as far as the texts of Mark and Luke are concerned. It may even be doubted whether it is contained in Matthew's expression; comp. Matt. xxvi. 64: "*Henceforth* [from now] ye shall see the Son of man *coming* in the clouds of heaven." The expression *henceforth* does not permit of our thinking of the Parousia. But this saying is very similar to the one before us. Others apply this promise to the fall of Jerusalem, or to the establishment of the kingdom of God among the heathen, or to the descent of the Holy Spirit. But inasmuch as these events were outward facts, and *all* who were contemporary with them were witnesses of them, we cannot by this reference explain τινές, *some*, which announces an exceptional privilege. After all, is the Lord's meaning so difficult to apprehend? *Seeing the kingdom of God*, in His teaching, is a spiritual fact, in accordance with the inward nature of the kingdom itself; comp. xvii. 21: "The kingdom of God is *within you*" (see the explanation of this passage). For this reason, in order to enjoy this sight, a new sense and a new birth are needed; John iii. 3: "Except a man be *born again*, he cannot *see* the kingdom of God." This thought satisfactorily explains the present promise as expressed in Luke and Mark. To explain Matthew's expression, we must remember that the work of the Holy Spirit pre-eminently consists in giving us a lively conviction of the exaltation and heavenly glory of Jesus (John xvi. 14). The τινές, *some*, are therefore all those then present who should receive the Holy Spirit at Pentecost, and behold with their inward eye those *wonderful works of God*, which Jesus calls His kingdom, or the kingdom of God. In this way is explained the gradation from ver. 26 to ver. 27 in Mark and Luke: "Whoever shall give his own life shall find it again, not only at the end of time, but even in this life (at Pentecost)." If this explanation be inadmissible, it must be conceded that this promise is based on a confusion of the fall of Jerusalem with the Parousia; and this would be a proof that our Gospel as well as Matthew's was written before that catastrophe.—Ἀληθῶς must not be connected with λέγω: *Verily I say to you.* It should be placed before the verb, as the ἀμήν is in the two other Syn.; and Luke more generally makes use of ἐπ' ἀληθείας (three times in the Gospel, twice in the Acts). It must, then, belong to εἰσίν: "*There are certainly among you.*"—The Alex. reading **αὐτοῦ**, *here*, must be preferred to the received reading, ὧδε, which is taken from the other Syn.

4. *The Transfiguration:* **ix.** 28–36.—There is but one allusion to this event in the whole of the N. T. (2 Pet. i.), which proves that it has no immediate connection with the work of salvation. On the other hand, its historical reality can only be satisfactorily established in so far as we succeed in showing in a reasonable way its place in the course of the life and development of Jesus.[1]—According to the description of the transfiguration given in the Syn. (Matt. xvii. 1 et seq.; Mark ix. 2 et seq.), we distinguish three phases in this scene: 1*st.* The personal glorification of Jesus (vers. 28, 29); 2*d.* The appearing of Moses and Elijah, and His conversation with them (vers. 30–33); 3*d.* The interposition of God Himself (vers. 34–36).

1*st.* Vers. 28, 29.[2] *The Glory of Jesus.*—The three narratives show that there was an interval of a week between the transfiguration and the first announcement of the sufferings of Jesus, with this slight difference, that Matthew and Mark say *six days after*, whilst Luke says *about eight days after*. It is a very simple explanation to suppose that Luke employs a round number, as indeed the limitation ὡσεί, *about*, indicates, whilst the others give, from some document, the exact figure. But this explanation is too simple for criticism. "Luke," says Holtzmann, "affects to be a better chronologist than the others." And for this reason, forsooth, he substitutes *eight* for *six* on his own authority, and immediately, from some qualm of conscience, corrects himself by using the word *about!* To

[1] No one seems to us to have apprehended the real and profound meaning of the transfiguration so well as Lange, in his admirable *Vie de Jésus*, a book the defects of which have unfortunately been much more noticed than its rare beauties. Keim might have learned more from him, especially in the study of this incident.

[2] Ver. 28. ℵ* B. H. Syr. It^aliq. omit και before παραλαβων.—The Mss. vary between Ιωαννην και Ιακωβον and Ιακωβον και Ιωαννην.

such puerilities is criticism driven by the hypothesis of a common document. The Aramæan constructions, which characterize the style of Luke in this passage, and which are not found in the two other Syn. (ἐγένετο καὶ ἀνέβη, ver. 28; ἐγένετο εἶπεν, ver. 33), would be sufficient to prove that he follows a different document from theirs.—The nominative ἡμέραι ὀκτώ, *eight days*, is the subject of an elliptical phrase, which forms a parenthesis: "*About eight days had passed away.*" It is not without design that Luke expressly adds, *after these sayings.* He thereby brings out the moral connection between this event and the preceding conversation.—We might think, from the account of Matthew and Mark, that in taking His disciples to the mountain, Jesus intended to be transfigured before them. Luke gives us to understand that He simply wished to pray with them. Lange thinks, and it is probable, that in consequence of the announcement of His approaching sufferings, deep depression had taken possession of the hearts of the Twelve. They had spent these six days, respecting which the sacred records preserve unbroken silence, in a gloomy stupor. Jesus was anxious to rouse them out of a feeling which, to say the least, was quite as dangerous as the enthusiastic excitement which had followed the multiplication of the loaves. And in order to do this He had recourse to prayer; He sought to strengthen by this means those apostles especially whose moral state would determine the disposition of their colleagues. Knowing well by experience the influence a sojourn upon some height has upon the soul,—how much more easily, in such a place, it collects its thoughts and recovers from depression,—He leads them away to a mountain. The art. τό denotes the mountain nearest to the level country where Jesus then was. According to a tradition, of which we can gather no positive traces earlier than the fourth century (Cyril of Jerusalem, Jerome), the mountain in question was Tabor, a lofty cone, situated two leagues to the south-east of Nazareth. Perhaps the Gospel to the Hebrews presents an older trace of this opinion in the words which it attributes to Jesus: "Then my mother, the Holy Spirit, took me up by a hair of my head, and carried me to the high mountain of Tabor." But two circumstances are against the truth of this tradition: 1. Tabor is a long way off Cæsarea Philippi, where the previous conversation took place. Certainly, in the intervening six days Jesus could have returned even to the neighbourhood of Tabor. But would not Matthew and Mark, who have noticed the journey into the northern country, have mentioned this return? 2. The summit of Tabor was at that time, as Robinson has proved, occupied by a fortified town, which would scarcely agree with the tranquillity which Jesus sought. We think, therefore, that probably the choice lies between Hermon and Mount Panias, from whose snowy summits, visible to the admiring eye in all the northern parts of the Holy Land, the sources of the Jordan are constantly fed.

The strengthening of the faith of the three principal apostles was the object, therefore, of this mountain excursion; the glorification of Jesus was an answer to prayer, and the means employed by God to bring about the desired result. The connection between the prayer of Jesus and His transfiguration is expressed in Luke by the preposition ἐν, which denotes more than a mere simultaneousness (whilst He prayed), and makes His prayer the cause of this mysterious event. Elevated feeling imparts to the countenance and even to the figure of the entire man a distinguished appearance. The impulse of true devotion, the enthusiasm of adoration, illumine him. And when, corresponding with this state of soul, there is a positive revelation on the part of God, as in the case of Moses or of Stephen, then, indeed, it may come to pass that the inward illumination, penetrating, through the medium of the soul, even to its external covering, the body, may produce in it a prelude, as it were, of its future glorification. It was some phenomenon of this kind that was produced in the person of Jesus whilst He was praying. Luke describes its effects in the simplest manner: "*His countenance became other.*" How can Holtzmann maintain that in him the vision is "æsthetically amplified." His expression is much more simple than Mark's: "*He was transfigured before them,*" or than that of Matthew, who to these words of Mark adds, "*and His countenance shone as the sun.*"—This luminous appearance possessed the body of Jesus in such intensity as to become perceptible even through His garments. Even here the expression of Luke is very simple: "*His garments became white and shining,*" and contrasts with the stronger expressions of Mark and Matthew.

—The grandeur of the recent miracles shows us that Jesus at this time had reached the zenith of His powers. As everything in His life was in perfect harmony, this period must have been that also in which He reached the perfection of His inward development. Having reached it, what was His normal future? He could not advance; He must not go back. From this moment, therefore, earthly existence became too narrow a sphere for this perfected personality. There only remained death; but death is the offspring of the sinner, or, as St. Paul says, *the wages of sin* (Rom. vi. 23). For the sinless man the issue of life is not the sombre passage of the tomb; rather is it the royal road of a glorious transformation. Had the hour of this glorification struck for Jesus; and was His transfiguration the beginning of the heavenly renewal? This is Lange's thought; it somehow brings this event within the range of the understanding. Gess gives expression to it in these words: "This event indicates the ripe preparation of Jesus for immediate entrance upon eternity." Had not Jesus Himself voluntarily suspended the change which was on the point of being wrought in Him, this moment would have become the moment of His ascension.

2*d*. Vers. 30–33. *The Appearing of Moses and Elijah.*—Not only do we sometimes see the eye of the dying lighted up with celestial brightness, but we hear him conversing with the dear ones who have gone before him to the heavenly home. Through the gate which is opened for him, heaven and earth hold fellowship. In the same way, at the prayer of Jesus, heaven comes down or earth rises. The two spheres touch. Keim says: "A descent of heavenly spirits to the earth has no warrant either in the ordinary course of events or in the Old or New Testament." Gess very properly replies: "Who can prove that the appearing of these heroes of the Old Covenant was in contradiction to the laws of the upper world? We had far better confess our ignorance of those laws."—Moses and Elijah are there, *talking with Him.* Luke does not name them at first. He says *two men.* This expression reflects the impression which must have been experienced by the eye-witnesses of the scene. They perceived, first of all, the presence of two persons unknown; it was only afterwards that they knew them by name. Ἰδού, *behold,* expresses the suddenness of the apparition. The imperf., *they were talking*, proves that the conversation had already lasted some time when the disciples perceived the presence of these strangers. *Οἵτινες* is emphatic: who were no other than . . . Moses and Elijah were the two most zealous and powerful servants of God under the Old Covenant. Moreover, both of them had a privileged end: Elijah, by his ascension, was preserved from the unclothing of death; there was something equally mysterious in the death and disappearance of Moses. Their appearing upon the mountain is perhaps connected with the exceptional character of the end of their earthly life. But how, it is asked, did the apostles know them? Perhaps Jesus addressed them by name in the course of the conversation, or indicated who they were in a way that admitted of no mistake. Or, indeed, is it not rather true that the glorified bear upon their form the impress of their individuality, their *new name* (Rev. ii. 17)? Could we behold St. John or St. Paul in their heavenly glory for any length of time without giving them their name?

The design of this appearing is only explained to us by Luke: "They talked," he says literally, "*of the departure which Jesus was about to accomplish at Jerusalem.*" How could certain theologians imagine that Moses and Elijah came to instruct Jesus respecting His approaching sufferings, when only six days before He had Himself informed the Twelve about them? It is rather the two heavenly messengers who are learning of Jesus, as the apostles were six days before, unless one imagines that they talked with Him on a footing of equality. In view of that cross which is about to be erected, Elijah learns to know a glory superior to that of being taken up to heaven,—the glory of renouncing, through love, such an ascension, and choosing rather a painful and ignominious death. Moses comprehends that there is a sublimer end than that of dying, according to the fine expression which the Jewish doctors apply to his death, "from the kiss of the Eternal;" and this is to deliver up one's soul to the fire of divine wrath. This interview, at the same time, gave a sanction, in the minds of the disciples, to an event from the prospect of which only six days before they shrank in terror. The term ἔξοδος, *going out*, employed by Luke, is chosen designedly; for it contains, at the same time, the ideas both of death and ascension. Ascension was as much the natural way for Jesus as death is for us. He might ascend with the two who talked with Him. But to ascend now would be to ascend without us. Down below, on the plain, He sees mankind crushed beneath the weight of sin and death. Shall He abandon them? He cannot bring Himself to this. He cannot ascend unless He carry them with Him; and in order to do this, He now braves the other issue, which He can only accomplish at Jerusalem. *Πληροῦν*, to *accomplish*, denotes not the finishing of life by dying (Bleek), but the completion of death itself. In such a death there is a task to accomplish. The expression, *at Jerusalem*, has deep tragedy in it; at Jerusalem, that city which has the monopoly of the murder of the prophets (xiii. 33).—This single word of Luke's on the subject of the conversation throws light upon the scene, and we can appraise at its true value the judgment of the critics (Meyer, Holtzmann), who regard it as nothing more than the supposition of later tradition?

Further, it is through Luke that we are able to form an idea of the true state of the disciples during this scene. The imperf., *they talked*, ver. 30, has shown us that the conversation had already lasted some time when the disciples perceived the presence of the two heavenly personages. We must infer from this that they were asleep during the prayer of Jesus. This idea is confirmed by the plus-perfect ἦσαν βεβαρημένοι, *they had been weighed down*, ver. 32. They were in this condition during the former part of the interview, and they only came to themselves just as the conversation was concluding. The term διαγρηγορεῖν is used nowhere else in the N. T. In profane Greek, where it is very little used, it signifies: *to keep awake.* Meyer would give it this meaning here: "persevering in keeping themselves awake, notwithstanding the drowsiness which oppressed them." This sense is not inadmissible; nevertheless the δέ, *but*, which denotes an opposition to this state of slumber, rather inclines us to think that this verb denotes their return to self-consciousness through (διά) a momentary state of drowsiness. Perhaps we should regard the choice of this unusual term as indicating a strange state, which many persons have experienced, when the soul, after having sunk to sleep in prayer, in coming to itself, no longer finds itself in the midst of earthly things, but feels raised to a higher sphere, in which it receives impressions full of unspeakable joy.

Ver. 33 also enables us to see the true meaning of Peter's words mentioned in the three narratives. It was the moment, Luke tells us, when the two heavenly messengers were preparing to part from the Lord. Peter, wishing to detain them, ventures to speak. He offers to construct a shelter, hoping thereby to induce them to prolong their sojourn here below; as if it were the fear of spending the night in the open air that obliged them to withdraw! This enables us to understand Luke's remark (comp. also Mark): *not knowing what he said.* This characteristic speech was stereotyped in the tradition, with this trifling difference, that in Matthew Peter calls Jesus *Lord* (*κύριε*), in Mark *Master* (*ῥαββί*), in Luke *Master* (*ἐπιστάτα*). And it is imagined that our evangelists amused themselves by making these petty changes in a common text!

3*d.* Vers. 34–36.[1] *The Divine Voice.*—Here we have the culminating point of this scene. As the last sigh of the dying Christian is received by the Lord, who comes for him (John xiv. 3; Acts vii. 55, 56), so the presence of God is manifested at the moment of the glorification of Jesus.—The cloud is no ordinary cloud; it is the veil in which God invests Himself when He appears here below. We meet with it in the desert and at the inauguration of the temple; we shall meet with it again at the ascension. Matthew calls it a *bright* cloud; nevertheless he says, with the two others, that *it overshadowed* this scene. His meaning is, that the brightness of the central light pierced through the cloudy covering which cast its mysterious shadow on the scene. If with the T. R. we read *ἐκείνους*, only Jesus, Moses, and Elijah were enveloped in the cloud, and the fear felt by the disciples proceeded from uneasiness at being separated from their Master. But if with the Alex. we read *αὐτούς*, all six were enveloped in an instant by the cloud, and the fear which seized the apostles was

[1] Ver. 34.—ℵ. B. L. some Mnn., επεσκιαζεν instead of επεσκιασεν.—ℵ. B. C. L some Mnn., εισελθειν αυτους instead of εκεινους εισελθειν, which is the reading of T. R. with the other Mjj. and the versions.—Ver. 35. ℵ. B. L. Z. Cop., ο εκλελεγμενος instead of ο αγαπητος, which is the reading of T. R. with 18 Mjj., the greater part of the Mnn. Syr. It[aliq].

caused by their vivid sense of the divine nearness. The former meaning is more natural; for the voice *coming forth out of the cloud* could scarcely be addressed to any but persons who were themselves outside the cloud.

The form of the divine declaration is very nearly the same in the three accounts. The Alex. reading in Luke: *this is my Elect,* is preferable to the received reading: *this is my beloved Son,* which is taken either from the two other narratives, or from the divine salutation at the baptism. It is a question here of the elect in an absolute sense, in opposition to servants, like Moses and Elijah, chosen for a special work. Comp. xxiii. 35. The exhortation: *Hear Him,* is the repetition of that by which Moses, Deut. xviii. 15, charged Israel to welcome at some future day the teaching of the Messiah. This last word indicates the design of the whole scene: "Hear Him, whatever He may say to you; follow in His path, wherever He may lead you." We have only to call to mind the words of Peter: "*Be it far from Thee, Lord! this shall not be unto Thee,*" in the preceding conversation, to feel the true bearing of this divine admonition.—We find here again the realization of a law which occurs throughout the life of Jesus; it is this, that every act of voluntary humiliation on the part of the Son is met by a corresponding act of glorification, of which He is the object, on the part of the Father. He goes down into the waters of the Jordan, devoting Himself to death; God addresses Him as His well-beloved Son. In John xii., in the midst of the trouble of His soul, He renews His vow to be faithful unto death; a voice from heaven answers Him with the most magnificent promise for His filial heart.

Matthew mentions here the feeling of fear which the other two mention earlier.—The word: *Jesus only,* ver. 36, is common to the three narratives. It is a forcible expression of the feeling of those who witnessed the scene after the disappearing of the celestial visitants; see on ii. 15. Does it contain any allusion to the idea which has been made the very soul of the narrative: The law and the prophets pass away Jesus and His word alone remain? To me it appears doubtful. —The silence kept at first by the apostles is accounted for in Matthew and Mark by a positive command of Jesus. The Lord's intention, doubtless, was to prevent the carnal excitement which the account of such a scene might produce in the hearts of the other apostles and in the minds of the people. After the resurrection and the ascension, there would no longer be anything dangerous in the account of the transfiguration. The risen One could not be a king of this world. Luke does not mention Jesus' prohibition; he had no reason for omitting it, had he known of it. The omission of the following conversation respecting the coming of Elijah may be accounted for, on the other hand, as intentional. This idea being current only amongst the Jews, Luke might not think it necessary to record for Gentile readers the conversation to which it had given rise. Besides, i. 17 already contained a summary of what there was to be said on this subject. This entire scene, then, in each of its phases, conduced to the object which Jesus had in view—the strengthening of the faith of His own. In the first, the contemplation of His glory; in the second, the sanction of that way of sorrow into which He was to enter and take them with Him; in the third, the divine approval stamped on all His teaching: these were powerful supports for the faith of the three principal apostles, which, once confirmed, became, apart from words, the support of the faith of their weaker fellow-disciples.

The objections to the reality of the transfiguration are: 1. Its magical character and uselessness: Why, asks Keim, should there be a sign from heaven on this grand scale, when Jesus always refused to grant any such prodigy!—But nowhere, perhaps, does the sound reasonableness of the gospel come out more clearly than in this narrative; glorification is as much the *normal* termination of a holy life, as death is of corrupt life. The design with which this manifestation, which might have been concealed from the disciples, was displayed to them, appears from its connection with the previous conversation respecting the sufferings of the Messiah.—2. The impossibility of the reappearing of beings who have long been dead (see on ver. 30).—3. A real appearing of Elijah would be an actual contradiction to the following conversation (in Matthew and Mark), in which Jesus denies the return of this prophet in person, as expected by the rabbis and the people. These are the arguments of Bleek and Keim.—But what Jesus denies in the following conversation is not a temporary appearance, like that of the transfiguration, but Elijah's return to life on earth in order to fulfil a new ministry. This is what John the Baptist had accomplished (i. 17).—4. The silence of John, who must have conceived of the glory of Jesus in a more spiritual manner.—Is it to be believed that this objection can be raised by the same critic who blames John for the *magical* character of the miracles which he relates, and denies their reality for this reason? The transfiguration, along with many other incidents (the choice of the Twelve, the institution of baptism and the Lord's Supper, etc.), is omitted by John for the simple reason that they were sufficiently known through the Syn., and did not necessarily enter into the plan of his book.—5. "The artificial character of the narrative appears from its resemblance to certain narratives of the O. T." (Keim). And yet this very Keim disputes the reality of the appearing of Moses and Elijah, on the ground that apparitions of the dead are not warranted by the O. T.! But how is the existence of our three narratives to be explained? Paulus reduces the whole to a *natural* incident. He supposes an interview of Jesus with two unknown friends with whom He had made an appointment on the mountain. The reflection of the rising or setting sun on the snows of Hermon, followed by a sudden clap of thunder, occasioned all the rest. But who were those secret friends more closely connected with Jesus than His most intimate apostles? This explanation only results in making this scene a got-up affair, and Jesus a charlatan. It is abandoned at the present day. Weisse, Strauss, and Keim regard the transfiguration as nothing but an invention of *mythical* origin, designed to represent the moral glory of Jesus under images derived from the history of Moses and Elijah. But they can never explain how the Church created a picture so complete as this out of fragments of O. T. narrative. And how could a mythical narrative occur in the midst of such precise historical notes of time as those in which it is contained in the three narrations (*six* or *eight days after* the conversation at Cæsarea, on the one hand; the eve of the cure of the lunatic child, on the other)? And Jesus' strict injunction forbidding His apostles to publish an event which never took place! We must pass here, as everywhere else, from the mythical theory to the supposition of imposture. And Peter's absurd speech—would the Church have been likely to make its founder speak after this fashion? Lastly, others have regarded the transfiguration simply as a dream of Peter's. But did the two other apostles have the same dream at the same time? And would Jesus have attached such importance to a disciple's dream as to have strictly prohibited him from relating it until after His resurrection from the dead? All these fruitless attempts prove that the denial of the fact has also its difficulties.

From innocence to holiness, and from holiness to glory; here we have the normal development of human existence, its royal path. The transfiguration, at the culminating point of the life of Jesus, shows that once at least this ideal has been realized in the history of humanity.

This narrative is one of those in which we can most clearly establish the originality and superior character of Luke's sources of information. Certainly, he has neither derived his matter from the two other evangelists, nor from a document common to all three. This is evident from these two expressions: *eight days after*, and *the elect of God* (ver. 28 and ver. 35). The details by which Luke determines for us the precise object of this scene, and the subject of Jesus' conversation with Moses and Elijah, as well as the picture he gives of the state of the disciples, are such inimitable touches, and are so suggestive for purposes of interpretation, that criticism must renounce its mission as a search after historic truth, or else decide to accord to Luke the possession of independent sources of information closely connected with the fact.

The transfiguration is the end and seal of the Galilean ministry, and at the same time the opening of the history of the passion in our three Gospels.

5. *The Cure of the Lunatic Child:* ix. 37–43*a*.—The following narrative is closely connected with the preceding in the three Syn. (Matt. xvii. 14 et seq.; Mark ix. 14 et seq.). There was a moral contrast which had helped tradition to keep the chronological thread.

Vers. 37–40.[1] *The Request.*—The sleep with which the disciples were overcome, as well as Peter's offer to Jesus, ver. 33, appear to us to prove that the transfiguration had taken place either in the evening or during the night. Jesus and His three companions came down from the mountain the next morning. A great multitude awaited them. Nevertheless, according to Mark, the arrival of Jesus excited a feeling of surprise. This impression might be attributed to a lingering reflection of glory, which still illumined His person. But a more natural explanation of it is the violent scene which had just taken place before all this crowd, which gave a peculiar opportuneness to the arrival of the Master. Matthew omits all these details, and goes straight to the fact.—The symptoms of the malady, rigidity, foaming, and cries, show to what kind of physical disorder it belonged; it was a species of epilepsy. But the 42d verse and the conversation following, in Matthew and Mark, prove that in the belief of Jesus the disorder of the nervous system was either the cause or the effect of a mental condition, of the same kind as those of which we have already had several examples (iv. 33 et seq., viii. 26 et seq.). According to Matthew, the attacks were of a periodical character, and were connected with the phases of the moon

[1] Ver. 37. א. B. L. S. omit εν before τη εξης.—Ver. 38. The Mss. are divided between επιβλεψαι and επιβλεψον.—Ver. 39. א. D. some Mnn. It. Vg. add και κρασσει before και σπαρασσει (taken from Mark).

(σεληνιάζεται). Mark adds three items to the description of the malady: dumbness (in the expression *dumb demon* there is a confusion of the cause with the effect; comp. viii. 12, 13, 14, 23, for examples of similar confusion), grinding of the teeth, and wasting away. These are common symptoms in epilepsy.

The disciples had found themselves powerless to deal with a malady so deep-seated (it dated from the young man's childhood, Mark ix. 21); and the presence of certain scribes (see Mark), who no doubt had not spared their sarcasm either against them or their Master, had both humiliated and exasperated them. The expectation of the people was therefore highly excited.—What a contrast for Jesus between the hours of divine peace which He had just spent in communion with heaven, and the spectacle of the distress of this father, and of the various passions which were raging around him!

Vers. 41–43*a*. *The Answer.*—The severe exclamation of Jesus: *Faithless and perverse generation,* etc., has been applied to the disciples (Meyer); to the scribes (Calvin); to the father (Chrysostom, Grotius, Neander, De Wette); to the people (Olshausen). The father in Mark acknowledges his unbelief; the scribes were completely under the power of this disposition; the people had been shaken by their influence; lastly, the disciples—so in Matthew Jesus expressly tells them when the scene was over—had been defeated in this case by their want of faith. All these various explanations, therefore, may be maintained. And the expression, γενέα, *generation,* the contemporary race, is sufficiently wide to comprehend all the persons present. After enjoying fellowship with celestial beings, Jesus suddenly finds Himself in the midst of a world where unbelief prevails in all its various degrees. It is therefore the contrast, not between one man and another, but between this entire humanity alienated from God, in the midst of which He finds Himself, and the inhabitants of heaven whom He has just left, which wrings from Him this mournful exclamation. Διεστραμμένη, *perverse,* an expression borrowed from Deut. xxxii. 5.—The twice repeated question, *how long . . . ?* is also explained by the contrast to the preceding scene. It is not an expression of impatience. The scene of the transfiguration has just proved, that if Jesus is still upon the earth, it is by *His own free will.* The term *suffer you* implies as much. But He feels Himself a stranger in the midst of this unbelief, and He cannot suppress a sigh for the time when His filial and fraternal heart will be no longer chilled at every moment by exhibitions of feeling opposed to His most cherished aspirations. The holy enjoyment of the night before has, as it were, made Him home-sick. *Πρὸς ὑμᾶς, amongst you,* in Luke and Mark, expresses a more active relation than *μεθ' ὑμῶν, with you,* in Matthew.—The command: *Bring thy son hither,* has something abrupt in it. Jesus seems anxious to shake off the painful feeling which possesses Him; comp. a similar expression, John xi. 34.

There is a kind of gradation in the three narratives. Matthew, without mentioning the preceding attack, merely relates the cure; the essential thing for him is the conversation of Jesus with His disciples which followed. In Luke, the narrative of the cure is preceded by a description of the attack. Lastly, Mark, in describing the attack, relates the remarkable conversation which Jesus had with the father of the child. This conversation, which bears the highest marks of authenticity, neither allows us to admit that Mark drew his account from either of the others, or that they had his narrative, or a narrative anything like his, in their possession; how could Luke especially have voluntarily omitted such details?

We shall not analyze here the dialogue in Mark in which Jesus suddenly changes the question, whether He has power to *heal,* into another, whether His questioner has power to *believe;* after which, the latter, terrified at the responsibility thrown upon him by this turn being given to the question, invokes with anguish the power of Jesus to help his faith, which appears to him no better than unbelief. Nothing more profound or exquisite has come from the pen of any evangelist. It is the very photography of the human and paternal heart. And we are to suppose that the other evangelists had this masterpiece of Mark's before their eyes, and mutilated it!—We find these two incidents in Luke mentioned also in the raising of the widow of Nain's son: *an only son* (ver. 38): *and He gave him to his father* (ver. 42). "They belong to Luke's manner," says the critic. But ought not the original and characteristic details with which our Gospel is full to inspire a little more confidence in his narratives?—The conversation which followed this miracle, *and which Luke omits,* is one of the passages in which the unbelief of the apostles is most severely blamed. This omission does not prove, at any rate, that the sacred writer was animated with that feeling of ill-will towards the Twelve which criticism imputes to him.

6. *The three last Incidents of Jesus' Galilean Ministry:* ix. 43*b*–50.

1*st.* *The Second Announcement of the Passion:* vers. 43*b*–45.[1]—We may infer from the two other Syn. (Matt. xvii. 22, 23 ; Mark ix. 30–32), more especially from Mark, that it was during the return from Cæsarea Philippi to Capernaum that Jesus had this second conversation with His disciples respecting His sufferings. Luke places it in connection with the state of excitement into which the minds of those who were with Jesus had been thrown by the preceding miracles. The Lord desires to suppress this dangerous excitement in the hearts of His disciples. And we can understand, therefore, why this time Jesus makes no mention of the resurrection (comp. ix. 22). By the pronoun ὑμεῖς, *you,* He distinguishes the apostles from the multitude: "You who ought to know the real state of things." The expression θέσθε εἰς τὰ ὦτα, literally, *put this into your ears,* is very forcible. "If even you do not understand it, nevertheless impress it on your memory; keep it as a saying."—The *sayings* which they are thus to preserve, are those which are summarized in this very 44th verse, and not, as Meyer would have us think, the enthusiastic utterances of the people to which allusion is made in ver. 43. The *for* which follows is not opposed to this meaning, which is the only natural one: "Remember these sayings; *for* incredible as they appear to you, they will not fail to be realized."—The term, *be delivered into the hands of men,* refers to the counsel of God, and not to the treachery of Judas.—They can know very little of the influence exercised by the will on the reason who find a difficulty in the want of understanding shown by the disciples (ver. 45). The prospect which Jesus put before them was regarded with aversion (Matt. v. 23), and consequently they refused to pay any serious attention to it, or even to question Jesus about it (Mark v. 32). Nothing more fully accords with psychological experience than this moral phenomenon indicated afresh by

[1] Ver. 43. The Mss. are divided between ἐποίησεν (T. R.) and ἐποίει (Alex.).

Luke. The following narrative will prove its reality. The ἵνα, *in order that*, ver. 45, does not signify simply, *so that*. The idea of purpose implied in this conjunction refers to the providential dispensation which permitted this blindness.

2*d*. The question: *Which is the greatest?* vers. 46–48.[1]—This incident also must belong, according to Matthew and Mark, to the same time (Matt. xviii. 1 et seq.; Mark ix. 33 et seq.). According to Mark, the dispute on this question had taken place *on the road*, during their return from Cæsarea to Capernaum. "*What were ye talking about by the way?*" Jesus asked them after their arrival (ver. 33); and it was then that the following scene took place in a house which, according to Matthew, was probably Peter's. We have several other indications of a serious dispute between the disciples happening about this time; for example, that admonition preserved by Mark at the end of the discourse spoken by Jesus on this occasion (ix. 50): "*Have salt in yourselves, and be at peace among yourselves;*" then there is the instruction of Jesus on the conduct to be pursued in the case of offences between brethren, Matt. xviii. 15: "*If thy brother sin against thee . . .;*" lastly, the question of Peter: "*How many times am I to forgive my brother?*" and the answer of Jesus, xviii. 21, 22. All these sayings belong to the period of the return to Capernaum, and are indications of a serious altercation between the disciples. According to the highly dramatic account of Mark, it is Jesus Himself who takes the initiative, and who questions them as to the subject of their dispute. Shame-stricken, like guilty children, at first they are silent; then they make up their minds to avow what the question was about which they had quarrelled. Each had put forward his claims to the first place, and depreciated those of the rest. Peter had been the most eager and, perhaps, the most severely handled. We see how superficial was the impression made on them by the announcement of their Master's sufferings. Jesus then seated Himself (Mark v. 35), and gathering the Twelve about Him, gave them the following instruction. All these circumstances are omitted by Matthew. In his concise way of dealing with

[1] Ver. 47. ℵ. B. F. K. L. Π. several Mnn. Syr. read ειδως instead of ιδων.—B. C. D., παιδιον instead of παιδιου.—Ver. 48. ℵ. B. C. L. X. Z. some Mnn. It[plerique], εστιν instead of εσται.

facts, contrary to all moral probability, he puts the question: *Which of us is the greatest?* into the mouth of the disciples who address it to Jesus. All he regards as important is the teaching given on the occasion. As to Luke, Bleek, pressing the words ἐν αὐτοῖς, *in them,* supposes that, according to him, we have simply to do with the thoughts which had arisen in the hearts of the disciples (comp. ver. 47, τῆς καρδίας), and not with any outward quarrel. But the term εἰσῆλθε, *occurred,* indicates a positive fact, just such as that Mark so graphically describes; and the expression *in them,* or *among them,* applies to the circle of the disciples in the midst of which this discussion had taken place.—Jesus takes a child, and makes him the subject of His demonstration. It is a law of heaven, that the feeblest creature here below shall enjoy the largest measure of heavenly help and tenderness (Matt. xviii. 10). In conformity with this law of heaven, Jesus avows a peculiar interest in children, and commends them to the special care of His own people. Whoever entering into His views receives them as such, receives Him. He receives Jesus as the riches which have come to fill the void of his own existence, which in itself is so poor, and in Jesus, God, who, as a consequence of the same principle, is the constant complement of the existence of Jesus (John vi. 57). Consequently, for a man to devote himself from love to Jesus to the service of the little ones, and so make himself *the least,* is to be on the road towards possessing God most completely, and becoming *the greatest.*

The meaning of Jesus' words in Matthew is somewhat different, at least as far as concerns the first part of the answer. Here Jesus lays down as the measure of true greatness, not a tender sympathy for the little, but the feeling of one's own littleness. The child set in the midst is not presented to the disciples as one in whom they are to interest themselves, but as an example of the feeling with which they must themselves be possessed. It is an invitation to return to their infantine humility and simplicity, rather than to love the little ones. It is only in the 5th verse that Matthew passes from this idea, by a natural transition, to that which is contained in the answer of Jesus as given by Luke and Mark. It is probable that the first part of the answer in Matthew is borrowed from another scene, which we find occurring later in Mark (x. 13–16) and Luke (xviii. 15–17), as well as in Matthew himself (xix. 13–15); this Gospel combines here, as usual, in a single discourse elements belonging to different occasions. Meyer thinks that in this expression, *receive in my name,* the *in my name* refers not to the disposition of him who receives, but of him who is received, in so far as he presents himself as a disciple of Jesus. But these two notions: presenting oneself in the name of Jesus (consciously or unconsciously), and being received in this name, cannot be opposed one to the other. As soon as the welcome takes place, one becomes united with the other.—The Alex. reading ἐστί, *is,* is more spiritual than the Byz. ἔσται, *shall be,* which has an eschatological meaning. It is difficult to decide between them.

3*d. The Dissenting Disciple:* vers. 49 and 50.[1]—Only in some very rare cases does John play an active part in the Gospel history. But he appears to have been at this time in a state of great excitement; comp. the incident which immediately follows (ix. 54 et seq.), and another a little later (Matt. xx. 20 et seq.). He had no doubt been one of the principal actors in the incident related here by himself, and which might very easily have had some connection with the dispute which had just been going on. The link of connection is more simple than criticism imagines. The importance which Jesus had just attributed to *His name* in the preceding answer, makes John fear that he has violated by his rashness the majesty of this august name. When once in the way of confession, he feels that he must make a clean breast of it. This connection is indicated by the terms ἀποκριθείς (Luke) and ἀπεκρίθη (Mark). This incident, placed here in close connection with the preceding, helps us to understand some parts of the lengthened discourse, Matt. xviii., which certainly belongs to this period. These little ones, whom care must be taken not to offend (ver. 6), whom the good Shepherd seeks to save (vers. 11–13), and of whom not one by God's will shall

[1] Ver. 49. ℵ. B. L. X. Δ. Z. some Mnn. read εν τω in place of επι τω (εν perhaps taken from Mark).—ℵ. B. L. Z. Itaaliq., εκωλυομεν instead of εκωλυσαμεν.—Ver. 50. C. D. F. L. M. Z. add αυτον to μη κωλυετε.—They read καθ' υμων and υπερ υμων in ℵcb B. C. D. K. L. M. Z. Π. several Mnn. It. Syr.; καθ' υμων and υπερ ημων in ℵ* A. X. Δ. some Mnn.; and καθ' ημων and υπερ ημων in T. R., according to ℵca E. F. G. H. S. U. V. Γ. Λ. and most of the Mnn.

perish (ver. 14), are doubtless beginners in the faith, such as he was towards whom the apostles had shown such intolerance. Thus it very often happens, that by bringing together separate stones scattered about in our three narratives, we succeed in reconstructing large portions of the edifice, and then, by joining it to the Gospel of John, the entire building.

The fact here mentioned is particularly interesting. "We see," as Meyer says, "that even outside the circle of the permanent disciples of Jesus there were men in whom His word and His works had called forth a higher and miraculous power; these sparks, which fell beyond the circle of His disciples, had made flames burst forth here and there away from the central fire." Was it desirable to extinguish these fires? It was a delicate question. Such men, though they had never lived in the society of Jesus, acquired a certain authority, and might use it to disseminate error. With this legitimate fear on the part of the Twelve there was no doubt mingled a reprehensible feeling of jealousy. They no longer had the monopoly of the work of Christ. Jesus instantly discerned this taint of evil in the conduct which they had just pursued.—In Luke, as in Mark, instead of the aor. ἐκωλύσαμεν, *we forbade him*, some MSS. read the imperf. ἐκωλύομεν: "We were forbidding him, and thought we were doing right; were we deceived?" Their opposition was only tentative, inasmuch as Jesus had not sanctioned it. This is the preferable reading.

The answer of Jesus is full of broad and exalted feeling. The divine powers which emanate from Him could not be completely contained in any visible society, not even in that of the Twelve. The fact of spiritual union with Him takes precedence of social communion with the other disciples. So far from treating a man who makes use of His name as an adversary, he must rather be regarded, even in his isolated position, as a useful auxiliary.—Of the three readings offered by the MSS. in ver. 50, and which are also found in Mark (*against you—for you; against you—for us; against us—for us*), it appears to me that we must prefer the first: "He who is not *against you*, is *for you*." The authority of the Alex. MSS., which read in this way, is confirmed by that of the ancient versions, the *Italic* and the *Peschito*, and still more by the context. The person of Jesus is not in fact involved in this conflict,—is it not in His name that the man acts? As a matter of fact, it is the Twelve who are concerned: "he followeth not *with us;*" this is the grievance (ver. 49). It is quite different in the similar and apparently contradictory saying (Luke xi. 23; Matt. xii. 30): "*He who is not with me, is against me.*" The difference between these two declarations consists in this; in the second case, it is the personal honour of Jesus which is at stake. He opposes the expulsions of demons, which He effects, to those of the Jewish exorcists. These latter appear to be labouring with Him against a common enemy, but really they are strengthening the enemy. In the application which we might make of these maxims at the present day, the former would apply to brethren who, while separated from us ecclesiastically, are fighting with us for the cause of Christ; whilst the latter would apply to men who, although belonging to the same religious society as ourselves, are sapping the foundations of the gospel. We should have the sense to regard the first as allies, although found in a different camp; the others as enemies, although found in our own camp.

Mark introduces between the two parts of this reply a remarkable saying, the import of which is, that no one need fear that a man who does such works in the name of Jesus will readily pass over to the ranks of those who speak evil of Him, that is to say, of those who accuse Him of casting out devils by Beelzebub. After having invoked the name of Jesus in working a cure, to bring such an accusation against Jesus would be to accuse himself.

Nowhere, perhaps, is the fitting of the Syn. one into the other, albeit quite undesigned, more remarkable. In Matthew the words, without the occasion of them (the dispute between the disciples); in Luke the incident, with a brief saying having reference to it; in Mark the incident, with some very graphic and much more circumstantial details than in Luke, and a discourse which resembles in part that in Matthew, but differs from both by omissions and additions which are equally important. Is not the mutual independence of the three traditional narratives palpably proved?

END OF VOL. I.